Richard Aldington & H.D.

MANCHESTER
UNIVERSITY PRESS

Richard Aldington & H.D.

Their lives in letters
1918–61

EDITED
WITH AN INTRODUCTION
AND COMMENTARY BY

CAROLINE ZILBOORG

MANCHESTER UNIVERSITY PRESS
MANCHESTER AND NEW YORK

DISTRIBUTED EXCLUSIVELY IN THE USA BY PALGRAVE

Copyright introduction and commentary © Caroline Zilboorg 2003

All other material copyright as acknowledged

Published by Manchester University Press
Oxford Road, Manchester M13 9NR, UK
and Room 400, 175 Fifth Avenue, New York, NY 10010, USA
www.manchesteruniversitypress.co.uk

Distributed exclusively in the USA by
Palgrave, 175 Fifth Avenue, New York, NY 10010, USA

Distributed exclusively in Canada by
UBC Press, University of British Columbia, 2029 West Mall, Vancouver, BC, Canada V6T 1Z2

British Library Cataloguing-in-Publication Data
A catalogue record for this book is avalaible from the British Library

Library of Congress Cataloging-in-Publication Data applied for

ISBN 0 7190 5972 0 *paperback*

First published 2003

11 10 09 08 07 06 05 04 03   10 9 8 7 6 5 4 3 2 1

Designed in Fournier with Fairfield display
by Max Nettleton FCSD
Typeset by Koinonia Ltd, Manchester
Printed in Great Britain
by Bookcraft (Bath) Ltd, Midsomer Norton

FOR TOM

MY PARTNER
IN NUMEROUS ENTERPRISES

Contents

List of illustrations

Preface

This single-volume edition of correspondence brings together for the first time a selection from the nearly 1,200 letters exchanged by two important modernist writers: Richard Aldington and H.D. (Hilda Doolittle). The letters published here span nearly fifty years and chronicle their relationship in specific and compelling detail. Beginning in 1918 and continuing until 1961, the correspondence between them documents the fraught passions of their courtship, marriage, and subsequent separation. The letters also reveal their participation in the development of modernism, their experience of the Great War, their often flamboyant bohemian lives in the 1920s and 1930s, as well as their experience of the Second World War and its aftermath. The cast includes a host of illustrious characters; Ezra Pound, D.H. Lawrence, Amy Lowell, Wyndham Lewis, Bryher, Havelock Ellis, Sigmund Freud, Roy Campbell, Lawrence Durrell and numerous other friends and acquaintances are vivid presences, as are historical and literary figures, ranging from Homer and Euripides through Balzac and Malarmé to Swinburne, William Morris, Wilde, Joyce and T.E. Lawrence. The notes and extensive commentary in this new edition are designed to provide the necessary background and context for both the scholar and the general reader interested in the story these letters contain.

The surviving correspondence begins in April 1918, when Aldington left for the Western Front for his second tour of duty during the First World War. In late 1920, Aldington destroyed the very early letters (June 1916 to March 1918) as well as H.D.'s letters between 1918 and 1920. Part I of this book includes Aldington's side of this early correspondence – that is, all 92 of the extant letters from this period – and is a revised version of my book, *Richard Aldington and H.D.: The Early Years in Letters* (Bloomington: Indiana University Press, 1992).

After 1920, H.D. broke off the correspondence, which did not resume until 1929. H.D.'s letters during this time have apparently not survived, and by late 1933 their correspondence again breaks off. A few letters from Aldington during and immediately following their divorce in 1937–39 chronicle yet another stage of their relationship, but his second marriage in 1938 effectively concluded this period. After the Second World War, however, when Aldington had returned from America to live permanently in France and H.D. had settled in Switzerland, the two writers resumed their epistolary relationship, which continued with intimate regularity until H.D.'s death. This final series of sometimes daily letters comprises the bulk of their interchange and is the only group to contain both sides of the correspondence. The sheer number of letters after 1920 has made a selection necessary, and a representative group of 133 letters is included here in Part II, a revised and expanded version of my book, *Richard Aldington and H.D.: The Later Years in Letters* (Manchester: Manchester University Press, 1995).

Because these letters are personal as well as literary, and because they cover such an extensive period of years and shifting intensities of feeling, they depend on and reveal the authors' intertwined and separate lives. The following selection of letters and my presentation of them thus comprise a kind of biography. The book draws extensively on unpublished correspondence by Aldington, H.D. and their contemporaries, and offers evidence upon which any subsequent understanding of Aldington's and H.D.'s relationship must to a degree depend. This volume is thus appreciably different from Janice Robinson's *H.D.: The Life of an American Poet* (Boston: Houghton Mifflin, 1982) or Barbara Guest's *Herself Defined: The Poet H.D. and Her World* (London: Collins, 1985) or Charles Doyle's *Richard Aldington: A Biography* (London: Macmillan, 1989). Additionally, this is a dual biography, the biography of a relationship. Further, except for rare and noted exceptions, I have chosen not to base my commentary on the authors' fictional treatments of their own experiences. H.D.'s autobiographical novels – especially *Bid Me to Live* (1960), *Asphodel* (1992) and *Paint It Today* (1992) – are at times virtual *romans à clé*, but they are nonetheless artistic representations and not to be read 'straight'. Aldington's famous war novel, *Death of a Hero* (1929), contains passages based very closely on his own experiences at the front, but is also a carefully crafted as well as highly satiric modernist fiction and not to be taken as a factual account of his own life. While both writers also produced compelling memoirs, these too must be read in context: Aldington's *Life for Life's Sake* (1941) is notable in part for its omissions, while H.D.'s *End to Torment: A Memoir of Ezra Pound* (1979) and her *Tribute to Freud* (1974) are idiosyncratic and personal accounts of H.D.'s inner world. In other words, *Richard Aldington and H.D.: Their Lives in Letters, 1918–61* is grounded in primary materials and depends on the immediacy of the two voices, which tell their own story to each other and to us.

I have included whole letters throughout this book in an effort to preserve their context as well as their character, and in Part II I have tried to include clusters of letters in order to focus on specific topics and to suggest the nature of the writers' relationship at a particular time. My commentary – both in the notes which follow each letter and in the sections of biographical text which fill in the gaps between letters or clusters of letters – is intended to make a readable volume while emphasizing the overarching narrative in which these letters are imbedded.

Some information that the reader of this correspondence might want is no longer available. For instance, Aldington often refers to volumes in the library he and H.D. shared, but these books were separated, lent, sold, and have otherwise failed to survive as a collection. Books in H.D.'s later library are now at the Beinecke Rare Book and Manuscript Library at Yale, but it contains few volumes before the early 1920s; the same is true of Bryher's library, which includes many of H.D.'s books and is now housed in a building dedicated to it on the grounds of the Schaffner family's home in East Hampton, New York. Although the late Alister Kershaw kept several books Aldington owned at the time of his death in 1962, Aldington's library has not been preserved.

The reader might also have been aided by Aldington's military service record, but this, too, is unavailable. German bombing of London during the Second World War destroyed many early records at the Ministry of Defence. H.D.'s side of the early correspondence, as recounted in my introduction, is also unavailable.

I have chosen to translate most of the foreign language material in the letters, excepting the most obvious French phrases. Aldington especially used French often and at length, frequently idiomatically. Additionally, his command of French in the teens was nowhere near so good as it would become in the twenties and during his later years, when he lived entirely in France.

I have refrained from correcting the authors' grammar, punctuation or spelling except where it seemed essential for clarity or a graphical error. Aldington was an excellent speller and a stickler for correctness of expression; his letters stand here virtually as he wrote them. H.D., however, was a notoriously bad speller and often omitted letters or words. I have chosen in most cases not to draw awkward attention to her mistakes by the use of [*sic*] but have generally allowed her errors to stand. I have not attempted to standardize her American and British spellings; her use of one or the other (or both within a single letter) seems important evidence of her expatriate identity. I have, however, silently inserted commas when it appeared necessary for clear sense: H.D. frequently includes parenthetical or appositional material with only one of the required commas; I have provided the other, usually the second in the pair.

Acknowledgements

I could not have completed this book without the help of the following libraries. I am especially grateful to the staff at the Beinecke Library at Yale (which holds Aldington's letters to H.D.) and at the Morris Library at Southern Illinois University (which holds H.D.'s letters to Aldington). Special acknowledgement is made to libraries for permission to quote from or publish material in their collections; they are cited in the book by the letters indicated.

Yale: The Beinecke Rare Book and Manuscript Library, Yale University
BL: The British Library
UL: The Brotherton Library, University of Leeds
UCLA: The University Library, University of California, Los Angeles
The University Library, Cambridge University
Special Collections, University of Chicago
The Fales Library, New York University
Firestone Library, Princeton University
Grasselli Library, John Carroll University
HRC: The Harry Ransom Humanities Research Center, University of Texas at Austin
HU: The Houghton Library, Harvard University
HL: The Huntington Library, San Marino, California
Rare Book and Special Collections Library, University of Illinois, Urbana-Champaign
The Imperial War Museum
UIL: The University of Iowa Libraries, Iowa City
Lakeland Community College Library
The Lily Library, Indiana University
Lincoln Library, Lake Erie College
Special Collections, Middlebury College
The Ministry of Defence, Hayes, Middlesex
University Libraries, University of Minnesota, Minneapolis
SIU: Morris Library, Southern Illinois University
Mugar Memorial Library, Boston University
Olin Library, Cornell University
PRO: The Public Record Office, Kew, Richmond
UR: The University of Reading Library, Reading
The Royal Signals Museum, Blandford Camp, Dorset
TU: The Rare Book and Manuscript Collection, Temple University
UV: Special Collections, University of Victoria

All of Aldington's letters to H.D. are published here by permission of the Yale Collection of American Literature, the Beinecke Rare Book and Manuscript Library, Yale University. All of H.D.'s letters to Aldington are published here by permission of the Morris

Library, Southern Illinois University. All letters from H.D. and Aldington to Amy Lowell are at HU; all letters from Aldington to Frank Stewart Flint are at HRC; all letters from Aldington to John Cournos are at HU; all quotations from H.D.'s letters to John Cournos are from unpublished letters at HU unless otherwise noted; all letters to Clement Shorter are at UL. All letters from H.D. to Ezra Pound, from H.D. to George Plank, and from H.D. to Norman Holmes Pearson are at Yale. All letters from H.D. and Aldington to Bryher are at Yale; all letters from Bryher to H.D. are at Yale; all letters from Bryher to Aldington are at SIU. All letters from Aldington to Glenn Hughes and from Aldington to Brigit Patmore are at HRC. 'Refuge from War', by Harriet Monroe, first appeared in *Poetry* © 1918 by the Modern Poetry Association, and is reprinted by permission of the Editor of Poetry.

A portion of the Introduction appeared in somewhat different form in the *H.D. Newsletter* as 'H.D. and R.A.: Early Love and the Exclusion of Ezra Pound', Vol. 3, No. 1, 26–34.

Special acknowledgement is made to the following for permission to publish or quote from previously unpublished material: the late Alister Kershaw, literary executor for Richard Aldington; Catherine Aldington (for the Aldington Estate); H.D./Aldington letters © 2002 by the Schaffner Family Foundation, literary executors for H.D. and Bryher; all Bryher material is quoted thanks to the Schaffner Family Foundation; New Directions; Indiana University Press; Dundas and Wilson, Trustees, Ltd., agents for the estate of Cecil Gray; David Wilkinson; and Ann Monroe Howe, literary executor for the estate of Harriet Monroe. Thanks are also due to staff of the Paul Nash Trust.

When I first read Aldington's letters to H.D. during the summer of 1987, I had no idea that I was beginning a project which would involve more than fifteen years of work and result in many personal as well as intellectual rewards as well as three scholarly books and a novel. The late Alister Kershaw, Aldington's friend and literary executor until his own death in 1995, was unstintingly supportive in granting permissions, answering questions, reading drafts, and offering his friendship in person and in regular correspondence. The late Perdita Schaffner, H.D.'s daughter and until her death in 2001 H.D.'s and Bryher's literary executor, has been a pleasure to work with and invariably generous in giving permission to quote and publish. I am also grateful to Catherine Aldington, Aldington's daughter and current literary executor, who has been interested in my work from the very beginning, and to Peggy Fox at New Directions for permission to include the letters from H.D. which appear here.

Friends and colleagues who have offered me specific support over the years in everything from checking a reference in an archive to detailed talks late into the night include especially: Jane Augustine, Gemma Bristow, Hugh Cecil, Diana Collecott, Shelley Cox, the late Fred D. Crawford, Susan Stanford Friedman, Norman T. Gates, Eileen Gregory, Cathy Henderson, Dominic Hibberd, Donna Hollenberg, Cassandra Laity, A. Walton Litz, Allison Meinhold, Thomas Nevin, Sharon Ouditt, the late Louis Silverstein, Angela Kay Smith, Robert Spoo, the late Martin Taylor, David Wilkinson, Patricia Willis, and Patrick Quinn. I am grateful to all those who contributed to this book by participating in The Richard Aldington Centenary Conference, held in July of 1992 in Montpellier, France, especially to Alain Blayac and Frédéric-Jacques Temple.

I am also grateful for the financial and institutional support I have received while working on this project at Princeton in 1987 while I was a participant in A. Walton Litz's Summer Seminar in modernist poetry funded by the National Endowment for the

Humanities. The NEH also supported my research with a Travel Grant in 1988. In 1991 I spent a month at Yale as the first recipient of the Beinecke's H.D. Fellowship. In 1992–93 my work was supported by a Visiting Fellowship at Clare Hall, Cambridge. During that year, and subsequently as a Life Member of Clare Hall, I have benefited from the support of colleagues both at the college and in the larger Cambridge community, among them Terri Apter, Michael Black, David Lloyd, Mary Joannou, Jane Marcus, Trudi Tate and Jay Winter. I owe a special debt of thanks to the staff at Manchester University Press for their commitment to this new edition of these letters.

Finally, I am deeply grateful to my children (Austin, Tobias, Elodie and Miranda Nevin) and to my husband, Thomas Nevin, for their abiding interest in my work. Their unfailing encouragement and respect for my research and writing has been more important than even they know.

Introduction

Richard Aldington began to write almost daily letters to his wife, Hilda Doolittle Aldington (H.D.), as soon as he entered the British army on 24 June 1916. She wrote to him nearly as frequently, and the intense correspondence between them continued until his demobilization in mid-February of 1919. They wrote to each other less often from mid-February through April of 1919 and sporadically into the 1920s, resuming a limited exchange of letters between 1929 and 1932. They resumed the correspondence in 1937, their letters becoming more frequent and continuing, often twice a week, until H.D.'s death on 27 September 1961.

Not all of these letters have survived, but the astounding number (nearly 1,200) which have reveal the development over a span of more than forty years of two complex people who never ceased to care deeply about each other. The missing letters are also a part of the story, for as the late Alister Kershaw, Aldington's literary executor and a close personal friend, has suggested, while Aldington 'wasn't in the habit of piously preserving every letter he ever received ... hers would have been infinitely precious to him.'[1] H.D. similarly valued Aldington's letters; in her autobiographical novel *Bid Me to Live* (1960), Aldington appears as the character Rafe Ashton, who brings back to Julia (H.D.) on his leaves all the letters she has written to him.[2]

In light of Kershaw's statement, Aldington's purposeful destruction of letters from H.D. seems uncharacteristic, but in the early 1950s H.D. reported to her friend and admirer Norman Holmes Pearson that 'during the first war she had written Richard every day, and he had sent back the letters periodically for her to keep, along with his to her. "There was a trunkful." When she left the apartment, she left the books + letters behind; then when they met for the first time [after 1919] in Paris [in May 1929] ... , she asked what had become of them, + he said he had destroyed them all.'[3] On the basis of Aldington's letters to H.D. during the war, it is easy to imagine her concern about the revelation of their private contents. Aldington in his turn may also have felt that the intimacy and loss the letters recorded were too powerful for him to preserve. Thus he apparently did destroy their letters of 1916 and 1917, which he would have recovered from H.D.'s flat along with books and other papers she had stored there, as well as her letters to him after March of 1918, which he would have had with him when he moved to a cottage in Hermitage, Berkshire, in December of 1919. When at the end of 1920 he moved to Malthouse Cottage in Padworth, his charwoman's daughter recalled over sixty years later:

> ... he left a lot of papers, and all the things that were left behind him saying what will happen to him in wartime. ... Saying about his wife and all the things about his wife. My mother destroyed those. Really, they were letters about him and his wife ... to Mr Aldington ... from her to him. ... there were piles and piles of papers left. He left the whole lot behind and Mother said, 'What's that?' ... and he said to my mother, 'Would you burn that for me?' So she said, 'Yes, certainly.' And she said [to the daughter, then

aged eleven], 'Well, look at this!' And then, in the end, she destroyed them.[4]

Such destruction of correspondence and papers, however upsetting to future readers, was also for Aldington a natural part of the cleaning up occasioned by his numerous and sometimes unanticipated moves from one residence to another. For example, Aldington left Malthouse Cottage precipitously in August 1928, for Italy: his friend Alec Randall was recovering from typhoid fever near Rome and his wife wired Aldington with an urgent invitation to visit him during his convalescence.[5] Aldington had planned to host Glenn Hughes, an American scholar interested in imagism, during September; in his absence, he lent Malthouse Cottage indefinitely to Hughes and his family. He periodically requested papers from Hughes during the winter of 1928–29, but he did not decide to give up the cottage until the end of November 1928, effective at the end of February 1929.[6] As a result Aldington disposed of and relocated his books, papers and other possessions from a distance and left much to be burned at the discretion of others, for he remained on the continent throughout 1929. If all the early letters between Aldington and H.D. were not burned by Mrs Brown in 1920, it seems likely that they were destroyed during this later period.

The first section of letters in this book is thus one side of the correspondence: Aldington's letters to H.D. between April 1918 and December 1920. This was a pivotal and important time in both writers' lives, a dramatic and intense period personally, socially, and historically. These years would test their love for each other and challenge their ideas of art and the future, calling into question all of their earlier decisions and commitments. The early letters are deeply embedded in their biographies – not merely literary, philosophical, or topical exchanges – and an overview of both writers' lives before 1918 seems in order.

Aldington was born in Hampshire on 8 July 1892. He and his two sisters and brother grew up in the south of England in Portsmouth, Dover, and the surrounding country-side. His childhood does not appear to have been a particularly happy one: in his memoir, *Life for Life's Sake* (1941), he repeatedly and at length details the constraining middle-class life that oppressed him as a boy, experience that he treated bitterly and with under-standable censure in 'Childhood', a poem which first appeared in *The Egoist* in 1914.

His parents were not really sympathetic to his nature, although each had enough awareness of the young Aldington's personality to realize his developing values and misunderstand them. His mother appears to have been especially difficult in this respect. A domineering woman who aspired to 'culture' as socially defined at the turn of the century, May Aldington seemed to her son throughout his life an affected, pretentious, and hollow person whose sentimentality and materialism came to represent all that he abhorred in England. She wrote several romantic novels, and evidently drank to the point of being unpredictable and unreliable. Aldington's deep hostility toward her developed into his notion of the 'bad' mother who appears regularly in his fiction: Mrs Winterbourne, for example, in *Death of a Hero* (1929); Mrs Withers in *The Colonel's Daughter* (1931); Mrs Reeves in *Seven against Reeves* (1938). Aldington developed simultaneously an ideal of the 'good' mother, based not so much on direct experience as on wide reading of both early twentieth-century psychology (Havelock Ellis, for instance) and literature, English, continental, and classical. This notion of the 'good' mother was also an imaginative response to the feminism with which he was in close contact after he moved to London.

Aldington's father, in contrast, appears to have been a rather weak man for whom his son felt an abiding affection and intellectual affinity. A middle-class solicitor, Albert Aldington had little business acumen or ambition, and his son resented his lack of direction and consequent hypocrisy. But Aldington also saw him as a victim of Victorian English culture, and respected his wide and independently acquired knowledge of history and letters. His father made some effort to launch Aldington's literary career, and on 7 June 1910, wrote on his behalf to St Loe Strachey, editor of *The Spectator*:

> I have a son between 17 + 18, of whom one of our greatest living writers [George Bernard Shaw, to whom Aldington's mother had sent a sample of his work] has declared that 'he has literary ability enough for anything', + as I am therefore anxious to obtain for him an atmosphere that would be congenial, it has occurred to me that possibly you might be able to find him a position that would be mutually satisfying.
>
> As an old lover of the classics I can vouch for the boy's ability in that direction. His knowledge of French is good, of art excellent, of English literature, for his age quite remarkable. His productions, particularly in poetry are equally distinctive, + withal, he is tall, muscular + can do a twenty mile walk any day of the week.[7]

Albert Aldington's large library with its strong collection of Elizabethan and Romantic poets as well as classical and European authors was a rich treasure for the young Aldington; it was there he grounded himself early in literature and the past.

The other solace of Aldington's childhood was nature. He relished the countryside in the south of England, its flowers, hills, chalk cliffs, and sea. As a youth, he became a great walker, setting out on long hikes over the downs and through the villages in the rural South Foreland. His approach to nature was at once sensual and scientific, imaginative and precise. He enjoyed swimming and dreamy afternoons in the sun as well as counting the miles he walked and collecting butterflies. These two tendencies – the passionate and the analytical – come to characterize his responses to all aspects of life: literature was simultaneously a personal, private, emotional experience and something to take a well-reasoned public stand on; love was intimate, sexual, and overwhelming as well as spiritual, and yet something one could analyse and consider responsibly.

There is obviously a potential conflict here, and it was one which Aldington never fully resolved in his relationships with others, in his own art, or in his critical and biographical work. He was increasingly conscious of these tensions in his personality, yet the gusto with which he approached life, often combining seriousness with humour, his sensibility with sense, made him many lasting friends and not-so-lasting lovers. His own account of himself in 1929 in response to a questionnaire sent out by *The Little Review* captures these contrasting aspects of his personality while it conveys the apparent arrogance and even off-handedness of this man who was emotionally private and scrupulously truthful about his own feelings as well as sensitive and widely read:

1. What would you most like to do, to know, to be? ...
2. Why wouldn't you change places with any other human being?
3. What do you look forward to?
4. What do you fear most from the future?
5. What has been the happiest moment of your life? The unhappiest? ...
6. What do you consider your weakest characteristics? Your strongest?
7. What things do you really like? Dislike? ...
8. What is your attitude toward art today?

9. What is your world view? ...
10. Why do you go on living?

Aldington responds:

1. A. To write a poem.
   B. Greek.
   C. Ninon de Lenclos.[8]
2. Because 'tis better to endure those ills we know than to fly to others that we know not of [*Hamlet*, act 3, scene 1].
3. Telling England what I really think of it.
4. Having to take a job.
5. A. Losing my virginity. B. Lying with a virgin.
6. A. Honesty. B. Independence. C. Ha! ha! D. He! he!
7. A. Women's. B. Puritans.
8. Enlightened benevolence.
9. Despair.
10. Pour écraser l'infâme [to crush the infamous].[9]

Aldington's hellenism, his knowledge of French literature and language, his love of Shakespeare, his feminism, his respect for art, his enjoyment of sexuality and personal freedom, his hostility toward England and hypocrisy, his forthrightness and privateness, however masked by brash humour, are all readily apparent here. Almost twenty years earlier, when at eighteen he first came to London in the autumn of 1910 to attend University College, his character was well-formed and his academic knowledge advanced; the experiences he would have in the next decade deepened and complicated the man who appears above in *The Little Review* in 1929.

Aldington completed only one year at University College before his family's financial indiscretions forced him to leave to earn his own living. The academic year was not particularly intellectually quickening for him – he had already covered more ground on his own than most entering students – but he pursued Greek with diligence and enthusiasm; Aldington always worked intensely with care, precision, and a clear plan. He pursued and mastered Greek, Latin, French, and Italian in this fashion. After leaving University College, he received for a while a small allowance from his parents, which enabled him to support himself as a journalist and to begin to publish his poetry in British periodicals. He lived simply during the summer and autumn of 1911, and began to associate with London's bohemian fringe. Late in 1911 Aldington met Brigit Patmore; through her he met Ezra Pound, who had come to London in 1908, and soon after Aldington attended a party at Patmore's where he met H.D.

H.D. did not become publicly known as 'H.D.' until Pound, as *Poetry*'s foreign correspondent, signed her poems 'H.D. "Imagist"' before sending them off to Harriet Monroe in the early autumn of 1912. In January 1913, H.D.'s first poems appeared in *Poetry*, where Aldington's work had appeared two months previously. In the table of contents, she is listed as 'H.D., "Imagiste"', although the poems in the text are attributed merely to 'H.D.' She never again appears as 'H.D., "Imagiste"'; when Monroe publishes her a second time in February of 1914, she appears as 'H.D.' both in the table of contents and in the text. 'H.D.' was a literary persona, however, like the others she variously assumed (Rhoda Peter, D.A. Hill, Delia Alton, John Helforth), and when Aldington met her at Mrs Patmore's, she was Hilda Doolittle, just as after her marriage she was always Hilda Aldington.

H.D. was born in rural Bethlehem, Pennsylvania, on 10 September 1886. When she was nine, her father, Charles Doolittle, left his position as Professor of Astronomy and Mathematics at Lehigh University for a comparable position at the University of Pennsylvania; the family moved to Upper Darby, five miles west of Philadelphia. Here H.D. grew up in the countryside near a busy city, attending private schools in Philadelphia, then commuting for university to Bryn Mawr College for a year and a half (October 1905 through January 1907). In 1908–09, she enrolled at the University of Pennsylvania in the college course for teachers, but she did not pursue the programme.

From a previous marriage, Charles Doolittle had two sons, and with his second wife, Helen Wolle Doolittle, produced three more, one older than H.D. and two younger. H.D. thus defined herself in a predominantly masculine and professional household. She was sympathetic with her mother as the only other female and as a woman also defined by her relationships with the males in the fa}Ilm/Her mother appears, however, to have been somewhat passive and busy, having put aside her own interests in painting and music in order to assume the more conventional roles of wife and mother to a large family. She was a maternal and warm woman, religious but not fanatic, and at least passively supportive of her daughter in her intellectual aspirations and later unconventional life. H.D. was her father's favourite child, yet Charles Doolittle seems a preoccupied and cerebral figure in H.D.'s childhood. A serious man of real prominence in his field, he worked hard at odd hours in the Flower Observatory, and apparently had little time for active family life. He, however, actively encouraged his only daughter's formal education, particularly in science and mathematics, and must have approved an independence of spirit and seriousness of purpose that characterized the maturing H.D., who could romp with ease through the fields and woods near her home, hold her own with her brothers, and pursue academically French, German, Latin, and Greek as well as literature and the natural sciences.

The essentially rural experience of H.D.'s childhood fostered the intense sensitivity to nature which she shared with Aldington. She enjoyed the independence she gained as the result of being the only girl among boys in a large family in which she was encouraged both to excel physically and intellectually and to develop a spiritual response to the world. Particularly close to her brother Gilbert, two years her senior, she also had many female friends in the neighbourhood and at school, but seems to have sought out particular friends who became confidantes for periods of time, sharing with her chosen friend especially intimate and private experiences of a personal and often spiritual nature.

Thus H.D. like Aldington valued self-reliance and freedom. Her need for confidantes, however, distinguishes her from him in a significant respect, for although Aldington valued intimacy and deeply enjoyed close relationships, he seems to have been more self-contained than H.D., less willing to reveal himself to others, more controlled, less emotionally raw. This important difference explains in part why Aldington appears to have developed few intimate friends by the time he met H.D. in 1911; it also speaks to the difference in experience that H.D., six years Aldington's senior, brought to their relationship.

An account of Aldington's youth is an account of solitary experience and mentors: parents, occasionally sensitive teachers, older men who shared with him their libraries and wider knowledge of art, language, nature, history, and Europe. An account of H.D.'s life before 1911 is often an account of intense relationships with other people: her parents (who both seem to have been closer to her and more powerful influences in her life than Aldington's in his), her brothers, and particular friends. The most important of these early friends were Ezra Pound and Frances Gregg.

H.D. met Pound in 1901; she was fifteen and he a year older and already a freshman at the University of Pennsylvania. The two shared excellent educations which they both valued, having gained them both formally and informally, and a special sensitivity to poetry. They were young, exuberant, and independent people who enjoyed each other's company at social gatherings and during solitary walks in the woods. Just as later H.D. would turn repeatedly in her writing to her relationship with Aldington, fictionalizing him not only in *Palimpsest* (1926) and *Bid Me to Live* but in numerous other works and even in *Helen in Egypt*, the long poem published just before her death in 1961, so Pound also figures prominently in her writing throughout her life: he is the central figure in *End to Torment*, a memoir written in 1958, a character in *Helen in Egypt*, George Lowndes in *Hermione*, written in 1926–27. H.D.'s relationship with and eventual engagement to Pound (which seems to have been, like his engagements to other women, periodically official and unofficial) were interrupted several times by his work at Hamilton College, his term of college teaching in Indiana, and his travels in Europe, but she maintained an intense relationship with him into 1912. When H.D. left America for France in July of 1911, she travelled with Frances Gregg and her mother, and finally saw for herself the Europe which Pound must have described to her in great detail. In September she left the continent for England where she again, after Frances Gregg's departure for America in the autumn of 1911, resumed her close friendship with Pound.

H.D.'s relationship with Gregg began in 1910 when they met in Philadelphia and continued through the autumn of 1911. Like Aldington and Pound, Gregg is fictionalized in H.D.'s work, appearing as Fayne Rabb, for example, in *Hermione*, which is also dedicated to her. Gregg, for a time a student at the Pennsylvania Academy of Fine Arts, shared with H.D. an interest in poetry, but her relationship with H.D. seems to have been more sensual than intellectual, more passionate than cerebral, in contrast to H.D.'s relationship with Pound, which appears to have consisted of a great deal of emotionally charged philosophical discussion of themselves and of literature and art. H.D.'s friendship with Gregg was sexual in a way not evident in H.D.'s romantic friendship with Pound. If we can trust H.D.'s own fictionalized account of her relationship with him in *Hermione* as well as her memories of him in *End to Torment*, Pound was not finally an effectively passionate lover; despite some physical exchanges of intimacy, it seems unlikely that they ever slept together.[10] H.D.'s lesbian relationship with Gregg, on the other hand, seems to have fulfilled her sexually, at least for a time.[11]

Both friendships were fraught with difficulties, however, for all three participants had powerful personalities which tended to vie with each other for dominance rather than complement each other in mutual fulfilment and balance. Neither relationship permitted H.D. much independence and in their intensity evidently embroiled the partners in psychological tensions instead of evoking complementary and shared thoughts and feelings. Matters were made increasingly complex for H.D. by the intermittent and overlapping pace of these two friendships and by the simultaneous romantic attraction Pound and Gregg briefly shared with one another.

By the time Aldington and H.D. met in late 1911, they were both free and independent writers on their own in London. Through Pound, Aldington was beginning to meet other young poets and artists and to establish himself as a participant in England's modernist movement. Brigit Patmore and Aldington were having a passing affair.[12] She was not happy with her insensitive and impecunious husband, and had sought out young bohemian artists as an alternative society. Born in 1883, she was two years older than Pound, three years older than H.D., and nine years older than Aldington; she was thus seeking out interesting if younger contemporaries who had chosen less conventional paths for themselves than she had initially begun to follow. Patmore was also consciously rebelling against a philandering husband and a traditional married life. That she was a mother with two young sons gave her a privileged status as an experienced woman, enabling her to create a salon of sorts and to live her life with a measure of freedom not conceded to unmarried women in 1912. She enjoyed the full advantage of her special position.

H.D.'s affair with Frances Gregg was essentially over: early in 1912 Gregg began a lifelong romantic friendship with John Cowper Powys, and in April married his close friend Louis Wilkinson. She did invite H.D. to join her and her new husband on their European honeymoon, but Pound with some effort dissuaded H.D. from accompanying them. By 1911 Pound had begun courting Dorothy Shakespear, whom he married in April of 1914, and his relationship with H.D. had become more fraternal than romantic. Aldington, H.D., Pound, and Patmore met often in London in the early months of 1912. H.D. had decided to remain in England and to work on her writing; a small allowance from her parents gave her a measure of security and permitted her to spend long hours reading at the British Museum and relishing a city rich in art and literature. Patmore found her charming and sexually attractive, and probably encouraged her own lover in his attentions to H.D. out of a genuine willingness to foster romantic relationships but also impulsively as a way of loving H.D. vicariously through him. Aldington needed little outside encouragement, and H.D. responded to him as a colleague, an intellectual equal, and a romantic partner. Pound liked to introduce people; he liked to bring young artists together, to quicken one person with another, to send new work to editors, to electrify the chemistry of a gathering. He was often brilliant in doing all these things; he was more awkward in his reactions to the consequences of what he had done: initially cordial working relationships with editors often became after a time impossible, and he alternatively perplexed and outraged friends and acquaintances when he no longer controlled their activities. From his perspective, people seemed to have changed, or to be different from the way he had initially perceived them, or to be acting oddly. He never quite grasped that H.D. and Aldington were falling in love with each other, but he was finally willing to accept, even if he could not understand, their partnership.

In the spring of 1912 Aldington was working hard to establish himself as a literary critic and poet and was also regularly writing articles on subjects of more general interest. With the small monthly allowance from his parents, he managed to support himself. After H.D. left for a visit to France in May of 1912, an enamoured Aldington soon joined her. Pound was also in Paris that summer and the three sometimes toured the city together, although H.D. and Aldington were clearly at this point close companions and their relationship was deepening. They went regularly together to museums and their shared experience of both visual and literary art was an obvious element in their romance. H.D. showed her diary to Aldington, and during these months in Paris, it occasionally even became a joint enterprise: on 28 May 1912, Aldington wrote humorously in the diary about the art they were seeing; on 4 July, in response to a painting (probably a copy of the original in Florence) they had both seen in the Louvre, he composed a sonnet, 'Angelico's Coronation', and dedicated it 'To H.D.' In the octave he remarks on the Christian painting's attraction for him, its delicacy and calm; in the sestet, he rejects the peace of Fra Angelico for a hellenic life and love:

> ... the blithe wild earth,
> Scurry of satyr-hooves in dewy lands,
> Pan-pipes at noon, the lust, the shaggy fur,
> White bosoms & swift Dionysiac mirth.[13]

H.D. and Aldington thought of themselves as 'Greeks'; on 15 June H.D. noted in her diary that they had spent the morning in the Luxembourg Gardens, 'R deep in Greek choruses – H – sketching cast of Gladiator –' They probably also consummated their love that summer. On 10 June, H.D. recorded in her diary that when Pound joined them for tea, she said to him, '"You see I am taking your advice." (The advice weeks since in Luxembourg gardens "You better marry Richard").' On the facing page is a poem by H.D. beginning 'I love you. ...' The diary also reveals the emotionally intense but formally conventional poems both H.D. and Aldington were producing. They are writing on the Greek or personal subjects that would become characteristic of their mature poetry, but in strict meter and rhyme, formal elements both would soon reject for the *vers libre* of early modernism.[14] After their return to London in August, H.D. and Aldington went back to their respective work. Probably in early September 1912 their now famous encounter in a tea shop near the British Museum occurred: H.D. showed her poems to Pound and he, impressed with what he read, signed them 'H.D. "Imagiste"' and sent them off in October to *Poetry*.

Three of Aldington's early poems, also written before Pound labelled him an 'Imagiste', appeared as imagist works in *Poetry* in November 1912; H.D.'s poems appeared in January 1913. The two were by no means established poets from this time forward, but their debut in *Poetry* was a significant introduction of their verse to serious readers who sensed a new awakening of poetry at the very beginning of the modernist movement. Both H.D. and Aldington had published poems in newspapers,[15] but neither had received the critical consideration both would receive from now on. The translations on which each would work – free, poetic, and impressionistic renditions of Greek verse, more precise and conventional translations of contemporary French prose – became parallel if not occasionally collaborative efforts from this point, and their shared discussions of books and each other's work became an integral part of their increasingly intimate relationship.

In October of 1912 H.D. left for another trip to the continent: to Italy to meet her parents, Margaret Snively, and her father, who had made the trip to Europe with them. The Snivelys were neighbors of the Doolittles in Upper Darby and Margaret had been a close friend of H.D.'s since girlhood. The Doolittles missed their only daughter, whom they had not seen for fifteen months, and were curious and probably somewhat concerned about what she was doing and her future plans. They landed at Genoa, where their daughter greeted them, on 14 October; on 18 October the group left for Florence, stopping at Pisa on the way.[16] The Doolittles and the Snivelys saw the sights; Mrs Doolittle bought H.D. a dress; H.D., Professor Doolittle, and Margaret took Italian lessons together until the end of November. On 2 December, the Snivelys left Florence for Nice, where Dr Snively, an Episcopalian vicar, had an appointment; Margaret remained there with her father until his death in January 1914, when she moved to England.[17] On 4 December 1912, the Doolittles took the train from Florence to Rome. On 5 December, they began their sightseeing, and Mrs Doolittle noted that there was 'mail for Hilda'.

In H.D.'s absence, Aldington worked furiously in London, managing before the end of the year to persuade A.R. Orage, editor of *The New Age*, to accept a proposed series of articles on Italy. With this small measure of security he left London for the continent, arriving in Rome in mid-December. H.D. and Aldington did not return to London until August of 1913, and their eight months of traveling essentially together, primarily in Italy but also in France, took thsem as far south as Naples. This period was not the family visit that Pound felt the Doolittles expected;[18] Aldington was increasingly in love with H.D. and she increasingly inclined to him, although according to Pound H.D. was influenced by her parents[19] and Aldington finally needed Pound's permission to pursue his courtship seriously.[20] Even as late as May 1913, Pound observed rather insistently that despite H.D.'s time alone with Aldington, 'she doesn't seem much more in love'; with patent obtuseness, Pound declared the next day, 'I think they *must* be in love.'[21]

They were in love. Pound is not a particularly reliable source for this period. H.D. in her few surviving letters to others from this time tended to write of the sights and climate she experienced and does not mention Aldington.[22] Aldington is similarly discreet in his many postcards to his father and sisters during his travels, never once mentioning the Doolittles or H.D. by name nor even indicating that he is courting someone; his postcards refer to his work, the sights he is seeing, the weather, his changes of address.[23] Both writers are also reticent about this period in their later autobiographical work. H.D. does not discuss this trip in *End to Torment*, for example, which focuses on her early relationship with Pound. In *Life for Life's Sake*, Aldington writes that he left London in December because of the fog as well as because of a postcard from 'a friend in Genoa' (clearly H.D.) telling him that in Italy the blossoming almond trees 'will be full out in a few weeks'.[24] He does not mention spending most of his trip abroad with H.D., but focuses instead on amusing characters, local sights, and the fine climate in conveying the beauty and delight he discovered during these months in the south. He indicates with only slight ambiguity that it is Italy he is in love with rather than a woman, writing that 'we can never quite regain the first fine careless rapture of discovering Italy. Perhaps the course of true love runs all the truer for not being smooth; and very possibly my enjoyment of these wanderings was made keener because I had been forced to wait so long, overcome difficulties and take risks. In spite of very high expectations I was not disappointed.'[25] While Aldington is writing here of his affection for Italy and his financial constraints, he is also equating the experience of Italy with the realization of his love for H.D. He implies that their relationship, despite their insecure finances and the presence of other people and even of other lovers, was like the almond trees on the postcard about to come into full bloom. Further, H.D. had for years identified herself with trees. Pound may well have called her 'Dryad' as early as the poem 'The Tree', which he wrote for her and gave to her bound together with the other poems in 'Hilda's Book' in 1907; surely Aldington called her 'Dryad' in 1913. Thus the 'friend's' postcard increases in significance and becomes an erotic invitation to join H.D. in Italy.

It is important to see the Aldingtons' marriage as a love match between equals. The Aldingtons' courtship deserves particular attention because of its misrepresentation by Pound and its at best oblique presentation by Aldington and H.D. themselves. A detailed account vividly reveals their love and its development. On 12 December 1912, Mrs Doolittle notes that H.D. was spending time with her 'English friends'; on 16 December, Mrs Doolittle writes, 'Hilda had tea with her English friends', Aldington presumably among them by this time. Mrs Doolittle's travel diary for 1912–13 is an important source for understanding Aldington's and H.D.'s early love. She was clearly an outsider, but her entries are regular and specific though brief and generally without commentary. The details reveal the texture of H.D.'s and Aldington's days and Mrs Doolittle's affectionate encouragement of their courtship. While Pound's version suggests all sorts of tensions within and without the relationship, Mrs Doolittle's diary conveys a much happier and smoother friendship. On 18 December, she noted that 'Hilda was feeling particularly well.' On 20 December, she mentioned Aldington for the first time: 'Hilda out with R.A.' H.D. seems to have spent much of each day sightseeing with Aldington, occasionally with her father and mother, but generally without them. By 24 December, Mrs Doolittle was calling him 'Richard'. When the Doolittles left Rome for Naples on 12 February 1913, Aldington followed two days later, and he and H.D. resumed their pattern of days out together at museums and local sights, then tea and dinner at which her parents might join them. When Professor and Mrs Doolittle left Naples for Venice on 6 March, she noted that 'H. and R.A. came on later train.' On 14 March, the Doolittles and Aldington took a boat to Capri, then travelled across the island to Anacapri, where they all stayed.

Throughout their travels Mrs Doolittle seems to have been quite close to her daughter. She evidently accepted and respected H.D.'s intimacy with Aldington, confining her maternal solicitude to buying H.D. nice clothing: she purchased her daughter a dress in Florence (25 October 1912), blue fabric for another dress in Rome (9 December 1912), and material 'for Hilda's new nightdress' in Capri (19 March 1913). On 23 March, Mrs Doolittle wrote 'make plans – Hilda remains here [at Anacapri] while we [the Doolittles] go to Sicily'. The Doolittles took the boat to Naples on 25 March, went on to Sicily, returning to Naples on 11 April, then taking the train to Rome. On 14 April, the Doolittles arrived for a brief stay in Bologne, finally reaching Venice on 17 April. H.D. and Aldington remained unchaperoned in Anacapri for six weeks; Mrs Doolittle's diary reveals no signs that she was the least upset with her daughter's decision nor could she have been the least deluded about the intimacy of H.D.'s relationship with Aldington. Mrs Doolittle regularly noted her correspondence with her daughter, and letters and postcards passed constantly between them throughout March and April of 1913. On 4 May, Mrs Doolittle wrote, 'Ezra P. – looked for us – found us here [in Venice] – we came back to the hotel together – he had dinner with us – stayed until midnight.' On 5 May, 'Ezra called this afternoon + had dinner again with us.' The impression conveyed is that Pound was rather lonely. On 7 May, H.D. and Aldington arrived in Venice, and during the next week they and Pound and the Doolittles spent time together; on 8 May, 'Ezra gave a gondola party this evening ... wonderful! Hilda and Richard in one + E + I in another – back 11:30–'. Professor Doolittle left for the United States on 15 May. On 21 May, Mrs Doolittle was again devoting herself to her daughter's wardrobe: 'Bought blue crepe for blouse for Hilda – have nearly finished it.'

Aldington seems to have grown quite close to Mrs Doolittle in late May and June. He and she and H.D. travelled together to attend a Bach festival at Verona on 30 May, moving on from there to Lake Garda on 4 June. On 5 June, Mrs Doolittle noted that she 'Had a long row on lake with Richard'; on 6 June, she was making and having a dressmaker make clothes for H.D.; on 7 June, 'Richard took me out boating'; on 10 June, 'after dinner Richard took us on the lake – moonlight + very beautiful –'. On 22 June 1913, they left the lake for Verona, where Professor Doolittle met them on 25 June; Aldington went with them part way, then continued on to Paris. On 6 July, H.D. left her parents in the Alps for Paris; her mother commented, 'I know H. will enjoy settling down for a little but we shall miss her.'

The Doolittles went on to tour Switzerland, Austria, and Germany; Aldington and H.D. spent the rest of July together in Paris. After their return together to London in early August, they moved into separate flats at Churchwalk, Kensington: H.D. lived at Number 6, Aldington at Number 8; Pound lived at Number 10. The Doolittles arrived in London on 4 September and were greeted by H.D. and Aldington. Professor Doolittle soon became ill, however, and the Doolittles stayed in town only long enough to celebrate H.D.'s twenty-seventh birthday on 10 September before going on to Bournemouth, where it was thought Professor Doolittle could best recover. On 19 September, Mrs Doolittle recorded: 'Eventful day. Richard and Hilda came for the day to talk about the future – Such a lovely time + I am happy for them both!' She added exuberantly that she felt 'happy + peaceful!!'

On 28 September, the Doolittles returned to London to 'prepare for [H.D.'s] marriage'. H.D. and her mother went shopping daily for 'towels +c.' and 'to get Hilda's things together' (30 September 1913). On 18 October 1913, in the presence of Pound and the Doolittles, Aldington and H.D. were married. Shortly after the wedding, her parents returned to the United States and the Aldingtons together moved into a flat of their own at 5 Holland Place Chambers; Pound soon moved, too, into a flat just across the hall.

Pound's intrusive presence during the Aldingtons' courtship and the early months of their marriage was disconcerting and sometimes awkward for them. The direct influence Pound had on H.D.'s formative work before 1908 was, like their engagement, long since over, and H.D. had grown into a poet in her own right. After the Greggs' departure for America in the autumn of 1911, she had begun regular and disciplined work on her poetry, spending daily hours reading in the British Library, starting on her translations as exercises in language, experimenting with free verse and classical material. A significant part of Aldington's and H.D.'s attraction for each other was their independently arrived at but shared ideas of poetry: its subjects, purposes, techniques, language, emotional effects. The many versions of Pound's initiation of imagism all suggest that when he read H.D.'s poems over the famous tea, they appeared new to him: he was apparently not familiar with them in earlier drafts, and his enthusiasm arose in part because of his genuine surprise at what he immediately claimed in his naming of H.D. and the movement as his own discovery and invention. It seems likely that he read Aldington's poems at the same meeting.[26]

The Aldingtons and Pound were active participants in the exhilarating literary ferment in this prewar period in London. Their many mutual friends – Ford Madox Hueffer (later Ford), Violet Hunt, May Sinclair, Frank Flint, John Gould Fletcher, John Cournos, Brigit Patmore – contributed to the development of early modernist verse in the many informal discussions about art which occurred not only in tea shops but in Soho restaurants, at evening parties at Brigit Patmore's, and at each other's flats. Still, Aldington and H.D. were working together intimately in an atmosphere of mutual exchange and influence that was particularly important to them personally and to the shaping of their poetry. In his desire to direct and to control, and sometimes by his mere presence, Pound was an intruder. Aldington recalled in *Life for Life's Sake* that in the spring of 1912, 'Ezra had been butting in on our studies and poetic productions, with alternative encouragements and the reverse, according to his mood',[27] and H.D., too, remembered in *End to Torment* her disconcerted surprise when she discovered Pound examining the apartment across the narrow hall from the Aldingtons'; he was looking for a place to live with Dorothy Shakespear after their wedding: 'I found the door [to the opposite flat] open one day before they were married, and Ezra there. "What – what are you doing?" I asked. He said he was looking for a place where he could fence with Yeats. I was rather taken aback when they actually moved in. It was so near.' She added rather pointedly, 'But we went soon after [in January 1915] to Hampstead. ... After that we did not see much of Ezra and the Kensington group.'[28]

Initially with Pound's help, but soon quite independently of him, Aldington and H.D. established themselves as writers in these prewar years. *The New Freewoman*, owned and edited by Dora Marsden with help from Harriet Shaw Weaver, had become interested in imagism through Pound's influence. Rebecca West devoted an article to the movement in the issue of 15 August 1913; the next issue (1 September 1913) included poems by Aldington, H.D., and other imagist poets as well as an article by Hueffer ('On Poetry') and 'In Meter' by Pound, in which he discussed Robert Frost's *A Boy's Will* and verse by D.H. Lawrence and Walter de la Mare. More of Aldington's poems appeared on 15 September, and he began to write book reviews for *The New Freewoman* with the 1 October issue. Thereafter Aldington wrote topical articles on English life, new art, and modern literature. Pound also appeared as a regular writer of columns on art and poetry, and although H.D.'s work did not again appear in *The New Freewoman*, even three stories by Frances Gregg were published there on 1 December 1913. Aldington and H.D. had found in this periodical a very small but influential outlet for their ideas and work, and by the end of the year Aldington had carved out a place for himself on its staff.

In January of 1914, *The New Freewoman* changed its name to *The Egoist* and Aldington was listed as assistant editor on its masthead. Pound continued to exert influence at the paper, but his work came to appear here less and less often, and Aldington's regular reviews and translations begin to reveal his wide interests in continental (particularly French) and classical literature as well as in modernist writing. Poems by Aldington appeared in *Poetry* in January 1914; two poems by H.D. appeared there in February. In the same month, with Pound as editor, *Des Imagistes*, an anthology of imagist poetry, was published in the United States; Aldington and H.D. were well represented with several poems each.

The Aldingtons had come to know Amy Lowell, also represented in *Des Imagistes*, primarily through correspondence. By the spring of 1914 they were exchanging letters regularly, and Pound's control of the imagist movement as editor, advertiser, and general advocate was waning while his place in the Aldingtons' personal life was becoming increasingly cumbersome. In a letter in Aldington's hand but signed by both him and H.D., Aldington wrote to Amy Lowell that Pound lay on their couch and claimed he had 'cerebral gout'. Aldington added only half humorously, 'Perhaps Ezra is a little cracked.'[29] When Lowell visited London in the summer of 1914, she met the Aldingtons frequently and plans began for a second imagist anthology. Pound refused to participate, explicitly in reaction to Amy Lowell, whom he rejected out of hand on account of her corpulence, patrician Boston background, and inconsistently strong verse. Psychologically, Pound needed to maintain a control that true group effort denied, and he redirected his energies elsewhere with some superiority and hostility. Aldington points out additionally in *Life for Life's Sake* that Lowell 'was fed up with Ezra. So were others.'[30]

In fact, Aldington was chiefly in charge of the subsequent imagist anthologies that appeared in 1915, 1916, and 1917. While some of the contributors were American (Lowell, H.D., and Fletcher), most of the poets whose work appeared in these collections were either British (Aldington, Flint, and D.H. Lawrence) or were living in England at the time.[31] Through Amy Lowell, the Aldingtons met Lawrence in July of 1914, and their intellectual and personal friendship with him became important for both of them.

The Aldingtons' marriage seems to have been a good one in 1914 and 1915. They managed to extricate themselves in large measure from past relationships and to work and love together as a couple. H.D. became pregnant in August of 1914 and, despite the war, Aldington did not feel immediately threatened: Britain had no military draft at the time. He published his first book of verse, *Images*, in 1915, and both he and H.D. turned more and more toward a rural life beyond the intense war atmosphere of London. They moved in January of 1915 from Kensington to a larger flat in Hampstead, and their letters to others during this period speak of frequent trips to 'the country', generally to Surrey (where James Whitall had a house) or Rye (where Aldington's parents lived) or west toward Devon and Cornwall and the country Aldington had known affectionately in childhood. The new place in Hampstead also offered them more than a physical distance from central London. Aldington wrote to Amy Lowell on 1 February 1915: 'We like it much better out here as we have a larger flat with a real bathroom & a kitchen. I surprise my useless American wife with my skill & accuracy in cooking potatoes & mending chairs – they are admirable avocations for clearing one's mind & in this clearer atmosphere, away from Kensington squabbles & intrigues I feel more hopeful.'

In May, the Aldingtons' child was born dead, an extremely traumatic experience which continued to haunt them both for years. This was a pivotal time in their marriage and deserves attention at length not only in the context of the Aldingtons' immediate personal lives but in terms of the larger social events which were inextricably related to both H.D.'s and Aldington's understanding of the child's death and their relationship at this point.

Britain declared war against Germany on 4 August 1914, and the continental Europe with which Aldington identified himself – particularly France and Italy – became embroiled in battles whose horror soon outbalanced the instant patriotism and enthusiastic enlistment of huge numbers of men in the late summer. The Battle of the Marne occurred on 5–12 September; First Ypres followed in October. The Germans bombed the Yorkshire coast on 16 December; the first airship raid on England came on 19 January 1915. Aldington had no hallowed respect for British institutions nor any special political objection to Germany, but he felt an obligation to the other men of his generation who were fighting and dying. For Aldington the war would always be a personal experience, and although he had little in common with his fellow soldiers, he would always feel a deep bond of male companionship and respect beyond intellectual affinity with those who had participated in the Great War.

The declaration of war created a somewhat different situation for H.D. She loved her husband deeply and supported his responses to the war, but she was an American woman, and the United States would not enter the war for three more years. Like Aldington, she had no strong political feelings, but direct participation in the war was not for her as a woman either an opportunity or a direct threat. The possibility of returning to the States for the duration became a constant question intensified by her husband's impending conscription in 1916. Thus the war introduced tensions into their marriage, for it stressed their differences in nationality and gender; it also replaced the social and intellectual atmosphere of prewar London, which had nourished their relationship, with a political and military consciousness antithetical to both their natures but directly affecting them.

The first years of their companionship occurred during an era of feminist ferment to which both of them were sympathetic. Suffragette riots and demonstrations characterized the period, and the issue of votes for women came to a head early in 1912. The House of Commons rejected the franchise on 28 March 1912, and a second time on 6 May 1913. *The New Freewoman* was a clearly feminist paper, which was not founded as a platform for early modernist literature but as a forum for feminist and related causes. *The New Freewoman*, like its predecessor in 1911, *The Freewoman*, and its successor *The Egoist*, published articles on birth control, female and male sexuality and sexual orientation, childbirth, women's economic situation, free love, and the suffragette movement. These were all issues in the air and in the press, and H.D. and Aldington not only knew about them but characteristically responded to them in personal terms.

Years later, in one of his six novels, *Very Heaven*, Aldington reveals through a central character much like himself the effect of the feminism of this period on a man's notion of womanhood. The young Christ Heylin addresses the woman with whom he has fallen in love:

> Let's admit that the attraction between us is a sexual one. If it weren't for our sex, we'd be no more than friends. It's the fact of sexual desire which compels us to seek each other, which gives us this sense of ecstatic happiness. I'm not going to fall into the common literary sublimation, and pretend to myself and you that I want you and adore you for something you're not. I don't want you to be a blessed damosel or even a sweet girl graduate in golden hair. You're not a violet by a mossy stone or one of the brightest stars in all the heavens. Under that pretty blue gown of yours is the naked body of a human woman. I rejoice in it. I'm glad you're a real woman, I want you as a woman. I know that you are exquisitely and wonderfully made of millions of cells, that your heart keeps them alive by beating blood to them, that there are subtle chemical processes in you, that you have periods, that you have a womb and ovaries and breasts. And all that is the true wonder, the real beauty, the miracle of wonders, that you are you![32]

This sort of awareness in all likelihood informed Aldington's attitudes toward sexuality and female identity in the early years of his marriage to H.D.; he was certainly no traditional or conventional male. The atmosphere of conformity and the impression of a nation in uniform encouraged both Aldington and H.D. to turn inward, to withdraw, to retreat. Neither had an affinity for large groups anyway; both could be aloof and shy, though they had good friends during these years: John Cournos was friendly with both of them, though particularly close to H.D., while Frank Flint became Aldington's intimate intellectual companion and confidante.

The baby's death resulted in a breakdown of the conventional unit of father, mother, and child and bound H.D. and Aldington more intensely to each other as individuals who had shared a painful experience. They were both private people, but Aldington did write to Amy Lowell of their loss on 21 May 1915; after a paragraph about business matters, he confesses: 'I have been rather distressed, because Hilda was delivered of a little girl still-born, about 2. am. this morning. She (Hilda) was in a good nursing home & had an obstetrical specialist. I haven't seen the doctor, but the nurse said it was a beautiful child & they can't think why it didn't live. It was very sturdy but wouldn't breathe. Poor Hilda is very distressed, but is recovering physically.' The experience also made Aldington aware of how fragile H.D. could be. Her distress was natural, of course, but he sensed as well as shared her acute grief while realising that he was somehow tougher, more able to handle emotional pain. From this point on in their relationship, Aldington assumed a role as protector not evident earlier. He was always a champion of H.D.'s poetry when she was more hesitant about its strengths, but now he became aware that she also sometimes needed someone as a buffer between her and the harshness of reality, the brutality of experience that could harm her more easily than it could him. By nature more practical and organised than she, he seems to have decided upon a conscious retreat from London into the country. When H.D. left the nursing home on 11 June, they immediately drove to Surrey, not returning to London until late August. That winter, however, they gave up their flat in Hampstead and moved to Devon, where they remained until after Aldington entered the army.

Aldington had considered enlisting in the national wave of patriotism following Britain's declaration of war, but because of a hernia operation in 1908, which he mentioned to a soldier supervising the crowd at the gates of a local armoury, he was told that it was unlikely that he would be passed as medically fit to train with the first troops going abroad. This brief vision of military bureaucracy and masses of men milling about was sufficient to deter him in any event; for a short while, he still felt disposed to serve, but by December of 1914, he felt personally threatened and oppressed by the war atmosphere. He wrote to Lowell on 7 December:

> This war is killing us all, Amy. As Gourmont says our word is 'wait'; but the daily waiting, the anxiety, the constant strain is making us all 'old.' Only just over four months! And those last four months seem immeasurably longer to me than all the rest of my life. I cannot concentrate my mind for long enough on beautiful things to be able to write good poetry – there is too much at stake in Belgium and France for me to forget them long. For this is the great war, the war of democracy against autocracy, of the individual against the state, of the Anglo-Latin civilization against the Prussian, even of vers libre against academic meters! ... If we lose I don't see the use of my going on with my work – logically I should have to become a professional soldier. So you see, I can't work well at present.

If 1915 was a transitional year during which the Aldingtons withdrew in large measure from the intensities of bohemian London and turned inward and toward each other, 1916 promised imminent conscription and more challenging changes in their situation. The war atmosphere may have threatened Aldington's creative powers, but actual combat would threaten his life. Many options, all disruptive, presented themselves: the Aldingtons both seriously considered going to the United States for the duration.[33] Aldington persuaded his father, then working as a minor official in the ministry of munitions, to try to get him immediately into officers' training, where impersonal army life might be less brutalizing, but his father could do little.[34] Aldington made a variety of legal arrangements granting H.D. power of attorney should he be wounded, declared missing in action, or killed, and wrote a will.[35] They debated whether he should enlist so as to have perhaps some choice in how he would serve, or wait until the eventual passage of the conscription act and take his chances.[36] H.D. considered leaving for Philadelphia alone when her husband entered the army; she feared the possible forced labour scheme that might compel able women without families to work in factories or otherwise support the war effort.[37]

In February of 1916, the Aldingtons moved from Hampstead to a small cottage in north Devon. They had little money, but found the country an escape of sorts. H.D. wrote to Amy Lowell: 'You see, this war period, our *joint* income is about 3 pounds a week –

we live here extremely comfortably on it.' The pressures of war still intruded, however, and H.D. continues: 'I can not write you what I think, feel + know about this terrible war. We are all weakened by this continual strain!' Before she closes, referring to her baby's death, she adds that she finds that things have been particularly stressful since she was 'ill' the previous year.[38]

In March a draft of the Military Service Act of 1916 was passed; in May *Some Imagist Poets, 1916* appeared; on 24 May conscription of married men began. By June 1916 there were 1,400,000 British troops on an eighty-mile battlefield in France. With conscription imminent, Aldington accepted the inevitable, and in order to be with his friend Carl Fallas, 'so that at least … [they each] should have someone to talk to',[39] Aldington and Fallas enlisted together at Lynton in late May. After a brief respite, he and Fallas were inducted in late June as infantry privates in the Eleventh Battalion of the Devonshire Regiment and sent to train in Worget Camp in Wareham, Dorset.

The period between February and June of 1916 was a particularly significant one for H.D.'s and Aldington's marriage. H.D. was recovering somewhat from the trauma of losing their child and was preparing her first volume of poems for publication; Constable accepted the book by the end of February, although because of paper shortages it did not appear until the autumn. She and Aldington took long walks on the Devon hills, and in the spring and summer regularly swam naked with friends in the sea nearby. John Cournos frequently visited from London and introduced them to his acquaintances, Carl and Florence Fallas, who lived in the neighbourhood. Both Aldingtons responded sensitively to the raw nature surrounding them and enjoyed the independence and freedom of

Aldington in May 1916, shortly before he entered the army. This is one of two photographs Aldington had taken the day he went to Lynton to enlist with Carl Fallas

rural life. They were writing poetry and working together on translations. There seems to have been an aura of abandon about these months as well as an atmosphere of impending doom; a sense of frivolity and danger; a combination of productive mental and physical exertion and self-indulgence. This period was the beginning of H.D.'s flirtatious letters to Cournos, in which she told him in turn how much she cared for her husband and how close she and Cournos were to each other spiritually and sensually. Aldington was alternately resigned and frantic. On the one hand he was concerned about H.D. and made practical plans for their present and future life; on the other he was no longer able to protect her from their inevitable separation or his own anticipated suffering.

While H.D. was fragile and easily emotionally shaken in that experiences often affected her unusually deeply and over a long period of time, she was also a perceptive woman of great intelligence whose good sense could often co-exist with, if it could not curb, her intense emotional responses. She was domestically impractical, a poor speller, and impulsive, and sometimes seemed to function on an airy plane that at best could be called 'spiritual', at worst childish and irresponsible; but she was also an energetic and well-disciplined poet with a broad sense of humour and the intelligence to understand both people and ideas. She was stronger than those who tried to protect her sometimes thought she was; she could if necessary rise to the occasion that demanded her inner strengths.

Aldington, in contrast, was more practical, also intelligent but more assertive, firm, and clear about his convictions. The sensitivity and passionate joy he brought to experience were aspects of his character he tended to save for private and intimate sharing. He was vulnerable and capable of deep emotional responsiveness, but tended to cover his sensitivity with good humour, camaraderie, and hard work. He was tender and sensual, but preferred to shelter this part of his nature not out of concern for his public appearance but out of a sense of self-protection.

And he was young. At twenty-three he was literary editor of an influential journal, a poet whose work appeared regularly in America and England, co-editor of several anthologies of imagist verse, a budding literary critic and translator; he was a married man, ready to assume the responsibilities of fatherhood, and felt that everything he cared about would soon be destroyed or put in limbo for an indefinite period, perhaps never again to be recovered. Many of the lofty ideas he and H.D. shared about art and relationships seemed irrelevant or unrealisable in the world of 1916. They had always believed in 'free love', in their own union as greater than any other relationship, even a sexual one, either could have. They were not prepared for the emotional havoc such naive ideas can create when put into action. If Aldington's affair with Flo Fallas during that spring and summer was foolish in retrospect, it was not merely impulsive; rather, it can be understood as an attempt to put into practice – as time seemed to be running out – an idea both he and H.D. were convinced was realistic and fair.

Aldington's attraction to Flo Fallas seems to have been almost exclusively sexual. Soon after he met her in March of 1916, he wrote to Frank Flint about how erotic she appeared to him, but he also shared his resolve not to sleep with her, feeling that such an act would disturb H.D.[40] By June he wrote Flint that he and Flo had twice consummated their attraction, but he was jocular, sharing with Flint his fleeting panic when the postman knocked at the Fallas' door while he and Flo were in bed together. He did not mention her again in letters to Flint; indeed a deep respect and love for H.D. are repeatedly conveyed. The affair was disturbing to H.D., but Aldington evidently did not consider his feelings for Flo Fallas so serious as his wife sometimes suspected them to be.

H.D.'s letters to John Cournos reveal her response. She was not initially hurt, but felt that if the affair with Flo were something that Aldington wanted or needed, then she approved. She did not at first consider it a serious attraction or a threat or a particularly disturbing fact. By the autumn, however, she was fearful that perhaps it was a more serious relationship, although there was little evidence for this conclusion and Aldington assured her that her concern was unfounded. She wrote Cournos that Aldington had written to her: "'Hang Flo & damn Carl. ... For God's sake, love your Faun.'" [41]

Neither H.D. nor Aldington fully realized the repercussions an affair might have. It introduced further tensions into an already difficult situation and resolved nothing, although it did partially assuage some of Aldington's frustrations with the military by providing a fleeting distraction. While Aldington was apparently fairly open and he hoped clear with H.D. about his feelings for Flo Fallas, H.D. was more concerned than she felt she could let him know; she felt ironically that she had to protect him from the brutality of soldiering and war and serve as a peaceful, comforting, and inspiring centre for him. She wanted to be supportive at a time when much of his identity was stripped from him. Their relationship was precious to them both, and the fact of Aldington's affair, with whatever feelings he may have had for Flo Fallas, faded away.

Army life was devastating to Aldington. He felt isolated from the other men, not superior so much as unbridgeably different. As a professional poet who managed to earn a living by exposing his soul in language and who shared his ideas and perceptions of literature and life with others through the relatively safe medium of the written word, scrubbing filthy floors and peeling potatoes was anesthetizing labour. The long hours of physical drill left little time or energy for reading or writing, and while he soon came to appear extraordinarily physically fit, he also seemed hurt and emotionally hollow. As he had anticipated in his letter to Amy Lowell, the army brutalized the poet in him. He wrote to Flint in July, 'I am on the go from 5:30AM to 7PM & have only time for one note as a rule & that goes to H.D.' [42] In the same month he wrote Cournos that he hoped by diligent work and perhaps through the influence of friends to gain a promotion that would keep him in England for further training. He continued only half jokingly: 'There is just a chance; and I do want to live, for my own sake, of course, but also for H.D.'s. What would she do without me?' [43] Later in July in an undated letter he wrote Cournos again:

Yesterday I had a horrible experience, which please don't tell H.D. In the morning I was down for Officers Mess Fatigue. I had to beat carpets, clean windows, polish forks and spoons and, worst of all, scrub floors. I don't mind scrubbing like tables &c. which Carl [Fallas] and I do for our beat every morning. But at this fatigue I was put to scrub the stone floor of one of the filthiest kitchens I ever saw in my life. It was deep with grease, soot and mess of all kinds. The bucket was greasy & the scrubbing rags so unspeakably filthy & slimy that it made me nauseated to touch them and I shuddered every time I had to plunge my hand into the pail of loathsome, greasy water. For a while it broke me, old chap, and I'm not too ashamed to tell you that for a moment or two I just bent my head & sobbed. It was so bitter a humiliation, so sordid a Golgotha. ... I am very glad that I am not an officer, very glad. It is so much better to be hurt than to hurt.

Do please keep this from H.D. I wouldn't have her know for worlds...

Aldington needed here to share his experience with one of the few people he now thought of as his close friends; the others were Frank Flint, Alec Randall (whom he had met at University College and who now worked in military intelligence) and H.D.

Simultaneously, however, he wanted to hide his suffering from H.D., to protect her if he could, identifying himself with her, for he would have avoided his own pain if it had been possible. What he could not avoid himself, he could at least try to prevent from hurting H.D. He continued to feel overwhelmingly reduced by the military experience. He wrote to Cournos on 14 August 1916: 'You must try to forgive my silence. On weekdays I have so little energy after work that I can only write one letter & that nearly always goes to H.D. ... don't, *don't* let yourself be shoved into this. Better retire to U.S. for 6 months or so, than get this soul-destroying mechanism on to you.'

Aldington was always closer to Amy Lowell than was H.D., although he often found her presumptuous and overbearing, and he even confided in her during this period. On 30 June, he wrote her of his entry into the army: 'I am afraid poor Hilda is very lonely without me; I feel the separation very keenly.' In August he wrote: 'H.D. has been truly wonderful: her affection and unselfish devotion have been the prop of my existence.' He thanked her for a recent letter which 'helped me to get through a hard day'; he told her that there was much about the details of his life that he felt he could not share with her because of military security, but he reiterated his desolation amid army routine, concluding: 'I look at the flowers of a wild rose which grows in the hedge of a field at the far end of the camp. There is still much for me – clouds, rain and sky, distant hills and trees, the early morning sun & the quiet twilight, red poppies & yellow daisies in a deserted corner of the camp – and on Saturday & Sunday afternoon, the wild flowers & scent and deep peace of country lanes. These things are poignant in their beauty, so exquisitely indifferent to humanity, as, perhaps, a poet must be!'[44]

H.D. also confided in Lowell her feelings about her husband's military experience and its affect on him and their relationship. On 31 July 1916, she wrote, 'You cannot imagine how starved he is – how eager for news of people and books.' In August H.D. confessed that when Aldington visited her during his weekends off, 'it is hard for me to face his tragic eyes alone!'[45] On 13 October, H.D. wrote, 'let me thank you again for placing R.'s work for him. You can not realize what this means to him – and as my one struggle is to make him feel he is not being forgotten, is not dropping out of the world, (our world) you can hardly over-estimate my sense of gratitude to you.' H.D. was more open with John Cournos about her feelings and Aldington's adjustment to the military. After a weekend visit from her husband, H.D. wrote:

> It is curious and wonderful and tragic to watch his developement [*sic*]. One thing is sure: he has not been hurt by all this brutal regime – only at first, it was terrible – his eagerness and his fear to speak of books, of people, of the beauty we all love. And last night was terrible – the rending, as it were, of spirit & flesh – but this morning he was calm and beautiful – and said he knew now he could come back to life – that he wouldn't lose his hold. He had hallucinations at first – I think his suffering must have been awful. But I feel I have given him hope again – and he cares so intensely, so deeply that his very love may help him to live – may bring him back. ... I have suffered so in imagination that perhaps this agonny [*sic*] of mind has recalled – redeemed as it were my own sanity – Richard's beauty.[46]

H.D. and Aldington felt deep respect and affection for each other, but they also psychically seem to have identified themselves each with the other, almost symbiotically equating their experiences and emotional and spiritual selves. For example, on 4 August 1916, H.D. wrote Cournos that she had beside her 'a beautiful letter of Richards [*sic*] which has given me great hope'; she quoted from it at length: '"The world, the great herd

Aldington in uniform, probably taken in Devon or in London
during the autumn of 1916

of men hates beauty: we who love beauty can but die for it, or live, if necessary. The
world, our world, is beautiful, but if we are the Sampadaphoroi (*tourch bearers* [*sic*]) we
must be equal to the least soldier who dies at his post. Yours is a great task ... be strong,
swift and brave; there is no hope but be strong."' At about the same time she noted in an
undated letter to Cournos, 'It is hard for me to face this spiritual loneliness of R. alone.'
On 9 August, she wrote:

> R. seems to grow spiritually stronger – we must be patient, very patient and tender. He is
> strange and even with me closed into himself – and then suddenly some curious feeling,
> some intense longing, some little sign of affection. He is *born*, but at times not conscious of
> his spirit-and he suffers when we think him indifferent or merely glad! – He says at first he
> cried, desperate tears, when he looked over toward Corfe Castle [the town where H.D.
> was staying] – He is like a wounded animal: – He is like some great, beautiful, clean,
> sensual beast, captured galled with chains. –

In another undated letter at about the same time, H.D. wrote explicitly to Cournos about
her relationship with Aldington: 'With R. I feel older, mature, not maternal, I hope, but
mature, ready to help, desirous only to obliterate myself if my help is not wanted! I feel
him Greek and masculine and intellectual and strong and perhaps at times cruel. I feel

H.D., probably taken in 1917 at 44 Mecklenburgh Square

him very passionate and terribly sad, and in the midst of a new growth which is tearing and causing him pain.'

The Aldingtons lived these difficult months at a high emotional pitch, and their experience was intensified by their proximity and frequent visits during the summer and autumn of 1916. Called up at the end of June, Aldington was sent for initial training to Wareham in Dorset. Within a few weeks, H.D. gave up Woodland Cottage, Martinhoe, Parracombe, in north Devon, where the Aldingtons had been living since February of 1916, and in July took rooms in the town of Corfe Castle to be near her husband. She stayed in the small village in the shadow of the ruined twelfth-century fortress into the autumn. Because he efficiently performed his military duties, Aldington was selected for additional training as a noncommissioned officer; he was reprieved from the trenches for a few additional weeks and so did not go to the continent in August as he had first anticipated. After the six-day leave following his basic training, which he and H.D. spent in London,[47] he went to a camp near Manchester in mid-September for further training while H.D. returned to Corfe Castle, where Aldington later also returned to complete his training.

H.D. analysed at length her relationship with her husband in the letters she wrote to Cournos during the autumn of 1916. This correspondence conveys clearly the tensions and intimacy of the Aldingtons' marriage. Her self-analysis is important, too, for it reveals the complex personality to which Aldington was responding in his later letters. On 13 September 1916, H.D. wrote: 'I have faith in my work. What I want at times is to feel faith in my self, in my mere physical presence in the world, in my personality. I feel my work is beautiful, I have a deep faith in it, an absolute faith. But sometimes I have no faith in my own self.'[48] In an undated letter written in the same month, she described her husband as 'a golden, clear naked Greek', and on 3 October she stated that 'Richard is the very core of my life.' Yet in an undated letter in the early autumn she acknowledged the tensions between them: 'I am often unhappy to think that my complicated nature has led R. to think I am unhappy'; she continued, 'I seem to have separated love and peace in my mind.'[49] Despite the Aldingtons' love and respect for each other, H.D. felt that she was not always communicating clearly with her husband while he, in turn, was sometimes confused by her. On 16 October, H.D. wrote to Cournos that she felt torn between 'a sort of beautiful serenity' and 'that miserable hypersensitive[,] nerve-wracked, self-centered self'. During late September and October, the Aldingtons seem to have become more physically intimate. The affair with Flo Fallas appears to have subsided by mid-September after the Aldingtons' visit to London during his leave. If they had not been sleeping together at the height of the affair during the summer of 1916, it would seem that they were now sexually close to each other. It was during late September that H.D. found her husband a 'naked Greek', 'masculine', and 'very passionate'; she wrote to Cournos with coy humor on 16 October: 'R. writes he can only come in the afternoon for the present – a new rule – but hopes to have the "sleeping out" granted again later!'

As Aldington neared the end of his training as a noncommissioned officer, H.D. became briefly ill and her letters to Cournos were disjointed and visionary. On 31 October, she wrote that she saw people as colours; on 1 November, she stated, 'I know R. will die or else something in him will die', and insisted that she had seen 'his god, his Daemon'. In an undated letter from this time in which she mentions her illness, she compared Aldington to Jesus Christ while simultaneously identifying herself with her husband. She mentioned considering going to America, but added, 'I feel now if I leave England, something in him will break.'

Once Aldington was definitely slated to go to France and H.D. had made the decision to remain in England, once she had decided to move to London, a resigned acceptance and comparative peace evidently resulted. There is a gap is her correspondence with Cournos at this point, perhaps because she was seeing him often, for he soon took an apartment above hers, but when the letters resume at the end of 1917, H.D. was no longer so open with him and no longer used her letters to him confessionally. The tone of her letters and her relationship with him had changed.

The emotional and physical instability of H.D.'s life seems at this point to have depended in large measure on Aldington's military situation, but a new stage in both their lives was about to conclude this rough period of transition. In December H.D. moved into rooms at 44 Mecklenburgh Square,[50] a flat she was to keep throughout 1917 and into the summer of 1918. By 8 December Aldington had been promoted to lance corporal[51] and on 21 December he was shipped overseas.[52] He spent the last week of 1916 in a tent at a base camp two miles from Calais. For the first half of 1917 he served in a pioneer battalion on the Lens-La Bassée front, billeted most of the time about 2,000 yards from Loos.[53]

The winter and spring of 1917 were a relatively calm period for the Aldingtons despite –

or perhaps even because of – their separation from each other. The months of military training in 1916 had been particularly difficult because of a duality in the Aldingtons' lives. Understandably reluctant to give up their earlier intimacy and literary work, both Aldington and H.D. attempted to maintain two lives at once: during the week Aldington was a soldier while on duty, but in the brief free evening hours, on weekends, and during his longer leaves in the early autumn and before he left for France, he tried to maintain or resume his former life. When he was called up in June, his name – now with the addition of H.D.'s – continued to appear as assistant editor on the masthead of *The Egoist*; not until June of 1917, long after H.D. had in fact assumed all of her husband's responsibilities on the paper, did Aldington relinquish the title. At that time, deeply involved with her own writing, H.D. was finding the task too demanding, and at Harriet Shaw Weaver's suggestion, both gave up the position to T.S. Eliot.[54]

Aldington tried to maintain old patterns as well as to begin new intellectual projects during the summer and autumn of 1916, but the demands on his time and stamina were overwhelming. He found it difficult to write more than one letter a day; in an undated letter, H.D. wrote to Cournos that at camp Aldington 'only gets about ten minutes to read after they are in bed'. Aldington took with him to Wareham in June a volume of Heine's poetry, intending to pursue German, the weakest of his many languages, at a time he felt ironically appropriate. The book was confiscated in suspicious horror by his commanding officer.[55] On 1 October 1916, he wrote to Amy Lowell and enclosed 'several poems which register various moods of depression or otherwise', and he customarily mentioned to her their ongoing work on the last imagist anthology of this period, which appeared in 1917. H.D., too, wrote to Lowell at length about the business of the anthology, and she was working hard as well on her own poetry, which she regularly shared with her husband as she wrote. Her long poem 'The Tribute', a work dedicated to her husband, was written in the early autumn of 1916.

Personally, the Aldingtons were naturally unable to establish a clear or predictable life together in late 1916. They saw old friends: Flint and his family were living that summer in Swanage on the coast near Corfe Castle; on 1 October Aldington wrote Lowell that they saw John Gould Fletcher and his wife in London during his September leave; both Aldingtons wrote affectionate letters to Cournos during this time. On 4 October, H.D. also wrote Lowell that 'we see Lawrence occasionally. He seems very ill.' But Aldington was concerned about H.D. and resurrected the plan of her going to America, where she would be safer and life more stable. Ironically, the plan to leave England merely further disrupted their lives. H.D. wrote to Lowell on 3 November 1916: 'I may be returning to the U.S. in a few weeks. ... I am packing etc. R. has received promotion [to corporal] + may be moved any time. He begs me to leave England –' Yet nine days later on 12 November she wrote Lowell again: 'I do not know my plans from week to week. I had made all arrangements to return when R. found he would be kept on in England for a time at least. I will stay in England as long as he does though I am not able to see him as before.' Their frequent visits and subsequent separations at the end of afternoons or weekends together were emotionally wrenching for them both. In December Aldington was evidently no longer in Dorset, but had been shifted for yet additional training and to wait shipment abroad. On 8 December he wrote Lowell that 'H.D. won't know I've gone till I'm "across" – I think it kinder to spare her the tedium of another parting.' Yet even this plan did not work out: on 21 December H.D. wrote Lowell, 'I am waiting at Waterloo to say goodbye to R. He leaves England to-night.'

The atmosphere of the last half of 1916 was further intensified by the news from France. The war was not going well for the Allies. The Battle of the Somme officially began on 1 July and continued through 18 November 1916, with heavy casualties and slight gains. Trench warfare was well established and news of its horrors was reported daily. With the institution of conscription in May, the home population in Britain became even more aware of the war effort with its routine intrusion into their lives. By the beginning of 1917, it was clear that the war would last for a long time. Bread rationing began throughout the United Kingdom on 2 February, while the United States did not declare war on Germany until 6 April, and American troops did not actually land in France until the end of June 1917.

After Aldington's departure for the front in December of 1916, H.D. was able to settle back into a life of relative calm despite the deprivations of war. The first half of 1917 she spent in London, seeing friends (D.H. Lawrence, Cournos, Fletcher) and writing. Aldington in his turn settled into life at the front, finally adjusting somewhat to the inevitable routine and labour of the military machine. The relationship became an epistolary one, shifting of necessity into the realm of the written word, where each felt comfortable and probably more in control of their life together than during their unpredictable meetings and separations of the previous year. On 24 January H.D. wrote Lowell, 'I hear from R. often.' Aldington wrote to Cournos on 9 February, 'I go on from day to day, living spiritually on letters', and to Flint on 22 February, 'know that I respect *always* poems & H.D.'s letters'.

Aldington also, however, managed to continue to produce some literary work during periods when he was not actually in the trenches. In a typical month, a soldier in the British Expeditionary Forces served four days in 'the front line' (the first of three parallel lines of trenches), four days in 'support' (a short distance behind in the second row of trenches), eight days in 'reserve' (in the third line of trenches), and the remainder in 'rest' (usually at a large base camp a march of fifteen miles and a train trip of about forty miles from the trenches).[56] The Pioneer Corps, in which Aldington served in 1917, 'was a relatively low-stress environment';[57] his duties involved digging and repairing trenches, preparing graves, and making the numerous crosses to put on them.[58] So while Aldington was constantly within earshot of artillery and the threat of bombardment, he enjoyed some leisure since, at least for the first months of 1917, little military action occurred in the Cambrai and La Bassée area, where he was stationed.[59] The Battle of Arras began with a British attack on 9 April, and Aldington was directly involved in an area midway between La Bassée and Cambrai, but much of the fighting on the western front occurred to the south during this period, near Reims in Champagne (from 16 April to 7 May) or to the north at the Third Battle of Ypres, also known as Passchendaele (between 31 July and mid-November 1917).

Aldington wrote with some pride to Flint about his literary work on 19 November 1916: 'I've written 12 poems & 3 essays [in the five months] since I've been in the army.' H.D. comments on his mood and his writing in a letter to Lowell on 4 March 1917: 'He is quite happy in a philosophical way and doing more work than he has had for some time'; on 29 March H.D. wrote that she was working on putting together a volume of Aldington's poems and assured Lowell that 'R. is cheerful + managing to do a little writing between guns. He is seeing a good deal of the terrible side of things, but keeps his head and is very fine about it all.' Aldington's letters to Cournos during the first half of 1917 frequently concern literary matters; on 2 February he writes that 'there is only one's work & one's friends as a consolation in these worse than dark ages!' On 14 February, he wrote Cournos again in the same vein: 'I rather welcome the idea of getting out another book myself' and encouraged Cournos and H.D. in the project to select the best of his poems from 'the 3 [imagist] anthologies & all my m.s.s & stuff published in mags. &c.'

The military experience, however, was grim, and Aldington endured the life of the average British Tommy with a forbearance that was a mixture of humour and resentment. The tone of protest that characterises Aldington's retrospective treatment of the army in *Death of a Hero* and in *Life for Life's Sake* is echoed in the memoirs of many British veterans.[60] In *Death's Men: Soldiers of the Great War*, Denis Winter generalises about the soldiers' response to the military machine, a response that Aldington certainly shared: 'Faced with the impossibility of sustaining dignity in a situation so often degrading, most accepted the official line and compensated with that sad or boisterous humour and vulgarity which pretended that such an acceptance did not matter since it did not touch the real man and related only to a temporary and unimportant phase of the man's life-span.'[61] So long as Aldington felt that the war would indeed end within a period of months and so long as he could insist on his identity as a poet-critic through literary work and reading, he was able to maintain a relatively good-humoured equilibrium. Years later Walter Lowenfels would recall this aspect of Aldington's psychology, remarking that 'he was brave enough never to tout [*sic*] ammunition in his gun at the front in World War I, refusing (he once told me in Paris, 1930) to participate in that massacre – a secret he never shared with his fellow officers, being there, as he was, when he was one of the pre-war Imagist poets, part of the ever-young avant garde movement of his youth.'[62] Aldington's first months in France in 1917 reveal this phase of his response.

The experience of military life was indeed degrading. Clothing in the line was worn at least a week at a time, and 'food supplies were too little, erratic, dull and unbalanced'.[63] The soldier was also regularly exposed to the weather: bitter cold in winter, deep mud during the seasonal changes, heat and dust in summer. Soldiers were reduced to occupying themselves with elementary and life-sustaining chores, seeking animal comforts when possible and writing home. Aldington scraped and burned lice from the seams of his uniform; ate the cold tinned beef, occasional warm stew, and bread and jam that were the soldier's staple fare; shaved in cold and dirty water shared with others in his area of the trenches; avoided the latrines whenever possible as locations the Germans soon discovered and frequently aimed at. He suffered the digestive ailments of his diet and the standard intestinal and influenza infections rampant at the front. Amid the other odours of the trenches, mustard gas was difficult to detect and, with the stronger chlorine and phosgene gases, was a constant threat. The bronchial difficulties from which Aldington suffered for the rest of his life are surely attributable to his frequent encounters with gas, though he was never incapacitated by a gas attack just as he was never wounded. Like other soldiers, Aldington discovered that the quickest and the most immediately effective response to a gas attack was often not the gas mask but a piece of clothing (a glove, a vest) soaked with urine and pressed to one's face.

The literary work and reading Aldington was able to do while in France boosted his spirits in early 1917, and despite months in the army, he was still a fresh combatant for whom military experience at the front was somewhat new. The efficient British postal system kept him in close contact with H.D. and the few friends he had time to write. Denis Winter notes the impressive operation of the mails: 'Letters and parcels from home were received with equal regularity. Nothing ever took longer than four days, even though

Aldington in uniform, probably taken in Devon or
in London during the autumn of 1916

name and regiment were the only permitted addresses. ... mail was delivered punctually
even in the very front line, where it would come up on top of the ration sandbag.'[64]

Aldington's comparative good humour was bolstered by the possibility of a commission
as well. By 8 May he wrote Cournos that he had completed all the necessary paperwork
involved in the application and was eagerly awaiting orders to return to England for
officers' training. Many infantry soldiers put in as much as a year at the front without
home leave; Aldington would depart for England in early July, after six months in
France, for an extensive period of training, followed by a long leave and additional
training before he returned to the front in the spring of 1918.

H.D. remained Aldington's primary concern and intimate correspondent throughout
the first half of 1917. About to leave for France on 20 December 1916, Aldington wrote to
Cournos, 'Please look after H.D. in my absence. Try to cheer her up.' On the same day
he wrote to Flint, 'Look after H.D. won't you?' Well aware that he might be killed at the
front, he masked the seriousness of his situation with jocularity in a letter to Lowell on 4
January 1917: 'If I get flipped, you'll give an eye to H.D. won't you? She is my chief
concern & if it were not for her I should enjoy this experience immensely.' In contrast,
Aldington also fantasized about a time after the war when he and H.D. could again travel
to Italy together in sensual escape. He shared this idea with Flint on 29 January 1917,
imagining wandering about Rome 'with H.D. whose gusto for antiquities fits in
gloriously with mine'. H.D. was writing poems for a second volume of verse and busy
with *Egoist* work, but Aldington was concerned that she not feel too keenly his absence,
which might become permanent. On 22 January he wrote to Flint to amplify what he had
meant earlier in asking his friend to look after his wife: 'For the Lord's sake don't

interrupt H.D. if she is having a good time with anyone – when I said "Look after H.D."
I meant help her to have a good time & not bother about me. I didn't want to make you a
kind of Argus! Take H.D. out if you can, to theatres, & get her to meet new & amusing
people. And if you can devise any sort of "affaire" pour passer le temps, so much the
better.' Aldington missed H.D. deeply, yet felt impotent in the relationship from the
imposed distance and deprivation; the sums she received as a soldier's dependent seemed
embarrassingly small to him, and he regularly sent her additional money from his own
pay. He felt that she needed him financially, emotionally, intellectually, and sexually,
and that he could not in his present situation satisfy her needs. He tried to encourage
others, vague and specific, to fulfil his former roles, and simultaneously felt an exclusive
and intense connection with her. On 3 May 1917, he wrote Cournos about his anticipated
homecoming for officers' training: 'I want you to break this tactfully to H.D., so she can
make all due preparations for the event. I had an idea that I'd just stroll into 44 & say
"Hullo," but it occurs to me that the shock might be too horrible even for the most
affectionate spouse. ... I would like to see you and H.D. when we arrive. ... Please don't
tell *anyone* but H.D. I don't want to see *anyone* for a couple of days. ... tell H.D. as
quietly as possible, so as not to over excite her.'

When Aldington returned from the front in early July 1917, he was sent immediately
to a camp at Lichfield near Birmingham for a short period of reassignment before several
weeks' leave. While he was eager to come 'home' to 44 Mecklenburgh Square, he was
also eager for time alone with H.D., and she joined him for a few weeks, taking a room at
Brocton, a village about twelve miles northwest of Lichfield. This was an idyllic time for
them both: a reprieve from anxiety about the physical dangers of war, an escape from
London and the impinging acquaintances of the city's literary life, an interlude between
the trenches and the next phase of their relationship. Ironically, the calm on the western
front that had characterized the first half of 1917 abruptly ended soon after Aldington left
France, and news of the 'big push' of the Third Battle of Ypres began at the end of July
and continued through late October when, amid appalling carnage, British troops reached
Passchendaele, and into mid-November, when the battle finally concluded. The atmosphere of Aldington's leave and training period in England was one of brief escape,
limited reprieve from devastation. Aldington and H.D. both knew that he would return
to the front, but unlike their anticipation of the previous summer, now they also knew
from direct experience what this return would mean for them, and the knowledge
threatened and unsettled them both.

By late July Aldington had left Lichfield for a few weeks' leave, which he spent with
H.D. in London. He looked after some matters of literary business, writing on 21 July to
Edmund R. Brown of the Four Seas Company in Boston, which eventually published
two collections of his war poetry in 1919 and 1921, and on 29 July and 4 August to Martyn
Johnson, editor of *The Dial*, which began to publish his series of six articles, entitled
'Letters to Unknown Women', on 14 March 1918. Aldington and H.D. attended a party
given by 'Ezra Pound and his satellites'[65] and saw T.S. Eliot, who appeared to H.D. 'very
nice – very quiet + not at all the sort E.P. usually gets hold of'.[66] Yet these busy summer
weeks in town seemed awkward to the Aldingtons.

Like most men back from the front, Aldington felt disconnected from civilian life,
oddly different from other people not directly involved in the war, somewhat resentful of
their ongoing ordinary life, the continuity and apparent independence of their experience
while his own was disrupted and at the mercy of the military. H.D., too, identifying

herself with her husband, was consciously distancing herself from the literary life she had known. On 10 August, she wrote Amy Lowell that imagism was essentially over and the poets who once called themselves 'Imagists' were developing in different directions; of her own verse she wrote, 'I, too, am going through a transition'. On 19 September she wrote to Lowell that she had earlier been discouraged about her writing, 'but with R. back again + you still keeping my memory green, I am tempted to have another fling!' She continued to try to define their separation from London and their former friends: 'We are rather out of touch with things in London.' She objected that Pound 'seems untouched by all the realities that are torturing us all'. She noted their separation from *The Egoist* now that they were no longer editors, insisting that 'we are on quite friendly terms with all these people but think it best to lie fallow a bit'. On 14 November she confided in Lowell: 'I don't *really* feel friendly with E.P. nor does R. – he just does not matter.' While Aldington enjoyed the conviviality of old friends in London in July, H.D. continued, 'we don't really care – and, in sober mood, on our return to town, do not expect to see that gang at all'.

Aldington left London in late July for the camp at Lichfield to begin his officers' training course. H.D. soon took rooms off the market square in the nearby town, where she remained except for occasional visits to London until he was commissioned on 28 November. This period of rural retreat was in many ways restorative to both of them. H.D. returned to her poetry with renewed energy, spending the weeks peacefully alone and welcoming her husband each weekend. Aldington enjoyed this time of predictable routine, and wrote in relative good humour to Amy Lowell on 18 November 1917: 'All my time is taken up at the Officers' Training School, and the week-end, when I do get away, is too delightfully lazy for me to spoil with writing.' But this concern about his creative work was a problem for Aldington that would persist throughout the war, and he discussed it at length with Lowell here:

All writing is distasteful if one is without leisure – for one must have time to live. ... I cannot write as I could once, though I have captured a certain stern ideality, have regained a serenity by leaving any kind of journalism or publicity for the anonimity [*sic*] of my present life. After all in the general futility of things it matters very little whether I use my superfluous energies to write poems or to make stories and tales & jokes for the soldiers ('rough men' as The Little Review in its daintiness calls them) who are my companions.

But don't think that I haven't ambition or the desire to make beautiful things. I have lost a great deal, I am handicapped in ways you cannot imagine, but this abrupt withdrawal from the rapid current of my life into something alien & painful may, perhaps, be as salutary for me as prison for the author of De Profundis! One sees the importance of the 'literary life' and the supreme importance of literature, the one imperishable record of the human soul, the means of multiplying personality, the expression of destiny.

Most of the things I thought about poetry two years ago I still think; but in the present pause in my intellectual life I am not sure whether it is the final pause or a period preceding intense creation. In any case I do not complain.

In the same important letter, Aldington recounted biographical information Lowell had requested and concluded with a reaffiramation of his intimacy and identification with H.D.: 'Hueffer, Yeats & Lawrence have all taught me something, but apart from any personal feelings, H.D.'s poetry is the only modern English poetry I really care for. Its austerity, its aloofness, its profound passion for that beauty which only Platonists know, make it precisely the kind of work I would like to do myself, had I the talent.'

The war's power to damage Aldington's creativity drove him closer to H.D. and encouraged him to emphasize her spiritual and artistic sensibilities, the elements of her nature which seemed to him to transcend his traumatic and reductive experiences in the military. Her art, as evidenced in this lettser to Lowell, became particularly precious to him as he turned more and more to translation in the last year of the war. Aldington was also to a degree suffering from the shell shock which would make him especially emotionally sensitive after demobilisation in 1919. He wrote to Flint on 7 September 1917, sharing his pleasure that H.D. was staying in Lichfield 'only 3 miles from here. She has a room in the Place de la Ville overlooking the statues of Boswell & Johnson. ... Each weekend I get a sleeping out pass.' He qualified his joy, however: 'I think I shall just lie down and sob if I get into another artillery barrage.' For all these reasons, the Aldingtons seem to have been particularly close during these months away from London. In March of 1917 D.H. Lawrence had written to Amy Lowell that he found H.D. 'very sad and suppressed' in her letters to him;[67] the calm and restraint of the first half of 1917 was replaced in Lichfield with healthy if serious reflection and some joy. The period probably fulfilled H.D.'s expectations when she wrote to Flint at the end of August that she was looking forward to moving to Lichfield. She was gathering books to take with her and wrote that her husband was 'doing very well – but I am sick of single blessedness!'[68]

While away with Aldington in the Midlands, H.D. had kept her apartment in Mecklenburgh Square, but it had not been vacant. Dorothy Yorke (known to her close friends as 'Arabella'), an American woman whom John Cournos had courted unsuccessfully in the United States before the war, had arrived in London in the late summer of 1917. She and her mother had been touring in France, living in Paris, were compelled to leave because of hostilities, and now were casting about for lodgings in England.[69] The city was flooded with war workers and country people seeking employment because, with millions of men missing, dead, or fighting at the front, maintaining the family farm or local shop was sometimes impossible; accommodations were naturally in short supply. When H.D. left for Lichfield she wrote Flint that 'a beautiful lady has my room'.[70] Throughout September Cournos, still in the upper apartment at Number 44, resumed his courtship, but in early October he left London as a translator and journalist with the Anglo-Russian Commission to Petrograd. Although the intimate relationship that he sought with Yorke had evidently not been realized, he left with the apparent understanding that H.D. would watch over his friend in his absence. In late October D.H. and Frieda Lawrence moved into H.D.'s large room and Yorke moved into Cournos's smaller one upstairs.

The Lawrences, like the Aldingtons in 1916, had been seeking refuge in the country during the war. Living in Cornwall since December of 1915, in October of 1917 they were staying in a cottage at Zennor near St. Ives. A friend of theirs, the young London music critic Cecil Gray, had taken a neighbouring cottage, Bosigran, and joined them in Cornwall in the summer of 1917. They saw a good deal of one another, and after singing German songs one night with a light shining from their window, the Lawrences were compelled by the local police to leave the coastal area under suspicion as spies. When the Lawrences arrived precipitously in London, they moved temporarily into Mecklenburgh Square.[71]

When the Aldingtons returned to London at the end of November, the Lawrences moved in with Cecil Gray's mother at 13b Earl's Court Square, where they stayed until 18 December; they then moved on to Berkshire, where by January they had settled into a cottage at Hermitage owned by Lawrence's friend, Dollie Radford.[72]

Aldington had a month's leave before he was sent first to a camp at New Haven, then to Tunbridge Wells where he was stationed until he finally left for France in mid-April of 1918. He had several 'short leaves' in the first months of the new year and spent them in London. This period was a tumultuous one. Immediately after he left London on 28 December 1917, Aldington wrote to Flint and reflected on his changes in attitude since entering the army:

I didn't say much when you told me that you had to go into the army, but, believe me, I felt & feel it very much. There are many things I'd like to say to you, but don't know how. I wish I could save you many inevitable pangs, some of which you cannot foresee. Yet, in a strange way, I believe the miseries and deprivations and melancholies you will undergo, will benefit you as they have benefitted me.

Dear boy, you are sensitive and quickly wounded, proud and a poet – do you need any further composition for misery? I know you will feel most bitterly the separation from those who are dear to you. They will not understand your isolation & your pain, & it will seem to you as if your friends have forgotten you. Time, which passes so cruelly & monotonously for the solider, passes swiftly for them. But you will have compensations. You will feel the implacability of destiny, the hard reality of war – wh. no civilian can know – you will have the spiritual gain of suffering, of disruption of your life, of severed affections, of lost leisure. You will realise then how much you now enjoy and also you will come to hate and perhaps to love men, as never before. With death imminent & threatening you will find courage to support terror, & in the gaps of liberty allowed you to grasp at life with a zest you never before had. Rosy, not legal life, will tempt you!

Perhaps, things will be very different for you. Certainly your psychology will not immediately & exactly follow mine, as I have sketched it for you. But, when you do go, remember, if you feel lonely and betrayed by life, that I shall understand, as perhaps no one else, & can sympathise.

H.D. wrote Cournos on 28 December 1917 that she felt quite unsettled: 'I cannot work these days. ... R.'s very fine – but so broken at going away –'Aldington was also concerned about H.D.'s attitude toward her work and wrote Amy Lowell on 2 January 1918 that

unfortunately she has burned some most poignant lyrics and a long poem of about 10,000 words. I can't forgive her for it, but she said she thought them inadequate! The long poem – such as I saw of it – had beautiful passages. But she is so relentless. I think she has grown very much spiritually. Everything she writes has now that sure touch which seems to me immortal – the arrangement of simple poignant words in an absolutely original way yet perfectly inevitable, so that one wonders why one has not thought of it oneself. But she is frightfully reserved – I had to beseech her for hours to prevent her burning a lot more!

The atmosphere at Mecklenburgh Square during that December in London was extremely tense. Aldington met Arabella and immediately responded to her sexually, beginning an affair with H.D.'s knowledge that was consummated not only in Cournos's former flat but in the Aldingtons' own bed curtained off at one end of H.D.'s large room. As with Aldington's affair with Flo Fallas in 1916, H.D. seems to have been initially accepting, then upset: depressed, exasperated, and anxious. Her destruction of poetry on which she had been working for months and her husband's pleading with her at length to preserve it suggest H.D.'s self-doubt and frustration as well as Aldington's guilt and powerlessness. The Christmas season did not calm the turbulent climate but rather intensified the pain of Aldington's imminent departure: the irony of holiday celebration

H.D. and Aldington, probably taken in London during one of his leaves in late 1917 or early 1918

seemed at best ridiculous, at worst pathetic. The Lawrences and Cecil Gray were frequent visitors and did little to assuage the rising tensions. Lawrence quarreled with his wife, sometimes affectionately, often pointedly. Gray and Frieda Lawrence were sexually attracted to each other, but the height of their passion had evidently passed and Gray shifted his attentions to H.D. Lawrence and H.D. felt an artistic bond with one another as fellow artists who responded instinctively to spiritual aspects of experience, but despite H.D.'s sense of erotic chemistry between them, Lawrence's personal reserve prevented any sexual consummation of the relationship.[73]

Additionally, both H.D. and Aldington knew that their good friend John Cournos would be angry with them, as indeed he was, when he returned from Petrograd in early April of 1918. H.D. suggested the persistent tensions at Mecklenburgh Square when she wrote to Cournos on 25 January 1918: 'Things are strange here ... Dorothy is *quite* well & happy & working. You need not fear for her. ... R. has not yet had orders – is waiting in England. But far from London. I may go to Cornwall for a little while. But will return the moment you write you may come back.' She did not tell him about her husband's ongoing affair with Dorothy Yorke, nor any details of the visit to Cornwall that she was considering. A week later she reiterated her intentions and reassurances, but was no more specific: on 2 February, she wrote, 'I want to go to Cornwall & live very, very quietly for some time. I feel I can *work* there. ... D. is quite well – is busy & seems happy.'[74]

With her husband's lover living upstairs; with Miss Elinor James, the landlady, quite displeased with the goings on in her house; with Aldington occasionally home on short leaves and weekends; and with Gray urging her to come away with him, H.D. was unable to work in London. Her capacity to work productively was always a barometer of her emotional state, as was her capacity to love, to be in love, to express love emotionally and sexually; just as Freud would assert in his own writing and she would affirm in her own relationship with him in the 1930s, the healthy individual was characterized by her ability to love and work ('lieben und arbeiten'). However, H.D. wavered in her inclination to go off with Gray. Periods in the country had regularly assuaged for her the difficulties of wartorn London (in 1916 in Devon, in 1917 in Lichfield), and now the idea of spring and summer in Cornwall seemed to promise her a period of quiet in which she could write and perhaps also love. But she did not love Cecil Gray, and there was something retaliative that was not attractive to her in beginning her own affair in response to her husband's.

Aldington was acutely aware of H.D.'s continuing unrest and its affect on her work worried him. Still in England, he wrote to Amy Lowell on 3 March 1918: 'Hilda has done a certain amount of work, but naturally feels unsettled through my being away for so long – two years now. She needs tranquility for her work & the raids in town, though comparatively harmless, are rather noisy & disturbing to a person with fragile nerves. She will probably go to the country when I leave.' More open with Lowell than was H.D., still Aldington was seldom intimate and here conceals much of the cause of his wife's distress.

In fact, much remained unsettled, inconclusive, and unclear in the Aldingtons' lives on the brink of his return to France and the beginning of the surviving correspondence between them. Cournos's imminent return was somewhat unnerving: both Aldingtons were about to lose an intimate friend who had also been a frequent correspondent. H.D.'s hesitation about the trip to Cornwall was about to be resolved, but her relationship with Gray was no clearer to her and rather than consciously asserting her own will, she seems to have been reacting to the atmosphere at Number 44 and to Gray's own pleadings. Gray wrote to her from his room in West Hampstead on a Monday evening probably in early March:

Dear gray eyed One,

I was rather depressed and sad at not seeing you today, though perhaps it was really very wise of you all the same. But I think I rather resent, or fear, this cold, abstract, impersonal kind of wisdom of yours. It makes me feel that I have no hold over you – that at any moment you might simply cease to have any feeling for me – that I might no longer exist for you. But this is possibly only the exaggerated expression of my fear of losing you which is always very strong when I am away from you. You must try and dissipate this mistrust and apprehension. If only I could feel sure of you – as you put it yourself – 'secure.'

Forgive this rather maudlin exhibition, and do not think I am reproaching you. One of the things I love most about you is your detestation of any kind of falsity or deception in our relations. You do not pretend to love me any more than you do. That is something, at any rate, but it is not enough to keep me from being unhappy now and then. Why are you so elusive, so unapproachable? It is to a certain extent true of you what Lawrence and White in that ridiculous poem seem to imply – you refuse to give anything, you will only receive. Others must pledge themselves – you alone have the privilege of withdrawal, of non-committal.

Do not think that because I say these things I love you any the less, you crafty, subtle, perfidious Argive – that unfortunately is something over which I have no control. Hence my fury. My dear, my dear, I love you so. Never mind what I say, it really doesn't matter much.

A rivederci

Cecil

I shall come along tomorrow between 4 and 5.[75]

Such an insistent, petulant and rather possessive lover provided a stark contrast to Aldington, but certainly did not seem to H.D. to be clearly what she wanted. From Gray's letter, she appears to have been reluctant to respond to him as fully as he wished: willing to have him love her, but unsure whether or how much to respond to him; trying to assert some control over herself and her life.[76]

Yet she did eventually decide to go off to Cornwall, and Gray left London on 11 March with the clear hope that she would soon follow. In an undated letter postmarked 12 March 1918, Gray wrote her from Bosigran:

Dear Person,

I arrived last night at Penzance about 6 and drove out in a trap, getting here about 7:30. A very boring journey it was, and by the time I got to the house I was in a dreadful state of depression which continued to increase with the wind as the evening wore on. I do not know whether the wind or I howled the loudest.

The food problem is a very acute one here and I am thinking of shifting over to Tregerthan after my year's lease runs out here – ie. in May; but that can be decided when you come down.

And how are things with you. Are you also feeling grisly? And did you go away with Brigit? But I suppose you are writing me all this.

I have not yet made up my mind as to your status in my household, so have not yet broached the subject to the fisher. The only decided thing is that you must come, whether you want to or not, because I need you very, very much. It doesn't matter how soon you come; we can manage all right about beds and things like that. Nothing really matters very much.

My piano is in a dreadful state – can't touch it until the tuner has come. That adds considerably to my woes.

Forgive me if I can't write a more amusing or interesting letter, but I am still bouleversé, as I always am after a deracination; and cannot collect myself. Shall be better tomorrow.
much love, in fact all my love.
Cecil

P.S. Letters take two days to London from here so don't scold me for not writing earlier.

Gray's moodiness, depression and general pessimism here do not seem attractive qualities, nor does his arch authority in commanding H.D. to join him, whether she wants to or not. Nevertheless, H.D. did join Gray in Cornwall before the end of March, and Aldington addressed his initial letter to her there.

The Aldingtons' relationship with Cournos also figures in the immediate background as the correspondence from Aldington to H.D. begins. On 6 April 1918 Aldington responded to an angry letter from Cournos, which reached him at Tunbridge Wells. Aldington declared brashly and sincerely: 'I am not ashamed of anything I have done; I regret nothing. ... there are events which are stronger than we are; there seems a kind of fatality about it, a bitter irony. ... I am not excusing myself. ... We fell in love with each other, that is all. ... I accept full responsibility.' Aldington insists at once here on his own responsibility and on an ironic fate determining his life; about to leave for France once more, he asserts that he is in control of his actions while acknowledging his powerlessness in the face of forces beyond his control.

In this psychological context, his relationship with Arabella appears understandable as an emotional response to his impending departure for the front, experience of which he knows and dreads. In the affair, Aldington managed to escape – under the illusion of a free assertion of his will (his own 'responsibility') – the emotional demands of an intensely erotic and poetic life with H.D., a life which the dehumanising life of the trenches was about to deprive him of anyway, perhaps permanently. It is as if Aldington were committing a kind of suicide rather than allowing the military to kill him either in body or in spirit. Certainly this is the kind of destructive self-assertion that appears in the character of George Winterbourne, who commits suicide in France at the end of *Death of a Hero*. It is also possible to see Aldington's affair with Arabella as an unconscious attempt to make a mess of his marriage, to create in himself a guilt commensurate with the responsibility he insisted upon, a guilt which in turn would give purpose to the suffering his return to France would cause. Throughout his life Aldington was a vigorously independent man, and his struggle to assert some control over his experience, even (or particularly) at the cost of threatening relationships very dear to him, seems a characteristic reaction to the extreme pressure he was currently enduring.

H.D. was confused, frightened, hurt, and sympathetic in response to Aldington's actions and state of mind. When Cournos discovered the affair on his return from Russia, he wrote her as he had immediately written Aldington. She responded and shared with him her conflicting and complicated feelings:

> I was very anxious – Yet, as you say, there was nothing to be said! They *are* to be pitied – O, it was so terrible – you can't imagine. Though I was of it – still I felt detached. I don't know what will happen.
>
> ... I am not able to think of myself as a *person* now. I must move, act, & do as it is *moved* upon me to do & act. ... I am cut off from everyone in the old world. ... Lawrence seems not to exist and R. seems far & far. I do not even write – poor boy – I suffered so for him. I think him very strange & unbalanced now – his actions were quite unaccountable. I pray for him – indeed they both need our pity –[77]

Neither H.D. nor Aldington, however, was ever able to regain their intimacy with Cournos, and it is against the backdrop of H.D.'s relationship with Gray and Aldington's with Yorke that the story of the letters unfolds.

1 Letter from Alister Kershaw to the author, 1 February 1988.
2 H.D., *Bid Me to Live* (1960), London: Virago Press, 1984, 27.
3 Norman Holmes Pearson's notes toward a never-written biography of H.D. (Yale).
4 Taped interview by David Wilkinson with Mrs Gertrude Hilda Brown Cotterell, 10 December 1981, shared personally with me. The ellipses in the quotation indicate the omission of Wilkinson's questions and of the comments of Mr Brown, who was attempting to clarify his wife's responses; she had recently suffered a stroke and her statements were not always clearly articulated.
5 Sir Alec Randall, a reminiscence in *Richard Aldington: An Intimate Portrait*, ed. Alister Kershaw and Frédéric-Jacques Temple, Carbondale: Southern Illinois University Press, 1965, 119.
6 Letters from Richard Aldington to Glenn Hughes, 31 August 1928 to 1 March 1929 (HRC), chronicle the events of this period and Aldington's efforts to move his possessions out of his Berkshire cottage while he was in Italy and France.
7 Letter from Albert Aldington to St Loe Strachey, 7 July 1910, quoted by permission of Alister Kershaw and the British Library.
8 Anne de Lenclos (1620–1705) was well known for her liaisons with some of the most distinguished men of her time. She was also famous for her charm, intelligence, and good sense. She had a salon in Paris, befriended writers, and was portrayed as Clarisse in the novel *Clélie*

(1644–60), by Madelaine Scudéry, known as 'Sapho', who (like H.D. in her novella 'Hipparchia', 1926) portrayed people she knew as characters in Greek and Roman settings (in H.D.'s work, Aldington appears as Marius Decius, H.D. as Hipparchia). When Lenclos's lover left for the army, he requested from her a written promise of fidelity, but she was soon unfaithful. See *The Oxford Companion to French Literature*, comp. and ed. Sir Paul Harvey and J.E. Hazeltine, Oxford: Oxford University Press, 1959, 407–8, 667.

9 'Confessions', in *The Little Review*, Vol. 12, Spring (May), 1929, 11.

10 Penny Smith, in her perceptive article 'Hilda Doolittle and Frances Gregg' (*Powys Review*, Vol. 8, No. 22, 1988, 46–51), quotes a letter from Frances Gregg to her mother, Julia Gregg, on 18 August 1913. This letter further suggests the unfulfilled passion in H.D.'s relationship with Pound. Gregg commented on the '"expression of veiled resentment with which Hilda used so much to look at Ezra, – that resentment that is based in unsatisfied sexual desire"' (48). I am grateful to Louis Silverstein for having brought this article to my attention.

11 In an intimate correspondence with Eunice Black Gluckman, Aldington reflected on his own sexual past and on the sexual experiences of women he had known. He is discreet in these unpublished letters, writing that 'As a rule, I never speak about one woman to another' (8 August 1960) and reminding her that 'I always follow the rule of the Officers Mess, and never mention a woman's name nor drop any hints' (4 August 1958). Reflecting on homosexuality in both women and men, Aldington noted: 'I think women are quite often bi-sexual, having affairs with women without in the least losing their pleasure in men; and some of the women I've been with longest have gone to be with other women quite frankly, and with no disturbance. Both my wives did it …' (11 November 1960). Explicitly discussing oral sex, Aldington commented on what appeared to him its apparent universality, reflecting that all the women he had known had experienced orgasm through cunnilingus before their sexual experiences with him: 'I have never had any wife or mistress who had not already experienced it' (7 August 1961). In the apparent absence of another candidate for H.D.'s affections, and from Frances Gregg's remarks on H.D.'s unsatisfactory sexual relationship with Pound and Aldington's remarks to Gluckman here, it seems probable that H.D. and Gregg did indeed engage in physical and fulfilling sexual activity during the most intense period of their friendship in 1910 and 1911. I quote from Aldington's letters to Gluckman by permission of Alister Kershaw and the Beinecke Rare Book and Manuscript Library (at Yale).

12 Aldington recalled this early affair in letters to Brigit Patmore in 1928 at the beginning of their second, eight-year affair. In a letter dated merely 'Tues.', and likely written in late December 1928, Aldington wrote to her as 'you who first held my body'. In a letter dated merely 'Thurs.', and likely written early in 1929, he recalled their first 'honeymoon' as 'the good old days', then referred to their renewed intimacy at Port Cros in October 1928, as a second honeymoon, finally stating explicitly 'seventeen years ago I loved you'. (HRC)

13 I discuss this poem at greater length and publish the sonnet in its entirety in my article '*H.D. and R.A.: Early Love and the Exclusion of Ezra Pound*', in *The H.D. Newsletter*, Vol. 3, No. 1, 26–34.

14 All the quotations in this paragraph are taken from H.D.'s unpublished 1912 diary (Yale).

15 In *The Poetry of Richard Aldington: A Critical Evaluation and an Anthology of Uncollected Poems* (University Park, Pennsylvania: Pennsylvania State University Press, 1974), Norman T. Gates reprints Aldington's 'Song of Freedom', first published in the newspaper *Justice*, 29 October 1910, 5 (Gates, 227–8). Gates notes that 'this poem, written when Aldington was eighteen, is the earliest published poem' he has discovered (228). Gates reprints other early verse: 'In Memoriam: Arthur Chapman' (*Union Magazine*, Vol. 5, No. 3, December 1911, 254; in Gates, 228–9), 'Chanson of Winter' (*Evening Standard*, 6 February 1912, 3; in Gates, 229), and 'Villanelle' (*Evening Standard*, 8 February 1912, 3; in Gates, 230) are typical examples. Aldington continued to publish verse in the *Evening Standard*, the *Pall Mall Gazette*, and the *Westminster Gazette* during the spring and summer of 1912 before the appearance of his

'Imagiste' works in *Poetry* in November 1912. Publication of H.D.'s early work has yet to be so specifically chronicled, but in autobiographical notes she made for Norman Holmes Pearson, H.D. stated that she first published work in New York syndicated papers in 1910 (Yale). Such work was probably poetry; her cousin, Francis Wolle, in his memoir, *A Moravian Heritage* (Boulder, Colorado: Empire Reproduction and Printing Company, 1972), notes that during the autumn of 1910 H.D. lived for several months in Greenwich Village so that she could 'work at her poetry' (56).

16 This information and all subsequent details about this trip unless otherwise noted are drawn from the unpublished 1912–13 travel diary of Helen Wolle Doolittle, H.D.'s mother (Yale).

17 Letter from Margaret Snively Pratt to Bryher, 6 December 1968 (Yale).

18 Pound found them 'disconsolate on the piazza [in Venice] yesterday afternoon & spent the evening consoling them for the absence of their offspring' (Ezra Pound to Dorothy Shakespear, May 1913, *Ezra Pound and Dorothy Shakespear, Their Letters: 1909–1914*, ed. Omar Pound and A. Walton Litz, New York: New Directions, 1984, 220). In her autobiographical notes, H.D. recalled the period in Venice particularly: 'Ezra was there; general feeling of disapproval.' Her fragmentary comments on this trip suggest that it was essentially full and happy, however, despite the tensions she also remembers: 'Rebellion, stay on in Florence, go Venice, cheap third class, no food. Ezra takes on mother and dad' (Yale). Phyllis Bottome (in her memoir *The Challenge*, New York: Harcourt, Brace and Co., 1953, 381–5) found Aldington's and particularly H.D.'s relationship with the Doolittles unconventional. Drawn more to Aldington than to H.D. but interested in both of them as 'highly stimulating companions', in Rome in late 1912 Bottome was still 'violently shocked at their unkind treatment of H.D.'s simple and kindly parents' (381). Certainly H.D. was rebelling against her childhood and much that the Doolittles represented. By the time they arrived in Rome the dynamics of her relationship with her parents must have been complex; to an outside observer it is not surprising that her behaviour would have appeared 'shocking'. I am grateful to Louis Silverstein for having drawn Bottome's comments to my attention.

19 Pound wrote to Dorothy Shakespear on 8 May 1913 that H.D.'s 'family distresses her & seems to drive her more fawn-wards' (that is, towards Aldington, nicknamed 'Faun' by both Pound and H.D.; *Ezra Pound and Dorothy Shakespear*, 224).

20 Pound wrote to Dorothy Shakespear on 21 April 1913 that he expected to be amused by Aldington and H.D. together in Venice. On 29 April, Pound sent Dorothy a first version of 'The Faun' (published in revised form in *Poetry and Drama*, 2, in March 1914). In this poem he addresses Aldington as the faun, accusing him of 'sniffling and snoozling about among my flowers', but finally the speaker, conceding defeat, states, 'But take it, I leave you the garden' (*Ezra Pound and Dorothy Shakespear*, 207, 213).

21 Pound to Dorothy Shakespear, 8 and 9 May 1913, *Ezra Pound and Dorothy Shakespear*, 224, 226.

22 For example, in H.D.'s letters to Isabel Pound, Pound's mother, 5 and 30 December 1912 (Yale).

23 Aldington sent twenty-one postcards to his father and his sisters between 12 December 1912 and 25 June 1913 (TU).

24 Richard Aldington, *Life for Life's Sake: A Book of Reminiscences*, London: Cassell, 1968, 110.

25 *Life for Life's Sake*, 111.

26 In *Life for Life's Sake*, Aldington notes that Pound invited 'each of us' to the now famous tea and there 'informed us that we were Imagists' (122). On 7 August 1928 Aldington wrote Pound that he, Aldington, and H.D. should agree that officially 'The "movement" was decided upon by the three of us, in a Kensington tea-shop, to launch H.D.' (SIU). In a late letter to H.D. on 2 November 1955, he recalled imagism as '"une affaire de famille" between us three [H.D., himself, and Pound], mainly to boost your poems and to a less extent mine' (Yale).

27 *Life for Life's Sake*, 122.

28 H.D., *End to Torment: A Memoir of Ezra Pound*, New York: New Directions, 1979, 5.

29 Letter from Richard Aldington to Amy Lowell, 21 September 1914; all letters from Aldington to Lowell are at HU.

30 *Life for Life's Sake*, 126.

31 Aldington's and H.D.'s correspondence with Amy Lowell during these years makes clear that Aldington with H.D.'s help spent a good deal of time and effort soliciting poems for these anthologies, encouraging contributors to make alternative selections and to revise or expand the number of their submissions. It seems clear that Lowell was responsible for contracting with their American publisher and through her influence publicizing the volumes on her side of the ocean; however, Aldington – who was in England until late 1916 at a time when transatlantic mail was unpredictable and who thus had more direct and dependable contact with contributors and with their English publisher, Constable and Company – seems in fact to have done most of the actual work the anthologies entailed. A letter from Aldington to Lowell on 7 December 1914 is typical: he begins with three and a half single-spaced typed pages of numbered points which offer Lowell discussion and advice about matters of publication (HU).

32 Richard Aldington, *Very Heaven*, London: Heinemann, 1937, 245–6.

33 For example, Aldington discussed a plan for both Aldingtons to go to America for the duration in a letter to Amy Lowell on 28 December 1915; H.D. wrote to Lowell on 20 January 1916 that the plan would need to be postponed.

34 Aldington described his efforts either to avoid conscription altogether or at least to get into officers' training in a letter to Amy Lowell dated 5 January 1916, concluding, 'My father assures me that nothing can be done.' He further detailed his father's efforts on his behalf in another letter to Lowell on 6 May 1916 (HU).

35 Aldington discusses these legal details at some length in a letter to Amy Lowell on 6 May 1916 (HU).

36 Aldington's and H.D.'s letters to Amy Lowell in 1915 and 1916 recount this ongoing debate as the Aldingtons struggled to plan for the future.

37 Frank Flint detailed the reasons that he felt H.D. should remain in England and chance forced labour in a letter to Aldington on 23 November 1916 (HRC). Flint indicated that the decision to stay was finally H.D.'s, but that she discussed the matter at length with Alec Randall and with Flint himself and his wife Violet. I am grateful to John Wardrop for transcribing this letter for me from Flint's shorthand.

38 Undated letter from H.D. to Amy Lowell, February 1916.

39 *Life for Life's Sake*, 162.

40 Letter from Richard Aldington to Frank Stewart Flint, 27 March 1916.

41 Undated letter from H.D. to John Cournos, probably written 8 September 1916, in Donna Hollenberg, 'Art and Ardor in World War One: Selected Letters from H.D. to John Cournos', *Iowa Review*, Vol. 16, No. 3, Autumn 1986, 134.

42 Letter from Richard Aldington to Frank Flint, 6 July 1916.

43 Undated letter from Richard Aldington to John Cournos.

44 The heading of this letter has been cut off, evidently by military censors, but it is dated August 1916 in Lowell's hand.

45 Undated letter, dated in Lowell's hand August 1916.

46 Letter from H.D. to John Cournos, dated 'Sunday evening' and probably written in July 1916.

47 Letter from H.D. to Amy Lowell, 13 October 1916.

48 Hollenberg, 136.

49 Hollenberg, 136, 137.

50 Letter from H.D. to Amy Lowell, 1 December 1916.

51 Letter from H.D. to Amy Lowell, 8 December 1916.

52 Letter from H.D. to Amy Lowell, 21 December 1916.

53 Richard Aldington, 'Books in the Line', *The Sphere*, 12 April 1919, 26.

54 Letter from H.D. to Harriet Shaw Weaver, May 1917, quoted in Jane Lidderdale and Mary

Nicholson, *Dear Miss Weaver: Harriet Shaw Weaver, 1876–1961*, London: Faber, 1970, 138.

55 *Life for Life's Sake*, 167.

56 Denis Winter, *Death's Men: Soldiers of the Great War*, London: Penguin, 1978, 81.

57 Winter, 130.

58 Malcolm Brown, *Tommy Goes to War*, London: J.M. Dent, 1978, 147.

59 Winter, 213.

60 Winter, 42.

61 Winter, 43.

62 Walter Lowenfels, 'A Letter to Angela' (unpublished manuscript), quoted in Selwyn Kittredge, 'The Literary Career of Richard Aldington,' Ph.D. dissertation, New York University, 1976, 573.

63 Winter, 148.

64 Winter, 164–5.

65 Letter from H.D. to Amy Lowell, 19 September 1917.

66 Letter from H.D. to Amy Lowell, 14 November 1917.

67 D. H. Lawrence to Amy Lowell, 23 March 1917, in *The letters of D.H. Lawrence*, Vol. 3, ed. James T. Boulton and Andrew Robinson, Cambridge: Cambridge University Press, 1984, 104.

68 H.D. to Frank Flint, 30 August 1917, in 'Selected Letters from H.D. to F.S. Flint: A Commentary on the Imagist Period', ed. Cyrena N. Pondrom, *Contemporary Literature*, Vol. 10, Autumn, 1969, 584.

69 John Cournos, in his *Autobiography* (New York: G.P. Putnam's Sons, 1935), details his relationship with Yorke at great length. I am drawing on his account here as well as on information revealed in a taped interview with Yorke conducted by Walter and Lillian Lowenfels on 25 October 1964. I am grateful to the late Fred Crawford for having shared with me his typed copy of Miriam J. Benkovitz's transcription of this interview.

70 H.D. to Frank Flint, 30 August 1917, in 'Selected Letters', 584.

71 H.D. went down from Lichfield to London briefly to see that the Lawrences were settled in her flat (Autobiographical Notes, Yale), but she remained 'off in the country still', as she wrote to Lowell on 14 November 1917, seeing her husband regularly on the weekends until his training ended and he received his commission on 28 November.

72 Keith Sagar's *A D.H. Lawrence Handbook* (Manchester: Manchester University Press, 1985) is an invaluable resource for determining Lawrence's precise whereabouts, and I have drawn on his work here as well as on Mark Kinkead-Weekes' *D.H. Lawrence: Triumph to Exile, 1912–1922* (Cambridge: Cambridge University Press, 1996).

73 H.D.'s novel *Bid Me to Live*, probably begun as early as the summer of 1918, chronicles the events of December 1917 and the first months of 1918 in great autobiographical detail. While I have attempted as much as possible here to rely on letters and other primary sources in my account, it is this novel itself which most explicitly conveys the experience of the group's interaction. Specifically, I am relying heavily here on H.D.'s account of her relationship with Yorke, Gray, and Frieda and D.H. Lawrence, although Aldington, in *D.H. Lawrence: Portrait of a Genius But* ... (London: Heineman, 1950), gives his own brief, more general, and rather detached account of the Lawrences' departure from Number 44 (199). Yet throughout his biography Aldington clearly indicates Lawrence's attitude toward women, which H.D. examines at length in her novel and which I draw on here. Aldington writes: 'there can be no doubt that he had a great attraction for many women, all the more so since his innate puritanism kept them at a distance. ... yet he considered his own marriage inviolable, and *noli me tangere* [don't touch me] in a snarl was about all that the others ever got' (106). It is this same characteristic recoiling that H.D. attributes to the Lawrence character in *Bid Me to Live* (81–2), even quoting his own expression, also cited by Aldington: 'noli me tangere' (82).

74 Hollenberg, 141.

75 This and the following letter from Cecil Gray to H.D. are at Yale.

76 D.H. Lawrence satirized H.D.'s vacillation here in his fictional portrait of Julia Cunningham, who hesitates to go off with Cyril Scott (the Cecil Gray character) to his 'house in Dorset' (*Aaron's Rod* [1922], Cambridge: Cambridge University Press, 1988, 47). Despite unsympathetic treatment, Julia's concerns ('compromising herself' in the eyes of others; her concern for her husband, Robert; her reluctance or inability to consider her own feelings and to make her own decisions [45–55]) do indeed seem to be H.D.'s in her relationship with Gray.

77 Hollenberg, 144. This letter is merely dated 'Monday' and was probably written on 7 April 1918, not sometime in 1919 as Hollenberg suggests.

Part I: the early years

[Letterhead:] E.F.C. Officers Rest House and Mess.[1]

19 April 1918

Dearest Dooley/[2]

Arrived here [in France] last evening after a stormy passage, though I am happy to say I was not sea-sick! Some ways it is good to be back with the B.E.F. [British Expeditionary Forces] though it looks as if most of us are in for a hot time. I guess there's not really much chance of coming through this time, yet I feel very calm about it all, kind of indifferent you know!

I am at an I.B.D. [Infantry Base Depot] waiting to go up the line, which I presume will be pretty soon. Only address is: 9th Royal Sussex, J. Depot, 32nd I.B.D., B.E.F. France. I shall be 9th Royal Sussex all the time now; I know their Division quite well – they were next to us last year at Loos. It is a pukka [genuine] infantry batt. – no pioneer business this trip![3]

Have just heard a rumour that we are going up the line to-morrow.[4] Don't know if it's true, but I must run along & see if it's true. There are one or two things I want to buy.

I hope C.G. is all right & that he'll be left undisturbed.[5]

Love from
Richard.

1 Aldington is writing from the officers' area of an Expeditionary Forces Canteen.
2 One of Aldington's pet names for H.D., derived from her maiden surname, 'Doolittle'.
3 For the first half of 1917, Aldington served as a lance corporal in a pioneer battalion and was stationed for six months near Loos in the Cambrai-La Bassée region of the western front. Pioneer battalions were intended to perform as manual or infantry units whenever the occasion arose, and were accordingly trained in both functions. In their manual capacity they worked with the Royal Engineers field companies and were responsible for building and repairing trenches and dugouts and maintaining roads, railways, and tramways, work often undertaken in forward areas under heavy fire. In their infantry capacity they were used to consolidate captured positions and were often involved in defending these positions against enemy attack. Aldington's duties had also included making wooden crosses and digging graves.
4 Aldington is at a base camp from which he will go 'up the line' to the trenches.
5 Cecil Gray (1895–1951), the young British musician and music critic who was H.D.'s lover. Gray first met the Aldingtons in London in December of 1917. At twenty-two he was an aspiring composer and music critic three years younger than Aldington and nine years younger than H.D. Born in Edinburgh and privately educated, Gray lived with his mother in London during the war and periodically took a cottage by himself in Cornwall to work on his music at a distance from the intensity of city life. He had met the Lawrences, his country neighbours, early in 1917, and had returned to London with them in October. He visited them at 44 Mecklenburgh Square before the Aldingtons' return to London from the north in late November 1917, and continued the flirtation with Frieda that had begun in Cornwall. In mid-March of 1918 he left London again for Cornwall, where he remained through July. He then returned to London in part to escape conscription but also under pressure from the volatile Phillip Haseltine (Peter Warlock), a misogynist who disapproved of Gray's retreat to the country with H.D. in bizarre, bawdy, and insistent letters to Gray throughout the spring and summer of 1918 (BL). Gray remained in London through the end of the war, never serving in the armed forces in any capacity, and left England for Italy in September 1919, as soon as continental travel, limited by the war, was again allowed. Gray drank heavily, had many fleeting relationships with women,

and was generally a passive and removed observer of experience rather than an active or successful participant. In a letter to a friend identified only as 'Jack' on 16 October 1921, Gray analysed his character: he found 'drink and women, the two substantial realities of existence on this planet – ... my exploits and adventures have not even the justification of inner necessity. After each one a feeling of distaste and disappointment comes over me' (BL). In a notebook of random jottings, Gray continued his self-analysis in an entry in 1922: 'I experience the greatest difficulty in transmounting the gulf between feeling and action. I have never really managed it, except through alcohol. Hence, no doubt, the great hold this resource has over me. For example, I make love to a woman, but all the time the essential I is standing apart, watching, analysing, contemplating in utter detachment and isolation' (BL). Gray's compositions were not well received, and as a music critic he was contentious, judgmental, and facetious, promoting the work of friends, principally Warlock and Bernard van Dieren. To the writers he came to know through the Lawrences he appeared at best introspective, calm, wry, and removed from passion at a time when the lives of the Aldingtons and their circle were intensely and even debilitatingly emotional. Gray was not in fact a figure of sanity, however, but a neurotically disengaged man apparently incapable of mature commitment or deep response. His draft category in the spring of 1918 exempted him from military service.

᪥ 2 ᪥

23 April 1918

Dearest Dooley/

This is just to let you know that I got to the battalion on Sunday afternoon [21 April]. So far we are on rest, several kilo[metre]s behind the line, but are expecting to go up in a day or so.[1]

There is plenty of work here, so I've had no time to write at all. In fact I've only written to you & A. since I've been out here.[2] Life is much better this time than before. Yet I'm hoping for something in the shape of a blighty one at the earliest possible moment![3]

How are you? I hope to hear from you soon. My address is 'D' Coy, 9th Royal Sussex, B.E.F. How is Gray? Still free I hope.

Will write more when I get a chance.

Love from
Richard.

1 The Ninth Royal Sussex Battalion was in training behind the lines at La Comte from 19–29 April.
2 Dorothy ('Arabella') Yorke (1891–1971), Aldington's lover. Born in Reading, Pennsylvania, Yorke met John Cournos in 1910 in Philadelphia, where she was then living with her mother, her father having left the family some years before. Yorke and Cournos began an intermittent relationship of periodic engagements and separations. When she and her mother arrived in London from Paris in the summer of 1917, Mrs Yorke volunteered to do war work in the countryside; Cournos then invited Arabella to take over H.D.'s flat at 44 Mecklenburgh Square while H.D. went north to be near her husband. On the Aldingtons' return to London at the end of November, Yorke moved upstairs to another room in the same house. Cournos stresses the course and importance to him of his relationship with Yorke in his *Autobiography* (New York: G.P. Putnam's Sons, 1935). Aldington's affair with Yorke probably began in December of 1917. It was a passionate relationship on both sides, intensified by the conflicting emotions each felt for their other partners: both Aldington and Yorke were aware of violating other ongoing relationships. H.D. portrayed Yorke as Bella Carter and John Cournos as Ivan, in *Bid Me to Live*. Yorke was dubbed 'Arabella' apparently by the Aldingtons or perhaps by the Lawrences during their brief stay at Number 44 in the autumn of 1917. An artistic woman,

Yorke was a fine seamstress and periodically, probably with Aldington's encouragement, an illustrator (nine full-page fashion illustrations by Yorke appear in *The Art of Lydia Lopokova* [London: Cyril Beaumont, 1920]) and a translator (of Renée Dunan's *The Love Life of Julius Caesar*, New York: E.P. Dutton, 1931). In later years she resumed a correspondence with Cournos and, responding to the publication of *Bid Me to Live* in 1960, reflected on her experience with the Aldingtons. She objected to H.D.'s portrait of her as 'an illiterate bunny-brained whore' (29 September 1960), though she later called herself 'a rather uneducated person (in fact totally so)' (2 October 1965). She admitted, too, that H.D.'s resentment of her was understandable: 'Of course I think she had plenty of cause to hate me' (29 September 1960), but in the same letter adds her own resentment of H.D., who she felt had 'no body'. Yorke is also bitter in these letters toward Aldington, who left her in 1928, recalling the years in which they had lived together after the war, insisting defensively that she had 'worked *for*' him, '– typed, read proofs, took dictation, cooked, washed + made his shirts to save money' (14 January 1965). In these late letters to Cournos (from which I quote by kind permission of his step-daughter-in-law, Isabel Satterthwaite, whose family owns the letters), Yorke appears resentful and petty, an old and lonely woman who failed to secure Aldington's full intellectual or emotional attention and never quite understood why. She died in a nursing home in Reading, Pennsylvania, where she spent her last years, having outlived all of her early circle of companions.

3 'Blighty' is England or home; a 'blighty one' is Great War slang for a wound which will cause one to be shipped home, a lucky wound.

❧ 3 ❧

6 May 1918

Dearest Dooley/

I am O.K. Hope you and Cecil are all right. Are you still happy in Cornwall?[1]

I am right in the line in temporary command of a company, which means a lot of work & responsibility. However, that helps to pass the time.[2]

When I have done my 10 days trip up [in the trenches] (5 of wh: has passed) I am going to the base for a course, which lasts until June 15![3] I am not really pleased as I was hoping to get wounded. I saw in the paper yesterday that Carl Fallas is wounded. Lucky little pig![4]

There is no time for more. So, au revoir.

I love you – too much.

Richard.

I haven't had a letter from you yet.[5]

1 Throughout his correspondence with H.D., Aldington is careful to shelter her from his deep frustration and despair with the war and military life. His letters to others during the war years often provide a stark contrast to the sometimes jaunty and restrained tone of his letters to H.D. For example, he writes to Alec Randall on 2 May 1918:

> You see I am still alive though horribly fed-up. It is not within the compass of any language to express to you how fed-up I am with a Gargantuan disgust at this démodé folly. Sometimes when I wake up from my somewhat rare slumbers I am more than surprised to find what pestilential surroundings I have.
> But really this life is brutish & tries my patience almost beyond endurance. The horrible thing is that one has nothing, absolutely nothing to live for. (HL)

In mid-March of 1918 H.D. had left London to join Cecil Gray at Bosigran Cottage near St Ives in Cornwall.

Bosigran Cottage, Cornwall, where H.D. stayed with Cecil Gray during the summer of 1918

2 Aldington received his commission as a second lieutenant in the infantry on 28 November 1917.

3 Probably Étaples or another large base camp near Calais.

4 Carl Fallas (1885–1962). The Aldingtons came to know Carl Fallas and his wife Florence through John Cournos, when the Aldingtons and the Fallases lived near each other in Devon in 1916. Fallas was a journalist, a minor novelist, and a friendly if rather passive man; his wife was livelier and very attractive. Aldington began a brief affair with Flo in May of 1916, just before he was called up into the army. He and Carl enlisted togather in the Eleventh Devonshire Regiment and trained and served together during Aldington's first tour in France in 1916–17. After H.D. left Devon and after Aldington returned to England in July of 1917 for officers' training, the Aldingtons' acquaintance with the Fallases essentially ceased, although Aldington maintained a sporadic correspondence with both Carl and Flo throughout his life.

5 The extreme tensions of the months immediately preceding this correspondence evidently made H.D. resolve not to write to her husband despite his letters to her since the end of his last long leave in late December 1917.

🖎 4 🖎

11 May 1918

[On this date Aldington sent a field postcard similar to the one reproduced as letter 12, indicating that he had received a letter from H.D.]

🖎 5 🖎

17 May 1918

Dearest Dooley/

My exquisite one – can you know how cool & lovely the memory of you is to me? Recently I have been very close to the place where I wrote 'Reverie' and I remembered, I remembered many things.[1]

No doubt things seem very tragic & bitter to you, but what seems to me the great bitterness is my own apathy. Back here once more everything goes; I ask myself often what am I living for? Why do I trouble to hide from a shell or bullets? Only the mere weakness of the flesh. There really isn't anything or anybody I care for. My loneliness is complete. But it is not a beautiful loneliness. It is a loneliness haunted with horror and regret.

I suppose in a way I care for Arabella, & in a way I care most terribly for you. But nothing is real; there is nothing I really want. Isn't that rather sad?

O my dear Dooley, I would so like to be gay & witty, contemptuous of 'ordinary' people – how I envy Gray his contempt – but there are too many dead men, too much misery. I am choked and stifled not so much by my own misery as by the unending misery of all these thousands. Who shall make amends for it?

How silly all this is! But you are silly to think that our love would ever be broken. Don't I long sometimes to throw myself at your knees & call passionately to you?

But what will happen who can tell? And I do not want anything any more, except perhaps sleep.

> Sleep, what have the gods to give but sleep
> After warring & after loving?
> The closed eyelids shall forget to weep
> And the heart its roving.[2]

Or some such nonsense.

Yesterday I found some lilac in a ruined garden and its beauty was too poignant. Isn't it the uttermost cruelty of the gods to sprinkle flowers in hell – some gainless glimpse of Proserpine's veiled head?

I am glad you have the beauty of those Cornish hills & the tranquility & comfort of a pleasant house – you must think of yourself as Fred's 'Friend of Paul' in his house in Spain, meditating on Lucretius & the vanity of things.[3]

Really, Dooley, I want to come back to you very much. Someday perhaps we will run away together – some unsuspected isle in the far seas. But now you are more unreal than the memory of the shadow of Narcissus in a pool. I *belong* no more to the life that is in tranquil places, but just to this odd distorted existence.

Yes, work at Greek if it helps you – I nearly said 'what is Greek'![4]

I should like very much to kiss you.

Your
Richard.

[In the margin of page 1: I have been 18 days in the trenches & am wearied out.][5]

1 Aldington's poem was first published in *Reverie: A Little Book of Poems for H.D.* (Cleveland: Clerk's Press, 1917). The poem conveys poignantly his feelings about both love and war:

> It is very hot in the chalk trench
> With its rusty iron pickets
> And shell-smashed crumbling traverses,
> Very hot and choking and full of evil smells
> So that my head and eyes ache
> And I am glad to crawl away
> And lie in the little shed I call mine.

And because I want to be alone
They keep coming to me and asking:
'How many billets have we in such a trench?'
Or, 'Do you know the way to such a redoubt?'

But these things pass over, beyond and away from me,
The voices of the men fade into silence
For I am burned with a sweet madness,
Soothed also by the fire that burns me,
Exalted and made happy in misery
By love, by an unfaltering love.
If I could tell you of this love –
But I can tell only lovers,
Only irresponsible imprudent lovers
Who give and have given and will give
All for love's sake,
All just to kiss her hand, her frail hand.

I will not tell you how long it is
Since I kissed and touched her hand
And was happy looking at her,
Yet every day and every night
She seems to be with me, beside me,
And there is great love between us
Although we are so far apart.

And although the hot sun burns in the white trench
And the shells go shrilling overhead
And I am harassed by stupid questions,
I do not forget her,
I do not forget to build dreams of her
That are only less beautiful than she is.

For there are some who love God,
And some their country and some gain,
Some are happy to exact obedience
And some to obey for the sake of a cause –
But I am indifferent to all these things
Since it was for her sake only I was born
So that I should love her.

Perhaps I shall be killed and never see her again,
Perhaps it will be but a wreck of me that returns to her,
Perhaps I shall kiss her hand once more,
But I am quite happy about Fate,
For this is love's beauty
That it does not die with lovers
But lives on, like a flower born from a god's blood,
Long after the lovers are dead.

Reason has pleaded in my brain
And Despair has whispered in my heart
That we die and vanish utterly;
I have seen dead men lying on the earth

Or carried slowly in stretchers,
And the chilled blood leaped in my heart
Saying: 'This is the end, there is no escape.'

But for love's sake I brush all this away
For, since I do not know why love is
Nor whence it comes, nor for what end,
It may very well be that I am wrong about death,
And that among the dead also there are lovers.

Would that we were dead, we two,
Dead centuries upon centuries,
Forgotten, even our race and tongue forgotten,
Would that we had been dead so long
That no memory of this fret of life
Could ever trouble us.

We would be together, always together
Always in a land of many flowers,
And bright sunlight and cool shade;
We should not even need to kiss
Or join our hands;
It would be enough to be together.

She would stoop and gather a flower,
A pale, sweet-scented, fragile flower
(A flower whose name I will not tell,
The symbol of all love to us).

And I would watch her smile
And see the fair flowers of her breast
As the soft-coloured garment opened from her throat.

I would not speak, I would not speak one word
Though many ages of the world's time passed –
She would be bending by the flower's face
And I would stand beside and look and love.

Not far away as I now write
The guns are beating madly upon the still air
With sudden rapid blows of sound,
And men die with the quiet sun above them
And horror and pain and noise upon earth.

To-morrow, maybe, I shall be one of them,
One in a vast field of dead men,
Unburied, or buried hastily, callously.
But for ever and for ever
In the fair land I have built up
From the dreams of my love,
We two are together, she bending by the pale flower
And I beside her:
We two together in a land of quiet
Inviolable behind the walls of death.

2 Unidentified. It is possible that these lines are a part of a poem Aldington never finished or published.

3 In Frederic Manning's philosophic tale 'The Friend of Paul', which appeared in *Scenes and Portraits* (1909), the central character, Serenus, has retreated to his country house after the death of his wife and child; there he tells visiting friends of his near conversion by Paul at Corinth and his abiding affection for the holy man.

4 It seems that H.D. has finally written to Aldington and that letter 5 is in some measure a response to the details she has written him of her work on Greek translation and her situation in Cornwall.

5 On 1 May Aldington's battalion was stationed near St. Maroc; D Company, in which he served, was in 'Chalk Pit Alley'. The battalion was in the trenches near Loos until 19 May when the Ninth Royal Sussex moved into rest at Brébis.

➴ **6** ➴

20 May 1918

It is more difficult not to love you when I am away from you than when I am with you. Really, it is true that one has many lovers but only one love. And I gave you everything, so that I have only desire and consideration to give to others. But I wonder if I was your love or just one of your lovers?

To-day I have looked at whole trees all green with spring and fields and I have seen an old French woman I used to know out here who nearly wept over me & gave me tea & cognac![1]

But still, though things are kind, I am terribly indifferent. The truth is: I love you & I desire – l'autre [that is, Arabella]. Really I can never be happy without you; and very often it seems I couldn't be happy without her. Folly to talk of happiness when this horror goes on. But on remâche ses idées [one broods over one's ideas] in the long nights of watching. The stars are very powerful instillers of truth. Somehow, Dooley, I have made a great mess of my life. But I would have been content if I hadn't made you suffer so much. And then, and then, I must look after A. C'est de la démence [That is the pure folly of it]. I find it hard to write to her. Do you realise what that means? It is a psychological point which gives me distress.

Out here I really don't know what one lives for. I don't pretend it is all misery and horror; there are moments of rest, compensation, gaiety even. But there is constant wear – & having lost somehow the pearl & essence of life there seems no point in keeping on. Je vis en bête [I live instinctively]. Do you think there is any point in keeping on? Twice last week I tried to get killed – and was unlucky or lucky, whichever you like.[2]

Isn't this folly? Do be happy with Cecil. I shall get over this someday.

R.

1 Probably the owner of the bookshop at Grenay, whom Aldington writes about in 'The Bookshop at Grenay' in *The Sphere*, 19 April 1919, 54. When Aldington returned to the section of the front where he now is after an absence of over a year, he recalls in his article that 'Madame' greeted him with joyous surprise and invited him into her kitchen as if he were a relative. An excerpt from this sketch is reprinted as a part of my article 'Richard Aldington in Transition: His Pieces for *The Sphere* in 1919', *Twentieth Century Literature*, Vol. 34, No. 4, Winter 1988, 498.

2 Aldington's attempted suicide here anticipates George Winterbourne's successful effort when he stands up in the trenches at the end of Aldington's popular war novel, *Death of a Hero* (1929).

7

28 May 1918

Dearest Dooley/

I often think of you in the hours about dawn and hope you are happily sleeping. It is a great comfort to know that you are safe and well and not too unhappy. It seems a long time since I heard from you, but of course time does drag in the front line; so perhaps it is not so long as I think. Have done ⅔ of our time up here – I shan't be sorry when we are relieved.

Have you any news of Yeats & White over this Irish business? I do hope Yeats has managed to steer clear. I notice Mrs Gonne is under arrest.[1] Some people have odd ideas of happiness. Mine is to be let alone – an impossible ideal.

I suppose where you are there is sea & a clean wind & flowers, and inside books & white linen and more flowers. And I suppose you don't really feel happy – I mean that you are probably a little bored sometimes, not enjoying every hour? I feel that I wouldn't ever want to 'grouse' if I could be clean and quiet and undisturbed again. One goes over & over things – what am I living for? What do I hope? And then even if the war did end & I got out how could I live? I'm too [old] to learn a trade or profession now & I don't feel like writing any more. Even if I did it wouldn't amount to much.

Well, I am a grouser, Dooley, don't you think? Anyhow you mustn't think I'm nothing but a grouser, for I keep pretty cheerful. We all had our photographs taken in tin hats the other day – I'm going to send you a copy as soon as some arrive. That will be in about a fortnight I expect.

Do hope you are well & happy. Remember me to Hulun when you write.[2]

Richard.

1 William Butler Yeats (1865–1939), the Irish poet, and his friend James Robert White (1879–1946), who helped to organize the Irish Citizen Army during the transport workers' strike in Dublin in 1913. Both men were acquaintances of the Aldingtons. In late May of 1918, a bill to establish an Irish parliament and executive was being hotly debated, and Aldington is probably referring to the discovery of a German intrigue in Ireland on 16 May. On 18 May, a proclamation was issued to apprehend those allegedly involved; 150 Sinn Feiners were arrested in Dublin and interned under the Defense of the Realm Act. Maud Gonne MacBride (1866–1953) was arrested in Dublin on 22 May 1918 for complicity in the plot and interned in Holloway Jail for six months.
2 Evidently a private nickname for Gilbert Doolittle (1884–1918). Two years older than H.D., Gilbert was the brother to whom H.D. felt closest. When the United States entered the war, he enlisted in the Army Engineering Corps and was sent to France as a captain in the summer of 1918.

8

31 May 1918

Dearest Dooley/

This is just a short note to tell you that I am quite all right. I thought possibly you might be wondering as there is another offensive beginning.[1]

I am not in the very front line, but about 1000 yards back. Soon we should go out for six days rest & if all is well I shall probably not go in with the battalion next trip. This will take me almost to the end of June. So you see things are not too bad.[2]

I have one or two French books up here which I manage to read for half an hour at a time. In a fit of optimism I nearly wrote to Crès & the Mercure for their list, but it hardly seems worth while. 'Patience & endurance' are all that is really necessary.[3]

Cornwall must be very lovely now if the days are as full of sunlight there as they are here. Extraordinarily pitiless and ironic these bright days are here, but get more physically comfortable – no mud, & nights are warm. We have no blankets, – just a trench coat. Yet I sleep very well.

Remember me to Cecil.

> Your
> *Richard.*

P.S. I had my photograph taken about 10 days ago – I am sending you a copy.[4]

1 The Germans reached the Marne on 27 May 1918, and by 4 June the Allies had mounted a counterattack at Château-Thierry.

2 Aldington, now in the third line of trenches, is anticipating a period of additional training which would keep him at base camp for the first two weeks of June; his training actually lasted from early June through mid-July.

3 Georges Crès of *La Nouvelle Revue Française*; founded in 1909, the influential French review of literature and the arts also had a publishing house. *Le Mercure de France* (1890–1965) was a famous literary and artistic monthly which featured original work by writers of all schools and nationalities. Aldington's friend Remy de Gourmont was an editor from 1895 until his death in 1915. I have not been able to identify the quotation here.

4 Several times Aldington sent H.D. photographs from the front, but it is not clear exactly which one he is referring to here.

◈ 9 ◈

> 1 June 1918
> 11 pm

Darling

Just a word to you to-night, in a hurry to catch the ration limber.[1]

Your letter melted much bitterness of heart. I thought you did not write because you did not care. And I wanted you to care so much.[2]

It is horrible here – you probably know where I am.[3] But yet I have not forgotten to love you. You write sweetly & I pardon your reserve. If only I had more than myself to give.

My sweet, you seem so beautiful and tranquil – any flower makes me think of you. No more time. To-morrow.

> Richard.

1 The ration limber, an articulated two-wheeled cart often joined to other similar carts, brought warm food to the lines, but it also transported mail.

2 Aldington apparently received a brief note from H.D. on 11 May (see letter 5), but it is not until now that H.D. responds to his letters with personal and detailed letters of her own.

3 Aldington is in the line north of Loos. Although his battalion commander characterized the period from 25 May to 1 June 1918 as 'a fairly quiet tour' in the line, he also noted on 31 May that 'about 400 gas projectors [were] fired on to Battalion' and that 'casualties were rather heavy' (the war diaries of the Ninth Royal Sussex Regiment, PRO).

1 June 1918
11:30 pm

Dearest Dooley/

I have just sent you a little note saying how glad your letter made me; I wanted to get if off at once in case anything should happen to prevent my writing to you later.[1]

Ah yes, I do think of our days together. What strange, despised creatures we were & yet what a treasure we had. At times I think of some statue we looked at together or remember some book we both cared for. How could there ever be anyone but you?

Maupin. It was in London, I think, that we read it.[2] But how far, far away that time is. In such a way people spoke of The Golden Age. I wonder what is gained through this deprivation & suffering? After all we have scarcely known each other for two years. It is a lot.[3]

'Friends' you say.[4] Not verse now, only prose?[5] Once when I threw myself at your feet I felt your heart beat so wildly I was frightened. Friends – I would like you to kiss me passionately just for one night, to realise once with you, my Beatrice, the great frisson with the woman I love best.

Oh, I know the world is a queer place, & those who love each other best hurt each other most. Perhaps it will be only 'friends', but I cannot bear to think it yet; I shall think 'lovers' until you tell me 'no' with your own lips. But, as I told you I have changed, through misery, through routine, through the strain of things. Perhaps I may get back equilibrium, some sort of life, even write again, but 'never glad confident morning again'.[6] One acquiesces in the death of a flower but it is hard to admit that the flower of one's unique life dies as surely & nearly as quickly as the summer lilac.

Isn't it strange. I know the date & what time it is; but none of us knows which day of the week it is. All days are alike. I think it is Friday or Saturday.[7] But, really now, aren't days of the week a superfluity?

Do you get enough money, enough to eat & buy clothes & books?[8] Won't you let me give you 'of my scant pittance'?[9] (you can see, can't you, how hard I'm trying to make up to you!) Ah, but I'm nearly crying as I write, my wife, my Dooley. I am so proud that you have my name – please, please won't you keep it, whatever happens, in memoriam as it were?[10]

I shall go on writing until dawn if I don't stop. For a while thinking of you I forget the horror.

I never forget you.

Richard.

1 Aldington is aware of the possibility of his imminent death, but tends to refer to it euphemistically throughout his correspondence with H.D.

2 *Mademoiselle de Maupin* (1835), a novel by Théophile Gautier, explores in detail the subject of physical beauty and contains much erotic description. The preface was one of the first declarations of 'art for art's sake'.

3 Aldington is referring to the time since he entered the army on 24 June 1916. Not since then have he and H.D. lived together the life he is idealizing here.

4 H.D. has evidently suggested in her letter that she and Aldington exclude the sexual from their relationship and think of their marriage as merely a partnership between 'friends'.

5 In late 1917 H.D. had destroyed the poetry on which she had been working for some time (see Introduction) and is now, it would seem, beginning to write the autobiographical novel which will eventually become *Bid Me to live* (1961). She writes to John Cournos on 17 July 1918: 'I

have begun really seriously on a novel.'

6 Robert Browning, 'The Lost Leader' (1845), line 28. In this poem Browning laments the 'leader's betrayal of literature for material wealth and earthly glory. The 'leader' is specifically Wordsworth, who had accepted a Civil List pension in 1842 and become poet laureate in 1843, but the identity of the 'leader' is intentionally ambiguous, and Aldington's quotation is in the spirit of the poem: the experience of the war has destroyed his confidence in the transcendent power of both his marriage and literature.

7 1 June 1918 was, in fact, a Saturday.

8 In addition to a small allowance from her parents, H.D. received a small sum as a soldier's dependent and a few pounds sporadically in royalties from her own *Sea Garden* (1916), from Aldington's *Images* (1915) and from the various imagist anthologies.

9 In 'Meditation', which appeared in *Images of Desire* in 1919, Aldington echoes this phrase, referring to the 'scanty pittance' he felt capable of earning as a poet (*The Complete Poems of Richard Aldington*, London: Allan Wingate, 1948, 146).

10 H.D. did keep Aldington's name; throughout her life she was known personally as Mrs Aldington or Hilda Aldington.

➢ II ≪

2 June 1918

My dear Dooley/

I hope you don't mind my writing to you so often. You must tell me if it causes any difficulty in your new ménage[1] and I will then abridge my correspondence. But I shan't stop writing until you tell me that you don't want to hear – & perhaps not even then!

On the day after to-morrow I am being sent down the line for a five weeks course. I may not last anything like that time as I should be sent for if reinforcements were badly needed. But at least for a little I shall be back of the line. Better keep the same address if you write – letters will be sent after me. I don't particularly want to go – I'm more or less at home now with this battalion, but as it's an order I can't refuse. It makes a change anyhow, though I am more or less indifferent.[2]

I think of you perhaps too much and wonder if I shall ever see you again. Arabella sends me very kind letters & seems genuinely grieved to have me gone. But I can't tell. In any event I don't really care, but sometimes I would give everything just to touch your little finger as I did that first day at Brigit's.[3] It's queer to be living in memories so early in life.

I can't quite give up the idea that we shall be together again. There is of course the complication of Cecil and Arabella, but they seem – to me at least – to fade into the arrière-plan [background] when we two are concerned. Ah, Dooley, we have not been as happy as we might – somehow I have failed. Of course it makes no difference that we have had other lovers – though sometimes it hurts, hurts. But out of this present utter darkness of mine, this confusion & complete lack of direction & interest, there is one thing that seems to matter – you.

The little less & what miles away! Why didn't you love me passionately *before* Arabella & not after?[4] Don't you know that it's you, you I wanted & want life, everything with? The bitter irony of it! Like St. Augustine I repeat to myself bitterly: 'too late have I loved thee O pulcritudinem antiquam!'[5]

Infinite problems circle about us, but, dear Dooley, let us at least keep a certain tolerance, a certain tenderness for each other. Here I am in this wretched dug-out & there you are in Cornwall. What the next year will do for us, god knows. Perhaps it is very wrong of me to write you love-letters – perhaps I ought not to disturb you. You are very reticent – you do not tell me if you are happy with Gray. It is a great consolation to me to know that there is someone to look after you now & in the future, if by chance I should not be able to do so.[6]

How one wanders in words – half expressing half one's thoughts. I write rather my meditations than a letter – chiefly writing because for a time I concentrate on the memory of you, all I seem to possess now. Why should one agonise with hope? I won't ask anything of you, anything of some things I was going to ask. I'll just finish & go up & listen to the guns a bit.

Richard.

1 H.D.'s relationship with Cecil Gray in Cornwall.
2 Aldington is about to be transferred to the base camp near Calais where he will receive additional training. Letters to a soldier at the front needed only his rank and regiment to reach him.
3 Aldington is recalling the day they met at Brigit Patmore's house in late 1911.
4 The Aldingtons' sexual life together was not always one of equal or mutual passion.
5 'Pulcritudinem antiquam' literally means 'beauty of long ago', but here Aldington clearly intends 'my first and true love'. It is likely that the quotation comes from Augustine's *Confessions*.
6 This was one of Aldington's constant concerns.

☞ 12 ☜

9 June 1918

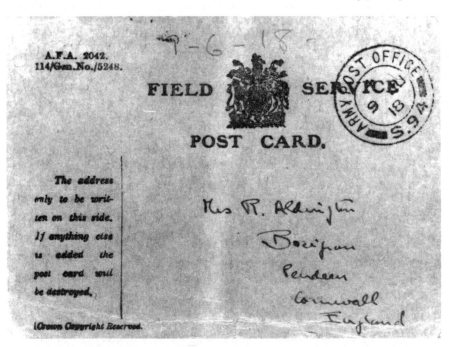

Form postcard indicating that Aldington has received a letter from H.D. dated 31 May 1918. At critical times, when troop movements were occurring that needed at all costs to be kept secret, no correspondence was allowed except for field postcards such as this one, in which a soldier crossed out sentences he did not want

I am quite well.

~~I have been admitted into hospital~~

{ ~~sick~~ } ~~and am going on well.~~

{ ~~wounded~~ } ~~and hope to be discharged soon.~~

~~I am being sent down to the base.~~

I have received your { letter dated _31·5·18_

{ ~~telegram~~ „ _____

{ ~~parcel~~ „ _____

Letter follows at first opportunity.

~~I have received no letter from you~~

{ ~~lately~~

{ ~~for a long time.~~

Signature
only } Richard

Date_____ 9·6·18

Wt. W1566-R1619-18539 8000m. 6-17. O. & Co., Grange Mills, S.W.

⁂ 13 ⁂

12 June 1918

Voici presque deux années, mon amie, que je subis cette vie immonde de soldat.
Pendant tout ce temps nous ne nous sommes pas vus que par bribes de temps. J'avais
vingt-trois ans quand je te quittait; or dans un mois j'aurais vingt-six. A-tu [*sic*] bien
compris ce que cela veut dire? C'est que le temps passe, ma chère, et nous sommes
toujours plus loin.[1]

Je veux bien un peu te gronder. Ta lettre m'a l'air un peu malhereuse [*sic*]. Mais
qu'est-ce que tu as de t'affliger ainsi? Tu es libre, tu as un amant sy[m]pathetique, tu as
– à ce qu'il paraît – une bonne maison, des fleurs, des livres, de quoi manger, des
livres, de la musique – enfin, tout ce qu'on peut souhaiter. Or, je crains que la Destinée
ne te prépare quelque sale coup pour te faire regretter ces temps. Ah, je sais bien que tu
es de celles pour qui le bonheur n'existe pas. Sais-tu pour quoi? Tu exiges de la vie plus
que la vie ne pent te donner. Vraiment, ton ardeur de perfection te fait bien
malheureuse, pauvre petite.

Mais j'ai l'air assez prètre [*sic*] de te sermoner ainsi. Chère enfant – car, somme tout,
avec tout ton beauté et sensibilité tu n'est [*sic*] qu'une enfante – combien je te plains.

55

Combien je voudrais te faire douce la vie! Tu te sens déracinée. Mais lequel de nous n'est pas déraciné? Il faut bien se trouver quelque but dans la vie ou l'existence n'est qu'un sinistre farce. Je te conseille les livres de Renan; je ne sais pas de livres qui sont aussi confortants [*sic*] pour un esprit sensitif. Mais je sais bien que tu ne te fiches pas mal de la philosophie.

Je divague. Vraiment, je ne sais pas au juste ce qu'il faut dire à toi. Je t'ai déjà un peu expliqué mes sentiments à ton égard. Je me trouve toujours au même point – je t'aime, je vais t'aimer pendant tout ma vie, mais, mais, tu l'as très bien dit – mon corps avait faim d'une femme qui fusse de la terre comme moi. Et toi aussi tu avais besoin d'une spiritualité moins grossière que la miènne. Mais, je te previeu que tu ne peux jamais rompre le lien qui te jouis [*sic*] à moi. Je n'entends pas le lien tout legale et vulgaire de la marriage – je veux dire celui de l'amour que nous avons eu chacun pour l'autre. Notre union qui était parfait en beaucoup de choses manquait à certains égards – comme tous les unions à ce qu'il paraît. Je sait parfaitment que presque tous les torts sont à moi. C'est vrai que je t'ai traitée fort mal. Mais, que veux-tu, les hommes sont cuistres. Je crois que je t'ai moins fait de la pèine que n'importe quel bourgeois auquel tu aurais pu très bien te lier. Est-ce que je me flatte?

Le temps coule très doucement ici. Puisque nous sommes à trente kilos de la ligne nous moquons les Boches, bien que la position de Paris ne semble pas des plus gais à ce moment. Mais nous avons tout un mois à vivre – c'est beaucoup. Il y a tant de choses qu'on peut voir dans un mois, surtout quand il fait beau temps. J'ai des livres et un lit de fer dans un pavillion. Je travaille de sept heures du matin à cinq heures du soir. Je lis, j'écris, je regarde pousser l'herbe et les feuilles de cinq à dix, ou onze. Je sommeil [*sic*] de onze à six. C'est parfait. Le dimanche j'assiste au service de L'Eglise Angleterre et je prends un vif plaisir a constater la bêtise de tout cela. J'ai tout l'après-midi de Samedi et Dimanche à moi. C'est beaucoup. Mais je ne m'ennuis pas du tout.

Enfin, je dois me taire. J'ai trop bavardé. Mais si on est tranquil – je ne dis pas heureux – on prend l'habitude de trop parler. Puisses-tu te trouver de la tranquillité!

Pardons à ton vieux amant tous ses torts et tous ses petitesses et ne te souviens que de cette partie de lui que tu as aimé autrefois – Atthis!

Bonne chance. Mes amités à G.

Richard.

P.S. Quand tu écris à un soldat du B.E.F. tu n'as qu'à mettre un timbre de 1 penny, comme auparavant.

[Translation]

It's almost two years, my girl, that I have endured this foul soldiers' life. During all this time we have seen each other for only scraps of time. I was twenty-three when I left you; and in a month I will be twenty-six. Do you understand what that means? It means that time is passing, my dear, and we are always further apart.[2]

I really want to scold you a little. Your letter seems to me a bit unhappy. But why on earth do you worry about things so? You are free, you have an amiable lover, you have – or so it would appear – a nice house, flowers, books, something to eat, more books, music – in sum, everything you need to make you happy. But I'm afraid lest Destiny is preparing you some dirty trick to make you miss these times. Ah, I well know that you are among those people for whom happiness does not exist. Do you know why? You ask of life more than life can give you. Really, your ardour for perfection is making you very unhappy, poor girl.

But I seem like a priest to preach thus to you. My child – for, above all, with all your beauty and sensitivity, you are only a child – how much I pity you. How I would like to make life sweet for you! You feel yourself uprooted. But which of us is not uprooted? One really needs to find some purpose in life or existence is nothing but a sinister farce. I recommend Renan's books to you.[3] I do not know any other books which are so comforting for a sensitive spirit. But I well know that you don't give a damn about philosophy.

I digress. Really, I don't rightly know what to say to you. I have already somewhat explained my feelings with regard to you. I always find myself at the same place – I love you, I am going to love you for my whole life, but, but, you have already said it well my body hungered for a woman who was earthy like me. And you, too, needed a spirituality less gross than mine. But, I warn you that you will never be able to break the bond that joins you to me. I don't mean the utterly legal and common bond of marriage – I mean rather that of the love we each have had for the other. Our union which was perfect in so many ways was lacking in certain respects – as all unions are it would appear. I know perfectly that almost all the wrongs are mine. It's true that I have treated you very badly. But, what do you want, men are absurd. I think that I have given you less pain than any other bloke you could have hooked up with. Do I flatter myself?

The weather is very mild here. Since we are thirty kilometers away from the line, we mock the Boches, although the position of Paris does not seem very gay at this moment.[4] But we have a whole month to live – that's a lot.[5] There are so many things one can see in a month, especially when the weather is good. I have books and an iron bed in a house. I work from seven in the morning until five at night. I read, I write, I watch the grass and the leaves grow from five till ten, or eleven. I sleep from eleven to six. It's perfect. On Sundays I attend an Anglican Church service and I take a lively enjoyment in observing the foolishness of all this. I have the whole of Saturday and Sunday afternoon to myself. That's a lot. But I don't get bored at all.

Finally, I must stop writing. I have prattled on too long. But if one is at peace – I don't say happy – one gets into the habit of talking too much. I wish you could find peace!

Let's pardon your old lover all his faults and all his pettiness and remember only that part of him that you used to love – Atthis![6]

Good luck. My regards to C[ecil].

Richard.

P.S. When you write to a soldier of the B.E.F. you only have to put on a 1 penny stamp, just as before.

1 Aldington routinely wrote in French to his good friend Frank Flint as an academic exercise and as a way of privileging intimate information. Writing in French seems to serve both purposes here as well as two additional ends: the effort it requires apparently assuages somewhat the boredom and dislocation Aldington felt at the front while simultaneously restraining his real irritation with H.D.'s most recent letter. Later letters to her in French seem to function similarly.

2 Aldington entered the army on 24 June 1916; his birthday is 8 July.

3 Ernest Renan (1823–92) was a French historian, Hebrew scholar, philologist, and critic. He published his well-known *Vie de Jésus* in 1863, the first volume of *Les Origines du Christianisme*

(1863–83), in which he treats the Christian tradition critically, eschewing exegesis and dogma for a psychological and biographical approach. Renan was very attractive to intellectuals at the end of the nineteenth century because of his admiration for scientific progress and romantic spiritualism.

4 Paris was constantly threatened, though never occupied, by the Germans in 1914–18.

5 Aldington is away from the trenches at base camp for additional training until mid-July.

6 In a poem by Sappho, of which five stanzas and parts of two more survive, she writes of Arignota, now married to a man in Sardis, who remembers with affection her former lover, Atthis, who has deserted her for the awkward and less sophisticated Andromeda. Aldington's own poem, 'To Atthis', after Sappho's, appeared first in *Glebe*, Vol. 1, No. 5 (1914), 19, then in *Des Imagistes* (1914), and bears reprinting here:

> To Atthis
> (After the Manuscript of Sappho now in Berlin)
>
> Atthis, far from me and dear Mnasidika,
> Dwells in Sardis;
> Many times she was near us
> So that we lived life well
> Like the far-famed goddess
> Whom above all things music delighted.
>
> And now she is first among the Lydian women
> As the mighty sun, the rose-fingered moon,
> Beside the great stars.
>
> And the light fades from the bitter sea
> And in like manner from the rich-blossoming earth;
> And the dew is shed upon the flowers,
> Rose and soft meadow-sweet
> And many-coloured melilote.
>
> Many things told are remembered of sterile Atthis.
>
> I yearn to behold thy delicate soul
> To satiate my desire. ...

❧ 14 ❧

13 June 1918

Dearest Dooley/

Yes, I was interested to get Hulun's letter. I have written to Gilbert 'toot sweet' to say how-do. No doubt he's fearfully pleased at being in France – I wonder how long it will last? There are umpteen Yanks in these back areas so I may just possibly run across him. He has – or will have – my address, anyhow.[1]

It must be charming for you to know so many of your family are here or on the way. Specially nice, too, if they get wounded & come down to Cornwall to convalesce!

Thank you for the card of Newlyn. It used to be a very 'arty' place, where R.A.s. instructed their pupils in the obviously picturesque. There is a man who does pictures of naked boys in boats – they always suggest Newlyn to me.[2]

Ah, it was so sweet of you to write to me. And to send me your love & speak of Italy[3] – I kiss your hand, dear, and cannot tell you how happy I am to know you think of me a little.

There is a most mysterious ruined castle in this village, an immense thing on a great mound – rather like Corfe – with a 50 foot moat still damp with water.[4] All the approaches are overgrown with tall grass, shrubs & trees, so that one has to force a way through like the prince in the 'Sleeping Beauty'. Inside the front courtyard which is now a tiny field of grass & shrubs there is an immense peace and a deep solitude. The tower of the donjon is vast – twice as broad & thrice as high as those at Corfe & immutable as time itself. I don't think I have ever felt so deep a sensation of mystery and seclusion as I got from this place.

Time is slipping by only too quickly. Already it is a week since I came & there is only a month now.[5] How I shall hate going up the line again! But – as the Tommies [ordinary British soldiers] say – 'we've done it before'. Really, I've been awfully lucky, for these courses are supposed to be for officers who are 'tired' after many months of hard fighting. And I still haven't hit a German. Every morning in the line I used to watch through glasses for Boches & then shoot at them & dodge down when they shot back. But all was wasted – neither side scored a hit!

By the way I am sending you 3 more of my photographs – one for Hulun, one for Amy[6] & one for the Four Seas Coy.[7] Do you mind sending them on? I don't think they will he stopped by the censor puisqu'il s'agit d'un militaire [since it is a picture of a soldier]. Also, there is no harm in letting Hulun know my address – the censor can cut it out if he damn well likes. One mustn't respect these beastly officials too much. I have Samain's 'Contes' which I am going to send you when I am through.[8] They remind me a little of Imaginary Portraits,[9] though they haven't the same 'maestria' [mastery]. Here is something will please you: 'Oui, tout tend vers la Beauté, tout lutte, tout s'efforce, tout s'épuise pour la réaliser; mais comme elle est infinie, ceux-la seuls s'en approchent le plus qui doivent le plus à la Douleur.'[10] And there is a wonderful description, more Wilde than Wilde, of an aesthetic Renaissance duke, qui 'avait développé jusqu'à l'accuité son aptitude originelle à s'émouvoir de la beauté des choses, et à cet effet il rassemblait sans cesse autour de lui les éléments des plus délicates jouissances.'[11] And there is a story of a sad faun which will make the Dryad cry.[12]

Au revoir, chère belle fantôme, souviens-toi un peu de moi.[13]

Love from
Richard.

1 Gilbert Doolittle had just arrived in France and, like Aldington, is in a 'back area' – that is, at one of the large base camps near Calais, Boulogne, or Rouen, about forty miles from the actual front.

2 Landscape artists, many of them 'R.A.s', members of the Royal Academy, frequently took their students to Newlyn, just west of Penzance on the southern coast of Cornwall.

3 Throughout the war and after, Italy and the time Aldington spent there with H.D. on their 'honeymoon' in 1912 and 1913 would represent to him, and to a lesser degree to her, escape, freedom, art, the past, and an ideal time in their relationship before the war. In this vein Aldington recalls Italy, both real and idealised, in 'Theocritus in Capri', an essay collected in *Literary Studies and Reviews* (London: George Allen and Unwin, 1924):

We all have a few nooks of enchantment in our memories to turn back to for consolation and pleasure. In the creation of them perhaps more depended upon the inner man than upon outward events; the determination to find beauty and at least momentary happiness will find some satisfaction almost everywhere. Youth, spring in a Mediterranean island, Greek poetry, idleness – those were the simple factors of an enchantment whose memory will only end with life. It was of no importance that youth was qualified by penury, that the spring was a mere phenomenon, the result of sidereal motions, that the island was the tourist-ridden Capri and the Greek poet – Theocritus – had never attempted to describe it. Such contingencies have no effect upon a happily constituted mind. ...

... the mood did not vanish nor the happiness fail. It was an enchantment, a plentitude of beauty sufficient to sweeten much bitterness, though, like all enchantment and all beauty, it faded too soon into the past. (241, 245)

4 The Château de Fressin near the village of Azincourt. Aldington writes about visiting this castle in his article for *The Sphere*, 'The Château de Fressin' (3 September 1919, 260), and invests the experience with a good deal of mystic emotion: 'It was like Beaudelaire's [sic] dream of order and luxury – the order of natural life untroubled by the poisonous activities of stupid men, the luxury of silence. I will not say it made me in love with death, but it reconciled me in a quarrel with life.' The Château reminds Aldington of Corfe Castle, the ruined twelfth-century fortress which towers above the village of Corfe Castle where H.D. lived for several months in the summer and early autumn of 1916 when Aldington was in basic training in nearby Worget Camp in Wareham, Dorset.

5 Aldington has been in base camp for additional training since 6 June 1918.

6 Amy Lowell (1874–1925), the American poet and critic. The Aldingtons first met Lowell in the summer of 1914. She came to England because of her interest in imagism and took on the movement as a crusade, publicizing it in the United States and supporting it financially through small personal gifts to writers but particularly through her sponsorship of the imagist anthologies which appeared in 1915, 1916, and 1917. She corresponded regularly with both Aldington and H.D., primarily about literary matters, but the Aldingtons often shared with her details of their daily life. As a large, older, socially conservative, and occasionally obtuse woman, Lowell was at times a figure of ridicule for young writers, though she was also for the Aldingtons a useful patron and a friend.

7 An American firm in Boston which published Aldington's first book of poems, *Images (1910–1915)*, in 1916. The volume had appeared the year before in England. In 1919 Four Seas published *War and Love (1915–1918)*, a combination of two books (*Images of War* and *Images of Desire*) that appeared separately in England in the same year. In 1921 Four Seas published *Images of War* in a single volume edition.

8 Albert Samain (1858–1900), the French poet who helped to found the *Mercure de France* in 1891, was influenced by the symbolists and by Greek sources. He wrote several tales published posthumously in *Contes* in 1903. Amy Lowell devoted a chapter to his work in *Six French Poets: Studies in Contemporary Literature* (1915).

9 Walter Pater's *Imaginary Portraits* (1887). Aldington later included several essays from this collection in his edition, *Walter Pater: Selected Works* (London: Heinemann, 1948).

10 'Yes, everything tends toward Beauty, all fights, struggles, exhaust themselves to realize it; but as it is infinite, those solitary ones approach closest to it who owe the most to Sadness.' Aldington is quoting from 'Rovère et Angisèle' (see *Oeuvres de Albert Samain*, Vol. 3, Paris: Mercure de France, 1920, 157).

11 Who 'had developed to the point of acuity his original aptitude for exciting himself with the beauty of things, and to that end he assembled around him ceaselessly the elements of the most delicate enjoyments'. Aldington is quoting a description of Rovère, the son of the Duke of Spoleto, in 'Rovère et Angisèle' (see *Oeuvres de Albert Samain*, Vol. 3, 113–14).

12 Probably 'Hyalis le petit faune aux yeux bleus', although a faun also figures as a character in 'Xanthus ou la vitrine sentimentale'.

13 Goodbye, my beautiful phantom, think a little bit of me.

18 June 1918

Ma chère femme,

Je me porte très bien. Je suis ni blessé ni malade (malheureusement) et voici quelques jours que je n'ai pas reçu de tes nouvelles.

Mes jours se rassemblent tellement que je ne crois pas qu'il y a grand chose à ajouter à ce que je t'ai déjà dit. Mais ici on a la paix – ce qui est beaucoup. On regrette sa liberté quelquefois, mais somme tout on s'y habitue à la fin.

C'est aujord'hui [*sic*] l'anniversaire de Waterloo. Je parie que tu ne l'avais pas rapellé – dis? Il y a precisément cent trois ans que La Vieille Garde faisait sa suprême attaque – tiens, je devient heroique genre Victor Hugo. Espérons du moins que cela ira mieux pour les français aujourd'hui.

Je ne sais pas au juste pourquoi j'écris puisque j'ai l'esprit tellement vide qu'il ne me reste rien à dire. Alors, faut bien dire au revoir, n'est-ce pas?

Richard.

[Translation]

My dear wife,

I am very well. I am neither wounded nor sick (unfortunately) and for some days now I have not heard from you.

My days are such that I don't think that there is anything of great moment to add to what I have already told you. But here we have peace – which is a lot. One misses one's freedom sometimes, but over all one finally becomes accustomed to it.

Today is the anniversary of Waterloo.[1] I wager you didn't remember it – tell me? It is precisely one hundred and three years since The Old Garde launched its final attack – goodness, I am becoming heroic in the style of Victor Hugo. Let's hope at least that this present situation will go better for the French.

I don't know exactly why I write since I have a spirit so empty that there is nothing left for me to say. So, it's best to say goodbye, isn't it?

Richard.

1 The famous battle in which the Duke of Wellington defeated Napoleon in 1815. Aldington's interest in this battle eventually led to his biography *The Duke: Being an Account of the Life & Achievements of Arthur Wellesley, 1st Duke of Wellington* (New York: Viking, 1943).

20 June 1918

Dear Dooley/

All your letters seem to be coming backwards! Last night I had the one saying you didn't want to write any more and to-night I have your 'third installment'. The others will come on later from the batt'n [battalion headquarters], so I shall be able to piece them together. I am very interested in the little girl in the garden & the German conversation seems very thrilling to me[1] – someday I must learn German.[2] Really it is very kind of you to send me these letters – like of [*sic*] sort of realistic fairy tale 'to be continued in our next', though I hope I shan't be here for 1001 days.[3]

Amy's lecture is dreadful, but I am very touched by it – the poor old thing was really trying to please me & to help me. It isn't her fault that she can't see how very foolish she is – 'vanity of vanities' blinds her. The whole 'lecture' is laughable – my chief concern is to conceal it now I've got it![4]

I don't like my article on Sappho at all – it's bad prose & contains not one original idea.[5] Je m'en fiche [I don't care].

These days I am learning to write all over again. My method may amuse you. I write on a sheet of paper a line of French prose upon which I 'meditate' until out of the confusion of my sensations & thoughts & emotions something definite frames itself. This I translate as briefly & clearly as possible in two or three prose paragraphs, upon which I work at odd minutes and half hours during a week or so. I've done 8 so far, 6 of wh: I sent to Flint[6] with the remark that he might pass them on to you. I am trying to avoid 1. All complaint & self-pity, 2. All excessive depression, 3. Any lack of candour with myself, 4. Everything that is not at least abstractly true. I am rather proud of this paragraph: 'There, lingering for a while beside the marble head of some shattered Hermes it (the soul) shall strew the violets of regret for a lost loveliness as transient as itself. Or, perhaps, by some Homeric sea it shall watch the crisp foam from a straight wind & gather sea-flowers exquisite in their acrid restraint of colour & austere sparseness of petal.'

Richard.

Please *note:* Correspondence for soldiers of H.M. Forces needs *only one penny* stamp.

1 H.D. did not routinely keep her early manuscripts and the stories which she is sending to Aldington here were never published and apparently have not survived.

2 Aldington was never so comfortable with German as H.D. was (she had studied German throughout her years at Friends' Central School, from 1901 through 1905), but he was not the ignoramus he implies here. In *Life for Life's Sake,* Aldington notes that when in training in Dorset in the summer of 1916 he took with him a copy of Heinrich Heine's *Buch der Lieder,* which he planned to read to 'brush up' on his German (182).

3 An allusion to the continuing fairy tales in *1001 Arabian Nights.*

4 I have been unable to determine whether Aldington is referring here to something Amy Lowell has recently published or to something she has written in a recent letter to one or the other or both of the Aldingtons.

5 As part two of a series of six articles entitled 'Letters to Unknown Women', which appeared in *The Dial* between 14 March 1918, and 17 May 1919, Aldington's essay 'To Sappho' appeared in the 9 May 1918, issue (No. 766, 430–1).

6 Frank Stuart Flint (1885–1960), fellow imagist poet and translator. Publishing as F. S. Flint and often called 'Franky' by both H.D. and Aldington, Flint knew both writers well but was particularly close to Aldington and remained his closest male friend and confidant throughout the war and into the 1920s. Unlike other artists in the Aldingtons' circle, Flint did not support himself by his art but with various civil service jobs. His stable home life (he had two children by his first wife, Violet, who died as a result of childbirth in April of 1920; soon afterwards he married her sister Ruth) set him somewhat apart from his literary friends, as did his steady if small income and his established literary reputation. His first book of verse, *In the Net of Stars* (1909), contained a few poems in free verse; his literary articles for *The Egoist* and other journals and publication of poems in all four imagist anthologies established Flint as a serious modernist artist. He was also a well-regarded translator and Britain's most prominent authority on twentieth-century French poetry in the years before the war. His translation, *The Mosella of Decimus Magnus Ausonius,* appeared as Number 6 in the first Poets' Translation Series in February 1916. Flint came to know the Aldingtons in London and became especially close to

them during the summer of 1916, when he and his family took a cottage not far from them at Swanage in Devon. H.D.'s letters to Flint (a selection of which, edited by Cyrena Pondrom, appeared in *Contemporary Literature*, 10, Autumn 1969, 557–86) show that the two were close if jaunty friends who shared with each other details of their personal and professional lives between 1912 and 1917, after which time their relationship faded. Aldington's letters to Flint are characterized by a boyish jocularity and a serious sharing of experiences, emotions, and ideas, and reveal an intimacy not found in his letters to anyone else. Aldington often wrote to Flint in other languages, privileging information as well as sharpening his linguistic skills; letters in French, Italian, and Latin occur throughout their correspondence. Flint is probably the only contemporary whom Aldington consistently admired in the 1910s and 1920s for his professional achievement and personal qualities. Ironically, as Flint produced less and less literary work, in the 1920s Aldington replaced him as England's foremost authority on French literature.

⪼ 17 ⪻

21 June 1918

Dear Dooley/

The first 'installment' has come to join the third which arrived yesterday.[1] I am expecting the second tomorrow to make the sequence complete. I am very glad you are sending them especially if it is any help or pleasure to you to write them. Certainly it gives me pleasure to hear from you.

I think I like the third better than the first. Yes, the third is charming and touching and somehow the little German conversation makes it quaint and like a fairy-tale. The first one is – shall we say – un peu cinglant [rather bitter]. But it's astonishing what a thick, thick skin one grows – dodging whizz-bangs, I suppose, helps one to this indifference.[2]

Harriet's letter & the extract from Poetry are, I suppose, some sort of a belated 'tribute'[3] – can't you see them unctiously quoting Choricos if I happened to stop a whole one?[4] I am genuinely pleased, though, that some American lad has found even a rhetorical consolation in my words. But I don't really believe he thought of anything *but* shells when shells were falling. Perhaps I am mistaken.

I can't see you writing a 'Deirdre' – no, no, sharp edges not mist.[5] Yet it is perhaps good that you should add the stimulus of music to your great gifts – yes, excellent, you will do beautiful things. Why not assassinate H.D. since Amy has mangled her?[6] The combinations of the alphabet are quite numerous. Or a name – something Anglo-Boche?

Ah, well; time passes. Will you post the enclosed to Harriet, please?[7]

With love from
Richard.

On second thoughts I'm going to ask you to type the enclosed – for old acquaintance sake? – and to send them to Harriet for me. Will you, please?

1 An 'installment' of prose H.D. has recently begun; see letter 16.
2 'Whizz-bangs' were German flat trajectory bombs whose detonation was preceded by an audible 'whizz'.
3 In 1912 in Chicago, Harriet Monroe (1860–1936) founded *Poetry: A Magazine of Verse*, which she edited until her death. The journal was dedicated to modern poetry which, if it were truly good, would also, Monroe was convinced, be democratic and speak to a wide audience. Her notions of poetry and its purpose owe a good deal to Whitman, and it is revealing that among the poets she published she was especially fond of Edgar Lee Masters and Vachel Lindsay.

Monroe was not enthusiastic about H.D.'s verse, but thought very highly of Aldington's work.

Monroe sent Aldington with her letter a copy of her review of his *Reverie: A Little Book of Poems for H.D.*, which appeared in *Poetry*, Vol. 12, No. 1, April 1918, 44–5:

An American soldier now in France writes, in acknowledging a copy of the new *Poetry:*

Certain poems, like the *Choricos* of Aldington, have shuddered with me along night roads, and through their bold beauty have saved me from terror at moments when one of the great shocks – the explosion of an enemy shell, the sudden presence of pain or awful agony, the nearness of death – fell without preface upon me.

I remember once particularly, in the drab of light of a cloudy dawning, when I saw near the edge of a road a poilu quietly lying. I should have fainted, I think, from the sheer tragedy of the incident, had I not heard, singing in my head, Aldington's invocation to death.

Such a letter proves, more sharply than any review, the value of a poet's work. No later lyric by Aldington can ever dim the Greek-marble-like beauty of *Choricos*, but neither can that poem dim the more tender and human beauty of Reverie. The contrast of moods in the two poems bridges the gulf between youth and manhood. *Choricos*, which was first printed over five years ago in the second number of POETRY, was written while the poet was still in his teens. It presents the feeling of adolescence, that high and impersonal exaltation not uncommon when noble youth confronts the thought of death:

> Thou art the silence of beauty,
> And we look no more for the morning;
> We yearn no more for the sun,
> Since with thy white hands,
> Death,
> Thou crownest us with the pallid chaplets,
> The slim colorless poppies
> Which in thy garden alone
> Softly thou gatherest.

Since writing it, the poet has experienced love and war – love at its highest, war at its most terrible. He has compassed life, from extreme to extreme, and after that there is no longer question of youth or age – life moves in the larger rhythms of eternity.

> All men love for a flash, a day,
> As I love now,
> But all men do not always love so long
> Nor find in love the excuse for life,
> The sanction for the bitterness of death.
> Not far away as I now write
> The guns are beating madly upon the still air
> With sudden rapid blows of sound,
> And men die with the quiet sun above them
> And horror and pain and noise upon earth.
>
> To-morrow, maybe, I shall be one of them,
> One in a vast field of dead men,
> Unburied, or buried hastily, callously.
> But for ever and for ever.
> In the fair land I have built up
> From the dreams of my love,

We two are together, she bending by the pale flower
And I beside her:
We two together in a land of quiet
Inviolable behind the walls of death.

This tiny book of nine brief poems contains 'no murmur against Fate.' The poet accepts war, as he might accept a cyclone, in anguish and bitterness of spirit but without revolt. He feels no élan, no conviction of war's necessity or righteousness, but he takes his place in the ranks and does his part with a grim and resolute stoicism. And out of his despair, out of his hunger for beauty, comes a lyric note clearer and richer than anything we have heard from him since those earliest poems, and an exaltation of spirit as noble and impassioned, and perhaps more humane.

We are of those that Dante saw
Glad, for love's sake, among the flames of hell,
Outdaring with a kiss all-powerful wrath;
For we have passed athwart a fiercer hell,
Through gloomier, more desperate circles
Than ever Dante dreamed:
And yet love kept us glad.
H.M.

4 First printed in *Poetry* in November 1912 (Vol. 1, No. 2, 39–40), 'Choricos's title appeared in Greek, 'XOPIKOS':

The ancient songs
Pass deathward mournfully.

Cold lips that sing no more, and withered wreaths,
Regretful eyes, and drooping breasts and wings –
Symbols of ancient songs,
Mournfully passing
Down to the great white surges,
Watched of none
Save the frail sea-birds
And the lithe pale girls,
Daughters of Oceanus.

And the songs pass from the green land
Which lies upon the waves as a leaf
On the flowers of hyacinths.
And they pass from the waters,
The manifold winds and the dim moon,
And they come
Silently winging through soft Cimmerian dusk,
To the quiet level lands
That she keeps for us all,
That she wrought for us all for sleep
In the silver days of the earth's dawning –
Proserpina, daughter of Zeus.

And we turn from the Cyprian's breasts,
And we turn from thee,
Phoebus Apollo,
And we turn from the music of old,

And the hills that we loved and the meads,
And we turn from the fiery day,
And the lips that were over-sweet;
For silently
Brushing the fields with red-shod feet,
With purple robe
Searing the grass as with a sudden flame,
Death,
Thou hast come upon us.
And of all the ancient songs
Passing to the swallow-blue halls
By the dark streams of Persephone,
This only remains –
That in the end we turn to thee,
Death,
We turn to thee, singing
One last song.

O death,
Thou art an healing wind
That blowest over white flowers
A-tremble with dew;
Thou art a wind flowing
Over far leagues of lonely sea;
Thou art the dusk and the fragrance;
Thou art the lips of love mournfully smiling;
Thou art the sad peace of one
Satiate with old desires;
Thou art the silence of beauty,
And we look no more for the morning,
We yearn no more for the sun
Since with thy white hands,
Death,
Thou crownest us with the pallid chaplets,
The slim colourless poppies
Which in thy garden alone

Softly thou gatherest.
And silently;
And with slow feet approaching –
And with bowed head and unlit eyes,
We kneel before thee;
And thou, leaning towards us,
Caressingly layest upon us
Flowers from thy thin cold hands,
And, smiling as a chaste woman
Knowing love in her heart,
Thou sealest our eyes
And the illimitable quietude
Comes gently upon us.

5 Yeats's play 'Deirdre' (1917), which was based on the Irish myth of Deirdre of the Sorrows.
6 Aldington suggests that H.D. abandon the persona that Amy Lowell has misrepresented (see letter 16). H.D. herself often had reservations about her pen name, using others from time to time (for instance, *Nights* appeared under the pseudonym 'John Helforth' in 1935, and 'Delia Alton' was a pseudonym H.D. seriously considered when she was preparing *Bid Me to Live* for publication in 1960). She wrote to Lowell about her name as a literary identity on 5 March 1917: 'My signature is "H.D." for poetic purposes. *Please* let it be *just* that. I have always wanted to keep R's and my literary personalities absolutely distinct. ... I must keep *H.D.* clear from R.A. R. has his career + it is best for him not to have me as an appendage.'
7 Aldington probably enclosed 'Prayers and Fantasies I–VIII', dated 'France, 1918', which appeared in *Poetry* in November 1918 (Vol. 13, No. 2, 67–71):

I

To have passed so close to annihilation, and (which is worse) to have become stained so inalterably with the ideas and habits of masses – this leaves me immeasurably discouraged, out of love with myself.

Now I am good only to mimic inferior masters. My thoughts are stifling – heavy grey dust from a scorched road.

For me silence; or if speech, then some humble poem in prose. Indeed I am too conscientious – or shall we say too impotent? – to dare the cool rhythm of prose, the sharp edges of poetry.

Nymphes de Parnasse! Encore un Pégasse raté!

II

Touch once again with the lips of thought the fair rigid limbs of goddesses men imagined beside the inland sea. Give the life of our blood to one among them, and worship in her oval of tremulous gold the beauty of that body whose embrace would murder us with ecstasy.

Recall from Orcus the Foam-born, lady of many names; make for her a broidered throne among the dusky colonnades of the soul.

Death, a fierce exaltation, sweeps from the lips of the conqueror; but from hers, gently, a frail kiss, breathes a savor of life.

III

Slowly, too slowly, the night, with its noise and its fear and its murder, yields to the dawn. One by one the guns cease. Quicker, O dawn, quicker – dazzle the hateful stars, lighten for us the weight of the shadows.

The last rat scuttles away; the first lark thrills with a beating of wings and song. The light is soft; deliberately, consciously, the young dawn moves. My unclean flesh is penetrated with her sweetness and she does not disdain even me.

Out of the East as from a temple comes a procession of girls and young men, smiling, brave, candid, ignorant of grief.

Few know the full bitterness of night, but they alone will know the full beauty of dawn – if dawn ever comes.

IV

Life has deceived us. The thoughts we found so vivid and fresh were dull and crass as the prayers muttered to a worn rosary by an infidel priest.

The joy we felt in beauty, our sense of discovery at the touch of some age-green bronze; even the sick horror at some battlefield where the flesh had not quite fallen from the shattered bones – all this was old, a thousand times felt and forgotten.

And is the kiss of your mouth then but the reflection of dead kisses, the gleam of your breast a common thing? Was the touch of your hand but a worn memory of hands crumbled into cool dust?

V

And in the end one comes to love flowers as women, and women as flowers. Beauty recoils from excess. Imitate the wise Easterns, and let a few sprays of blossom decorate the empty chamber of the soul and spread their fragrance through its recesses.

Ah! To retain this fragrance, to make permanent this most precious of essences, this mingling of suave and acrid perfumes – something wild and tender and perverse and immortal!

I will make for myself, from tempered silver, an Aphrodite with narrow hips and small pointed breasts, and wide brow above gay, subtle eyes; and in her hand shall be a perfume ball sweet with this divine fragrance.

VI

Escape, let the soul escape from this insanity, this insult to God, from this ruined landscape, these murdered fields, this bitterness, this agony, from this harsh death and disastrous mutilation, from this filth and labor, this stench of dead bodies and unwashed living bodies – escape, let the soul escape!

Let the soul escape and move with emotion along ilex walks under a quiet sky. There, lingering for a while beside the marble head of some shattered Hermes, it strews the violets of regret for a lost loveliness as transient as itself. Or perhaps, by some Homeric sea, watching the crisp foam blown by a straight wind, it gathers sea-flowers, exquisite in their acrid restraint of color and austere sparseness of petal.

There, perhaps, among flowers, at twilight, under the glimmer of the first stars, it will find a sensation of a quiet, almost kindly universe, indifferent to this festering activity.

VII

The gods have ceased to be truth, they have become poetry. Now only simple pure hearts and those who are weary of doubt believe. Why not pray to the gods, any god? Perhaps even from the immensity of space will come a gently ironic echo.

'Dionysios, lord of life and laughter, from whom come twin gifts of ecstasy, hear me.

I pray the noble Iacchos of reverent mien and wide tolerant eyes, to look mildly upon me and to show me the mystery of beauty, the mystery of vineyards, the mystery of death.

And I pray the young Dionysios, the bearer of the fawn-skin, the charioteer of leopards, the lover of white breasts, to show me the mystery of love.

And grant that nothing ignoble may render me base to myself; let desire be always fresh and keen; let me never love or be loved through ennui, through pity or through lassitude.'

VIII

The moon high-seated above the ridge, fills the ruined village with tranquil light and black broken shadows – ruined walls, shattered timbers, piles of rubbish, torn-up ground, almost beautiful in this radiance, in this quiet June air. Lush grass in the tangled gardens sways very softly, and white moths dart over the bending sprays.

Somehow to-night the air blows clearer, sweeter – the chemistry of earth is slowly purifying the corrupting bodies, the waste and garbage of armies. Sweetness, darkness, clean peace – the marble rock of some Greek island, piercing its sparse garment of lavenders and mints like a naked nymph among rustling leaves.

Heavy-scented the air to-night – new-mown hay? – a pungent exotic odor ah! phosgene. ...

And to-morrow there will be huddled corpses with blue horrible faces and foam on their writhed mouths.

23 June 1918

My dear Dooley/

This letter will be written in rather a hurry as I feel I'm sickening for 'pyrexia' wh: will put me to bed for a couple of days. I daresay you've heard of it, this new mysterious disease which is going over Europe, especially the armies, like the old plagues. Fortunately it is quite harmless & only lasts a few days – one has a dreadful head & back ache, legs like lead, a high temperature & a rapid pulse. Then it goes as suddenly as it came. I'm one of the last to get it here & I guess I shan't have it badly.[1]

I am very happy to get your letters and to live with them either your child's or girl's life or something we lived together. That scene in Paris. I had almost forgotten it, but now I remember it all so clearly, so plainly. Perhaps I exaggerated a little the odd sensation of Margaret's regret.[2] Yet it was there, and she was there or seemed to be. One's nerves play these games, induce these hallucinations. Just as to-day any over-weary Frenchman, struggling on, battling long after all strength has gone, may see Joan of Arc on her white horse in the barrage-smoke. These eidola have no existence in themselves, but are real because of the emotion that creates them. (Am I writing dreadful nonsense? I feel so damn queer – it wouldn't surprise me now if the war ended!)

I think, rather against you, that Death does settle nearly everything. Somewhere back in my mind is a memory of some stately prose Elizabethan discourse on death. I cannot remember the words but this is how I should write them: 'O kingly, O pontifical death, at whose touch, Midas-like yet priestly, all the vain efforts of man crumble into the golden dust of oblivion; Death, that receivest into thy great Commonwealth not only the stately dames & great lords of history but the most humble, the most childish, the weakest and most despised of mankind. By thy graves, O Death, all must bend in sorrow, & in thy sepulcres all must at last rest. Thou art that Basanos [transliterated Greek; touchstone] whereby we may test the vanity of all flesh & prove what fools' baubles be those crowns, those lands, that honour, those riches, that lust, that beauty, those busy affairs wherein the jewish race of man doth so agitate & afflict him. Over all thou triumphest, O Death, for whatever be the play thou speakest the funereal prologue & all our histories & pomps are summed up by thine inevitable 'Hic Jacet' ['Here Lies'].

Isn't that Sir Thomas Browne with the genius cut out?[3] Yet it is true and I for one am 'too timid, too frail in hope' to deceive myself (as I think) with any talk of Islands of the Blessed.[4] 'Dust hath closed Helen's eyes',[5] and not all Homer's rhetoric nor all the tears that have been shed for her will ever make that dust pure red & white again or give that heart one thrill of the many kisses of the young prince.[6]

Ah, well one can go on for pages enwinding the sadness of one's heart in more or less picturesque rhetoric. I'm going along to the Doc. now & shall find out if I'm in for a slight or a serious do. It feels very slight to me.

Au revoir – l will go on writing something each day when possible.

Richard.

1 Known to doctors as P.U.O. ('pyrexia of unknown origin') and to soldiers as 'trench fever', pyrexia was a virus carried by lice and characterized by chills and fever. In Aldington's battalion between 11 June and 23 June 1918, five officers and 250 men of other ranks were hospitalized because of an outbreak of influenza (the war diaries of the Ninth Royal Sussex Regiment, PRO).
2 Margaret Lanier Cravens (1881–1912) was a young American ex-patriate and Ezra Pound's patron, to whom he introduced Aldington and H.D. in Paris in the spring of 1912. H.D.,

Aldington, and Pound were shocked when she committed suicide in June 1912 shortly after the announcement of her friend Walter Rummel's sudden engagement to Thérèse Chaigneau. Robert Spoo's edition of the Pound-Cravens correspondence (*Ezra Pound and Margaret Cravens: A Tragic Friendship, 1910–1912*, Durham: Duke University Press, 1988) discusses the impact of Cravens's suicide on Aldington and particularly on H.D., who chronicled her response at the time in two sonnets to 'M.L.C.' written in the summer of 1912 and published in Spoo's book.

3 Sir Thomas Browne (1605–82) was a British physician and miscellaneous writer, an antiquarian known for rhetorical elegance in the grand style.

4 Unidentified quotation, but the imaginary islands Aldington refers to are those western isles thought proverbially to be the home of good people after death.

5 A line from Thomas Nashe's 'In Time of Pestilence':

> Brightness balls from the air;
> Queens have died young and fair;
> Dust hath closed Helen's eye.
> I am sick, I must die.
> Lord have mercy on us.

6 Paris, Prince of Troy.

⚶ 19 ⚶

24 June 1918

Just to say that I'm all right & that the little fever is progressing normally. Have to stay in bed a couple of days, that's all; which, as you can imagine, I don't mind in the least!

Will write more to-morrow.

Richard.

P.S Have you heard anything from the Dial about paying for those articles? I must write to them.[1]

R.

1 *The Dial*, the American periodical edited at this time by Martyn Johnson, accepted six articles from Aldington, which appeared under the title 'Letters to Unknown Women': 'To the Slave in "Cleon"' appeared 14 March 1918 (226–7); 'To Sappho' appeared 9 May 1918 (430–1); 'To Helen' appeared 6 June 1918 (525–6). Aldington is probably awaiting payment for these three. The other articles in the series appeared after this time: 'Heliodora', 28 December 1918 (598); 'To the Amaryllis of Theocritus', 22 February 1919 (183); and 'To La Grosse Margot', 17 May 1919 (510).

⚶ 20 ⚶

26 June 1918

Well I've got over my little fever fit and am walking about again, rather slowly as my head feels a little queer still & my legs shake a bit. But I'm better, much better; very terribly tired of the war though & rather tending towards discouragement. There is just the hillside & its trees & the white bend in the road that one seems to cling on to frantically as the man in Notre Dame clung to the bending lead gargoyle.[1] In the end of course one must let go but for the time being …

Your letter of the 20th came to-day with its virginal mood, pellucid & wistful. A little convalescent in texture, perhaps, and so rather fitting in with my present state. Of course as always the heart of another is a dark forest; I cannot 'place' you, especially at this distance. I mean have you, at last, really found out something of what you want or are you just wrapping in Attic parables an almost legitimate repulsion to me? You liken me to Antinous, to Meleager – ah, but I am very far from that now – a kind of mixture of Le Feu of Barbusse & Remy's Diomède, blood & fire annihilating that elusive, perhaps imaginary, freshness.[2]

But I'm not in a proper state to write coherently to-day – very little things irritate me & entirely divert my thoughts. Someone spoke to me & I've quite forgotten all I was going to write. So it must just go – do you know how easy that renouncing things becomes? (You say 'Keep young'; you say, 'we must not meet for years.' Then, lady, say how be young away from the fountain of all youth – your eyes?)

Presently I shall go for a little walk down the village street and come back for tea, speak outworn trivialities, & so gradually to bed. They say the Italians have beaten the Austrians – what does it matter? A few Sou [?] thousand more widows and 'loverless' – nothing, a mere nothing.

I haven't heard from Gilbert, but I think I know where he is, a good way from here, in a very charming place. No chance of our meeting I think.

Please go on writing. I like to get your angle of vision.

Richard.

1 Quasimodo, the hunchback who loved Esmeralda in Victor Hugo's novel, *Notre Dame de Paris* (1831).

2 Antinous (c. 110–30 C.E.) was Hadrian's beloved. His death by drowning in the Nile was thought to have been a suicide or a ritual sacrifice. He was mourned extravagantly by Hadrian to such an extent that he was deified. Meleager was the first century B.C.E. Greek poet and philosopher, known for his erotic verse and as the first editor of the Greek Anthology. *Le Feu: Journal d'une Esconade* (1916), a realistic novel by Henri Barbusse (1874–1935), was one of the most widely read works of the First World War; it detailed the soldier's experience in the trenches, behind the lines, and on leave. *Les Chevaux de Diomède* (1897), a novel by Remy de Gourmont, appeared in installments in *The Egoist* in 1914.

≈ 21 ≈

29 June 1918

I'm glad you got those two books but they were sent off a long time ago – before I left the line in fact.[1] Gyp is not much – one gets tired of her in no time. She is the Frenchwoman comme il faut [a proper lady] – a horrible type.[2]

I never hear from Mrs Shakespeare – is she ill or something.[3]

Frank didn't mean any ill by his question.[4] Clearly, someone has made the suggestion to him – Hutton, I fancy.[5] But he hasn't replied to my letter – perhaps the gods have put him in the army as punishment.

Sanity, yes that is worth having. What exactly does it mean? Giving things & people & ideas that correct relative importance. That is why a sane man always looks a little mad to other people. But if Gray can give you sanity from that marmoreal calm of his, then indeed he is not one who gives nothing. You must beware, though, of staying too long in Cornwall. Don't you think an occasional 'bout' in town would be good, or are you utterly fed up with London? μηδὲν ἄγαν [nothing in excess] you know. You have been quite fourteen weeks in Cornwall now.[6]

My flu left me very spiritless & unpoised, & I am only just getting back that sense of self-satisfaction so necessary to comfort. I have written nothing for a week & have no desire to; à quoi bon noircir du bon papier blanc [to what good purpose blacken good white paper]?

The woods here are still lovely, but 'lack a somewhat' as friend Pound would have remarked in his exquisite classic English.[7]

Au revoir

Richard.

1 Aldington left the trenches on 4 June for additional training at the base camp where he now is.

2 Pseudonym of Marie-Antoinette de Riguetti de Mirabeau (1850–1932). Her light and witty books include *Petit Bob* (1868), *Autour de Marriage* (1883), *Mademoiselle Loulon* (1888), and *Le Marriage de Chiffon* (1894).

3 Olivia Shakespear (1864–1938) was the mother of Dorothy Shakespear, Ezra Pound's wife. She had many literary friends and Aldington had met her through Pound in 1912.

4 Frank Flint had just entered the army and evidently wrote Aldington in late May asking if the Aldingtons had parted ways. Aldington wrote back on 2 June 1918: 'I knew of course that there would be "facheux bruits" [angry noises, gossip] about H.D. and myself. We are "parted" to the extent that I am in France and she in Cornwall. But we are not "parted" in any other sense. We write to each other comme toujours. You – et le monde – are very blind if you think anything could ever part us two.'

5 Edward Hutton (1875–1969), writer, translator and editor. The Aldingtons probably first came to know Hutton personally at Constable's (where he was employed from 1913 to 1928), and they evidently worked closely with him on H.D.'s *Sea Garden* (which Constable published in 1916) and on the imagist anthologies (which Constable published in 1915, 1916, and 1917). Hutton was an author in his own right, however, specializing in Italian literature, history, and art, and the Aldingtons may well have been familiar with his work as early as their first trip to Italy, for he wrote several travel books on Italy in the early years of the century. Hutton served in the Foreign Office dealing with Italian affairs from 1916 through 1918, and edited *The Anglo-Italian Review* in 1918 through 1919.

6 If Aldington is being precise, H.D. arrived in Cornwall on 23 March 1918.

7 Ezra Pound (1885–1972) first met H.D. in 1901, when he was a student at the University of Pennsylvania. She inspired early poems, later gathered into *Hilda's Book* (printed at the end of *End to Torment*, 67–84). They were periodically 'engaged' during Pound's years at Hamilton University, his return to the University of Pennsylvania, his brief term teaching in Indiana, and his trip to Europe in 1908–10. By the time Pound sailed again for England in early 1911, their rather vague romance was essentially over. Pound's very early influence on H.D. was intense, and he certainly influenced her ideas of poetry when she later met him in London in the autumn of 1911. There, Pound introduced H.D. to his widening circle of artistic friends, and at a party at Brigit Patmore's late in 1911, Pound introduced H.D. to Aldington. Patmore had earlier introduced Aldington to Pound.

Pound was at his best during these prewar London years, and the Aldingtons both before and after their marriage were indebted to his energy and imagination. He labelled their poems 'Imagiste' in the autumn of 1912 and was responsible for their publication soon after in *Poetry*. Pound was instrumental in securing Aldington his position as literary editor of *The Egoist* in 1913, and continued to serve the Aldingtons as a sort of literary godfather through the publication of *Des Imagistes* in 1914. But before the tensions stemming from Amy Lowell's appropriation of Imagism and the anthologies of 1915, 1916, and 1917, Pound was for the Aldingtons clearly a troublesome force, never quite understanding either their love for each other or their continued poetic development. They were always to feel a deep affection for him, but he became an interloper, an unmanageable enthusiast whose depressions and manic vitality they could not share. Both Aldingtons maintained an intermittent correspondence with him throughout their lives and valued his friendship and the attention he had given them. H.D. would reflect at length on her relationship with him in *End to Torment* (written in 1958); Aldington would write sensibly, perceptively, and affectionately about him in *Life for Life's Sake* (1941), concluding in words H.D. also might have written: 'We have come to differ over a lot of things but ... I can't go back on the Ezra of 1912–1914' (111).

Aldington is here in Letter 21 making fun of Pound's idiosyncratic locutions. Aldington early perceived that Pound's witty and sometimes bizarre phrasing was a result, conscious or not, of a mistranslation of a foreign phrase into English (as in *Des Imagistes*), of an amusing mishearing (as in Pound's later references to New Directions as 'Nude Erections'), of peculiar orthography, cryptic shorthand, or coded elision (as in Hamadryad for H.D. or H.D. for Hilda Doolittle), or even of mistyping or gross typographical error, which Aldington in the late 1920s generously attributed to Pound's typewriter itself, which by some fluke of circumstance Aldington inherited, probably when Pound left England for Italy in 1920.

⇗ 22 ⇖

1 July 1918

Where was I in my discourse?[1] Somewhere about 'life', I fancy. Once at 44[2] I tried to get at what was moving in me, by talking about 'keeping in touch with common humanity.' That is not quite what I mean, but it is somewhere near it. The attitude I am getting at is very hard to define. One acts & yet at the same time one reflects on action: one does the ordinary things that quite common people do, simply because one is convinced that what happens to humanity happens to oneself, that the things which quite stupid poor men do are the real things of life. The man who sows the wheat, the man who grinds the grain, the man who kneads & bakes the bread – just to take one instance – these people are exceedingly important. One's art must take note of them, be at least sympathetic towards them. Why is it Ezra, for instance, seems to us so utterly dead? Just because he has cut himself off from this common humanity – which is fundamentally the same which Christ walked with and Plato talked with & Villon played the scoundrel with.[3] Don't mistake me; I am a thousand miles from the philanthropic man, the man who wants to reform the world, the democrate. No, and I would by no means be blind to all the misery & treachery & petty lusts & cruelties of this 'common humanity'. But I think one should realise one's own clay, be part of the drab or golden pageant, be at ease with common men as well as with exceptional men. That is very hard for such as we, yet we cannot but gain by it. For that is the true romance, that the great living truth which makes vital our love of beauty, our knowledge of dead worlds – here, I mean, on this earth.

I seem always to be describing loops about my subject, always shooting à peu près [near the mark]; but I think perhaps you will get me. For myself I see clearly that I want to avoid the dead-egotism of Pound, the very foolish paltryness of Chelsea, the ridiculous splurging of Chicago, the diseased strength of the Cubists, and the mere belly-worship of the bourgeois, the mere struggle with poverty of the poor.[4] What is left then? Why just that full consciousness of life I speak of, that almost fanatical sincerity I am seeking. Oh, yes, books are good and it is good to know all about Gothic churches & the philosophy of Lucretius[5] – but it is good too to know how a soldier puts

Aldington enclosed this photograph with his letter of
1   July 1918

together his marching order, how a blacksmith shoes a horse & why we do not grow as
much wheat in the west of England as in the east. And beyond all this knowledge one
should be sincerely interested in common lives, realise I mean what these people do.
They are the salt of the earth; we, I don't quite know what we are, not
'unacknowledged legislators' certainly![6] We are, perhaps, a kind of unauthorised
priesthood, the go-betweens of the spirit & the flesh. We interpret humanity to itself, &
ourselves. It doesn't matter at all whether anyone ever reads what we write. The great
point is to think rightly & clearly – and all these things shall be added unto you.[7]

Thus, I now know that Alexander the Great was an imbecile; but he was a very
brilliant imbecile. He did things which were perhaps not worth doing; but if anyone
thinks the handling of armies an easy thing let him take charge of a company for a
week. What I mean is this: that Alexander was not a great man – he added nothing to
the world – but he cannot have been a fool. One must understand even Alexander, just
as one must understand the scrub-woman.

At once, you will see that there is a tremendous lot to be learned. One knows nothing
of these things. Could you make a pair of shoes? Can you hoe a row of turnips? Do you
understand, say, the difference between municipal government in the United States & in
Italy? Oh _not_ dull, because these are people's lives & we live in this world, not in Sirius,[8]
certainly not in 'Chelsea'. The problem of expressing these things is infinitely difficult –
much more than, say, the record of one's ecstasy before an 'old garden'![9] I am trying to
approach it obliquely, through little prose poems,[10] feeling my way & waiting for the
illumination which may or may not come.

But there I am. We have before us the warning of certain futile personalities and I feel it is better to do nothing & seek something than to do something & seek nothing. What is James Whitall[11] seeking, what Ezra Pound? Lewis,[12] Joyce,[13] Lawrence[14] are all seeking something – wrongly, because haughtily, with a 'what a great man I am' gesture – but they are seeking; they are not dead.

So it is up to me, isn't it? But, yes, life first.

Richard.

1 Aldington is talking to himself in this letter as much as to H.D., although he does touch on the idea of 'sanity' that he refers to in the previous letter (see letter 21). He is here trying to make sense of his military ('common') experience, yet he does not identify himself with the ordinary Tommy; by his values he distinguishes himself from the soldier. A letter such as this one makes H.D.'s later fictional treatment of Aldington as the quintessential military man seem particularly unfair: Aldington appears as Marius Decius in 'Hipparchia' and as Captain Rafton in 'Secret Name', both sections of *Palimpsest* (1926).

2 The Mecklenburgh Square flat H.D. had rented since 1 December 1916. She gave up her lease at the end of July 1918.

3 The French poet François Villon (1431–?). In his first known poem, the *Lais* or *Petit Testament* (1456), he suggests that he is driven from Paris not because of theft (as was in fact the case) but because of his betrayal by the woman he loved. His longer autobiographical poem, *Testament* (1461), recounts his disappointments in love, his poverty, and his periods of imprisonment. Both works include witty bequests to a variety of friends and acquaintances.

4 Chelsea was a district in the southwest of London, which flourished as a bohemian community of artists at its height in the generation before the Aldingtons'. Chicago Aldington associates with *Poetry* and its editor, Harriet Monroe, whose philosophy included a Whitmanesque belief in the democracy of art that Aldington is clearly rejecting here. Despite his emphasis on the importance of the artist's awareness of common humanity, Aldington's position shares a great deal with Pound's insistence on art as aristocratic in the latter's 'Editorial' in *The Little Review* in May 1917; Aldington is, however, rejecting in large measure Pound's conclusion that 'there is no misanthropy in a thorough contempt for the mob' (Vol. 4, No. 1, 6). The cubists Aldington understands as emphasizing form at the cost of content; their work for him thus had a modernist power without meaning and was ultimately ridiculous.

5 T. Lucretius Carus (c. 99–55 B.C.E.), Latin author of the calmly reasoned *De Rerum Natura*.

6 In *A Defense of Poetry* (1840), Percy Bysshe Shelley states that 'poets are the unacknowledged legislators of the world'.

7 This is not a direct quote, but is sufficiently biblical in phrasing to suggest divine justice or retribution.

8 Literally the dog star, in Egyptian mythology identified with Isis.

9 One of Aldington's earliest poems was the relatively simple 'Au Vieux Jardin' which first appeared in the second issue of *Poetry* in November 1912. It later appeared in *Des Imagistes* in 1914 as 'In the Old Garden'.

10 On 1 January 1919, Aldington enclosed in a letter to Bryher a prose poem dated June 1918 and entitled 'ESCAPE'; the brackets are Aldington's:

Escape, escape! From the monstrous sin of this insanity, from the chains of restraint, from this ruined landscape, these murdered fields, these fetid striations across the body of earth, from this insult to God, this murder & bitterness & agony, from this harsh metallic death & more disastrous mutilation, from this filth & this labour, this stench of unmasked bodies, this resentment & trickery & slavishness – escape, escape!

Let the soul escape & move with emotion along ilex walks in the company of lyric women, with tenderness, with delicacy. There, lingering for a while beside the marble head of some shattered Hermes it strews the violets of regret for a lost loveliness as transient as itself. There, perhaps, by some Homeric sea it watches the crisp foam of a straight wind & gathers sea flowers exquisite in their acrid restraint of colour & austere sparseness of petal.

There, remote from turbulence, it lies at twilight among flowers that simulate the drooping asphodel and at the first glimmer of frail stars it catches for a moment some [inkling] of harmony, a sensation of a quiet, almost kindly universe, indifferent to [the festering] activity [of perverted intelligence.]

Yes, the escape is perfect & complete; the spirit moves more easily from the flesh, hoping eagerly for some complete separation which will render it all liberty & return to it that tranquility which formerly it enjoyed as a right.

11 Brought up as a Quaker in Philadelphia, James Whitall (1888–1954) came to England just before the war. Through John Cournos, whom he had known in the United States, he met the Aldingtons in August of 1914. Whitall's independent income and his taste for traditional writers (such as George Moore, Conrad, and James) separated him from the Aldingtons, but his expatriate status and his Philadelphia roots, as well, probably, as a religious background much like H.D.'s, drew him particularly to the American poet. Aldington shared with Whitall the plan for the Poets' Translation Series in its earliest stages, and both Whitall and H.D. helped him to translate *The Poems of Leonidas of Tarentum*, which became Number 5 in the first series. Despite vague literary ambitions, Whitall never completed any original poetry or prose, but came to make his career as a translator of French and later, for a period, as a reader at Heinemann's. In *The Egoist* of August 1915, Aldington printed Whitall's translation of Judith Gautier's *Le Livre de Jade*, her translation of Chinese lyrics by, among others, Tu-Fu and Li-Po. Whitall's good friend, the American wood engraver George Plank, also became a close friend of the Aldingtons, particularly H.D. Whitall lost touch with the Aldingtons after the war, but gives a warm and affectionate account of their friendship in *English Years* (London: Jonathan Cape, 1936, 54–9).

12 Percy Wyndham Lewis (1882–1957), writer and artist. Lewis was probably introduced to the Aldingtons by Pound and was one of the central figures in vorticism, futurism, and *Blast* in the years before the war. Lewis appeared to them as the dramatic, flamboyant, gifted, but irascible man that he indeed was. Aldington admired Lewis's art and writing, and praised his work in *The Egoist*, which published Lewis's first novel, *Tarr*, in instalments in 1915. Lewis served with the British Expeditionary Forces in France during the war, for which Aldington always respected him while deploring his misogyny and his degradation of sexuality.

13 James Joyce (1882–1941), the Irish novelist who lived most of his life on the continent. Joyce's work appeared in *Des Imagistes* in 1914, and although his formally experimental modernism was very different from Aldington's more realist modernism, Joyce's *Portrait of the Artist as a Young Man* was serialised in the *Egoist* in 1916.

14 David Herbert (D.H.) Lawrence (1885–1930). The Aldingtons first met Lawrence at a dinner given by Amy Lowell in July 1914, soon after his marriage to Frieda von Richtofen Weeks, who had left her English husband and three young children for Lawrence the year before. He published *Sons and Lovers* in 1913, *The Rainbow* in 1915, and a collection of poems, *Look! We Have Come Through*, in 1917. He contributed poems to the imagist anthologies of 1915, 1916, and 1917, and came to know both H.D. and Aldington as fellow writers. After the Aldingtons left Kensington for Hampstead, the Lawrences, who themselves moved to Hampstead in August of 1915, became close friends. H.D. developed a particularly intimate relationship with Lawrence, which evidently had its source in their similar, intense and spiritual response to beauty, especially in nature. They shared their poetry with each other, and when the Aldingtons moved to Devon in February of 1916, an intimate correspondence began between Lawrence and H.D. The Lawrences had moved to Cornwall at the end of 1915, to a cottage near Penzance, where they later met Cecil Gray. Singing German songs one evening with a

light shining from improperly closed curtains, the Lawrences were accused of being enemy spies by the local authorities and were forced to leave the coastal area. The Lawrences were virtually destitute when they arrived in London in mid-October of 1917. On 20 October they moved into H.D.'s flat at 44 Mecklenburgh Square. H.D. came down from Lichfield briefly to settle them in, but they essentially occupied her room in her absence. As soon as Aldington received his commission on 28 November 1917, the Aldingtons returned to London and the Lawrences moved out of Number 44: until 18 December into Cecil Gray's mother's house in Earl's Court Square and then to Hermitage, near Newbury in Berkshire. It was through the Lawrences that the Aldingtons met Cecil Gray in December of 1917. During these weeks before Christmas, when Dorothy Yorke began flirting with Aldington, H.D. drew particularly close to Lawrence, even – if we can trust *Bid Me to Live* –- indicating to him that she was willing to develop their relationship physically. He was not interested, was even perhaps already impotent as a result of his tuberculosis, and in his characteristic way withdrew from the corporeal with distinct unease. They may have corresponded during the winter of 1918 and during the time H.D. was with Gray in Cornwall. Lawrence, however, who had come to know Yorke during his weeks at Mecklenburgh Square, remained consistently fond of her, and his relationship with H.D. seems to have gradually faded away by late 1918. Lawrence left England to live permanently on the continent at the end of 1919. Aldington grew increasingly close to the Lawrences in the 1920s and wrote a personal biography of Lawrence (*Portrait of a Genius But* ...) in 1950.

⇗ 23 ⇖

4 July 1918

Recently I have been reading Zarathustra.[1] Not with very much pleasure, though. Nietzsche is a kind of epigramatic Carlyle. He tries to be apocalyptic & often only achieves apoplexy. I suspect all thought which needs such tumultuous obscurity. Emotion may be difficult in expression (Mallarmé,[2] Dante) but pure thought must be clear (Renan, Plato). What is well thought is well expressed; but what is well thought can only be clear. Somehow I feel that obscurity always masks a weakness – in Mallarmé, for instance, a fundamental sterility; in Dante (who is not often obscure except in the Paradiso) an ignorance of psychology. (& *you* might add 'of astronomy!')[3] But then one has to find a hair line to divide the mystic from the obscure. I get lost here & have to fall back on Renan and France and the Greeks.

Yet after all obscurity is a vice. No man writes obscure advertisements; few, except intentionally through calculation, write obscure love letters. So if a man writes confusedly, dear Dooley, surely we are not unjust if we say he has been thinking confusedly? Surely that gives one a line on which to approach the moderns – doesn't the obscurity of, say, a Marinetti,[4] just mask the nullity of ideas, the void of talent? I had an idea of analysing James Joyce's new prose, but refrained in view of the ultimate futility of all things. (So that is why I work these things off on you!) Where Joyce thinks clearly he is really marvellous. That scene by the sea-shore in 'Ulysses' has amazing passages – & amazing rot too.[5] But like all of us he lacks a guiding principle. He doesn't really believe in anything except himself; & that is fatal. Scepticism is of its essence sterile – one sees it in Remy de Gourmont,[6] where a nature abnormally rich is reduced to comparative poverty by the vice of cynicism. Joyce tries instinctively to make up this void with an astonishing *verbal* energy. His sentences are like spectres, grotesque, phosphorescent, clanking rusty chains of phrases from their boneless limbs.

He has a little of Job, a good deal of Blake & even something of Leautréamont[7] in him. And Flaubert! [in margin] He is incredibly selfish but not confident. He is, I think, more interesting (yet more repellent) than any of 'us youth'. Perhaps he has escaped the blight of Dostoievski which has consumed Mackenzie[8] & is consuming Lawrence & will consume Lewis. Melodrama masked as intensity, rhetoric walking as thought, & eloquence (shades of Slonimski!)[9] posing as energy.

There are moments when I doubt even the Greeks; clearly Aristotle ruined the poetry of the 17th and 18th centuries (in France especially) but perhaps that was only because the poets misunderstood the 'Poetics'. On the whole, Racine is more boring than Hugo, but less repulsive because more sincere. Yes, I suppose the 'Greeks' are our norm, the inventors of our criticism, the dictators of our taste. For us Europeans I mean. Perhaps future Americans working from the East instead of the West may escape this tyranny;[10] but we cannot or if we do we fall into the grotesque, the obscure, the flatulant.

For, after all, the Greeks alone of European nations, succeeded in solving the great problem – they coincided life & art, so that the prose which Pericles talked to the mob is really the best Greek prose, & the poetry which Sophocles wrote for the mob is the best poetry. But since then the arts have abandoned life, or, when touching her, have been making prostitutes of themselves. Can the theory of the intellectual élite really stand? Granted Plato did not talk to slaves; but with his 40,000 free Athenians &, say, 50,000 colonials, he had the largest intellectual audience any man ever had. You remember Remy over calculated that the audience of a French intellectual was about 4000, of whom more than half were foreigners – Germans, Russians, Spaniards, Americans & English. And the little Greek states offered more than 20 times that number!

But why continue in this strain? I feel sure you've had more than enough, & I'm only sowing discouragement before one of the few authentic children of the Muse now living.[11] Your cuckoo song had charm & certain of your inevitable vivid phrases;[12] but it has not the virtú [moral excellence], the sublime essence, of your best work. (True, French critics now recognise 'quintessentialism' as a literary vice,[13] but I think our literature needs it.) But you, how are you going on? Are you in a cul-de-sac? You have gathered your garland of sea-flowers, exquisite, unique;[14] but another such garland, however exquisite, will have lost something, the novelty which is a condition of beauty. You destroyed your work of a year & perhaps rightly, I don't know.[15] You had some poems which were fine & vivid & inevitable, though bitter. But how are you going on now? Prose? No![16] You have so precise, so wonderful an instrument – why abandon it to fashion another perhaps less perfect? You have, I think, either to choose pure song or else drama or else Mallarméan subtlety. Which will you choose? I am anxious to know. Perhaps you will send me a copy of anything you write. I shall seize on your tendencies with how avid a critical 'goût' [appetite]!

Richard

This is now the *8th* Corps. Letters should be so addressed until the 13th, when they should go to 9th R. Sx. again. Always put regiment on.[17]

---

1 Nietzsche's *Also Sprach Zarathustra* (1883–92), in which the author posits his idea of the 'superman' who will survive the loss of transcendental illusions.

2 Stéphane Mallarmé (1842–98) was an influential French symbolist poet who wrote among other works *Après-midi d'un Faune* (1876), an eclogue which inspired Debussy's prelude. His poetry was characterized by obscurity resulting from elaborate symbols and metaphors and

experimental syntax and rhythm. He attempted to evoke an ideal beauty based on an emotional and mystical apprehension of reality. Despite or perhaps in part because of his obscurity and certainly because of his compression of ideas and language, he appealed to the imagists.

3 Aldington recalls that H.D.'s father, Charles Leander Doolittle (1843–1919), was a professor of astronomy at the University of Pennsylvania and first director of the Flower Observatory.

4 Filippo Marinetti (1876–1944), Italian futurist writer and artist. Aldington reviewed Marinetti's lectures in London in *The New Freewoman* as early as 1 December 1913 (Vol. 1, No. 2, 226) and once brought him to Yeats's flat for a poetry reading (*Life for Life's Sake*, 108). Marinetti's bombast and passionate rejection of the past seemed ridiculous to Aldington, whose reverence for history and practical nature were antithetical to Marinetti's modernism.

5 The Proteus episode of Joyce's *Ulysses* (1922), which appeared in *The Little Review* in May 1918.

6 Remy de Gourmont (1858–1915) was a French critic, essayist, and fiction writer who held considerable prestige among the symbolists. In 1889 he joined the group that founded the *Mercure de France*, to which he contributed regularly until his death. Disfigured by lupus, he became a semi-recluse during the last years of his life and relied heavily on correspondence for his friendships. Gourmont's encyclopedic knowledge (much like Aldington's own in his mature years) and brilliant mind were combined with eclectic curiosity. His sensitivity to language and the mysticism and sensuality in his work made him very appealing to both of the Aldingtons.

H.D., Aldington, and Pound came to know Gourmont's work through Flint, whose discovery of contemporary French literature before 1910 was initiated by his correspondence with the editors of French journals and the writers they published. In 1912 Aldington and Pound also began to exchange letters with Gourmont. In part on the basis of conversations with H.D., N. Christophe De Nagy indicates that they began reading *Le Problème du Style* in the early months of 1912 (*Ezra Pound's Poetics and the Literary Tradition*, Basel, Switzerland: Francke Verlag Bern, 1966, 118). Pound's relationship with de Gourmont is amply discussed in Richard Sieburth's *Instigations: Ezra Pound and Remy de Gourmont* (Cambridge: Harvard University Press, 1978), but the French writer's influence on H.D. and Aldington has received little attention.

Both Pound and Aldington were instrumental in translating and publishing Gourmont's work in his last years. Aldington developed a personal and affectionate friendship with him, and attempted to secure funds for him in his final poverty through critical praise and publication of his writing. *The Horses of Diomède*, for example, was serialized in *The New Freewoman* and *The Egoist* in 1913–14. In part through Aldington's influence, *The Little Review* even published a special Gourmont number in March 1919, to which he as well as others contributed essays. Aldington published *Remy de Gourmont: A Modern Man of Letters* in 1928 and in 1929 his translation *Remy de Gourmont: Selections from All His Works*. He published his translation of a selection from *Lettres à l'Amazone* (1914) and the posthumous *Lettres Intimes à l'Amazone* (1928), Gourmont's sensitive and reflective correspondence with Natalie Barney, with a substantial introduction in 1931 (*Letters to the Amazon*, London: Chatto and Windus). It is on Aldington rather than on Pound that Gourmont had his greatest impact and through Aldington more than through Pound that Gourmont's thought and writing reached the English and American public.

7 Comte de Lautréamont, the pseudonym of the French writer Isidore Ducasse (1846–70). The hallucinatory quality of his prose anticipated French surrealism and impressed Remy de Gourmont.

8 Compton Mackenzie (1883–1972) was a prolific British writer of both poetry and novels.

9 The Polish-American philosopher Henry Slonimski (1884–1970). The Aldingtons met Slonimski in London in early 1912 and again in Paris later the same year. In *Life for Life's Sake* Aldington recalls the impression Slonimski made:

> Slonimski talks books better than most people write them, but though you listen spellbound and enchanted by his grave elegant voice and marvelous gift of finding the right phrase, the brilliant image, the books vanish with the sound of his voice. In another age he would have been appreciated. ...

... He made philosophy as attractive as a Persian tale. He had wide literary culture and a sensitive aesthetic appreciation. He presented philosophical ideas so poetically that what for me was the dark forest of abstractions became temporarily real and living; and he talked of poetry so profoundly that it took on fresh significance. (118–19)

10 Aldington refers here to Pound's lovely free 'translations' from the Chinese in *Cathy* (1915). Other Americans (James Whitall, Amy Lowell) were also interested in the Eastern literary tradition, as was the English writer Allen Upward (whose translations from the Chinese often appeared in *The New Freewoman* and *The Egoist*). Aldington tended to find English enthusiasm for the East, as evidenced in English enthusiasm for Rabindranath Tagore, fatuous and insincere, and he satirized such attitudes freely (see *Life for Life's Sake*, 108–9).

11 Aldington always had the highest esteem for H.D.'s work and responded throughout their lives with encouragement and praise for her literary gifts.

12 H.D.'s 'Cuckoo Song' was published in *Hymen* (1921):

Ah, bird,
our love is never spent
with your clear note,
nor satiate our soul;
not song, not wail, not hurt,
but just a call summons us
with its simple top-note
and soft fall;

note to some rarer heaven
of lilies over-tall,
nor tuberose set against
some sun-lit wall,
but to a gracious
cedar-palace hall;

not marble set with purple
hung with roses and tall
sweet lilies – such
as the nightingale
would summon for us
with her wail –

(surely only unhappiness
could thrill
such a rich madrigal!)
not she, the nightingale
can fill our souls
with such a wistful joy as this:

nor, bird, so sweet
was ever a swallow note –
not hers, so perfect
with the wing of lazuli
and bright breast –
nor yet the oriole
filling with melody
from her fiery throat
some island-orchard
in a purple sea.

Ah dear, ah gentle bird,
you spread warm length
of crimson wool
and tinted woven stuff
for us to rest upon,
nor numb with ecstasy
nor drown with death:

only you soothe, make still
the throbbing of our brain:
so through her forest trees,
when all her hope was gone
and all her pain,
Calypso heard your call –
across the gathering drift
of burning cedar-wood,
across the low-set bed
of wandering parsley and violet,
when all her hope was dead.

13 Aldington calls himself a 'quintessentialist' in a letter to Amy Lowell on 1 February 1915. In a letter to Lowell on 24 January 1915, Frank Flint implies that Lowell thought of renaming the imagists as 'Quintessentialists', evidently in anticipation of the imagist anthology of 1915. The term here may simply denote imagism after Pound left the movement.

14 H.D.'s first volume of poems, *Sea Garden*, appeared in the autumn of 1916.

15 Aldington regrets this destruction in a letter to Amy Lowell on 2 January 1918.

16 Aldington's antipathy to prose shifted dramatically by 1920. His early espousal of free verse depended in part on a rejection of prose. His own preference for poetry over prose in the hierarchy of art was a conviction held by many writers in the years before the war. He developed this early position in 'Free Verse in England' in *The Egoist*, 15 September 1914 (351–2). He clarifies his increasing sympathy with prose as art and its relative relation to verse in 'The Art of Poetry' in *The Dial* in 1920 (August, LXIX, 168) and in an exchange with T.S. Eliot, 'Prose and Verse', in *The Chapbook* in 1921 (April, No. 22, 21). Aldington's attitudes toward the relative merits of poetry and prose depend on a wealth of fine distinctions and definitions, but his reservations about H.D.'s interest in writing prose is not personal here. It is worth noting, too, that like H.D., Aldington would soon draw on his experiences during the war years both in poetry and in his prose fiction.

17 H.D.'s tendency to be inaccurate in practical details is frustrating to Aldington: he is eager to receive her letters without delay and her impracticality is antithetical to his pragmatic nature. His letters abound in reminders such as this one.

⤚ 24 ⤙

7 July 1918

Dearest Dooley/

Yesterday I didn't write you because I wanted to write you a love-letter and I felt somehow that it would make you unhappy, would infringe the bounds of your compromise, and insult that sovereign pride & modesty behind which you entrench yourself. So you see not being able to feign moods there was nothing left for me but silence.[1]

Your last letter was delightful, but the little pencil note scribbled on the back made me happy. No, I haven't really been ill at all – only a couple of days in bed with 'Spanish influenza' – but it is so good to know that your dear loyal heart responded when you thought I was ill. You must be careful not to get this Spanish influenza – it affects one queerly & leaves one weak & terribly depressed. It is a sort of physical expression of our war lassitude.[2]

You will be pleased to hear that Beaumont is printing my war poems (just the war poems) under the title of 'Images of War'. Paul Nash is illustrating the book which will be a kind of edition de luxe – just 200 copies, 50 of which will be coloured by Nash himself. Nash has done illustrations for Bombardment, Barrage, Dawn & Fatigues & in each case has interpreted the 'image' rather well I think. I gather from Beaumont that others are being done.[3]

I haven't heard from Brown & don't particularly care what happens in America, now that I can thus publicly register my denunciation of the machine-made war.[4]

If you have used the Dial money, please don't trouble to send it. I will be delighted for you to have it; I only wanted to be certain that they had paid, since these distant editors are a little apt to swindle one. Did you acknowledge cheque? And what do you mean by cheque returned from Nutt wrongly endorsed? Please let me know *at once* – if a cheque of mine is not honoured I run the risk of a court martial. I can't understand at all what it is – Nutt has said nothing to me &, so far as I know, all my self cheques have been paid by Cox.[5]

Thank you for doing the typing of my 'proses'; will you tell Harriet [Monroe] to pay up 'toot sweet', for these be parlous times & I rather like to enjoy anything I earn while I'm still alive to do it![6]

To-morrow is my birthday. I think my 21st & 25th birthdays have been my happiest – last year at Brocton you know. Mysterious girl! You didn't want to come, do you remember? What was the counter-attraction?[7]

I had a long letter from Flint, very apologetic &c. He means well & you know there is a certain gain in his having written to me thus clumsily – he will – with his naïveté – immediately contradict anything that may be said.[8] The greatest danger is Cournos who is going about London in that damned Jew way of his, hinting here & hinting

Illustration by Paul Nash, accompanying the poem 'Bombardment', *Images of War*, p. 30

there & implying that I have committed some deed of revolting treachery.[9] Alec,[10] Flint & Mr. Whitall all wrote in one week asking what Cournos & I had quarrelled about. Now, I really don't mind whether John speaks well or ill of me, but I do think he might at least say that we've quarrelled about art or the Bolsheviks or any old thing instead of being such a bloody fool. Selah [so be it]!

I am so glad to know that you are writing poetry again. As they said in the 18th century: 'I am consumed with impatience to peruse your works, Miss Biron.' Do let me have them at once, before I go up the line again, so that I can read them in the comparative tranquility of this place.[11]

Have you read Stendhal's 'de l'Amour'? It is extremely thoughtful & has remarks of great penetration. Speaking of America – where he'd never been – he says: 'Des jeunes filles de la gaité la plus folle et la plus innocente y deviennent, en moins d'un an, les plus ennuyeuses des femmes.' How often you have made the same remark about American girls in America! And Stendhal adds that the Germans are the same. He says it's the climate & the Bible! Perhaps. But in America I think the population is being emancipated from the Bible by the climate. What do you think?[12]

I have just re-read the pencil postscript to your last letter and it emboldens me to say that I am tenderly and passionately in love with you as always. I don't care whether you believe me or not; I know myself. How the most brilliant of women are the slaves of conventional ideas! C'est désespèrant [It's disheartening]! Never mind, I shall just go on loving you & hoping for things to 'pan out'. I suppose the psychology of each sex is incomprehensible to the other. My fault is really, I suppose, that I treat women as equals, instead of pretending that I consider them superior & secretly despising them.[13]

Dear Dooley! Here I am plunged in a disquisition which needs a hundred pages to bring to a clear point. And so au revoir. And I kiss your dear white hands tenderly and your mouth qui ne m'aime plus [that no longer loves me].

Richard.

Illustration by Paul Nash, accompanying the poem 'Fatigues', *Images of War*, p. 13

1 In an earlier letter H.D. has evidently outlined the terms of their current relationship. She has apparently decided that she and Aldington should maintain a correspondence about literary matters and avoid the personal. See letter 10.

2 The pyrexia Aldington refers to in letter 18. This was a common name for the virulent influenza strain that swept through Europe and America in 1918 and 1919.

3 Cyril Beaumont (1891–1976), bookseller, publisher and aficionado of the ballet, published Aldington's first collection of poems after the war, *Images of War: A Book of Poems*, in April of 1919. Paul Nash (1889–1946) was the illustrator whose stark, stylized woodcuts accompanied these poems. Aldington was very impressed with his work and wrote Beaumont on 5 July 1918: 'Nash has very fine imagination – the drawing of the Ypres front is A1. ... Nash's drawings are simply splendid – they give me great satisfaction & I'm quite proud to think that he has used anything I've written so admirably' (UIL). Nash later illustrated covers for Aldington's *Death of a Hero* (1929) and his collection of war stories, *Roads to Glory* (1930). Beaumont's edition of *Images of War* was indeed quite elegant. Only forty-six pages, it included twenty-seven poems, eleven of which were illustrated by Nash, including 'Bombardment', 'Barrage' and the prose poem 'Fatigues'; 'Dawn' was not illustrated. The coloured woodcuts are particularly effective in conveying the brutality, terror, and irony of the war in various shades of blue, green, orange, yellow, brown, and grey against the black and white of the woodcuts themselves. Nash's maroon cover is also dramatic, with modernist woodcuts of slashes and crescents that suggest explosions.

4 Edmund R. Brown, editor at the Four Seas Company in Boston, published Aldington's *Images Old and New* (1916), *War and Love (1915–1918)* (1919) and *War: A Book of Poems* (1921). Each of these was essentially a republication of a collection of poems published previously in England.

5 Aldington's reaction here may seem excessive, but his experience of war made him hyper-sensitive to the legal consequences of even the most minute act that might involve him with civil or – in this case – military bureaucracy. David Nutt was a London bookseller, with whom Aldington had a running account; Cox and Company was Aldington's bank.

6 Aldington here refers to the prose poems on which he has been working and which he earlier asked H.D. to type for him in letter 17.

7 Aldington turned 26 on 8 July 1918. He recalls here the time he spent with H.D. just after he returned from his first tour of duty at the front in early July 1917. He was stationed at Lichfield and H.D. had taken a room in the village of Brocton. See Introduction.

8 That is, gossip to the effect that the Aldington's marriage is in trouble.

9 John Cournos (1881–1966), an intimate friend of the Aldingtons until this time. Born in Kiev, Russia, in 1891 Cournos emigrated to America, where he later met and fell in love with Dorothy Yorke, known as 'Arabella'. In the spring of 1914 the Aldingtons met him in London, where he was working as a journalist and translator, although he contributed one poem to *Des Imagistes* in 1914 and more of Cournos's work appeared in the imagist anthologies in 1915, 1916, and 1917. Like the Aldingtons he published work with Charles Bubb at the Clerk's Press in Cleveland, Ohio. He also wrote regularly for *The Egoist* and published essays on art as well as literary criticism for other periodicals in which Aldington's and Pound's work also appeared. Although he did not contribute to either of the Poets' Translation Series, Aldington kept Cournos in mind as a potential translator of Russian and Hebrew authors. He was particularly close to H.D. and his relationship with her became especially intimate during 1916 and 1917, when they viewed each other as souls with transcendental affinities; the relationship remained 'spiritual', however, not physical, although it clearly had sensual elements. He was a frequent visitor when the Aldingtons lived in Devon and introduced them to friends he knew in the area, most notably to Carl and Florence Fallas. Cournos was living in a room on the top floor when H.D. took a flat at 44 Mecklenburgh Square in January of 1917. In the late summer of 1917, Cournos met Yorke by chance in London, where she had recently arrived from France

84

with her mother. Yorke's feelings for him had never been so intense as his for her, but she now needed him as one of the few people she knew in London. He invited her to stay in H.D.'s large room at Mecklenburgh Square, for H.D. was on her way north at the end of August to stay near Aldington for several months while he was in officers' training near Lichfield. In October of 1917 Cournos left England as a translator with the Anglo-Russian Commission to Petrograd. When he returned in late March of 1918, Yorke told him of her affair with Aldington. He was furious and blamed both H.D. and Aldington for what he saw as the violation of a trust. His relations with the Aldingtons grew increasingly strained after late 1917, and he satirized both of them in his autobiographical novel, *Miranda Masters* (1926). Aldington had many Jewish friends and his criticism of Cournos in Letter 24 is not so much personal as representative of the anti-Semitism of the period.

10 Aldington first met Alec Randall (1892–1977) when they were both students at University College, London, in 1910–11. Randall always remained on the fringe of the bohemian and artistic circles to which Aldington introduced him. More conventional and political than Aldington, Randall nevertheless became one of his few close friends. When Aldington gave up his position as part-time secretary to Ford Madox Hueffer (Ford) in 1914, he managed to turn the job over to Randall. Randall married in 1915, and he and his wife, Amy, a physician, took a flat at 3 Christchurch Place in Hampstead near the Aldingtons, who from January 1915 rented a flat at 7 Christchurch Place. The Aldingtons and the Randalls were thus neighbours as well as friends for all of 1915 until the Aldingtons moved to Devon in early 1916, and both Randalls became particularly close to the Aldingtons during H.D.'s first pregnancy and the birth and death of their child in May 1915. When H.D. left Cornwall in September of 1918, she went to stay with Amy Randall in Hampstead. From 1915 Randall served in the Foreign Office as an officer in the British Army, and after being demobilised in 1919, he joined the diplomatic service. A Roman Catholic, he served as Britain's ambassador to the Vatican in the 1920s, and remained a good friend of Aldington's throughout his life.

11 Aldington alludes here to the naughty and erotic memoirs of Armand Louis de Gontaut Biron, Duc de Lauzun (1747–94). The first edition of the memoirs appeared in 1821; Aldington described Biron as 'a sort of romantic madcap' in his introduction to C.K. Scott Montcrieff's translation, *Memoirs of the Duc de Lauzun* (London: George Routledge & Sons, 1928, v). Aldington is hoping to read H.D.'s work in the relative calm of the base camp where he is undergoing further training before returning to the trenches.

12 'Stendhal' was the pseudonym of Henri Beyle (1783–1842), novelist and critic. He published his well-known study *De L'Amour* in 1822, in which he divides love into four types: passion, social experience, controlled self-indulgence, and physical pleasure. Aldington quotes Stendahl that 'Young girls of the wildest and most innocent gaiety become there, in less than a year, the most annoying of women.'

13 In *All Men Are Enemies* (1933), Aldington expands this idea. The central character and his attractive older female cousin discuss the equality of women and men: 'They had quite a long and heated argument about it, an instinctive attitude of equality clumsily and hesitatingly opposing the hereditary "English contempt masquerading as chivalry – put them [women] on a pedestal and make it your footstool"' (*All Men Are Enemies*, London: Heinemann, 1933, 38).

≽ **25** ≼

8 July 1918

Dearest Astraea/[1]

It is strange how utterly empty one's mind becomes sometimes. To-day – by way of a birthday present from the ironic gods – I have not observed in myself a single glimmer of intelligence. Everything has been dull and indifferent. The effect of routine & the crushing heat I suppose. We have been displayed all day for the benefit of an old general whose ideas are detestable to me but whose influence on my unfortunate country is great and decisive. He has amazing gifts & great though banal eloquence. He came & preached the doctrine of action, of efficiency, of duty – everything that is contrary to us who worship thought, and freedom & reverie! I realised when I stood beside him that here for the first time since I had landed in France was a man who was my intellectual equal – and yet, malheur sur nous [unfortunately for us], we are at opposite poles. C'est triste, effroyablement triste [It's sad, dreadfully sad].

Well, perhaps one must not worry about these things, yet that is why the war continues.

> There, violet-wreathed as your own Attic hills,
> And golden-sandalled as your own white isle,
> Your spirit for a moment stooped to mine.
>
> Too long had I been starved of beauty,
> Too long done violence to myself,
> Mocked at by the thing I held most dear,
> Too long suffered the insult of authority.
>
> But the echo of your song
> Pierced me to tears & left me faint
> With the misery of old memories.
>
> I am exiled, even as you, & miserable.
> But for your sake, white violet of the Muse,
> Violets shall be dear to me & dear
> The sparse woods sweetened with the violet's breath.[2]
>
> R.

Just to amuse you & show I sometimes think of other things than shells & bayonets!

Your letter of 14th July to hand – I can't contradict you in any way or think too much about these things now.[3]

The Faun sends kisses to his dear Dryad.[4]

[The following poem was included in the letter to H.D., 8 July 1918]

The Faun Captive

> A god's strength lies
> More in the fervour of his worshippers
> Than in his own divinity.
> Who now regards me or who twines
> Red wool or threaded lilies round the brows
> Of my neglected statues?
> Who now seeks my aid
> To add skill to the hunter's hand
>
> Or save some pregnant bitch or ewe
> Helpless in travail?
> None, since that fierce autumn noon
> I lay asleep under Zeus-holy oaks,
> Heavy with sirupy wine & tired

With the close embraces
Of some sweet wearer of the leopard skin –
That noon they snared & bound me as I slept
And dragged me for their uncouth mirth
Out of my immemorial woods & crags
Down to their bastard hamlets.

Then the god's blood my father spilled
To get me upon a mortal stock, dwindled & shrank
And I was impotent, & weak
As the once desireable flesh of my human mother;
I, that should have been dreaded in wan recesses,
Worshipped in high woods, a striker of terror
To the wayfarer in lonely places,
I, a lord of golden flesh & dim music –
I a captive & coarsely derided!

Ai! I could bite the brown flesh
Of my arms & hands with shame & grief.

I am weary for the freedom of free things,
The old gay life of the half-god
Who had no dread of death or sorrow.
I am weary for the open spaces,
The long damp sands acrid with many tides,
And the infinite wistfulness of evening seas.
I am weary for wooded silences,
The nymph-rapt hours of heat,
The slow cool lapse of moonlit nights,
The solitude of the mysterious stars
Pearlwise scattered upon the domed breast
Wherewith the Great Mother suckles the earth;
Ah, weary for my brown clean streams
And cold petals of woodland flowers
Scented with dew & delicate as a kiss.

Here they grow careless, thinking me a coward
But soon I shall break these thongs
And kill, kill, kill in sharp revenge;
Then out of doors by the lush pastures
To the heath, the foot-hills & the hills,
To the wild-rose kisses of the deathless girls
Who laugh & flash between the sombre trees,
Out to the unpeopled lands no foot oppresses,
The lands that are free, being free of man.[5]

1 Aldington's pet name for H.D., Astraea (the starry maid), is another name for the constellation
Virgo, the zodiacal sign under which H.D. was born. Astraea is associated with Justice, who
used to live among people in the Golden Age, retired to the Mountains in the Silver Age, and
fled to the heavens during the wickedness of the Bronze Age, where she may yet be seen on

starry nights. Ovid gives a brief account of her in his *Metamorphoses*, I, 149–50.

2 Aldington never published this poem. I discuss this work as well as 'We are those ...' (see letter 32) in my article 'Two Poems for H.D.', *Journal of Modern Literature*, Vol. 16, No. 1, Winter 1989, 176–9.

3 Aldington must mean '14th June'. H.D. appears to be writing to Aldington regularly at this point, and it would seem that her letters are attempting to shift and redefine the grounds of their relationship. Aldington's response is reactive and generally accepting.

4 Aldington was called 'Faun' by H.D. and Pound, while 'Dryad' is a pet name for H.D. used by Pound and Aldington, recalling her association with trees as early as 1905–07, when Pound included 'The Tree' in a series of early poems written for H.D. and bound together as 'Hilda's Book'. The collection is included at the end of *End to Torment: A Memoir of Ezra Pound by H.D.*, ed. Norman Holmes Pearson and Michael King, New York: Directions, 1979, 67–84.

5 This poem, with some revision, was finally included in *Images*, second and revised edition, London: The Egoist Press, 1919, a volume later reissued by Allen and Unwin. In the published version, 'pregnant bitch or ewe' in line 9 becomes 'pregnant ewe or bitch'; the comma is omitted after 'impotent' in line 22; the break between lines 28 and 29 is omitted; in line 41 'the domed breast' becomes 'the domed breast of The Great Mother'; line 42 is omitted; 'Ah' in line 43 becomes 'oh'; 'cold' in line 44 becomes 'wet'; 'soon' in line 47 becomes 'one night'; in line 50 'and' is inserted after the comma; in line 52 'between' becomes 'among'; and in line 53 'unpeopled' becomes 'unploughed'. The poem first appeared as 'The Captive Faun' in *The Nation* on 31 May 1919 (Vol. 25, No. 9, 265).

⤜ 26 ⤛

9 July 1918[1]

'A spirit beyond all tyranny.' That is a spirited phrase and would be a fine epitaph for the William Wallaces & George Washingtons of the world – but how few deserve it. They say Madame de Staël was the only person who ever dared to tell the Emperor Napoleon to his face that he was a tyrant. Anyway I am sure I do not deserve it. But it was 'like your gracious ways' to think of saying that.[2]

One has above all things to guard against vanity, the besetting sin of the French as hypocrisy is that of the English. Pride, I suppose, is legitimate, though it is not amiable in the successful but only in the unfortunate. The difference is, I think, between Rouchfoucald's 'amour propre' [self-esteem] & the determination of Shelley's Prometheus.[3]

It is curious, one talks of the possessive instinct of men for women but I believe it is stronger in women. I don't mean that I agree with the rather vulgar viewpoint of [George Bernard] Shaw; but to some extent the history of an impulsive or erotic man is simply that of successive enslavements & exceedingly painful emancipations from different women. Unfortunately, it seems as if another woman is the only means of escape. ... Of course I see with astonishing clearness (astonishing because I ought to be blind to it) that Arabella is trying hard – let us be genial I say also 'unwittingly' – to enslave me completely. I see perhaps the working of her instinct more clearly than she herself and I am appalled, yes positively appalled, at the degree of subjugation she intends for me.[4] Mind you I don't condemn her in the least; it is just what the majority of women – who live merely instinctively & sensually – try to do & usually succeed. One thinks of Flint and Lawrence with a shudder. Ford too, by Jove.[5] You are right; one must possess oneself. But that is exceedingly difficult, because one cannot be 'reasonably' in love – it would be tedious & bourgeois – and any 'amour-passion' [sexual love] at once betrays one into a state of abject submission. Therefore, one must live entirely apart from women – which is absurd – or else engage in this perpetual warfare of passion versus freedom. I cannot compass the cynicism of Diomède – who, himself, got into a horrible mess by falling in love with one of his mistresses – nor can I aspire to Petrarchan heights.[6] Life is that way. One must be like England – muddle through somehow.

I daresay this sounds devilish blunt – in any case, most of it doesn't apply to you – but I merely reciprocate.[7]

The case of Brigit is rather curious. She has now entirely dropped me. Why? Clearly because it was you she cared for. Therefore, as long as she thought I belonged to you she was charming & flirted most graciously – arguing, I suppose, that this prevented a more dangerous concurrance. Now, there is no point in being charming – as she believes – she shows her complete indifference. I don't say it's a great grief to me but in a way it is a grief to lose so old and so sweet a friend. Wounded vanity, eh? No doubt I seem unjust, but I believe I have caught the nuance of psychology here just as with Arabella. (Of course Brigit must now be getting into a ghastly state because of that ill-advised operation. You may remember [Havelock] Ellis' remarks on the matter – I think in an appendix to one of his volumes.)[8]

You will see that the problem from the male point of view is thorny with difficulties. Though it simplifies itself eventually into the ancient problem of eating one's cake & having it. Perhaps Euclid might be of assistance – & perhaps not.[9]

My dear, you saw, possibly earlier than I, the terrific possessive instinct which A. has. You have exercised extraordinary restraint in not mentioning it; though I've been aware of it for some considerable time. Me voici prèvenu en tout cas [I have been forewarned in any case]. But – forgive, if you can, this ultimate irony – I smile to think of you watching with so delicately aesthetic & appraising an eye the physical loveliness of *your* Cecil! Tu quoque, Brute? Is it the 'yours' or the 'loveliness'? A problem to be meditated.

I forsee that you are going to hate me very much for this letter. Even with the best & greatest of human beings we should employ a certain amount of humbug. But we agreed to cut it out, didn't we? Dangerous, most dangerous. I wonder if even our love can endure perfect frankness? From 'color che sanno' [those who know] I gather that is impossible.[10] How does it seem from your angle of the triangle – or perhaps one should say acute-angled rectangle?

Well, my dear, in about a week I shall be trotting up the same old line to the same old tinny tune of M.G.'s [machine guns] & whizz-bangs. One gains, if not philosophy, a sort of resignation. Certain pretentions to the good things of life have to be abandoned – & one 'accepts whatever comes with equal mind' (Landor?)[11]

With my love – that tempestuous monosyllable –

Your
Richard

1 This letter was enclosed with letter 27 on 10 July.
2 H.D. has evidently written Aldington that he has such a spirit. William Wallace (1844–97), a Scottish philosopher who was professor of moral philosophy at Oxford from 1882 until his death, specialized in German philosophy, particularly Hegel, whose work he translated. 'Madame de Staël' was Anne-Louise-Germaine Necker (1766–1817); she had a Paris salon that was both an intellectual and political meeting place for those who shared her antipathy to Napoleon, who exiled her three times, in 1803, 1806, and 1810. Aldington is quoting here from Coventry Patmore's 'Departure', stanza viii:

It was not like your good and gracious ways!
Do you, that have nought other to lament,
Never, my love, repent
Of how, that July afternoon,
You went
With sudden, unintelligible phrase,
And frighten'd eye,
Upon your journey of so many days,
Without a single kiss, or a good-bye?

3 The French moralist François, Duc de la Rochefoucauld (1613–80). His famous *Maximes* was published in 1665. Aldington is recalling here the character of Prometheus as portrayed in Percy Bysshe Shelley's *Prometheus Unbound* (1820).

4 Ironically, in Aldington's own life, falling in love with another woman tended to become his way of concluding for whatever reason an ongoing relationship. Evidently Arabella has in her letters asked for an exclusive relationship; that is, she wants to marry Aldington and to have a child with him.

5 Flint married early and by 1918 had two children. D.H. Lawrence fell in love with Frieda von Richthofen while she was married to Ernest Weekly; he insisted immediately upon marrying her, so she felt compelled to leave her husband and three children and to secure a divorce. Ford Madox (Hueffer) Ford (1873–1939) was an English novelist, poet, critic, and editor, whom Aldington first came to know well personally when he worked briefly as Ford's secretary in 1914. Ford married in 1894, but by 1908 he and his wife were estranged. In 1909 he began a relationship with Violet Hunt, but was unable to marry her since his wife would not grant him a divorce. In 1911, Ford publicized the false story that he and Hunt had married in Germany after he had assumed German nationality on the basis of his father's birth there. In 1912 his wife sued a newspaper for libel when it referred to Hunt as Ford's wife, and won the case, successfully embarrassing Ford and Hunt. In late 1914 Ford was with some difficulty naturalized as the English subject he had been since birth, in order to avoid service in the German army or internment as an enemy alien. He later served with the British Expeditionary Forces in France, about which he wrote five novels, *The Good Soldier* (1915), and the tetralogy, *Parade's End* (1950). His sensibility was modernist and he moved in London's literary circles, which included both writers of his own generation and artists of early modernism. He was influential in publishing their work in *The English Review*, which he founded in 1908, and later in the *transatlantic review*, which he founded in Paris in 1924.

6 Aldington recalls here Remy de Gourmont's treatment of Diomedes. Aldington also alludes to the male character's shift in courtly love literature from sexual to Platonic love, as Petrarch (1304–74) depicts in his sonnets to Laura.

7 H.D. has evidently written in her last letter about her relationship with Cecil Gray, whom she is beginning to find petty and possessive.

8 Born in Ireland, 'Brigit' (Ethel Elizabeth Morrison-Scott) Patmore (1883–1965) married John Deighton Patmore, grandson of the sentimental Victorian poet Coventry Patmore, in 1907. Her marriage was an unhappy one, and by 1918 she with her two sons was living apart from her philandering and economically irresponsible husband. Dramatically beautiful and sensitive, she enjoyed associating with artists on the bohemian fringe of London society. She had little money but was a resourceful, sensual, and dynamic woman three years older than H.D. and nine years older than Aldington. It was over tea at her house that she introduced Aldington to H.D. in late 1911. Throughout her life, Patmore would shift her sympathies back and forth between Aldington and H.D. primarily on the basis, it would seem, of erotic attachment. She and Aldington began a brief affair soon after they first met in 1911. Patmore was also, however, sexually attracted to H.D., as suggested in H.D.'s fictional treatment of Patmore as

Morgan in *Bid Me to Live* and in Patmore's two autobiographical fictions – *This Impassioned On-Looker* (1926) and *No Tomorrow* (1929) – and in her memoir, *My Friends When Young* (1968). It seems unlikely, however, that Patmore's relationship with H.D. was ever sexually consummated, in large measure because H.D. was not particularly responsive to her overtures. When H.D. and Aldington met, Patmore may have felt that she could preserve her relationship with both poets, but as the two writers became increasingly involved with each other, she discovered that she would have to reestablish her relationship with them on new grounds. She initially chose to align herself with H.D. as a woman with an unfaithful husband, becoming rather hostile toward Aldington as a result. This affection for H.D. and disaffection for Aldington lasted from at least 1917 until 1926, as evidenced in her letters to H.D. and Bryher during this period (Yale). By 1928, she and Aldington were lovers again in a passionate affair that lasted until 1936. In 1918 and 1919, both Aldingtons saw Brigit as an experienced mother and independent woman of the world.

In letter 26, Aldington refers specifically to Patmore's 'operation', an abortion she had in 1913. In autobiographical notes made for Norman Holmes Pearson, H.D. recalled that at the time of the Aldingtons' wedding, 'Brigit is having operation' (Yale). Exactly which of Ellis's works Aldington recalls as a gloss on Patmore's situation is unclear.

9 Aldington sardonically surmises that the famous Greek mathematician's geometrical theories and calculations may help him and H.D. out of their two triangles.

10 Here Aldington refers to Dante's *Inferno*, Canto 4, l. 131, where Aristotle is designated as the master of 'those who know'.

11 As Aldington nears the end of his six weeks of additional training at base camp, he quotes not Walter Savage Landor, but line 883 of Book 3 of John Dryden's *Palamon and Arcite*: 'With equal mind, what happens, let us bear.'

⚜ 27 ⚜

10 July 1918

I wrote the enclosed [letter 26] yesterday, kept it until to-day, thought very seriously of destroying it & then felt that it would be a pity as I had said several things I wanted to say as well as others it was unnecessary & perhaps unworthy to say. Cynicism, as our friend Oscar [Wilde] remarks, is the bank-holiday of sentimentality. Keeping that profound truth in your mind you will be able to gauge fairly nearly the mood of the letter. The remark about Gray is rather unforgivable, but since it was once written it seemed a lack of candour to erase it. Of course if you can interpret it you will observe the profound compliment underlying it, but I don't know whether you take the trouble to find out the *implied* sense of words & acts as well as their direct sense. Do you? One needs a certain tranquility, and perhaps a little indifference as well as intuition.[1]

And, you see, the discussion of most of these points is really rather academic. I mean I shouldn't look at the position quite so whimsically and carelessly if I thought there was a great chance of my ever having to face again the whole problem. That gives me a certain advantage and I can deal with the situation in a peculiar way which I can only describe as 'ante-post-mortem'. Pater's detachment, you know.

I am enjoying these last days here [at base camp] immensely – six weeks of summer in wartime is a generous gift of the gods. In the line, you know, one has no pleasure in these things; it is either hot or cold, wet or dry; beauty of earth there can be none; even the beauty of the sky becomes a sinister, sneering sort of thing. But here one recognises the great plan, the alternation of seedtime & harvest, the spirit of the earth. I say to myself that I do not envy you your Cornwall, your books, your sea, your leisure, your lover. For if life to me is often horrible and wearing & terrifying & exhausting, it has also moments of respite, poignant in their intensity. After a long period of revolt and depression I have reached 'un bel indifférance' [a beautiful indifference]; I take no more than the barest necessary interest in army work and am, as it were, preparing myself for something different & eternal. One gets to a certain point when any misfortune or discomfort or loss comes more or less naturally & is borne tranquilly. Perhaps it is because one gets purged of the necessity for unessentials. Of course it is much pleasanter to have money and books & friends & someone to love and an art; but one can do without all these things. Latterly I do not bother to write down my poems – I just think them sitting quietly in my tent. It is perhaps in this way that one should love – carefully discriminating between 'l'amour passion' and 'l'amour physique'. (You should read Stendhal 'de l'Amour'.)²

In the books I sent you I think you will like Samain's tales and possibly Gide's book – the latter seemed a little forced to me. The Renan has charming passages. I advise you not to bother with his correspondence with his seminary friend – it is tedious, parsonic & lowers one's estimation of Renan's character. Renan is a kind of artistic protestant – too obsessed with logic to be happy in Catholic sophisms, too refined in senses to fall into the ridiculous self-mutilating Calvin point of view. He interests me exceedingly, though the lack of force & determination is his great weakness.³

I have placed Nietzsche at last. He is not a modern but a 19th century Romantic, the last of the bunch. His tedious superman is no other than our friend Jean Valjean elevated to the intellectual plane.⁴ The sense of uneasiness one gets in reading Zarathustra is not because Nietzsche was mad or amazingly egotistic, but simply because he is out of date. He preaches the individualism of 1840 to the communism of 1920 – useless. We don't need a doctrine of violence, but a doctrine of common-sense. I would like to conduct friend Nietzsche through, let us say, the town of Loos as it now is.⁵ He would find that his violent effort towards more life had merely utterly annihilated it. And there are dozens, scores of such villages given over to the rats & the lice, sole benefactors of the superman ideal. No, let us get back to the sanity of Voltaire & plant each his own cabbages in his own garden.⁶ We do not need all to do the same thing. (God forbid that the majority of mankind should become artists.) Let us amuse ourselves tranquilly and try to refrain from assassinating our neighbors. I do not think the world at present is capable of any higher ideal.

Of course, when one looks coldly at the present state of affairs, one sees pretty clearly that this turmoil is very far from being appeased. Actual hostilities will not cease in this decade & the next will be a mass of tumult. It is possible that there will be a re-shuffle of the belligerents – Germany, Russia & Japan uniting against the Latin-Anglo-Saxon menace. It is, of course, a contest of jackals for the lion's skin.

So you must organise your life at least with the forethought that the present state of affairs will continue for some years. When people tell you that the war will be over soon it's simply a case of the wish being father to the thought.⁷

> Au revoir.
> With love
> Richard.

1 Aldington suggests that his comments on Gray reveal his own jealousy, which is an indication of his love for H.D.

2 Aldington here repeats his argument from letter 24. H.D. evidently shared Aldington's feelings at this time. Describing her physical situation in Cornwall, she wrote to John Cournos on 17 July 1918: 'The country is lovely – much finer than Devon. There is a pool below the house where I bathe almost daily now and I get nice food and have so much time to work. I am really awfully fortunate. Only I feel so detached, I really sometimes wonder where I am. I have never lived so completely in the imagination. And nothing much matters' (HU).

3 Aldington has earlier discussed Samain (letter 14) and Renan (letter 13), whose works he has posted to H.D. at least in part because he cannot take into the front lines the many books he has recently accumulated. He now also comments on André Gide (1869–1951), the French essayist, critic, novelist, and dramatist, whose early work was influenced by the symbolist movement. Gide founded the *Nouvelle Revue Française* in 1908 and was a strong influence on the literary avant-garde in his rebellion against convention and inhibition. It is unclear exactly which of his many works Aldington has sent to H.D.

4 The admirable peasant hero of Victor Hugo's novel *Les Misérables* (1862), who tries repeatedly to escape his past of petty crime by assuming various identities.

5 The French town near which Aldington was stationed during the first half of 1917 and where he fought in the spring of 1918.

6 François-Marie Arouet Voltaire (1694–1778), French poet, historian and philosopher, who argued deistically for religious tolerance and a transformation of political thought through rational criticism in the name of social justice.

7 Aldington, like many other soldiers, was convinced that the war would last at least until 1920.

❧ 28 ❧

12 July 1918

I am very glad that you see it is no solution of life merely to perpetuate one's species. Thinking of my mother & her narrow maternal instinct I once said – I think to you: 'Many women think they have solved the problem of life when they have gotten someone else to face it.' A little 'smarty' perhaps, but on the whole surprisingly true.

For, whatever may be the gift of parenthood it has ghastly pitfalls – the fruited individual forgetting, unlike the fruited tree, that it must blossom again. The danger, too, of living for & in one's child. 'I have not found happiness – I will see my child does; I have failed in life – my child shall succeed; the books I dreamed – my child shall write.' Eternal deception of Nature! From this attitude come the trammeling affection of parents, the insufferable tutelage, the attempts to solve in terms of their maturity and disillusion the problems of youth and illusion. And once again begins the revolt, the breaking away of youth, the dismay of the parents who find they have a swan not a duckling and vice versa. If you have a child, beware! I say unto you beware. You will try to make your child a poet and he will be a designer of coke-ovens; you will try to make him a lover of natural things and he will desire money. Children – haven't we said it? – are reactions from their parents. But you might try the experiment – a reaction from you would certainly be something interesting. (Perhaps the worst might happen – & the child would be a weak echo of you.)

Is this folly or wisdom? After all life and more life – that is the thing. One should refuse no experience which offers itself.

Yes, it is odd how we think simultaneously, but perhaps not so odd as you think. With minds somewhat similarly framed & equipped we are meditating the same problems; not extraordinary then if we sometimes arrive at similar conclusions or, rather, similar moods. All our thought is mood; we think we are dealing with the world with our minds when we are really dealing only with our emotions. So that when we reach one of those arid spots of life devoid of emotion, we have no ideas. That is why we are poets, not philosophers. The ἰδεα [semblance] comes to us on Psyche wings, irridescent, an image, things being thoughts for us & thoughts things. But for the philosopher it is not so. He deals with thought as a mathematician with numbers. That is why those who are in love with life are seldom mathematicians. Thought has no meaning for them till it is clad in mortal shape. Poets do not sing the eternal, as bad critics pretend, but the glory of the perishable – beauty, love, intoxication, flowers, moods, the sea, all things that are transcient and lovely. But for the philosopher ideas exist. Even Socrates, who was what we should call a Nihilist, believed in his ideas.

One has so carefully to distinguish between what is primary & what is only secondary, between the essential & the non-essential of life. Harund-al-Raschid, it is said, earned every day his food by making shoes. He kept in touch with reality. But the essential point to him (if I am not mistaken) was not the money he earned but the sense of – how shall I put it? – humanity gained. (Moreover, the wise Caliph, who had listened to poets' tales, knew that monarchs are sometimes dethroned.) The essential thing, after all, was the fun of shoe making when he was fed up with ambassadors, state affairs, harems and palaces & musicians and wars.[1] After all, if you examine life, you will see that in its collective as well as in its individual activity, ennuie is the enemy. Even the war is simply the expression of a continent weary of fifty years of peace – an absurd remedy for vacuity of mind, but one which satisfies the Mrs [Olivia] Shakespeares and the [Edward] Huttons & the Rupert Brookes of the world.[2] Nearly every man in this camp now frankly admits that he was wrong in his estimation of the amusement to be got from war. It is my misfortune to have foreseen its ennuie & yet to have allowed myself to be forced into it.

You speak of my desire not to come back from the war.[3] It is perhaps there all the time – a sense of a destiny to be fulfilled. Quem dei amant [whom the gods love], you know. But I have rid myself of morbidity and await what often seems the inevitable, tranquilly, almost with indifference. I do not despise my life, but I do not overvalue it. Perhaps something will set me free; perhaps not. In any case, I do not complain.

Will you send the enclosed to Bubb? I forgot for so long to write him.[4]

With all affectionate & tender thoughts,

Richard.

1 Harun-ar-Rashid (766–809), fifth Abbasid caliph, was the lavish patron of the arts who wandered around Baghdad in disguise. His court is the setting for the tales in *The Thousand and One Nights*.

2 Here Aldington compares Olivia Shakespear, Edward Hutton and Rupert Brooke (1887–1915), the English poet best known for *War Sonnets in New Numbers* (1914) and *1914* (1915) which contained a patriotic, sentimental view of war and lost youth.

3 Aldington is obviously responding here to a letter from H.D. in which she has raised the issue of his psychology. While Aldington was not suicidal, his fatalism here has a great deal to do with his efforts to make the war mean something; see Introduction.

4 Aldington enclosed a letter dated 12 July 1918 (UCLA), to the Reverend Charles Clinch Bubb, who at the Clerk's Press in Cleveland, Ohio, printed elegant editions of several works by H.D. and Aldington.

This photograph was sent in an envelope by itself. Aldington is in the front row, far right, with fellow officers; other ranks (including a sergeant, corporal and privates) are in the second and third rows. All the men are in field helmets and carry light kits

≫ 30 ≪

16 July 1918

Dearest Astraea/

To-morrow I set off on my travels again; the army has at least that advantage – one never stays long in the same place, though frequently the moves are so short that one merely has the trouble of shifting while remaining in approximately the same place. But to-morrow will be a real move.[1] It is sad to leave this lovely village where, though I've had some boredom & depression, I have had also hours of quiet reverie and have had some time for thought & self-collection. As I wrote you I have found a little of my soul that was lost. Very likely I shall lose it again up in that damnable landscape of war, that wrecked earth which is a blasphemy, an insult to the gods. But in any case I have found something here, if it be only a specious wisdom. Dooley dear, j'ai la tristesse des départs [I feel the sadness of leaving] – and this is my third trip up the line. I hope it may be my last.

But let us talk of pleasant things. Your correspondence has been a great help and a great pleasure. Through your letters I got into touch once again with that world of ideas which is my world just as much as the world of 'stupid poor men' is my world.[2] You have been an immense succour to me and I shall carry back with me a charming image of you in my heart. I hope you will sometimes write me when I am in the line even if I can't write to you anything of interest.

By the time this letter reaches you the papers – if you see them – will have informed you of events whose _noise_ is only too plain here. My luck, so far, has been good. This is the fifth great battle I have just missed. I mustn't boast, though, lest I find myself in it this time tomorrow![3]

Will you take charge of the enclosed letter which is all I have by way of an agreement with Beaumont.[4] I have written him that in the event of my becoming a casualty, the proceeds of the book & the copyright belong to you. But if you have the letter it will be rather more secure. Don't lose it, will you? I have told Beaumont to send you a copy of the book. Well, I must get to bed now.

Au revoir and my love

Richard.

1 After six weeks of training, Aldington left the bast base camp for the front line on 17 July 1918.
2 I have been unable to identify the source of this quotation.
3 Aldington was extraordinarily lucky in missing major battles of the war. The Battle of the Somme began a week after he entered basic training in Dorset on 1 July 1916, and concluded on 18 November 1916, a month before he was first sent abroad. While in France, he served just north of the most intense battle activity, and he left for officers' training in England just after a major offensive in Flanders began on 7 June 1917. He was in London on leave or in Lichfield during the Third Battle of Ypres, which started on 31 July and continued until mid-November of 1917. He left the trenches for base camp on 2 June 1918, two days before an important Allied counterattack at Château Thierry. The current 'great battle' is likely the beginning of the Allied advance which on 8 August 1918 culminated in the Battle of Amiens.
4 Aldington enclosed a letter from Cyril W. Beaumont dated 26 June 1918, in which Beaumont offered Aldington a royalty of 10 per cent on his *Images of War* (Yale).

≈ **31** ≈

18 July 1918

This photograph was sent in an envelope by itself and includes the same group in almost exactly the same pose as in the previous photograph (Aldington is in the front row, far right). Taken immediately after the earlier shot, this picture shows Aldington and his company in dress attire

20 July 1918

Dear Astraea/

Just to say that I am back in the line & quite all right. It is very quiet here, quite supernaturally so! There is no news. I had a book from Alec Randall which will be amusing to read.

Somehow I have no thought up here, being immensely lonely without flowers & trees & little creatures or else people I care for. If I could be completely alone in some quiet lovely place, or with 'my own kind' again! But that is too much to ask, isn't it? Everything seems too much to ask. It makes me angry sometimes to think of the many people we know who are important enough to be found interesting jobs, while I. But that's rather weak, isn't it? Yet am I an utter fool? I am useless at this soldiering game. I wonder if I'd be useless at everything?

How is Cornwall? I do hope you're happy & well.

> Your
> Richard

> We are those for whom the world has no use,
> Guiltless but unneeded.
>
> Was it our fault? All our fault?
> Our voice was clear when we spoke,
> Fresh and vivid our lives,
> Ourselves not unlovely, our thought
> Not without kindness for men,
> Not without strength.
> Was it our fault they did not care,
> Our fault they could not hear!
> Cast out and forgotten, contemned,
> Without root, without purpose, we drift,
> Without country – beauty has none –
> Without place; we were proud.
>
> O my beautiful,
> Your silver is scorned,
> Your ivory grace held nothing
> By those who root in the mud,
> The under-filth of the world.
>
> Come then, be silent,
> Glide guilty away,
> Either to silence and the dream
> We hold more precious than life,
> Or to silence & a great light
> That will not perish.[1]

1 Aldington never published this poem, which I discuss in my article 'Two Poems for H.D.', in *Journal of Modern Literature*, Vol. 15, No. 1, Summer 1989, 174–7.

Well, miss, I dunno what things be a-coming to, but us have got ourselves into a regular mess-up. Sicut erat in principio et nunc et semper [Thus it was in the beginning, is now and ever shall be].

There is a regular sou-wester blowing across France & I can imagine what Cornwall is like to-day – heavy cold seas breaking against the rocks with a flurry of white spray, great gusts of wind roaring over the hills and clouds of rain sweeping over everything, breaking the poor Dryad's flowers and spoiling her quiet sea-pools. Am I right? But perhaps after all the heat & windless days you will not mind the big winds blowing 'that the small rain down can rain'.[1]

I have heard at last from Gilbert, he was near the line but not actually in it. No doubt he has had his first dose by now – hope he likes it. Lieut. of Engineers isn't a bad job – they do very little fighting. The posts between the British & American E.F.s [Expeditionary Forces] seem singularly bad – perhaps they are afraid we shall tell the Americans the truth. Heaven forbid.

He says something about hoping to see you soon. If he gets a blighty leave & threatens a descent on Cornwall, you must either turn his flank by wiring for Brigit as chaperone or else attack his center by going straight up to London & keeping him there till his leave is o'er. Have pity on him also – et ille in Averno [and he in Hell]! He will probably be in love with his wife again by now.

I had intended to write more in addition to the letter I wrote you 2 days ago [that is, on 20 July], but once again a kind of mental apathy has seized me & my brain refuses to work. Not from unwillingness to face the problem but because my mind is tired with all this turmoil – & nothing much seems worth while. You spoke, I remember, of my losing all sense of responsibility with Arabella. Of course you are right, but then at least I can urge as an excuse that the times are out of joint, and if I am mad in my way other people are no less mad in theirs. Besides the very madness & extravagance of that passion is the one thing that redeems it from vulgarity. One must have the courage of one's illusions or else life is willed [?] a fit of 'shame & loathing'.[2]

Another thing – I didn't make A. 'promise to be chaste & faithful to me for 2 years'. I said if she stayed in love with me for 2 years it would get her round a danger-point when she might do something desperate. God knows I [am] not Sir. Parsifal.[3] I desired the woman (best be frank even if brutal, eh?) but I was not entirely selfish. Perhaps if you knew a little more of life, a little more of the brutality of men, you would not feel so contemptuous. Brigit has assumed that my motives are similar to those of Deighton's friends. So be it, but I protest energetically against that view and maintain that there was idealism & poetry even in the absurdities & cruelties of this affair. I am not an insurance broker, nor am I a soldier – mais assez, on peut bien se faire un idiot ainsi [but enough, one can easily become an idiot this way]!

Anyway here we are – you in Cornwall, A. in London, I in France.[4] I don't know who's having the worst time.

You speak of poverty – dear girl, try living in a hole 30 feet underground with a pint of water per diem for drinking & washing & bully [beef, tinned meat] & biscuit for food; do you think poverty really matters? And in any case if I survive the war the government will be bound to look after me to some extent.

What really troubles me nowadays is the semi-drying-up of my impulses to work, though I think I would get them again with idleness & tranquility. But I am very tedious & as bored as a child sometimes.

Richard.

P.S. The faun sends kisses to his dear Astraea, and never, never, NEVER forgets her, nor her girl laughter, nor all the sweet parts of her. When the faun is free again she will love him as she used to.

1 The second line of an anonymous medieval poem:

> O western wind, when wilt thou blow,
> That the small rain down can rain?
> Christ, that my love were in my arms,
> And I in my bed again!

2 I have been unable to identify the source of this quotation.
3 The pure knight in Arthurian legend who finally attains the holy grail. Aldington may also have in mind Richard Wagner's treatment of Parsifal's sexual temptations and purity in his opera *Parsifal* (1882).
4 Arabella Yorke was still living at 44 Mecklenburgh Square in July of 1918 (D.H. Lawrence to Cecil Gray, 3 July 1918, in *The Letters of D.H. Lawrence*, Vol. 3, 261), although she spent two weeks in June with D.H. Lawrence at Mountain Cottage in Middleton (D.H. Lawrence to S. Koteliansky, 20 June 1918, in *The Letters of D.H. Lawrence*, Vol. 3, 256).

⪫ 34 ⪪

24 July 1918

Dearest Astraea/

You must never feel discouraged because the social order of to-day has apparently no niche to offer you, because you appear to be a sort of outcast, 'déracinée' [uprooted] as you like to call it. Only in a very few short épochs has there been a place for the 'dreamer of dreams'[1] & even then he has been counted for other things than his dreams – in Athens for his criticism of gods & men, in Florence for his learning, in the Paris of Louis XIV for his support of the monarchy – Euripides, Poliziano[2] & Racine were not loved merely for their poetry but for something extraneous. You, who are purely a poet, would have felt the hostility of any age.

You lay too much stress on nationality – a thing invented by politicians. True the traditions of one's race & people are immeasureably important, but less important than the tradition of one's soil which in turn is far less important than the 'tradition of free minds'.[3] That universal 'Kultur' which belongs to any spirit wide enough to invent it is far beyond any limited 'Kultur' or a race.[4] There is more sympathy between a mad Chinese poet & ourselves than between us & a living Australian politician. We must, it is true, go into the lives of the 'common people', who are humanity, because they never change; but we must not fall into the error of confusing this love & this understanding with nationality. The people never changes – it applauds Barrabas & crucifies Christ & it is right to do so – and that humanity which Aristophanes laughed at & Petronius sneers at in his patrician way & Rabelais knew and even Browning has glimpses of, remains eternally, or at least as eternally as human life.[5] People who do natural things are less numerous in proportion than in times past, yet they are obviously our companions. And just as Christ loved fishermen & a money-changer and peasants & women of

99

strange temperament, because he was a poet; so do we. Authority and the man of solid virtue, the woman who never errs are nothing to us. We came into the world to interpret sinners (i.e. people who have vivid lives and temperaments) not the righteous, who are so because they are too unimaginative to do anything else.

Life is an adventure & death is an adventure. When Nietzsche told his disciples to 'live dangerously', he did not mean among bombs & projectiles & physical dangers but among spiritual adventures. To live according to one's character, to live against the world's way – isn't that to save one's soul?

Someday you are coming back to be my dear Astraea again and all these mad adventures we have been on will make us the richer for each other, make our love the sweeter & keener. You speak of not having a body – you are wrong; you have a beautiful and passionate body. I knew that the last times we were together. And someday you will come back to me with a passionate abandonment and we will live a most poignant adventure together.[6]

You are more wise than nearly all women. Don't be too bitter against me. Someday we will walk along & talk of the clouds & the fields as we did.[7] And the beauty of these things will enter us & feed our love. Ah, my Dooley, did you want me to be like 'Caesar's wife'?[8] To shut out the world of experience? Because I do not hate Gray perhaps you think I do not love you? Should I fear the ice who am fire? No, no; I love you & you love me & I know well that the time will come – & soon – when we will be lovers together again, & you will come to me naked & passionate, with a richer abandonment. My dear, dear beautiful child-wife, you don't think that our love could end? One epoch in it has been broken off; we have both suffered, you especially, but there will be new epochs. I don't mind what you say now – I know you must love me as inevitably as I must love you. Other people are nothing to us – just toys on the way. You have never looked into anyone else's eyes as you have looked into mine & I have never looked into anyone's eyes as I have looked into yours.

Yes, have faith and – 'escape me? Never!'[9]

Richard

1 Aldington is quoting from William Morris's *The Earthly Paradise* (1868–70), whose classical tales in narrative verse are preceded by a six-stanza apology in which Morris defines his limitations (he cannot console or distract the reader from life's brute realities):

> Dreamer of Dreams, born out of my due time,
> Why should I strive to set the crooked straight?
> Let it suffice me that my murmuring rhyme
> Beats with light wing against the ivory gate,
> Telling a tale not too importunate
> To those who in the sleepy region stay,
> Lulled by the singer of an empty day. (stanza 4)

2 Angelo Poliziano (1454–90) was an Italian poet known for his Latin odes, Greek and Latin epigrams, and Italian lyrics.
3 Unidentified, probably proverbial.
4 Germany proclaimed that it was fighting the Great War in order to spread its 'Kultur'; at this time, the term was frequently used satirically by the British press.
5 Aristophanes, the Greek comic playwright (c. 446–386 B.C.E.); Petronius, the first-century C.E. Roman author of the *Satyricon*; François Rabelais (1494?–c. 1553), the French physician and humanist writer who often drew on classical sources and portrayed in his work the range of

French society during his time.

6 Aldington insists here that it is H.D. who has initiated and defined the current terms of their relationship. Although in many ways Aldington's actions have caused her decisions, she is nevertheless the partner who is insisting on a distance between them. She has evidently in recent letters not only been angry because of his affair but has felt sexually inadequate and insufficiently compelling to her husband. Aldington's response here, which is both apology and reassurance, seems his attempt to insist on a future for their marriage.

7 Aldington enjoyed long walks in the English countryside, and when outside of London, he and H.D. regularly hiked long distances together. He discusses at some length his fondness for walking in *Life for Life's Sake*, 53–8. H.D., too, reveals her enjoyment of this activity in the long walk she details in chapter 9 of *Bid Me to Live*, in which Julia passes most of a day wandering in the rural hills of southern Cornwall.

8 That is, to be above suspicion of any crime or immoral behaviour.

9 Aldington is not threatening H.D. here; rather, he is quoting aptly from Robert Browning's 'Life in a Love', first published in *Men and Women*, Vol. 1 (1855):

> Escape me?
> Never —
> Beloved!
> While I am I, and you are you,
> So long as the world contains us both,
> Me the loving and you the loth,
> While the one eludes, must the other pursue.
> My life is a fault at last, I fear:
> It seems too much like a fate indeed!
> Though I do my best I shall scarce succeed.
> But what if I fail of my purpose here?
> It is but to keep the nerves at strain,
> To dry one's eyes and laugh at a fall,
> And, baffled, get up and begin again, —
> So the chase takes up one's life, that's all.
> While, look but once from your farthest bound
> At me so deep in dusk and dark,
> No sooner the old hope goes to ground
> Than a new one, straight to the self-same mark,
> I shall shape me —
> Ever
> Removed!

⤞ 35 ⤝

28 July 1918

Dear wild Dryad/

I'm so glad to know that you're going to 'the isles' [of Scilly], though I'm afraid this rain and rough wind will have spoiled a little the lilies of all kinds you were to live with. Two days ago I had a very sad little note from you but instead of answering it I just sent you a faun poem.[1] I'm so glad I did because I know now that the Faun & Dryad will always live & always love each other. You see sometimes the Faun kids himself he's dead & sometimes the Dryad kids herself *she's* dead — & then, like Toddy, they wake up from the 'burn-down-dead' and find themselves good & alive again.[2] I hope you'll like the Faun song anyhow.

I wish I'd known you were going earlier – it would have cheered me up lots. Are you staying with the little girl who knows H.D. by heart?[3] Or have you just got rooms? As you speak of Alec & Amy coming down that way I suppose you are not staying with yr: amie.[4] I wish you were in some pleasant house. (Apropos, will you remember I always keep a small balance for you at Cox's? You have only to mention that you need it & I'll send a cheque by return. Don't be proud about this, for I get more pay than I need & I can't use it more pleasantly than for you.)

Amy Lowell's letter strikes me as about the most offensive thing that was ever penned – she is in her fat Boston drawing-room having the impertinence to lecture me in the front line! It takes my breath away. She is absolutely past all decency – and that talking that rot about wishing she were in the trenches. She'd get so stuck in the mud she'd never shift. Amen![5]

Ah, my dear, how sweet and beautiful you are. Of course I will come to you after the war and we will be 'wild & free', and happy 'in the unploughed lands no foot oppresses, The lands that are free being free of man', I love you, best-beloved and dearest among all the daughters of the half-gods; you knew that though you forgot that Fauns are queer & wild, with 'maggots in their brains' sometimes! Dooley birds get maggots sometimes, only they just trail their wings & look kind of doleful – but it's the same thing in the end![6]

You must tell me more about this new admirer of H.D. She must be very wise since she can love your poems so much. Has she a name or is she just some belle anonyme? Is she truely of the sacred race or merely one to whom it is given to recognise the gods yet not be of them?[7]

I would like so very hard to kiss you again – that dear small mouth that was made to speak exquisite things just as your curved ears were made to hear 'the music of the spheres'. But perhaps I should not say this, for silence is most noble to the end. And yet I tremble with pleasure when I think that on the very day of my leaving this prison[the army] I shall kiss again the cool fragrant petals of your pale hands and hold against me the tiny points of your sterile breasts.[8]

Over me have swept great waves, yet the great ninth wave has so far missed me;[9] perhaps in the end I shall win through. But, like you, I have been a wanderer upon foreign seas and yearn only to return to 'the isles' that are mine by right.

R.

9th R. Sx. B.E.F. is correct address.[10]

1 That is, a love poem; unidentified.
2 Unidentified, but clearly a character in a children's story or folk song.
3 The 'little girl' is Bryher (1894–1983), who met H.D. in Cornwall on 17 July 1918; she was an inexperienced young woman of twenty-four, eight years younger than H.D. In her memoir *The Heart to Artemis*, Bryher recalls that she had learned H.D.'s *Sea Garden* 'by heart from cover to cover' (*The Heart to Artemis*, London: Collins, 1963, 187). Born Winifred Ellerman, Bryher was the illegitimate daughter of Hannah Glover and Sir John Ellerman, the wealthy shipping tycoon, who by 1918 was also a major shareholder in *The Times*, *The Sphere*, and a number of other established London journals. Her parents finally married after her brother's birth in 1909. Bryher grew up a pampered child in a Victorian household, living at 1 South Audley Street in Mayfair during the winter and at Eastbourne on the southern coast of England during the summer. She also travelled extensively with her family before the war. She loved and was loved by both her parents, but her dependence on them was forced and psycho-

logically complex. By 1918 she had renamed herself after one of The Scilly Isles and saw herself as a rebel, a potential writer, and an avant-garde artist, but much of the competence and experience she claimed were a pose. Intelligent and eager to read widely, she had led a sheltered life. She was in fact neurotically confident at the same time that she was frequently self-doubting, petulant and aggressive. She denied her femaleness and adulthood, feeling that she was really a boy trapped in a girl's body, and by her early twenties she was clear that her sexual nature was exclusively lesbian. Frightened of what she saw as the force of other personalities upon her, stubborn and in many ways unhappy, she responded to her insecurities by being intensely manipulative and by attempting suicide numerous times, acts which combined her tendency to over-dramatise and her psychic distress.

4 Alec Randall and his wife, Amy. By 'amie', literally female friend, Aldington conveys here a particularly intimate friendship. Aldington probably sensed the special attraction between H.D. and Bryher from H.D.'s recent letters, and the playful and erotic tone of letter 35 suggests that he is relieved by her beginning a new relationship.

5 Exactly which letter Aldington is referring to here is unclear. Amy Lowell wrote the Aldingtons regularly, sometimes insisting on a sympathy which they found presumptuous given her position of social and financial privilege and her physical distance from their experience.

6 In this paragraph, Aldington quotes from his own poem 'The Faun Captive', a draft of which he sent to H.D. on 8 July 1918 (letter 25). By 'daughters of the half-gods' he means dryads, who are not quite immortal but have a special semi-immortal stature. By 'Fauns' he means creatures like himself; by 'Dooley birds' he means creatures like H.D. Proverbially, whimsical or crotchety people had maggots in their brains.

7 By 'of the sacred race' Aldington means 'one of us', a colleague worthy of being considered a particularly close friend.

8 Aldington is using this word idiosyncratically here to mean 'pure'. He uses this word similarly, for example, when writing to the publisher Charles C. Bubb about the lesbian verses in *The Love Poems of Myrrhine and Konallis* on 29 July 1917: 'I wanted to express the intensity of passion ... ; I wanted something sterile and passionate and lovely and melancholy. ... Myrrhine & Konallis are simply the love of beauty, too sensual to be abstract, too remote from biological affection to be anything but sterile' (quoted by Norman T. Gates in 'Richard Aldington and The Clerk's Press', *Ohio Review*, Vol. 8, No. 1, Autumn 1971, 23).

9 Proverbially the largest or most destructive in a series.

10 Ninth Royal Sussex Regiment, British Expeditionary Forces. Aldington routinely reminds H.D. of his address, for apparently she repeatedly forgets and asks in her letters to him.

⁂ 36 ⁂

3 August 1918

My dear girl/

Mail, which had been delayed several days, has just reached me. You seem to be in rather a devilish mess, and in a way I am responsible. Distinctly unfortunate that this should happen now as I have been nearly four months in France & haven't much hope of getting back before November! There is the faintest possible chance of my getting back on duty before then and if so I could of course see you & possibly establish your 'alibi'.[1]

However, the chief point is yourself, your own health and well-being.

Do this:

1. Stay in Cornwall until you know whether Gray is going to be enlisted. (I think he will – most Grade III men are now.)[2]

2. When you are sure of your condition – which, by the way, you should establish

at once by consulting a doctor – you must tell Brigit and get her advice & assistance.

3. You must then leave Cornwall. If you stay where you are there may be all sorts of unpleasantness.

4. I don't quite know where to suggest your going – Brigit can help here.

5. You must not worry about the situation – I will accept the child as mine, if you wish, or follow any other course which seems desireable to you.

6. I enclose £5. I will send you as much of my pay as I can. Try & keep it by you for doctors &c. You will need it.

Of course I won't tell Arabella. I can see you must be feeling pretty rotten about things, but you must just feel that this is one more strange experience and not feel badly about it. Cheer up and eat lots – I expect you are frightfully hungry?

Can you give a guess at the date of conception? You see, the devil is that I've been corresponding with Gilbert & he knows I haven't been out of France! I wrote grousing about it only a few days ago. That's rather a blow isn't it? But perhaps that can be arranged – I can tell him I managed to wrangle a couple of days from the Corps School & that I didn't write it to him because of the censor, as I'd been asked to keep it quiet. Let me have as soon as possible the date on which you want me to have been in England.[3]

I really don't know what else to suggest. I am pretty powerless here, as you know. But I will do anything I can.

Brigit is the only trustworthy woman friend you have.

The money question is the most difficult. You can have any [royalty] cheques that come for me. And perhaps I can borrow some. If necessary I can refuse leave & send you the money I would have spent on that.

Anyway, you must keep on keeping on and not get hysterical or anything. These little matters are not really as grevious as they seem.

With love
Richard.

Address: 9th Royal Sussex. B.E.F.

1 H.D. has written Aldington that she thinks she is pregnant.
2 Cecil Gray's draft classification was Grade III. Men were periodically reexamined and reclassified throughout the war, and the British government regularly revised its draft standards as the demand for new troops at the front increased. Gray is about to be called up despite a grade which previously exempted him.
3 From later letters the date of conception would seem to have been 5 July 1918, while Aldington was at the Corps School back of the lines. It was sometimes possible to arrange leave during or at the end of such training sessions before returning to the trenches.

≫ 37 ≪

Sunday, 4 August 1918

Dearest Dooley/

I've been getting down to this proposition, and, though I'm anxious not to worry you about it, there are certain points in it which I must put before you since they profoundly modify our various relationships and since upon our present and immediate action depends the tranquility (I won't say happiness) of several lives.

I divide these points into two main headings: Natural and Social.

Let's take the natural first. We assume, do we not, that each man & woman is free to live his own life, to ignore any ordinary rules of conduct when he so chooses. We assume also that men & woman are at liberty to use this freedom in matters of sex. That is merely common-sense & the practice of most civilized communities. But in sexual relationships a woman's part is curious and difficult (so is a man's). That is to say a man has one 'mate' & many mistresses; a woman one 'mate' & many lovers. But there is a difference here somehow, for a man only loves eternally his spiritual mate, whereas a woman's 'mate' is the man to whom she bears children. Am I wrong? Formerly I stood first with you & remained first however many lovers you might have had. But doesn't this event cause a sort of volte-face? Gray becomes your husband & I merely your lover; because the emotions that bind lovers together are exquisite & sterile [pure] like poetry, but a child is a more ponderous link than any beauty. It is there, it cannot be ignored or explained away; it is made out of two people's bodies, is they, cannot be distinguished from them. Therefore I feel most deeply that it is no solution of the difficulties involved for me to pretend that this child is mine. Certainly it solves some immediate social difficulties but it does not solve the natural one, which to us should be the more important. For if I take that step, not only are we all three committed to a lie for the rest of our lives, not only is your child deprived of a real father, but there is immeasurable humiliation for you, humiliation for Gray & even for me. (My dear, my dear, don't let this cold language repel you; I am agonising for you; I will do anything, everything for you, but we must see this thing straight.) Every moment that child is growing within you makes you go further from me & nearer to Gray. Inevitably, you must come to love him more – is he not the father of your child? Inevitably, he must come to love you more – are you not the mother of his child? Inevitably I must drift further from you both – what part have I now that you have come together?

Oh, it is sad, bitter, biting sad, when our love was so deep, so untroubled really by our other love-affairs. But a child! It came to me last night as I lay awake and thought out the situation. The thing I proposed in my first letter [letter 36] is wrong, impossible, cruel – cruel to you, to Gray, to me, cruellest of all to the dear baby-thing you will bear. You have become Gray's; you have ceased to be mine.

You will think: 'This is selfishness, this is unkindness, this is cowardliness, this is mere ordinary jealousy.' No, dear, it is just truth. You must stay with Gray if he wants it. I think he will. If he behaves meanly then come to me. But now I have no 'right' to ask you, no natural or divine right. It's sad, it's bitter sad, but it's true.

Now let us look a minute at the social side. Two lovers meet, kiss, love & part; there is no contract socially, no bond is formed. They are free. But two lovers meet & there is a child – then there *is* a bond, the first social unit is formed, it is ruthless and iron. You & Gray & your child are a social unit, harmonious; any attempt to monkey with that unit only produces chaos. You may have as many more lovers as you choose, he as many mistresses; but you cannot escape that obligation; you ought not to have other children. I may be wrong in this – some people, like Isadora Duncan or Craig, were clearly fitted to disregard that social unit. But aren't we all too poor for that?[1]

I won't go into the disgusting & laborious laws of our country relating to marriage and illegitimacy. You may know that they are a disgrace. The only point is that your child will be given my name unless I repudiate it; that, if I do, it cannot afterwards be made legal. You see the difficulty? It's going to be rotten for Gray to have his child bearing my name; it's going to be rotten for the child also. On the other hand, if you were to divorce me for adultery (with A.) & desertion (!) the child would remain yours & still keep my name! If I divorced you the child would be handed to me & you wouldn't be supposed to have it!!! What a darned farce! I get quite silly when I think of it. The best thing we can do is to avoid the law altogether. You & Gray must live together at least for a time and, if afterwards, things alter you & the little one must come & live with me. It's damned hard luck on Gray, I admit, but then he must consider you & the child first, & it's really better for the child in the long run.[2]

You see I've argued myself round in a circle. It's going to be damnable for us all, because no one will believe that yarn about my going to Newhaven on leave. Who the devil would go to Newhaven on leave? And heaps of people – A. [Arabella], Mr. [James] Whitall, Gilbert, Beaumont, Alec, Amy [Lowell], Frank, Ezra, May Sinclair know perfectly well I've not been out of France since I landed. Best be honest and say what's happened and say that I'm eccentric enough not to commiserate but to applaud you, that even this makes no real difference to us. Damn it, Dooley, I am fed up to have lost you. I was an idiot to let you go away with Gray, but the omens were unfriendly. I never really thought you would have a child with him. And, Dooley, I can't ever really love this little one – there's our own sweet dead baby I'll never forget.[3] I should always hate this one for being alive. No, no; we *can't* act this lie. I won't. You are a free woman; act as such; be brave and tell the truth; you loved Gray because I had a mistress & you two have had a child. You have a right to have a child with anyone you want; but don't let's act this lie. Always, always I will be devoted to you; I will do all I can with my money &c. But this other life-long lie I will not act. I will not. Your people in America must be considered, of course, but the Atlantic is wide, the war lasts – you need say nothing to them, but must we sacrifice our lives for them? Even if you had to tell them the truth they will blame me (& rightly) not you. In any case we can't get around Gilbert; he knows enough of the army to know that such a leave as you speak of is impossible. The right thing to do is to have the child, not to pretend it's mine but of course not to flaunt the fact that it's Gray's. If Gray is exempted go away somewhere quietly with him & have the child – I will try to see you both before this happens (sometime in November or December) & we can talk things over quietly. If Gray is enlisted you must try to get Brigit to be with you. Someone you must have; perhaps America will be inevitable. If I am asked I shall say quite simply that the child is not mine, but that you & I are just the same to each other. (Which is true, as least as far as I am concerned.) We will get as comfortable a time for you as possible. You must just become a primitive creature and for God's sake have a *healthy* child! Don't go & compromise its life by worry, intrigue or bother. I will send you £5 a month as long as I am in the army, more if I can; Gray must try to do the same. That will help you to live cheerily, and if possible I will give you £20 extra towards nursing expenses.[4] Later on, if you and Gray wish to marry, we will discuss it. But the main thing at present is your own health, well-being & peace of mind. There will not be so much to trouble about if we face things squarely. *You are to tell Gray at once*; you understand? It is most unfair not to tell him. He can write to me if he wishes – you know I will be courteous and understanding. It's really more his pigeon [business] than mine, for, as I have explained above, I'm now secondary in your life. I only step in if he fails. But as an old friend I claim to do everything I can to help you through this rather rocky period of your life.

Write me freely, & never doubt my love.

God bless you, dear.

Richard.

1 The flamboyant American modern dancer Isadora Duncan (1878–1927) had a tempestuous
   affair with Gordon Craig (1872–1966), English scene designer and theatre producer, who was the
   illegitimate son of the actress Dame Ellen Terry and Edward Godwin.
2 Aldington's discussion of English laws relating to marriage, divorce and illegitimacy in this and
   subsequent letters is sound. There were no strict rules for divorce in 1918; a husband could
   divorce a wife on the basis of her adultery (establishing the affection of both parties and the
   opportunity), but a wife could divorce on the basis of adultery only when it was coupled with
   cruelty or desertion. 'Non-access' of the husband was sufficient proof of a child's illegitimacy.
3 The Aldingtons' child died at birth on 21 May 1915.
4 The costs of delivery and postpartum care.

⁓ 38 ⁓

5 August 1918

My dear/

Your letter postmarked Aug 1st has just come. I don't understand at all. Please see a
doctor at once. I've been living hell these last 48 hours, thinking of your anguish &
distress, thinking that this strange event had separated us perhaps for years. Please,
please, *please* find out & let me know. I can stand the truth – I've faced the whole
problem for us both. But I'm just grasping at the hope you may be mistaken.[1]

You will wonder why I seem to lay so great a stress on your having a child with G,
when I approve of your being his mistress. My dear, no man can take you from me by
being your lover & I'm only too happy for you to have a pleasant companion, a lover,
to keep you gay & well and interested while I'm here. But I do lose you if you become
a mother, naturally & inevitably. It was for precisely that reason I stifled my desire to
have a child with A. That desire was very great but it was madness – it meant binding
A. very closely to me or else behaving very cruelly. Am I right? You must really get
this affair put straight. One way or the other. I'll face *everything* with you & stick by
you, dear. Don't have any doubt of that. I spent terrible hours thinking how confused
you must be feeling. Have this child if you are pregnant – we will arrange things
somehow. Do get my attitude correctly – I'm not angry or jealous or 'honorable' or
any such bilge, but only profoundly grieved because I suddenly realised that your
maternity would naturally & inevitably cut you away from me & join you closer to G.
And I don't want to lose my Astraea – queer wonderful creature that she is! You've just
got to understand me properly here or you will be making a bad blunder in psychology.
I love you & I want you to be happy & have lovers & girl lovers if you want,[2] but I
don't want to lose you as I should if this happened. Gray would be a worm if he let you
go when you had his child in your womb. Now wouldn't he? You know he wouldn't
do such a thing; he wants to have you with him. And you & I would just be friends or
lovers, not imperishable sweet comrades as we have been.[3]

O my dear, I pray I don't hurt you by what I say. I want to be so tender, so all-
embracingly compassionate – but while this thing is in doubt I haven't the right.

Your

Richard

P.S. Shorter's article need not worry you. Why change H.D.? You are bound to get this sort of thing. Let them print your photograph – you don't care. What the devil do these people matter?[4]

1 Evidently H.D. has written that she may not be pregnant, that she is not certain.
2 Aldington knew about H.D.'s erotic relationship with Frances Gregg before their marriage (see Introduction) and is evidently aware of H.D.'s now potentially erotic relationship with Bryher.
3 There is no evidence to suggest that Gray ever wanted to marry H.D., to live with her for an extended time, or to participate actively in the role of father or provider for their child. It would seem that Aldington is projecting himself into Gray's situation here.
4 Clement K. Shorter (1857–1926) was a Fleet Street journalist of Aldington's father's generation. Aware of modernist movements in literature and art, he felt the obligation to befriend and encourage the new work of twentieth-century youth, but he was essentially old-fashioned and at best Edwardian if not Victorian in sensibility. He had strong literary tastes, and his many editions (for instance, *The Complete Poems of Emily Brontë* and *Wuthering Heights* in 1910 and 1911) suggest his enthusiasm for facts rather than elegance of expression or critical judgement. In 1900 he founded *The Sphere*, an illustrated weekly, which he edited until his death and for which he wrote a regular literary column. Shorter was an acquaintance of Sir John Ellerman's, and by 1918 had become a family friend. His first wife, the sentimental Irish writer Dora Sigerson, died in January 1918, and by the summer of that year he had begun his courtship of Bryher's girlhood friend, Doris Banford, whom he married in September 1920. It was through Shorter that Bryher secured H.D.'s address in Cornwall, and H.D.'s friendship with Shorter developed alongside her friendship with Bryher. *The Sphere* published eight articles by Aldington between April and September 1919 (excerpts from these appear in my essay, 'Richard Aldington in Transition', *Twentieth Century Literature*, Vol. 34, No. 4, Winter 1988, 489–506). For a more detailed account of Shorter's friendship with Bryher and the Aldingtons, see my article 'A New Chapter in the Lives of H.D. and Richard Aldington: Their Relationship with Clement Shorter', *Philological Quarterly*, Vol. 68, No. 2 (Spring 1989), 241–62. H.D.'s photograph was never printed in *The Sphere*, and while Bryher may have proposed something to H.D., Shorter never wrote an article about her in his column. He did mention Amy Lowell and discussed Carl Sandburg as an imagist in 'A Literary Letter' on 3 August 1918 (90), and on 5 October 1918, he included a photograph of the Aldingtons' fellow imagist John Gould Fletcher in a brief profile of his work.

8 August 1918

Have a bad cold – will write to-morrow.

Love – R.

Be gay & cheerful – all will come right.

This postcard photograph of Aldington and fellow officers was sent in an envelope with the message on the reverse. Aldington is standing in the second row, second from the right

~ 40 ~

9 August 1918

Dearest Astraea/

I have been hoping so much to have a letter from you but none has come. I suppose you have not understood my letters – it was only to be expected. Never mind. We will go on loving each other, won't we?

You'll write me soon I hope & tell me truthfully how you are. Remember, I still don't know.[1]

Dear girl, I do pray that you are happy *whatever* has happened; & be sure I want to do all for your happiness, not for myself.

I kiss you – and I want you so hard sometimes, often, always!

Richard.

1 Aldington is still unsure whether or not H.D. is pregnant.

Dearest Astraea/

Your two letters of the 7th & 8th have just come. I feel very confused and a little mad, yes, quite a little mad. Things seem so inextricably confused, so tragically in conflict that I cannot think except 'what does it matter? what does anything matter?'

I don't understand yet whether you are ill or just enceinte [pregnant] – either is sad. But the saddest thing of all is – us. Where are we? What are we doing? What do we want? I really don't know what I want, except perhaps to creep away by myself & try to construct the illusion of peace. The war is driving us all mad. But you, how is it with you? I feel in your letter pain & scorn. Yesterday I had one very similar from A. She 'will not write again until I answer'.

Put it I'm a pathological case – to be in love with two people is, I suppose, a disease still, I must try to carry on. If I don't, there's nothing for me but a revolver bullet.

I love you so much that it is an agony. I love Arabella. This is really madness. You see it would be all right if I didn't care, now wouldn't it?

I am so sorry you are ill. You must see the doctor & get to know what is wrong & then we will do all we can to get you well & to look after you. I am glad Gray will look after you, but I don't like him going to his mother. These mothers! They are only less imperative than their daughters!¹

Dear Dooley, you are a jolly good sport and I admire you immensely. You have a hell of a long furrow to plough if what you fear is true. But I will do anything I can. What can I do?

You speak bitterly of 'one afternoon' in my November leave. One afternoon! O my dear, my dear. What is there to say? 'Ah me, pain, pain. Pain ever, forever.'²

The news from the line is very good, don't you think? It ought to prolong the war quite a lot.³

I have two or three French scientific books to read; it helps to keep one sane. I have a work of materialistic philosophy 'Intelligence & the Brain', which is somewhat alarming. It appears that our aptitudes & characters are determined by 'lobes' & 'lesions'! Tiens [Really]!⁴

Let me know how you are getting on. Is it very hot in Cornwall? It's positively scorching here, but I have a pretty 'cushy' [comfortable, safe] sort of job.

Au revoir. I wish I didn't feel so damned discouraged about everything.

Richard.

P.S. If you see John [Cournos] please be very reticent about me – I don't care to have my affairs discussed with him.

I suggest it would be better not to see Arabella.

R.

1 Gray apparently left Cornwall in early August for his mother's flat in London in part to escape local conscription. Reflecting on Gray's death in 1951 from complications as a result of heavy drinking, Aldington commented in a letter to H.D. on 23 February 1952 on Gray's desire to avoid military service: 'Gray's heart was so bad in the war – perhaps for war purposes? – that I was much surprised he lived so long.' Aldington's distrust of mothers certainly has its roots in his unpleasant relationship with his own mother, although his relationship with H.D.'s mother seems to have been positive and warm. He is perhaps particularly sceptical here because of his

experience of Dorothy Yorke's mother, who was manipulative and imperious.

2 H.D. has evidently suggested in her most recent letter that they meet only 'one afternoon' during Aldington's anticipated leave in November 1918. I have not been able to identify this quotation.

3 The successful Allied effort at the Battle of Amiens began on 8 August and concluded on 11 August 1918.

4 I have not been able to identify the text Aldington refers to here.

≫ 42 ≪

12 August 1918

Dearest Astraea/

My long letter [letter 37], written a few days ago, has very likely hurt you. I realized that at the time but it seemed so essential to 'clear up the situation'. I gather from your last letter that Gray is still away, & that you haven't told him. Really, Dooley, it's damned unfair not to tell him. He's got to readjust himself to this state of affairs and I consider that he now has a sort of 'right' over you. If he fails you, o my dear, my dear, I am there 'semper eadem' [as always]. I wish I could comfort you, my pretty one, and have you sleep gently in my arms. Of course, dear, you will always be my lover, won't you? And we will have each other in spite of all your husbands & children & so on. That I never for a moment doubt, but somehow this other thing has to be settled somehow. I fear that your having gone 3 weeks over your time is a pretty sure indication. What do you think? Have you tried giving yourself several orgasms in one night? As you know, that helps a delayed period very much. I wish I were with you for I understand that delicate little part of yours so well – I could make you glad & perhaps start you going again. I wish you weren't pregnant, Dooley; & I'm still hoping you aren't; but I'm facing the whole thing as if you were. The American idea would perhaps be good, though it seems hard to have you go.[1] I don't know that the Scillies would be the best place for you – the doctor there is probably incompetent. But you must find out soon whether you are enceinte or no, & you must tell Gray. I feel rather annoyed with him – dash it, he might have been more careful. Though perhaps he didn't know *how* careful one must be.

You must write and tell me all that happens. I wish I could be more use to you, but chained here and depressed myself I feel very useless, as if I'd failed you. You must 'stick it' [keep on with it, hold out], Dooley; you are a dear wonderful creature & are made for great exquisite experiences. This is a hard time for you, but with courage you will come through & life will be good again.[2]

Tell me if you want more money. Anything I can do, count as done. Keep cheerful, exercise, eat, don't read too much, bathe, & don't forget to have a tremendous affair with yourself *at once* – the excitement of the spasms may start you. Have as many orgasms as you can, even if you don't want them – go to bed after lunch, say, and do it then. If that doesn't do any good, you can pretty certainly decide that you are enciente. Don't talk to your flower too often – it is a strain on the nerves. What I mean you to have is a sort of orgy straight off to stimulate you. Otherwise, only do it once or twice a week – & don't forget to think of me! I think of you when I have mine.

Your
Richard.

1 H.D.'s plan, in reserve since 1914, to go home to Pennsylvania for the duration of the war.
2 Aldington echoes here the title of D.H. Lawrence's first volume of poetry, *Look! We Have Come Through* (1915), whose erotic verse explores both the tensions and the affirmations of marriage.

➢ 43 ➢

14 August 1918

Dearest Astraea/

After I got your letter of the 8th I went & played a most strenuous game of 'table tennis', got very hot, had a bath, changed, meditated, and am now in as sane a mood as a sheep in wolve's [*sic*] clothing can be.

I like your letter. It is clear & firm and puts things well. But at once on reading it there came into my mind the chief cause of our unrest, the 'unknown' quantity. It is not these extraneous love affairs which separate us but the uncertainty of my tenure, the fact that for more than two years we have known each other only in snatches.[1] Dear one, above all things I want to be your lover, to help you if I can, not to hurt you. (There are nights when I simply writhe with shame & anguish thinking of the poignancy of those moments last December when you sat alone by the fire singing softly to yourself. That was terrible, terrible, Dooley; it was like some Greek tale – Oenoene.[2] It was the bitterness of all life. And that night my spirit was yours though my body was another's. I never deserved such love; but I pay a little for it every day with tears I shed inwardly, with pangs I do not speak of. My Dooley – 'and I am no more worthy to be called' your love.)[3]

You say I am a child of Zeus, and about me indeed there is a sense of Fate; what of life I deny the gods force upon me. But we have spoken of that.[4]

My dear, you, like me, like all artists, have a diverse nature, have not one personality but several. Therefore I am inadequate to you & Gray is inadequate to you. I believe you & I complete each other more closely than most people – at least, we did; the last 2 or 3 years may have changed us. But there is a side of me which, as you know, goes hankering after unredeemed sensualism; & there is a part of you which is always seeking something purer & more spiritual than me. You may reproach me with carnal tastes as I reproach you for 'living a world ahead' (which simply means ahead of me), but these tendencies in us remain, cannot be hidden.[5] We must look upon each other with the tenderness, the understanding, the tolerance of Rénan.

You speak of forming some new attachment.[6] There, you are presuming upon Fate. Love is a chance and one does not create it by imagining one is in love with a person. On the other hand, should you find someone with whom you were in love, it would be inevitable. I never worried about G. – I knew he wasn't human enough for you. But someday I may anguish over you as you over me. But your woman's instinct here deceived you; you didn't see that I *loved* you & *desired* the other. You would not take your mythology far enough; and you saw a 'rival' (horrid word!) in the nymph surprised in the brake. Yesterday I read this: Ἐγω γὰϱ ἀμπελίδος ὄϱχον ἐλάσας. εἶτα μοσχίδια συκιδίων παραφυτεύσας ἁπαλά, κ.τ.λ. and I knew, in a way, that it was your voice speaking. And then: τί σοι καλὸν εἴϱγασται.[7] It was a reproach, infinitely sweet, from the lost lips of Euridike, a reproach for my yielding to the powers of brute force, an exhortation to remember that clear light we used to speak of.[8] And do not think that this love of mine for you is just abstract, just 'literature'. You are young and beautiful and attractive and charming; and I love you also in the rich earth way, the desire of the flesh for the flesh, the look in your eyes when you love me, the touch of your chaste mouth upon my over-heavy, over-eager lips.

There is no doubt that I love you; there is no doubt that _were I free_ I would be with you, look after you, love you. But, alas, I am not free. There are still two more years at least for you to face without me, or with me at long irregular intervals. I shall be 28 then, a little bitter, disappointed, my work perhaps ruined, my mind infinitely agitated, myself useless for making money. Dooley, Dooley, I'm not worth the waiting for.[9]

And then as to Arabella. She is passionate & thinks, acts & lives by instinct. Perhaps she will be persuaded, but I fear that in the end there must be a break. I dread that, Dooley, partly from constitutional cowardice but partly also because she will feel so badly & perhaps act rashly. God forbid that I should exaggerate myself, but permit me the vanity of stating that this is the first time she has known a European who was both an artist and one who has that sense of 'decency' towards women which some Englishmen strive for but which is not common in the regions of the Boulevard du Montparnasse.[10] Forgive this self-gratulation. But if she comes to think I've behaved meanly she loses what little moral sense she has left. And, damn it, Dooley, I believe in women having all the lovers they want if they're in love with them – but I don't like to be responsible for the making of a halt. Your wisdom & your woman's instinct can help me here enormously. Don't think me a 'prig' – I don't deny that I am to blame in this matter. But – you understand?

Well, I must break this letter off abruptly – it is very late and I've been so interrupted that I fear I have been very incoherent.

Keep wise and cheerful. And get well, dear.

Love from
Richard.

1 That is, since Aldington entered the army in June of 1916, he and H.D. have spent only 'snatches' of time together.
2 A nymph of Mount Ida whom Paris loved before he met Helen.
3 Luke 15:19, 21; on his return home, the prodigal son declares to his father, '"I have sinned against heaven and before you; I am no more worthy to be called your son."'
4 Apparently H.D. has written that Aldington's sensibility is essentially Hellenic.
5 I have been unable to identify this quotation, but it seems proverbial.
6 H.D. may have written Aldington about her possible erotic response to Bryher, but it is more likely here that she has suggested that he may fall in love with someone else if he hasn't already fallen in love with Dorothy Yorke.
7 'For I cut down the row of grapevines, next I planted the tender stalks of figs, etc.' Aldington is quoting from Aristophanes' _The Acharnians_, line 995. He also quotes Plato: 'What fair thing have you done?' Cf. Plato's _Gorgias_, 521e.
8 When Eurydice, the beloved wife of Orpheus, died, he lamented her with songs on his lyre, seeking her in the underworld. On the condition that he not look back, he was permitted to lead her out, but looking back to see if she were following, he lost her irrevocably.
9 Aldington underlines 'were I free' four times, and reiterates in this paragraph his sense that the war will continue until at least 1920.
10 Aldington feels a particular responsibility toward Dorothy Yorke, in part because of her having been deserted by a former lover in Paris before coming to London in the summer of 1917. By 'Montparnasse', he suggests the bohemian Left Bank.

44

18 August 1918[1]

Dearest Astraea/

Having descended in the enclosed poem to a more than Rummelesque sentimentality I see nothing for it but to dump the result upon Walter. Perhaps sometime when you have nothing better to do you would type the enclosed & send it [to] Rummel, saying that if it inspires him to melody he is welcome to make any use of the work (free of all charge!) & if not, he has waste-paper baskets and razors. Apropos, I suppose they (W. & T.) are still at the Rue Raynouard? Quelle vie! Thank God we never sank into such iniquitous domesticity.[2]

Four months ago to-day I was on a charmed steamer midway between the two countries. Time does pass somehow, you see. I hope that before another 4 months have passed I shall see you again. Will you still love the fat and faithless faun? But one cannot arrange life or it becomes merely a system. We retain enough spontaneity not to know how we shall behave – yet I hope you will say again: 'Is this Richard?'[3]

Let me know how your health is and please allow me to pay *all* doctor's fees for you. See a specialist if necessary and tell him or her to send the bill to me. Please tell me about yourself. Write and let me see what you write – or have I lost that privilege?

I kiss your Dryad flowers,

Your
Faun.

1 Aldington addressed this letter to Cornwall, but it was forwarded from Pendeen on 22 August to London, where H.D. had gone to stay with Amy Randall, Alec Randall's wife, at 3 Christchurch Place, Hampstead, four houses down from where the Aldingtons had lived from the autumn of 1914 through the summer of 1915.

2 I have been unable to identify the poem to which Aldington refers here. Walter Morse Rummel (1887?–1953), an American composer and pianist, first met H.D. in Philadelphia or at Swarthmore, where he performed during the summer of 1910. She heard him perform again in Paris late in the summer of 1911 as well as that autumn in London. H.D. and Aldington, often together with Pound and his friend Margaret Cravens, saw Rummel frequently in Paris during the spring and summer of 1912. He and the French pianist Thérèse Chaigneau were married later that summer, and H.D. saw them in Paris in October and probably again with Aldington in Paris during the summer of 1913. Rummel's compositions and performances influenced Pound, but while always on amicable terms with the Aldingtons, a close friendship never developed.

3 Throughout his adult life Aldington had a tendency to gain weight; H.D. in contrast was always slender and tended to lose weight when under stress.

19 August 1918[1]

I love you, I think of you, I want you – wait for me.

Richard.

1 Like letter 44, this note was addressed to Cornwall and forwarded to London.

21 August 1918[1]

Dearest girl/

I understand so well how unhappy you must feel while there is this uncertainty. Once you know one way or the other things will be clearer and the courses of action more defined. Somehow I still think you are perhaps not enciente. If you were you would surely feel very well and contented; but if you are in pain it must mean that there's something more wrong than just pregnancy. You must go see a specialist in town – at my expense, please, dear. Have the bill sent to me. If you don't do this I shall feel you are 'cutting' me.

I think these interminable days are among the most abominable of my life. If only it did the slightest little good.

When you see Brigit you must be careful to let her know all about everything so that she can give you advice after proper thought. I don't know that it's necessary to tell Arabella – unless you particularly want to. The fewer people who know at present the better. Perhaps, if you find you are enceinte, it would be wise to speak to her. But it's entirely up to you – I have said nothing, have hinted nothing.

You must not be too generous in your desire to let everyone be 'free'; after all, 'freedom' does imply a voluntary admission of responsibility. G. cannot possibly evade the fact that he is the father of your child. Army or no army that fact remains.[2] You know, Dooley dear, I do want to do anything and everything for you, but it doesn't seem as if [I] have the 'right' to do much. This makes life seem very queer. O my dear, I do so want to do the right, the tender, the gracious thing – you know? – my heart is good enough. But I cannot quite see how. I wrote Brigit a curt little note – as we are not on particularly good terms – begging her to be very careful as to what advice she gave you, because I feel all your life's happiness depends on what happens now. I seem to bring unhappiness to everyone I care for – it drives me mad to think of such unhappiness falling on the little girl I saw in Brigit's room six years ago. I feel very angry with Gray sometimes – because it's just like a sloppy musician not to be precise and careful. God, I feel deadly sick to think what you are going through – poor dear, my dear little girl child Astraea. You have suffered too much already that this should come on you.

Keep a good heart, my dear; nature, in her infinite kindliness, is perhaps preparing for you some exquisite recompense for these bitter years. It is perhaps weak selfishness for me to regret that your child is not ours. But 'no man escapeth his fate by lamentation', and I must accept this, the bitterest thing that has ever happened to me.[3] Between you & me as always there is great love, a perfect love. I do not see the future clearly, yet I do know I shall never love anyone but you inevitably. Though we be oceans apart I never forget you. Be brave, be strong, have your child and I will try to care for it for your sake – if you want.

Sleep, dear; don't think; just be a happy mother.

Your
Faun.

---

1 Like the previous two letters, this letter was addressed to Cornwall and forwarded to London.
2 That is, whether or not Gray is conscripted.
3 I have been unable to identify this quotation.

Dearest Astraea/

You are very wise to be going to town – I insist on your going to a good doctor at once. There may be something seriously wrong with you and you must have it seen to at once. Do you understand? Give my name and address (B.E.F.) to the doctor & I'll pay his bill by return.[1]

Now for God's sake *don't* go live in some dull little room in town. Stay somewhere cheerful and let me make up any deficiencies in your accounts. Miss Weaver owes me a few pounds over the P.T.S. & I should be getting some money from the U.S.A. soon. Please do not go to any rotten little place.[2]

I see from your last letter that you are not at all happy and I am quite grieved at this. Moreover I am frightfully disappointed that your trip in Cornwall has not built up your health. I was hoping you'd get quite well again. You must forgive me if I am often forgetful of your physical fragility, but you know people of 'rude health' are very selfish in that way. And with the improvement in food & conditions one gets as an officer I have now become 'very fit' – very sunburned, not quite so fat, fresh and very 'male'! The last two months have been the most agreeable I've had for over two years. I've been very worried about you and about things generally – but what I mean is that life has been pretty cushy here and yet strenuous enough to be healthy.[3]

I don't see why you should run away from London because there's a chance of my getting leave. You needn't really worry – there's not much chance of my coming this year. And Arabella though jealous has amazing patches of sanity for a woman – and in any case why the devil shouldn't I do as I like? Are you going to make me waste 2 days leave travelling up & down from London to the Scillies?[4]

My dear, I get fed up with G. & van Dieren. It makes me think of what we used to call 'holy Ezra'. (Apropos, poor old Franky is a 'Tommy' in the Rifle Brigade at Falmouth! He's in a B1. battalion, so I guess mending roads & frightening Boche prisoners will be about the extent of his military excesses.) Of course it's damned rotten for a man of Gray's sensitiveness & talent to be shoved into the A.P.C. But he won't have more than two years of it and must look on it as imprisonment for art's sake![5]

I know I am glad to be out here now – there is an immense stimulation in these victories, especially when you are not fighting them! My present situation is ideal – I get all the excitement with a minimum of danger. I never thought the Allies had the brains or the guts to do what they've done. The Boche is really rattled – he's getting pushed all ways; there are rumours that he is retreating, retreating, retreating everywhere. I know it's all rot and so on, but it's like a bull fight or a fierce football match; and after one side has been conspicuously beaten & stuck it there is something pleasing in seeing them turn round & give the other man hell. They have a simple amplitude about things nowadays; if the Boche sends a shell over they send back 5, does he drop a bomb, a telephone message gets 10 dropped on him; does he raid with a company, we attack with a brigade. And so on. I feel pretty sure we shall drive him back to the Meuse next year, be in Germany in 1920 & have peace by the end of that year – i.e. in just over two years. I don't know if you read the papers, but perhaps you know the armies have taken 100,000 prisoners & more than 1000 guns in about six weeks? Stuff to give the troops, who by the way have the same cynical boredom in victory as they have in defeat. Of course most of us will get killed, but it will be an amusing experience. So you must cheer up and get through the next two years somehow and then we'll be happy ever after. Do you ever write anything nowadays? You are such a shy bird, one never hears anything of you.[6]

Au revoir, dear girl. I love you very, very much and I want you to love me – and I'll do *anything* to make you happy. Don't feel too sad; one does I know, and hates people who say 'be cheerful', but it's worth being cheerful on one's own. Anyway, we're not immortal, old thing; we're 'on leave' from eternity, so may as well have a good time.

Get *well* – take yourself in hand; you must. Hang it, you're young & sweet & fresh – 'I say unto you mourn not for the kingdom of heaven is at hand.'[7]

Richard

1 On the basis of postmarks on forwarded letters it would seem that H.D. left Bosigran in Cornwall for London before 22 August 1918. She evidently left somewhat precipitously, for she did not inform Aldington of her new address in time to avoid the forwarding of letters 44, 45, and 46. Letter 47 is correctly addressed, so Aldington has heard from H.D. that she is staying with Amy Randall in Hampstead.

2 The housing shortage in London in 1918 was serious. Having given up her room in Mecklenburgh Square in early August (H.D. to John Cournos, 7 August 1918) and realising that she cannot stay indefinitely with a friend, H.D. is in a somewhat awkward situation. Harriet Shaw Weaver (1876–1961) was the editor of *The Egoist*. The Poets' Translation Series included six translations that appeared initially in part or in their entirety in this periodical. The Egoist Press published the translations as pamphlets in 1915 and 1916. Aldington was general editor as well as translator of the first (*Anyte of Tegea*), fourth (*Latin Poetry of the Italian Renaissance*), and fifth (*The Garland of Months by Folgore Da San Gemignano*) volumes. The money Aldington expects from the United States is probably from *The Dial*, in which instalments of Aldington's 'Letters to Unknown Women' had appeared in March, May, and June.

3 H.D. was periodically ill, and her physical health was often related to her emotional state. She had not been well since returning to London from Lichfield in late November 1917. Aldington's boast here of good health and physical comfort cannot be taken very seriously. He is obviously trying to reassure his wife and to relieve her of having to worry about him. Officer or no, Aldington's experience at the front was far from pleasant.

4 While the Aldingtons are comfortable writing to each other, H.D. has evidently decided that she would prefer not to see Aldington in London and/or that she would prefer not to take the chance of seeing him and Arabella together – a possibility if the three of them were in London at the same time. H.D. is still considering a visit to the Scilly Islands with Bryher; however, she also wants to see Aldington during his next leave.

5 Bernard van Dieren (1887–1936) was an English composer unceasingly championed by Cecil Gray, who was also a personal friend. Flint has been conscripted into a battalion of men fit for service abroad in garrison or provisional units, but not for front line service. 'The A.P.C.' was the Army Pay Corps, which employed men trained in accounting or unfit for any sort of physical service.

6 The Allies were victorious at the Battle of Amiens (8–11 August), and on 21 August the Allies initiated the Second Battle of the Somme and the Second Battle of Arras, both of which were going favourably. During the summer of 1918 the war, which had been static and entrenched all along the western front, finally began to move forward in a series of Allied successes that would enable British forces to reach the Hindenberg Line by mid-September 1918. The Meuse is a river located in the Ardennes region of France, northwest of Verdun and southeast of Cambrai. The many months of stasis at the front had not prepared the soldiers for the rapidity of the war's conclusion, and Aldington's estimate here is typical.

7 John the Baptist says, 'Repent, for the kingdom of heaven is at hand' (Matthew 3:2), while Jesus repeats the same words later (Matthew 4:17); it is probably these words that Aldington is recalling, despite his misquotation.

Dearest Astraea/

I feel kind of baffled I admit. Wish I'd get brain fever or something and not have to think.

The only thing I am sure about is that I don't want you to have an operation [an abortion]. I beg and implore and beseech you not to. You are not strong enough; it is most fearfully expensive & difficult; it would harm you very much physically and do your mind irreparable harm. Please believe I am absolutely sincere in this; look at B. [Brigit]; she is not the gay sweet creature she used to be. But not you – no, no, no; I can't bear the idea and your being cut. Promise me you won't?

I don't know why A. wants to be married to me. Except that sense of possession. Psychologically she is right – I am not a lover but a husband. Too many scruples.[1]

This is absurd. What complications.

You felt she was hostile to you? I gathered that from an over-tone emanating from your last letter. A pity. Still it is only natural.

Yesterday, before I had your letter I wrote her saying that I intended to accept paternity of the child if you wished and that I would always want to see you because you are very dear to me. I tried to explain and more how it was that you will always mean a great deal to me and how she has given me so much. I admit ruefully that the present position is untenable; both flanks are gone & the center is wavering. Quey? Which is the best position to retreat to? (I'm afraid you were damned unlucky in marrying me, Dooley.)[2]

Now, look here, dear one; no hang it, I can't suggest that.

A. writes rather fiercely that she won't let me accept the child as mine! (Gesture of tigress preserving her young.) Good girl. But suppose I insist? It is rather charming of her, though, don't you think?

I don't know that I like the farm idea. A mother ought to suckle her child if she can and have it live near her. You would have fits all the time thinking it would get hurt if it was away from you. I know what mothers are. And your child *must* be brought up among gentlefolk.

As a matter of fact, dear, the whole problem is insoluble. I think the only possible solution is the one you suggest – to break with both of you and go live by myself. I shall be miserable, but I can get a post-office job after the war and that will keep me from thought & ambition. I care too much for both of you to take either without the other. Best quit. You will have your child; Arabella will marry someone; I will learn German and devote myself to philanthropy.

You can tell Arabella that it is not possible for us to marry since you are not able to divorce me (adultery alone is insufficient in England) and I refuse to divorce you. I will write her the same if she asks me, but she doesn't. I am rather surprised that you say she still persists in the 'all or nothing' attitude. Perhaps it is only logical and normal; yet granted the somewhat peculiar circumstances perhaps some concession might have been possible. Curious.

I have been very much at fault, weak and over-anxious not to wound. To you I have under-estimated my passion for A., to A. I have under-estimated my tenacious devotion to you. You might, if you choose, call me a liar & a blackguard; I should not feel it truthful to dispute it. I have said passionate and intense, no doubt foolish things to A., and have led her to expect more than it is in my power to give. To *want* to give everything is not the same as having the power; my nuances were not precise. I have made a mess of things. You, poor darling, are up against it; A. will be very angry with me (which I shall dislike) and will say bitter things (which will hurt me very much) and I shall feel very lonely & lost. But the only straight thing is to quit and see neither of you.

Cheerio,
Richard.

Later.

Have written A. the substance of this: ie. that I intend to accept the child as mine, but that I will not see either of you two again. It is the only possible solution.

I will send you the money I mentioned. Please accept the Dial cheque which I returned endorsed to A. yesterday.

R.

1 Aldington is apparently commenting on H.D.'s concerns in a recent letter. It would appear that H.D. and Dorothy Yorke have met in London and discussed their situation. Aldington was always essentially monogamous and had a strong tendency to bond with a partner against all others. His self-evaluation here is perceptive and anticipates his erotic relationships with women for the rest of his life.

2 While Aldington initially reassured H.D. that he would not tell Yorke about the pregnancy, it is clear here that he has told her, as he inevitably had to at some point. By 'Quey?' Aldington is likely thinking of the Spanish 'Que?' meaning 'What?'

🙟 **49** 🙜

1 September 1918

My dear Astraea/

I am sitting out of doors to write this in a deep lane with banks covered with sunny flowers. The wind and the clear sky give me sanity and calm. And I am more than ever convinced that what I wrote you yesterday is the only possible course for us to follow. It is true, as I wrote Arabella, that all the colour goes out of life, all the interest. But I gain calm and a certain liberty of the spirit and a sense of justice. I have still some evil hours to go through, to struggle with my loneliness, my affections, my sensuality. Yet I believe I can do this. The B.E.F. gives me at least a temporary protection under which I can 'grow a shell' to use your phrase. It is better for us all to live apart, and not to see each other. I don't think there is any necessity for me to see either of you in November.[1] I can go to Paris or not go anywhere, and by the time the war is over we shall all be pretty used to the state of affairs. You see there was a time when I cared so much, so very much. But now I don't care; I should not be strong enough, I know, to resist if I saw either of you, but from here, my 'Hindenberg Line', I can laugh at you – you can't come to me & I need not come to you unless I want. I think I am master of the situation? After the war, if there is an afterwards, it will be easy for me to evade you both.

I maintain what I said before: I will accept your child as mine and give it my name. It is too great a burden for a sensitive child to brand it with bastardy. And I won't have it. The little creature has done no harm and that at least we can do for it.

I will send you one third of my income whatever it happens to be.

I will not see Arabella any more than I will see you. It is all over, napoo, fini –

understand?[2] Neither of you. I can do without you, and I must do so and you will both have to do without me – which I guess you can do.

My present job is to get on with the war, which I shall do to the best of my ability. Afterwards I shall do what I think best – almost certainly it will not be literature, nor women. There will be plenty of jobs for discharged officers. So I have no particular worries about my future. I hope you will be happy and I hope Arabella will, and I hope you will both forgive me for having loved too much and now not at all.

Richard.

P.S. I endorse September cheque.[3]

Later.

Your letter of 26.8.18 has just come. I am sorry about the Lawrence business for your sake; but people are like that. I suspected the Gray business too. Artists! My God, quel canaille [what riff-raff].[4]

But I see no reason to alter what I have written above. Look on me as a sort of eternally absent friend; you can rely on my discretion and help at any juncture and in any circumstances.

I am deeply sorry for you, but I can do no more.

R.

1 Aldington anticipates a three-week leave in mid-November.
2 'Napoo' is an English corruption of 'il n'y en a plus', meaning finished, dead, gone.
3 Aldington regularly sent his army paycheck to H.D., who periodically sent him funds from her bank account.
4 After the Aldingtons' return to Mecklenburgh Square from Lichfield in late November 1917, D.H. Lawrence's relationship with H.D. became very intense. If we can trust *Bid Me to Live*, she and Lawrence maintained an intimate correspondence (their letters have apparently not survived) that continued throughout her time in Cornwall. Lawrence's failure to respond with equal passion to H.D.'s overtures effectively precluded this aspect of their relationship. In addition, Lawrence's affection for Dorothy Yorke, of whom he was consistently fond, probably led him finally to distance himself from H.D. Yorke visited the Lawrences for two weeks at their cottage in Derbyshire in June (D.H. Lawrence to S.S. Koteliansky, 20 June 1918, in *The Letters of D.H. Lawrence*, Vol. 3, 256). It was through Yorke, for example, rather than through H.D., that Lawrence probably knew, as did very few others, that H.D.'s child was Gray's and not Aldington's (D.H. Lawrence to S.S. Koteliansky, 7 April 1919, in *The Letters of D.H. Lawrence*, Vol. 3, 349). Aldington finds Gray no more faithful to H.D. than Lawrence has been.

🌺 50 🌺

2 September 1918

Dearest Dooley/

I hope you are feeling better all round and that Brigit has been a comfort to you.

You must forgive me if I write only a little letter or none at all; I am rather unhappy and exhausted with a great struggle.

Let me know how you are, if you want anything &c.

Don't trouble about L. and G. If I can I will provide for the child – I would rather, if it can be done, that you didn't take G.'s money.[1]

Richard

1 Feeling deserted by both Lawrence and Gray, H.D. is apparently considering asking Gray for money to pay for childbirth expenses and later maintenance. Despite pressure put upon him, primarily by Brigit Patmore and Bryher, Gray could never be coerced into giving H.D. any funds toward child support. Patmore's letters to H.D. and Bryher during the 1920s (Yale) chronicle the women's unsuccessful efforts to persuade Gray of his financial responsibility.

➢ 51 ➣

September 8, 1918

Just to say that I have not forgotten your birthday. Perhaps it would be too cynical to offer you congratulations, yet at least I can salute you with a gesture.[1]

Life is very strange and pitiful. These bitter days we are all three suffering, this pain and discontent seem very useless; one can only keep in mind the immense background of human misery and reflect that we are now in harmony with it instead of in contrast.

Of course one must not take things too tragically; there is something attractive in Anglo-Saxon imperturbability. Yet I have a precise sensation that what Browning would call 'the poetry of life' is over. No doubt I shall continue to live and act and perform all the little fruitless gesticulations of existence, but the flash has gone from the gun, the perfume from the flower, the ecstacy from music. I shall never again live in the old intense way, never be thrilled by beauty as before, never wait for a woman with a beating heart and dry lips, never *live* again.

O my dear, this is a sad bitter little birthday note, but you must accept it. We have become middle-aged before our time, and it is more gracious to leave the stage at once than to importune spectators with a diminishing charm. This moment comes into all lives. I did not think it would come so soon to me; I hope that it has not come to you. But directly we cease to live in ecstasy, youth has gone. I have had nearly ten years; and of many beautiful things given me by the Fates the most beautiful has been to love & to have been loved.

I am firm in my resolution and I have this one hope in life – that it will make things easier and more tranquil for you. I shall not see Arabella again, as I promised you; nor will I ever have another mistress. I will do all I can for you and your dear child – dear to me, because it is part of you – but you must not expect to see me again; the middle-aged like to avoid pain!

Richard

1 On 10 September H.D. celebrated her thirty-second birthday in London at dinner with her old friend May Sinclair (1863–1946), the English novelist who had given her address to her new friend, Clement Shorter, with whom she had begun to correspond in July 1918, and whom she had recently met after her return to the city.

➢ 52 ➣

20 September 1918

Dearest Astraea/

Thank you for your letter and for sending Amy [Lowell]'s. She makes one impatient and I intend not to write her again. The woman's a fool. Harmless, but a fool.

I haven't heard what address you are going to, so am writing via 3 C.C. Place.[1]

As you may remember I am here until October 8th, so naturally there is no news to give. I am dull but comfortable. May have more to report this time next month.[2]

I hope you are well and that everything is progressing well. Look after yourself and keep fit.

What are you doing about coal for the winter? I suppose you know it is strictly rationed? Don't forget to look after this.[3]

Love from

Richard.

1 3 Christchurch Place, where H.D. has been living for almost a month, although she is now planning on moving to a place of her own. In an undated letter to Amy Lowell sent from this address in September 1918, H.D. conveys her current situation and intentions. Although the letter is guarded and omits mention of much that is emotionally central to H.D. at this point, it deserves quotation in full:

> c/o Mrs Randall
> 3 Christchurch Place N.W.
> Hampstead
>
> Dear Amy,
>
> I was sure I wrote you and I had an idea R. too wrote, as he said your article was far, far too kind and he was awfully touched by your generosity. But word keeps coming from time to time of things not received, so I imagine you never knew how really touched we both were. How could you doubt that? – Now I hope this reaches you, as I appreciate your writing me, after my apparent neglect – also I want to thank you + for R., for the check. I will write again. This is just a scrap to catch the next post out.
>
> I have just got back from Cornwall + am hoping to go away again somewhere nearer London. Above address always will reach me – also 44; though I have given up my room there, books etc. still stay + post is forwarded. But I shall send you my country address as well.
>
> I am writing Fletcher – have not seen him yet. Will give you news of him. I dined with Clement Shorter last night. He is a fine old man – very generous + open-minded, though, of course, a bit conservative + old-fashioned. I think your book gave him his first impulse toward modernity. He thinks a lot of you, as you already know. I met the Bryher girl in Cornwall. She is about 24. I think, too, shows great promise. She simply worships you + your work. I go to see her this afternoon + will write you further of her. She comes from wealthy people. Do not tell her I told you as she is very queer about it. But her wealth could make no difference to *you*, nor to any real friend. She imagines any kindness + interest come *only* because her father is reputed 'the richest man in England'. Of course, one can understand, but if she is any good at all, her father's position won't hurt her. (Her name is not Bryher.) Of course, I did not know this when I met her, and my interest was genuine. Yours, too, I am sure is. – She was worried: Did I think Miss Lowell was offended etc. I assured her you would be pleased by her appreciation + now I will tell her I have heard direct from you. She wants to meet people who write. Clement Shorter + H.D. is the extent at present of her literary acquaintances. I will try to find people but you know how disappointing most 'writers' are – and everyone is in the war almost. I told her if she went to America, I was sure Miss Lowell would be very kind to her. She is wild to go away. But it seems impossible now – and her people are dead against it.
>
> The Lawrences are in the country. You probably hear from Lawrence. Flint is in the army – I don't know anything about him. I am forwarding the letter. R. has a jolly job now, back of the lines in signal work. No doubt you will hear from him. I have not seen the Pounds. London is rather more lively than when I left – more hope in the air, and food problems not so serious.
>
> Well, good luck. I will write again.
>
> Love to Mrs Russell + to you.
>
>> from
>> *Hilda.*

2 Aldington is still at base camp receiving special training in Signal School 8th Corps.

3 The British government introduced wide-scale rationing in 1918: sugar was rationed in January; in April ration cards were issued for meat, butter, cheese, and margarine; in July ration cards were replaced by coupon books and only tea, cheese, and bread were unrestricted. Coal was also rationed in 1918 and electricity and gas supplies reduced.

⚘ 53 ⚘

22 September 1918

Dear Astraea/

Have had a letter from your little friend Winifred Ellerman. She seems to have the right spirit, and I've encouraged her to work at Greek with the idea of her doing something for the P.T.S. [The Poets' Translation Series] if we can get it going again. Has she showed you any writing? It seems most enthusing to find someone who understands things; she realized what 'Captive' means, 'Syracuse, the quarries &c.'[1] Has anyone else, I wonder? Anyway, thank you for getting her to write – it was 'like your gracious way' once more. Perhaps you will bestow upon her with my blessing all the Bubb booklets if you care, if you haven't given them already.[2]

I have had some money from Miss Weaver for the P.T.S., some I will send Franky & your cheque I enclose herewith.

Hope you are getting on well, & that you are happy.

Love from
Richard.

1 Bryher has read Aldington's 'The Faun Captive', a draft of which he sent H.D. in July. Aldington wrote to Bryher directly on 22 September 1918, thanking her for her initial letter and elaborating on her understanding of his poem: 'You are the first person I know of who has understood that indeed it does mean "Syracuse, the whole expedition, the fight in the harbor, the quarries". It is the bitterness of that abominable captivity felt again, resentment against the invasion of one's spiritual life. For we, who care for beautiful things … , are in perpetual conflict, in which too often we are worsted' (Yale). In quoting Bryher's letter back to her, Aldington confirms her gloss on the poem, which recalls the destruction in 413 B.C.E. of the Athenian fleet in the harbour of Syracuse during the Peloponnesian War (Thucydides, *History of the Peloponnesian War*, Book 7, chapters 69–71).

2 Booklets of work by H.D., Aldington, and others, published by Charles C. Bubb at the Clerk's Press in Cleveland, Ohio. These included reprints from the first Poets' Translation Series as well as H.D.'s *The Tribute and Circe* (1917) and Aldington's *The Love Poems of Myrrhine & Konallis* (1917) and *Reverie: A Little Book of Poems for H.D.* (1917).

⚘ 54 ⚘

27 September 1918

My dear Astraea/

Your plans seem to me excellent and sensible, and you should pass a fairly comfortable winter I think. Take exercise & keep normal. The arrangements for food and warmth seem O.K. It is not precisely the ideal existence one formulates but it is the best you can do under the circumstances.[1]

Will you note that after Oct. 4, letters should be addressed 9th Royal Sussex, & the 'Signal School 8th Corps' discontinued. I go up the line on the 8th.

I am very glad to find that you are cheerful and, as you say, 'without resentment'. Yet, when you say that, I wonder if you have completely 'got' my attitude. God forbid that I should re-touch new wounds, but as I was catagorically definite with Arabella, so must I be with you. I want you to understand that in the actions & determinations I have taken I have been moved by affection for you rather than any bourgeois sense of duty. That is clear, isn't it? But I want you to understand also that this affection is purely that of friendship. Your friendship seems very valuable to me & I am anxious to retain it, but on no misapprehension. So far as you & I ever being lovers again or living together as husband & wife, you must understand that it is fini, fini, fini. Now I am not trying to force you into anything. I am proud that you should bear my name; glad if you correspond with me on matters of art & literature & life; happy to meet you as one meets an old friend. You are quite free to make any kind of 'liaison' you choose, providing some sort of elementary social camouflage is used; I don't wish to interfere with you in any way. Be as 'free' as you can in a world of slaves. If you care to give & accept friendship upon these terms, I am only too happy. It is purely up to you. But I cannot have you being pleasant to me if I feel there is any idea in your mind of the old relationship being renewed. Because that is now impossible. You may think me idiotic and affirming more than I can carry out. But women are not so essential to life as they imagine; and in any case – well, there's no need to be offensive, is there?

I think I've made my point clear, and made it so with as much consideration as is consistent with precision.

It is no use our being humbugs, my dear. Things can't ever be the same again, so why carry on with something patched-up, a makeshift? I have at last 'sorti mon beau tranchant' [got out my good cutting edge], as you see & cut the Gordian knot of this affair. Arabella knows precisely how I stand & we have now ceased to correspond except at rare intervals. But there is no necessity for you & I to adopt this severity, unless you are anxious to eliminate so eccentric a person from your circle. We have many points of common interest not at all affected by the state of our hearts. You don't need any reiteration of my admiration for your work (though, since we are being so devilish frank, it wouldn't hurt for you to improve your spelling & punctuation!) or for your personality and fine mind. So, as I have said, if you care to carry on, on this purely friendly basis, I am delighted. If not, it is up to you.[2]

Now then; I believe this is really the last postscript to this almost year-old affair. I am conscious of being less pleased with myself than I could wish, yet on the whole I have been fairly frank & not altogether inconsistent. Your going-off with Gray was of course a mistake – never, in future, have an affair with a man if you are not both in love with each other. If you had been in love passionately with G., all right; but just slipping off like that – wrong, dead wrong. Probably you will now write & say that you *were* passionately in love with G. In which case I shall just note down that all men are liars, especially women.

For myself, as I wrote you, there seems to be no particularly brilliant future. There is nothing I particularly want, and that is very dull. Yet I have gained a certain balance, a certain possession of myself, and a measure of certainty that no person in the world is essential to me. That is a great gain, for to put one's happiness into the hands of another is indeed a handing of hostages to the future.

You will, I hope, pardon the frankness and perhaps offensiveness of this letter – it is for the truth's sake. I hope to hear from you.

Ever yours
Richard.

1 Aldington directs this letter to H.D.'s new address, about which she has written him so that no
  letters are misdirected or forwarded. She has also evidently shared with him her plans for the
  next few months: she has rented Peace Cottage at Speen, near Princes Risborough in
  Buckinghamshire, and has asked her American girlhood friend Margaret Snively Pratt with her
  baby to join her for the autumn and winter. Pratt had been living in London with her year-old
  daughter while her English husband, Bernard Pratt, was fighting at the front. Years later Pratt
  wrote to Bryher about H.D.'s arrangement: 'I think the reason she had me stay with her in
  Speen before Perdita arrived was because I was so normal, not poetic' (Margaret Snively Pratt
  to Bryher, 3 February 1975, Yale). In leaving London for the country, H.D. was acting less
  impulsively than in her somewhat precipitous departure from Cornwall: she had an attractive
  cottage in a village that offered her the relative peace of rural England within a short distance of
  London. Her new friend Clement Shorter had a large country house nearby at Great
  Missenden. The situation seemed to both Aldingtons sensible and stable.
2 Aldington was more decisive in general than H.D., and more able to stick with a course of
  action once decided upon. H.D.'s palimpsestic method in her writing was also characteristic of
  her life: she was less able than Aldington to let go of friendships and experiences in fact and
  memory. Thus while she initiated the separation Aldington is defining here, the decision and
  responsibility he indicates are hers will be difficult for her to manage clearly and consistently.

> 55 <

30 September 1918

Dear Astraea/

Enclosed Oct. cheque.[1]

I have Miss What's-her-name's poems; I don't know quite what to say about them.
They leave me quite unmoved. I expect I have lost my flair for these things.[2]

No further news. I go up the line on the 8th. Address to battalion after 4th.

Ever yours
Richard.

1 Aldington routinely sent H.D. his army pay, which is the excuse for this letter. This and many of
  the letters which follow are occasioned by Aldington's excuses for the continued correspondence.
2 Bryher's poems, perhaps those which later appeared in *Poetry* in October 1920 (Vol. 17, No. 1,
  136–7), under the group title 'Hellenics': 'Blue Sleep', 'Eos', and 'Wild Rose', or similar poems
  inspired by Bryher's relationship with H.D. and imitative of the latter's style and subjects.
  These poems were signed 'W. Bryher', and Aldington is obviously exasperated here about
  whether to call Bryher 'Miss Ellerman', 'Miss Bryher', or 'W.B.', as she sometimes signed
  herself during this time in initials that echoed H.D.'s. In an undated letter to Bryher (probably
  written in mid-September 1918), H.D. indicates that Aldington is interested in seeing some of
  Bryher's work and writes: 'I am sending him the three poems you sent me. He will understand
  and appreciate them.' In the same letter H.D. urged Bryher to send Aldington the manuscript
  of her novel (see letter 56). She continued: 'He would be so pleased to see the MS. and is, I
  assure you, an impersonal + just (even if beautifully generous) critic.' (Yale)

> 56 <

6 October 1918

Dear Astraea/

I like your little friend's book. She is immature, but in some ways startlingly like you.
I hope you will see her sometimes & lead her in the right paths. Her liking Amy [Lowell]
so much is a weakness – let's hope she'll grow out of it. I've dropped notes to May

[Sinclair] & Brigit to ask her [to] tea – she may need to know pleasant women. Really, I have enjoyed her enthusiasms & I thank you for getting her to send me the m.s. book.[1]

I have not heard from you in answer to my long letter [letter 54]. But I feel sure you will see the wisdom of my plan. Don't think, because I wrote bitterly, that I will ever be anything but tender & affectionate to you. But can we do anything but be friends, dear friends? There must be no more humiliation for either of us.

I heard from Arabella yesterday; she is 'touchante' [touching], but I can see she still dreams of 'possession'. And that will not be. I will not sell my tatters of freedom, my mind, my love of beauty, for any other passion. No doubt she would be an excellent wife; but that is precisely what I don't want. You are not a wife; you are a dryad. And I am ever so safe by being married to you. None of these human women can then steal the faun from himself, because he is a wanton.

Don't think I am resentful. I have told you frankly that I wish things were different, but I accept fate – and you are, & always have been, free to do what you choose. You must not mind if, in the future, I see you without the child; I would not have asked you to look at Arabella's.

I am glad that you'll be comfortable at Speen. And I hope Margaret won't get on your nerves. Still she can give you many hints.

My dear child, you must save more than £10 – at least £50. I should be getting some money from my book – you must have that and the money from Poetry, if it comes.[2]

Flint says he may get me some stuff into a new Anglo-French review, so if he asks for any stuff of mine send him the 'Faun Captive' & the 'Fantasy in Three Movements.'[3]

Don't forget to write to 9th Royal Sussex again now. Leave out 'Signal School'.

Affectionately

Richard.

1 Bryher sent Aldington a draft of her autobiographical novel *Development*, published by Constable in 1920. Aldington was genuinely pleased with Bryher's prose and wrote more expansively to Flint on the same day as this letter to H.D.: 'Hilda has found a new Imagist, a girl in London who is mad about our work, and has a most wonderful mind. I have seen a m.s. of her prose. It is young (and foolish) in parts, but she has a superb gift of realisation of beauty & a clear imagist method of writing.' Aldington then quoted from *Development* at some length and concluded: 'A prose H.D. She has pages of quite magnificent stuff. Of course, the book is far too much concerned with literature; but she is now quite crazy about life & if she avoids certain obvious perils will do good work' (HRC). Bryher's affection for Lowell's work was untempered. Aldington wrote Bryher on 5 October 1918: 'You love an ideal Amy. I know her well, know how good she is; but she won't last you. ... You like her love of life more than her art. You are quite right; but someday you will strike the essential falseness there. Amy has not known great love or great grief. She is vivid and delightful, altogether miles above that deadly Georgian crowd; but she is not of the immortals. You can say I hate her because she has too many dollars & a motor car & a suite at The Berkeley. Not a bit; these things are extrinsic. She is just too comfortable' (Yale).

2 The book Aldington refers to is his forthcoming *Images of War: A Book of Poems*, published by Cyril W. Beaumont in early 1919. *Poetry* owed Aldington for poems it had accepted and would publish in November 1918 (Vol. 13, No. 2, 67–71), under the title 'Prayers and Fantasies I–VIII'.

3 Aldington was able to place several poems in *The Anglo-French Review*, which began publication in February 1919.

13 October 1918

Dear girl/

I am back at the Div: Rest Camp in another part of the line, but still many miles from the fighting. Still as this is unconquered land it is interesting to take trips to places now 'famous in story'. Strangely enough the country is not nearly so destroyed as the kind I have known before. The villages are wrecked, it is true; no life, except soldier's, exists over vast tracts, dotted with shell holes & crosses, pitted with the holes of myriads of field mines, where only the whirr of partridges & the noise of starlings break the silence. Desolation, yet not unpleasant. It fits my mood of tranquility and self-possession – a land that has lost much, yet is free. For as Landor says: 'If the souls of the citizens are debased, who cares whether its walls & houses be still upright or thrown down?' The converse also is true.[1]

I send you with this a book of songs I picked up on a battlefield, dropped by some poor lad who lost his life in this struggle. How bitter it is to reflect that the fight is for wealth & power & greed only, not for freedom, not for love, not for the future, not for anything true or great or noble. Yet somehow I grow to a mood of acceptation; not just timidity or resignation, but a knowledge that fools are many times too strong for the wise, & that we must use what little wisdom we can gather from the parsimonious gods to endure the pains unnecessarily inflicted on us by the carelessness of others. I feel ready for anything.

You must read the little book I send you. Some of it seems to me very beautiful, though I can only guess the meaning. This (p. 16) I like:

> Der tag ist nun vergangen
> Die güldnen Sternlein frangen
> Am blauen Himmelsfaal.[2]

which makes one think of the old Germany of romance & tenderness, apple-cheeked girls & young men called Johann Wolfgang or Ludwig von Beethoven – Ludwig who would not lift his hat to an emperor! This also I think very sweet and beautiful:

> Unsern Ausgang segne Gott,
> Unsern Eingang gleichermasson,
> Segne unser täglich Brod,
> Segne unser Thun und Lassen,
> Segne uns nut selgem Sterben,
> Und mach uns zu Himmelserben![3]

And there are quite a lot of other things worth reading, especially the Volksleider [folksongs] at the end.

I hope you are going on well. It is some days since I heard from you, but communication here is rather more complex than at the Signal School.[4]

Affectionately
Richard.

1 Aldington recalled this experience of returning to the front years later in a brief essay which he sent to his friend, Eric Warman, probably enclosed in a letter to him dated 19 November 1958:

> In the autumn of 1918 I was sent down the line to go through a course which was supposed to qualify me to be a Company Commander. The course was hurried at the end, and we

were told we had to rejoin our units at once, there had 'been another battle'. We knew what that meant. Although all officers, we had to march on foot the last part of our journey – all transport needed for the advance, that advance of which we had heard so often for so long that we no longer believed in it. We bivouacked the first night on the old Somme battlefield, between Bapaume and Cambrai, just where our old front line had been at the time of the March, '18, attack. I persuaded two or three of my brother officers to take a walk in the dim autumnal afternoon, with the flames of burning Cambrai and other towns or villages bearing witness that at last 'the advance' was a reality and not paper propaganda.

Forty years later I cannot forget what we saw. As far as we could see, just over against what had been our positions in March were battalion graves – every two or three hundred yards, the grave of a battalion. They were not ours, they were Germans. Over each was a huge cross bearing the date 21/3/18. Then in front was the grave of the Colonel or Major; behind him the regimental officers; then the N.C.O.s and men – fifty, sixty, a hundred, sometimes more. And looking over that ghastly dreariness of the Somme, we could see that these cemeteries, these battle burial fields, went on as far as the eye could reach. And Cambrai, burning, lighted our way back to camp, as we stumbled over the debris of the German army.

... Having seen that, I know what Death is. In that desolation nothing lived. Even the rats had been killed by the gas, and if birds drank the water of the shell-holes, poisoned with mustard gas, they died. There stood smashed guns and broken tanks like wrecks in that ocean of shell-holes. As had been the case a month or more before, on the old battle-line, the ground was covered with a bewildering chaos of abandoned German equipment – camouflaged German helmets, rifles, entrenching tools, bombs, gas masks, water-bottles, overcoats, hairy packs, cartridges. Here and there, occasionally, the equipment of one of ours, dumped by the stretcher-bearers or the burying parties. The utter silence, save for the faint hissing of the engine, the utter desolation, the ugliness, the sense of misery, the regret of all our lost comrades. (SIU)

I have been unable to trace Aldington's quotation from Landor.
2 The day has now passed / The little golden stars break / Upon the blue heavens.
3 May God bless our going out / And likewise our coming in, / Bless our daily bread, / Bless what we do and do not, / Bless us with blissful dying, / And make us Heaven's heirs!
4 Aldington left Signal School on 8 October 1918, and is now moving eastward towards the front line. The Allies were advancing rapidly in October of 1918 and Aldington is travelling through territory which was recently 'no man's land' between Allied and enemy trenches and territory recently occupied by the Germans.

☙ 58 ❧

14 October 1918

My dear/

A paper came, the first in four days. What does it mean? Can it be? Dare we hope? Is this torture, this age-long nightmare ending? I dare not hope it, dare not or I should give way utterly. When I heard that there was even a chance of peace – 'terms accepted' – I was dumbfounded. We had heard nothing. No newspapers, you see. This is a great desert. Miles & miles. No news. But that one newspaper – terms accepted. It can't be; I can't believe it. The hope, the chance overwhelms me. Some of them are talking of 'good times'. O, it is mad. We must pray to be sane. I went out & stood leaning my head on the cross over a dead German's grave and cried, yes cried like a weakling. It is too much. O my God, if only it is true.[1]

They speak of what they have lost. A brother, money, a mistress. I say nothing – I have lost my dreams, only my dreams. Yet I am thankful. Oscar Wilde came out of prison broken, penniless, almost friendless. I shall leave (if this peace comes) this harsher prison, no less broken than he, but with a good heart, a great heart. It does not matter if I must hold out my hand for bread to my inferiors, if I must be a beggar.[2] At least I shall be free & perhaps my lost dreams will come home to me. O to see with clear unafraid eyes once more the calm light upon calm waters, sun, wind & trees and the ecstacy of beauty, the presence of the gods. It will not matter if I be lonely & friendless & poor, shamed some ways & desolate, if only once more we have peace, if only once more we can feel the gods near, and the divine dreams return.

There will be people about you speaking foolishly & haughtily of 'victory'. Turn from them – remember, as I do, the myriad dead and give them, if you can, your tears, as I do. Perhaps yet the nations will be saved from utter destruction; perhaps greed will triumph & distrust & malice & ambition separate men. But at least we can hope and at least, thank all the gods, no man has died at my hands.

Affectionately,
Richard.

P.S. Tell me it is not all a lie. There is hope of peace?

1 Germany formally requested an armistice on 4 October 1918.

2 Aldington is acutely aware that he has no job, no means of support, waiting for him once he leaves the army.

⤜ 59 ⤛

20 October 1918

Dear Astraea/

We are out of the line for a few days rest, yet are in a village which has not seen Allied troops since August 1914. To-day we took down a board which said 'Sachen Strasse' & put up one which said 'Sussex Street'.

There seems to be no other news except that I have been made signal officer for the time being, the other signal officer having been wounded in the last 'show'. It is much pleasanter than being with a company.[1]

Have you seen Bennett at all? He is an officer in our brigade whom I asked to write to you when in town. You should have heard from him by now.

May Sinclair writes very pleasantly. She is of course full of 'victory'. I am sending her (ironically) a German helmet.

I have a little German testament for you, picked up at 'XYZ' –.[2]

I hope you are well. Will send you November check (post-dated) before we go in the line again.

Affectionately
Richard.

1 Aldington has been made an acting captain.

2 Because of military security, Aldington cannot reveal to H.D. his precise location.

23 October 1918

Dear girl/

I haven't written for a day or so, chiefly because I haven't had any paper. The advance is so rapid, that even here (10 miles behind line) we have been without everything except bare rations. Things are slowly improving, though, now.

I am glad you are happy in your new place. I trust you will keep well and strong and learn how to look after your child. Margaret can tell you many things of course.[1]

It is unfortunate that Gray is in his present position.[2] Of course, one respects his resolution, but I doubt its utility. He will probably be in 'durance vile' after we have got free again.[3] And there always remains the plain fact that once war starts one should help to keep its horrors from the people one cares for. Whether he serves safely in prison as a deserter or dangerously in France as a soldier, he will be equally cut off from his music; in the first case he is useless, in the second at least he is preventing his wife & child suffering the horrors that one sees here.[4] But I do not condemn him; I regret the circumstances & hope he will emerge untouched from his ordeal, whatever it may be.

Well, I have had a very long spell out of the line & don't so very much dislike going back to it again. At least there seems now some chance of a solution, though not that ideal solution one hopes for. I scarcely think it will last more than another year.

In addressing letters please omit 'D Coy' [D Company] – I am now on B.H.Q. as signal officer.[5]

Affectionately
Richard.

1 H.D. has now settled in at Peace Cottage near Speen, where she has been living for almost a month with her friend Margaret Snively Pratt.

2 Although Cecil Gray's military status (IIIB) protected him through July 1918, he became increasingly fearful about being forced into military service and evaded local conscription by leaving Cornwall before August 1918 for his mother's home at 13B Earl's Court Square, London. He must have been in hiding at this time.

3 With this familiar phrase Aldington suggests that even after the war's end, Gray may find himself in prison as a conscientious objector or merely as a draft evader, a deserter.

4 That is, H.D. and her unborn child, both of whom Aldington considers bonded to Gray in some spiritual way.

5 Battalion Headquarters, to which Aldington, as acting captain and highest ranking signal officer, was now assigned.

61

26 October 1918

Dear Astraea/

As I promised I am sending the November cheque. You must stick another penny stamp on it, or it will not be paid. Sorry I haven't one to put on.

It is quite interesting up here and I am hoping to see more interesting things soon.

There is no particular news to write. I had a very friendly note from Paul Nash, excusing himself for the delay in providing drawings for my book [*Images of War*]. Humbug, no doubt, but expressed with a 'sheen' of sincerity.

Au revoir,
Richard

62

27 October 1918

Dear Astraea/

Thank you for your letter of the 22nd. I am glad you are well, though, no doubt, you have bad moments sometimes.

I don't think you should take Amy Lowell too seriously. Whatever she may or may not have done to cheapen your work & reputation you are still too unknown for it to make the slightest difference to you. If you want to write, write; if you don't want to write, don't. But what Amy Lowell does, says or thinks is really of no particular importance to you.[1]

As to leave; it will probably be some weeks before I get it, but, if I do, it will be better in many respects for us to meet somewhere in town [in London]. I shall probably stay with my father & Molly & go down to Rye for a week-end's shooting & riding. It will not be wise for me to come to Speen for just one day; it would make Margaret very suspicious and would also arouse the curiosity of the villagers.[2]

I have rather lost count of time, so I don't quite know how long you have been enceinte – if it will embarrass you to come to town, we might meet on neutral territory, Brigit's perhaps.[3] But I will write you from town *when* I get there.

Of course, I shall not stay with Arabella; though I may meet her on terms of decorous & amiable frigidity.

Any news of Gray? He is a fool to resist. The war won't last more than a year & he'll never get to France. Why not put up with it? Still, he's free to do as he pleases.

Things are very interesting here as I wrote you, though sometimes too tragic. I saw a French child to-day – but, never mind, we won't speak of these things. Keep well & strong & happy.

A very pleasant compliment was paid your country to-day. The whole of our Brigade marched into a village with the bugles playing 'Over There', the American war song. Quite graceful don't you think?

I sent you the little cheque yesterday. I'm sorry it's so small.

Herewith letter from Nash explaining delay in publishing my book [*Images of War*].

Affectionately
Richard.

1 That is, to write poetry; the issue is not whether H.D. will correspond with Amy Lowell. The Aldingtons maintained a regular exchange of letters with Lowell, although by 1918 their letters had become less frequent than when the three were working closely together on the imagist anthologies. H.D. had been experiencing a difficult time with her work since early 1918, confronting now apparently for the first time the writer's block which she would periodically encounter later in her life. She had also resolved not to publish for a while, in part questioning the quality of what work she felt able to produce, in part as an act of protective retreat from the personal intensity of her life, which was at this time – and would continue to be – the emotional centre of her art. On the same day (22 October 1918) that she wrote Aldington about Lowell, she also wrote Lowell a letter which deserves quotation in full:

> Dear Amy:
>
> I am sorry my note seemed mysterious and queer. I believe Winifred Ellerman has written you. She had a romantic idea that she wanted to be on her own + I understood that – feel the same myself. I believe she is of German jew (as you suggest) extract. I have seen her only about three times.
>
> Its very sweet of you to suggest my publishing – but I hope not to do that again – for a long time, if ever. I want to keep in touch with literary people for R.'s sake until he is free of the army – and I hope to continue to be in touch with you always in a friendly way – But I suppose like Fletcher I am a pathological case + I may as well accept the fact. I am very, very anxious for R. to have his chance of a 'career' once the war is over – and I shall do everything to help but I have been putting off publishing poems – I don't really over-criticize my work – but what is good will be good in ten years. I am only writing you an ordinary little note.
>
> Miss Ellerman is very, very simple – an undeveloped, lonely child.
>
> I hope Mrs Russell is well – R. is up the line again but the news is awfully good.
> In great haste
> with love
>   always
>   *Hilda.*
>
> I have not seen Fletcher for six months – nor do I hear from him. I am very happy in the country here – beautiful beech forests – you really must visit me here one good day.

2 Aldington's father and sister Margery had a flat in London during the war. Aldington's mother maintained the family's home at Rye in Sussex.

3 Brigit Patmore was living temporarily in Brighton at this time.

⇗ **63** ⇖

1 November 1918

Dear Astraea/

Herewith blank cheque – only to be used if I am killed. It will save any trouble about duties &c. Just go to Cox's & find my balance & make out cheque accordingly. Don't forget to put another penny stamp on it.

You are entitled to a pension in the event I mention – see you get it.

We go over the top in a couple of days. Hence these gloomy words![1]

Cheerio! The war's nearly over, I think. So you'll be all right.

Richard.

1 From the front line of trenches into no-man's-land. Aldington was part of a successful British advance that began on 4 November 1918.

⇗ 64 ⇖

Dear Astraea/

I am very sorry you feel that way about things, but there are many reasons for it. I scarcely know what to say about it. We are fighting & advancing all the time – no rest, but we don't mind if only it's ending the bally [bloody] business. So you see I'm not very clear as to the best thing to say.[1]

No doubt I have changed. It is not my fault, but a misfortune over wh: I've no control. As to G. – I don't blame him. Influenza is rotten – had it myself in July.[2]

I shan't be back until the end of the month, & don't want to come specially. This is very interesting & exciting – new towns & villages every day, enthusiastic welcomes by French people, &c &c. And then what have I to come home to? I arrive at Victoria [Station] – where am I to go? What am I to do? Arabella puts one part of London 'out of bounds' to me – old sentiment puts another. You are hurt and unfortunate, I know; I sympathise deeply & do all I can. But my life also is ruined. I am the only man in this battalion who is not anxious about leave!

I will like to see you & talk quietly. I will try not to hurt you, but you must remember it is seven months now since I touched civilisation.

Don't let me hurt you. Keep proud. As to money it is not worth being proud about.

In great haste
Richard

1 Evidently H.D. has written that she feels Aldington has changed and that he is to a degree responsible for the problems they are now struggling with in their marriage.
2 Cecil Gray is apparently avoiding a confrontation with H.D., evidently refusing at this point to see her because he says is ill with the influenza that soon became epidemic in postwar London.

⇗ 65 ⇖

Dear Astraea/

I go on leave tomorrow & hope to reach London about the 16th or 17th. If you will write me and fix a date, place & time for meeting, I will be there. Only address will be 68 Queensborough Terrace, London, W2 [a private hotel in Paddington].

Affectionately
Richard.

⇗ 66 ⇖

Sunday

I am not seeing *anyone* to-day. Excuse my breaking appointment.

Richard

The relatively perfunctory nature of Aldington's letters in early November suggests the new plane he thought he had established in his relationship with H.D. The process which initiated this somewhat detached and practical but finally unstable territory began as early as 8 September (letter 51), exactly one month before Aldington was due to leave signal school and to begin his return to the trenches. With H.D. then in London and her plans to retire to Speen crystallizing, Aldington evidently felt that her situation had achieved a stability that did not depend strictly on him. Anticipating his return to the line, Aldington began the difficult task of once again getting his affairs in order to face the real possibility of imminent death: 'Dearest Dooley' (letter 50) and 'Dearest Astraea' (letter 60) of 2 and 20 September give way to 'Dear Astraea' and the somewhat jaunty 'Dear girl' or to no greeting at all. Aldington could not, however, have anticipated the armistice on 11 November, and was unprepared for the overwhelming emotional tension of his long awaited leave, which followed soon after. Just when he thought he had perhaps negotiated the terms of a peace, a workable, controllable stance from which he could deal with the problems of his marriage, he discovered, as letter 66 suggests, that he was by no means so much in command of his own responses as he had earlier supposed and had insisted to H.D. The three difficult weeks of Aldington's leave deserve detailed attention particularly because of the gap in the Aldingtons' correspondence caused by their proximity.

In *Life for Life's Sake* Aldington recalls his specific experiences during the last days of battle and the events that quickly followed the armistice. On 4 November 1918, he remembers, 'I was looking at the luminous dial of my watch in the gray dawn and giving my headquarter signallers the order to advance. As far as the eye could see to north or south a huge curve of flashing gunfire lit up the sky, and the old familiar roar and crash of drumfire beat on the ears' (175). He continues:

My job that morning of the 4th was not to kill Germans, but to see that as my battalion advanced I kept my battalion headquarters in touch with brigade and both flanking battalions with a minimum of break and delay. For this purpose my field service message book and those of the other relevant officers contained two pages of mysterious letters and numbers, showing my different positions and those of the other stations at quarter-hour intervals, until the final objective was reached.

I hadn't to worry about what was going on. What I had to do was to lead my little group of men forward for about five hundred yards, cross a road which my map assured me was there (it was), set up a lamp signal station at once, establish contact in three directions, send and receive any messages; and at 6:15 a.m. precisely move on to another point. These manoeuvres were carried out with such clockwork precision that, except when moving, we were never out of touch with the other stations for more than two minutes. I got through the German barrage with the loss of my corporal and one man, passed dead and wounded and surrendering Germans, and lost my knapsack. Our trench mortar bloke covered himself with glory. Somewhere, somehow he had pinched an old horse, and brought his clumsy mortar walloping into action at just the right moment to knock out two machine-gun nests which were punishing one of our companies. By 7:30 a.m., we had advanced two miles, captured six guns and two hundred prisoners, and could see the enemy retreating with undignified haste in the distance. Field guns galloped up, and went into action.

We had another weary week of marching and actions with rear-guards before our armistice, and when it came it was undramatic and undemonstrative. Yet it was not without deep feelings. There was an uprush of confused, poignant emotions – relief, gratitude, a stir of hope, a belief that this was the end of the war, an overtone of profound sadness as one thought of the silent ruined battlefields and the millions who never saw the day for which they had fought. And one's own insignificant little life, saved, but in ruins. (175–6)

The 'ruins' of his own life were, of course, deeper and more personal than this memoir reveals, and the arduous days of travel to England on his first leave in many months did not calm his nerves. Aldington recalled the details of his trip to London with vivid specificity:

There had been no leave for several months, and my name was at the head of the roster. On the morning of the 12th I was handed a leave warrant in the orderly room, with the laconic and somewhat cynical advice to get to rail head as best I could. During the long period of trench warfare, rail head had been only a few miles behind the line, but now it was at least sixty and nobody in front knew exactly where it was. The best bet seemed to hitch-hike to Cambrai by jumping an army truck, but unluckily I couldn't find one going that way. Heaven knows how many trucks I rode on that day or where we went, but for hours and hours I was driven over an interminable landscape of ruined villages, battered trenches, wrecked guns and tanks, and a huge amount of scattered equipment of all sorts abandoned by the fleeing Germans.

Somewhere in the early afternoon I passed through Quesnoy, which was full of Australian soldiers cleaning up the debris of war and some of the filth characteristic of places which had been German rest billets; and at dusk reached the headquarters of another Corps somewhere in the advanced Somme area. That night I slept, along with other officers returning on leave, in a large and rather chilly marquee tent; and some time on the next day got to Cambrai, only to find that the leave train had left and I should have to wait overnight.

Not long before, I had been among the first troops to enter Cambrai, while it was still being shelled and was on fire. The streets then were littered with dead men and horses, fallen telegraph wires and the debris of ruined houses. Even in that confusion I noticed two things: the Germans had invariably fired the beautiful old Flemish houses, and the glowing woodwork still showed the beautiful Renaissance designs of the carving; and as we went along the streets of unshelled houses, we could see that they had been looted and that in the centre of each room was a pile of clothing, books, pictures, broken furniture, torn cushions, and similar objects on which the Germans had urinated and defecated. I am quite sure of these facts, because I saw them myself. In 1917 on the outskirts of Lens we discovered the same peculiar form of German insult in trenches and dugouts they had been forced to abandon by the Canadian advance at Vimy. On that afternoon of the 13th of November I went round the town and verified what I had seen. I could not go into any house – that was forbidden – but I could see easily through the smashed ground-floor windows. Moreover, I could not find a single one of the old Flemish houses unburned.

That night Cambrai was full of officers returning on leave, and we were billeted in a large hospital which was not required for the wounded. It was still a strange and delicious experience to sleep in a real bed again, but about 5 a.m. we were roughly awakened by orderlies, who rushed in and shouted the sensational news that the German armistice commission had revealed the existence of a time bomb in the building due to explode in an hour. There was no need to urge us to dress rapidly. After a very quick breakfast we entrained in a hurry; the train moved out a couple of miles from town and waited. And waited several hours. I then had ample time to reflect that Cambrai had been in our hands for at least three weeks and that no time bomb could be devised to last for such a period; so evidently that was a little joke of the authorities to make sure we didn't oversleep and miss the train.

How slowly the train moved! At sunset we had only got as far as Pérone, whose ruins looked gaunt and tragical against a gray sky cut with a blood-red rift of light from the setting sun. We did not reach Boulogne until dawn of the 15th, and there I saw a curious and moving sight – French soldiers who had been prisoners of war since 1914. They still wore tattered uniforms of red and blue, which looked positively historic, they were so different from those of the later armies. The faces of these men were pinched and yellow with privation, and there was an eerie, slightly insane expression on them.

In all it took me about eighty hours to go from the Franco-Belgian border to London... (176–8)

It is apparently from Cambrai that Aldington wrote to H.D. on 13 November (letter 65), asking her to determine a time and place for them to meet, but when he finally arrived in London late on 15 November, he was physically and psychically exhausted and unprepared to see her for several days.

H.D. heard of the armistice on 11 November at Speen, where she and Margaret Snively Pratt and her one-year-old daughter had spent a relatively calm and insulated autumn. Although she had celebrated her birthday in London at a small party with her old friend May Sinclair and her new friend Clement Shorter, the older, rather staid editor of the illustrated weekly *The Sphere*, by the end of September she was settled in the tiny cottage in the country. She took walks in the neighbourhood and received presents of roses, nuts, and jam from the old-fashioned and gentlemanly Shorter, who often shared tea with her when spending weekends at his country house less than four miles from Peace Cottage. Bryher also came to tea perhaps once or twice, but H.D. did not have many visitors and tended to organize her days with Margaret Pratt according to her baby's schedule.

H.D.'s letters to others during this period reveal the tenor of her life during the fall of 1918. On 11 October she wrote to Shorter that she and Mrs Pratt 'are walking over to see your garden as soon as we get a good day. ... It rains + rains, but I love this country and the air is miraculously fine + bracing.' (UR) On the same day she wrote to Bryher, encouraging her epistolary relationship with Aldington: 'Do send him a line about books etc. He must not lose hold on his literary life + he gets so discouraged. ... We must all make an effort, once the war is over, to renew some interest in the real living beauty of the so-called classics.' H.D. was enthusiastic, it would seem, about her husband's plan for the second Poets' Translation Series, and looked forward to the communal effort. By mid-October H.D. was also past the first trimester of her pregnancy and evidently felt physically better than she had for some months.

The period was, of course, not without emotional strain for her. While it seems likely that she had told Margaret Pratt about her pregnancy, her tall, slender frame would allow her to conceal her condition from others until at least the middle of December, and she never told Pratt that the child was not Aldington's. Amazingly Pratt wrote to Bryher on 8 August 1962: 'I read of the death of Richard Aldington. I didn't know that he had another daughter. ... Did Perdita keep in touch with her father when they were both living in New York?' (Yale) The painful problems and shifting nature of the Aldingtons' relationship were intensely private matters for H.D. and she dealt with them alone and in personal letters to her husband; later, she would deal with them in her art. She must have anticipated his approaching leave in November of 1918 not only as a confrontation but as an opportunity for expression, a time both for a formal reworking of the grounds of their relationship and for an intimate sharing at this point impossible for her with anyone else.

The violence of world events had continued to impinge on H.D.'s private life as well. On 25 September 1918, her older brother Gilbert was killed in France in the Battle of St. Mihiel. She did not hear of his death until her mother wrote her, and she responded with deep sadness on 4 November 1918. H.D. felt real affection for her brother, but she was also distant from him and had not seen him since she left the United States in 1911.

H.D.'s relationship with Bryher was only beginning and its nature and boundaries were still unclear to them both. They were not often in the same place at the same time. They had been near each other in Cornwall in July, but Bryher was evidently at her parents' country house at Eastbourne in Sussex when H.D. moved into town in late August. Bryher remained in Sussex when H.D. moved to Speen at the end of September, then moved into London in October while H.D. remained in the country. Their friendship was thus primarily epistolary throughout 1918 and apparently focused on Bryher's literary work and travel plans: she was eager to visit America and still wanted H.D. to come with her to the Scilly Islands, which she had enjoyed since childhood; it was not until December of 1918 that the two women would imagine traveling together to Greece or that Bryher's planned American itinerary would include H.D. The friendship was between, on the one hand, an ingenue, a childish woman still living with her parents, a pupil eager to learn about literature and to meet the people who created it and wrote about it ; and, on the other, an experienced older woman (Bryher was twenty-four, H.D. thirty-two) living on her own, who was a poet, had published and been a part of a significant literary movement (imagism), who knew other writers and could tell her what to read and discuss writing with her.

H.D. found Bryher stimulating in her youth and novelty, but throughout 1918 she shared Bryher with Aldington: she sent him the younger woman's work at a time when she was not sending him anything of her own; she encouraged Bryher to participate in Aldington's plan for translations on which she was also working; she paralleled Bryher's writing with Aldington's, pointing out to her their shared subjects and sensitivities. H.D. apparently initially understood Bryher as a part of her marriage. She welcomed her as a person who did not exist as an intimate so much on her own terms as an alter ego: Bryher was H.D. unfettered with her pregnancy and husband; Bryher was a daughter, the un-born child whose birth H.D. anticipated with confused feelings; Bryher was Aldington, another literary mind inspired by her and writing out of the context of their friendship. But for all the psychological complexity of this relationship for H.D., Bryher was by no means H.D.'s confidante in 1918, and H.D. kept her at a distance. At the time of Aldington's leave in November, Bryher did not know her friend was pregnant, and H.D. did not tell her that the child was not Aldington's until after her birth.

On 11 November 1918, H.D. wrote Bryher that she was coming to London on Friday, 15 November, and suggested meeting her at her parents' home for lunch on the following day: 'Your enthusiasm has helped me – and once I hear from R., I will know definitely about my future work and life.' (Yale) The letter is chatty and indicates little of the apprehension H.D. must have felt. While implying to Bryher that Aldington will somehow define 'her future work and life', she also implies that it is merely details (logistics perhaps of his demobilization or their living arrangements) that need to be settled. The letter is replete with indecision but gives the impression of haste and good spirits rather than psychological equivocation: 'I shall probably come up this weekend or early next. I shall write you in a day or so when I decide. ... I find I am coming Friday.'

H.D. probably did have lunch with Bryher on Saturday, 16 November, and she had planned to see Aldington the following day when she received his note at the Lancaster Hotel, 66 Upper Bedford Place, where she apparently remained during the two weeks she spent in London before returning to Speen at the end of the month. Exactly what occurred when they did meet and how often they saw each other are not clear. Certainly they met privately, probably more than once, and Aldington saw H.D. at least once at the Ellermans', where he also met Bryher and Sir John Ellerman, her father. He wrote Amy Lowell on 8 December 1918 that Bryher was 'very enthusiastic about you & about us all & seems a person of decidedly fine temperament'. On Sunday, probably 24 November, H.D. wrote to Clement Shorter:

> I feel so very sorry but Richard was suddenly called away. He had hoped for another week, and we had made all our plans accordingly. I am feeling so tired with the continual rushing about we had last week that I will return at once to Speen. I wonder if you understand how really disappointed I am? And when I come to London again in a month's time, – will you let me have a little talk with you about work?
>
> With best wishes and sincere regrets on the part of Richard
> and Hilda Aldington (UR)

While Aldington's leave was due to end on 1 December, he managed to arrange an extra week, and H.D. is clearly making excuses for them both in her letter to Shorter. As is clear from Aldington's letter to her on 6 December (letter 68), she also hoped to see and probably did meet with Gray in London. Aldington could not now give her what she wanted and needed in terms of emotional support; he was required to return to the front and had no money beyond his army pay, which he was already sending her. Nor could he make decisions for her – which may in fact have been what she was asking of him. He had with deep reluctance but finally with committed acceptance agreed to define the relationship on her terms (see letter 48), and he felt he could not now renegotiate. On or soon after 24 November H.D. left abruptly for Speen and did not see Aldington again before his return to France.

≫ **67** ≪

1 December 1918

Dear Astraea,

I haven't forgotten you, you see. I was sorry you left town so suddenly, but I have no wish to interfere with your movements. Nor am I going to remonstrate any further on the subject of provision for your future; it is really up to you. No more than Cain am I my brother's keeper. Get from Gray what you want or what you can; and call on me in any emergency. I shall not fail you.

I am planning to restore the P.T.S. Are you willing to collaborate? The whole thing would be on a larger scale than before & I would pay a royalty on all successful translations. Let me know if this agrees with you & what choruses you would care to do.[1]

Affectionately
Richard

P.S. I have extension of leave until the 5th, but have not written 'W. Bryher'.[2]

1 As the third pamphlet in the first Poets' Translation Series in 1916, H.D. had translated selected choruses from Euripides' *Iphigeneia in Aulis*. For the second pamphlet of the second series she translated choruses from Euripides' *Hippolytus*, which appeared with her earlier work in 1919 as *Choruses from Iphigeneia in Aulis and the Hippolytus of Euripides*. H.D. wrote Bryher on 11 November 1918, 'I have an idea for some new Greek work'; this work was likely the translation of choruses from *Hippolytus*.
2 Aldington was probably hoping to remain in England so as to be demobilised quickly. Unluckily, two days after he finally returned to France, the War Office issued an order permitting all officers on leave to remain indefinitely in England and to be demobilised from there.

≋ 68 ≋

6 December 1918
E.F.C. Officers Rest House and Mess[1]

Dear Astraea/

I'm staying here on the way back to the division. Train is delayed 6 hours. Cheerful prospect.

Look here. I hate to bother you but I want my books away from Miss James. Will you have them at Speen or shall I store them somewhere? I want now a Greek dictionary, the epistolae of Alciphron sent out to me. If you will not be in town yourself could you drop Miss James a note and let Arabella get them? You see I am very much handicapped by not being able to get at my books, but I thought it better not to go to 44. There would have been too many explanations.[2]

As to yourself. I hope your interview with Gray was satisfactory and that you feel more tranquil about things. We will leave all discussion until you are well again. It is not kind to worry you about things when you are enciente. It was wrong of me to allow you to talk. Just try to think of nothing but getting through with this. Has Brigit fixed up that place for you?[3]

When you do start work again I should think that the choruses, or an entire play, would be your forte. We ought to get some big publisher to take up the whole [Poets' Translation] series.

Will you let me know about those books? Perhaps for the time being you could let me have your small Greek dictionary & keep my large one, as transport is not so difficult for you.[4]

Later I may ask for other books.

Affectionately
Richard.

1 Aldington is writing from an Expeditionary Force Canteen at a base camp in France on the way back to the Ninth Royal Sussex Regiment, now at Monchin in Belgium.
2 Although H.D. gave up her room at 44 Mecklenburgh Square in early August 1918, Miss Elinor James, the Aldingtons' landlady, had agreed to store their books, papers, furniture, and linen. Throughout his time at the front, Aldington had been working without reference books from his own library, often without any books at hand at all or only with whatever odd volumes he was able to purchase in French towns or to borrow from fellow soldiers. Any books he had at the front were expendable and were frequently left behind, lost during battle or while advancing, or sent to H.D. for safekeeping. He now realises that he will have both some time to work and some order in his life so that books and papers will not be routinely lost. He is

also aware of the necessity for literary work, as he must begin to find a position to support himself as soon as he is demobilized. He asks now for the letters of Alciphron, a sophist of the second or third century C.E.; these were supposedly written by ordinary Athenians during the fourth century B.C.E. and reveal Alciphron's wide reading of classical literature. Aldington intended to translate Alciphron's 'love letters', probably those written in the voices of courtesans, for the second Poets' Translation Series, although such a translation was never published.

3 Aldington here suggests that they defer any discussion of the future of their marriage. H.D. intended to move from Speen to a nursing home (a maternity hospital) in London before the baby's birth (due in mid-March). Brigit Patmore was making arrangements for H.D. to enter St. Faith's Nursing Home at the appropriate time.

4 H.D. owned a copy of the abridged edition of Liddell and Scott's *Greek-English Lexicon* (Oxford: Clarendon Press, 1916); it is now in the Bryher Library in East Hampton, New York.

≫ **69** ≪

12 December 1918[1]

Dear Astraea/

I heard from Miss Ellerman & am writing to her. Did you tell her to like the line 'Sleep that is whiter than beautiful morning' or did she find it herself? She says she likes 'Red & Black'; I hope she realizes what it means![2]

As to P.T.S. I would like to see [Edward] Hutton & talk it over with him. I would like to bring translations out in a uniform cover at 6d & 1/-. I want Latin, Greek, French, Italian, Russian, Spanish & perhaps modern Hebrew things. I want to be general editor, to make you Greek editor, Frank French, [Edward] Storer Latin, myself Italian, John [Cournos] Russian, and Ezra Spanish. I will undertake to 'manage' all these dissonant elements. I want to pay authors or other translators 10% on what they do, & I propose that you & I do at least ⅛ of the translations. They will be published three at a time or perhaps six, to attract notice. Moreover, in most cases they will be accompanied by the text.[3]

Now don't give this scheme away, as if it is known, it will be cribbed. I think Hutton could be trusted, but not Dent or any other publisher; I think Constable ought to do it as it will be the choicest piece of scholarship of modern times, if properly done.[4]

I will like to have the poems you speak of. I'm sorry I can't get you the German book as I am at a place called Monchin between Lille & Valenciennes. But if you write to Nutt, Shaftesbury Avenue, he will get it for you through Holland. It will cost more than published price but that is inevitable.[5]

It is not so bad here, but I'm trying to get away; have written some letters with that intention.[6]

I hope you have come to a satisfactory arrangement with Gray; your letter is a little vague on that point.[7]

Affectionately,
Richard.

1 After his return to the front, Aldington's letters took longer than previously to reach H.D. British troops were moving eastward rapidly and his letters are seldom stamped at the field post office on the same day on which he dated them. Additionally, H.D. was now spending a good deal of her time in town without having told her husband of her address, so his letters are forwarded to her from Speen. This letter was dated by Aldington 12 December 1918, postmarked

at the field post office on 16 December 1918, stamped for forwarding at Speen on 19 December, and redirected to the Lancaster Hotel, 66 Upper Bedford Place, London WC2.

2 The quotation is from Aldington's 'Noon', a poem in his lesbian sequence 'The Love of Myrrhine and Konallis'. The hetaira Myrrhine longs for her friend and declares, 'my eyelids are shunned by sleep/ that is whiter than beautiful/ morning, for Konallis is not here.' The poem is reprinted in Gates, *The Poetry of Richard Aldington*, 290. I am grateful to Gemma Bristow for helping me to identify this passage. Aldington hopes Bryher understands Stendhal's famous novel, *Le Rouge et le Noir* (1830), which depicts the French social order under the Restauration (1814–30). The central character, Julien Sorel, is a carpenter's son who combines an admirable sensibility with cold ambition. He eventually is condemned to death as a result of his passion for two women.

3 Despite the difficulties in their personal friendship, Aldington assumed that he and Cournos could still work together professionally. Similarly, he assumed that despite the problems in his marriage, he and H.D. could continue to be helpful to each other artistically as critics and fellow poets. Aldington was experienced in such management of personalities; his work on *The Egoist* (1913–17) and with first Ezra Pound and later Amy Lowell on the imagist anthologies (1914–17) had taught him a great deal about 'dissonant elements' and how to manage them. His later work on a final imagist anthology, which appeared in 1930, as well as his edition of *The Viking Book of Poetry of the English-Speaking World* (1941), attest to his competence as managing editor of the series he proposes here. The six translations eventually published included Aldington's *Greek Songs in the Manner of Anacreon* (No. 1) and H.D.'s *Choruses from the Iphigeneia in Aulis and the Hippolytus of Euripides* (No. 2) in 1919 and Aldington's *The Poems of Meleager of Gadara* (No. 6) in 1920. None of the translations included the original text.

4 Aldington is probably thinking of other contemporary efforts to define the canon by publishing a series of 'classics' for a wide audience, and hopes to publish either with J.M. Dent or with Constable and Company, which had published H.D.'s *Sea Garden* in 1916 and the British editions of the three anthologies *Some Imagist Poets* in 1915, 1916, and 1917. The democratic impulse to freeze and to interpret 'classic' works inspired *The World's Classics* series published by Oxford University Press, for example, as well as the Everyman series in the United States.

5 It seems likely that Aldington is referring to the choruses from Euripides' *Hippolytus* on which H.D. is now working and for which she has apparently requested a German translation or commentary. Aldington's current situation was not particularly conducive to scholarship – in *Life for Life's Sake* Aldington calls Monchin, a town five miles from Tournai, 'a straggling Belgian village' (178) – and he recommends that H.D. go to David Nutt, the London bookseller with whom he had an account.

6 Actually Aldington was quite frustrated by his life in the army after the armistice. He wrote Ezra Pound on 8 December 1918: 'I am teaching Tommies to read the newspapers & do multiplication sums. ... This education scheme is bullshit at its purest.' (Yale) He was doing everything he could to arrange demobilization.

7 Although H.D. apparently met with Gray in London in late November, no financial settlement or other formal arrangement was made then or later.

～ 70 ～

13 December 1918

Dear Astraea/

Re P.T.S. I enclose a rough draft of my proposal. Will you and Winifred Ellerman take it to Shorter and get him to lay the proposal before Constable & Co.? Don't let this Scheme out of your hands except to Shorter & make him promise not to give it away. If you will get him to take it to Hutton they should be able to wrangle it for us.

Remember we sold 3000 of the others [in the earlier translation series] with no advertisement & without any machinery of distribution.

I will deal with Miss Weaver & keep all these translators at work. I should use people like Whitall for dull things that have to be included, Amy [Lowell] for modern French &c. I want Greek & Latin work only from you; Greek & French from W. Bryher; French from Amy (she translates French well.) French & Italian from J.G.F. [John Gould Fletcher]; French, Italian & Latin from Flint; Latin & Italian from Alec [Randall]; Greek & Latin & [*sic*] Storer; Greek, Latin, French & Italian from myself. If we do Russian & German, Alec & John will have to find translators.

Can you do this at once? Get Miss Ellerman down, tell her I have got this plan out, with work for her to do; & together sit on Shorter's neck. Get him to persuade Hutton, & there should be no further difficulty. Lay stress 1. On unique plan. 2. Former success. 3. That this is work of permanent value. 4. Will bring kudos to a publisher. 5. Will not be a financial loss. 6. It is cheaper to get out 10 of these little books, which will always go on selling, than to publish one bad novel.

I need scarcely add that it will give us all something to work for.

Your translations [of selected choruses from Euripides' *Hyppolytus*] are here. Will write you more later.

Ever Yours
Richard.

P.S. We must have a pukka contract with Constable.

Scheme for Poets' Translation Series

Object: To give the public at small cost versions of choice, though often little known, poetry & prose.

Translations will be made by people who have produced work of some interest & distinction; their endeavour will be to rescue this literature from the philologists, to present it purely as a work of art, to 'give the words of the original as simply & clearly as possible'.[1]

Series will include not only authors who wrote in Greek & Latin but those who used the languages of modern Europe; new foreign authors as well as those of older times will be included. When complete the Poets' Translation Series will form a choice collection of Belles Lettres.

General Editor: Richard Aldington
Greek editor: H.D.
Latin   ”   : R. Aldington
Italian   ”   : R. Aldington
French   ”   : F.S. Flint
(if desired)
Russian ”   : J. Cournos
German ”   : A.W.G. Randall
List of Translators:
R. Aldington, H.D., F.S. Flint, Amy Lowell, W. Bryher, E. Storer, A.W.G. Randall, J.G. Fletcher and others.
 Following are proposed for publication in the series; others will be added:
Greek. Choruses from Ion, Hippolytus and Iphigeneia in Aulis of Euripides, Meleager,
Anyte, Sappho, Asclepiades, Anacreon, Leonidas, Aelianus, Alciphron (Love-Letters). (Nearly all complete.)[2]

<u>Latin</u>. Renaissance Latins (2 Vols), Mosella, Columella on Gardens, Gotteschalcus, Tibullus, Gallus, some of Ovidius, Commodian of Gaza, & other classic, silver & church Latinists.[3]

<u>French</u>. [François] Villon, du Bellay, d'Orléans, Remy de Gourmont, [Stéphane] Mallarmé (prose poems), Rimbaud, Laforgue, Samain, de Règnier, Ronsard (?), Marot, pre-Villon lyrists, Symbolistes & Parnassiens, living people, Spire, Vildrac, &c. (Flint will add to these.)[4]

<u>Italian</u>. Lorenzo di Medici (part of), Folgore da San Gemignano, Poliziano (songs), Cecco (sonnets), Cavalcanti (?), new versions of Trecento poets, Carducci (some), Leopardi (some), Molza & Bembo & the other 'pastorals' including Tuscan work of Navagero &c., the poetry from Il Decamerone, Boiardo (perhaps) and others.[5]

<u>Terms</u>. Books should be published at 6d. & 1 / – in neat coloured stiff paper covers; should be known as Poets' Translation Series; should be published at least 3 at a time; should eventually include not less than 50 vols & not more than 100. Series to be advertised as a contribution to modern taste, not as a stunt or any darned Amy Lowell business – no vulgarity.[6]

I pick my own books & my own translators; if the publisher knows better, let him find them. I accept suggestions from anyone if I think them good.

Granted all this I consider I can make a good show of this, bring kudos unto any firm & not lose their money but even make some, in view of the fact that these things will sell <u>permanently</u>.

<u>N.B.</u> The Egoist will do the above, but not on a big enough scale for me to give my time to it.[7]

R.A.

[The following is crossed out:]

Notes

1. With regard to Russian & German I need to consult Randall & Cournos to get out list.
2. With regard to prose, I can get out a list later when I have time to think.
3. Present lists are incomplete – I have no books here.
4. Within a month I can hand over enough work to make at least 6 vols.; thereafter can guarantee 5 per month at least.[8]
5. I should be general editor & <u>all</u> work would pass through my revision; I guarantee nothing obscene, Cubist &c. I would get a certain sum for my work as editor to cover expenses of correspondence, buying books &c, 10% per copy to all translators, including myself.

[The following note was written on a torn slip of paper and enclosed in letter 70.]

Any foreign books you may need, whether Greek or French – any of Renée Vivien for example –[9] you may need; order form David Nutt, Shaftsbury Avenue, W.C.1. & tell him to charge them to me. He will send you any catalogue you may want.

1 In the first number of the first Poets' Translation Series, Aldington described the purposes of the project: the translators 'will endeavour to give the words of these Greek and Latin authors as simply and clearly as may be' (Richard Aldington, *Poems of Anyte*, London: the Egoist Press, 1915, 7).

2 *The Ion* (c. 412 B.C.E.), a play by Euripides (c. 485-c. 406 B.C.E.), has a complex plot concerning the discovery of the parentage of Ion, son of Apollo and Creusa. The drama is considered one of the most beautifully writen of Euripides' plays. H.D. eventually published her translation as *Euripides' Ion* in 1937, but – as Aldington suggests here – work on this project began before the end of 1918.

In Euripides' *Hippolytus* (c. 428 B.C.E.) Theseus's second wife Phaedra's unrequited passion for her stepson Hippolytus is expressed in particularly powerful language; in his *Iphigeneia in*

Aulis (c. 405 B.C.E.) Agamemnon's sacrifice of his daughter is a plot on which the sometimes static choruses have little bearing. H.D. translated *Choruses from Iphigeneia in Aulis* in 1915 and it appeared as the third pamphlet in the first Poets' Translation Series in 1916. It was subsequently included in a slim volume entitled *Choruses from Iphigeneia in Aulis and the Hippolytus of Euripides*, which appeared in 1919 and is one of the six books in this scheme that was actually completed.

Born in Gadara, Meleager (fl. 100 B.C.E.), the Syrian poet and philosopher, wrote epigrams and other poems, many of them erotic, over a hundred of which appear in the Greek Anthology, the greatest surviving collection of classical literature and a work both Aldington and H.D. knew well. Aldington published his translation, *The Poems of Meleager of Gadara*, in 1920 as Number 6 in the second Poets' Translation Series. In 1930 he included this translation in his collection of translations *Medallions* (London: Chatto and Windus) and commented on Meleager's 'exceedingly rich, voluptuous poems', noting that he omitted only those which were revisions or which were so erotic that they 'could only be printed in an enlightened country' (13, 14).

Born in Tegea, Anyte (fl. early third century B.C.E.) was a well-regarded lyric and epigrammatic poet. Eighteen of her Doric epigrams, many of them in the spirit of Sappho, appear in the Greek Anthology. Aldington's translations of her work appeared as *The Poems of Anyte of Tegea* in 1915 as Number 1 of the first Poets' Translation Series. It was reprinted as part of the second series, and Aldington included it in his collection *Medallions*, calling her 'one of the great woman-poets of Greece' (3).

Born in Lesbos, the Greek poet Sappho (born 612 B.C.E.) lived in Mytilene with a group of female companions whose lives and marriages she celebrated in her verse. She was sensitive to nature and her subjects are usually personal, while her treatment is lyric, direct, melodious, and powerful. Edward Storer translated some fragments of Sappho for Number 2 of the first Poets' Translation Series.

Asclepiades of Samos (fl. 290 B.C.E.) was one of the greatest epigrammatic poets of the Alexandrine period, while Anacreon (born c. 570 B.C.E.), the Thracian poet, wrote witty and fanciful verse concerned mostly with pleasure. Aldington's translation, *Greek Songs in the Manner of Anacreon*, appeared in 1919 as Number 1 in the second Poets' Translation Series. When he reprinted this translation in *Medallions* (1930), he commented:

> This translation was entirely a 'war work,' as it was started in camp and finished, after a long interval, in the village of Taintignies near Tournai. A small and imperfect dictionary was the only one light enough to carry on active service; the translator is aware that this fact, added to lack of practice in Greek during those years and the general effect of unpleasant surroundings, rendered the translation less accurate and spirited than is desirable. (57)

Leonidas of Tarentum was one of the greatest Greek epigrammatists of the Alexandrine era. He wrote sad poems about the life of the poor, with whom he identified. Nearly a hundred of his epigrams appear in the Greek Anthology.

Claudius Aelianus (c. 170–235) taught rhetoric in Rome and wrote in Greek, publishing collections of excerpts and anecdotes of a paradoxical or moralizing character. His works were popular among his contemporaries and are known for their Attic purity of diction.

3 Aldington published his translation *Latin Poems of the Renaissance* (1915) as Number 4 in the first Poets' Translation Series. He did not complete a second volume, but included a much expanded collection of translations in *Medallions* (1930). Mosella had already been translated by Flint as Number 6 in the first Poets' Translation Series.

Lucius Junius Moderatus Columella was a first-century C.E. Latin writer on agricultural subjects. Book 10, dealing with gardening, of his *De Re Rustica* (60 C.E.) is written in verse as a tribute to Virgil.

Gottschalk (810–69) was a medieval monk who wanted to leave monastic life but was repeatedly prevented by the authorities until he became an itinerant preacher. What little verse of his survives apparently grew out of his enforced suffering and his sense that people are predestined to evil as well as to good, a heretical doctrine which finally led to his imprisonment. Albius Tibbulus (48?–19 B.C.E.) was a Roman elegist. Gaius Cornelius Gallus (c. 69–26 B.C.E.) was a friend of both Augustus and Virgil. Although once well-known for his love elegies, only one pentameter of verse by Gallus survives.

Publius Ovidius Naso (43 B.C.E.–17 C.E.) was during his life the leading poet in Rome. In the early twentieth century his *Art of Love* and *Metamorphoses* were well-known in many English translations; Aldington is probably proposing to translate Ovid's less popular works, such as the love poems in *Amores* or the epistolary verse in *Heroides*, which contains poems in the voices of legendary women writing to absent husbands or lovers.

Commodianus was a Christian Latin poet of the third, fourth, or fifth century C.E., known for his rough metrics in which quantity played little part.

4 Joachim du Bellay (1522–61) was a French poet and a Latinist rather than a Hellenist. Many of his poems had earlier been translated into English by Edmund Spenser. The Duchess d'Orléans was the Princess Charlotte-Élisabeth de Bavière (1652–1722). Her letters, written for the most part in German, provide political and social commentary on court life. Arthur Rimbaud (1854–91) was a violent and unstable poet of genius, who had a strong influence on the symbolists and on modernism generally, both in England and on the continent. Championed by the French poet Paul Verlaine (1844–96), Rimbaud is known for his exploration of the unconscious and for his experiments with rhythm and syntax. The French symbolist poet Jules Laforgue (1860–87) advocated vers libre and was an important early influence on T.S. Eliot. Henri de Régnier (1864–1936) was a French symbolist poet and novelist who advocated vers libre and drew on classical forms and themes. Pierre de Ronsard (1524–85) was a French renaissance poet and humanist who drew on classical authors as models. Clément Marot (1496–1544) was a French poet of the early Renaissance. The Symbolistes were French poets who rejected traditional conventions of theme and technique in their verse, advocating vers libre and emphasising sensory impressions and the role of images in poetry. The movement began about 1880 and reached its height ten years later. Among this group Aldington was particularly interested in Mallarmé, Verlaine, Rimbaud, LaForgue, Régnier, and Gourmont, all of whom he wants to translate here. The Parnassiens were an earlier group of poets, active between about 1860 and 1880, who admired the scientific positivism of the period, rejecting romanticism for restrained, objective, and impersonal poetry in rigid rhythms. Later Symbolistes rejected this movement, although several, notably Mallarmé and Verlaine, initially identified themselves as Parnassiens. André Spire (1868–1966) was a French poet, editor, biographer, and bibliographer, whose poems Aldington published in *The Egoist* and through the Egoist Press and with whom he corresponded between 1915 and 1955. The surviving letters between them are at SIU. Charles Messager Vildrac (1882–1971) was an individualist French poet and dramatist associated with the Abbaye commune and press.

5 Lorenzo de Medici (1449–92) was a Florentine poet-prince whose Petrarchan sonnets and other verse reveal a wide range of subjects and literary experiments with meter and form. A contemporary of Dante, Folgore da San Gemignano (fl. 1305–16) wrote a series of sonnets for the months of the year and another for the days of the week. Aldington translated *A Garland of Months by Folgore da San Gemignano* as Number 5 in the first Poets' Translation Series in 1916. Angelo Poliziano (1454–94) was among the poets whose work Aldington translated in *Latin Poems of the Renaissance*, in which two of Poliziano's poems, 'Simonetta' and 'Epitaph for Giotto, the Painter', appear. Cecco Angiolieri (c. 1260-c. 1313) was the first master of Italian humorous and realistic verse. Guido Cavalcanti (c. 1250–1300), a close friend of Dante, wrote about fifty poems and is particularly known for his difficult canzone on the nature of love. The Trecento poets were lyric thirteenth-century authors who wrote primarily in the Tuscan dialect, among them Cavalcante and Dante, although Aldington is probably thinking of many less stellar writers, such as Brunetto Latini (c. 1220-c. 1296) and Cino da Pistoia (c. 1265-c.

1337). Giosue Carducci (1835–1907) was primarily a classicist, but he also wrote ten volumes of poetry and essays on literary criticism and history. Giacomo Leopardi (1798–1837) was also well-grounded in Greek and Latin literature; his lyric poetry and moral dialogues in verse reveal a somber, even distraught personality. Francesco Maria Molza (1485–1544) was a minor poet. Pietro Bembo (1470–1547) had a great influence on his contemporaries, although his own poetry and prose, primarily in the form of dialogues, was essentially minor, imitative, and classical in impulse. Andrea Navagero (1483–1529) wrote highly regarded Latin verse often translated into English, while his few Italian poems are less well-known and Petrarchistic. Aldington translated several of his Latin poems in *Latin Poems of the Renaissance* and expanded his selection of Navagero's work in *Medallions*. Giovanni Boccaccio (c. 1313–75) wrote his great *Decamerone* in the early 1350s, a collection of a hundred various, primarily humorous tales. Aldington published his translation, *The Decamerone of Giovanni Boccaccio*, in 1930. Matteo Maria Boiardo (1441–94) was also a poet; his unfinished epic of Arthurian love, *Orlando innamorto*, was completed by Ariosto in his *Orlando furioso*. Aldington may be considering translating Boiardo's highly regarded Petrarchan lyrics.

6 While Aldington, H.D., and Pound initially welcomed Lowell's publicizing of imagism and praise for its principles and poets, they were embarrassed by her pushiness and tendency to appropriate control of the movement while not always embodying its tenets in her own work.

7 Aldington's previous experience in coordinating the English contributions to the imagist anthologies of 1915, 1916, and 1917 had given him experience in the business of editing, as had his work for *The New Freewoman* and *The Egoist* and his initiation of the first Poets' Translation Series of six titles. His practical mind and disposition to detail made the huge task he proposes here a logical direction for him to pursue. Nevertheless, because of failure to secure a contract with other publishers, the six translations which did appear as part of the second Poets' Translation Series were ultimately published by the Egoist Press.

8 Aldington intended to reissue several translations already published on a smaller scale by the Egoist Press as part of the first Poets' Translation Series. Among the works he mentions here, H.D.'s *Choruses from Iphigeneia in Aulis* was in fact reissued in an expanded volume with the choruses she was currently translating from Euripides' *Hippolytus* as Number 3 in the second series. Aldington's *The Poems of Anyte of Tegea* (Number 1 in the first series) was reissued with Edward Storer's *Poems and Fragments of Sappho* (Number 2 in the first series) as Number 2 in the second series. Aldington's *Latin Poems of the Renaissance* (Number 4 in the first series) was expanded and became Number 4 in the second series. Flint's *The Mosella of Decimus Magnus Ausonius* (Number 6 in the first series) was with his translation of *Columella on Gardens* formally advertised in *The Egoist* as Number 6 in the second series, but did not materialize. Four other volumes, among them translations by Storer and Randall, were also advertized but never completed.

9 Renée Vivien was the pseudonym of the poet Pauline Tarn (1877–1909), companion of Natalie Barney. Her French verse in very pure forms was influenced by Baudelaire, and she shared Barney's interest in Sappho.

꙳ **71** ꙳

15 December 1918[1]

Dear Astraea/

Thank you for your promptitude in sending the dictionary; I am afraid that, in this mess of Christmas, it will be some days before it arrives. I am handicapped here in all manner of petty ways – lack of ink & paper, no fuel to warm the room I work in, irritating little military jobs unsuspectedly thrust upon one. I have but one prayer: to get away from this hated uniform & this hateful race. I don't think I can live in London; even Paris seems too near England![2]

As regards my books I think they had better stay in London. You see if they are there I can go over them & pick out those I want to keep. Perhaps Alec could take charge of them; of course you are welcome to all you want for your own use, but I prefer that the majority should stay in London. Probably I shall not require many of them in which case I can distribute them.[3]

Alciphron is in the Teubner edition. Alec could find it in five minutes if he had the books.

Glad you are working. I like the new translations [of Euripides] very much – am making careful notes to send you. Let me know if anything happens in re the proposal for the new P.T.S.

May write to Fred.[4]

Ever yours
Richard.

1 This letter was addressed to Speen, postmarked 17 December at the field post office, and forwarded to the Lancaster Hotel in London.
2 In *Life for Life's Sake*, Aldington recalls that after his return to the front in early December of 1918, '…I spent twelve endless and miserable weeks, in bitterly cold weather, with a foot or more of snow, and no fuel except a bit of coal dust and an occasional tree which I bought from the estate of the local count … [who] charged about three times as much as his wretched trees were worth. However, we were glad to have them at any price, for without the wood we couldn't even have had our food cooked' (179). Eager to be demobilized, Aldington blamed the British for the war's physical, emotional, and spiritual effect on him. His anger never diminished and can be seen as the impulse behind most of his novels (notably *Death of a Hero* in 1929, *The Colonel's Daughter* in 1931, *All Men Are Enemies* in 1933, *Women Must Work* in 1934, and *Rejected Guest* in 1939). His eventual rejection of England for homes in the United States and France also has its roots in this wartime anger and blame.
3 Aldington is referring here to the books stored at 44 Mecklenburgh Square. H.D. went through them carefully, writing Bryher on 17 December that she had 'spent a rather discouraging morning over the books'. (Yale) Aldington periodically acquired an enormous number of books and because of his many changes of residence (he never owned a house and travelled frequently throughout his life), was periodically forced to dispose of portions of his library by selling volumes or giving them to friends. Aldington's decision to make a selection from his current library and to store the majority of his books in London does not necessarily indicate that he intends to separate from H.D. after his demobilization.
4 The Australian writer Frederic Manning (1882–1935), recently demobilized and living in England, who was both a poet and a classical scholar.

≈ **72** ≈

[17 December 1918][1]

Dear Astraea/

This is a very lovely translation, unique, personal, vivid. No one but you could have done it. I have marked a few minor corrections of punctuation, spelling & grammar, chiefly to preserve you from the fools who will see that & nothing else. Work of your sort must be utterly impeccable. Certain lines from their concision are ambiguous – expand them a little & make your meaning plain, unless the original demands ambiguity. Avoid inversion, the stocatto, & repetition 'why, why' &c or use them very sparingly. Note that your use of 'absolute' is incorrect & makes it a noun.

I need not apologize to you for these remarks. You, as an artist, know how much work on my part they mean! And I would not make them except that I want your work absolutely flawless. I think this translation an improvement on the Iphigeneia.[2]

May I have it for the P.T.S if we get it going?

Now, _don't_ touch this translation except to make the corrections marked.

Ever yours
Richard.

1 This undated letter was addressed to Speen and forwarded to H.D. at the Lancaster Hotel in London.

2 Aldington's criticism of others' writing was often specific and authoritative. H.D. was used to working closely with her husband and understood both the essential justice and the kind impulse behind Aldington's response to her compositions. In 'Heliodora', she gives a vivid account of their mutual effort, his criticism, and her ability both to 'take it' and to profit from it. 'Heliodora' first appeared in _Heliodora and Other Poems_ in 1924, though it was obviously written several years earlier. Aldington here finds H.D.'s current work superior to her 1916 translation of Euripides' _Choruses from Iphigeneia in Aulis_.

❧ 73 ❧

21 December 1918

Dear Astraea/

I was very glad to get the Dictionary & Bough. Thank you for sending.[1]

Will write Miss Ellerman in re P.T.S. You will have had my letter by now in connection with it.

You are very good to think so charmingly of my future, but really, dear child, you must think of your own. Keep warm & well fed this bitter weather. I must find out from Brigit if she has got that twilight-sleep place fixed up.[2]

You will forgive my not sending anything for Xmas. I'm sending to no one, as I can't afford it. Cheque of course will go off on Jan 1st.

I do hope that trip to Greece comes off. Some arrangement could be made about the child. Of course it will live & you will love it very much & you will be happy even if it is messy & noisy.[3]

I am sure you will be all right. And I'm glad you want to work again; it is the most satisfactory thing. I hope you will realise that my criticisms on your Hippolytus are meant in the right spirit.

Don't worry about 'Double Maitresse'. I can't work much here – too cold.[4]

Affectionately
Richard.

P.S. A. wrote she had seen you & you looked better & gayer. I am glad.

It was rather hard coming back here, but I keep as happy as I can.

1 Aldington is acknowledging the Greek dictionary H.D. has sent him, apparently along with one or two volumes of James Frazer's _The Golden Bough_, which appeared in a twelve-volume expanded edition in 1913. Part 4, in two volumes, entitled _Adonis Attis Osiris_, would have been of particular interest to Aldington in 1918.

2 Brigit Patmore was making arrangements for H.D. to enter St. Faith's nursing home to have her baby, due in mid-March. There H.D. could give birth with 'twilight sleep', a combination of morphine and scopolamine first introduced in Germany in 1907 as an anaesthetic during

childbirth. The medication was still considered novel in 1918.

3 H.D. has evidently written Aldington about Bryher's idea of traveling with H.D. to Greece after the baby's birth. On 17 December 1918, she had written Bryher in response to the plan: 'I am very, *very* excited about Delphi! But I must have two years preparation.' On 18 December 1918, she continued enthusiastically: 'I bought myself one of these modern Greek manuals – and it amused me so much, I thought you must have one. It will save us some time to ask fluently for "candles, matches and hot water", and as there will be none of the above-mentioned in the wilds of Arcadia and the crags of Parnassus, our energy will perhaps be wasted. But I should like to feel, should occasion arise, that I *can* say to my laundress in the vale of Tempe, "You don't put enough starch in my collar!"' The two women did make the trip in February of 1920, not returning to England until the summer. Aldington's reassurance here is apparently in response to a letter from H.D. in which she recalled their own child and shared her concern that she might not be able to love this baby. H.D., like Aldington, tended to perceive the coming child in the context of the one they had both lost. She wrote to tell Bryher of her pregnancy in these terms on 18 December 1918: 'Three years ago, I had a sad illness + lost my little child. I am expecting to have another towards the end of March. – Do not take this too seriously, as you know my views on the average parent, and if arrangements can be made, an old nurse of Mrs Patmore's children will take, at times, entire charge, so that I may continue my work.' In an undated letter in early January 1919, H.D. told Clement Shorter of her pregnancy and placed it in the same context: 'I am making arrangements to enter a nursing home in March or early April. I had a very sad confinement about three years ago and lost my child, so I feel it very wicked to worry yet about this one's life and future. ... Do not refer to this. I cannot talk about it, as I was so sad and ill the last time.'

4 Aldington has apparently asked H.D. to send him a copy of Henri de Régnier's best known novel, *Double Maîtresse* (1900), a psychological work set in the late seventeenth and early eighteenth centuries. It is characterized by an elaborate libertinism and written in a highly decorative, precious style.

⇜ 74 ⇝

24 December 1918

Dear Dooley/

I heard from A. that you had lunched together. She seems very 'triste', don't you think? I fear she is rather alarmed at the number of articles I send her to type!

Glad you & Shorter had such a good time. Perhaps you can do prose regularly for something after your confinement?

As to articles for Massingham. The 'Letters to Unknown Women' May Sinclair has, since she wrote me she would try to place them. I want to write 'critical dialogues' about books. I have actually done: 1. The Tenderness of Dante. 2. Les Chevaux de Dioméde. 3. A Soldier's Library. 4. The Scholar's Italian Book. Arabella has the first three & I have the last. I have planned tentatively these: 5. Anacreon. 6. Folgore da San Gemignano. 7. Scenes & Portraits. 8. La Double Maitresse. 9. Rimbaud. 10. Landor's Classical Dialogues. 11. Campion & Quantity in English. 12. Sea Garden. 13. Villon. 14. Alciphron's Love Letters. Of course I might not do all or any of these but I shall do some. An article on The Future of Poetry I am having sent to Harriet [Monroe]. I don't know whether these dialogues would suit Massingham. Perhaps he might have a look at them, though I thought Hutton would perhaps like one or two of the Italian ones for his [*Anglo-Italian*] review. Still there would be no harm in Massingham seeing them. I have done three dialogues & an article since I came back here, as well as several poems & poems in prose. So there is no doubt about *quantity* if the quality is O.K.[1]

I don't know about social or political articles. I did one about the election[2] but lost it somewhere. If I do any now I will send them.

Have you any news of P.T.S.? I am working, rather slowly, on Anacreon & Alciphron. It is good steady plodding. I hope the scheme comes off; it would be great fun. Of course, I want W. Bryher in it, but she must learn Greek & improve on her Lament for Adonis.[3]

I hear we are going to Tournai on the 7th Jan — always a little nearer Germany! I do hope I can get free soon.

Hope you are well and cheerful as your letters sound.

Affectionately
Richard.

1 Many of these essays were probably never completed. Aldington is hoping to publish work through Henry William Massingham (1860–1924), a well-travelled journalist who edited *The Nation* from 1907–23. Although Aldington was publishing his 'Letters to Unknown Women' in *The Dial*, he is, as was his legal right, also seeking English publication. It seems likely that 'A Soldier's Library' became 'Books in the Line' (*The Sphere*, April 12, 1919, 26). 'Quantity in English' probably became 'Campion's "Observations"' (*Poetry*, Vol. 15, No. 5 [February 1920], 267–71). 'The Poetry of the Future' appeared in *Poetry*, Vol. 14, No. 5 (August 1919), 266–9.

2 Polling took place on 14 December-1918; Lloyd George's coalition government obtained a sweeping majority.

3 Bryher's *Lament for Adonis: Bion the Smyrnaean* (London: A.L. Humphreys, 1918). Bryher's translation comprised only five pages of this fifteen-page book; the rest was made up of the Greek text, reproduced with acknowledgement from William Heinemann's Loeb Classical Library edition, and a five-page introduction. Bryher relied heavily on J.M. Edmund's translation in the Loeb edition and voiced as her own Aldington's principles of translation as expounded in the first Poets' Translation Series (see letter 70, note 12). She wrote: 'In this translation I have endeavored to recapture the spirit of the poem rather than to render it word for word into English, to use no archaic prose or needless inversion, and to reflect, as closely as may be, the thought of the poet himself' (5). Aldington reviewed Bryher's translation in *The Egoist* (Vol. 6, No. 1, January-February 1919); his approval is restrained: 'It is a pleasure to know that the principles of translating laid down in the prospectus of The Poets' Translation Series are being followed by other translators. That this "literary-literal" method has a distinct advantage over all others is proved by a very sensitive version of Bion's *Lament for Adonis* recently published [in November] by Miss Winifred Bryher. ... she is on the right track. ... The translation is not perfect ... but it contains beautiful phrases.' (10)

⁓ 75 ⁓

28 December 1918

Dear Astraea/

Do you mind concentrating your mind for a few minutes on the convolutions of bureaucracy?

Now then.

1. Was Miss Weaver's letter correctly worded. i.e. did it state catagorically that I was in the employment of The Egoist before August 4th 1914 & that she was prepared to re-employ me?[1]

2. Was the letter sent to the correct place, i.e. the Local Advisory Committee of the Department of Appointments (for officers *only*) as laid down in the procedure for Demobilisation of Officers?[2]

If the answer to either of these two questions is in the negative, will you communicate at once with Hutton & request him to inform you:

A. Exactly how the letter should be worded and

B. Exactly where it should be sent.

On receipt of above information will you hand it on to Miss Weaver with the
request

A. That she will write a letter in the correct form. And

B. That she will forward it to the correct address.

– – – – –

With reference to application already made – will you tell Hutton how it was
worded & where it was sent & ask him if it is valid or if a new application should be
sent. I am not sure whether 'Ministry of Labour' _is_ the Department of Appointments or
something different.[3]

All this is tedious & elaborate but unless the procedure is rigidly adhered to I shall
not be posted as a 'slip man' & shall hang on here until I am as old as Rip van Winkle.[4]

Thanks for card – will write more soon.

Affectionately,

Richard.

1 Aldington has asked Harriet Shaw Weaver to write a letter to the military authorities on the
  basis of which he might be demobilized.
2 This department arranged the release of officers who had jobs waiting for them. Demobilization was arranged by selected categories, regardless of rank. Men in occupations considered
  to be of national importance, such as miners, were the first to be released.
3 The Ministry of Labour was not the same as the Department of Appointments. The former
  concerned itself with the release of soldiers in nationally important occupations.
4 A 'slip man' was one for whom a productive job was waiting and who could be released, on the
  orders of his commanding officer, at the same time as men in 'pivotal' occupations. The 'slip'
  refers to an employer's certificate confirming occupation.

76

1 January 1919

Dear Astraea/

I am so pleased that you feel more secure about the future. No, I won't take any of
little Miss E's gifts, but I shall ask you to let the monthly £5 stand over this time. I had
so many stupid expenses here this Christmas – all kinds of things, Christmas cards,
charities, god knows what – that until I see my pass-book I don't quite know where I
stand.

Are you hurt by the alterations I suggested in your Hippolytus? Surely you are
beyond, far beyond, that amateur stage!

I have written John [Cournos] about P.T.S. Am working on Alciphron & making
lists of poets to be translated. I have also done some dialogues & articles which will do
to show as specimens in London. I hope that Hutton's efforts will be of some avail.

The French are only demobilising down to men of 40! So I don't think there is
much chance [of a speedy demobilisation] unless some special kind of appeal is made. It
is humiliating & maddening to be kept here, but there you are – were I wealthy, like
the Sitwells,[1] or merely syphiletic like [Wyndham] Lewis, the case would be different!

I am in correspondence with your little Ellerman friend & advise her about books &c. Have set her a P.T.S. job.[2]

Other things are as usual.

Hope you are fairly cheerful.

Affectionately

Richard.

1 Edith (1887–1964), Osbert (1892–1969), and Sacheverell Sitwell (1897–1980) were known for their extravagant personalities and freedom to experiment in literature because of family wealth.
2 Aldington advised Bryher about her translation in a letter he wrote her on 22 December 1918:

> Hilda writes that you are thinking of doing Theocritus. You have courage! Do you know what I think? That it would be better to leave him until you know more Greek & have read more Greek poets. If you start off with one of the greatest, the lesser poets, beautiful as they are, will not move you. Whereas, if you start by the lesser poets you will be all the more dazzled by the loveliness of Theocritus. I wish you would do an epigrammatist for the Translation Series: Will you? I will give you four to choose from: Plato, Lucian, Callimachus & Antipater of Sidon – just the epigrams in the Anthology. You will need Jacobs' Anthologia; (& for the time being you can have my copy, which Hilda will lend you) and the latest edition of Liddle & Scott's Lexicon (containing all the special anthology words) and a good Greek grammar. The Latin translation in Jacobs' will help you to be sure you have the precise literal sense, & for the rest I am secure in your own taste. You will find it a hard job if you are conscientious. The right word is never in the dictionary, & will elude one's search.
>
> Will you do this? I would so much like to have you in the Series. ...

On 1 January 1919, Aldington again urged Bryher to translate a minor poet: 'I wrote you about the translations, & gave you a choice of four beautiful poets, any of whom would dazzle this century. Lucian, Plato, Callimachus, Antipater of Sidon. Which is it to be? Plato is perhaps the most intense, Callimachus the most polished, Lucian the cleverest, & Antipater the most decorated! Indeed I want you to be a translator in this series, & I know your work will be a great help.'

❧ 77 ❧

2 January 1919

Dear Astraea/

Thank you so much for sending me 'Hymen'. It is delicate and fragile, with an air of much less maturity than your earlier work in Sea-Garden. There is a most exquisite child-like quality in the earlier songs, & the more sensual tone of the last three strikes one as a totally different impulse. The introduction of rime is not displeasing, because it is used with skill & tranquility; tho' 'sips' & 'lips' gives me just a faint displeasure.[1]

The prose descriptions between the songs do not interest me; I should very much like to see the procession as you describe it & to hear the music, but it is a little out of my 'galère' [present hell] to criticise this part of your poem. Yet, as they are part of your idea they should be retained. It seems a pity to waste it on 'Poetry and Drama', yet I cannot think of any other periodical which would take it. Show it to Shorter & ask him. If there is no English periodical, then I should certainly send it to Harriet [Monroe] with the prose part, as she'll then have to pay you more! I think that without saying anything to her you could publish the poems separately in the Sphere under separate titles. Here they are: 1. Song for Hera. 2. Ivy & Crocus. 3. Winter-Rose. 4. Hyacinthes. 5. Bride-Song. 6. Laurel. 7. Bridal Song. 8. Cyclamen. 9. Epilogue. If they would take the lot – as they ought – & print one each week, Harriet wouldn't know & you would get some money. (Excuse this commercialism!) Then I think it should be issued as a little book at 1/-, with a short note by someone or other, perhaps Willy Yeats. He would surely say a word if we asked nicely! That is my advice: Get Harriet to print the whole thing; the Sphere or some other English periodical the Songs; & issue it later in book form. It is worth this publicity, though, as you say, it hasn't the epic intensity of your other stuff. If you can't get an ordinary publisher, I will put up the money for the Egoist to bring out a few hundred copies, & we can probably get someone to do it in the U.S.A.[2]

Will write again soon. Am retaining the ms. for a day or so longer.

Affectionately
Richard.

P.S. Hippolytus I returned some time ago.

1 'Hymen' was first published in *Poetry*, Vol. 15, No. 3 (December 1919), 117–29; it was later collected with other poems in *Hymen* (1921). H.D.'s *Sea Garden*, her first volume of poetry, appeared in the autumn of 1916.

2 Harold Monro edited eight issues of the quarterly *Poetry and Drama* between March 1913 and December 1914, when publication was suspended because of the war. Aldington visited Monro at the Poetry Bookshop during his November leave and evidently discussed with him the periodical's revival. Monro began to publish the journal again under a new title, *The Monthly Chapbook*, in July 1919. In January 1920, the title was changed again, to *The Chapbook*, which continued until 1925. Aldington published here regularly after the war. While Monro was committed to new directions in criticism, poetry and poetic drama (he published Edward Storer's verse play 'Helen', for example, in the June 1914 issue), neither the whole of 'Hymen' nor individual poems ever appeared here, nor did parts of 'Hymen' appear separately in any journal. Despite Aldington's suggestion of William Butler Yeats, whose literary stature and interest in both poetry and dramatic forms would have made him a suitable champion, no note preceded the poem when it appeared in book form. In the end, Aldington did not need to 'put up the money', and the Egoist Press published *Hymen* (which included 'Hymen' as well as other poems) in England in 1921; Henry Holt published it in America in the same year.

~ 78 ~

3 January 1919

Dear Astraea/

Herewith your 'Hymen'. I have been over it several times & have corrected a few spelling errors & made a note or so. Words surrounded by a circle thus: (maidenhead,) are those I think should be either omitted or altered, you will see which in each case. I believe it may be taken as an axiom in poetry that in nine cases out of ten repetition of a word weakens the effect. Apropos the word 'maidenhead' – this does *not* mean virginity, 'maidenhood' but is an Elizabethan word meaning the sex of a maiden. Is that precisely what you wanted to say at that point? It is a trivial thing but worth considering.[1]

I think I like the thing more now I've got to know it & the prose intervals are more attractive to me. You must have it re-typed by a professional typist – your own copy is full of little blurs & errors which distract the attention & will cause mistakes in setting up the type. Moreover it looks better. Have it done in duplicate. The songs for the Sphere you can do yourself, but do them slowly & correctly, with a two-line space between each line – trivial but again necessary. And, moreover, don't submit your m.s. *ever* until I have been over it; you make little careless errors in spelling & syntax &c which fools pick up as a weapon against an original artist. Remember, H.D. cannot afford to be anything less than perfection.[2]

Richard.

1 H.D. kept the word 'maidenhead' in the stanza in which women sing:

> From citron-bower be her bed
> Cut from branch of tree a-flower
> Fashioned for her maidenhead.

Three stanzas later, H.D. used the word 'maidenhood':

> That all the wood in blossoming,
> May calm her heart and cool her blood
> For losing of her maidenhood

(H.D., 'Hymen', in *Collected Poems, 1912–1944*, ed. Louis Martz, New York: New Directions, 1983, 108). Since the original typescript of 'Hymen' has not survived, we cannot know exactly what revisions Aldington suggested nor what changes H.D. may have made as a result.

2 H.D.'s typing was oddly spaced and irregular; she frequently omitted words or letters, and her spelling was indeed very bad. Here Aldington is equating 'perfection' with 'H.D.', his wife's carefully fashioned literary persona. He is under no illusion that his wife is, can, or should be perfect, nor does he ever measure her as a person against any standards of 'perfection'. In fact, Aldington criticizes H.D.'s own 'ardour for perfection' in letter 13. Aldington is, however, voicing an aesthetic idea shared by his contemporaries. In March 1913, Pound wrote to Harriet Monroe about the lack of artistic standards in America: 'Who in America believes in perfection, and that nothing short of it is worth while?' In March 1915, Pound wrote to Monroe again on the same subject, insisting that the artist's 'only respectable aim is perfection' (Ezra Pound, *The Letters of Ezra Pound*, ed. D. D. Paige, New York: Harcourt Brace, 1950, 14, 56).

꙰ **79** ꙰

See inside also
B.E.F. 6 January 1918[1]

Dear Astraea/

Your choruses must be delayed or lost in the post – I sent them off before Christmas. They probably got submerged in that insipid mass of sentimentality.[2]

Have you another copy? I thought the choruses excellent, & only ventured on a few verbal alterations – mostly spelling & grammar! And inversions, of which you have too many.

I am glad that you feel more courageous. Your prospect is not pleasant & the courage you show is admirable. I cannot believe that so clear & fine a mine [*sic*] can be wasted, & I expect with confidence great things from you. One gets exceedingly depressed at times. And then exceedingly & unreasonably exalted. It is all very foolish. Of course, I am fretting about being demobilised, but when I am I really don't see how I'm going to make bread let alone butter to put on it. Frankly, we poets are anachronisms; the world has no place for us & the sooner we recognise it the better. Yet it is impossible for us, by reason of our temperaments, to succeed in any other capacity. We are fated to make a mess of our lives. When I see what a mess mine is in, I shudder. I see absolutely no solution anywhere, & very little but hardship, wretchedness & distress for the future.

Wherefore, I return to my writing table & continue my translation of Anacreon, remembering that the Royal Sussex never lost a trench![3]

Affectionately
Richard.

Later.

Your letter of Jan. 1st arrived. And from Miss Weaver. My God. All I can say is, My God. I am surrounded by fools and super-fools. Does she, do you, does *any* sane person imagine that the Govt. will release an officer to take up an appointment of £36 a year? Are you mad? Couldn't she have the sense to put a reasonable figure? I told her that there was nothing binding in it. Do you know what this means? That the application will certainly be rejected, that no effort on Hutton's part or my part or anyone's can alter it, that I shall be sent to the army of occupation & not be released, perhaps, for years?[4]

Well, I suppose it's not your fault; but it is the last straw. It's no use grousing is it? But my only chance of life is gone, wrecked. What a blasted fool the woman is. Tell her and her bloody paper [*The Egoist*] to go to hell, will you. I have [not] the patience to write to her.

Another two years of this hell!

Cheerio; be good.

R.

1 In fact, 6 January 1919.
2 That is, the Christmas mails.
3 Aldington had served with the Ninth Royal Sussex Regiment since early 1918.
4 Sixteen British divisions formed the Army of Occupation in 1918–19. If a soldier's unit was attached to one of these divisions, and he were not in a high priority demobilisation category, he would have been obliged to continue his army service. Reallocation of troops began in early February, 1919.

⤳ 80 ⤾

7 January 1919

Dear Astraea/

Excuse me for the hasty way I wrote you yesterday. My excuse is that I am on the verge of a complete mental collapse & the news from Miss Weaver simply stunned me, since I know that my release is now an impossibility. You could not expect the W.O. [War Office] to release an officer to take up a position at £36 a year. Now could you?[1]

And the worst of it is no other application can now be made.[2]

I have written Hutton & await a reply from him, before taking decisive measure. I will *not* endure another year of this.

Yours
Richard.

1 There is no question that Aldington is here suffering from 'shell shock' (what is now called 'Post Traumatic Stress Disorder'). Throughout these letters he tries to shelter H.D. from his nervousness, depression, and guilt, but occasionally – as here – he is frank and open, even desperate.
2 Late in 1918 the War Office changed the procedure for demobilization to the simple release of soldiers on the basis of length of service: those who had served longest would be released first.

81

9 January 1918[1]

Dear Astraea/

I have an idea. Do you think that Shorter could get me a hack translation job while I'm here? I mean the translation of some French novel or tedious memoir or something which a publisher is going to do & for which he would pay the ordinary translator rates. And could you find out 1. If Marshall Foch 'Principes de Guèrre' has been translated, 2. If not, whether any publisher would <u>give an order</u> for its translation by me. I have the requisite military knowledge as well as the power to put the French into English. If I could get the job it would help to pass time here & also get a little money.[2]

Excuse brief letter – I have such extraordinary head-aches these days that I can scarcely write.[3]

Your

R.

1 In fact, 9 January 1919.
2 Ferdinand Foch (1851–1929), maréchal de France, became General-in-Chief of the Allied Armies during the last year of the First World War. His *Des Principes de la Guerre: Conférences Faites en 1900 à L'École Supérieure de Guerre* (1917) was translated by Hilaire Belloc in 1918.
3 The word 'wright' is crossed out here and 'write' substituted. Aldington was plagued with intense headaches that began about this time and lasted well into the 1920s. They are a characteristic element of the experience of 'shell shock'. In *Life for Life's Sake*, Aldington recalled that after his return to the continent in December 1918, 'I began to notice some of the after-effects of the war. I slept badly, was subject to meaningless but unpleasant moods of depression, and was in a frenzy of impatience to get out of the army. And it seemed to me that my mind had deteriorated, because of the difficulty I found in concentrating on mental work' (179). Years later Aldington recalled his psychological and physical distress when commenting on Henry Slonimsky's difficulties with insomnia in a letter to him on 8 November 1941: 'A physical symptom naturally suggests a physical cause, but from my own experience I do believe that insomnia may have a psychological basis. I suffered rather badly from it February through May of 1919, after I was demobilised. True, my general health was rather poor after the hardships of two campaigns mostly on half or even quarter rations; but I think the real cause was a combination of public and personal disappointments and miseries' (SIU).

82

13 January 1919

Dear Astraea/

Sea-Heroes is the best of these pieces; needs a little working over. Be quite sure of the spelling & meaning of these words before sending the poem out.[1]

Who is 'she' in the third strophe? Greece, Carthage, England?[2]

I don't think I'd send it to Harriet [Monroe] – try one or two English papers first. Why shouldn't The Nation give you a showing? Don't despise these English weeklies. They are <u>read</u>. If you got your Hymen poems in the Sphere & then three or four others into The Nation, it would help you enormously, I mean in getting known.

Simaetha is quite good & should made a good link in a series. Thetis is a little weak in spots – it doesn't say much & the mood is uncertain. Still it has undoubted beauties. I think it needs more work.[3]

Just received the prospectus of 'Art & Letters', new series. *If* they can make a 'do' &

get their subscribers it might be worth while going on with them. I gave them a couple of poems. But I doubt very much if they get anywhere. The prospectus is largely my fault. I don't think Read put things as tactfully as he might![4]

Cheerio,
Richard.

1 H.D.'s poem 'Sea Heroes' was first published (as 'Sea-Heroes') in *Coterie*, No. 4, 1920, 44–6, and collected in *Hymen* in 1921. After a long period during which H.D. found it difficult or impossible to write, she was now working productively again not only on translation from the Greek but on her poetry. On 1 February 1919, after a hiatus in their correspondence, H.D. wrote Amy Lowell about her difficulty: 'It has been impossible for me to work for some time – but I believe I can now begin again. Richard's position out there was, for so long, so exceptionally dangerous – and my people at home were broken by my brother's death in France – and you can imagine being alone here + not able to get across to them, pretty well wore me to shreds. But the first shock over, my people seem strong again, and R. is safe – and I am seriously getting back to work.' While H.D. is not being fully open here about all the pressures which have made writing difficult for her, she acknowledges the period of unproductive work and suggests the beginning of a new period of creativity.

2 The reference for the pronoun in the third stanza of 'Sea Heroes' remains vague.

3 'Simaetha' was first published in *Contact*, No. 3, 8, in 1921 and appeared in *Hymen* later the same year. H.D. evidently agreed with Aldington about the weaknesses in 'Thetis': she revised the poem extensively (as evidenced in the typescript, Yale), did not publish it serially, and included only part of it in *Hymen*.

4 Edited by Frank Rutter with Charles Ginner and H. Gilman in 1917, this journal of visual and literary art suspended publication in 1918, then recommenced in 1919–20, edited by Rutter and Osbert Sitwell. Aldington may have met Herbert Read (1893–1968), the poet and literary critic, as early as his November leave in 1918; they became good friends during the years after the war. In 1917, Read's critical and aesthetic theories shaped the character of *Art and Letters*. When the periodical resumed publication in 1919, T.S. Eliot's theories became the dominant feature of the journal.

⇜ 83 ⇝

21 January 1919

Dear Astraea/

Thank you for your letters & for all you have been doing for me. The news is excellent.[1]

Now, Mrs Yorke is a good common-sense woman & offered to help, so I've sent her the forms with precise directions. She will take them to Weaver, get them filled in, & get them stamped &c.[2]

You are *not* to worry any more about this or about me; above everything you are not to stand in queues &c. You know perfectly well you shouldn't.

I'm am [*sic*] 'bucked' [encouraged] with Shorter's letter – I'll love to do some work for him; & I'll write Amy [Lowell] almost at once. I've finished rough draft of Anacreon & am carefully rewriting.

M.S. [May Sinclair] also has a small temporary job for me, so I'll be all right.

You have fixed up twilight sleep O.K.? Please be tranquil in your mind & let the child be a pleasure to you – I don't mean having it, which is as Euripides says, but afterwards. Don't feel that it is anything but fine to be a mother; because it is fine, and is one of those simple pure things that fools like Lawrence & Pound do not understand.[3]

So glad you have promise of work. It is splendid. You'll be O.K.

Enclosed Feb: cheque. I send it early, as an officer going on leave is taking mail. Excuse, therefore, hurried letter.

Yrs.

1 H.D. had been doing her best to arrange for Aldington's demobilization: she had written to Harriet Shaw Weaver at *The Egoist* about the possibility of Aldington's getting his old job back; she had spoken with Clement Shorter about Aldington's situation in the hope that he might employ Aldington in some capacity at *The Sphere* or use his influence to persuade other editors or publishers to give Aldington some formal contract for articles or translations. H.D. had also, evidently, visited the War Office in an attempt to see exactly what needed to be done to secure her husband's release.

2 Dorothy Yorke's mother, Selina Yorke, was a strong, forceful, even domineering woman who was very close to her daughter and anxious to look out for what she saw as Dorothy Yorke's interests. She is evidently filing the employment forms required for Aldington's demobilization.

3 In *Medea*, Medea tells her children, 'I laboured, travail worn, bearing sharp anguish in your hour of birth' (1030–1).

➢ 84 ᐸ

29 January 1919

Dear Astraea/

Thank you for sending me Myrrhine.[1] I have written Mrs Yorke to try to get that 'slip' through, but I rather fear it will be too late. The Adjutant has twice given me a very strong hint that they intend sending me to the army of occupation – a sort of revenge, I suppose, for my being a conscript. I've got fairly used to the idea, though, and I suppose it doesn't really matter. I had hoped to gain a little happiness and freedom, but fate was against it. Don't say anything to the Yorkes about this; there is the faintest chance that if the papers went through before 30–1–19 I might get out. A. will feel rather badly when she knows; and I must tell her myself so she can re-organise her life.

Now, my dear, as to you. You must cease to worry about me; you did your best & it's not your fault. You have your troubles to contend with. I think it improbable I shall get leave before you go to hospital, as they purposely keep me as long as possible, & I am not going to whine to them for special leave. You've got to consider that I am probably fixed here for many, many months to come; & you must organise your life without any thought of me. I will send you all the money I can; beyond that I can't do anything. Life has not treated either of us too well, but you've got to realise, which you still haven't, the utter soullessness of the military machine, and the impossibility of an artist securing even bare justice from it. And the harshness of that machine is the reflection of the harshness of commercial civilization; you must secure some means of providing for yourself & your child. I am helpless and I am poor: you knew that six years ago; whatever chance I had of 'making good' has practically disappeared, and you can only rely on me for a very few pounds. When, eventually, I am discharged, I shall be scarcely able to earn a pittance for myself, as this harsh system has robbed me of whatever gifts I had. What on earth do you think I shall be worth after 2 or 3 years more of this?[2]

There are the bare facts & you must face them. If Gray cannot or will not help you, then you must get work of some sort through your friends. What I can give will be totally inadequate.

I wish you 'the best of luck' in your coming ordeal; this time you go over the top while I watch helplessly.[3] If it is any good saying it I would ask your forgiveness of the pain I have caused you, as freely as I forgive the pain you have caused me.

Richard.

1 H.D. has sent Aldington a copy of his *The Love of Myrrhine and Konallis, and Other Poems*. Aldington had written to Bryher on 1 January 1919: 'Yes, I would like a copy of Myrrhine, as my wretched batman lost my last & only copy when we moved our quarters.'

2 As H.D. arranges to enter St. Faith's nursing home in mid-March in anticipation of the baby's birth, Aldington reflects on what has happened to them both since they decided to marry in 1913.

3 Aldington's jaunty phrases here echo the curt and understated exchanges among World War I soldiers before they left the trenches to attack. He thus parallels H.D.'s coming childbirth with the male experience of going into battle.

Between 1 December 1918, and 29 January 1919, Aldington wrote H.D. seventeen letters. It seems likely that additional letters and notes were written between the end of January and 24 February 1919, but if so none has survived. He received his demobilization papers during the first week of February and recalled in *Life for Life's Sake* that his long trip back to England, like the experience of returning home just after the armistice in November, was a

> fantastic and uncomfortable journey, beginning with seven miles in the mess cart through deep snow. There was a slow, all-night train journey in an unlighted, unheated train, lacking window glass and doors. I had been cold in the trenches, but seldom as cold as during that interminable, frosty night [of 8 February 1919]. We sat packed together stamping our feet and beating our hands to keep them from frost-bite. At dawn we stopped at Armentières, which was a strange sight. The splintered trees and telephone wires were festooned with thick hoar frost, and the ruins looked black in the dead-white snow. We stumbled over to a shed where we were given bowls of hot soup, and the cases of frost-bite were evacuated to hospital. (182–3)

On 9 February 1919, Aldington reached Tournai, where he was able to write briefly to Ezra Pound:

> By enormous efforts I've managed to secure release on the very last day it was possible! Damned close shave. Am now at Tournai, which I leave tomorrow evening, for a nice 12 hour ride to the Base in frozen cattle trucks! I expect to cross on Wednesday [12 February] – then have to report to Crystal Palace [a Victorian exhibition hall in south London used as a demobilization centre at this time], I should with luck be free on Friday [14 February]. Will trot along to see you. It gives me shivers to think how nearly I got caught for the Army of Occupation – never again will I trust a woman [that is, Harriet Shaw Weaver] to do anything really important.
>
> I have got a chance of one or two jobs in town, but I want to come & talk things over with you &, if possible, to re-commence our ancient war on les cuistres [the pedants]. (Yale)

Aldington left Tournai on 10 February, and by 'late in the afternoon we detrained at Dunkirk, and we were sent to what was optimistically called an Officers' Rest Camp, which consisted of canvas tents pitched in the snow' (*Life for Life's Sake*, 183). On 11 February, Aldington finally arrived in London and later recalled: 'I walked from Charing Cross to an Italian restaurant in Soho, and as I was very tired I rented a room there for the night' (*Life for Life's Sake*, 183).[1]

Lodgings in London were if anything more difficult to come by in the months immediately following the armistice than in the months preceding it, and Aldington was compelled for a while to keep his room at the Hotel du Littoral on Moor Street across from the Palace Theatre. He felt somewhat embarrassed about the neighbourhood: Moor Street is a block in length and on three of its four corners stood public houses; at Numbers 6, 9, and 14 were wine merchants; other buildings contained printers, hairdressers, a confectioner; and at Number 15 stood the Italian restaurant of Mario Missaglia. Moor Street was clearly not a residential area, and Aldington felt compromized that as a demobilized officer and a promising writer he could neither find nor afford anything better.

Aldington was also exhausted and rather disoriented. Despite the eagerness to resume meaningful work that his January letters to H.D. and his February letter to Pound reveal, he spent 12 February sleeping and attempting to wash the filth of the trenches from his body, which would take months to recover physically from the war experience. In a letter to Amy Lowell on 5 January 1920, he recalled that upon his return to England he was 'covered with boils ... through bad water, exposure &c. I was really very depressed in health. ...' And the headaches and troubled sleep he mentioned to H.D. in letters 80 and 81 persisted.

While he recalled in a letter to Amy Lowell that on 13 February 1919, he 'started work',[2] and while he wrote to Clement Shorter on 15 February that he was 'just demobilised' and eager to meet with him, Aldington left London on 17 February to spend several days at Rye in Sussex with his family. He returned to town sometime after 21 February, but as letter 85 implies, he did not see H.D. during these first weeks after his release.

The terms of the Aldingtons' relationship seem very unsettled from early December, when H.D. abruptly left London for Speen. Subsequent letters suggest that both Aldingtons were comfortable with an intimate, ongoing professional friendship. Additionally, they were bound to each other by their shared past, and various domestic tasks continued to define H.D.'s role as she sorted through her husband's books and ran errands for him in his absence. Aldington's letters also imply their agreement that nothing about their relationship could be decided definitely until after the baby's birth. H.D.'s letters to Bryher during this time also imply a similar suspension: nothing about the future can be determined until after the child's arrival. Such vagueness must have been both unnerving and reassuring to the Aldingtons: neither wanted to force the other to face some ultimate rupture, while the lack of settled terms meant that a resolution of their difficulties was still a slim possibility. In the weeks before the baby's birth, Aldington wanted to protect H.D. in whatever ways he could. In her turn, H.D. wanted Aldington to feel economically and professionally secure before any final confrontation.

Their relationship was further complicated by the differences between the experience of writing to each other and the experience of being in close proximity if not actually physically in each other's presence. Thus much of what was apparently settled between them in letters – that Aldington would never again see either H.D. or Arabella Yorke, that H.D. would expect nothing but financial assistance from Aldington – was in fact disregarded by both of them when Aldington returned on leave in November 1918 and for good in February 1919.

For her part, H.D. was almost eight months pregnant in early February and was beginning to feel cumbersome. On 1 January 1919, she wrote to Bryher about an approaching visit to London: 'As you know, I am not feeling awfully fit, so would prefer, if possible, to talk with you quietly up in your little room.' H.D. continued for a while, however, to make frequent trips into town, and probably called on Bryher there on 4 February and again the following week.[3]

The snows Aldington experienced on his way home through France also fell at Speen, and a pampered pony and its small cart were H.D.'s only means of transportation between Peace Cottage and the local railway station. By mid-February, she began to feel like staying put. On 14 February she wrote Bryher: 'I feel better but still inclined to crouch a bit over the fire. Let me know about your coming. We could have a little tramp across the common + a quiet talk. ... I am converting the big shawl – your gift – into a warm bed wrap for *myself*.'

H.D. was continuing her rewarding work on new poems and translations from the Greek, work she regularly discussed with Bryher who, in turn, was sharing with H.D. chapters of her own nearly finished novel, *Development*, as well as her early attempts at translation (of Antipater of Sidon). These exchanges were emotionally as well as intellectually quickening for H.D., and her letters to Bryher during this period reveal her excitement with this fresh burst of creativity. Certainly her relationship with Bryher nurtured her artistic work; her departure from Cornwall and separation from Cecil Gray must have relieved some tensions for her, and probably her rather settled life with Margaret Pratt in Speen also encouraged her writing. In a letter to Amy Lowell on 1 February 1919, H.D. attributed her renewed energy to a release from tensions caused by the war, but the reasons she gives Lowell are surely only a half-truth (she was always guarded with Lowell). It would seem that Aldington's own renewed energy for creative work, which dominates his letters to H.D. after his return to the front in December 1918, clearly struck a responsive chord in her; however obliquely and ironically, they were once again working together.

Also ironically, it was still only with Aldington that H.D. was fully open about the now soon approaching birth. Arabella Yorke knew Gray was the father, and it seems likely that Brigit Patmore may at this point have known, too, but Bryher did not know. H.D., like Aldington, felt uneasy about the deep intimacy that still bound them closely to each other, yet she chose not to share with Bryher the details of their estrangement while she made clear to her new friend that she wanted to remain aloof from her husband. In late January H.D. wrote Bryher about Aldington's interest in working for *The Sphere*, commenting that he 'seems duly touched and appreciative [of her efforts on his behalf]. But I must keep impersonal + detached!' H.D. again wrote Bryher in February 1919: 'My mind is so full of ideas – and I am not at all peaceful or at one with myself.'4

It seems clear that H.D. did not find it easy to maintain a distance between herself and her husband, yet she was wary about alternatives. Aldington's shattered nerves coupled with his self-protective determination to preserve the distance they had finally agreed upon made him wary as well. H.D.'s friendship with Bryher had grown more intense between the time of Aldington's November leave and his demobilization; Aldington's relationship with Yorke had not dissolved after all, and Yorke was persistent in her desire to continue the affair and to marry him if possible. Both H.D. and Aldington had thus other potential relationships with which to replace, as it were, their relationship with each other, yet these alternative relationships were secondary to both H.D. and Aldington in February of 1919. Both Aldingtons also had chores to do: Aldington needed to reestablish himself as a writer and H.D. had to go through the process of having her baby. Both were agreed that these tasks took precedence over working out their emotional relationship.

1 Aldington dates the stages of this journey specifically in a letter to Amy Lowell on 17 June 1920.
2 Aldington to Lowell, 17 June 1920.
3 Undated letters from H.D. to Bryher, probably written on 1 February 1919 and in mid-February, 1919.
4 Undated letters from H.D. to Bryher, probably written on 30 January 1919 and 1 February 1919.

85

24 February 1919
Hotel du Littoral
Moor St W.

Dear Astraea/

I hear you are not feeling too famously; you must keep strong and hopeful, for I think you will have a good chance of a fine literary career. Let me know if I can do anything for you in the way of sending out m.s.s &c.[1]

As to type-writer. I intend buying another second-hand so you had better keep the one you have. It still goes, doesn't it?

No news particularly. I see few people – they are all so very discouraging. But I'm sending out quite a deal of work to U.S. Dial has promised more pay. As soon as you are well I want you to write some articles for them – I know I can get them to print them.

Keep cheerful & courageous. I <u>know</u> there is happiness & a fine life for you. This is a harsh test, but remember your Greeks at Marathon![2]

Richard

1 Aldington would have heard news of H.D. from Brigit Patmore or from Bryher. Apparently there was some agreement that he and H.D. would not see each other until after the baby was born. It is not clear at this point whether H.D. is actually ill or whether she is simply feeling tired and awkward in the last weeks of her pregnancy.

2 The Greeks routed the army of Darius at Marathon in 490 B.C.E., thereby winning the first campaign of the Persian wars.

86

1 March 1919
52 Doughty St W.C. 1.[1]

Dear Astraea/

I hope you are feeling better. Brigit & Miss E. [Bryher] let me know from time to time & I'm glad to hear you are getting better than you were. Please get well soon; I feel very miserable when I think of you lying ill.[2]

There is so much for you to come back to; everyone speaks so admiringly of you & your work. On Friday I saw Massingham and he asked me for work by you. I said I would ask you to let him see your Hippolytus; so if you will ask Brigit to send it to me I will retype it & send it to him. Could you make her send it soon? This week I have some Anacreon in the Nation; but you should be there too.

You must let me do anything I can for your work – it seems all I can do.

I have this studio for a month & must then find another place. And I'm very happy to be back. Please forgive my being happy when you are so ill. And please keep brave – you have a wonderful life to come back to and all the really worthwhile people will stick to you.

Richard.

1 Aldington was able to rent a studio here for the month of March. This letter is addressed to H.D. at 2 Hanger Lane, Ealing W.5.; she had just moved into a pension near St. Faith's nursing home in this London suburb in anticipation of her baby's birth.

2 H.D. was ill at this time with the influenza that became epidemic after the war. The flu itself was debilitating, but brief in duration and not usually serious; the pneumonia that often developed in patients weakened by influenza, wartime deprivation, and the harsh weather was, however, serious indeed: by 1920, the epidemic had become worldwide, and influenza and its complications were responsible for twenty-two million deaths.

By the end of March Aldington had been demobilized for six weeks and had begun to reestablish himself as a writer and to shape his professional future. He still had no dependable income, no 'job', but he was working hard on a great many projects and publishing in a wide variety of journals. He wrote Amy Lowell on 19 April 1919 that despite his initial enthusiasm for the second Poets' Translation Series, 'I feel that the translation *series* must be left for a bit. I would like to do it, but I just can't afford to!' Aldington pulled out all the stops in February and March 1919, calling on and writing to old friends (Pound, Flint, Lowell, May Sinclair, Harold Monro) and cultivating new acquaintances (Shorter, Bryher, Sir John Ellerman, Herbert Read, T.S. Eliot) in energetic, even frenzied efforts to place individual articles, poems, and translations and to find permanent employment. His social schedule seems as a result to have been quite hectic: coming into London from a visit with his family at Rye, he dined with Shorter on 17 February; he called on Henry Massingham, editor of *The Nation*, on 24 February; he met with Bryher on 10 March; on 21 March, he dined with Sir John Ellerman at his home; on 26 March he spent the evening with Harold Monro; he spent the following evening with Shorter and Austin Harrison, editor of *The English Review*; on 12 April he dined with Frank and Violet Flint; on 16 April, he attended a dinner party with May Sinclair and Hugh Walpole at the Albemarle Club.[1]

The result of these efforts encouraged Aldington. On 31 March 1919, he wrote Lowell the reasons for his essentially abandoning his Poets' Translation project:

> The attempt to get out the series was provoked first because I wanted to get back the 'feel' of literature again after so long an absence & secondly because Miss Bryher & Mr Shorter were so keen on it [in response to Aldington's own enthusiasm]. I have talked it over with them & with Hilda & am coming over to your opinion: that the attempt is ill-advised at present & probably beyond my power to carry to a successful conclusion. Hilda, W.B. & I will therefore probably publish our translations as individuals though, if possible, with the same publisher.
>
> ... I agree with you that the whole project could be more trouble than it is worth. I see that quite well now. I didn't see it in Belgium because I was in such a condition of wretched nerves that *any* sort of hard slogging work seemed desirable.

Aldington also came to realize that his other writing was demanding nearly all of his time, and in the interests of reestablishing himself and making a living, he would need to put aside most translation work for a period. In his letter to Lowell on 31 March, he described his current work: 'I'm "critic of poetry" for the Pall Mall Gazette, I have got reviewing for The Anglo-French Review & I'm doing a series of articles on French poets for them; I'm doing 6 articles on life in France [during the war] for The Sphere. [Holbrook] Jackson has promised to use my work regularly in To-Day & [Austin] Harrison has promised to give me a show in The English Review.' He wrote to Lowell on 19 April 1919, that his translation of Anacreon, which he had been working on in the trenches, was due to appear in parts in *The Nation*, *The New Age*, and *To-Day* and that *The Anglo-French Review* had accepted a set of articles on modern English poets. He wrote to Shorter on 8 March that *The Express* had accepted an article and that he was considering writing something for *The Saturday Review*. His two books of poetry were also in the process of being published: early in 1919 Beaumont issued two limited editions (one of thirty, the other of two hundred copies) of *Images of War*, while Allen and Unwin issued an expanded edition in December; in June 1919, Elkin Matthews published *Images of Desire*. The Egoist Press published *Images* in September 1919, a volume which included poems in both *Images of War* and *Images of Desire*. Before the year was out the Four Seas Company in America published a similar combined volume, *War and Love (1915–1918)*.

Bryher's father, Sir John Ellerman, and Clement Shorter, whom Aldington had come to know through H.D. and Bryher's family, were crucial figures in enabling Aldington to move from his prewar position as a poet associated with an influential but small, elite journal (*The Egoist* never had a circulation of more than a few hundred readers) to a position as a writer with a broad range who could produce articles as well as verse and translations for general as well as specialized periodicals with wide circulations. Shorter published six of Aldington's articles on his experiences in wartime France in *The Sphere*, but much more importantly Shorter introduced Aldington to a number of older men, established journalists mostly of Aldington's father's generation, who were willing to take him on as a regular contributor. Probably sometime in late March or early April Ellerman wrote on Aldington's behalf to Bruce Richmond, editor of *The Times Literary Supplement*, in which Ellerman held a large block of shares. On 19 April 1919 Aldington wrote Lowell that 'strictly, *entre-nous*, there is a chance of my getting on The Times in a literary capacity. But there's nothing settled.' On 5 May 1919 he wrote to Lowell briefly: 'I've been taken on by Times Litt. Supp. as their critic of French literature.'

Aldington's efforts to establish himself were in part a result of his sense that work was essential to steady him emotionally after his experiences of the war years. He was also responding naturally to the practical problem of earning a living, and part of that challenge was the hope that he might need to support not only himself but a woman and a baby.

In early March 1919, H.D. was exhausted by her bout of influenza, but recovering steadily and amazingly rapidly. Despite her nervousness and emotional and physical vulnerability, she had deep inner resources, mental and physical, on which she could rely in times of intense stress. Throughout her life it was not so much during periods of tension and pressure as after that H.D. needed to rely on others for help. Her severe depression after the death of her baby in 1915 was characteristic of this pattern of response. In an undated letter to Bryher in March 1919, H.D. wrote from St. Faith's that 'the doctor said I have had pneumonia – of a sort – it was your fruit and flowers that persuaded me to pull through. I feel much better. ...' Despite this gracious acknowledgment of Bryher's presents, H.D. certainly 'pulled through' for many reasons. In the same letter to Bryher, who was away from London at her family's country house for most of March and April, H.D. discouraged Bryher from visiting her and wrote of Aldington's Anacreon and Bryher's novel as well as of Bryher's own health and the health of her parents. H.D. thus seems to have been in good spirits just before her baby's birth. Aldington evidently was visiting her and she recalled in *End to Torment* (41) that on 30 March Ezra Pound visited her as well.

On 31 March 1919, H.D.'s daughter, Frances Perdita Aldington, was born, a plump and healthy child to whom H.D. became immediately attached, for the baby evoked deep maternal feelings. Years later H.D. would recall: 'P arrived with a bird-black mop or cap ... she was two weeks late, so had time to grow and was a very pretty baby, really grown up.'[2] Despite H.D.'s earlier decision, urged upon her in large measure it would seem by Bryher, to place the child in a nursery after leaving St. Faith's, H.D. began to breastfeed her daughter, though she stopped after several days, commenting to Bryher: 'I think feeding Perdita weakened me a little – I have had to give it up + expect to get strong soon.'[3] On 19 April 1919, H.D. again commented to Bryher about the baby: 'Perdita is so very good.

She stays with me most of the day. I am relieved about her "home" [the nursery] – but don't know what I shall do.' Just before she left St. Faith's, she again shared her misgivings with Bryher: 'Everything seems to be going all right, but I *will* be so glad when tomorrow is over. I grow weaker as the parting comes – but I *know* it is best to leave Perdita for the time. She gets more charming – that is the trouble. ... I am torn between a desire for a little place with Perdita + fairy books + Noahs [*sic*] arks and dolls, and a wild adventure.'[4] Bryher, however, was firm and clear about what H.D. ought to do: 'I hope you will be sensible over Perdita and remember you were not given poetry to sit and worry over an infant in a solitary cottage. I am very jealous for your poetry and I will even fight Perdita about it. She will be much healthier and happier for the next year or two in a home. '[5]

Bryher was also now demanding and directive in other ways in her relationship with H.D. While much of H.D.'s emotional and physical energy was going into the experience of motherhood and the recovery from illness and childbirth, she was also striving to come to new terms with her husband: she wrote Bryher on 10 April 1919 that once out of the nursing home, 'I think I can get R. out of his bombastic Victorianism! At least I will give it a try – and if pressure from outside is too heavy, I fear I shall be forced to shout the truth to everyone! I can't stand this virtuous + abused wife business. I really can't. But I will be diplomatic for the present.'

By 'the truth' here H.D. apparently means the nature of the Aldingtons' 'open' marriage. It seems that she has by now told Bryher about Aldington's affair with Arabella, in part perhaps to account for the current tensions in their marriage. H.D. wanted Bryher to understand that her husband's affair was not to be treated in a traditional ('Victorian') fashion, though of course she was deeply hurt by the extent of his feelings for his lover. On 13 April H.D. wrote Bryher that she and Aldington 'had quite an interesting talk. You must not let him discourage you. He is really so interested and grateful for any intelligence – as you + I – he feels the general futility of most people + feels someone who knows Greek + Elizabethans is really a trouvaille [a find]!' On 19 April H.D. wrote Bryher again about her husband: '... R. came. He was in such a strange state of duality. He is so puzzling. But I want to see more of him. I can't rest now till I understand.' Her future to a large degree depended on whether or not she and her husband would continue in some manner to live together, and in March and April of 1919 they were still trying to define what their marriage might continue to be. On 18 April H.D. wrote Bryher: 'R. comes tomorrow after all – so I can get future plans more definite with his help.' But Bryher was growing increasingly hostile toward Aldington, forcing H.D. into a position of having to defend him and apologize for her relationship with him. Bryher was going through a difficult period in trying to separate herself from domineering parents about whose wealth and social position she felt quite ambivalent. Years later H.D. recalled that Bryher 'had talked of suicide from the earliest days, when she came to see me, before Perdita was born'.[6] Bryher was also struggling to think of herself as a writer and to finish her autobiographical novel *Development*, which she was revising and completing in the early months of 1919. Her behaviour with H.D. during this spring can be understood as neurotic, but was nonetheless also unquestionably selfish and manipulative.

H.D.'s letters to Bryher in the first weeks of April 1919 are constantly encouraging in evident response to Bryher's own self-doubt and deep insecurities; they suggest how careful and controlled H.D. had to have been to focus on Bryher and her needs at a particularly difficult time for H.D. herself. H.D.'s letter to Bryher on 10 April 1919 opens: 'I think the chapter [of *Development*] excellent – really a good contrast. Do go on as well as you can. We will try to get away somewhere *as soon as possible* – then you must work. You will get ideas once away – ' Bryher wanted H.D. to come away with her: to the Scillies first, then to Greece, Egypt, the United States. In the same vein, H.D. continued on 13 April: 'Don't get discouraged – everything *must* come right – there is a lot of work for us all. Only keep well – and have patience – ' And on 19 April: 'I think I am getting things clear in my head – There are great times ahead, I am sure. The two chapters are *excellent* – quite in the same scale of intensity – that is what I hoped for. You have only to go ahead now. This is splendid!'

Bryher's own feelings about Aldington were clearly hostile by the time H.D. was ready to leave St. Faith's. As if to force H.D. into an increasingly dependent relationship with her, Bryher now took evident glee in alienating Shorter, who for all his conventionality had been kind and helpful to both her and H.D., and in confronting Aldington, ironically on ground on which she was least strong and he most secure. On 21 April Bryher wrote H.D.: 'I am most disturbed that Mr Aldington is applying the pedantic method to your poems. To my eyes, at least, it lowers his mind. ... Please don't alter a word to please him. ... He has no right to do other than accept thankfully your poems.' On 22 April, the day H.D. left St. Faith's, she wrote H.D. that she had told Shorter that she was thinking of sending *Development* to a publisher other than the one to whom he had spoken at length on her behalf, after reading the manuscript and advising her about it, and continued: 'I have had many pages from Clement [Shorter] who says he hates the sight of me, I have been so cruel to him, and he will never again read a line that I have written.' Then she wrote about Aldington:

> I have had an amusing letter from Mr Aldington. I have evidently annoyed him very much. (This relieves my mind.) He takes refuge in saying that I shall grow wiser with age which is no right weapon to use and one feels his extreme contempt curling about the lines. But I won't give in to his theories and he can't afford to talk about wisdom increasing with years and to publish 'Images of Desire' on top of it. Also one would imagine from his letter that I had never taken pen in hand before. I am so amused that he is reading the studies [Havelock Ellis's studies in sexuality]. I trust they do him good.

Bryher here discounts Aldington's greater experience in life and literature on the basis of poems in *Images of Desire* which H.D. felt and must have indicated to Bryher were inspired by Aldington's relationship with Arabella Yorke. Generously one may construe Bryher's alienation of Aldington as a misguided protection of H.D., but her tone and timing here reveal a snide cattiness and self-centredness that have completely obscured for her any sense of what problems her nastiness to Aldington may have caused for his wife.

1 The sources for this information are Aldington's letters to Shorter (17 and 24 February, 8 and 22 March 1919, UR); Aldington's letter to Martyn Johnson (17 February 1919, HRC); Aldington to Charles Bubb (21 February 1919, UCLA); Aldington to Frank Flint (27 March and 17 April 1919, HRC); and Aldington to Herbert Read (28 March 1919, UV).
2 H.D. to Norman Holmes Pearson, 2 March 1951 (Yale).
3 H.D. to Bryher, 10 April 1919.
4 H.D. to Bryher, 21 April 1919.
5 Bryher to H.D., 22 April 1919.
6 H.D. to Norman Holmes Pearson, 26 September 1946, in *Between History and Poetry: The Letters of H.D. and Norman Holmes Pearson*, ed. Donna Krolik Hollenberg, Iowa City: University of Iowa Press, 1997, 58.

Doughty St.[1]

Dear Astraea/

I've told her. It was very hard and I suffered very much, because – well, you understand. As usual after a 'scene' I can't sleep – have just made a meal of eggs & tea at 4.a.m.! Shall go out when the light comes & get breakfast. Dooley, I feel terribly responsible. Do you understand.

But deep down I feel calm. I wish I could go away for week-end in a motorcar.[2]

Don't worry about me. I shall be all right. Only *live*.[3]

The enclosed letter from the Nation makes one very proud – I hope it will please you a little.

Yrs

R.

1 This letter is undated, but was clearly written in March 1919.

2 A great deal has happened to both H.D. and Aldington that goes unrecorded in his brief letters. Here he indicates that he has broken off his relationship with Arabella Yorke. Apparently this rupture was something he and H.D. had discussed in person and which he promised her he would do. H.D. was ill in early March with the influenza sweeping the country, but by 8 March Aldington wrote Clement Shorter that 'Hilda is very much better but rather weak' (UL). On 17 March, Aldington wrote Shorter again: 'I saw Hilda yesterday in her new place. She is of course very weak but I feel more hopeful about her than before. She is more cheerful. And her courage is truly wonderful; she should have been a soldier' (UL). By mid-March, then, it seems that the terms of the Aldingtons' relationship have once more shifted. On 31 March Aldington wrote to Amy Lowell that he had read recent poetry she had sent him 'in the train going to see Hilda' (HU). Thus despite earlier resolutions Aldington and H.D. were seeing each other and developing a new closeness in the final weeks of her pregnancy.

For her part, H.D. had the added stress of her illness in early March and then the news that her father had died in the United States on 3 March 1919, partially as a result of the tensions of the war years and in response to her brother Gilbert's death in late September 1918. She had moved from Speen to the pension in Ealing in early March, then when she developed influenza, had moved earlier than planned into St Faith's Nursing Home nearby. While Bryher suggests in her memoir *The Heart to Artemis* (191–3) that H.D. in her rented room was essentially alone, deserted, and nearly unconscious and that Bryher single-handedly saved her from death, such does not quite seem to have been the case.

For his part, Aldington felt acutely responsible for the pain he was causing Arabella and longs, as he indicates in this letter, for emotional peace. He reiterates this desire in his letter to Lowell on 31 March 1919: 'I'd like to go away & lie in the grass & rest & sleep for a month or two; but of course I can't' (HU).

3 Despite Aldington's rather jaunty change of tone here, he admitted with some chagrin to Lowell on 31 March 1919: 'you see I'm not at all well; my nerves have got in such a state that I have a sort of "sympathetic" neuralgia in my neck & arms; I sleep badly; I have a "trench throat" & cough; I have ague directly I get cold. This sounds a devil of a grouse, but it's true; only for Heaven's sake don't mention it to Hilda' (HU). These physical effects of the war were systemic and persisted for some time. As late as 12 October 1925, Aldington wrote Ezra Pound: 'It is just three months since I got rid of the last boil on me back caused by drinking water full of corpses of several nations' (Yale). Aldington was acutely aware of the war's deep psychological effect on him as well. On 17 March 1919 he wrote Shorter about his sense of dislocation: 'I wonder if you realize what a gulf there is in my generation between the men who fought and those who didn't? It's a strain being with them; I feel as if I were calling across an enormous ravine to them. Of course I've got to get used to meeting them, but honestly I shrink from it. I can't quite

tell you why, except perhaps that we others have seen all the misery & pain & hunger & despair & death of the world & they, in this favoured comfortable England, have not' (UR). Despite his confessions to others, however, Aldington remained anxious that H.D. not know the extent of this distress.

≈ 88 ≈

Wed. [2? April 1919]
Hotel du Littoral[1]

Dear Astraea/

I got the typewriter all right after all; thank you for letting me have it.[2]

I like your daughter quite well; she is very attractive with her long hair and oriental features. I think you like her more than you say.[3]

Shorter has sent me duplicate proofs of two articles, so I am sending them on to you.[4]

Let me know of anything I can do for you.

Affectionately
Richard.

1 Aldington had to give up the studio flat he rented for March (it belonged to someone who needed it back), and he returned to the Hotel du Littoral on 1 April.

2 Apparently the one he and H.D. jointly owned, stored in all likelihood at 44 Mecklenburgh Square.

3 Frances Perdita Aldington was born 31 March 1919. Aldington has obviously visited H.D. soon after the baby's birth and astutely seems to have sensed her mixed but essentially positive feelings about her daughter. He himself 'liked' the child, despite his earlier reservations. Significantly, H.D. permits him to see Perdita during this early visit; when Bryher first visited H.D. after the birth, H.D. would not let her see the baby (Bryher to Brigit Patmore, 3 April 1919, Yale).

4 Probably 'Books in the Line' and 'The Bookshop at Grenay', which appeared in *The Sphere* on 12 and 19 April 1919 respectively, the first two of six articles Aldington wrote for *The Sphere* in 1919.

≈ 89 ≈

5 April 1919
Authors' Club
2. Whitehall Court, S.W.1.

Dear Astraea/

Thanks for yr: note for £1. There will be lots of change![1]

I think it would be better for me to come along later next week. May S. [Sinclair] wants to see you. She has sent me a cheque saying: 'Will you get H. some little thing with enclosed, considering me for the time being as a sort of aunt.' It is very charming of her. So I don't think you can refuse, especially as you'll need *all* the money you can get. Will you drop May a line & tell her when to come see you? Why not make it Tuesday [8 April]? I'm seeing her this p.m. & will arrange that tentatively.

I will come see you Thursday [10 April], if that will suit.

You are not in Nation this week. Will be next I suppose.[2]

Yrs
Richard.

1 H.D. routinely asked Bryher and Brigit Patmore to bring her envelopes and stamps; it would seem she has made a similar request of Aldington here.

2 H.D.'s translation of selected choruses from Euripides' *Hippolytus* (lines 199–233, 740–85, 1282–96) appeared in *The Nation*, 19 April 1919, 80–1.

⤜ 90 ⤛

Thursday [17? April 1919]
Hotel du Littoral
Moor St. W.

Dear Astraea/

I don't mind abstractly what C.K.S. [Clement Shorter] does or says – the only thing is that the quicker & more dignified we are about it, the less conscious or self conscious, the less we shall be troubled. C'est un situation qu'il faut accepter mais dont il ne faut pas se vanter.[1]

I'm sorry W.B. worried you with it. I told {her/him}! not to.[2]

I will of course try to get you a room. Will a week be long enough? Try to get a feeling of *leisure*. It is excellent after these years of worry. There is time enough. Anyhow I'll see what can be done.[3]

I have been to 'Times' with a recommendation from Sir John [Ellerman]. They are actually considering giving me a job! Don't mention it to anyone – will let you know later if it 'pans out.' And don't be too sanguine.[4]

Affectionately
Richard.

1 It is a situation that we have to accept but which we need not boast about. Aldington was well aware that he and H.D. were friendly with Shorter in some measure because he could be so helpful to them. They could not afford to be less than polite and conciliatory. It is unclear, however, exactly what problem Shorter seems to be causing here.

2 Aldington is aware of Bryher's confusion about her sexual identity. It seems likely that H.D. has shared with him Havelock Ellis's view of Bryher's nature. On 20 March 1919 Bryher had written H.D. that she had discussed her confusion with Ellis: 'we got onto the question of whether I was a boy sort of escaped into the wrong body and he says it is a disputed subject but quite possible …' (Yale). In *Development*, Bryher writes repeatedly of her desire to be a boy.

3 Aldington is arranging to get a room for H.D. at the Hotel du Littoral. Apparently it is only at this point that H.D. has definitely decided to be with Aldington after leaving St. Faith's. She does not, however, want to remain long in London after she leaves the nursing home. As soon as the baby is settled in the nursery, H.D. intends to visit Cornwall with Bryher for a few weeks. On 19 April 1919 Aldington wrote to Amy Lowell of their plan: 'Hilda is better of her pheumonia & has a little daughter – very delightful little creature. But Hilda is terribly ill and thin – the strain of all these years has told on her. She comes out of hospital on Tuesday & will stay with me in town, but she will soon go to the country, probably with W. Bryher. I have to stay in town for the purpose of "getting into" these infernal periodicals.'

4 Aldington was applying for the position of reviewer of French literature at the *Times Literary Supplement*, a 'job' which he indeed got and held from May of 1919 until the early 1930s.

After Perdita's birth, Aldington visited H.D. often in the nursing home: on 10 April (letter 89), on 13 April (H.D. to Bryher, 13 April 1919), on 18 April (H.D. to Bryher, 19 April 1919). On 22 April, H.D. left St Faith's for the Hotel du Littoral, where Aldington had found her a room as she had requested. H.D. was still physically weak but was feeling stronger each day. She settled Perdita in her nursery on the day she left St Faith's. On 23 April, Bryher returned to London from the country and that afternoon H.D. visited her at her parents' home at 1 South Audley Street. By 26 April (letter 91), H.D. had left the Hotel du Littoral for the Ellermans' and had made a definite and final rupture with Aldington. What occurred between the Aldingtons during those few days at the Hotel du Littoral was difficult and painful for them both. Sometimes less intensely, sometimes more so, they were always to regret their parting.

H.D.'s relationship with Bryher and her intense maternal feelings for Perdita contributed to her responses to Aldington during these crucial days; Aldington's responses to H.D. were influenced by the tensions which resulted from his war experiences and by his continuing if vague relationship with Arabella Yorke. While Aldington was clear that H.D. had indeed left him, apparently he never understood quite why. When later in the 1920s he heard rumours that she was afraid of him, he was shocked and mystified. On 7 August 1928, he wrote Pound, 'H.D. won't know me because (so I'm told) she thinks I want to harm her – Christ knows why, since I feel perfectly benevolent and wouldn't hurt her for anything.'

H.D. apparently decided to leave Aldington soon after she arrived at the Hotel du Littoral, and she was clearer about the reasons for the rupture. She had not officially registered Perdita at the time of her birth, and the issue of her legitimacy depended on Aldington's appearing as the father on her birth certificate. Aldington, always and particularly in times of stress, was a martinet about order and detail: H.D.'s work had to be perfectly spelled, punctuated, and typed; forms for demobilization had to be completed correctly and promptly; letters had to be properly addressed and stamped. With his emotional and professional life in chaos and his physical health precarious, he clung, however pedantically and irrationally, to the fact that he was not Perdita's father and that to claim so on an official document was illegal. Such a false claim, if discovered, could cause criminal action against H.D. by the courts or, if he chose, civil prosecution by Aldington himself, and the adultery revealed in such action would certainly be grounds for divorce, if that were what he wanted. But that was not really what he wanted. It appears that he wanted insistently to do the right thing, morally and legally, and they were not the same. In 1929 H.D. recalled their parting in a letter to Pound: 'I put down a lot of myself after Perdita's birth. I loved Richard very much and you know he threatened to use Perdita to divource me and to have me locked up if I registered her as legitimate. This you see, was after he had said he would look after us, up to the point at least, of seeing me on my feet again. I was "not on my feet" was literally "dying".' Although from all available evidence H.D.'s account here seems rather exaggerated, one can perhaps pardon the melodrama in her memory of an experience so emotionally painful. H.D. continued her recollections: 'But R and A [Arabella] had told me they didn't want to marry and I suppose their turning on me afterwards [that is, in a confrontation at the Hotel du Littoral] when I was actually crippled, has put me out of touch with my own integrity. ... suddenly they were howling at me, screaming illigitimacy and what not, and they started it. I mean I wanted A. and R. to be "happy", as R. was too forceful for me and too éxigent.'[1] Amid this argument, H.D.

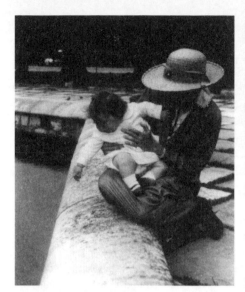

H.D. and Perdita, taken in Kensington Gardens, probably by Bryher, late in 1919

recalled in a letter to John Cournos, Aldington 'literally called up Bryher and said "Hilda must get out of here at once." '²

H.D.'s leaving Aldington was both an emotional and to her a reasonable decision; rationally, she was willing to make the 'trade-off': Bryher for Aldington. It was a decision about which she was to have mixed feelings for the rest of her life. H.D. understandably felt a measure of guilt as well as regret. She sensed the effects of the war on Aldington, but felt powerless to help him. In the above letter to Pound, she declared, 'it was madness in London [in April 1919] to see him look out at me through a strange great hulk of strange passion and disintegration'. She recalled in a letter to Glenn Hughes in June 1929 'the horrible years of the war and the dreadful break-down he [Aldington] had then, and that I in a different way, shared in'.³ She defended herself to Pound, however, in an earlier letter: 'I was quite unprepared for the experience. I mean the terror of feeling that that wadge of bird-feathers and petticoats [Perdita] HAD to be protected. The freedom of my spirit ... [*sic*] went. I was no longer free.'⁴

Aldington did not want H.D. to leave him, but if what she wanted was divorce, he must have felt that the 'facts of the case' should be clear; such a conviction seems yet another reason for his wanting Gray's name on Perdita's birth certificate. Aldington also felt caught between H.D. and Arabella. Earlier (see letter 6) he felt that he loved and wanted both women and was unwilling to choose between them; he now felt incapable of choice. In 1929 in a letter to George Plank, who had known both the Aldingtons when they were still living together, H.D. remembered that at the Hotel du Littoral, 'He appealed to me, "I shall go mad between the TWO of you, it MUST be one or the other." It seemed feasable all round to step out completely.'⁵ The Aldingtons' final argument – which certainly had much to do with Bryher and Dorothy Yorke as well as with Perdita's need for a family – ultimately seems to have reduced itself to the formal and symbolic act of registering the child. In the above letter to George Plank in 1929, H.D. wrote that in 1919 'Richard had begged me to come back. ... When I went back to R., he simply said "now you will register this child as [Gray's] ... I will just take that slip of paper to the court, and there will be no difficulty about divorce."'

H.D. was aware of the irrationality of this reduction of the complex issues of their relationship, and sought advice – certainly from Bryher, also from professionals. She wrote Plank rather cavalierly, 'The doctor and lawyer said the only thing was to consider it shell-shock, and get on with my life. Well … [*sic*] that was all right. Out of the frying pan into the fire. There was Br [Bryher] to look after and Perdita.'[6] She also told Plank that Aldington 'was, I am quite certain, all but "certifiable" [as insane] that season just before I finally left him.'[7]

Bryher was surely counseling H.D. to leave her husband. She insisted on referring to Aldington as 'Cuthbert' throughout the twenties, a name used during the war to indicate cowardice; Bryher also suggested by it a self-centered Englishness, the stuffiness, pretension, rigidity, and hypocrisy of the quintessential English gentleman. In a letter to H.D. in 1924, Bryher wrote, 'I don't like the idea of your having anything to do with Cuth – there is no trusting him.'[8] Years later in a letter to Norman Holmes Pearson on 10 March 1960, Bryher wrote that she was discouraging H.D.'s idea that Aldington might accompany her on a trip to America. Bryher felt that her role was to make H.D. feel the impossibility of their being together again; she wrote Pearson: 'It is actually the repetition of the time that she cut everything and left Aldington' (Yale). Bryher could be dramatic, possessive, and manipulative, and H.D. did not then feel 'free', as she later wrote to Pound; she left Aldington and 'cut everything' in April of 1919.

1 H.D. to Ezra Pound, undated letter, probably written in April 1929.
2 H.D. to John Cournos, dated merely 4 February and probably written in 1925, HU.
3 H.D. to Glenn Hughes, 'Sunday', June 1929, Yale.
4 H.D. to Ezra Pound, 20 February 1929.
5 H.D. to George Plank, 4? February 1929.
6 H.D. to George Plank, 1 May 1935.
7 H.D. to George Plank, 4? February 1929.
8 Bryher to H.D., 26? August 1924, Yale.

≈ 91 ≈

26 April 1919
Authors' Club
2, Whitehall Court, S.W.1.

Dear Dooley/

Herewith letter that came for you.[1]

I'm sorry you feel ill; but things could not go on as they were. No doubt you think me selfish and unkind. I can't help it if you do. I've done my best to be amiable all round & the result has merely been chaos. I shall see a lawyer & hand the matter over; if you do the same with H.A. it will save us both much worry.[2]

Meanwhile, old thing, don't take things too damn seriously! I'm not going to have my existence poisoned by too much scrupulosity. And I *do* seriously want you to be happy somehow in your own way.

Yrs
R.

1 Aldington is forwarding H.D.'s mail to her after her precipitous departure.
2 By 'H.A.' (Hilda Aldington) Aldington means H.D.'s married self. Although H.D. sought legal counsel, there is no evidence that Aldington saw a lawyer at this time.

In May 1919, Aldington was taken on as critic of French literature at the *Times Literary Supplement*. In June, H.D. and Bryher traveled together to Cornwall and the Scilly Isles for several months; Perdita remained at a nursery in London. Unable to find other lodging, Aldington remained at the Hotel du Littoral until the end of the year; he was seeing Arabella, dining often with his old friend Frank Flint, meeting his father for occasional meals, working hard. Cecil Gray stayed in London until September, then left England for Italy. Aldington went to Cornwall for a few weeks alone in the summer of 1919; in the autumn, he and Ezra Pound, who was about to leave England permanently for Paris and then Rapallo, visited H.D. at 16 Bullingham Mansions, Church Street, Kensington, where she had taken a flat after her return from Cornwall. In autobiographical notes H.D. made in the 1950s for Norman Holmes Pearson, who was then contemplating a biography of her which he never completed, she wrote that in the autumn of 1919 'Richard comes to lunch at Bullingham Mansions and Ezra drops in. I finally exclude both from flat.' She recalled this meeting in writing to Pound in 1929, noting that Aldington 'walked in calmly'.[1] They were not to meet again for nearly ten years, and their correspondence essentially ceased, though there was some indirect communication, through Bryher or Amy Lowell, for the rest of the year and into 1920. In late 1919, Aldington left London for Berkshire. The D.H. Lawrences had lived at Chapel Farm Cottage in Newbury, and had suggested Aldington take it over when they left for Italy. In December he moved in, bringing Arabella Yorke and her mother with him. H.D. and Bryher remained in London throughout the autumn and into the winter of 1919; in February 1920, they departed with Havelock Ellis on their long-anticipated trip to Greece.

1 H.D. to Ezra Pound, undated letter, probably written in April 1929.

➤ **92** ➥

28 January 1920
Chapel Farm Cottage
Hermitage
Newbury, Berks.

Dear H.D.,

This is just to wish you 'bon voyage' and some peace in the sunlight of your Hellas.[1]

Has Constable answered your letter? If they have not taken the book, tell them to send it to me & I will get it published.[2]

What are you working at? Bring back poems from Crete. Don't ever forget that you are the 'grandest of the rebel poets'.[3]

Franky has written a long article on poetic style, contrasting [John C.] Squire with H.D., to the great detriment of the former. It will appear in Monthly Chapbook for March. I will save you a copy.[4]

Yrs
R.

Thanks for the Samain – could you add 'Au Jardin de l'Infant'?[5]

1 Bryher and H.D. left England for Greece on 7 February 1920, a trip of several months.

2 Apparently H.D. was hoping that Constable, which had published *Sea Garden* in 1916 and the imagist anthologies in 1915, 1916, and 1917, would publish Bryher's novel *Development*, as indeed they did later in 1920. She may also have hoped that they would be interested in *Hymen*, but the Egoist Press finally published this volume in 1921.

3 I have not been able to trace this quotation. It sounds very like something Aldington would have written about H.D. in one of his frequent reviews, but perhaps it was only something he said about her which never made its way into print.

4 Flint's article, 'Presentation: Notes on the Art of Writing; on the Artfulness of Some Writers; on the Artlessness of Others', appeared in *The Chapbook*, Vol. 2, No. 9, March, 1920, 17–24. In the first part of his essay Flint delineated fourteen 'Axioms' about the nature of poetry, points which echoed the imagists' various manifestos. He then briefly characterized Squire's work before devoting the last two pages of the article to H.D. He praised her 'sincerity' and natural form, quoted section two of 'Sea Gods', and noted the precision of her word-choice and phrasing, her 'sharp and fresh and clear' impressions. He concluded in words Aldington himself might well have written: 'She has a secret which you are only allowed to guess at, and she calls forth the same wonder and longing that are announced by the beauty of the flowers and the seasons. She may be the most exquisite English poet we have' (24).

5 Published in 1893, Albert Samain's *Au jardin de l'Infante* was a very successful collection of sonnets and elegiac verse. Aldington is once more borrowing back books from their shared library, still in H.D.'s possession.

Part II: the later years

A year before H.D.'s death in 1961, Bryher wrote to Norman Holmes Pearson about H.D.'s relationship with Aldington: 'Hilda is so much more influenced by the whole Aldington saga than we realize.'[1] Indeed the turbulent and enduring affection H.D. and Richard Aldington felt for one another influenced both writers throughout their lives: it had nourished their early Imagist verse and would contribute autobiographical material to their novels and later poetry; indeed, it created intense suffering and important affirmation which shaped their understanding of experience, memory and modernist art.

The letters included in Part II follow the lapse in communication that began at the time of H.D.'s trip to Greece in Febrary of 1920. As Aldington's letters in Part I suggest, there are many reasons for the distance that came between them, but during the decade that followed their differences were certainly exacerbated by H.D.'s relationship with Bryher. Despite extensive travel before the war, Bryher was in 1920 still an inexperienced woman, sheltered by her family from social and sexual relationships. Both dependent on her parents and, in her own eyes at least, rebellious against everything they stood for, Bryher thought of herself as a writer, a bohemian, 'a *boy* sort of escaped into the wrong body ... just a *girl* by accident'.[2] She revealingly saw this 'inversion', this trans-sexuality, in childish terms, and seems immature in her understanding not only of sexual expression and identity but of what it meant to be a writer or a friend or a responsible adult. The sexologist Havelock Ellis, who was friendly with both women, cautioned Bryher about her naive and possessive behaviour as early as 1919:

> As regards Mr and Mrs A., I quite understand your attitude, and (as I have told Mrs A.) since you were simply championing her cause, it would not be reasonable of her to be mortally offended. I am sure she isn't. But she was certainly hurt. That I also entirely understand. It is by no means wise always to show what one feels. With more knowledge of the world I am sure you won't. It is especially unwise to show one's attitude too plainly when the intimate private affairs of other people are concerned. It does no good + may do harm. You see you didn't much hurt him, whom you don't like, but you did hurt her whom you do like! Mr A. has behaved well to you so that it is not your part to be anything but polite + kind to him, reserving your feelings ... on matters in which you are not concerned, except indirectly. Mrs A. has an extremely sensitive and nervous temperament, a beautiful nature + much more experience than you; she can be a most helpful friend to you. But if you wish to keep her, it is absolutely necessary to share her as much as possible, not to put too much strain on her because she is not strong enough for it, + not to absorb too much of her time – or she might fly away.[3]

Despite this advice, Bryher would strive for years to recast H.D.'s relationship with Aldington as a part of her efforts to bind the older woman to her.

When in early December of 1919 Aldington finally left London for Berkshire, where he and Arabella set up household as man and wife, he evidently gave up all hope of any sort of reconciliation with H.D. He felt well-disposed towards her, regretted their parting intensely, admired her poetry, missed their literary and once intimate companionship – and with some anger and understandable bitterness blamed the war and, by extension, the British. H.D. in her turn cast her lot with Bryher: the infant Perdita was settled at the Norland Nursery in London, where H.D. visited her regularly; Bryher continued to live with her parents at 1 South Audley Street but was a frequent visitor at Bullingham Mansions, and when she travelled, she took H.D. with her.

When wartime travel restrictions were lifted towards the end of 1919, an immediate dispersal of literary modernists occurred: D.H. and Frieda Lawrence left England for the continent in 1919; Ezra and Dorothy Pound settled in Paris by the end of 1920; and Cecil Gray soon began an extended stay in Italy. Havelock Ellis accompanied H.D. and Bryher to Greece in February 1920 and remained with them for several weeks; the women themselves did not return to England until May. Aldington remained in the countryside at Hermitage until November of 1920 when he moved to nearby lodgings at Malthouse Cottage in Padworth, south of Reading. He and Yorke continued to live here until they left England for the continent in 1928.

For H.D., the 1920s were an unsettled period during which she travelled extensively (not only to Cornwall in 1919 and Greece in 1920, but to America in 1920–21 and Egypt in 1922) before essentially setting up residence in Switzerland. Perdita remained in England, but from time to time would join her mother wherever she happened to be. H.D.'s mother and her maternal aunt joined the household entourage for extended periods while H.D. and Bryher were in California during the winter of 1920–21 or in H.D.'s flat in Territet, Switzerland. Her life and Bryher's became increasingly intertwined.

The months in America were a kind of honeymoon, an adventurous sweep across the country during which the two women were independent explorers on their own. The California idyll provided a period of isolated calm during which they swam nude together at Carmel and took photographs of each other in which their naked bodies were silhouetted against rocks and sea or enveloped by lush vegetation. In Chicago they visited Harriet Monroe of *Poetry* and later Marianne Moore in New York, where H.D. also renewed her friendship with William Carlos Williams and through him met the young writer Robert McAlmon, whom Bryher persuaded to join her in a marriage of convenience. She had contemplated such a union since at least 1919, when she shared her idea with Havelock Ellis, who had serious reservations.[4] Bryher's plan now was to marry in order to veil her relationship with H.D. (whom she often referred to in print and socially as her 'cousin') and to gain a degree of mobility and freedom which marriage (and the supposed presence of a man in her life) would permit. She arranged to pay McAlmon an allowance (similar to the one which by the mid-1920s she regularly paid to H.D.), but had no intention of sleeping or living with him. When she visited London, he was to appear as the devoted husband as a ruse for her parents. Elsewhere, he was welcome to visit her, but both agreed that he would spend his time where and as he wished. For him, the marriage meant financial security and Paris.

The union did not work out quite as Bryher in her naiveté had imagined, although it did allow her a degree of independence from her family. McAlmon was increasingly frustrated by Bryher's complex psychology. Initially delighted by her enthusiasms and unconventionality, he soon became bored and irritated by what he came to see as silly plots and amusements. He grew angry at what he felt was Bryher's unfair treatment of H.D., whose work he actively encouraged and supported, and he began to drink heavily and to seek out the company of women in London pubs and Paris bistros. His own literary aspirations were never fully realized, but he did record in his memoir *Being Geniuses Together* (1938) and in unpublished novels vivid accounts of H.D.'s life with Bryher in the 1920s.[5] H.D., although sometimes hysterical, is portrayed as admirable and sympathetic. In contrast, Bryher generally appears as a mental case who talks often judgmentally and at length about people and experiences because she is finally incapable of positive action. In 'Some Take Their Moments', McAlmon writes that

Peace was not to be for Gail [H.D.], because of her temperament, and because of outside circumstances ... At first Garrick [Bryher] had got at her through her pity and own despair; but she then thought Garrick so desperate that helped to freedom she would make no demands. Now however she felt Garrick as a strange rodent creature, sucking blood from her veins, emotionally, intellectually, spiritually. ... Gail felt driven and possessed. She couldn't say what she thought. She could not have a simple impulse which was uncritical [that is, uncriticized]. Nevertheless she was powerless. Garrick had her, in several ways. There was the child, and Garrick's money. There were Garrick's real or acted dementias and terrors, and looking at Garrick's taut, hungry face and blankly expressionless eyes, Gail was torn with pity again. Moreover she needed a companion herself. Andrew [Aldington] wasn't there for her. ... Soon there would be no world for the two of them but each other, and Garrick, by seeming to solace and pamper Gail, had her way about most things. ... [Gail] struck out felinely at Garrick often, but Garrick liked her attacks because they proved her nervously wrecked and at Garrick's mercy.

When 'Gail' longs to see her daughter, 'the Lump' (one of Perdita's actual nicknames), the women return to England:

Instinctively the child liked Gail ... Garrick didn't like it that the Lump appeared to like people spontaneously. She had decided that the child was 'her twin' ... She grew obstinate and sullen when Gail wanted to lift and caress the baby. 'The doctor tells you not to lift heavy things. You will break something inside you. Don't be a fool, Giraffe. A child shouldn't be fussed over anyway.'

'Let me alone. It is my own child. Can't I have one simple emotion? Let me alone', Gail wailed when Garrick talked so.[6]

McAlmon is here broad, gothic and vitriolic, but Pound, too, was concerned, and his correspondence with McAlmon confirms the situation McAlmon conveys in his 'fictional' and nonfictional reconstructions. McAlmon wrote in 1926 about his sense that he should leave his marriage, but he offers reasons for staying on: Bryher 'was so upset and tragic' and 'Nerves. My own, and Hilda's, and Bryher's tied-up child-fright. For that reason I want H.D. to "relieve" herself in prose, essays, what not. And she doesn't anymore with pums [poems]. She's scary about her prose, rightly perhaps, but she's scary about many things and always has been. A claustrophobia, family, income, child, etc., etc.'[7]

Like McAlmon, the American expatriate journalist Louise Morgan Theis also saw Bryher at first as amusing, but her patience soon wore thin. Her unpublished autobiographical writings convey the world in which H.D. found herself in the 1920s and against which the resumption of her correspondence with Aldington needs to be understood. To Theis, Bryher appeared childish and dowdy 'in order to escape the publicity she loathed and feared'. Theis found Bryher's flat on Sloane Street 'strictly utilitarian and comfortable, with no ornament of any kind. The drawing-room looked like a men's club room and the bedrooms might have been in a good middle-class hotel.' McAlmon ('an extraordinary character, a mixture of kindness and cruelty, beauty and ugliness ... , genius and stupidity, charm and quarrelsomeness ...') lived there as well, but usually left the flat after a late breakfast and did not return until after midnight unless he was hosting a party. Theis recalled that

On Sundays, when Bryher went to her parents, I used to lunch with 'H.D.', the celebrated Imagist poet, in her tiny flat directly across the street, where she worked all day in solitude. She was really a member of the household, for she came to dinner and sometimes lunch and breakfast daily, and after breakfast took a walk in Hyde Park with Bryher. Sunday dinner with H.D. was not exactly a culinary privilege, for she was no cook ... However, H.D. was ... an enchanting personality and her talk was ... rich and witty ... Perdita ... was brought up chiefly by Bryher, H.D. being too absorbed in writing to be a really capable mother and teacher ... Bryher was remarkably successful with children, getting on to their plane of thought and experience without any difficulty and winning their confidence. At the same time she considered them a nuisance because they meant hard work to deal with, and she was never partial to hard work of any kind.

Theis finally corroborates McAlmon's view of Bryher: 'H.D. did not come to either [McAlmon's or Bryher's parties] because she could not bear crowds and noise. When Bryher remonstrated with her, she always made the same logical defense. "I can't write the poems you expect of me unless I have hypersensitive nerves. You won't get the poems if my nerves are blunted by noise. I can't be sensitive to beauty and not sensitive to noise." '[8] Theis was more open about Bryher in a journal she kept in 1933. Commenting on the story of Sir John Ellerman's Jewish ancestry, she added 'I heard this from Winifred who possibly may have made it up. She makes up many things in that fantastic world of her own ... She told me many times that she felt greatly drawn towards the Jews and felt more Jewish than English. John [her brother] is completely, as ever, under her thumb. The only maternal feeling she has is centered in him ... . Normal things have become abnormal to her and the other way around. She has constantly tried to prove to John that he is more girl than boy ... .' Theis then remembers a dinner with Bryher and Robert McAlmon at Sloane Street in the mid-1920s:

Winifred used to call him the Kitten, H.D. was Horse and I was the Leopard. H.D. was late that evening and had not come over for dinner. Winifred, who never used these names in Bob's presence, said absent-mindedly to me, 'I wonder how Horse is now.' Bob took a full glass of red wine and dashed it into the hearth, flung his napkin down and looking at her as if he could kill her, said 'You are never to use those foul names in my presence again.' ... He said that Winifred was five years old physically and mentally, that she was still in the nursery, that she could [only] have people about who were wooden toys on strings that she pulled. That she must have a nightlight; whenever any stranger came near she must shout 'Nanny, Nanny.' It is perfectly true, though she has her father's mind, a mind that would have done great things in the city, she has never used it, and she has refused to leave the protection of the nursery stage of life! This was my first real insight into her character.

Theis's sympathies are with McAlmon by the 1930s, as well as with H.D. and with Sir John and Lady Ellerman, Bryher's parents. The following is Theis's final comment on Bryher: 'All her vast money is being used in sinister ways. She is completely abnormal, but believes that her abnormality is the normal. That is the real danger. She used to tell me how "abnormal" and queer and unlike other people her father and mother were. They both are, as a matter of fact, very simple, direct people of a thoroughly sound and normal type.'[9]

While Bryher could be absolute, authoritative and meddling, she was also interesting, energetic and witty. She manipulated H.D. throughout the 1920s, the most intense period of their relationship, but H.D. gained from her not only financial security but a life separate from the literary London she had settled into before and during the Great War. This relative isolation served Bryher's ends in constructing and maintaining her possessive relationship with H.D. by distancing her (physically, sexually, socially, intellectually, perhaps even emotionally) from her predominantly male friends (Aldington, Pound, and Lawrence), but it also created a safe space for H.D., a primarily female world apart (in residences in elegant neighbourhoods both on Lake Geneva and in London) in which she could, as much as was possible, begin to recuperate from the trauma of the war years.

Bryher was also quick to join in the craze for psychoanalysis popular among intellectuals beginning in the early 1920s. In the months immediately after the war, she and H.D. were both drawn to Havelock Ellis and his interest in and acceptance of the range of sexual behaviour recorded in his seven-volume *Studies in the Psychology of Sex*. Ellis's sympathies did not generate a theory, however, although they affirmed Bryher's sexual nature (her lesbian interest in women as well as her antagonism to men as sexual partners either for herself or for others) and H.D.'s bisexual desires (her repeated choice of male lovers but erotic response to women). By the late 1920s, Bryher and H.D. had shifted their allegiances to Freud, whose theoretical terminology soon informed their understanding of themselves and others. Bryher's letters from this period and later confirm her near obsession with complexes and fixations, inhibitions and phobias, repression and the subconscious. She jumped to analyse others, to arrange psychiatric sessions for her friends, to make authoritative judgements in psychoanalytic language which also functioned as a personal, even exclusive code that, like her animal nicknames, she shared with H.D. Bryher met Freud in Vienna in 1927; in November of the same year she met his colleague Hanns Sachs in Berlin, with whom she began analysis in the spring of 1928. H.D. did not start her own formal psychoanalysis until 1931 when she began sessions with Mary Chadwick in London.[10]

H.D.'s life in the 1920s was to a degree circumscribed by Bryher and their mutual decision to distance themselves from bohemian, literary London and to establish a counterpart of their own. This world was in some measure a solitary retreat, but it was also an alternative artistic space which had at its centre Paris or, by the late 1920s, Berlin. H.D.'s erotic life during this decade followed a parallel pattern; her lesbian love for Bryher with its 'forbidden' qualities set up a secret and exclusive world, while her continuing relationships with men drew her back, on the one hand, to London and her former life, while on the other they initiated a series of different heterosexual relationships which were at some level ancillary to her relationship to Bryher, who often encouraged them, in part because of her fondness for intrigue and in part in order to control them and to bind H.D. to her.

Specifically, H.D. developed an obsessive but unrealized passion for Peter Rodeck, a man she met on the boat to Greece in 1920. Alone on deck one evening, she experienced a surreal conversation with him. This fantasy embodied her heterosexual desires for several years. In December 1926, however, H.D. met Kenneth Macpherson. Early in 1927, they became lovers and began to make films together in Territet. Conveniently, McAlmon decided in December of 1926 that life with Bryher was overwhelming, and he left for America. In June 1927, Bryher divorced McAlmon and on 1 September of the same year she married Macpherson. This non-sexual union served to mask his relationship with H.D. and was happier than Bryher's first marriage; she and Macpherson had more in common, and his interest in film fascinated her. Together with H.D. in July 1927, the three founded *Close-Up*, the first periodical seriously to discuss this new art. Bryher had been thinking for some time of legally adopting Perdita, a condition she insisted upon as a necessity to 'protect' her from Aldington and as a prerequisite to funding her education and an independent life (Bryher wanted no possible interference from 'outsiders' in situations which concerned her money). In the spring of 1928, the child who had always thought of herself as Aldington's daughter became Frances Perdita Aldington Macpherson. By the autumn of that year, H.D. found that she was once again pregnant; this time, there was no question of keeping the child and recapitulating her experiences of 1918–19, and in November she had an abortion in Berlin. Her relationship with Macpherson still had intensely passionate moments and they would continue to work together on films, but his nature was predominantly homosexual, and by now H.D. was probably also having an affair with a new lover, Stephen Guest, who spent the Christmas of 1928 with her in Switzerland.

Such unconventional sexual relationships expressed and complicated the tensions and complex psychologies of the two women who were still struggling to establish a life for themselves. Bryher's friendship with H.D. was never a settled 'Boston marriage'. Neither was sufficiently self-confident, independent or traditional to accept such a model of lesbian life. Bryher's need to control conflicted finally with H.D.'s need for both physical and emotional separateness. Bryher's childish nature (which could often charm others and drive her to new enthusiasms) did not encourage deep or mature sexual understanding or expression. H.D.'s own sexuality was an integral part of her womanhood. She may have appeared 'spiritual' or even 'repressed' to herself, her lovers and her analysts, but her sexuality was a defining element both of her female nature and her art. In contrast, Bryher often appears as an imp, an inexperienced child of indeterminent gender whose various enthusiasms and demands are passionate but fleeting. Freud may in the 1930s have found H.D. a classic bisexual, an interpretation she develops in her memoir *Tribute to Freud* (1956) and in her letters to Bryher during the period of analysis; certainly such an interpretation would have gratified Bryher who was never, no matter how hard she tried, able to induce in H.D. her own antipathy to heterosexual men. But H.D.'s friendships, her relationship with Aldington primary among them, in which sex often played an important part, were more enduring and important to her than Bryher ever understood. H.D.'s affairs with Macpherson (whose sexual confusion she explores in her experimental novella *Nights*, written under the pseudonym John Helforth in 1935) and with Guest (who was simultaneously having an affair with Brigit Patmore) are finally rather messy arrangements whose significance for H.D. seemed ultimately to lie in their impossibility, their restlessness, their connection to other people in her circle. Underneath all of these tensions and present relationships ran the current of her abiding interest in Aldington, with whom she recognized that she had experienced perhaps yet another impossible relationship but one which she needed at some level to return to and to renegotiate in both her life and her writing.

While H.D. and Aldington did not write to or see each other between 1919 and 1929, H.D. at least was eager for information about his health, his work, his lovers, his attitude towards her. In part, her curiosity, kept secret from Bryher, in news or gossip about her husband was a means of continuing to work out her separation from him in ways that did not involve Bryher, who had her own distorted version of Aldington as a threatening, blustering, sexually repellent Englishman. H.D.'s interest seems also to have been entirely genuine: she continued to love Aldington and perhaps to need him; she may well have needed to reassure herself of the real Aldington, the alternative to the myth she pretended to share with Bryher in her presence and in their correspondence. Thus H.D.

joked with Bryher about the version of Aldington Bryher created, but privately tried to define and nourish her own understanding of the man she continued to care for deeply.

Evidence of this duality and of the depth of H.D.'s feelings for Aldington appears in her correspondence with Brigit Patmore between 1922 and 1925. In 1918, Brigit allied herself with H.D. in a process of rejecting Aldington which may well have started earlier when he began his affair with Dorothy Yorke. Like H.D., Brigit must have felt spurned by Aldington's passion for another woman. Additionally, she had come to H.D.'s aid during her pregnancy with Perdita. Bryher initially accepted Brigit's status in H.D.'s life, indicating her approbation by the nickname 'Mimosa'. Brigit's affections shifted after 1926, when she realised that Aldington was unhappy in his domestic arrangements and that there was still chemistry between them. This shift probably coincided with Bryher's finally acknowledged hostility towards her, which seems to have surfaced at the time of the publication in 1926 of Brigit's *roman à clé*, *This Impassioned On-Looker*, in which Bryher is portrayed as a spoiled child while H.D. clearly has the author's sympathies. Bryher's rejection of Brigit is also evident in her trying to pass her on to McAlmon as a woman who would pacify him and simultaneously fulfil what to Bryher seemed their shared and flagrant animal needs. McAlmon at least has left a record of his outraged feelings in this situation. He wrote to H.D. in 1930: 'I have a curiosity as to why Bryher did not think I had a perfect right to want freedom from an artificial circumstance of hysteria, backwash of other people's lives … . Certainly the presenting of the mangy Brigit to me … gave me a grand idea of what she thought would suffice to keep me in leash.'[11] Earlier, however, Brigit wrote regularly to Bryher about Cecil Gray (from whom both wanted child-support payments, which were never forthcoming) and occasionally snidely mentioned Aldington (when she encountered him at a London poetry reading, she commented that 'R. looks common somehow – coarsened – an inclination of middle waistcoat button to protrude').[12] With H.D., however, Brigit shared any news she could discover about Aldington, ostensibly because of the possibility of a legal separation. But H.D. insisted to Brigit, 'It is only a matter of separation. I never drempt of divorse [*sic*]'; she felt uneasy about Aldington, but 'Perhaps [her response was] just a PHOBIA', and she urged Brigit to 'Keep friendly [with him] if possible and try to find out any "dirt".' In response to Brigit's writing that she once saw him coming out of the British Museum but did not speak with him, H.D. wrote, 'I am still rampantly curious to know what he is up to. He turns out such quantities of articles now. I can't think how he does it.'[13]

H.D. also turned to her friend the American artist George Plank for information and a renewed if displaced connection with Aldington. After having seen Plank in London, she wrote to him on 31 March 1925:

> Please do not think now or ever that I want you or anyone to 'spy' … on Richard. It is and has been always my very deep affection for him that has kept me from asking questions. I would myself write him as he asked me (through Miss Weaver) to do some ten months ago. But how do I know who will open that letter? What possible guarantee have I that it is not some lawyer's trick or some try-on of sorts? I myself would be too easily trapped, though this may be the most innocent and heart-rending of attempts to get in touch with me again. But what do I know? I have to protect the little girl first, don't I?

She concluded defensively, 'I just had to tell you in a hurry, before I had time to think about it, how much it means to be getting in touch with the London (which I suppose means indirectly Richard) I knew and loved for so many years and in which I so intensely suffered.' H.D. continued to see Plank as a confidant. On 4 February 1929, she wrote him that 'You were the first person ... that I have even SPOKEN to about R. I except Br [Bryher] of course, but she was younger and rather out of the "vibration" .... I would do anything for Richard, go through any divorce proceeding that he wanted. He asked me before [in 1919] NOT to do it ...' H.D. concluded by stressing the privacy of her feelings about Aldington: '... in speaking or writing to Bryher, don't let her know as she has always been very (justly) hard on R. and I must just joke about him to the two of them [Bryher and Kenneth Macpherson] if I speak at all. Not that K. isn't exquisite always ... [*sic*] they just don't understand.' Further evidence of H.D.'s continuing interest in Aldington appears in her work during this period; as she turned seriously to prose for the first time, she began the series of related *romans à clé* which included *Paint It Today*, *Asphodel*, and *Palimpsest*, all of which feature central male characters who are thinly veiled versions of Aldington.[14] She wrote to Plank that she hesitated to show her writing to their mutual friend James Whitall, now a reader for Heinemann's, who was urging her to let him consider her work for publication: 'something holds me back ... the things I write are all indirectly (when not directly) inspired by my experiences'.[15]

Life for Aldington in Berkshire was much less eventful, but had tensions of its own. His relationship with Arabella Yorke was in some ways fulfilling. H.D. is probably correct when she suggests in her autobiographical novel *Bid Me to Live* that Aldington (Rafe Ashton) found Arabella (Bella) 'a star-performer' in bed.[16] But Aldington needed to distance himself from both the war and his marriage to H.D. and attempted to obliterate both finally not so much with sexual indulgence as with hard work. The 1920s were a prolific period for Aldington as he began to define himself as a literary critic, translator and mature poet. By nature a driven writer, in 1925 he collapsed from overwork, a problem that was to plague him throughout his life. Rest brought with it a full recovery, however, and during this period the short 'modernist', 'Imagist' lyrics which he continued to write throughout the war soon gave way to longer, more dramatic verse influenced by such nineteenth-century authors as Robert Browning, Walter Savage Landor and William Morris. His literary and personal differences with T.S. Eliot, his close friend during the early 1920s, can be attributed in part to his preference for a realistic over an experimental modernism.

Aldington's personal life was more geographically settled than H.D.'s; Malthouse Cottage, a small building at the end of a lane next to the River Kennet and the Avon canal, was simple and rustic. Aldington described it as 'a tumble-down affair ... [whose] strategic position

Malthouse Cottage, Padworth, Berkshire, where Aldington lived with Arabella Yorke, 1920–28. This picture, taken by the author in 1988, shows a bay window added in the 1970s as well as a wooden addition to the left; on the right, the cottage is attached to the malthouse itself.

... was superior to its accommodation ... . It was really beautiful in the late spring and summer. On summer evenings we had dinner out of doors, and watched the light fade and the stars comes out as we sipped yellow Puglian wine from tall tulip glasses.' He added that he doubted 'if the gay twenties with their hip flasks and hangovers enjoyed life as much'.[17] Aldington's income was limited but sufficient; Arabella cooked, typed, and sewed his shirts, and he relied for his reading on his own large library, which included numerous review volumes of French literature, and on the subscription to the London Library which his friend May Sinclair generously gave him. He limited his smoking, while drinking a pint at the Butt Inn by the bridge at the other end of the lane was a special occasion. Aldington went regularly up to London on Wednesdays to stop by the *TLS* office about his work and to dine with friends as varied as the editor Bruce Richmond and Virginia Woolf; for the rest of his social life, he depended on his rural neighbours and on visitors (among them D.H. and Frieda Lawrence, F.S. Flint, T.S. Eliot, and Harold Monro of the Poetry Bookshop).[18] Intensive work kept him alone at his desk much of the time, but he remained a serious walker and continued to explore the local countryside and further afield on brief trips to the south-west. Aldington also began in 1926 a brief and to him disturbing affair with a local woman, Jessie Capper.

In her *roman à clé*, *Several Faces*, Capper offers a vivid portrait of Aldington (as Anthony Sommerville) at this time: 'He looked the typical Englishman, in whom foreigners believe, tall, broad, blue-eyed and fair-skinned ... . he resembled a boxer and a footballer ... superficially' but he also had a 'curious conflict between the heavy jaw and fine forehead, and between the brooding expression of his eyes and the satiric twist of his eyebrows ...'. Capper's love for Aldington was passionate and only initially requited. Aldington and Yorke apparently shared the same feelings about the 'openness' of their relationship that he and H.D. had agreed upon earlier; Capper's Valentine (Arabella) declares that 'Adultery *isn't* wrong – at least not necessarily', adding that it is much more important to be faithful in 'heart and mind' than in 'the body'. Anthony argues for 'sex experience', mocking the old-fashioned notion of 'Two virgins making a perfect marriage'. He is not being frivolous, however, when he points out that 'a man always feels a certain tenderness for a woman whom he has known in that way', introducing from the very beginning of his affair with Barbara (Jessie Capper) the fact of his own past allegiances. H.D. specifically haunts this relationship; when Barbara is distraught at the idea that she may have come between Valentine and Anthony, he declares in words Aldington himself could well have used to describe his relationship with Arabella:

> 'There is no question of "coming between". Valentine is very dear to me. We love and understand each other. But – I loved a woman once before I knew Valentine – not just a passing affair – she filled every channel of my being. When we parted, I thought I should die. Something did die in me. I can never give that love to anyone again. I don't give it to Valentine... . I only tell you this (and even now it hurts to remember) so that you should realise that even Valentine does not fill the whole of my life.'

As if reflecting on H.D.'s rejection in 1919, Anthony continues philosophically if perhaps sophistically: ' "The cardinal sin in love is not infidelity but jealousy." '[19]

Capper's passion for Aldington soon became cloying. In her novel, Anthony tries to explain to Barbara that he cannot see her constantly for he has commitments not only to Valentine but to his own work. He finally rejects her, characteristically in a letter, because ' "I ought to have realised that after many years of perfect happiness with one woman, I could have nothing but friendshisp to give another .... [Now] one's capacity for love is deeper but its scope is more restricted than at twenty .... I have only a husk of myself to give.'[20] Here Anthony confesses what H.D.'s Bella indicates to Julia (H.D.): that Rafe '"doesn't really love me. He isn't there. When he is with me, he is thinking of you .... he loves my body but ... it's you he cares for."'[21]

Towards the end of the decade, Aldington grew increasingly restless – with his isolation in rural Berkshire, with his finally dull relationship with Arabella, and with his gruelling round of translations and reviewing for the *TLS*, writing which left little time for creative work. Years later he recalled that '1928 was for me a watershed year of activity and change, ... which sent me moving in another direction, ... for it seemed to me that I had completely recovered from the effects of ... the [western] front and that retirement was no longer indicated.'[22] Aldington would never fully recover from his experience in the trenches nor would he ever for long periods be happy amid the social frenzy of a large city, but he was eager to escape from English provincial life and to return to poetry, particularly verse which in length and form would allow him to deal with personal issues and the impact of the war. Without as yet knowing it, he was ready to turn from lyric to narrative and from poetry to prose, to begin the war novel which would result in his publication of *Death of a Hero* in 1929. He was taking longer trips away from Padworth: the fortnight walking holidays alone in Devon in the early 1920s gave way at the end of the decade to months with Arabella in Italy and France. On 28 March 1928, they left England for Paris and in April invited Jessie Capper to join them.[23] This time abroad was a pivotal experience of conflicting feelings and what Aldington called in his memoirs 'an exuberant mood', 'a second youth'. Not only was he involved with both Arabella and Jessie, but he had reinitiated a more serious affair with Brigit Patmore earlier in the year and it was much on his mind. In *Life for Life's Sake* he noted that 'One result of idling in Paris that spring – by which I mean I didn't work more than four hours a day ... was a sudden and unpremeditated access of writing poetry. One of the things I wrote pleased me ...'.[24] This was *A Dream in the Luxembourg*, the long erotic poem which he published in 1930 and dedicated to Brigit. She had left her husband in 1926, and beginning probably in 1927, Aldington had begun to see her in London and she in turn had visited in Padworth. Capper portrays her as Rachel Armitage '... about forty-five and rather startling in appearance with her brilliantly henna'd hair and her dusky circled eyes, but she had great charm of manner and immense vivacity, which gave the effect of wit to her scintillating conversation'. In *Several Faces*, Valentine tells Barbara that '"Rachel looks like a whore, and some people thinks she lives like one, but she isn't at heart. She's had a hell of a life ever since she was twenty-two with a vile husband who drank and gambled and knocked her about. She stuck to him till her two sons were old enough to stand alone and then she left him. She hasn't a penny of her own .... Her boys adore her."'

Valentine later reveals to Barbara that she is aware that Anthony and Rachel have been sleeping together, but '"That isn't what I mind – it's trivial, it's nothing. What I can't bear is that Anthony shouldn't want me".'[25] In 1964, Arabella told Walter and Lillian Lowenfels 'I knew all about his affair with Brigit.'[26] By the time Jessie left Paris that spring, she had come to accept Aldington's rejection.

Aldington and Arabella returned to England by late June, but by the end of August they had left again, this time to visit Aldington's university friend Alec Randall, who was recovering from typhoid in Rome.[27] They remained in Italy through the summer, then in early October Aldington and Arabella travelled to France where they met Brigit and the

Lawrences, whom they had invited to join them on the Mediterranean island of Port-Cros off the coast to Toulon. Their plan was to spend the winter together in an old French fortress, a *vigie*, lent to Aldington by a friend.[28] The eight weeks there were fraught with tension and high-pitched emotion of all sorts. Lawrence was gravely ill, spent long periods confined to his bed, irritable, uncomfortable and unhappy. Frieda was conducting a passionate but brief affair with Joseph, an Italian servant. Arabella was bored, frustrated and increasingly marginalized by Aldington's blatant attraction to Brigit. Arabella finally confronted Aldington's waning interest in her; the *ménage à trois* which had included Jessie Capper in Paris in the spring had not apparently included much sexual activity on anyone's part, but now Aldington was sleeping with both Arabella and Brigit in the same house.[29] He had also begun to write the searing war passages of his first novel, battle scenes that he embodied in a vitriolic indictment of the English values which in his mind had sent so many men to die pointlessly. When the weather was fine, he and the women at the *vigie* could bathe in the sea; as autumn approached with its mistral, the house grew more confining and matters came to a head: in mid-November, Frieda accompanied the seriously ailing Lawrence back to the mainland for medical attention; Arabella took up with Joseph, in whom Frieda had lost interest, and together they travelled to Paris; Aldington and Brigit left the island and began to construct a life with each other that would continue more or less loosely for the next eight years.

By the end of 1928, after a brief Christmas in London with Brigit, who had gone to visit her sons Derek and Michael for a few weeks, Aldington had returned to Paris and wrote her of having met Robert McAlmon at the Dôme:

> ... he strikes me as a bit of a rough-neck, kinder unkulchered, and a bit more aster prairies an' cocktail bars than the West End – but .... . The point is ... BOB SAYS THAT both H.D. & Bryher want a divorce!?!! ...
>
> Bob says Bryher hates me so much that she would like to cut off any shadow of hold I have on Hilda; that they wanted both to have the divorce years ago, but they thought I'd be mean about the child (my God!), and he advises me to write to H.D., through Sylvia Beach, & ask her (H.D.) to divorce me .... .
>
> Bob says: 'Tell her (H.D.) you want to marry someone.'

Aldington continued to feel that McAlmon was 'crude' and enjoyed assuming 'a pose of brutality and vulgarity', but wrote to Patmore that

> McAlmon's account of H.D. & Bryher – *ex parte* of course – is rather agonizing. Apparently, *awful* scenes, with H.D. screaming, & McAlmon trying to make peace. He says 'Bryher is a rodent, a little rodent gnawing and gnawing at H.D.'s vitals' ... I just hate to think of *our* Hilda giving up like that. My fault, perhaps. Yes, my fault. Understand, Darling love, I don't ever want to see Hilda again; she made me too unhappy .... . But she was fine; &, if I were rich, I would smash Bryher, & give Hilda enough money to get away from her. Hilda is heavy on my conscience .... . McAlmon said: 'You don't need to worry about H.D. – she don't give a f – for anythin', & she wants to be miserable!' But what did rather touch me was that he also said that Bryher used to abuse me & say I was a great, fat, hulking, coarse brute, trampling on people's feelings, & determined to harm H.D. as much as possible; & that Hilda never said a word against me.[30]

McAlmon himself wrote to H.D. from Paris in the autumn: 'I did meet Aldington with Brigit Patmore and felt that life was repetitive, but he was not the fat repulsive thing B. [Bryher] had taught me to suspect. Sentimental and soft but not unlikable. And really fond of you, really bowled over by your quality. The man hasn't one fiftieth of the calculation that B. has, nor the malice.'[31]

Aldington now began to re-establish his intellectual and social life as an expatriate. He decided to settle with Brigit in Paris; she would be conveniently near London so that for short periods she could cross the channel to visit her sons, while he could begin to involve himself in the urban bohemia so vital on the continent. Early in 1929, he and Brigit travelled south to visit Ezra and Dorothy Pound at their home in Rapallo. Aldington's holiday here was convivial; he met Yeats and his wife, who were living briefly on the Italian coast, and confided in Pound, returning in a way to the roots of their friendship before the war. Indeed, Aldington sought him out as a kind of godfather both to his re-entry into the literary world of avant-garde exchange and to his resumption of a passionate relationship with Brigit.

By February 1929 H.D. had begun to hear rumours of Aldington's changed situation and wrote to Plank of her feelings:

> I hear that R. is all right ... . At least, he is not in any way materially in danger ... . I am glad that I wrote [you] when I did, otherwise I should have slurred things and been casual, and underneath I am not at all CASUAL ... .
>
> It is lovely of you to write about the 'core' of R. being beautiful ... [sic] for that is what so shocked me. When I heard this, I suddenly felt 'why Richard is alive, he is in the world, I might hear about him', just as if he had been dead all this time. The psychic shock to me has been so terrible and so, so beautiful. Richard is actually in the world among people I might meet and talk to. I have persistently cut myself away from anyone I 'might talk to' ... .
>
> It is like my mother dying [in 1927]. I suddenly felt, O my dear how lovely you are. You know, like flowers opening in a corner of a garden, a great bush of white lilac that you had forgotten was there. My love for Richard is like that.
>
> Richard may be a be-sotted fat sentimentalist ... [sic] nothing can cut across what my 'psychic' self or 'core' feels toward him.[32]

By 1 March, Aldington and Brigit had returned to Paris.[33] Within two weeks, he felt at last able to write to H.D. once more.

1 Letter from Bryher to Norman Holmes Pearson, 22 March 1960, Yale.
2 Letter from Bryher to H.D., 20 March 1919, Yale; my italics.
3 Letter from Havelock Ellis to Bryher, 16 August 1919, Yale, quoted by permission of Havelock Ellis's executor, François LaFitte.
4 *Ibid.*
5 These accounts have generally been regarded as biased by scholars sympathetic to Bryher. Of course, McAlmon is presenting the situation from his own point of view, but he was initially attracted to Bryher and his accounts offer the careful reader vivid and often witty insights as well as privileged information about a friendship which in many ways determined H.D.'s relationship to Aldington not only in the 1920s but probably at least until 1946.
6 Robert McAlmon, 'Some Take Their Moments', 1–4, Yale.
7 Letter from Robert McAlmon to Ezra Pound, 3 May 1926, Yale.
8 Louise Morgan Theis, 'Ellerman Recollections', unpublished typescript written in the 1950s, 6, 8, 9–10, Yale. The period on which Morgan is reflecting is approximately summer 1925 through summer 1927.
9 Louise Morgan Theis, unpublished typescript entitled 'Business Journal', 28 July 1933, 27–8, 31–2, 34, Yale.
10 I am indebted to the late Louis Silverstein, whose unpublished 'H.D. Chronology' has been extremely valuable in dating specific events both here and throughout this book.

11 Letter from Robert McAlmon to H.D., 30 October 1930, Yale.

12 Letter from Brigit Patmore to Bryher, 2 February 1922, Yale.

13 Letters from H.D. to Brigit Patmore, 18 February 1925 and 29 November 1924, Yale.

14 *Paint It Today* was written in 1921, but not published until 1992 (ed. Cassandra Laity, New York: New York University Press); *Asphodel*, written in 1921–22, also only appeared in print in 1992 (ed. Robert Spoo, Durham: Duke University Press). At the urging of Robert McAlmon, who seems from his own unpublished *romans à clé* to have been aware of all of these fictions, H.D. published *Palimpsest* in 1926 (Paris: Contact Editions).

15 Letter form H.D. to George Plank, 31 March 1925.

16 H.D., *Bid Me to Live* (1960), 47. H.D. repeats the phrase 'star-performer' several times in this text.

17 Richard Aldington, *Life for Life's Sake*, 222.

18 Aldington himself provides many details about this decade in *Life for Life's Sake*, but I am grateful here and throughout my discussion of Aldington's life in Padworth to David Wilkinson, who lived in Malthouse Cottage from 1971 through 1992 and who has shared with me in conversation and letters much information about Aldington's experiences at the cottage.

19 Jennifer Courtenay (pseudonym of Jessie Capper), *Several Faces*, London: Victor Gollancz, 1930, 223–4, 256, 265.

20 *Ibid.*, 280. Capper includes 'Anthony's' letter in its entirety; from style as well as subject and situation, it seems likely that she is quoting here from an actual letter from Aldington, although no letters from Aldington to Capper appear to have survived.

21 H.D., *Bid Me to Live*, 102.

22 Richard Aldington, *Life for Life's Sake*, 290.

23 Aldington's departure can be dated from his letter to Pound, 17 March 1928, Yale; Capper recalls this invitation in *Several Faces*, 299.

24 Richard Aldington, *Life for Life's Sake*, 291–2.

25 Jessie Capper, *Several Faces*, 317–18, 320.

26 Walter and Lillian Lowenfels, Interview with Dorothy Yorke, Maya Landing, New Jersey, 25 October 1964, typescript by Miriam Benkovitz shared with me by the late Fred D. Crawford and quoted by permission of Isabel Satterthwaite.

27 Letter from Aldington to Glenn Hughes, 31 August 1928, HRC. Aldington added that he was leaving Hughes an introduction to Brigit Patmore, who would be in England through September but would then join him and Arabella in France.

28 In a letter on 14 September 1928 (HRC), Aldington wrote Glenn Hughes that he intended to stay on the island until 20 December, when he would probably settle in Paris for an extended period. Even at this point, before leaving Italy for Port-Cros and before his separation from Yorke, Aldington was considering giving up Malthouse Cottage. Although he had not yet begun the intense autobiographical writing that would become Part III (the war section) of *Death of a Hero*, Aldington seemed ready at this point to make a final break with England.

29 Reflecting on the awkwardness of Port Cros in her interview with Walter and Lillian Lowenfels, Yorke commented that Aldington 'was having an affair … [*sic*] he left my room and went to Brigit's'. Yorke added bitterly that the ménage in Padworth had lasted until 'he got sick of me'.

30 Undated letter from Richard Aldington to Brigit Patmore, probably written in early December 1928.

31 Letter from Robert McAlmon to H.D., 16 October [1928], HRC.

32 Letter from H.D. to George Plank, 18 February 1929.

33 Letter from Aldington to Glenn Hughes, 1 March 1929.

93

14 March 1929
c/o Barclays Bank
Rue du Quatre Septembre
Paris (5)
France

Dear H.D.,

Just before I left Rapallo, Ezra told me he had received from you a letter (he did not show it to me) in which you spoke of me. He answered without consulting me. I gave him one or two messages for you; and since then I have heard nothing.

You know, of course, that Arabella and I have separated, that I have sold my books, and have returned to a freer life.

I was 'out of the world' and in comparative solitude for so long that I scarcely heard any news of you. When in Paris in December I was amazed and startled to learn that you had been dreading all these years that I would do, or might be induced to do, something (unspecified) to harm or annoy you. Dooley, how could you have thought that? Try to believe me when I say quite simply that nothing and no person could persuade me to be vindictive to you or to do anything intentionally to harm you. I have never allowed anyone to speak against you in my presence; I have always said you are a fine poet and a noble-minded woman; I have never consulted a lawyer or have done or said anything which could reasonably alarm you. It hurt me deeply to think that you may have been suffering so unnecessarily from I know not what suspicions and fears about me during these years. Try to believe that my feelings are only those of regret and tenderness.

Will you not let me hear from you?

Ever yours,
Richard

94

20 March 1929
Select Hôtel
Place de la Sorbonne
Paris 5
France.

Dear Astraea,

I am very glad I wrote to you, although Ezra assured me that it would be a 'mistake'! He is, as of old, a curious mixture. I think he thinks he means well, but he is strangely deficient in judgment and knowledge of people.

First let me deal with this divorce business. There is no hurry so far as I am concerned. I do feel, though, that since we have not lived together for so long, it would be more dignified to make the legal separation. I do not think I shall marry again, and certainly I am anxious not to imitate so many of our distinguished confreres who marry for a living. I did not know that a divorce from Paris could be made legal in England. The reason I dwelt upon the English courts to Ezra was because I thought that otherwise an ambiguous position resulted, i.e. that we should be divorced out of the British Empire but not in it. A sort of Ford [Madox Ford] and Violet [Hunt] position.[1]

But I cannot agree to your being the 'guilty' party or defendant. If anyone was in the wrong it is I, and it is you who should bring the action against me. Of course, I would share the expenses. There is, of course, the question of your passport; but I think that's all right. Apart from the fact that it is obviously right and just and convenient that I should be the 'guilty' party, there is Perdita to think of. I know that she has been adopted, but we don't want anything said or done which would hurt her. But I leave it to you to decide which method you prefer. The one thing I feel strongly is that a continental divorce which is not valid in the British Empire is really a worse position for us both than no divorce at all.[2]

I stayed too long in Padworth, blockaded chiefly by economics and partly by other things. It would not have gone on anything like so long, if I had not felt a morbid horror of inflicting any more pain.[3] Only when I felt myself on the verge of spiritual death did I make the decisive step. Down at Port-Cros last autumn with the Lawrences – my dear, you can imagine it. Lawrence, acrid, violent, bitterly resentful of my health, creating a monstrous atmosphere of emotional hatred which was utterly unnecessary. Up in that lonely Vigie, a mile from the nearest house, it was like a series of demented scenes from some southern Wuthering Heights. Most fortunately I kept my head and my temper and a certain aloofness; but I emerged with the conviction that Lawrence is really malevolent and evil. I hope I never see him again. He is merely a Cournos of genius.

'Happy', 'prosperous'? Well, it is true I have worked very hard these ten years, and have made myself a sort of expert on French literature, but at the expense of qualities which I value more. My latest break back to life is an attempt to do something more creative. I am weary of the sterility of reviewing, translating and editing. And the Times is very destructive to one's alertness towards modernity. I have written a good deal of 'poetry' (very much soi-disant) in the past year, but am not very content with it. It is different from the old stuff, but, I think, definitely worse. I know I am supposed to have 'made money' out of my books and articles, but only in the past three years have I made more than five hundred a year. I am giving A [Arabella] 20 pounds a month until she can find work – but when will that be? Rather rashly have turned to novel-writing as a less dreary way of earning a living. I showed the first 30,000 words of a novel to Donald Friede (of Covici and Friede), and he wrote me last week that it is 'great in the fullest sense of the meaning of the word'. I'm sure it's not that, but if he can publish it with moderate success it will be an easier and more entertaining method of hack writing than what I have been doing. One has at least the delusion of writing creatively.[4]

There is a man named Glenn Hughes now in Paris on a Guggenheim Travelling Scholarship to write a book on the Imagists. The idea of this may weary you, but I feel he ought to get some sort of statement from you. He has seen all the Imagists except the Imagist! Luckily I was at Rapallo when he went to see Ezra, and I sent him to [John Gould] Fletcher first – consequently I think he has a fairly correct idea of what happened and will not be stampeded into accepting everything Ezra tried to force on him. Ezra may have 'invented' Imagism but, after all, you wrote the poems.[5]

I was in a very bad state when I came out of the army, my blood poisoned with bad water, and my nerves completely shattered. Recurring nervous crises culminated in what I – and the local doctor – thought was a series of heart attacks. A specialist said it was 'complete nervous exhaustion'. I got better, and incidentally horribly fat, but really I have only had any sort of tranquillity of mind in the past four months. I have managed to get myself 22 pounds lighter, which is something![6]

Friede has promised to send me some extra copies of my Collected Poems, which are very nicely printed, and I will send you a copy. I will also send along a poem which Nancy Cunard is printing in a limited edition.[7]

Of course I shall not tell anyone, either here or elsewhere that we have exchanged letters. It is none of their business in any case.

Don't live too much alone, Dooley. It is good sometimes to come into the world and be distracted. But, there, I've lived so long in the country that I'm sick of it, and the mere spectacle of people moving in the streets is a constant entertainment.

Always yours
Richard

1 It is likely that Aldington counted among those who married 'for a living' both Robert McAlmon and Kenneth Macpherson, whose marriages of convenience to Bryher in 1921 and 1927 provided the men with financial security while serving Bryher's personal ends. Aldington is apparently under the false impression that Ford had in fact divorced his wife in Germany 1911, but that such an act was not legally accepted in England.

2 H.D. gave up her American nationality and became a British subject when she and Aldington married in 1913. Frances Perdita Aldington Macpherson (b. 1919) was adopted by Bryher and her second husband on 11 May 1928. Neither Perdita throughout her childhood nor any but H.D.'s most intimate friends (Bryher, Brigit Patmore) knew that Aldington was not the child's father. In notes probably made in the early 1960s, Norman Holmes Pearson recorded that Bryher told him that 'Beaver never knew about Pup' (Yale). That is, that even H.D.'s mother ('Beaver') did not know that Aldington was not Perdita's ('Pup's') father. H.D. evidently did wish to pursue the matter of divorce at this point. In response to a letter from her, Aldington wrote on 30 March 1929 that he had perhaps established official French residence because he had had an identity card 'for over a year'; he added: 'since hearing from you that a "world" divorce can be obtained in either Paris or Switzerland I am rather against London'.

3 That is, breaking off his relationship with Dorothy Yorke.

4 At the cost of attention to his poetry, Aldington served as the reviewer of French literature for the *Times Literary Supplement* until the early 1930s, translating and introducing an impressive number of French works during this period, among them his extensive efforts for the Broadway Translations published in London by Routledge, including *French Comedies of the XVIIth Century* in 1923 (works by Regnard, Lesage, Marivaux and Destouches); Choderlos de Laclos' *Dangerous Acquaintances* in 1924; *The Fifteen Joys of Marriage* in 1926; and Voltaire's *Candide* in 1927. Beginning with 'The Berkshire Kennet' in 1923, Aldington turned away from from short 'Imagist' lyrics towards longer and more narrative poems whose philosophical tendencies became increasingly developed and explicit. For example, 'A Fool i'the Forest' (1924) takes up forty-three pages in *The Complete Poems*. But Aldington later wrote enthusiastically about his long poems of the late 1920s – *The Eaten Heart* (1929) and *A Dream in the Luxembourg* (1930) – so exactly which poetry he is now disparaging is unclear. His present discontent with verse, however, signals an important shift in his creative focus from poetry to prose. He began work on his first novel, *Death of a Hero*, at Port-Cros during the winter of 1928–29 and finished it in April 1929 in Paris. This very successful book was published in October 1929 and drew on his experiences in England and in the trenches during the First World War, although only the third and most powerful part, set in France and Belgium during the last years of the war, can really be said to be autobiographical.

5 Glenn Hughes (1894–1964), an American professor at the University of Washington, first contacted Aldington in 1925. Hughes had arranged to visit Aldington to discuss the book on Imagism (which became *Imagism and the Imagists*, published by Stanford University Press in 1931). When Aldington left England in August 1928, he invited Hughes and his family to take the Padworth cottage in his absence. Hughes stayed in Malthouse Cottage until the expiration

of Aldington's lease in November and soon after went to the continent. In response to a letter in which H.D. apparently told Aldington that she was reluctant to participate in this project, he wrote to her on 30 March 1929, 'Never mind about Hughes and his Imagist book. ... Perhaps it is just as well that you should remain a somewhat mysterious and distant figure to him, a sort of Chthonian deity like Iphigeneia.' The 'story' of Imagism is complex, for from its earliest beginnings in the autumn of 1912, an understanding of the movement has depended almost exclusively on a history of its advertisement and reception rather than on an account of its practices or actual events and writers. The letters in this volume make clear, however, the extent to which the movement, such as it was, was an advertisement of Aldington's and especially H.D.'s poetry. Scholarly treatment of Imagism, beginning with Pound's own discussion of the alleged principles of the movement in *Poetry* and the *Egoist* in 1913, has essentially involved a discussion of what various other scholars have thought the movement to be rather than a consideration of the poems themselves or an account of who, as Aldington insists here, 'wrote the poems'. Aldington and H.D. were both aware that the translations and modernist poems which they were writing independently and sharing with each other during the summer and autumn of 1912 were written without a set of explicit or rigid principles and that these poems, codified and publicized as 'Imagiste' by Pound, became the illustration of the school invented after-the-fact which, as Pound's movement, sponsored a modernism that increasingly excluded them as it went on to feature male authors and such different writers as James Joyce and T.S. Eliot.

6 Aldington details these experiences at greater length in *Life for Life's Sake*. In 1925, having just finished his biography of Voltaire, Aldington describes collapsing while on a long walk. Afterwards, 'As long as I remained in bed, I felt perfectly well; but the moment I got up and made any physical exertion I felt like a sick puppy somebody has just trodden on.' He quotes a London specialist as diagnosing '"rapid nervous exhaustion"' and ordering '"absolute rest and change"'. Aldington comments finally: 'This psychological disturbance, simulating a real [that is, physical] illness, was a strong indication of inner discontents and disharmonies. ... I ... set them down as after-effects of the war. No doubt that was an important factor, but there were others. I failed to see that by devoting myself to literary studies to the extent of over-work I was frustrating a whole series of impulses. ... Above all I was irritated and oppressed by having to spend nearly all my time in England ...' (267, 268–9).

7 In 1929 Aldington's *Collected Poems* were published in London by Allen and Unwin and in New York by Covici, Friede. The writer and socialite Nancy Cunard (1896–1965) was a vigorous champion of various causes, among them modernism and Black literary and musical expression; her Hours Press published *The Eaten Heart* early in 1929.

As they began to re-establish their relationship, Aldington and H.D. wrote to each other at length about mutual friends, their work, and their immediate life in Paris and Territet. On 30 March 1929, apparently in response to H.D.'s psychoanalytic evaluation of both Lawrence and Cournos, Aldington offered his own interpretation, attributing their characters to '... some very deep inhibition and thwarting. Lawrence is a homosexual who won't admit it, and that makes the vindictive bitterness. In Cournos it is the Jew ... and American inferiority complex, and class inferiority, &c &c. Lawrence, of course, is a great writer, and that makes it all the more tragic.'

In the same letter, Aldington informed H.D. that he had written 50,000 words of *Death of a Hero*; on 3 April, he reflected that '... I should have finished my novel on Port-Cros if Lawrence and Arabella hadn't been such pigs, banding together in a sort of jealous hatred to create an atmosphere which made writing impossible. I fought them for eleven days and wrote 30,000 words, but had to stop finally. I'm now half way through Part 2, which is rather difficult, and then I believe Part 3 will rush as easily as Part 1 did. I know pretty well where I'm going, and I've got the last page done to write towards.' On 5 April 1929 Aldington offered to send H.D. a copy of the Prologue and Part I.

The two writers soon began to exchange books, not only their own work but those by other writers in whom both were interested. In early April Aldington sent H.D. a copy of his *Collected Poems*, for example, while she sent him a copy of *The Bacchae* in response to his request for her assistance in translating Euripides; on 30 March Aldington wrote that, having sold his library when leaving Padworth, he would be 'grateful for any guidance you can give me in making these versions. ... If you have any spare Greek grammars or technical books on the language of the Attic dramatists could you lend them to me?' With such a request for help on a translation project, Aldington recapitulated, probably unconsciously, the professional co-operation he sought from H.D. in late 1919 when, soon to be demobilized, he wrote her from Belgium and suggested that they work together on the Poets' Translation Series.[1]

As part of the process of self-affirmation in the other's eyes, they also exchanged photographs. On receiving hers, Aldington wrote on 3 April, 'I am very happy to see from the snapshot that H.D. is still H.D.' On 30 March he justified his own photo, taken in Rapallo in February: 'I send the portrait partly from vanity, that you may see the reports of my corpulence have been somewhat exaggerated', and added on 3 April, 'When I met Ezra in Rome last year he informed [me] that "all Europe" knew I was fat, and he was graciously pleased to add that on ocular evidence he considered the rumour exaggerated. Then, a little later someone else (NOT Ezra) told me that you had felt a sort of humiliation about it! Hence my anxiety to clear the matter up! What beastly lies people invent.'

Aldington then touched on Italy, always for both of them a country which recalled their courtship there in 1913: 'Italy seems awfully dead to me now. I went there a lot, and was tremendously stimulated in 1922, my first trip out of England after the war. But when Fascism came along and destroyed Italian life, it seemed to destroy for me the old Italian beauty. And I realised later how much the beauty of the world is something we create. Pompeii and Anacapri in 1926 were so different from 1913. I had meant to stay a month on Capri, but left after four days.'

Aldington finally tried to sum up for H.D. his present condition:

I am so very, very glad, dear Astraea, that you feel able to write to me and to receive letters from me. It has given me a healthier inner life. I find it hard to speak about this, for fear of hurting you. All I will say now is that I do thank you.

Paris is stimulating – not because of the people at the Dome or even from the intellectual life of the French, but because it has the energy and movement of a great city and at the same time an easier way of life than that of London. I don't like London much now. Perhaps I may go back there one day, but at present I feel I shouldn't mind at all if a sentence of perpetual exile had been pronounced against me. How does one understand the English? Is there anything to understand? Mysterious problem! I know only that at present they offend and exasperate me. It may be that if there is to be a genuine internationalism in the future we must all begin by hating our countries as countries. In England I feel responsible for public woes and injustices – here I feel absolved. I simply can do no creative work in England.

You will be amused to know that I have taken to dancing. I dance very badly but I enjoy it. That too is a sort of Catharsis. I can see, of course, how very easily it might become a stupefying drug! But it's like the movies – an art which isn't an art. The dancing has been very good for me – I had got myself into an absurd cul-de-sac, feeling too much of an outcast, too removed from ordinary human life and gaiety, an Orestes-like sense of undefined guilt! Your letters have helped me so much to get rid of all that.

1 For a discussion of what such a project meant to them both and especially to Aldington, see my essay 'Joint Venture: Richard Aldington, H.D. and the Poets' Translation Series', *Philological Quarterly*, Vol. 70, No. 1, Winter 1991, 67–8.

⚘ 95 ⚘

8 April 1929
Select Hôtel

Dear Astraea,

I found your letter here when I came back from a walk in the Tuileries and along the quais. It is very beautiful now, with the plane trees just budding, and the willow branches long strips of green, and the chestnuts holding out rather droopy little leaves.

It is good that you can write freely. There is much I should like to say, but you know how tongue-tied I am. What I should like so to say is that I believe I can say quite truly that I am and always have been spiritually staunch to you. That looks rather solemnly ineffective now it's written! But I should like you to feel that.

The things you tell me scarcely surprise me, although in a way they do. I have always felt that Lawrence and Cournos were mean-spirited, rather kicked dogs, you know; and that they were glad to be rather hypocritically nasty to people who seemed to have – did have – so much more than they. Cournos in a way has more excuse. And what you say about Lawrence is marvellously true – i.e. his trying to prove that everyone is not 'normal'. I feel that his trying to prove to me on Port-Cros that I was going mad is a rather serious symptom!

The discussion at the party was of course dastardly, purely dastardly. On the other hand, people will and do say dastardly things. And one must try not to bother about it. I think the 'come back' is this. If the people who say such things are strangers or mere acquaintances, then one says nothing. If, though, they are supposed to be friends, then one should get very careful evidence of what was said, and who said it; and then one should write a letter to the supposed friend asking for an explanation. It brings either an indignant denial or an abject apology. One can pretty easily see whether either is sincere, and act accordingly. Do you happen to know who were the people involved in this particular case? If it is anyone I know, I should rather like to be on my guard.[1]

When I think of us, how little we asked from the world, how unthinkingly we gave what we had to give, how entirely our errors or misfortunes were our own from which we alone suffered, and then think how almost savagely we were both treated – well, I am not pleased with humanity. I am so glad that we have endured, beaten out our storms, come to some sort of open sailing. For you it was much harder, but your courage was greater.

And I think it is important that we should succeed as artists. I don't mean the kind of success which comes from intrigue &c, but that we should do what we want to do, and by sheer power of achievement wring an admission of what we have done. And what we shall do. I feel we still have plenty to do. That is why I was so glad to know that you have two novels 'in hand'. Don't make the mistake of disparaging your work, Dooley, you know it's damned good. If anything is worth doing, it is above all things worth creating something lovely and strong and vital.[2]

Dancing? Mine is entirely unscientific! And I don't venture beyond the ordinary jazz shuffles. I made my knees ache banging them together with the Charleston. I don't know if there's anything very new. I went to a negro cabaret called the Plantation, and latterly to the Bateau Ivre, Cigogne and Coupole – all very ordinary and Montparno [Montparnasse]. But fun, quite fun.

The movies in Paris are dead rotten compared with London, especially the alleged highbrow ones, which are merely twenty year old films leased cheaply. The French films all suffer from the fact that they will make them a series of pictures instead of a motion. They entirely neglect rhythm. But all this you know far better than I – for I am among the readers of Close Up! But I shall like to have the last number, which I only looked at on the stall at the Ursulines.[3]

I don't believe that Untermeyer photograph was 'meant malicious', unless Mrs U was responsible. Untermeyer admires your poetry sincerely, and spoke of you very simply and naturally and nicely to me in London some two years ago. But I'm glad you're having a chic one done for the Imagist history. There is scheme on foot to get a Man Ray one of me.[4]

Montparnasse is dreadfully full. Last night I was out with a small party, and after finding eight restaurants shut we finally had a poor but expensive meal at a Russian restaurant. I expect Montparnasse bores you. Remember I have been practically in isolation for nearly ten years, so find these things rather amusing. I admit that the spectacle of so many ratés [drop-outs, failures] is depressing.

To-morrow I shall get brown paper and string, and send you the books I have before announced. The Hours Press book [*The Eaten Heart*] is rather nicely bound.

Are you staying the spring at Territet or going north or south? I shall stay here until I have finished this book [*Death of a Hero*].

Always yours
Richard

1 Exactly what rumours H.D. is concerned about are unclear here, but Bryher tended to encourage H.D.'s paranoid tendencies and evidently H.D. is concerned about her artistic reputation and what people might say about her renewal of a friendship with Aldington, the exact terms of which are defining themselves in 1929. Robert McAlmon described Bryher's 'tactics': '… she

tackled Hilda, and always produced results. By merely mentioning experiences of the war years or an unhappy episode in Hilda's past, and dwelling upon it long enough she soon had the highstrung Hilda acting much like a candidate for the straight-jacket' (*Being Geniuses Together: An Autobiography*, London: Secker and Warburg, 1938, 29). H.D. was, of course, eager to keep the intimacy and intensity of her real feelings about Aldington from Bryher and, logically, from others generally.

2 In 1929 H.D. had written several novels which she had not tried to publish as well as *Palimpsest* (1926) and *Hedylus* (1928). Perhaps it is these works Aldington means here, or H.D. may have written him of manuscripts she now felt ready to publish.

3 In 1927, Bryher and Kenneth Macpherson began to publish the film journal *Close-Up*, which included poems and articles by H.D.

4 I have not been able to identify Louis Untermeyer's photograph here. He included no photographs in his *Modern American Poetry: A Critical Anthology*, first published in London by Jonathan Cape in 1921 and subsequently revised. In the first edition, he mentioned in his biographical sketch that H.D. had 'married one of the most talented of the English members of this [Imagist] group (Richard Aldington) in 1913' (327), a statement later omitted. In the third edition in 1926, Untermeyer described H.D. as 'the only true imagist', further establishing H.D.'s critical reputation as 'only' an Imagist, then continued: 'Her efforts to draw the contemporary world are less happy. She is best in her reflections of clear-cut loveliness in a quietly pagan world. ... H.D., in most of her moods, seems less of a contemporary than an inspired anachronism' (405). These comments are apparently intended to be kind, but are finally trivialising and unfair. Untermeyer concluded perceptively, however: 'This is a woman responsive to color and pain, aroused by loveliness, shocked by betrayal ...' (406). Man Ray (1890–1976), the innovative American photographer who settled in Paris in 1921, had photographed H.D. in 1922 and again in 1925; he photographed Aldington in 1929. A picture by Man Ray of each writer appeared in Hughes's *Imagism and the Imagists*.

⁓ 96 ⁓

14 April 1929
Select Hôtel

Dear Astraea,

I think quite surely I shall be here in May, & I should be glad to see you. I wonder if the Louvre is not exceedingly public? But if we go to the rooms of classic art we shall surely not meet any 'modern', even dead!

Would it not be well for us to delay any decisive step in the divorce business until we have talked it over. I feel that it is as essential to your personal dignity and independence as to any possible addition to my freedom or happiness. I feel that a false position should be set right as decently and honourably as the world allows. I have told you that there is no hurry, but I do feel the action is necessary; & I should greatly prefer to be the 'guilty' party. If you can divorce me, are you not exonerated even to the most conventional persons?

Some of your last letter puzzles me – we have been out of touch so long that I don't always follow your elliptic expressions, as I can still follow Ezra's. What do you mean by my 'friends' being 'loyal' to you? I can assure you that I don't & won't allow them to be anything else before my face, but I can't answer for what they say or do behind my back, can I? If you are worried about any possible vindictiveness from Brigit, be at rest. She was desperately hurt when you dropped her without saying why, and to this day does not know the reason – for that 'conveyed' was inadequate, childish and untrue. We have talked of you, but she has never said or implied anything resentful or vindictive – to me, anyway. I feel a 'mystery' about it. How you & Brigit can ever have got separated just dazes me. When Brigit ceased to see or write to me in 1919, from a feeling of loyalty to you, I acquiesced most happily, and often thought of the beautiful affection and friendship between you. When Brigit wrote me in 1926 to ask for assistance after the Deighton collapse, I at once got her a book to do for my 18th Century Series, but did not see her until 1928. In our first interview we talked much of you, & only then did I learn with a shock that you two no longer 'met' …! However, so far as you and I are concerned, I feel you may need some assurance about Brigit's attitude. All I can say is that she suffered very much when you ended the friendship, that she does not know why you did it, that I do not think she bears any vindictive feeling to you, & that in any event I should allow neither of you to influence me against the other.[1]

I thought it best to speak frankly. I am not trying to hurt you, but to clear things up a bit. Of course, I don't suggest your meeting Brigit again. Why should you, when you have decided you don't want to?

If you come to Paris & see Hughes, you will learn from him how sadly I have degenerated in the past year – so true it is that the professorial mind is forever closed to the perception of a spiritual Renaissance! After doing no creative work for two years, I have in one year written 2 long poems [*A Dream and the Luxembourg* and *The Eaten Heart*], nearly two short ones, renewed & altered my poetic style, renewed my feeling for life, & written 70,000 [words] of a novel! Hughes, of course, preferred the respectable Times reviewer and Routledge editor! So much for the judgment of the 'world'! I imagine it is general – Tom Eliot, Flint, Herbert Read, Bonamy Dobrée, &c, have ceased to write to me. It is true I have not written to them. I have learned once again that in spiritual as in material crises one stands absolutely alone. I find that loneliness or aloneness alternately desolating and highly stimulating. I have written the poem of the former – I want some day to do the poem of triumphant aloneness, 'the mind its own place'. But how one needs time, that elusive dimension.[2]

I have finished Part 2 of my novel, & shall begin Part 3 after two days holiday. I imagine I shall be expunged from the Times for publishing it – if anyone in England cares to read it, which I doubt. However, the contract with Friede is signed, sealed & delivered, for this & the next one.

Let me know how you progress with your own books.

Always yours
Richard

1 In 1924 Brigit's husband, Deighton Patmore, lost his large fortune; in 1925 she left him and set up house with her oldest son, Derek. Provided with a small allowance by her husband, she took a job selling programmes at Wyndham's Theatre and remained in straightened circumstances throughout the late 1920s. Her translation for Aldington's '18th Century Series' was Jean François Marmontel's *Memoirs* (London: Routledge, 1930).

2 The poem of desolating solitude is probably *A Fool i'the Forest: A Phantasmagoria*, London: Allen and Unwin, 1924.

22 April 1929
Select Hôtel
Place de la Sorbonne
Paris 5

Dear Astraea,

I have been slow in answering your last letter because I have been working desperately hard on my novel. It is a big-scale affair, covering three generations, and needs a wide swing. I have now done close upon 90,000 words, and don't see how I can finish it with less than another 30,000.

Then Nancy [Cunard] came to town, and that always means starting the evening about midnight. I never knew such energy. Admirable, but exhausting to her friends.

Otherwise there seems no particular news. Oh, Ezra is in Paris – I saw him at the Deux Magots, the day before yesterday. He is going to England, so maybe you'll see him there.[1]

Did I tell you I had a long cable from Friede confirming the idea of doing the Greek plays?[2] I'm to begin as soon as the novel is finished. Apropos this, there is one point where I'd like to ask your advice. I have a feeling that it would be good to transliterate proper nouns directly, i.e. Alkestis, not Alcestis; Herakles, not Hercules. I think we agree on that? But in obscure and geographical names it is sometimes difficult to know the precise nominative. Do you know any dictionary where one can find them in Greek? Liddell and Scott is useless for that purpose. For instance, the other day I wasn't quite sure whether King Telephus ought to be Telephos or Telephon. Telephon looked ridiculous, so I chose Telephos. Tell me if you know any dictionary or handbook.

It is curious that people write you how fond they are of <u>me</u> – they don't write it to me, who would be happy to receive an intimation of the sort! Perhaps they do it like the sneezing baby in Alice.[3] But I'll write to some of them later. I was silent because I deliberately uprooted my life and wrenched away from what I thought was stifling me and they probably thought was a career beginning to be successful. Well, I thought I could do better than endless (quite skilled) translations and T.L.S. reviewing. I thought if I got free I could do some creative writing. I have done some and am doing more. But I felt angry with England and its deadening effect, and I wanted to make good before re-approaching anyone there. I wrote to Eliot and he replied in the strain of Mr Chadband.[4] I admit I was peevish about it, but I cared quite a lot for Tom. A man called Hal Glover,[5] who writes plays and is a friend of Arabella's, did what I thought was the right thing, and what I expected of anyone who called himself a friend. He wrote a letter, a very decent letter to which I immediately responded, and we correspond regularly. No one else took the trouble to write. Why should I write, as if apologetically, to them? I've nothing to apologize for.

Don't you find that a sort of moral discouragement and reprehension emanates from the English? They all try to discourage an artist with himself, and they're abominably jealous of anyone who succeeds, however slightly, in the arts. I get tired of being with people who are always trying to show me what a poor boob I am. I really got sick of it. If you knew, dear Astraea, how these people have subtly and indirectly tried to keep me back. It's not a delusion, nor am I suffering from Wyndham Lewis persecution mania![6] I just don't trust them, and when they write you how fond they are of me, well, I believe in puddings when I eat 'em!

However, all this is very unimportant!

As I think I told you, I am fixed here until my novel is finished, and I believe that will not be until June. The typist makes manifold errors in copying the part already done, and that takes hours to rectify. I think I shall probably stay here until July, do a French translation I contracted to do, and a few Times articles if possible. Then, if my money will stand it, I shall buy a small car, and go through some of the French country. Try to find some small place by the sea, and work over Alkestis, and bathe and make excursions. All things I have long wanted to do, but have never had the means or time. Then back to Paris for September and October. I very much want to see some of the smaller French towns and the medieval French architecture. And I have other plans. I am getting towards forty, I have worked very hard and still work hard, and I think I ought to do some of the things I want to do before I get too old to enjoy them. There is Spain, there is Greece – and Sicily. I have not yet seen Sicily.[7]

I feel very regretful if I hurt you and stirred up sad feelings by mentioning Brigit. I feel there was a misunderstanding, an error, and thought perhaps I could clear it up. Perhaps that was presumptuous. I felt only regret that it should be so. I won't mention it again. Only, don't think that Brigit feels any resentment against you.

Let me know if and when you decide to come to Paris, and let us meet – at the Louvre if you wish.[8]

Pilate's Wife is I think a good title, and suggests at once an interesting theme to me. I think it might go big, as your ex-countrymen say.[9]

Au revoir, and write when you think of it.

Always yours,
Richard

1 In late April, H.D. travelled from Switzerland to Paris; after her visit there, she planned to go on to England.
2 Donald Friede (1901–64), the American publisher.
3 That is, only to annoy or tease.
4 T.S. Eliot (1888–1964) and Aldington had become good friends in the 1920s despite their differences in temperament. Aldington initially served as a mentor for Eliot, but after the publication of The Waste Land in 1922 their unequal acclaim and increasingly divergent ideas about poetry and the functions of art in the modern world created an intellectual distance between them which, particularly for Aldington, intensified the unbridgeable differences in their personalities. The Reverend Mr Chadband, to whom Aldington compares Eliot, is the hypocritical and barely literate clergyman in Charles Dickens's Bleak House, whose pedantic style of oratory depends on obvious, even ridiculous distinctions.
5 Halcott Glover (d. 1949), the English dramatist and novelist, was a good friend of Aldington's throughout the 1920s. Like Aldington, Glover had served at the front in the Great War, and it is to Glover, in a prefatory letter, that Aldington dedicated Death of a Hero.
6 Julian Symons writes in his introduction to The Essential Wyndham Lewis: An Introduction to His Work (London: André Deutsch, 1989) that 'There were times ... when Lewis's behaviour would have offended anybody. A desire to dominate, distrust of rivals, resentment of those who provided the financial patronage he needed, contempt for most women and many men, and suspicion of others' motives and actions, were features of his character.' Even the sympathetic Symons calls Lewis a 'paranoiac', and adds that because of 'his extreme individualism' and 'radically critical' philosophy, 'By the end of the twenties Lewis was isolated in the British literary scene' (5).
7 The French translation is probably Remy de Gourmont: Selections from All His Works (New York: Covici, Friede, 1929), the only translation from the French which Aldington published during this year. Aldington reviewed anonymously for The Times; his articles are identified

and reproduced on The Times Literary Supplement Centenary Archive Database. Aldington's translation of Euripides' *Alcestis* was published in London in 1930 by Chatto and Windus.
8 H.D. had suggested this meeting place in a letter written in early April.
9 H.D. had written Aldington about her current novel. The work contains a great deal of auto-biographical material in the guise of a historical fiction. The protagonist, Veronica, is an Etruscan woman in exile in Palestine, Pilate's wife and Fabian's mistress. She loves both Mnevis, the priestess of Isis, and Fabian, who follows the cult of Mithra. Mnevis brings Veronica to a belief in Jesus as Christ at the novel's end because Christianity includes women as Fabian's cult cannot. Thus Veronica, like H.D. in 1918, is torn between male and female relationships and world-views. *Pilate's Wife* remained unpublished until 2000 (ed. Joan A. Burke, New York: New Directions).

⇜ 98 ⇝

26 April 1929
Select Hôtel
1 Place de la Sorbonne
Paris 5

Dear Astraea,

I posted my last letter to you just before your charming present for Brigit arrived. We went and telegraphed to you immediately. I am glad to know that you will be in Paris soon, and that you feel able to see us. Be sure we are with you.

I wired you again to-day – feeling that the intervening Sunday would delay letters – to beg you to see Brigit and me separately or together without Ezra. By all means bring your Swedish friend, if you wish, but don't, don't let's meet under the false auspices of Ezra. I would even say don't see him until you have seen us first. He has the most foolish ideas about us both, and his chief feeling is one of self-importance in engineering the meeting. I feel it would be odious to you and to me and to Brigit. Brigit feels this very strongly. After we have met and established the understanding I know we shall, then Ezra's imbecilities won't matter. But I say quite definitely I won't meet you if Ezra is to be there the first time – afterwards doesn't matter. But this is our affair, and it is important for us to be straight and simple and direct, and if Ezra's there he won't allow us to be simple. Ezra makes me shut up and say nothing and retire behind forty barriers![1]

Forgive me if I seem too categorical about this, but I know it's important. Ezra has nothing to do with the deeper relations between you and me and you and Brigit. He simply doesn't exist there. And his 'view' was so perspicacious that he prevented me from writing to you for weeks, when I ought to have written to you. Apart from Ezra arrange the meeting and meetings how, when and where you choose, just as you want, dear Dooley, and you will find Brigit and me only eager to respond to you in the way you wish.

I write in haste to catch the mail, but feel sure you will see the point.

With all good wishes, dear Dooley, and much affectionate eagerness to see you again (sans Ezra!)

Richard

1 Pound's relationship to Aldington and H.D. as a couple was always complex, and it does not seem surprising that Aldington wants to exclude Pound from this initial meeting with H.D. Aldington is perhaps made particularly uneasy because of the role Aldington had asked the

older poet to play in fostering his relationship with Patmore. H.D.'s 'Swedish friend' was Kenneth Macpherson's sister, Eileen. H.D. described her somewhat cryptically in a letter to Pound probably written on 25 April 1929: 'She is really half-English, half-Swedish, a very odd girl and worth while but incarcerated in her Nordic self and when the other busts out, it DOES bust. It is just possible you might find her attractive. … she is due in from London [in the] afternoon, May 1st' (Yale).

As they prepared to meet in Paris, H.D.'s feelings, like Aldington's in these letters which attempt to re-establish their relationship, were mixed and intense. When she sent Aldington's correspondence from 1929, 1930 and 1931 to Norman Holmes Pearson in 1951, she called it in an understatement not 'impersonal' and commented:

> I had never [before] read these letters in a batch, and I must say they gave me a sense of that time and scene. ... Richard's lot reads so much more vividly than any of his novels, it might be a little commedia dell'arte piece. The letters are not very discreet, but that is their charm. ... I had a sort of authentic Rossetti feeling about that Paris and Italy lot of letters, almost 'dear Liz, come back...' [sic]. There is also a real, dynamic, perfectly English and inimitable Byronic feeling about the décor. I don't think Richard ever really knew what he was or what he did to people. ...[1]

H.D. very much wanted to see Aldington again, a desire implied in her earlier correspondence with Brigit Patmore and George Plank. She reflected on Aldington's letters when she wrote to Plank on 1 April 1929: 'He said he felt he MUST write, so that is that. Nothing will be any different, I will never "go back" naturally, nor would he, I imagine. ... he comes back to life, apparently, having crawled out of his particular bog and his words bring me such peace and the assurance that everything has been for the best.' There were, from H.D.'s point of view, at least two 'practical' issues that needed to be resolved when she and Aldington met: whether, when, and where they might be legally divorced and Perdita's status as her own child, beyond Aldington's legal power or emotional intentions. Less important, but certainly a matter about which H.D. must have wondered, was Aldington's willingness to maintain and even assert the social ruse that their separation was merely an amiable growing apart and that Perdita was their child together and in no measure illegitimate or irregular.

For bohemian artists whose personal lives were in so many ways unconventional, both Aldington and H.D. remained surprisingly concerned about what the social world at large might think of them. They were self-protective for a variety of reasons. For Aldington, always economically marginal, the reasons were to a degree pragmatic; he could not afford to alienate those on whom his professional career depended. As he became increasingly reliant for his livelihood on the network of English and American publishers and journalists who backed his projects, offered him translations and editing tasks, advertised his fiction and – often from a distance – oversaw his work into print, Aldington needed to maintain good relations with his colleagues. Further, the projects which he conceived frequently depended on friends and acquaintances – *The Imagist Anthology* of 1930 is a typical case in point, but so were his translation series and his *Viking Anthology of Poetry of the English-Speaking World* (1946). No matter what personal differences separated Aldington from those to whom he had once been close (H.D., of course, but also John Cournos and D.H. Lawrence among others), he was always careful to distinguish what he might feel personally and sometimes say in private or in letters to a few intimate friends (among them H.D.) and what he would maintain socially, publicly or in print.

Not morally hypocritical but socially pragmatic, Aldington could not afford to be otherwise; he was impulsive in his own romantic relationships and often unwise, impractical and foolish in his choice of lovers (if such matters are ever wholly questions of choice or can be judged in rational terms, which for Aldington they definitely could not be). As Aldington's letters to H.D. reveal, he was also shrewd: he was quick, particularly towards the end of his life, to spot the potentially libellous remark in his own work but especially in the writings of others; he was a compendium of knowledge on such matters as how one might avoid exorbitant customs charges on items mailed from foreign countries or on how to get a driver's license almost anywhere in the Western world; he was acutely aware of the legal ins-and-outs of literary situations and of such personally significant matters as the relations between men and women (i.e. divorce, illegitimacy, alienation of affections, adultery).

In part, Aldington's concern about social and legal correctness stemmed from his position as an outsider, a man without a university degree from a middle-class background (his father was a solicitor, his mother ran an inn in Sussex). Aldington's understandable social sensitivity and defensiveness as a young man became in the mature writer a concern with public correctness (for example in dress, manners and appearance generally) and an often justified sense of persecution as he defended unpopular causes, flaunted convention in his romantic associations or took on the establishment in his fiction and biographies.

H.D. was also a social interloper as an American in England, but her awareness of herself as an outsider depended less on any real or perceived social difference than on gender. As a woman she was vulnerable physically, socially, economically, legally and intellectually. In *Bid Me to Live*, she explicitly states her position. Julia reflects on Rico's emphasis on 'experience', and on 'sex-emotion and understanding':

> It might be all right for men, but for women, any woman, there was a biological catch and taken at any angle, danger. You dried up and were an old maid, danger. You drifted into the affable *hausfrau*, danger. You let her rip and had operations in Paris ... danger.
> There was one loophole, one might be an artist. Then the danger met the danger, the woman was man-woman, the man was woman-man. (135–6)

In addition to these practical and social concerns, H.D.'s personal feelings about seeing Aldington again were complicated by her relationship with Bryher. Throughout their lives, Bryher manipulated H.D.'s awareness of her real vulnerability as a woman (a female expatriate, a woman writer, a mother, a wife, a single woman) in order to increase H.D.'s dependence on her. In part, Bryher projected her own insecurities onto H.D. Bryher would consciously attribute her sense of others' rejection of her or interest in her to their perception of her wealth. In Bryher's eyes, H.D. was also in danger of being misperceived, misunderstood, but the reasons were different: H.D. was economically unstable (actually, H.D. was increasingly economically secure as a result of her brother's careful investment of her inheritance); H.D. was emotionally fragile, physically delicate. While H.D. was unquestionably highly-strung and potentially nervous, she was also more durable (and thus less dependent on Bryher) than Bryher liked to think. H.D. further needed a privacy and separateness from Bryher, which the younger woman was reluctant to allow. H.D. was thus in an awkward and stressful situation for innumerable reasons when she met Aldington again in Paris on 1 May 1929.

Anticipating the experience and hoping to avoid meeting Pound in Paris (evidently H.D. shared Aldington's concerns), she wrote to her old friend:

> Please give me fair warning if you could or should be able to see me somewhere [in Paris in May]. I mean I am very old and very, very tired. I put down a lot of myself after Perdita's birth. I loved Richard very much. ... I mean, anything in the way of a shock brings that

[experience of 1919] back and I go to pieces ... [*sic*] that is why I kept away from you all. I was growing a sort of wall between myself and myself and when I heard R[ichard] and A[rabella] had parted, for some reason the wall fell down. All of me has been growing like an éspalier tree, trained and supported and blossoming too, but trained against a wall. One side of me is rich and creative, the other has not yet had time to let the Sun get to it ... [*sic*]

... I am so old, and look so different. I am so ashamed of myself, of my face and even my body sometimes ... [*sic*] I seem to remember always the indignity of being unsheltered and then the treachery of the betrayal. It doesn't make any difference to my LOVE and I will always love Richard. But you see it built up a wall ... [*sic*] and this side and that side of the wall are so very different. ...

... I want R. to know that THIS time, I want to make up for anything he may have thought disloyal in me. ...

I heard it 'whispered' that H.D. was 'hanging on to Aldington out of spite'. I am not. I was hanging on because I was 'winged', I had no place in the air and no place on earth. Now maybe I have a place in the air and a place on the earth ... [*sic*] and I want to make things as right as I can for R. or anyone he happens to love or wanted to marry.

About Bgt [Brigit]. I hadn't seen her for a long time as Bryher could not stand her. ... I have no feeling at all ... [*sic*] only here I am, with a very static and 'classic' and peaceful relationship with Bryher and Macpherson. I admit, I am at times very lonely, not that they do not understand, they just ARE not of that cycle and I was made by that pre-war London atmosphere and cycle. ... Br, between ourselves, has been in a very difficult way and is going through a trying 'analysis'. She is a 'border line case', so that sometimes I seem actuated by weakness in giving in to her. ... Br looked after Perdita and as that seemed to be the only thing I was hanging on for ... [*sic*] I looked after Br. ...

I couldn't bear to see you ... [*sic*] not just for the moment. I should cry and cry or else I should present a quite convincing sort of tin exterior ... [*sic*] that wouldn't get either of us anywhere. Just write me now and again ... [*sic*] it will do me more good. When I get a little used to things and to myself and to the idea of things being 'there' for me still the other side of the wall, I will be more presentable. It is a shock to me really to find I love Richard.

I suppose something of him has been there all the time ... [*sic*] it seemed fogged over. ... I am so glad he is working.[2]

H.D. was very agitated about the visit to Paris and unsure of herself in relation to her friends from the London 'cycle'. She wrote to Pound again on 21 April 1929:

I go to-morrow to the sleeping-car people and will try to get through [to Paris] about Tuesday, April 30, or possibly the Monday. I will write you at once but <u>do not let people know</u>. I will try to see you and may not even be able to see Richard. But I have been writing R. Things are rather odd. ... I expect I will be seeing R. and will write him but am writing you first. I will see you first anyhow. I will probably go to:

Auberge du Navigateur

49, quay des Grands Augustus

Paris VI

... I am very nervous about going and not very happy. ... I think it best not to see Bgt. this time but do not get me 'wrong' about that. I must see clear and am there for such a very tiny little while. R. wrote me that I had 'hurt' Bgt. horribly and all that. Well. ... [*sic*] I can hardly go into it now, but I sent back word through R. that of course I was sorry and would like to see Bgt. later if I came to Paris. But I cannot face seeing her until I <u>DO</u> get the thing straight a little with R. first.

On 25 April H.D.'s plans were more clearly in place and she wrote to Pound again: '... we are due May 1st. I may not be able to face seeing R. and B. the first day so have written Bgt. that I may be delayed until the 2nd.' After arranging to meet Pound for tea on the day of her arrival in Paris, H.D. added: 'But I feel so much better hearing direct from Bgt. and R. However, it is like a sort of tidal wave, the wave is gone and I am happy and at peace with myself, but something of the original shock comes back thinking of R. again.'

The events of the past, particularly the incidents of 1917–19 and her own and others' interpretation of these experiences, made H.D. very tense as she conveys in these letters to Pound through the powerful metaphors of the 'wall between myself and myself' and the 'tidal wave' whose aftermath is both calm and trauma. H.D.'s language itself, riddled with violent words such as 'treachery', 'betrayal' and 'disloyal', and the more concrete 'shock' as well as the repeated 'love', reveals her state as she prepared to see Aldington again for the first time in nearly a decade.

The time together in Paris apparently went well for both writers. They managed to see each other frequently, and Brigit Patmore left unexpectedly for a few weeks in London on 4 May.[3] In an undated letter to Patmore probably written on 8 May Aldington described his situation:

Quite a good séance with H.D. and Egon [Eileen Macpherson, Kenneth Macpherson's sister who joined H.D. in Paris] last night. I was met at the hotel by Egon, who said H.D. had gone on because she was tired. We discovered her in the remotest recess of the Rotisserie with her back carefully turned on the world. She was very nervous and high-laughing at first, but got better as things went on. Apparently, they had a lovely time with Ezra & Henry [Crowder, the black jazz musician] in the taxi. Henry said: 'Pray, Ezra', & Ezra invented a long prayer about Jordan, & Henry kept shouting 'Halleluia!' and uttering his marvellous laughs. They did want to come to the Plantation!

After dinner I took them to the Cigogne, & H.D. actually danced, with Egon & with me. Egon is a marvellous dancer. ... She said: 'How pleasant. You don't dance like an English-man.' I said: 'That's because I don't know any steps.' The negro has gone from the Cigogne, & the band is already getting bad. Some perfectly awful French commercial travellers came in, so we got a taxi & went to the Soufflet, which was nearly empty. So I gave the band 10 fr., & they played all the jazz we could think of, & none of those damned tangos. I liked Egon much more, & think she is very good for H.D. She doesn't seem inhibited as H.D. is. We said good-bye very respectably at midnight. They leave to-morrow morning.

Still, the visit was naturally also stressful for Aldington. In addition to resurrecting for him many complex feelings towards H.D., this meeting was also threatening to Brigit. As in the letter quoted above, Aldington is careful with Brigit not to suggest that he and H.D. are sexually attracted. Rather, in this case, he implies that any passing flirtation that may have existed was between himself and 'Egon'. He adds, for instance, at the end of this letter, 'Egon said I looked "beautiful"! Are you jealous? Please be – a little!' In a letter written to Patmore on 14 May 1929, he admits bluntly that 'it has been rather a strain seeing H.D.'

It was certainly stressful for H.D., but it was also restorative. On 30 May 1929, she reflected at length in a letter to George Plank:

I did get over to Paris on the first of May and things were very odd, very lovely and most inexplicable. I mean Richard was exactly as he was before the war, it was as if some landslide had taken place in his being, which in fact it has. We saw much of each other though always with others ... [*sic*] I was afraid of too much intimacy and he was altogether charming and dear. If we ever DO manage a separation, it will be simply because we are so fond of one another that we want to feel unhampered by any past or any legal obligation. ... He says he was 'dead' for ten years. ... Things are absolutely right and much fear and suppressed phobia is removed from me. I will feel straight with things again.

... It is strange to think of him 'back' again. He speaks so beautifully of the past and the ridiculous little times we used to have. Instead of forgetting, all his memories and loyalties seem to have been strangely embalmed ... [*sic*] a funny way to put it, but there they all are, perfectly fresh and untouched, the minutest details startlingly preserved, and fresh and fragrant with none of the intervening dust. ...

From London, H.D. wrote Plank again about her time in Paris: 'R. is so odd, so reflexive. He was on his own for a bit, his lady [Brigit] had gone to London, and then it was that we had those marvelous miraculous times together. I was with a girl [Eileen Macpherson] who loved him and he is so quick to respond. It was all so unexpected and beautiful ... [*sic*] then he is with someone else and becomes another person, rather watchful. ... The Richard we knew IS there, O so beautifully. ...'[4]

Clearly H.D. was very happy to have renewed her friendship with Aldington; she was delighted by his personality and by the remembered experiences which linked them both to a shared past. She was also surprised – by Aldington's charm, discretion, sensitivity, vivacity, gentleness, kindness. The impression she had formed of him during the intervening decade was quite at odds with the reality she discovered in Paris; the tensions in their relationship as a result of his affair with Yorke, of Perdita's birth and of his shell-shock during the last year of the war had dissolved, and H.D. found that the boorish, dangerous and cowardly Englishman whom Bryher had led her to believe she had married was a totally inaccurate representation of Aldington.

H.D. could not, however, write to Bryher as she wrote to Plank. The two women had developed in their correspondence during the 1920s a highly coded language and a mannered, gossipy intimacy which depended on an agreed-upon mythology. H.D. did not violate these conventions in her reports from Paris. Her letters to Bryher during May 1929 thus convey a vivid but slanted impression of the visit as H.D. tries both to reassure her friend and to provide nearly daily summaries. As soon as she got settled, H.D. wrote Bryher that while waiting in the hotel for Eileen Macpherson to arrive from London,

R. and Bgt. came in to call. They both seemed half-people, nothing to fear, R.A. oddly devitalized, neither good nor bad but seemed wanting to be 'friendly', very Anglais and hating Angleterre, hating and hating it. E. [Ezra Pound] came at the same time and I had to hide E. and let them escape. E. took me to a place on the Isle [Ile de la Cité], very pretty and high up and there I told E. all details. He was terribly nice, very big and bulky and fat and very kind. He told me R. had fallen for Nancy [Cunard] and N. had re-vitalized him but N. was bored with him more than a day on end and that he had 'winged' Bgt. in the hunt for N. ... E. was full of dirt ... E. is coming to take Egon and me out to dinner but so far there is no Egon. Bgt. and R. take us to dinner to-morrow. R. is making much money but E.P. says his work all badly received in States and elsewhere, 'he is where he was 15 years ago'. R. seems oddly young and harmless, I could not believe that mild flanneled Anglaise [*sic*] was the former Villain in military medals. ... Mrs Mimosa [Brigit], E. tells me, is still carrying on with Stephen [Guest]. She is going back to London for a week on Monday [6 May]. But returning ... [sic] I told her I was leaving on Wed. [8 May] so Cuth

[Aldington] will have all his poetic raptures for Nancy. ... R. is dead afraid still of London divorce. I told him it could be done, he said 'there is risk for <u>you</u> because of your Cheeeeild'. ... Mrs Mimosa, E. says, is really too bored to marry or not to marry. She just doesn't care. But E. says R. is making the 'English gentleman' gesture. Well, E. was quite nice. ... He was really very kind ... [sic] and gave me nice quiet tea and did not insist on love making. He was rather nice, really. So terribly ridiculous and grown fat with such amazing 'impossible clothes'. ...

   ... it was seeing R. and Bgt. just made them non-existent. I am so, so glad I felt as I did. R. is so just 'not there'. ...[5]

H.D. seems eager in this letter to reassure Bryher that Aldington is insignificant. She stresses rumour and confirms impressions that she and Bryher have agreed upon between them: that Aldington has uncontrollable sexual desires which seek fulfilment in ridiculous women or in those who do not return his affections; that all men are eager to 'make love' to H.D, but she is not interested; that H.D. and Bryher are somehow superior to most other people in taste and knowledge and manners; that Aldington is a benighted Englishman of limited imagination and artistic merit. Further coded elements in this letter also serve to allay any fears Bryher might have: Pound is 'fat', a word H.D. and Bryher use literally but also to discount someone as beneath their serious notice; Aldington is 'Cuth'. But H.D.'s emphasis on Aldington's 'nonexistence' for her seems a gross untruth, as her later letters to Plank reveal, and much of what she continues to write to Bryher needs to be understood in the context of what she apparently felt she could say and what she also apparently felt she had to say.

   On 2 May, H.D. wrote to Bryher again: 'Acorn [Eileen Macpherson]. ... arrived on top of E.P. and with no luggage (grève) [H.D. alludes here to the current rail strike] and ran into E.P.'s arms. The hotel has since thought the worst and as she had no sign of a bag, and as E.P. came up to our rooms, we are all ready for further complications and compilations re law courts. E.P. was like a golliwog and Acorn fell for him in some odd way, he rather mothered her like a big dog with a small doll.' H.D. described their lunch together, then continued: 'I am invited with Egon to dine with the Mim and the Cuth. I have warned Egon that she must slime over them. "They sound very middle class" said Egon profoundly and she IS right. E.P. is not that; they exude a suburban Noel Coward atmosphere. ...' It seems difficult to believe that Aldington in Paris seemed in any way 'suburban', but such a description would certainly have conveyed to Bryher that he was not a threat. H.D. wrote again on 5 May that Egon's current lover, 'Marc', whom she had come to Paris to see, was being insensitive to her. She continued:

I had a lovely dinner in Duval and a good little prowl along the quay. Then came home and as I have had NO sleep since arrival, went to bed. At 10, there was violent ringing and the Proprietor came up to tell me I must descend as 'Monsieur Aldington was on the telephone'. ... I had a long talk on telephone with R. who wanted Egon and me to come to a party. I said no, I was too tired and he went on and on 'O my darling you must' and so on. I rang off finally and went back to bed. At about 11, was wakened again but would not answer the telephone, finally after long wait (I thought I would be in peace at last) bang on the door. I feared Egon might have been taken ill or something so I opened it ... [sic] full onto Nancy looking like a goddess, beautiful and all glitter, 'you must put on your clothes and come.' Mimosa was slinking in the background. I had a sudden feeling that Nancy was 'hep' to everything, that R. had been saying nice things and that she wanted to sting Mimosa. Perhaps it was just an illusion, but suddenly, I SAW Nancy, so tall and beautiful and a sort of dynamo vibration. I was half asleep and said 'come in'. Nancy started to and Mimosa said, 'O no, I am sure we will tire her. Come, we must leave.' But Nancy wasn't having any. She came straight in, sat down and offered me [a] cigarette, started on how sorry she was that I wouldn't come, how sorry she was not to have known I was coming [to Paris], how if I could not stay, I must make special effort to let her see me later etc. etc. I don't know if she was just touched that Egon and I liked the nigger [Henry Crowder] or what. It appears that the nigger (R. told me on telephone) didn't want the party unless Egon and I came. At any rate, Nancy seemed to be the 'other side' of Mimosa, everything that Mimosa had done to slur it all over and to snub Egon was brilliantly righted by Nancy. N. said 'and your friend ... [sic] how indeed exquisite a creature. We ALL love her.' Mimosa looked sulky and said 'yes ... [sic] of course' though up to now she had snubbed Egon and never said a word about her to me. I felt very upset having them burst in but got quite a case on Nancy and I felt Nancy was rather working for 'us' as per (if necessary) against Mimosa. ...

... 'We' are a great success. I will try to see Sylvia [Beach]. Bob [McAlmon] is out of town but it appears is getting on and friendly. I will ask Sylvia. I met Florence Martin who is going to States. Egon loved her. Other people too ... [sic] but we have not met half E. [Ezra] and R. wanted, as I was too inhibited and did not like sitting too much at bars just now. ... I do, do miss you but had no idea I could so enjoy Paris.

The specific details of H.D.'s letters to Bryher – the snippets of conversation, the brief images (Nancy Cunard in the corridor, Brigit Patmore in the background) – convey with humour and vivacity some of H.D.'s experiences, although the dimension of the visit that included Aldington is both muted and distorted. H.D.'s extensive attention in these letters to Eileen Macpherson's romantic difficulties with Marc even creates the false impression that H.D. has come to Paris to supervise 'Egon''s love life. Her final letter to Bryher from this period continues in the same vein, beginning with a long, rather catty paragraph about Marc and his faithlessness towards 'Egon', then shifting once more to the subject of Aldington:

... I may see R. with Egon for dinner. Egon is now in great form. I long to see you, was so unhappy this morning, but after good lunch and red wine at the Rotisserie on the corner (E. showed us) I feel much cheered up.

[Glenn] Hughes was very respectful and seemed shocked at R.A., did not tell me anything, but general attitude was one of disapproval. Sylvia tells me now that it was thought I had been divorced after the war and that Mrs Yorke had been everywhere saying that she was Aldington's mother-in-law. Sylvia was much surprised when I spoke of divorce, as Arabella and her mother have made it clear that A. was legally married. It is rather a bore I do think and high time I jumped in.[6]

Bryher encouraged H.D. to write in this vein; Bryher's letters to Paris even determined H.D.'s responses and prevented her from sharing the depth of feeling, mostly positive, evoked by the reunion with Aldington. On 30 April 1929 Bryher wrote characteristically to H.D.: 'I expect by the time it [H.D.] gets this, it will be whisking its kitten whiskers and thoroughly pleased with the idea of the plate of "dirt" it will have presented to it in lordly fashion no doubt by E.P. To say nothing of R.A. and his gossip.' On 4 May Bryher wrote again in the same manner; her letter begins 'Dear Kitten' (in Bryher's network of nicknames, H.D. was often 'Kitten' or 'Kat' as well as 'Giraffe' and 'Horse', while Bryher herself was 'Dog') and concludes 'Love from both Dogs' (that is, from Bryher and Kenneth Macpherson); the letter is signed 'Fido':

It's a bad Kat and a naughty Kat, flirting with Cuthbert, sniffing bins [picking up gossip], going to all sorts of ash dumps [bars] and whisking its whiskers. We flung up our hands over your letter and sniffed! disinfected paws, sniffed, groaned and went to see a Harry Piel [film].

As far as we can gather all you are up to, is, flirting with C. and separating him from M. [Mimosa, Patmore]. Bad, naughty, sixteen-year-old Kitten.

The rest of this letter includes household details and light-hearted humour about whether or not Lady Ellerman thinks Bryher has a chaperon when she travels. This context essentially forbids any serious analysis of H.D.'s experiences with Aldington. It is not surprising that H.D. turned to Pound, to Plank, even to Glenn Hughes to express her feelings. In an undated letter from this period, she wrote to Hughes: 'I am so happy this time in Paris + everything delights me.' Reflecting on her visit in another undated and startlingly confessional letter to Hughes written shortly after her departure, H.D. commented specifically on her response to Aldington: '... the most important thing, is that I was terribly happy in Paris. I have the greatest feeling of joy and tenderness in Richard though any serious renewal of an "alliance" other than delightfully superficial and intellectually very poignant, is out of the question. I want people to know how I do feel about Richard and how happy I was seeing him look so well and happy after the horrible years of the war and the dreadful break-down he had then, and that I in a different way, shared in' (Yale).

1 Here H.D. alludes to Elizabeth Siddal, known to her circle as 'Lizzie', and her relationship with Dante Gabriel Rossetti, whom she married in 1860 after a long courtship occasioned in part by Siddal's ill health. Like H.D. in 1915, Siddal's pregnancy in 1861 resulted in a still birth which seriously depressed her. In 1862 she took a lethal overdose of laudanum. Siddal served as a model for Rossetti's paintings beginning in 1850; after her death, he continued to paint her from memory (for example as Dante's Beatrice). Haunted by his dead wife, Rossetti idealized her, although she was later displaced in his affections by other women. H.D.'s letter to Pearson appears in *Between History and Poetry*, 103.

2 Letter from H.D. to Ezra Pound, probably written on 18 April 1929.

3 Aldington indicates Brigit's plans in a letter to Glenn Hughes (6 May 1929) and recalls her departure in a letter to her (15 May 1929).

4 This letter is dated merely 'Thursday' but was written from London probably in late May or early June just before H.D. returned to Paris and saw Aldington again.

5 This letter is dated merely 'Wed. 6:15' but is obviously written soon after H.D.'s arrival in Paris on 1 May 1929.

6 This letter is undated, but seems to have been written on 6 or 7 May 1929; H.D. wrote here 'I hope to get off Thursday' (that is, 9 May) and 'I will write again to-morrow and that will be the last.' Her 'last' letter has apparently not survived.

≫ 99 ≪

14 May 1929
Select Hôtel
Place de la Sorbonne

Dearest Dooley,

It is quite all right about Egon's name. I quite see all your difficulties, and sympathise. I think it will be best if we are rigidly discreet about it, and do not even tell Brigit. I advise that you continue the 'half-Swedish, educated in England' idea. There are quantities of Scandinavians in the quarter.

While we are on the topic of difficulties – I heard last night confidentially that Nancy proposes to go to London *with* Henry [Crowder]. It is very imprudent of her, and may end in ructions. I feel it might cause difficulties for you if you got in any way involved. But I also think that you could easily manage to see Nancy alone.

I had rather a crise de nerfs after you and Egon left. The excitement of seeing you again, meeting her, the agitation of having Brigit go to London, the terrific reaction after the tension of writing that last novel rather bowled me over. There were other complications too. However, I knocked off all 'drink' and coffee, went to bed early, rested by day, and feel much better. The last part of the novel was very painful, as I had to relive all the experiences in the trenches. However, thank heaven I've got rid of it. I am most interested to know what you will think of the novel. My 'heroines' are drawn from Valentine Dobrée and Nancy, who said I might, and there is a satirical onslaught on my family which ought to amuse you.[1]

The MS is with Chatto and Windus, who wired me yesterday that they would telegraph their decision to-day or on Wednesday. I thought that sounded hopeful. So I sent them a 50 word cable with my terms! As Frank [Flint] says I seem to be 'developing a transatlantic business sense'!

About the Imagist Anthology. I have written to [William] Carlos Williams and [James] Joyce and [John Gould] Fletcher. You, Frank and I are certain. Frank has backed down on writing to [Ford Madox] Ford, so do you mind writing him? The point to make is that the anthology is meant as a last one and to show that several people connected with the movement are still alive. Say that we want to have him in since he always sympathised with us and appeared in the first anthology. Keep me very much in the background. The terms are 15% royalty and 250 dollars advance, to be divided equally among contributors. Right to reproduce poems in book form returns to the poets in one year. MS should be sent to you as early as possible, and certainly not later than beginning of July.[2]

When the time comes I think it would be best if you tackle Ezra. Shall you see him in London? If so, you might get hold of him and talk him over. Best there to leave me out, and make it your idea. But say nothing at present. It is important to get Joyce first.[3]

Yesterday I saw Janet and Solita and Djuna Barnes for a few minutes. Djuna is not so nice as last year, looked a bit ill and sullen. I think you might like Solita. She writes novels (I've never read one) but she is a sensitive little thing. I know very little about her really, but have always liked her.[4]

I shall of course write to Egon. In fact I shall write as soon as I finish this. It is essential for her to feel free and unrestrained and able to give full play to her sense of rhythm. Her dancing is marvellous. I only wonder that I had the cheek to dance with her!

Are you seeing any movies? To-night I go to see Journey's End, and I must also see that Jeanne d'Arc film. George Davies (a little literary 'fairy') told me it was on somewhere.[5]

Brigit seems to be having a good time in London, seeing lots of people, going to the theatre and out to dinner.[6]

Do write a lot of real H.D. poems for the anthology. I have been through mine with Nancy and we have picked out fourteen of the best, including the Eaten Heart. They give me a far better show than any of the earlier [Imagist] anthologies. If you have any translations from the Greek, include them. And might it not be good to include a descriptive page from one of the novels you've been working at? I would like you to be represented well and show the great vitality and beauty there is in you.[7]

With great love, dear Dooley,

Richard.

1 In an undated letter probably written on 29 April 1929 Aldington wrote H.D. that he had 'only one more chapter of my novel to go'. It would seem that he had finished *Death of a Hero* either during H.D.'s visit (that is, between 1 May and 9 May when Aldington wrote Brigit that H.D. had left Paris) or since her departure. Although we do not have H.D.'s response to this letter, apparently she accepted Aldington's contention that Nancy Cunard and Valentine Dobrée (d. 1974, wife of the English academic Bonamy Dobrée) were the models for George Winterbourne's wife Elizabeth and mistress Fanny. While parts of *Death of a Hero* are autobiographical (the battle scenes, for instance, and the portrait of George's family, which is recognizably a brutal satire of Aldington's own parents, particularly his mother), it is a misreading of the work to see George's love life as Aldington's indictment of Arabella and H.D. Despite the pain caused by his relationship with each woman, he never blamed either of them for the war or for his own suffering during 1914–18.

2 Aldington and H.D. obviously discussed this project when they met in Paris. The anthology, published in London by Chatto and Windus in the spring of 1930, was a collection of poems solicited from all those who had contributed to *Des Imagistes* in 1914 and to the subsequent anthologies, *Some Imagist Poets*, in 1915, 1916 and 1917. *Imagist Anthology 1930* finally included verse by Aldington, John Cournos, H.D., John Gould Fletcher, F.S. Flint, Ford Madox Ford, James Joyce, D.H. Lawrence and William Carlos Williams. There were two forewords, one by Ford, the other by Glenn Hughes, but no editor's name was indicated. The idea was apparently suggested to Aldington in 1929, perhaps in part jocularly, by the young poet Walter Lowenfels, whom the older writer befriended in Paris.

It seems clear from this and later letters to H.D. that Aldington himself served as editor for this project, although Ford is often given credit; Arthur Mizener writes that Ford 'helped Richard Aldington with his anthology of Imagist poets, collecting material and writing the preface' (*The Saddest Story: The Biography of Ford Madox Ford*, New York: The World Publishing Company, 1971, 195). Aldington and H.D., however, did most of the 'collecting' and Aldington was obviously in charge (Williams, for example, blamed Aldington for typographical errors in a letter to Louis Zukofsky quoted in Paul Mariani, *William Carlos Williams: A New World Naked*, New York: McGraw-Hill, 1981, 303).

Aldington was perhaps best suited of all of the contributors to edit such an anthology. He had the editorial experience and was well qualified for the task of negotiating contracts; by 1929, he knew his way around the publishing world. His knowledge and experience would be useful to H.D. later as they had been to her and others of their friends in the past. A collection of poetry seldom generated much financial return, and Aldington was not merely a money-seeker – as this sort of talk of money and copyrights may sometimes make him appear – but he was well aware that publishing is a business and that he – and most other writers – needed the income they earned from their writing.

3 Predictably, Pound finally refused to contribute to this collection as he had refused to participate in the Imagist anthologies edited by Lowell and Aldington.

4 Janet Flanner (1892–1978), the writer best known for her wide-ranging weekly essays ('Letter from Paris') for the *New Yorker*, which she began contributing in 1925; Solita Solano (1888–1975), Flanner's companion, also a journalist; Djuna Barnes (1892–1982), a friend of Robert McAlmon's, whose novel *Nightwood* (1936) established her reputation as an experimental modernist. All three women were part of a supportive expatriate lesbian network that flourished in Paris at this time.

5 *Journey's End*, not James Whale's film (released in 1930) but the anti-war play by R.C. Sherriff

on which it was based; Carl Dryher's *La Passion de Jeanne d'Arc* (1928). I have been unable to identify George Davies.

6 While Aldington seems detached in his mention of Brigit here, when she went periodically to London to visit her sons during this period (1929–33), she and Aldington regularly exchanged letters of torrid passion, a startling counterpoint to Aldington's letters to H.D. Of course, Aldington wanted H.D. to see his relationship with Brigit as less important to him than it probably was. Similarly, what he wrote Brigit is a declaration of love deeply felt but in context only part of Aldington's busy and complex emotional life at the time. For example, on 13 May 1929, Aldington wrote to Brigit 'My life is filled with happiness because of you. It is Brigit & Brigit only who is the perfect lover, the perfect companion and the perfect woman. I am completely happy with you, dear, and want only you. There is nothing so lovely as you in the world' (Norman T. Gates, ed., *Richard Aldington: A Biography in Letters.*, University Park: Pennsylvania State University Press, 1992, 104). On 16 May 1929 Aldington wrote Brigit with the same insistent excess (between paragraphs in which he discussed the publisher's impending cuts in *Death of a Hero* and the warm weather he and Lowenfels enjoyed while eating ice-cream near the river): 'I miss you every hour of the day, I wake up in the night and want you. I just live for your letters. Dearest one, do you know how much you are beloved, how much I want your beautiful presence and your touch and your kisses? … Dear love, my arms are about you and I kiss you so tenderly and passionately' (HRC). Aldington is not at his most eloquent in these letters to Brigit, though some of them certainly succeed in their obvious intention to be erotic. The elegance and sincerity of his letters to H.D. are of another order, but with both women he is for a variety of reasons selective in what he writes.

7 Aldington was represented in the anthology by three poems: 'The Eaten Heart'; 'Passages Toward a Long Poem', a series in ten parts which was eventually reworked as the eleven 'Short Poems' included in *The Complete Poems of Richard Aldington*, 291–301; and 'Sepads: A Modern Poem', a pastiche dedicated to Walter Lowenfels and excluded from *The Complete Poems*. H.D.'s contributions to the anthology included 'In the Rain', 'If You Will Let Me Sing', 'Chance Meeting' and 'Chorus Translations' (from *The Bacchae*), all poems later collected in *Red Roses for Bronze* (1931).

⫷ 100 ⫸

20 May 1929
Select Hôtel
Place de la Sorbonne
Paris 5

Dearest Dooley,

I hope Walter Lowenfels' letter didn't scare you. I am quite all right, but got into a very nasty taxi smash on Saturday. I was driving in the Bois [de Boulogne] when another car hit us smack in the side at about thirty miles an hour, and our car capsised. Everyone else is in hospital, and pretty dicky [ill]. I escaped with miraculous luck. I got a few cuts on the head, feel a bit sore and stiff all over, and have a tendency to faint away if I walk; but I'm perfectly O.K., eating well, and sleeping not too badly. The woman who was with me is pregnant (NOT by me!) and was telling me all about it and asking my advice when the smash happened. She was too ill to see anyone to-day, poor darling, but she's being looked after.[1]

Don't tell Egon about this. She's so sensitive, she'll think I'm injured &c. But, in fact, I'm devilish tough, and the whole affair made less impression than one heavy shell during the war. I was glad to find that I have perfectly recovered my nerve. I wasn't in the least scared and shall be as well as ever on Wednesday.[2]

214

So, darling Dooley, don't worry.

This has rather put me off buying a car. I think I'll stay here until first week in July, and then go to some seaside place in France. I'd just love to have a couple of months bathing. My novel is to be published October 4th. If it sells, I think I'll go to Marseille, and take a boat to Athens. I'd love to see a little of Greece. And then spend the winter in Sicily or Spain.

Be sure I will say nothing to Brigit of you and Egon. I see all your difficulties, and you can count absolutely on my discretion. Nancy is going to England early in June, but only for a fortnight. I saw her on Saturday afternoon (before the smash) and she was most charming, and spoke very sweetly of you and Egon. You must know her better – she is one of the world's rare and beautiful spirits.

I quite agree with what you say of Brigit's social activities. But the real difficulty is this – Derek is a homosexual, and knows quantities of effeminate pederasts, the kind of men who simply make me sick. It's so absolutely different in women, something quite normal and natural. But these little vindictive half-men are intolerable, especially to me, since I have lived and suffered with real men, and know how magnificent they are. Out of loyalty to Derek, Brigit accepts and is influenced by these miserable little scented worms, and that makes a rather difficult situation. I WON'T accept them. Out of loyalty to the dead I won't accept them. Varus, Varus, give me back my legions![3]

Did you know that Flossie Martin is the wildest little amateur whore in Montparnasse? I was shocked – yes shocked! – to see you quote her name. It should never come within a mile of you. Bob [McAlmon] knows some ghastly people.[4]

[Glenn] Hughes is a well-meaning ass. It doesn't matter what he writes.

I'll write to Mrs Russell.[5]

I read the translation of the 'Persians Are Coming'. It's all right – but … Doesn't go deep enough. I very much want to read No News on the Western Front.[6]

There seems to be a mild demand starting for my 'works'. I have notice from Routledge that they are setting up permanent stereotyped editions of my translation of 'Liaisons Dangereuses' and my biography of Voltaire. The first edition of each of these was 2,200 copies, so a reprint is rather encouraging. When artists are opposed and maligned as you and I have been, dear Dooley, the only thing is to smash opposition by a ceaseless Dionysian energy. Get out book after book, and get them better. You would laugh if you knew my grim determination to impose myself. And I'll do it, you see. Now I've got rid of Arabella, nothing can hold me back. I'm finishing off Boccaccio this month, then the Alkestis and Gérard de Nerval, the Imagist anthology, and then a new novel and more poems. Yesterday I mailed a 1,200 line poem to New York.[7] You keep on, my darling. You've got a rare wonderful genius, and you can impose it. It's the most marvellous help to me to feel that you're 'with' me. Whatever happens, don't let us get separated again.

I'm going to drop a note to Egon. I think that I won't say anything at all about the accident. Not even that the faun bumped his horns![8]

With love to you,

Richard

1 In a brief note dated Sunday 19 May Lowenfels had informed H.D. that Aldington 'was in a collision of taxicabs, last night' (Yale). The injured woman was Valentine Dobrée. H.D. commented on this incident in her letter to Norman Holmes Pearson on 3 May 1951. She felt that Aldington's correspondence during this period contained 'a real, dynamic, perfectly English

and inimitable Byronic feeling'. She concluded: 'I don't think Richard ever really knew what he was or what he did to people – there is Valentine in a taxi-smash (not the Lady V. of Ezra's canto) "pregnant but not by me". I think you will laugh. I did.' (*Between History and Poetry*, 103).

2 Aldington is being rather glib: he was not seriously injured, but his comments to H.D. here echo his reassurances from the front a decade earlier and are not to be completely trusted. He was always eager to shelter H.D. from anything that might upset her, especially about his own health. On 25 May 1929 Aldington continued, 'The girl who was with me is recovering. I was awfully scared – thought she might have a miscarriage &c.' While on 20 May he contrasts the accident with his war experiences, here he recapitulates one of his main concerns while in the trenches – that a woman, pregnant 'NOT by me', will be unable to bear a healthy, full-term baby. His worry contextualizes the accident as the war and parallels 'the girl' with H.D., both during her pregnancy with Perdita in 1918–19 and during her first pregnancy with Aldington's child. Such parallels abound in these early letters of renegotiation and suggest the intensity of complex feelings, often veiled or suppressed, which Aldington brought to his renewed friendship with H.D.

3 Aldington's position is complex here, and two separate issues are at work: homosexuality and the war. Derek Patmore had an unusually intimate relationship with his mother (about which he writes unselfconsciously in his *Private History: An Autobiography* (London: Jonathan Cape, 1960) and in his preface to Brigit Patmore's *My Friends When Young* (London: Heinemann, 1968), a posthumous memoir which he edited). Derek associated with a coterie of homosexual men who, like himself, fulfilled the stereotypes of the period. Additionally, he was apparently in love with Aldington, as evidenced, for example, by his admiring and hostile comments on Aldington in his preface to his mother's memoir and, more explicitly, by a photograph he chooses to include in that volume: lounging on a rock, Aldington poses nude while Brigit, looking a bit startled (she is also naked but submerged to the shoulders in the Mediterranean), stares at the camera from the sea. It appears likely that Derek took this picture; he was an amateur photographer with pretensions to artistry who later became an interior decorator. He seems the voyeur of this intimate triangle.

Aldington's resentment of Derek (as a spoiled child whose stylized behavior would have impressed Aldington as both smarmy and affected) is complicated by Aldington's understanding of male relationships during the war. The 'real men' he refers to are bonded together in common adversity, and while this bond is certainly homoerotic, it is not explicitly sexual nor did it manifest itself in effeminate gesture or homosexual stereotype. Paul Fussell writes of the essential chastity of these relationships in his chapter 'Soldier Boys' in *The Great War and Modern Memory* (London: Oxford University Press, 1975, 270–309). In his substantial introduction to his anthology of homoerotic poems from the First World War, Martin Taylor elaborates Fussell's perceptions and suggests the range of experiences that these male friendships included (*Lads: Love Poetry of the Trenches*, London: Constable, 1989, 15–58). Aldington himself insisted on the beauty of the bonds among men in wartime and on their purity; reflecting on such relationships, he wrote in the preface to *Death of a Hero*: 'Through a good many doubts and hesitations and changes I have always preserved a certain idealism. I believe in men, I believe in a certain fundamental integrity and comradeship, without which society could not endure. How often that integrity is perverted, how often that comradeship betrayed, there is no need to tell …' (*Death of a Hero*, London: World Distributors, 1965, 8). While 'men' here to a degree means 'humankind', in the context of the war and of the novel, Aldington is emphasizing relationships between males. He is even more explicit on this subject when through the voice of the novel's unnamed narrator he elaborates:

> Friendships between soldiers during the war were a real and beautiful and unique relationship which has now entirely vanished, at least from Western Europe. Let me at once disabuse the eager-eyed Sodomites among my readers by stating emphatically once and for all that there was nothing sodomitical in these friendships. I have lived and slept for months,

indeed years, with the 'troops', and had several such companionships. But no vaguest proposal was ever made to me; I never saw any signs of sodomy, and never heard anything to make me suppose it existed. However, I was with the fighting troops. I can't answer for what went on behind the lines.

No, no. There was no sodomy about it. It was just a human relation, a comradeship, an undemonstrative exchange of sympathies between ordinary men racked to extremity under a great common strain in a great common danger. There was nothing dramatic about it. ... Very few of these friendships survived the Peace. (30–1)

Aldington thus contrasts comradeship with sodomy, soldiers with 'effeminate pederasts', an 'exchange of sympathies' with the 'demonstrative' behaviour of 'these miserable little scented worms'. For Aldington, homosexual men like Derek Patmore embodied the mendacity and hypocrisy that, in fact, he saw as the cause of the war and the primary threat to honest emotion – between men or between men and women.

Aldington concludes by translating from Suetonius, *De Vita Caesarum*, II, xxiii. When Augustus discovered that the general Varus had lost three Roman legions as a result of having gone too far into the Teutoburg Forest in 9 CE, he cried 'Quintili Vari, legiones redde!' The slaughter resulted from Varus' incompetence.

4 In *Being Geniuses Together*, McAlmon chronicled his ardent night-life in this city of expatriates, artists, intellectuals, musicians, prostitutes and hangers-on. He called Florence Martin a 'one-time follies girl' (82) who, one evening at the Dome, elected herself 'Queen of Montmartre, Maharanee of late nights, long-distance, and marathon and Queen-bee of drinkers. She hailed everyone with hearty and often excretive hilarity, sure that each comer was there to provide her with drinks, unless she had money. On these rare occasions she would buy everybody drinks and make them drink them whether they would or not' (108–9). McAlmon continues: 'Flossie was a dashing bit of colour, of the Rubens type. Her orange hair was piled neatly above her clear, baby-smooth skin. ... She was capable of a forty-eight hour drinking bout, and after a little sleep was ready to begin again, and to keep up this routine for weeks' (109). It is worth remembering that Paris in the 1920s included Flossie Martin as well as the more serious Richard Aldington. Aldington's letters to H.D. during this period accurately reflect a different world from the one depicted in *Being Geniuses Together*, and indeed Aldington's life – the life of a creative writer who worked daily at his art – was considerably more sober than McAlmon's, but both Aldington and H.D. experienced the Paris McAlmon describes and in limited doses were exhilarated by it.

5 Ada Dwyer Russell (d. 1952), Amy Lowell's intimate companion from their meeting in 1909 until the poet's death in 1925.

6 Aldington is looking forward to the forthcoming English version of Erich Maria Remarque's *All Quiet on the Western Front* (1929), which A.W. Wheen translated for Putnam later in the year. Unlike H.D., Aldington could not read German easily and is translating literally here from the original title *Im Westen Nichts Neues*. H.T. Porter-Lowe translated Bruno Frank's *Politische Novelle* (1928) as *The Persians Are Coming* in 1929. The novel focuses on the disintegration of its central character, Carl Ferdinand Carmer, whose suffering during the war leads to a political career. Haunted by memories of the trenches and the loss of his wife (who died as a result of her nursing experience near the front), Carmer is finally murdered by a prostitute in Marseille. Frank, however, presents the war only briefly and in retrospect and seems more interested in the atmosphere of the post-war Weimar period.

In response to this letter, H.D. sent Aldington a copy of the English translation of Remarque's novel; he thanked her on 25 May 1929, adding, 'I was scared of it (on account of my own book) but – forgive conceit! – now I've read it I'm not scared at all. My book is better. Cry "Out upon you, faun!" but it's true!'

7 Routledge published Aldington's translation of Choderlos de Laclos as *Dangerous Acquaintances* in 1924; Routledge's edition of Aldington's *Voltaire* appeared in 1925. Aldington's translation

of Boccaccio's *Decameron* was published in New York by Covici, Friede and in London by G. P. Putnam in 1930; his translation of de Nerval's *Aurelia* was published by Chatto and Windus in 1932; his 'new novel' became *The Colonel's Daughter*, published by Chatto and Windus in 1931. The 'more poems' were few, and probably included only some of the lyrics which Aldington placed in the section entitled 'Short Poems' in his *Complete Poems* of 1948. He would later write both *Life Quest* (1935) and *The Crystal World* (1937) – long, reflective poems with some narrative threads – but in the late 1920s he wrote little verse except for short poems related in subject and themes to his war novel and short stories. The '1,200 line poem' is probably *A Dream in the Luxembourg*, published in 1930 by Chatto and Windus in London and by Covici, Friede in New York as *Love and the Luxembourg*.

8 Here Aldington's language recalls the privileged world of their early love: he is the faun; H.D. is the dryad; together they inhabit a Hellenic space apart from mundane reality. So long as they are 'with' each other at this spiritual level, they can transcend, overcome or escape the surrounding forces that attempt to impinge on or even destroy both their art and their relationship.

⁊⌃ IOI ⌃⌃

6 June 1929
Select

Dearest Dooley,

There's a postal strike on here, so heaven knows when you'll get this. Your second letter to Ford 'strikes the right note', as they say; and I've sent it on. Carlos Williams has written accepting. You will deal with Ezra, won't you? Everyone else has accepted – barring Ford. I must write and tell Friede.

The last few days I have been staggering at the final pages of Boccaccio. 250,000 word translations are wearisome to the flesh and spirit, but it's got to be done. I've only one more day's work now. Then must get at the Aquila Press book and Alkestis. I'm a bit scared about these Greek plays, but I suppose I can learn by doing them.[1]

A young American poet said yesterday: 'If the American critics weren't so ignorant they'd know it's insane to boost the poets they do when there's a great poet like H.D.' He picked out 'The Sea Shrine' and 'What are the islands' as the two best things in Sea Garden and Hymen. He also said, in which I rather concur, that you are best of all in middling long poems, about three to six pages. Brigit brought me from London my copy of The Tribute and Circe. I was amazed (which isn't perhaps polite!) to find how good The Tribute is. Did you ever print it in book form?[2]

The girl who was with me in the taxi smash was Valentine Dobrée. She got a nasty bang in the tummy as well as a very bad bruise with black eyes. She stayed in bed a week and then went back to England to see her own doctor. She's a nice girl, but a little frightening to me. Rather terrifyingly highbrow – you know the sort of thing, the English upper class disdain put into intellectual and spiritual things. That's where Nancy's so wonderful; she is completely free from any snobbery of any sort. By the way, Nancy goes to London this week. I just feel sick inside when I think of the possible complications.[3]

It is very nice to have Brigit back. For the first couple of days she carried traces of London affectations and snobberies in speech and manner, but that soon wore off and she became her natural self again. She is busy writing a first chapter and plan of a book which an American publisher wants her to do. It's a bit on the smart aleck line, but she might be able to do it successfully.[4]

Get to Paris as early as you can. I want to go to the seaside, either Atlantic or Mediterranean coast of France, and bathe and walk and work for a couple of months. But I shall certainly wait until after your visit. Do you know any small French coast villages, not 'plages' [beach resorts]? I thought we'd go to La Rochelle first, and then explore the coast in motor-buses. If there's nothing to be found there, I think we'll go back to beloved Toulon and find a place in one of the small (very unspoiled) villages between Marseille and Cannes. Brigit was scared by an octopus which tried to eat her at Port-Cros, so I believe she'll be happier with Atlantic bathing.

I'm writing to Egon. It'll be fun to see her again.

I was impressed by 'Im Western' [*All Quiet on the Western Front*], but I was also struck by the delight in brutality for brutality's sake, which it has. Admitted that the whole business was so brutal that its brutality can't be exaggerated, still the work of art demands a sort of restraint, and the choosing of typical rather than exceptional horrors. Moreover, I also think that he concentrates too much on battles and too little on the dreary spaces between battles. However, that may be a difference of experience. But there can be no doubt whatever that it's a great book and a great thing to have done.

My book is a bigger and different sort of affair, covering three generations – you know my weakness for the historical method! More than half the book is pre-war. The style abruptly changes with the war, and becomes impersonal instead of semi-humorous and occasionally prose-poetic. The war part is quite calm and impersonal. I'll bring you the MS when you arrive, if you'd like to see it. The book is filled with faults, which I (naturally) think more interesting than the perfectly slick 'modern' novel. I think that playing the fool a bit in the opening part makes the subsequent tragedy more poignant. But I could write a stinging attack on it myself!

Even if Ford stays out, I think our anthology is now an accomplished fact. Which is all to the good. I agree with what you said to Ford – that the Imagist movement was a mere curtain-raiser. I have confidence in you and in Richard, even![5] Ezra, with all his gifts and charms and sweetness, has somehow thwarted himself, somehow denied himself experience. We've got awfully banged, but we aren't frustrated and haven't shirked experience. But the early Imagist discipline was an excellent thing. It gives us power over words and confidence in using them. I hope you will be able to get out a novel next year soon after the anthology. Do try to.

Love to the Dooley-bird,

Richard

1 The Aquila Press, a small London publisher which soon went bankrupt, had initially asked for Aldington's translation of Gérards de Nerval's *Aurelia*, later published by Chatto and Windus.
2 *The Tribute and Circe: Two poems* was published by Charles Bubb in 1917; 'Circe' was included in *Hymen* (London: The Egoist Press, 1921), and both poems were included in *Collected Poems of H.D.* (New York: Boni and Liveright, 1925).
3 Aldington is apparently anticipating problems caused by the presence of Cunard's black lover.
4 Brigit's autobiographical novel *No Tomorrow* (New York: Century, 1929), which includes characters based on H.D., Aldington and Bryher.
5 Apparently Aldington is here quoting H.D.'s letter to Ford. At what point after this sentence he ceases to quote is not clear.

By 19 June 1929 H.D. had returned to France from Switzerland; by early July she had settled in London for the summer. Her second brief visit to Paris was apparently more relaxed than the earlier one in May, yet there was less opportunity for Aldington and H.D. to meet; Brigit was also in Paris and she and Aldington were busy preparing to leave for their summer in the south. On 23 June 1929 Aldington invited H.D. to accompany him and Brigit 'to see the Grands Eaux' the following day; 'We shall leave Paris [by taxi] about 11, lunch at [the town of] Versailles, then go to the gardens, & leave as soon as the display is over.' Indicating that he would also like to meet H.D. more privately, Aldington added '... and can I see you to-day some time? Let me know.' H.D. evidently enjoyed the water display and the gardens; on 30 June Aldington wrote to her, 'I was so happy that you "got" Versailles – that rather lovely intellectual-aristocratic order and the melancholy of long vistas.' But there was little time for the two writers to see each other alone: by 30 June, Aldington and Brigit had left Paris, visited Chartres, toured La Rochelle and moved on to Châtelaillon Plage where they remained until 16 July.

Aldington's *Imagist Anthology, 1930* remained a demanding project throughout the spring and summer of 1929 and, as he apparently intended, defined much of his correspondence with H.D.: the collection required a great deal of letter-writing to prospective contributors and necessitated a frequent exchange of information between the two writers who were now once again working together; the project simultaneously provided a fresh basis for their friendship (they were artistic collaborators, joint editors, business partners) and diffused other, more emotional bonds between them. The collaboration gave Aldington and H.D. time to renegotiate their relationship while establishing it on the relatively safe ground of former friendships with other authors and past achievements in Imagism; Aldington, perhaps naively, thought of it as a neutral project which emphasized professional respect among writers who had developed and changed in important ways. Discussion of the anthology soon replaced any mention of possible divorce or personal events in either's life. On 25 May Aldington wrote to H.D. characteristically, 'Yes, write to Ford care Sylvia Beach, & say "if you have no poems, can you give a few pages of prose, as Joyce is doing, to show your latest development? The idea is not to revive Imagism, but to show how the 'old group' of us have made good in spite of the critics." Or words to that effect.' By 30 May H.D. had written to Ford as Aldington suggested and sent him the letter for approval; he responded, 'Your letter to Ford is excellent, and I've posted it to the Beach.' He then directed, 'When you see Ezra in London will you say "Ezra, a canto?" I think you can deal with him.' Evidently H.D. did broach the matter with Pound, but he refused to participate; on 13 July Aldington wrote to H.D., 'You don't surprise me about Ezra – in fact, from the first I felt he would make difficulties. Don't say anything more about it. I shall not write to him. Bill Williams is taking up the matter of Ford and Joyce, and if they come in we can go ahead without Ezra. ... Ezra is jealous of both you and me. Like Joyce, he wants disciples not friends.' Aldington's approach to editing was in part to delegate tasks but to remain in charge himself – an effective process, although in writing it may often make him seem authoritative and arbitrary. H.D., however, understood his greater practical skills and business acumen, and on this project she apparently co-operated happily as she had when they had worked together earlier.

The effort expended on the anthology was comfortable for both of them, but Aldington must have been aware that he did not really need H.D. to bring the project off; both
must have sensed that he was seeking her out in this professional capacity in an attempt to
renew common ground for a relationship which, if they could re-establish it, would
transcend any particular project or professional partnership. Aldington justified H.D.'s
involvement in the anthology rather awkwardly on 7 July 1929: 'Forgive me if I dumped
too much of the letter-writing about the Anthology on you. It was the best tactics,
because it is harder to refuse a woman and because everyone is slightly annoyed with my
making a living by writing and not sticking for ever in Padworth. ... I have re-read your
poems more carefully, and think them very good indeed.' Aldington appreciated H.D.'s
help, and wrote to her on 27 July, 'Thank you so much, my dear, for the noble way you
have worked for the anthology. I hope you will not have to write any more letters about
it.' But the work continued throughout the summer. On 6 August Aldington indicated
the increasing complexity of corralling contributors when he asked H.D., 'Have you got
the Lawrence poems? It is important to have these. I would write to [Martin] Secker
[Lawrence's publisher] myself, were it not that my intervention would probably do more
harm than good. Will you try to get the MS of Lawrence as soon as possible? Both Bill
Williams and Fletcher have sent extra MSS. I have written to Bill Williams, asking him to
keep Ford up to scratch; so I hope you'll receive both poems and introduction soon.
Hughes sent a very nice little Introduction, so I suppose we'll have to use that too!' By 15
August the project was becoming a headache; Aldington wrote H.D. rather acerbically
that 'Lawrence's poems are rotten. Tant mieux [so much the better], we only want his
name.' He continued: 'we can't possibly publish that abominable composition of
Cournos's. It simply won't do. Put it all on me. We don't want him in the anthology.
Fortunately, Flint will be out of it too probably.' Aldington concluded: 'It's a pity everyone's so bad-tempered. Donald Friede made a very lucrative offer for an additional
limited edition, signed by everyone concerned. Can't you see us trying to persuade these
people to write their names 500 times? It would have given us all an additional 30 pounds
at least each but I've refused. "No more anthologies" for me!'

While it would appear that both Aldington and H.D. hoped to see each other again,
they made no specific plans and were apparently content that their relationship remain
epistolary. The new friendship which Aldington and H.D. had negotiated was delicate
and tenuous; both were romantically involved with other partners during this period
(Aldington primarily but not exclusively with Brigit Patmore and H.D. primarily with
Kenneth Macpherson but also with Stephen Haden-Guest and in a different and more
complex way with Bryher). Moreover, they moved in different social circles and physical
space: Aldington in southern France and Paris saw invited guests or urban café society;
H.D. was either in London or Berlin or in Territet near Montreux. Both finally preferred
the relative seclusion of their respective retreats (rural France, Switzerland) to the bustle
of their chosen expatriate cities (Paris, London).

H.D. was also wary of Aldington's physical presence; she was excited to see him in
Paris in May and June 1929, but actually meeting him and spending time with him were
emotionally exhausting for her. H.D.'s response was exacerbated by Bryher's hostility to
Aldington and H.D.'s own sense (probably correct) that Aldington would have responded to her sexually if she had in any way indicated an interest. Her own erotic
response to him also probably made her uneasy. Aldington in his turn hesitated to write
anything to H.D. which might frighten her, which might appear to her frequently

Aldington bathing in the Mediterranean with Brigit Patmore in the early 1930s

H.D. in the early 1930s, looking as she must have done when she and Aldington met in Florence

Aldington in the south of France in the early 1930s

H.D. in Switzerland in the mid-1930s, probably taken by
Kenneth Macpherson, possibly a still from one of his films

H.D. in the mid-1930s

Aldington, a formal portrait by Howard
Coster in the mid-1930s

nervous mind to threaten her; he very much wanted her 'with' him, and was acutely aware of how easily she might be scared off or influenced by Bryher to reject him a second time. Thus interspersed with work connected with the anthology are his frequent pleas that she maintain a special relation with him. On 25 May he declared 'I want to say, dear Dooley: "Let's make a pledge that whatever happens you & I will never get out of touch again." Do you agree? You're so rare and beautiful, & it's made me so happy to be good friends again.' In the same letter, however, Aldington also admits that Brigit will soon return to Paris from London and asserts awkwardly and blandly that 'It will be nice to have her back.' The intimacy with which he writes to H.D. about their unique bond suggests an abiding affection that occasionally approaches the exclusive familiarity of lovers. His tone when writing about Brigit suggests the difficulty he may simultaneously have had in developing an attitude and a language with which to redefine his relationship with H.D. while Brigit was, ostensibly, his sole partner. It is in this unspoken but clear context that he wrote H.D. on 26 August 1929, 'Please don't let anything separate us.'

With the business of the anthology eventually coming to an end, Aldington tried to initiate another formal bond. Recommending Friede to her as a publisher, he wrote on 15 August 1929, 'I do wish you were "in" with him. What I'd like is for us to collaborate on something. What can you think of? I do wish it could be done – it would put a lot of things right, I think.' Perhaps more practically, Aldington offered his services as unofficial agent for H.D.'s writing. On 7 July, for example, he wrote 'If you are not tied up with Houghton Mifflin, I wish you would let me submit a volume to Covici, Friede. Friede was part of Liveright when they took your Collected Poems, and the new firm has had an enormous success. ...' Throughout the early 1930s Aldington continued to urge H.D. to let him submit her writing – poems, novels, translations – to his own publishers in England and America. H.D. was periodically interested in his offers, but apparently also typically hesitant. On 10 January 1930 he reminded her, 'Of course, dear Dooley, I will always do anything I can to arrange for profitable publication of your work. Just tell me what you want, and I will try to do it.' On 23 June 1930 he urged her to submit something for the series of Dolphin Books to be published by Chatto and Windus; on 11 July he asked her again and amplified: 'In confidence as brother to brother, I may tell you that the original idea [for the series] was mine. Chattos are enthusiastic and will push the early numbers well, so that for every reason I should like you to be in early. If you have no original work to send in, what about The Women Poets of Greece, omitting Sappho (as done too often) and Anyte? Does that tempt you? ... I wish you'd splash in with the Greek ladies.'

As late as 5 June 1931 Aldington reiterated, 'I wish you would do a complete tragedy which Charles [Prentice] could use as a Dolphin. ... I have an idea ... of doing Prometheus and Philoctetes. It struck me in re-reading the plays that either the Antigone or Electra of Sophocles would suit you. ... But you might complete your Iphigeneia and Ion. Those choruses were beautifully done.'

Yet H.D. never published anything in this series that should have in many ways attracted her. Still, Aldington evidently felt that if he could maintain a professional link with H.D., then the waxing and waning of their more personal relationship would be protected from the various forces that buffeted it. H.D., in her turn, was hesitant to allow Aldington to forge these professional bonds for just the reasons he was most eager to negotiate them; once she committed herself to ongoing work with him again, she could not easily withdraw or protect herself from the many attractions which figured in this friendship – their shared past, Aldington's erotic appeal for her, his wit and literary sense, his sensitivity to nature and art, his knowledge of history and intellectual resourcefulness – all forces which would continue to bind these two writers to each other and which play a clearly important role in all their correspondence.

Another significant issue in the letters of 1929 was Aldington's *Death of a Hero*, whose publication in August placed its author in a distinctly different relation to his peers. From the time of the publication of the first Imagist poems in 1912, Aldington, H.D. and Pound consciously identified themselves with a new sort of writing, a literary modernism that would be revolutionary not only in subject but in frankness of tone and freshness of language. The result, the Imagists stressed, would be a literature which would also be technically different from the writing that had preceded them. Just what those technical differences would be (beyond the 'right' word and a proclaimed spareness of style) remained undefined.

By the 1920s, however (and certainly after the publication of *The Waste Land* and *Ulysses* in 1922), the dominant strain of modernism was characterized by technical virtuosity and exploration of the limits of earlier literary conventions (narrative, time, traditional notions of logical coherence and patterns of linguistic expression). Unlike H.D., Aldington increasingly distanced himself from such experimentation; his first principle of literary excellence remained the 'right' word – that is, writing should communicate clearly, should (by extension) be accessible to a wide, educated readership. Thus he was from the very beginning of his literary career intensely concerned with the matter of audience. For instance, he engaged in translation projects in part to make otherwise inaccessible writing available to a larger public. His letters to H.D. reveal a concern with all sorts of technical details of publication, among them typesetting, publicity, reviews, even 'sales' as one criterion of artistic success – not because the public 'knows best' (he was always sceptical about the standards of the masses), but because a well-executed piece of writing was successful in so far as it communicated and was in fact read.

His practical mind (like Eliot's, but unlike Pound's or Joyce's or H.D.'s) was thoroughly equipped to negotiate contracts, advertise, translate, and edit anthologies and made him all the more aware of the processes of book production. His diplomatic skills and willingness to engage himself with the mechanics of publication made him additionally sensitive to the issue of sales. Unlike Eliot, Aldington never earned a salary on which he could live. Unlike Pound and Joyce, he never had angels; unlike H.D., he had no inherited investments and no Bryher, no friendly millionaire to support his art. Aldington lived throughout his life away from the subsidies and patronage that made crucial economic differences for his contemporaries. The success of his first novel suddenly gave him a new status in the world of serious and popular writers and a measure of financial security which he had never known before.

Aldington himself was uneasy about the novel's artistic merits; having sent H.D. a set of proofs from his American publisher, he thanked her on 30 June 1929, 'Most noble of you to "plodge" … through my interminable inferno. The last part is the least bad. It would all have been much better, but for Lawrence and Arabella.' He was also dealing with the technical and moral matter of censorship and added in the same letter that 'Chattos [are] making an awful fuss about "obscenities". Now want to drop asterisks, and have me slash. I haven't refused point blank, but fight hard to keep my asterisks. I want to show the idiocy of "moral" censorship and the humbug of alleged freedom of the press in England.' Aldington initially hoped that H.D. would help him to arrange for a German translation of *Death of a Hero*, but soon realised that his publishers both in America and in England were sufficiently enthusiastic about the book so that he could leave the matter to them. On 7 July 1929 he wrote H.D. that 'Friede is going to advertise it and me so extensively in the U.S.A. that it is bound to be noticed, and of course if the Literary Guild takes it, there'll be a rush.' Promising to send H.D. copies of the English proofs, he commented on 13 July that she would find this edition of the novel 'much more cut on moral grounds than the American edition – sometimes a whole page has been cut, and all the love passages are sadly mutilated'. He added, however, that 'It is so important to me to be published by Chatto and Windus that I have simply allowed them a free hand. But I am going to insist on the asterisks.'

The 'rush' Aldington anticipated in July materialized in September. He had discussed with H.D. the process of writing the novel, his relationship with his publishers, the galleys and page proofs as he received them during July and August; now his correspondence contained enthusiastic reports of the novel's success. Aldington was genuinely amazed and understandably delighted; his earlier defensiveness and apprehension were replaced by amusement and satisfaction, and he shared his pleasure with H.D. On 9 September 1929 he wrote that 'The American publishers are booming the Hero vigorously. I received 21 preliminary notices this morning, including one about me and darling Nancy drinking gin fizzes at the d'Harcourt!' Three days later, preparing to leave Provence for Paris, he continued:

> Great excitement about the novel. Sixty-five clippings from the U.S.A. since Monday, and premature but excellent reviews from Joe Krutch and the N.Y. Times. The Syracuse Herald says 'strong, salacious stuff'! But what really is encouraging is the following:
>
>> 'Dear Mr Aldington,
>>   Thank you for the letter and the book. I have already read a lot of it, and I will certainly write something about it. So far I like best the brutal, savage parts. You are magnificent with the characters whom you detest.
>>   Yours sincerely,
>>   Arnold Bennett.'
>
> I hear you chuckle here! But Bennett is the most influential critic in England, and the very nearly most influential in U.S.A. An early and favorable notice from him is worth a 1000 copies in each country. That is one more reason for being nearer to London, so that I can cable 'quotes' to Friede for ads. He has certainly got me amazing publicity in almost every state of the union. 41 clippings arrived in one bunch, and we all got frightfully excited, and snatched them from each other.

There was more good news to report on 1 October: 'Dr. List of Leipzig came to Paris especially to buy the rights, and gave me quite good terms – a 10% royalty with an advance of 100 pounds. He will print a first edition of 5000, and publish in February.' Aldington continued:

> Thank you for congratulations over novel. It is officially listed a best-seller in London, New York and Philadelphia. Chattos printed a first impression of 5000, and ordered a second impression of the same number within a week. I dined with H.G. Wells last night, and he was very sweet about it. He thinks it will go to 100,000. There were three printings before publication in America. Of course the more sickly and self-conscious highbrows are against it because it happens to be alive, but when a book is selling thousands a week one rather smiles at all that.

After October 1929 Aldington's and H.D.'s correspondence is characterized by gaps and clusters of exchange until February 1932 when it stops altogether for nearly five years. There are thirty-two surviving letters from Aldington between 14 March 1929 and the end of that year; there are only seventeen letters between the beginning of 1930 and the end of this period of correspondence in 1932. There are many reasons for this pattern. Neither H.D. nor Aldington wanted a divorce, so that matter as a practical issue could not justify their correspondence. If they were not to separate legally, on what basis were they to continue their relationship? *The Imagist Anthology, 1930* was neither a critical nor a financial success; aside from negligible royalty cheques of a pound or so at infrequent intervals, once their collaboration on this project concluded, there was little either writer could say on the subject. No other collaborative project materialized, no joint translation, for example, nor could Aldington persuade H.D. to seek his help in submitting material for publication.

In fact, H.D. was having serious problems with her writing, feeling increasingly unable to produce work that pleased her or to write at all. Ironically, just as Aldington found his voice in fiction, H.D. began to doubt her own artistic powers. Her 'writer's block' led her finally into analysis: first with Mary Chadwick in London, then with Hanns Sachs, and finally in 1933 and 1934 with Freud in Vienna. The success of *Death of a Hero* and Aldington's subsequent work in fiction (he published two volumes of short stories – *Roads to Glory* in 1930 and *Soft Answers* in 1932 – and three more novels – *The Colonel's Daughter* in 1931, *All Men Are Enemies* in 1933 and *Women Must Work* in 1934) understandably did not draw him and H.D. closer: his success was economic and to a large degree popular; the aesthetic merits of his fiction were of a different order from H.D.'s strengths as she struggled in both experimental poetry and prose to work and rework painful autobiographical material.

There were also other factors which separated the two writers.

Aldington was by no means so relaxed or confident as he generally suggested to H.D. He still had bouts of nervousness and needed sustained periods of solitude both in order to work and to maintain a degree of inner peace which could withstand the turbulence he often experienced when he examined the world at large. In sum, he had needs of his own which probably frightened H.D. during this time as they had during the war years and after his demobilization in 1919. It was apparently more than that she was unwilling to take on Aldington's insecurities, to which she had herself contributed; in all likelihood a relationship that would involve such psychological intimacy was threatening to her and would demand that Aldington assume a physical presence in her life (or she in his) that she was not willing to consider. In any case, he never asked it of her. The hints in his letters of his continuing uneasiness remain fascinating indications of what he does not develop in his correspondence: they may be an invitation that H.D. could not and would not attempt; they certainly indicate an opening that H.D. did not take and underlying difficulties that his situation with Brigit at the time did not assuage. Anticipating H.D.'s second visit to Paris, he wrote her on 9 June 1929, 'I feel awfully tired, somehow, with the strain of writing the novel and those years of incessant hack work, and getting away from Arabella, and the excitement of getting the novel accepted. I must go to the sea and rest directly you leave.' In an undated letter written from Châtelaillon Plage probably in early July 1929 Aldington commented 'It is quite pleasant here. ... Sea bathing is so good for one's nerves.' On 7 July he continued, 'There has been a heavy gale off the Atlantic for 36 hours here – you know how a prolonged howling of wind and waves gets on one's nerves. I wish it would stop. It's just as bad this morning. If I were not held here by lines of communication, economic reasons &c., I should feel inclined to start for Capri tomorrow.' Aldington's language in these passages ('incessant', 'prolonged howling', 'held here', 'lines of communication') recalls his war experience of confinement in the trenches during long periods of constant shelling. 'Capri' is the antidote, a place which was not only physically attractive to Aldington and H.D. but which invariably for both of them recalled their love during their courtship in 1913 and came to represent both peace and a fantasized reunion. But Aldington did not leave southern Brittany for Capri but for Fabrégas near Toulon; on 26 August he wrote H.D. 'I feel better down here than I've ever felt since 1916. But I do wish you were somewhere near, so that we could meet sometimes.'

Other elements also characterize these letters of the late 1920s and early 1930s. In France and Belgium in 1918–19 Aldington had often included in his correspondence passages of natural description, frequently of pleasant surroundings, which served to obscure the mundane and unattractive realities of wartime. Now, similar passages perform more complex functions. Obviously, they obscure Brigit and the other women in Aldington's life whom he does not mention. They substitute for all the things he feels he cannot write about his daily activities or his emotional experience. They additionally offer a neutral subject to which both writers could freely respond. They also offer a landscape which substitutes for the physical space which it becomes increasingly clear that H.D. and Aldington will seldom share in person; that is, it becomes less and less likely that they will be comfortable in each other's presence. Aldington's life during this period involved a great deal of adventurous touring and moving about, while H.D.'s travels predictably took her from London to Territet and back again with occasional trips to major cities such as Florence, Berlin or Vienna or on a cruise to Greece. Bryher and Macpherson would go off to Iceland, but H.D. remained for the most part settled in one or the other of her flats. Aldington's passages of natural description serve further, then, as a kind of travelogue for H.D., a glimpse of a world that she enjoys intensely but which she ultimately prefers to experience at one remove. Thus Aldington writes to H.D. from Fabrégas on 27 July 1929:

> Have you ever seen the country between Bordeaux and Toulouse? It is Roman, a sort of French Campania, and most lovely. I did wish you'd been along to see and rejoice over it. It is your sort of country – rich vineyard plain, with sparse hills, scattered with olives and cypress. I'm going back there someday.
>
> Here it has been very hot, but is now much cooler. Mistral blowing – rather lovely with bright blue sky and sea and little white wave caps. Such butterflies, Dooley! Large swallow-tails – two kinds – and a very handsome velvety black and white one, and a gorgeous fritillary. There is a large bush with long blue spikes of blossom, rather like a large tree-lupin, which is covered with intoxicated insects. The cicadas sing all day in the pines – churr, churr, churr. Then at night there are crickets, including those beautiful bell-note ones which you used to vow were tree-toads. ...

Aldington's sensitivity to nature, his enthusiasm for sensual detail and his scientific eye, often combine in passages such as this one with yet another element: an allusion to shared past experiences. Perhaps it was this tendency that caused H.D. disparagingly to call Aldington 'sentimental' when she wrote to George Plank and others; certainly it was also a psychically important element to her in Aldington's correspondence, and her later letters to him suggest that she invariably responded to him in kind, joining in the coded discussion of their past together, affirming it, renewing it, recreating it. Thus on 10 January 1930 Aldington described for H.D. his trip through the Italian countryside on the way to Tunis, but emphasized that first 'I went up to Anacapri, and drank some wine at the Pensione del Lauro. The Signorina Maria del Tommaso was still there, considerably increased in girth and with two large children. She did not recognise me. I thought very tenderly over old times.'[1]

Such moments punctuate a correspondence that grows increasingly sporadic with only brief passages of intimacy or openness; Aldington's letters are never dull, but in the 1930s they often begin with indications that he is glad to hear from H.D. and include stock references to the weather while closing with the formulaic hope that she will write when she gets a chance. He wrote once in June and again in August 1931, then not until 21 February 1932, after which time the correspondence breaks off.

The period between 1929 and the resumption of their correspondence in 1937 was tremendously busy for both Aldington and H.D. and deserves summary if only to fill in the background to their meeting again by chance in a London bun shop in 1936. Both apparently accepted that they were more comfortable writing than seeing one another. H.D. evidently felt no pressing need to arrange a rendezvous, and Aldington generally seems to have concurred, although occasionally he longed to see her again, pleading for example from Algeria on 23 February 1930, 'Darling, can't you come to Paris soon – in March or early April? I want to see you most awfully. Please do come, if you can. It would be so lovely to see you. I am being horribly successful, and will blow any amount to amuse you! There, isn't that a proposition?' Even Aldington's final jocularity does not belie his urgency here. Still, they managed to meet only once more: in Florence in 1931. Aldington and Brigit were spending the winter in Italy and had settled in Florence by December 1930. On 13 February 1931 Aldington wrote H.D. to suggest that she pretend to be his sister-in-law while visiting, apparently to explain their shared name. Brigit was away for at least part of the time, and Aldington and H.D. spent most of a few days together. Aldington introduced her to Thomas MacGreevy, the young Irish poet, and all three dined out one evening. Years later in a letter to Aldington MacGreevy recalled H.D.'s 'smiling attempts to get you to marry me to somebody who remains no more than a name to me, Alida Monro [Harold Monro's wife]'. Perhaps Aldington and H.D. also saw Norman Douglas, whom she hoped would be in Florence then. On 17 March 1931 Aldington reflected elliptically, 'I was sorry indeed not to see you again in Florence, but I did not want to embarrass you in any way; so I left it to you.' Despite lighter moments, then, this meeting seems to have involved all of the tensions and apprehensions on H.D.'s part of the two previous encounters in Paris. Aldington and she remained friendly, however, but much occupied with their separate busy lives.[2]

The early 1930s was the period of H.D.'s intense involvement with film. She was both writing for *Close-Up* and making films directed by Macpherson, among them *Borderline* with Paul and Eslanda Robeson in 1930. By 1931 Bryher and Kenneth had built Kenwin, a bauhaus villa at Burier-la-Tour not far from Territet; this was to be Bryher's home throughout H.D.'s life, and H.D. and Perdita were frequent residents. In 1932 H.D. took a Hellenic cruise with Perdita and visited Delphi for the first time. Her affair with Macpherson essentially ended in 1931 when his homosexual liaisons displaced his attraction to her. She was upset but disentangled herself from this emotionally implosive relationship. In 1935 in London she entered analysis with Walter Schmideberg, which continued through 1938. Her experimental writing included poetry and prose: she published *Red Roses for Bronze*, a collection of verse and translation in 1930, and stories in two collections, *Kora and Ka* and *The Usual Star*, in 1934 as well as the novella *Nights* in 1935. In 1937 she published her translation of Euripides' *Ion*, begun in 1916 and finished in 1934 and 1935. She had no male lovers during this period, and although in 1934 she met Silvia Dobson, who was to become a lifelong friend, H.D. checked any physical expression of the erotic chemistry between her and this much younger woman (Dobson was twenty-six and H.D. was now forty-eight).

For Aldington's part, the period between 1929 and 1937 spanned the duration of his involvement with Brigit Patmore, a relationship that in many ways defined his daily life during these years, although he also had intense relationships with other women. Brigit was a frequent presence in his life, but she was often in London while he was on the continent, and when both were in England they generally maintained separate establishments, she with her sons, he at a London hotel. The popularity of *Death of a Hero* made its author also popular; he was, especially at this point in his life, the man who H.D. later said to Pearson 'was so handsome + had such a beautiful voice that he ravished all women + men at first glance'.³ Louise Morgan Theis interviewed him for *Everyman* in 1930 and was impressed with his exceptionally broad shoulders and his bronzed skin and hair which 'gleam with vitality'. She continued: 'His clear blue eyes shine with the excitement of living. He gives the impression of exuberant health and well-being, of a man who spends the greater part of his time in the open air. One is struck with his irrepressible good humour as well – his smile is always just below the surface, and his habitual expression is one of repressed amusement and mischief.' Theis wrote about Aldington again in 1933: 'He makes excellent company, for his good humour is as inexhaustible as his memory, and his tact and sympathy are unfailing.'⁴ This portrait accurately conveys Aldington's social and public self; his private self, which occasionally surfaces in the letters to H.D. between 1929 and 1932, is more guarded and vulnerable and prey to bouts of sadness and 'nerves'. This outgoing persona also contrasts with the personal and sexual man whose life was lived independently, with Brigit or with other women, primarily through letters.

Aldington's correspondence with H.D. falters primarily because she did not write him back, for her own reasons. Aldington, a prolific correspondent, was always careful to respond to letters from friends; it is very unlikely that he would have left a letter from H.D. unanswered. His correspondence to her indicates that by 1932 she was not writing regularly and that he often felt as if he were writing into a void. He would cease to write at all in part because he had other, more responsive correspondents who nourished his inner life.

A model of reserve when it came to kissing and not telling, Aldington was invariably discreet; he states in *Life for Life's Sake* that he consciously created 'certain reticences' in his 'Book of Reminiscences', and when he writes here of the 1930s, for example, his traveling companion is always an unnamed partner included in a ubiquitous 'we'. At this time, as he travelled throughout Europe, seldom spending more than a few months in one spot, Brigit was the companion, but Aldington had another life comprised of his relationships with women who sought him out in response to his writing. He scrupulously destroyed their letters to him, but we have evidence that these correspondences and the relationships they engendered were important and enduring both to him and to the women involved. He seldom actually saw these women. His own life was a hectic, sometimes frenetic series of trips. For periods he took a cottage in the south of France (most often near Le Lavandou in the summer), but he was in London sporadically (generally for a month or so in the autumn or winter), and he spent long periods in Italy – in Florence and as far south as Sicily. He was in Spain and Portugal in November 1932 and again in April 1934; he spent the summer of 1932 at Anacapri; he was in Switzerland (where he did not see H.D.) and Austria during the summer of 1934, and spent the spring of 1935 in Tobago and the summer in Connecticut. His travels, exhausting even to try to chronicle, were abetted by his acquiring a driving license and a car in 1930. He went everywhere, exploring the French and Italian countryside, staying in small hotels and sampling the local cuisine, often with friends such as Douglas and Orioli or his publisher at Heinemann's, A.S. Frere. And everywhere he went, he wrote, rigorously spending his mornings at his desk, writing not only fiction and correspondence but regular articles for such London periodicals as *Everyman, The Sunday Referee* and *The Evening Standard.* Aldington himself commented only half jocularly about the delicate balance of this nearly compulsive travel and writing: 'whenever I stopped for more than a few days, a miserable tendency to start working asserted itself, so I decided to push on'. But there were always addresses at which he could be reached.[5]

Among the women who sought him out in the early 1930s were the novelist Irene Rathbone, the young poet Eunice Black, and Marjorie Pollard.[6] His erotic correspondence with these women and his brief affairs with them in London or during their short visits to the south of France while Brigit was in England visiting her family were intense moments which Aldington apparently kept secret. Both the exchange of letters and the few occasions when they slept together were romantic elements which he deeply needed throughout his life. Black, for example, recalled her experience: 'I wrote my first fan letter to Richard in May 1932. ... Apart from the flattery, he must have liked my writing [to him], or he wouldn't have gone on answering and being drawn closer – until we met in London [in 1933] and were lovers. I was young and a "colonial" – from South Africa, so the whole thing of meeting and loving Richard was like Apollo descending, but in this case the god didn't disappear. We remained close and dear friends to the end of his life. ...' Black also recalled her impression of Aldington in the early 1930s: '... then he was happy, secure, pleased with his world-wide reputation, but he was never boastful or arrogant, in fact he was always humble and amazingly shy'. Aldington himself disingenuously confessed to Marjorie Pollard that he felt diffident, perhaps especially with women: 'It seems idiotic to be shy at my age, but ... [that] is one reason these letters are such fun – I can talk as I probably shouldn't be able to for weeks directly.'[7]

Aldington's relationship with H.D., itself often romanticized both in his work and in his responsiveness to her in his life and letters as a spiritual partner whom he had lost with the war, needs to be understood in the context of this other 'secret life'. Aldington's letters to these other women frequently seem more significant than any actual physical expression of sexual love between them (although in *Was There a Summer?*, her autobiographical poem about her visit to Le Lavandou in August 1931, Rathbone makes it very clear that Aldington was a wonderful lover). This private correspondence is itself erotic, designed to arouse both writer and recipient, as Aldington discusses his own sexual experiences (without naming names), responds to the other's personal confessions, imagines having tea naked before a fire, reflects in sensual detail about having kissed or touched. Such letters fulfilled needs unmet in his more mundane relationship with Brigit, who in 1930 was an ageing forty-seven to Aldington's still dashing thirty-eight. Aldington enjoyed playing the role of the older or at least more sexually experienced and worldly-wise partner; he was charmed and invigorated by youth at the same time that, without in any way being paternalistic, he enjoyed the role of initiator, leader, educator. Finally, he may have needed these relationships because they were primarily epistolary, since (as perhaps for anyone who cares deeply for language and literature) the very acts of writing and reading contained for him an erotic dimension.

H.D. would later need Aldington in some of the roles he played for other women – as a literary resource, for instance, or as an experienced traveller or sensual observer of the natural world or even as a flirtatious and inaccessible lover who because of their own past sexual relationship shared a knowledge of her body as well as of her mind. In the 1930s, however, she was not particularly receptive to these levels of experience with Aldington, although there are suggestions in his correspondence with her that he was ready to be flirtatious, to shift the level of discourse to the kind of erotic exchange that occurs much more expansively in his letters to other women. For instance, on 10 January 1930 he wrote to H.D. from North Africa that 'Tunis is really fun. The French have left the old town quite untouched. ... It is really very "picturesque", and you would love it.' He went on to report his progress on translations and his official position as '"critic in chief"' of *The Sunday Referee*, but interrupted his discussion of work to insert a single-sentence paragraph: 'On second thoughts Tunis is no place for you! Those veils!' He then returned to reporting on the sales of *Death of a Hero*, only to interrupt again before closing with another one-sentence paragraph: 'I enclose a Tunisian beauty' – a postcard of an attractive woman rather seductively veiled. With this picture Aldington initiates a rather curious habit apparent in the later letters of sending H.D. erotic postcards of actual women or women in art. These pictures reveal his interest in and affirmation of her lesbian attitudes, her bisexual tendencies, but they also function ironically as a kind of heterosexual flirtation (Aldington seems definitely interested in arousing H.D.) as well as allying the two writers in their sexual responsiveness to female beauty. Moreover, it seems likely that H.D.'s sensitivity to women played a role in the erotic chemistry between her and Aldington from the earliest days of their courtship in 1912; thus Aldington's postcard does not introduce a new element into their relationship (he assumes she will enjoy, understand, be amused by the picture) but functions as part of the intimate and continuing bond between them to which H.D. may not respond in the 1930s but to which both will return in the letters of the 1950s.

Aldington spent the autumn and winter of 1936 in London. In December, he wrote from Sadler's Wells to his close friends A.S. and Pat Frere to tell that he had fallen in love with Netta McCulloch Patmore, the wife of Michael Patmore, Brigit's son. Aldington admitted that he was his 'own worst enemy' in matters of the heart, confessing the details of this affair: he had fallen in love with Netta five weeks earlier (that is, some time in October 1936), and now felt in emotional upheaval, not knowing whether he was 'coming or going' and unsure of Netta's love for him, since she still felt affectionately towards Michael and tied to him and her marriage. Aldington continued in a subsequent letter on 21 December 1936: he and Netta had made love, but they were still trying to keep their relationship secret from both Michael and Brigit, struggling to decide what to do and sustaining their affair primarily through letters and flirtatious meetings. At one point that winter H.D. had even accidently come upon them in a bun shop; she had found Netta 'very young + quiet, [the] antithesis to B.P. [Brigit Patmore]', but it must have been a tense encounter. Aldington wanted to marry Netta and have a child; Netta was reluctant to go through two divorces (hers from Michael and his from H.D.) and to make open a relationship which would obviously hurt and anger both their other partners (Michael and Brigit) and alienate the entire Patmore clan (that is, Derek as well as his brother and mother). Netta evidently proposed that they continue their affair as it was while pretending to go on with their public companions; Aldington rejected this alternative, writing to the Freres that Netta 'accused me of "pride" when I refused the position of spare-time lover and sugar-daddy'.[8] In Aldington's first letter to H.D. in five years he struggled to explain the extremely awkward situation.

1 Aldington is here specifically recalling his experiences with H.D. during the spring of 1913. He reminds her of the halcyon time during their courtship, before their marriage, before Imagism, before the war. They had stayed, of course, at the Pensione del Lauro where Signorina Maria del Tommaso had served them. Aldington draws on this experience (both the 1913 idyll and the 1929 return visit) in his novel *All Men Are Enemies*, in which he explores a situation that vividly parallels his relationship with H.D. In this novel he portrays the war symbolically as the force which separates the two lovers, who as deeply hurt and painfully experienced people are finally reunited on Capri at the story's conclusion.
2 Letter from Thomas MacGreevy to Aldington, 29 September 1961, SIU. The details of this brief visit are suggested in Aldington's letter to H.D. of 13 February 1931 and in another dated merely 'Tuesday' but probably written 17 February 1931.
3 This statement is taken from undated notes Norman Holmes Pearson made while interviewing H.D. in Switzerland in the late 1950s (Yale).
4 Louise Morgan (Theis), 'Writing a Best-Seller in Seven Weeks', *Everyman*, 21 August 1930, 101, and 'Richard Aldington's Message', *Everyman*, 11 March 1933, 305.
5 *Life for Life's Sake*, 6, 3, 327.
6 There were probably other women among Aldington's lovers at this time, but we know of Rathbone because she wrote about the affair in her long poem *Was There a Summer?* (1943). We know about Eunice Black (later Gluckman) because of Aldington's letters at Yale. Letters from Aldington to Marjorie Pollard are now at SIU.
7 Letters from Eunice Black Gluckman to Norman T. Gates, 30 April and 30 July 1978, SIU, and quoted by permission of Harriet Dash; letter from Aldington to Marjorie Pollard, 12 May 1933, SIU.
8 Letters from Richard Aldington to A.S. and Patricia Frere; the first is dated merely December 1936, the second 21 December 1936. Photocopies of both are at SIU; the originals are privately held. The letter from H.D. to George Plank is dated 27 January 1937.

⫷ 102 ⫸

15 January 1937
c/o William Heinemann
99, Great Russell St,
London, WC.

On board the MS Lafayette, approaching England.
Dear Dooley,
    In a few days you will almost certainly receive the 'evidence' of my adultery. You will probably be surprised to find the co-respondent is Netta Patmore, Michael's wife, the girl you met in the tea shop.[1]
    Dooley, we're madly in love with each other. And believe me, the marriage with

Michael was not a real one — you know what I mean.[2] It's been going on for a year, with each of us trying to be 'honourable' and suppress our feelings, with the obvious result. In October we told each other, and lived undying moments of happiness and agony. There were terrible scenes with Brigit and Michael. Twice Netta nearly came away with me, and twice drew back.

It all came to a crisis on 16 Dec. when after a whole day together she said that she loved me utterly but felt bound to Michael and would not leave him. In complete despair I left everything and went to America. Dooley, I lived three weeks of bleakest hell. And then the miracle happened. Netta cabled me to come back and marry her. I was in South Carolina, and I've been travelling night and day since noon of the 7th. In two days we shall be together, and nothing but force majeur will part us.[3]

It was a staggering coincidence that you should come into that shop and speak as you did when we were there. If one were superstitious, how easy to see the hand of Fate! We want to marry and have a child. As soon as the legal 'evidence' is ready for both sides we shall leave England and live abroad. If you will set me free to marry her, I shall bless you indeed.

Should one praise one woman to another? 'Never do the immortal gods fail to know one another when they meet' — she belongs to 'our lot,' not to that futile milieu she was in. With me she can live the adventurer's life for which she was born, and not be just one more angel-in-the-house, servant-in-the-kitchen.

I am giving Brigit part of my income. I think she acquiesces. It is horrible to have to hurt other people.

Dooley, I trust you. I felt you ought to know about this. Forgive me if anything in this letter gives you pain. Lovers are selfish. They have to be. The world is against them. Don't be against us. Let us have our life together.[4]

Won't you let me have a word from you, care of Heinemann?

With love,
Richard.

1 Netta McCulloch Patmore (1911–77) had married Michael in 1935.
2 Aldington implies here that Michael, like his brother Derek, was homosexual.
3 These events as Aldington recounts them here are elaborated upon in his long autobiographical poem *The Crystal World* (London: Heinemann, 1937).
4 Aldington comments on his relationship with Netta by echoing the poet Coventry Patmore's proverbial formula for the ideal Victorian woman. Michael Patmore was Coventry Patmore's great-grandson. The ideas in this letter are a predominant theme in *The Crystal World*, but they were certainly not new ones for him and appear explicitly even in the title of his third novel, *All Men Are Enemies* (1933).

H.D. was stunned by Aldington's request for a divorce. For many years, it was she who had considered this possibility, rejecting it finally because it seemed so complex and because she wanted to keep Perdita's name ands her own irregular situation (her affair with Gray and subsequent lovers and her relationship with Bryher) out of the courts. She shared her feelings with George Plank on 27 January 1937:

> I had a thunder-bolt by way of letter from R.A. He is apparently trying to play a sort of trump-card. He says he <u>wants to marry</u> the young wife of Brigit's <u>younger son</u>! ... I am perfectly willing to do this [that is, grant him a divorce] + am consulting experts to see if divorce is feasible, but psychically I fear a catch + think the State of Denmark pretty rotten. ... [Brigit] is apparently on the war path + frankly, to me, the whole thing looks tricky + shady to a degree, not to mention incest.
>   ... My mind is cold like ice but my heart thumps when I even think of it – can't sleep ... what 'doings'.

The decision was made that H.D. would divorce Aldington for adultery and that not Netta but Arabella Yorke would be the co-respondent. Evidently H.D. was advised by her lawyers that this course would be best; to accuse Netta would publicly damage her reputation and would certainly fail to explain H.D.'s and Aldington's separation for eighteen years. English lawyers would not look favourably on H.D.'s affair with Cecil Gray in 1918 while Aldington was fighting on the Western Front nor on her illegitimate child who, although registered in Aldington's name, could not have been conceived by him in his absence. H.D. knew she would need to focus attention on Aldington's infidelity with Arabella in order to obscure her own subsequent affairs with men and her lesbian relation with Bryher. Arabella herself, however, was understandably unwilling to oblige either Aldington or H.D. by showing up in an English court or giving legal testimony by proxy. She recalled years later that 'A little lawyer trotted up the steps [of the flat in Paris where she lived in 1937] and tried to hand me a paper which I wouldn't take. He came a number of times and finally threw it in the door and disappeared.'[1]

H.D.'s lawyers suggested that she look for corroborating evidence of Aldington's affair with Arabella, and on 1 February 1937, H.D. wrote to Jessie Capper, whom she had met through Havelock Ellis in 1932, explaining Aldington's 'thunderbolt, just two weeks ago':

> I am only too anxious to clear things up. The case is to be given the discretion of the court, as it is called. Unless I am fully assured that there will be no publicity, I won't enter it at all. The person whom R. proposes that I 'cite' is this child Netta. I have, nevertheless, to account for the years, and though Arabella and Brigit may not even officially be mentioned, my barrister wants as much light on the whole situation as possible. It is all damnably painful to me, the one person, in a sense, out of it all these years. I look on it as a damn torturing form of analysis, an outer analysis of psychic facts that I so painfully tried to clear up for myself in my psychoanalytic work. I think the thing I fear most is the English law-courts. ... It's pretty hard as I have been alone almost the whole time, and am not intending to re-marry so have not that sort of protection. Certainly, I want to stand alone, do not ask, in a crinoline, protection. But it is a strange fatality that I should get my inner life clear with such excruciating pain (the analytical work), only just as I am recovering from that, to have another sort of search light turned on me. I feel like Saint Joan or an Antoinette simply putting my head to the axe.

... Well, Netta may be 24 [she was, in fact, twenty-five at this point] but the glimpse I had of her in that tea-shop ('Nell Gwyn', of all things) might put her anywhere between 22 and 28, more likely the former, a slight young little thing with no hat, no vamp, little if any make-up, a nicely tailored little dark costume, rather on the tiny, petite side. ... I feel like the leader of a Greek chorus, watching the antics of the players. The play is commedia dell'arte, Don Juan if you will or the Beggars' Opera. Or is it truly dignified, is there actually a touch of madness, Oedipus about it?

... It's a terrible thing to go back 20 years, especially since it seems all that [her leaving Aldington] happened yesterday. I suppose that is what the war did to us, took away our youth and gave us eternal youth. Richard acts as if he had arrested development, though, I must say. (Yale)

Obviously H.D. was indeed shaken by Aldington's request, but her response was complex. She felt that the divorce recapitulated her past and her psychoanalytic work, especially her sessions with Freud; she simultaneously felt that a variety of practical steps had to be taken, and she was quick to embark upon them (writing to Capper, consulting lawyers, making decisions about whom to name as co-respondent). But she also kept her sense of humour, so that her frequently wry wit often punctures her more serious efforts in the letters of this period to express (in psychoanalytic but also in very literary terms) her feelings towards a challenging situation.

Brigit was also devastated by Aldington's decision both to leave her and, with Netta, to destroy her son's marriage. Writing from Nice on 12 January 1937 she attempted to explain the situation and her response to Eric Warman, a young writer who was primarily Aldington's friend but whom they had known mutually. She had seen Warman on 7 January but had not mentioned 'certain happenings' for she 'hoped against hope that it wouldn't be necessary'. Now she confessed:

Richard has left me + not just with 'another woman' but with my son Michael's wife Netta. ... Michael had been terribly run down with overwork + trying to steer her through all sorts of emotional strains. She said up to the last moment – i.e. Thursday [7 January] – that Michael was the one she loved + that she was taking him away to a cottage in Dorset where they'd both been so happy. Then on that evening, Frere-Reeves [A.S. Frere] of Heinemann's rang her up + arranged for her to go somewhere + R was going to meet her – straight back from USA.

So Derek got us tickets + Michael + I came down here. There was no one else he'd go away with at the moment.

It would be easier to bear if it had been anyone else + Mickie too feels that but for his wife I'd still be happy. ... He's exceedingly courageous + sweet + wise but refuses to allow himself to be divorced. He says if there's to be a divorce he will cite R as co-respondent. And how can I possibly ask him [Michael] to take the blame? He's too young to spoil his life in that way.

... don't think I'm bitter against R. ... other people can believe what they like. It's strange to have to protect my son's name in connection with the fair name of someone I thought was my husband – I mean that in its deepest + most enduring sense.

... I wonder what I did that was so very wrong. In a way Mickie's burden is more than mine because he can't believe that R could do this to him – he's got two deceptions. (SIU)

Brigit hints here at the problem that Aldington implies: that there were sexual difficulties in Michael's and Netta's marriage attributable to Michael's homosexual tendencies, although Brigit suggests that Michael's inattention was attributable to his being 'run down with overwork'. Brigit is clearly unwilling to accept Michael's homosexuality as grounds for divorce (a case Aldington was ready to try to make) and adumbrates what will be a messy court battle with Aldington named as co-respondent in Netta's adultery.

Money was also an issue; Aldington had already agreed to settle an income on Brigit, although he was under no legal obligation to do so. Brigit for her part continued to feel affection for Aldington, but was torn by her attachment to her son; she wrote Warman again on 4 February 1937: 'I don't want to stamp Richard out of my life. ... [Yet] I can't just keep quiet about everything as I would if it concerned only myself. Michael has got to be protected from all the false rumours and humiliations ...' (SIU). When the divorce proceedings got under way, they were more difficult than Aldington imagined. After leaving England in February for Italy, he and Netta settled in April at Le Canadel in the south of France where Aldington wrote Warman on 7 August 1937 that he was 'disturbed by legal rumours from the divorce court. You cannot imagine how idiotic and unreal all these laws and procedures are. It is quite fantastic, and bears no relation to the actual facts' (SIU). He amplified in another letter to Warman on 18 August 1937:

> I'm having a devil of a time with lawyers, and the whole thing is in a frightful mess, owing to my trying to do what is called the right thing. The Patmores want their pound of flesh, and then some. It is extraordinary how people with highly refined feelings and aristocratic pretensions are so damn keen on money. Not to mention revenge. The idea seems to be to make as big a scandal as possible, to get the case reported if they can, and to cause me as much direct and indirect expense as possible by involving me in a defended suit in which I shall have to pay costs and by claiming fantastic damages, in spite of the fact that Brigit is being paid an income! Directly anything with common-sense in it is suggested to the lawyers, they have expensive conferences, and then say it's illegal.[2]

Both Aldington (in the case of Netta's divorce from Michael) and H.D. (in the case of her divorce from Aldington) made long, legalistic, official and not entirely truthful (and, in some instances, untruthful) statements. In a 'Memoir to Counsel', Aldington alleged, for example, that Brigit 'seduced' him in November 1912, when he was 'still a virgin male' and that the effect of 'this early seduction' made him her victim.[3] Similarly, in June 1937 H.D. spent several sessions with her lawyers crafting a statement about her past in which she contended that she was twenty-seven and Aldington thirty-seven at the time of their marriage in 1913 (she was in fact twenty-seven but Aldington was only twenty-one); that Aldington was conscripted in 1917 (he actually enlisted in 1916); and that she had discovered Aldington's affair with Brigit in 1931. She also alleged that the reason she was finally seeking a divorce was that she had 'recently learnt that she [Brigit] had been passing off as Mrs Aldington in Austria, London and New York, and that he [Aldington] had since run off with her daughter-in-law Mrs Netta Patmore who was now also passing off as Mrs Aldington'.[4]

Such complicated statements and slow court proceedings disturbed everyone. H.D. sent to Bryher at the time of her lengthy deposition a copy of a statement in the form of a letter to her lawyers that indicated her frustration. H.D. was attempting, she stated, 'to account for the years quite simply', but in fact she was creating a fiction that would, on the one hand, protect her privacy (even from her lawyers) and, on the other, convince the court of her innocence and suffering. She developed, for example, a series of substitute names: Jessie Capper was 'Jenny'; Bryher and Kenneth Macpherson were Renne and Neil Patterson, although Perdita was adopted by Mrs Macpherson; Cecil Gray was called

'Vane', the same name H.D. would use for Julia's lover in *Bid Me to Live*. Additionally, H.D. superimposed upon this material several literary 'readings' of the events, some of which elaborate on the images she used in her letters to Plank and Capper:

> I have lived with a subterranean terror, an octopus eating out my strength and vitality for almost eighteen years. ... I was frozen ... as a deer in the forest or a rabbit or hare is frozen. ... I was dead. Richard did not injure me or hound me, as in a sense he injured Arabella, as probably he has injured this Brigit and this Michael. Richard made a good job of it in my case. He killed me.
>
> ... I have looked on at this, as at a play, seeing the insides of houses, rooms, sliced off, in cross-section. ... Arabella was Mrs A., of course. Everybody is Mrs A. It is a sort of Greek chorus. I suppose I might be presumed to be the leader of the chorus, who has been asked to step out (vide Richard's letter) to play before the fall of the curtain, the Deus ex.
>
> I am willing to be goddess or leader of the chorus. But through all those years and during my married life, I never took part in the usual wrangling and bickering that is presumed to exist between wife and mistress. I never would play that role. Seeing the characters as in a play, my sympathies are inclined to go with Arabella, with Brigit. (Michael is just ridiculous. He does not exist. He is just that boy who shot himself in the last act of [Chekhov's] the Sea Gull). I don't presume Michael is [really] like that at all. I just see him and Netta as those two young people in the Sea Gull. ... and the livid mistress, that older woman is Brigit, of course, and the part of the talent[ed] man who was not yet a genius is only too easy to cast [as Aldington]. Myself, I was the original Sea-Gull, I presume, in period costume.[5]

Aware of the complex process of fictionalizing in which she was engaging here, H.D. comments in her statement that 'The facts are so complicated that if I begin fabricating on top of the facts, I can do nothing.' But in reality H.D. was 'fabricating on top of the facts', a process which here illuminates her own artistic method of moving from autobiographical experience to fictionalized expression as she renames people to make them characters in a drama, as she struggles to impose on experience the right literary form – her own, finally, but even that derived from other sources, in this case Greek drama and Chekhov's play. As she is living the experience of the divorce, H.D. is making art of it because, for her, art was a way of coming to terms with experience, of distancing herself from her material, of recreating life so that it could be understood, so that it had meanings not necessarily apparent while living it. Interestingly, it was during this time that H.D. managed to break through the writer's block which had led to her psychoanalysis in the early 1930s. H.D. wrote Silvia Dobson on 11 March 1937 about the recent ease and extent of her writing (Yale).

H.D. also had expedient reasons for portraying herself melodramatically here as 'frozen', 'dead'. In an earlier undated letter to her lawyers, probably written shortly after hearing from Aldington in January, H.D. insisted on her authority, justifying it in part because of stress: 'My head is like ice, my chest has been like a black crater. I cannot endure this nerve-strain much longer and I want to put this matter clearly and finally. ... I will add nothing ... nor will I be cross-examined nor interviewed except as regards the bone-bare facts ...' (Yale). She emphasized further in the statement she sent to Bryher that 'I won't be cross-examined and bullied. If I am, I won't enter into this case at all. ...' H.D. was probably not so distraught as these melodramatic legal statements suggest, but she was certainly startled and upset.

Netta's divorce from Michael came to court in November 1937, and Aldington was required to pay 'damages', which included court costs and a portion of his income to

Brigit for life. Despite H.D.'s formal filing of the 'Statement of Facts' on 21 June 1937, her case would not be finalized for nearly a year. Aldington and she were not now writing to each other, and she was once again a primed audience for Bryher's interpretation of the situation. Aldington wrote her, as he had in 1929, in part in response to 'rumours' and in part because he had a suddenly pressing problem.

1 Interview with Walter and Lillian Lowenfels, 25 October 1964.
2 This letter appears in Gates, *Richard Aldington: An Autobiography in Letters*, 150–1.
3 Aldington included this document in a letter sent to the Freres on 20 January 1937. The letter appears in Gates, 144–7; the document is privately held, but photocopies are at SIU. Aldington in fact was not a virgin when he began to sleep with Brigit in 1911, and it is silly to think that Aldington was in any way victimized by 'early seduction'.
4 This document, entitled 'Statement of Facts', is dated 21 June 1937, and was submitted to the court shortly thereafter; a copy is at Yale.
5 This undated statement at Yale is labelled in H.D.'s hand 'Bryher', but it is clearly not written for her but for H.D.'s lawyers. It seems on the basis of internal evidence to have been composed at about the same time as H.D.'s 'Statement of Facts', which was submitted to the court – that is, in late June 1937.

≈ 103 ≈

24 February 1938
Villa Koeclin
Le Canadel
Var France

Dear Dooley,

I have just heard that you have been greatly distressed by a rumour that alleges that I have said there was some 'trick' in the matter of the deed concerning Perdita. The assertion is too ridiculous, and I'm surprised that you gave it any credit and that you didn't immediately suspect its source.[1]

I don't think I have mentioned the matter three times in the last fifteen years and then only in the strictest confidence. For many years by my silence or in so many words I tacitly admitted paternity in order to spare you in any way possible.[2]

What I said about the deed was this:

(1) That I was at first a little startled by the request to sign it, since I thought it might in law be considered a kind of perjury. As soon as Sir John [Ellerman]'s lawyer explained the situation, I signed the deed at once without hesitation.[3]

(2) That it suddenly occurred to me at the time (and was subsequently alleged to me) that you had been fearful lest I might use the situation to interfere between you and your child. Upon which my comment was that it had never crossed my mind before that you, who knew me, would think me capable of such baseness; and that, had I known, I should have sent you a reassurance at once.

I am very sorry indeed that you have been troubled by this canard, and I can only assure you that it is self evidently a lie. What possible 'trick' could there have been in a matter of this sort which was put to me so frankly and openly by Sir John's lawyer?

You may be interested to know that Netta is having a baby about the end of June and that we are coming to Lausanne for this spectacular event. The clinic we looked at there seemed excellent and so much cheaper than London. If you are in Territet at the time, it would be nice to see you.[4]

And do stop worrying about that silly lie.

Ever,
Richard

1 The 'source' of this 'rumour' was probably Bryher, whose pattern was evidently to insist on Aldington as a threat, to stir H.D. into a state of agitated nervousness, then to offer to interpose on H.D.'s behalf as her protector.

2 Aldington always conveyed the impression that Perdita was his own child and not H.D.'s with Cecil Gray. Although he had grave concerns about the legality of his name on Perdita's birth certificate, H.D. had registered the baby as his in 1919. Aldington was, however, invariably careful to separate what was legally correct from what was morally or socially acceptable; even his own family as late as the 1950s thought Perdita was his daughter.

3 The legal point which concerns Aldington here is that, since Perdita is not his child, she cannot really be adopted with his consent. In other words, by signing the legal document, Aldington wondered at the time if he was in fact lying (perjuring himself) by acknowledging a false paternity.

4 Aldington and Netta eventually decided to have the baby in London.

Aldington remained with Netta in southern France into May 1938 when they left for Switzerland. H.D. was also in Lausanne that spring, but she and Aldington did not meet. She was in London on 13 May 1938 when the divorce petition was presented in court and granted, pending a six-month waiting period. In early June, Aldington and Netta travelled to England in order to hurry the absolute decree along as well as to assure the baby's British nationality. On 9 June Aldington rang up to ask if he might visit H.D. in her flat to discuss the problem that afternoon. H.D. was startled and between answering the telephone and his arrival wrote to Bryher, 'He begs to see me, and I like a fool said I would. ... why do I see him? Very much better for the UNK [unconscious], I thought, better to get him in perspective. ... Silvia [Dobson] is due at 3, R.A. at 4 ... [sic]'. On 10 June H.D. recounted the visit to Bryher:

> I am weak, dead, limp. Cuth came at 4 by the strike and stayed till after 6, just sitting in my big chair and drinking old and stale and staler china-tea. He must have had ten cups, and smoking. It appears that the baby would be 'heimlos' if born in Switzerland, that they would have to have stamped on Netta's passport 'illegitimate child'. ... R.A. said he had no money ... and ... he was pledged for life to support Bgt. by installments. ...
>
> Well ... [sic] all this was very good for the UNK. Silvia was here. ... She left, as pre-arrangement, after about a quarter hour.
>
> R.A. wore a tight wedding-ring and told me all about Netta's pelvis being too small!

To George Plank on 16 June 1938 she reflected humorously on Aldington's visit: 'R.A. turned up HERE. ... He is very fat. I never knew anyone make such a muddle of anything. The baby is expected any minute, "Netta has such a small pelvis", he announced. "I am very anxious – she may have to have a caesarian." I said, "Good. It will spare her a lot of bother." He seemed to think this was not the right remark – but as a matter of fact it is.' H.D. wrote to Plank more generously and nostalgically on 20 June: 'I am sorry the amazing maze + rootlets and moss beds + logs of the past make it impossible to contemplate seeing R. again; though it is not for lack of sentiment to the past. It or her [Aldington's marriage or Netta], rather, make a quagmire or quick-sand of what might have been introspective vistas – meadow-land + trees. But I truly wish him well + would always be glad of news if you happen on him or them.' H.D. had earlier decided to 'cover half or more of my share' of the divorce costs; now, because of Aldington's settlement with the Patmores, H.D. agreed to pay the remaining charges. Jessie Capper recounted the details of the hearing, at which she was a witness: 'It is all rather a complicated story, but there didn't seem to be any other alternative. ... I knew R.A. and Arabella lived together as man and wife but were not in fact married ...'.[1] Years later, in a jaunty letter to his brother about his legal affairs, Aldington recalled the experience as 'a slap-up, A.1., London (Eng) affair. I well remember going before some judicial moron for the absolute [decree] (called himself Master, I think, but looked to me as if he'd just dodged out of the Old Bailey dock) and his one concern was not with rights and wrongs, but the costs. "I must be assured that the costs will be paid." The barrister at my side gave me a weary look, for he knew H.D. was being backed by a woman friend whose dough runs into millions. Said millions kept the whole show out of Ye Press. ...'[2] The divorce was finalised on 22 June 1938.

241

1 Letters from H.D. to Bryher, 2 February 1937, and from Jessie Capper to Havelock Ellis, 19 August 1938, Yale.
2 Letter from Richard Aldington to Paul Anthony Glynne ('Tony') Aldington, 2 November 1961, SIU.

⫸ 104 ⫷

24 June 1938
Astor Hotel
Princes Square
[London] W2

Dear Hilda,

We both want to thank you for your generosity in applying for that absolute. It has come through just in time and we are to be married on Saturday morning. On Sunday evening Netta goes into the nursing home. It's rather like a movie. I'll let you know about the child. Let me know if you'd care to see it, as you suggested.

I am asking Heinemann to send you a small souvenir which I hope you'll accept with love from us both,[1]

Richard

1 Aldington and Netta were married on 25 June 1938; Catherine Aldington was born on 6 July. I have found no evidence that H.D. ever saw Catherine as a baby; it seems unlikely that she really wanted to. The 'souvenir' was probably a copy of Aldington's *The Crystal World*.

After Catherine's birth, Aldington and Netta moved briefly to a cottage in Hampshire, but returned to the south of France by the end of the summer. He was acutely aware of the possibility of war, and his letters during this period often discuss political matters and his plans for himself and his new family should hostilities break out. Increasingly, rather than remain in France or return to England, he considered leaving Europe for the United States. In January 1939 the situation looked grim, and he with Netta and the baby left Provence for London; on 11 February they departed from London for America. There he settled at first in New England but maintained regular contacts and eventually an apartment in New York. He finished his fourth novel, *Rejected Guest* (1939), and turned his attentions from fiction to his memoirs (*Life for Life's Sake* was serialized as 'Farewell to Europe' in the *Atlantic Monthly* in 1940) and from journalism to academic lectures at several eastern universities.

There are apparently no surviving letters from H.D. to Aldington during the period immediately following their divorce, but they kept in touch now, and seemed well-disposed towards each other, if cautious and a bit distant. For her part, H.D.'s life continued much as before as she alternated residence between England and Switzerland. On 20 July 1939 Aldington wrote her from the cottage in Rhode Island where he was spending the summer. Thanking her for a recent letter, for which he was especially grateful 'as I hadn't heard from you for so long', he began somewhat formally 'Dear Hilda' and apologized: 'I had a feeling that in some way I had unwittingly offended you. This was the last thing I wanted to do, as you have been so particularly kind and generous.' He then filled her in on his experiences since February 1939. The letter is chatty and contains details of Aldington's travels in New England, including the charming natural descriptions which had become characteristic of his correspondence with her. He wrote of 'deer, foxes, woodchucks, only too vigorous skunks, and multitudes of squirrels, chipmunks …'. He sent her news of his writing and of his year-old daughter, who would become a frequent subject in his letters: 'Catherine is a very healthy young woman, with blue eyes and dark hair, and singularly like the photographs of me at her age. She is just beginning to say words and to totter about holding on to her pen, and creeps with incredible energy. She is an amiable infant and very little trouble. I like her very much indeed.' Aldington continued to feel badly about not having been able to pay court costs: 'I feel very much ashamed at not having paid you my share of Goddard's fees, but lawyers, doctors and Patmores between them relieved me of all of my savings.' He concluded jauntily but finally rather impersonally, 'With all good wishes from us both'.[1]

England's declaration of war on 3 September 1939 caused Aldington to write H.D. in a less guarded and more intimate vein.

1 This letter appears in Gates, 163–5.

4 September 1939
c/o Viking Press
18 East 48th St
New York City
USA

Dear Hilda,

Here we are all reduced to rags by the nervous strain of the past few days. Right up to Saturday night the Americans kept broadcasting rumours of peace negotiations and believed in them. I had no such hopes, but that doesn't make the fact of war any the less crushing. Two European wars in a life-time are a bit too much. Especially as England and France begin in a worse position than last time with no allies and the potential enmity of Italy and Russia if Germany scores early successes. It is a hopeless outlook, for what will be left when it's over?

The Americans are screaming so violently about neutrality and [protesting] that nothing will induce them to take part that I begin to think they will be in it within a year.

I am a little uneasy at the thought of your being in Switzerland, which may not be able to keep neutral. However, as the Swiss are professional neutrals they have a better chance than most small nations. But what of Perdita? Were you able to get her out from England? Let me know.[1]

If you decide to come to America, for heaven's sakes come on an American ship. The first British passenger ship has already been torpedoed, and heaven knows how many more will have been by the time you get this.

After the hectic flood of radio 'news' up to and just after the declaration of war, there is a most sinister absence of news to-day – nothing but the moronic programs of the American radio which are incredible until one has heard them.

What we shall do I can't imagine. Considerably more than half my earnings came from English and Continental royalties and journalism; and that will cease immediately. I have been trying to get a job either in a university or in Hollywood, with no success so far. But in the face of the universal disaster in Europe one's own fate seems peculiarly unimportant. But I don't like the idea of Catherine's suffering.

Let me know how you are.

All good wishes,
Richard

1 Perdita was living in London. She did not come to her mother in Switzerland; rather, H.D. left the continent in November for England.

Only one letter from H.D. has been preserved from this period. Clearly, she and Aldington were communicating at irregular intervals between 1939 and 1941, but Letter 106 is the first letter from H.D. to Aldington to have survived from all the correspondence the two writers had exchanged since 1912.

≈ 106 ≈

31 October [1939]
Hilda Aldington;
British Passport; returning:
Flat 10
49 Lowndes Square
London SW1

Dear Richard,

Thank you for your letter of October 13.[1] I have been put off leaving [Switzerland] by an attack of grippe. There is much of it here, from the poor men in the mountains, snow and rain, sleet and cold, inadequate shelter, all the rest and a larger frontier to guard than one realizes. Bâle or Basle (I think you knew it) is a garrison frontier town now, with machine guns in private houses and an arrangement for general transportation of civilians to this lake-side [Geneva]. Also hotels, schools, etc. are being prepared in case of any big offensive. I heard from my Austrian-British friends that they got through [to England] all right, but it took a long time. There are waits of 2 and 5 hours and even [if] one spends the night at Boulogne, and at that, one never knows from day to day from which port the boats will go. So the crossing will be none too easy. However. ... I am desperately home-sick for my own rooms and surroundings. I came here [to Burier-la-Tour] in August [to visit Bryher] with the lightest of summer outfit[s]. I hear from English friends near Boston and in N.Y. that they are over-come with increasing nostalgia [for England]. However, I think it is probably different with you as you are busy and successful, with your lectures, and you have your heart's desire there.[2] Let us hope the book [*Rejected Guest*, just published] and books go on being well received. I saw a notice, very good, in the Manchester Guardian and one in the [London] Times not so good, but funny and publicity. No doubt you saw these. You speak of censorship of news, but here we devour papers from USA, 2 or 3 weeks old; they give such a good general historical long-distance view of things. We listen-in to German and French (Swiss) and French from London. The English from London, once a week, is lamentable. We hear German from Paris, and it is getting more and more difficult to switch on to what one wants, because of clever Berlin propaganda breaking in across the lines and even blurring them out altogether at important moments. It is heavenly here now, with the mountains across the lake in snow and with sun. But as I say I am anxious to get back. Thank you for your friend's address, I will make a note of it – I do not expect to leave but the chief difficulty is getting passage, even if one did want to.[3] I do not paragraph, as I am sending this clipper [airmail] and the lighter, the better.

If there is anything special I could do for you, in London, will you let me know.

All very-best wishes for your work and happiness,

Hilda/

1 On 13 October 1939 Aldington wrote to H.D. to acknowledge a letter in which she had reassured him that she and Perdita were both safe. He continued to be concerned: 'I can't imagine why, but I was haunted by the apprehension that you might have tried to get through [from Switzerland to England] early in September and have got involved in the French mobilization.'

2 Aldington's letters to H.D. during the summer of 1939 indicate little about his relationship with Netta; however, he wrote regularly about his work, American life, and his baby daughter. By 'heart's desire' here H.D. may mean his second marriage in general terms, or she may be alluding to the fulfilment of Aldington's wish to have a child. Sending her a photograph of Catherine, Aldington wrote H.D. only half jocularly on 9 August 1939, 'I am selfish enough to be pleased that she loves me more than anyone else in the world, because that is how I feel about her!' Fatherhood had also apparently increased his sensitivity to H.D.'s affection for Perdita. From this period on, his letters reveal a concern for Perdita as well as for H.D. herself. He signed the above letter 'Always', then added in a postscript, 'Can I do anything for Perdita? If she wants to write, I have a good deal of influence.'

3 Here H.D. means that she does not intend to leave England for the United States; she is planning as soon as possible to leave Switzerland for London. In case Perdita and H.D. wanted to go to America and needed help with visas, Aldington had given her the address of his friend Paul Willart, the former head of Oxford University Press, who had just been assigned to the Foreign Office.

✑ 107 ✑

30 April 1941
Jamay Beach
Nokomis, Florida

Dear Hilda,

I was very glad indeed to get your letter and to know that you are surviving the ordeal in apparently good spirits. Evidently some letters have been lost. I did not receive the one you speak of, and two or perhaps three of mine did not get through. I'll send this by air mail.

Here is a summary of our existence. In June last year I signed a contract with the Viking for my reminiscences, an anthology of British-American poets, and a third book yet to be written.[1] In the middle of the month we moved to a place on the Connecticut River, about seven miles from Old Lyme, very beautiful – I love that river. I worked very hard, for the Atlantic bought my memoirs for serialisation on condition the book was done by September, and at the same time I was taking books weekly by the armful from Yale for the anthology. I finished the memoirs in August and at the end of October we spent a week in New York and then moved on to Washington, where I worked every day at the Library of Congress.

Washington is a really nice town, but of course you must know it.[2] I liked the big boulevards with trees and the very opulent public buildings. When we had time we often drove to Mount Vernon partly for the sake of seeing the old house, but chiefly for the gardens and the magnificent view over the Potomac. I hadn't time to do sight-seeing, since I was working overtime to get the anthology done before America actually gets into the war. In this I succeeded, and turned in the script on the first day of February.[3]

I hope you will like the anthology if it ever gets to you. It has 1250 pages of text, with nearly 1300 poems picked by over 300 poets from Beowulf to Dylan Thomas (b. 1914)!! I have picked five poems of yours, more than any recent poet except Lawrence. They are Sitalkas, 'Never more will the wind' from Hymen, Lethe, Mid-day and Cities.

Of course they will be paid for, and the publishers are now sending out letters for permissions. That is a big job as there are over 250 copyright poems, and on my advice the Viking are writing to the publishers (in this way they can arrange for a number of poets in one letter) and asking the publishers to communicate with the authors. They are paying pretty well so there shouldn't be much trouble.

This paragraph is entirely confidential, and in fact it must be kept quiet until the public announcement. The Literary Guild of America has bought the anthology for its September or October choice, and the first printing will be 100,000 copies. Unluckily the money return to me is not as good as that large number seems to imply. The cost of producing such a book is tremendous – we estimate our permission fees to copyright poets and living poets without copyright whom [we] are going to pay too, will run to $3500 or more.* And to compete with the Oxford Book we have had to cut the price to $2.50.[4] My share of the Literary Guild will be only $2000, and royalties on the first 50,000 of regular sales will be only about another $5000. I don't despise this, indeed I'm very relieved about it, but $7000 isn't very much on a sale of 100,000. I should say that the book will not be an American giant, but will be printed on a rather expensive thin paper, on the lines of the Nonesuch Blake.

I don't know how to get you a copy of my memoirs and of the anthology when printed.[5] I sent copies of the memoirs to England, and not one apparently has turned up. My theory is that such frivolous freight as books just doesn't get put on board ship, and quite right too. Perhaps Atlantic transport will improve if the Americans really cooperate as they apparently mean to do. Probably even you don't realise how cautiously the President has to move, and what a tremendous barrage of persuasion has to be put up before each step is taken.

We left Washington by car on March 2nd, and came to this island off the west coast of Florida, about 60 miles south of Tampa. It is a most attractive place, with nearly five miles of sand beach and hardly a person ever visible. Yet we have a nice little cottage with all the American gadgets and I have a wooden hut with shelves and a desk to work in. At the end of May we are going to New Mexico to spend the summer with Frieda and her Capitano, and then return here in October – I have taken the cottage for another year from then.[6] Both rent and living are much cheaper here than in the north, and this seems the best temporary solution of our problems, providing that I can write here. Later there will be the problem of Catherine's education, and she is bound to pick up a Southern accent.

Catherine enjoys life here very much, running on the sands, bathing and picking up shells, and playing with another little girl. She is well and sunburned and beginning to say 'cute' things. Americans are awfully nice to small children, in fact they spoil them. Why so many of the children are horrid is a mystery. Do you remember the small American boy at [the] Bargello and 'sup'm raare'?[7] I'm glad to say Netta is very happy here. We got into rather a stuffy upper-class set in New England (and you know what that means) which made her restive.[8]

Do you ever hear anything of Tom Eliot? I saw Frank Morley[9] in Washington, and he said Tom was Fire Lootenant or an Air Warden – I forget which. Now he will probably write something cheerful. By the bye, among the latest refugees here is André Spire, the French poet we used to know.[10] The Nazis have stolen all his property, but he sounds very cheerful. I ran into two of your old friends (forget their names) when I lectured in Philadelphia in January – they spoke of you with great affection and admiration. I have Norman [Douglas]'s address, and mean to write to him. He ought to get out of Portugal, not healthy for him. Robin Douglas [Norman's son] wants to get him over here, but I can't see Norman crossing the ocean at any time, least of all now.[11]

I do hope you and Perdita will be all right. I worry about you sometimes. Try to write more often – Air Mail letters seem always to come through. Give my love to George Plank. And if there is anything I can do for you, please let me know.

With all good wishes,

Richard

* Total cost of producing book about $40,000!

1 Viking published both *Life for Life's Sake: A Book of Reminiscences* and *The Viking Book of Poetry of the English-Speaking World* in 1941 and *The Duke: Being an Account of the Life and Achievements of Arthur Wellesley, 1st Duke of Wellington* in 1943.

2 H.D. was not so widely travelled nor so familiar with the United States as Aldington generously suggests here. In fact, Aldington's penchant for information and extended visits to America (in 1935 and from 1939 through early 1946), with sojourns in Connecticut, New York, Washington, Florida, New Mexico and California and much scenic travel by car, made him something of an authority on the country.

3 The war caused serious paper shortages that limited book publication in England; Aldington rightly anticipates similar problems in the United States after December 1941.

4 Arthur Quiller-Couch's *The Oxford Book of English Verse*, first published in 1900, had gone through numerous editions and was still in print.

5 Because of paper shortages, Heinemann did not publish the anthology in England until 1947; Aldington's memoirs, which might have been printed in London at the same time, did not appear until Cassell published them six years after Aldington's death in 1968. Evidently *Life for Life's Sake*, which was discreet but also candid, seemed in 1947 too revealing about the wide cast of personalities whom Aldington knew before 1940; by the 1950s, Aldington's literary reputation was in question and publishers were doubly wary of publication.

6 Frieda Lawrence was living in Taos, New Mexico, with her lover, a former Italian army officer, Angelo Ravagli. During his visit Aldington was appalled at the emotional bickering and primitive conditions of the small artists' colony burgeoning on the site where his friend D.H. Lawrence was buried. Aldington's later correspondence with H.D. often refers to the 'chaos' he experienced there.

7 Aldington here recalls his experience with H.D. in Florence in 1913. The child who expected to see 'sup'm raare' at the city's National Museum was an anecdote Aldington frequently repeated in his correspondence.

8 Even such a passing comment as this one suggests that Aldington and Netta may not have been entirely happy living together in 1941 and anticipates the reasons for their separation nine years later. Netta never apparently understood the long periods of isolation (both at a desk and beyond the urban social fray) that were necessary to Aldington as a writer. Nineteen years younger than her husband and quite different in personality, Netta was happier when they lived in a popular and busy city and could associate frequently with other artists and intellectuals.

9 Morley (1899–1980) was co-founder of Faber and Faber and during the war an editor at Harcourt, Brace.

10 André Spire (1868–1966), the French Jewish poet. For a discussion of Aldington's friendship with Spire between 1915 and 1955 see Marie Brunette Spire's 'Richard Aldington and André Spire in Correspondence', in *Richard Aldington: Essays in Honour of the Centenary of His Birth*, ed. Alain Blayac and Caroline Zilboorg, Montpellier: Presses de l'Université Paul Valéry, 1994, 51–64.

11 Norman Douglas was isolated in Portugal, to which he had escaped from Italy and France after 1939, until he managed to get to England early in 1942.

H.D. spent the war in England, living for most of the period with Bryher in London where, for the first and only occasion, the two women shared a home for an extended time. The Blitz, rationing, and war conditions generally made the experience both thrilling and enervating for H.D. After a particularly brutal night of bombing, she wrote Marianne Moore, 'I am glad you are spared all this but somehow sorry, too, as our fervour and intensity gives new life to the very bones.' She returned often in her letters to this idea that the war was both threatening and affirming, writing again to Moore that '... every morning is a sort of special gift; a new day to be cherished and loved, a DAY that seems to love back in return ... life should always have been like that, the wasted days, years! Every new morning is like a return from a bout of fever ... and strangely I personally, and others who have been able to stick it, seem to feel more alive and physically stronger than for years.'[1] Similarly, she wrote to Pearson, 'I feel about 20 years older and 50 years younger, old values return ...'. Describing her experience in London to Pearson's wife, H.D. commented, 'There just comes a moment when one cannot absorb any more intensity or drama – and yet I would not have missed this time for anything.' H.D. also felt a loyalty to England, justifying to a girlhood friend in America her decision to remain in London for the duration: '... if one has taken joy and comfort from a country, one does not want to leave it when there is trouble about'.[2]

From its beginning, H.D. also felt that this war recapitulated her experiences in 1914–18, thus investing the experience with highly charged personal significance. She was working very productively – during this period she wrote *The Gift* (in 1941–44), a number of unpublished short stories (among her papers at Yale), *By Avon River* (in 1945–46), and *Trilogy* (in 1942–44); and she drafted (in 1944) the memoir which later became *Tribute to Freud*. The fresh energy and frameworks for thinking through her own experiences which surfaced in her letters to others during the period of her divorce from Aldington in 1937–38 allowed her to break the writer's block of the early 1930s. She had left behind the iterative, constricting style of *Red Roses for Bronze* for the first completed draft of *Bid Me to Live* in 1939; now she was writing intensely and at length in both poetry and prose.

As her above letter to Pearson attests, H.D.'s renewed creativity and understanding made her feel increasingly independent and confident, ironically just at a time when she was living most dependently with Bryher. This situation occasionally frustrated H.D., who reflected in a letter to Pearson on 26 August 1943 that she saw herself moving on while Bryher seemed to be sliding backwards; more explicitly, while on a visit alone to Stratford on 20 July 1945 she wrote to Silvia Dobson that 'I think separation [from Bryher] is good, in fact a necessity' (Yale).

With the end of the war, however, H.D. felt dislocated and uneasy. Her interest in astrology, mysticism and spiritualism, which had flourished during the war years, became finally obsessive and cast the extraordinary experiences of wartime London and the ordinary experiences of daily life into unrealistic relief. On 27 December 1945, anticipating a visit to the United States to lecture at Bryn Mawr College, H.D. wrote to Pearson that 'I am pretty breathed out ... want to be private and at least partially alone, a "room of my own".' As the time drew near for her to leave England, she became increasingly distressed. In early 1946, she climbed to the roof of her apartment house and threw a fur coat, a gift from Bryher, into the street; during the spring, she became extremely withdrawn, silent, destructive of her own papers and bookplates, eventually

Aldington in Hollywood, California, in about 1945, shortly before he
returned to France

moving the furniture in her flat into the hall, eating very little, and apparently no longer
recognizing those around her.[3]

For his part, Aldington, despite his periodic claims in letters that he found America a
beautiful country and one where he could write, was not ultimately happy in the United
States and was kept there primarily by the exigencies of war – its atmosphere, physical
dangers, and the German occupation of France, where he had lived since 1928 and where
he would continue to live from 1946 until his death in 1962. He enjoyed the warmth and
peace of a year in southern Florida, but the rural isolation evidently frustrated Netta,
Catherine needed regular schooling, and he needed a larger income. Aldington moved
his family west, but finally found the demands on him as a writer in Hollywood, where he
settled in October 1942, excessive and trivializing. A year after the fighting in Europe
ended, he and his family left California in April 1946; by mid-May the Aldingtons were in
Jamaica near Netta's mother, where they remained until August when Aldington, Netta,
and Catherine, now a youngster of eight, left America for France.

1 Letters from H.D. to Marianne Moore, the first undated but probably written in June 1940, the
second dated 24 September 1940, the Rosenbach Foundation.
2 Letters from H.D. to Norman Holmes Pearson, 19 November 1941 (*Between Poetry and History*,
20), to Susan Pearson, 12 September 1944 (Yale), and to Viola Jordan, 10 November 1941 (Yale).
3 These details come from Silverstein's 'Chronology', which draws heavily at this point on privately
held notes made by Silvia Dobson, and from a letter from Bryher to H.D., dated 29 September

H.D. wearing a characteristically large hat in Switzerland
in the mid-1940s

1946, in which Bryher attempts to explain what has happened to H.D., who apparently does not remember her breakdown; this letter is printed in full in Guest, *Herself Defined*, 278–9.

➢ 108 ➢

2 September 1946
c/o American Express
1 Rue Scribe
Paris

Dear Dooley,

You were coming to America.

I sent the books you asked for, and they were returned with a notice that you were not coming.[1]

I wrote you, but think I put wrong address.

Nothing from you.

We went to Jamaica, hated it, flew in here a few days ago by yankee clipper plane.[2]

I have contracts for books with French themes, and expect to be here for some time. At present we are at Hotel L'Aiglon, Boulevard Raspail, which you may remember as a place for American studes [students]. It is at any rate clean. (Your Hotel Quai Voltaire is in the hands of the Brit. army, damn them.)

Is there any chance of your being here? It would be so nice to see you, and Netta has a great admiration for you and would like to meet you again.

Try to 'make it', as they say. Paris is still in a mess, but still wonderful, and a million times better than America with all its money and morality and monkeys and morons ... .

Ever

Richard

1 In 1945 H.D. accepted an invitation from Bryn Mawr College to give a series of lectures on poetry during the spring of 1946. Early in 1946, however, she suffered a major emotional breakdown, and instead of going to America, she flew from London to Küsnacht, near Zürich, where she was treated at the Privat Klinik Brunner at Seehof. By October 1946, H.D. had essentially recovered, but she remained at the clinic through mid-November, when she moved to a residential hotel in Lausanne.

2 On 25 September 1946, he explained his situation to H.D.:

> Our decision to return to Paris was taken when we found that Jamaica was quite impossible – a kind of darky republic full of mysterious political intrigues and unpleasant obi, with a few despairing British officials trying to keep civilisation alive. We had to separate and come by different planes, as the trans-Atlantic crossing is in complete confusion and as badly organised as everything else is. But Paris has proved quite delightful, and I have spent many pleasant hours walking about. ... The town is shabby and weather-beaten, but still a relic of civilisation. It makes one think of what Rome must have been after Alaric – with the public buildings and libraries and statues and paintings still almost intact, but a nation on the way out.
>
> ... I have five books planned to do here, and need only to rescue my library from the Customs and to find a large quiet room to begin work.

⇗ 109 ⇖

4 November 1946

Hôtel L'Aiglon

232 Boulevard Raspail

Paris 14

Dear Dooley,

Your letter sounds ever so much stronger than the others, and I feel you are getting better rapidly.[1] However, you must not hurry away, but see that you are properly established in health before leaving. Unless one is well, people can be so destructive. I have just been reading a book called Goethe et l'Art de Vivre,[2] and I am most interested to see how the old man protected himself against intrusion. He met bores with a frigid exterior and a series of 'hem! ahem!' 'so! so!' which petrified them. I love the story of a man invited to 'tea' who found Goethe and his intimates sitting in complete silence each with a bottle of red wine. The stranger was about to address himself to the Geheimrath [privy counsellor], when his neighbour hushed him with the terrific warning: 'die Excellenz denkt' [his excellency is thinking]!

I don't know Sara Lawrence – is it at Colorado Springs?[3] There are fashionable schools there, and some nice people, but it is terrifying. I met your cousin Francis [Wolle] at Boulder (Colo) in 1942. He was very nice, and so was the university [of Colorado] out of season. But those places are 5000 feet up in the Rockies and must be dreadfully cold in winter. I like Colorado and all those western states from the point of view of landscape and natural grandeur, but the people are really awful, even in

Boulder which is comparatively high-brow and civilised.

The story of Ezra is very painful, but I think it is absurd for you not to be told.[4] During the war (as you probably know) he broadcast for the Mussolini government in the most violent terms, screaming like Hitler (so I'm told), telling England it would be wiped out, cursing the Jew Roosevelt and all the rest of the nonsense. (He wrote me in 1940 that 'Churchill will be hanged on the London Gold Exchange'!) After the boys landed in Sicily Ezra saw he had pulled a terrific boner and tried to get away to Switzerland, but was arrested by the Italians on the frontier and sent back. When the yanks got into Rapallo, a man came up to some G.I.s and announced he was an American stranded in Italy. They were very friendly until they heard his name, whereupon they put him under arrest. General Clark kept him from summary execution and eventually sent him home, and he was put on trial in Washington as a traitor to the U.S. Just before the trial he broke down, and the doctors humanely announced that he was suffering from paranoia and must be confined as not in a fit state to plead. When I last heard he was in St. Catherine's Hospital, Washington, D.C. Several attempts were made to get me to declare myself one side or the other and to contribute to his defence funds. I eluded them all, as I think most were from F.B.I. agents provocateurs or communists. I was denounced to the F.B.I. as 'a friend of Pound's' in 1942, but was not molested beyond a long interview with a couple of cops, awful-looking thugs who took voluminous notes. I know nothing of Olga and Dorothy or the child. I have made several inquiries, but can learn nothing.[5]

You shouldn't worry too much about old Ez, who is quite safe, humanely treated, with his economic problem solved pro tem. at any rate. It was rumoured that he 'could not read' (he never could) but was writing a book. He was unlucky to have this [label of] traitor gummed to him, when none of the six yanks who broadcast for Hitler have even been indicted.

I don't understand the complaints of your UNESCO friends about Paris. The food is expensive but delicious as of old. The traffic is about 75% of pre-war, and cars hoot like hell as they always did. (As a driver I can tell you [you] have to in a town without automatic traffic lights). Actually, Paris is wonderfully free from Americans and other foreigners, and well worth the high prices due to the fact that the franc is frantically over-valued. The Americans want to pillage France with their damned money as they have pillaged England, and I hope the French can stop them. After years of being insulted in U.S. for being British it is pleasant to be in a town where the British (pro tem) are still immensely respected and popular, and the Americans are not. The common American man is really an awful lout, the very antithesis of the Americans who come to Europe because they like it. Ezra was quite right about all that, but why O why did he have to be such a donkey?

Don't go lecturing in America if you can help it. The process is most exhausting, and they are used to professional lecturers with the gift of gab. A young man named [John] Arlott, who runs the overseas poetry programmes of the B.B.C., is probably coming to spend a weekend with me this month. I shall tell him you have some lectures which you are prevented by ill health from giving in the U.S., and I'll let you know what he says. You don't have to appear in person. They have highly trained 'readers' and 'narrators' who speak your prose and verse, are recorded, and then broadcast to U.S., India, West Indies, Overseas generally. You can sit calmly at home and listen to your own masterpieces on the air.[6]

I am glad you liked the little photograph of Catherine. It is Hollywood's idea of a passport photo, and rather in advance of the rest of the world, I thought.

With love from us all,

Richard

1 The letters to which Aldington refers here have apparently not survived. He did not even learn of H.D.'s serious illness until 25 September 1946, when he wrote to her that 'it was a great shock to hear from Bryher that you had been so ill, and this made poignant the very charming little note from you she sent on to me this morning. I hope you will take very great care of yourself, rest and eat the good Swiss "essen", and keep out of the cold and foggy north [i.e. England] as long as possible.' On 4 October 1946, learning that H.D. was leaving the clinic, he reiterated: 'I hope your transfer to Villa Kenwin means that you are recovering. I had no idea of your illness until Mrs Macpherson [Bryher] wrote me, and it was a great shock to me for I had imagined you settling down to happier times now that the latest bout of world insanity is over.' Aldington was probably not informed of the exact nature or extent of H.D.'s nervous collapse. At the end of this October letter, he urged her to resume work; he suggested 'an editorial job', as Greek reader in the Viking series, for which he had recently completed *The Portable Oscar Wilde* (1946). He gave her specific advice about including her own translations, avoiding copyrighted material and writing an introduction for the average reader, then encouraged her further to pursue work of the sort he had been doing: 'Why don't you write a novel with a story made intelligible to ordinary people? I know it's very hard. Or a biography?' This advice, based on this own experience, was probably the only sort he felt he could give her; Aldington is not so much being egotistic here as unsure of H.D.'s capacities and needs. She had evidently written him that she needed money, but her sense of financial insecurity was a misapprehension – perhaps a part of her unstable psychological state. Aldington wrote H.D. on 9 October 1946: 'I have just had a letter from Bryher in which she tells me that you are mistaken about your finances, which is good news; and that you must not work too hard for a bit, which is not such good news.'

2 Written by Comte Robert d'Harcourt in 1933.

3 Here Aldington confuses Sarah Lawrence College in Bronxville, New York, with Colorado College in Colorado Springs. Apparently H.D. has mentioned to him that she may still at some point lecture on poetry in the United States, though evidently not at Bryn Mawr.

4 It would appear that Bryher was now being especially protective of H.D. It was Bryher's nature to cast herself in the role of intermediary between H.D. and others, between H.D. and 'the public', even between H.D. and 'reality'. Perhaps the physicians at the Brunner Clinic had advised against informing H.D. about Pound, but it seems just as likely that Bryher had taken it upon herself to prevent H.D. from knowing about this and other potentially distressing matters. In contrast, Aldington saw H.D. as more psychologically durable than she appeared to Bryher, and he often felt – as here – that it was his role to inform her of facts, however brutal, although he was certainly aware of H.D.'s sensitive temperament and is careful to be tactful and diplomatic.

5 Aldington is telling H.D. the story as he knows and recalls it. Despite some errors of fact (Pound was at St Elizabeth's Hospital, not St Catherine's), Aldington is relating what happened essentially as it occurred and was reported at the time. The breakdown conveniently just before the trial seems contrived, but not by Aldington. It seems likely that Pound had been 'paranoid' for quite some time; the doctors (and Pound's lawyers) decided on this label at a strategic moment. For a detailed account of Pound's broadcasts, his internment at Pisa and subsequent incarceration at St Elizabeth's, see Humphrey Carpenter, *A Serious Character: The Life of Ezra Pound*, London: Faber, 1988, and Wendy Flory, *The American Ezra Pound*, New Haven: Yale University Press, 1989. Aldington remains concerned about Olga Rudge (Pound's mistress and the mother of his daughter, Mary, also called Maria, the 'child' he refers to here) and Dorothy, Pound's wife.

6 It seems unlikely that H.D. ever wrote any essays on poetry suitable for presentation over the radio or at a university, although it is apparent from her letters to others in 1945 and 1946 that she was giving serious thought to the substance and form such 'lectures' would take.

⇌ IIO ⇌

13 December [1946]
Au Croissant
Rue de Bourg
[Lausanne]¹

Dear Richard,

I expect to be [at the] Alexandra [Hotel in Lausanne], for most of the winter. I had to sub-let the Lowndes Square flat, because of the 'squatter' scare.² I cannot leave it empty. The bank is the most permanent address: Lloyd's Bank, Knightsbridge, 16 Brompton Road, S.W.1. I had a little <u>fracas</u> with my last passport, as I put the place of your birth as Dover, + the one before that, as Sussex (Rye), though I didn't think either was right. Perhaps you will let me know. I also put 'former husband', instead of 'divorced husband'. However, they [the Swiss authorities] are letting me stay on. I am sorry to hear of your mother, but I have two friends whose mothers, poor things, have gone the same way.³ It is probably war-strain — there is quite an epidemic! I have myself found a narcotic in mid-Victorian or mid-Bismarkian German romances. I found some books I had at school, <u>Immensee</u>⁴ and some [Hans Christian] Anderson + a large-print Grimm, + they have removed pro tem the political onus from my mind. I shudder when I see photographs of Russians in Dresden, + friends who were in Vienna said the Russians had crowded out the beauty spots with triumphal columns. I never got to Dresden, but I was very happy in Vienna, 1933–1934, for a few months. Here, they have woven cedar, juniper + pine from window to window, the whole length of the rue de Bourg, + Christmas-trees on street corners! It gives the town a legendary appearance. We have, market-days, pots of violets, cyclamen, Christmas-roses + mimosa – a touch of Italy + the south of France, plus this northern, gabled, Gothic atmosphere. I liked Zürich after London, but it has less vivacity + variety. We did have a wonderful picture exhibition – collected from Austrian galleries + private owners, some amazing Bruegels and Rembrandts that I had never seen. I agree with you about what little 'modern art' I have seen.⁵ I am glad [your sister] Margery (or Molly, as you used to call her) is happy. I remember [your sister] Pat, only as a little girl, with Tony, still younger. Do you see them? You did not tell me whether you were in England, or not.⁶ I have such very despairing letters from London friends, the usual bad food and no cigarettes unless they walk miles, for a small, daily ration. Here, I am so very lucky. I have only sampled one vintage, not beer but Johannesburg, with an Austrian friend, at the foot of rue de petit chéna (I think is its name) + I must say the <u>Palmiers</u>, where he took me, has the real pre-war atmosphere. I will ask him if they still have Münich beer! I have noted your new address.⁷ I do hope you will be comfortably warm there! With love to you all,

Hilda/.

1 H.D. is here writing characteristically from a local restaurant, in this case a patisserie of some renown, which Aldington acknowledged in a letter to her on 11 December 1946, recalling the Munich beer once obtainable upstairs.

2 Because of the shortage of housing in England after the war, unoccupied apartments in London were in danger of being occupied by 'squatters'.

3 On 11 December 1946, Aldington had written to H.D., 'My mother is still alive and still very nearly as belligerent and capricious as of old. Poor Tony [Aldington's brother, a solicitor] has a terrible time trying to keep her quiet. He has authority from me to pay her anything he deems needful out of royalties of mine in his keeping, but she complains bitterly it is too little. Between ourselves he keeps her short on account of the whiskey bottle, but of course it is widely reported that we starve our poor mother.'

4 A lyrical novella published by Theodor Storm in 1850 about love, frustration and resignation.

5 Aldington had commented on the mediocrity of modern painting in his letters to H.D. of 2 and 11 December 1946.

6 Aldington did not pass through England on his way to Paris, but was in close touch with his relatives, primarily through a renewed friendship with his brother. On 11 December 1946 he had written H.D. that Tony was a successful provincial lawyer in Dover, while 'Margery is married to the ex-manager of an Indian railway, has a nice house in Rye, and helps Patty – poor Patty – who has never got far in life. They are both rather bigoted Catholics – result of my father's flirtations with the Scarlet Woman who sitteth on the Seven Hills of Babylon with the cup of her abominations etc'.

7 Aldington had recently moved into a flat at 162 Boulevard Montparnasse in Paris, where he remained until July 1947.

⇗ III ⇖

20 January [1947]
Hôtel
Lausanne

Dear Richard,

Thank you so much for your letter. I hate to bother you again, but would you give me the name of the place where you were born. There was great trouble about getting money out [from England], as last summer there was such a racket with exchange, people more than paid for holidays by crossing into Italy, into France and so on, changing money back and forth and most of the arrears had to be paid up, for some reason or another, by the Swiss banks. Well – that meant when I finally got Lloyd's London to send money, that I had to pass a sort of examination and though 'independent', they wanted name etc. of former husband. I gave your name as Richard Edward Aldington, think that is correct, but as I wrote, I had put different place-names on old passports for your town of birth, said RYE, and another time DOVER. However, it does not really matter, but something might come up again. Now the just adequate allowance is coming for six months, and as they will find I am most prim and careful, I will get another six months, for the summer.[1]

I am so sorry that you have been ill.[2] A few, but very few people from Paris turned up here, all with doctors' certificates, because they were ill with some sort of bronchitis. They said they had the same difficulties getting allowances, as we, in England. The result is, as someone remarked, Switzerland is no longer an 'occupied country', occupied that is by the English. There is certainly a different atmosphere here and I feel more the Italian quality or the French even when I get down to the lake in the sun. It is wonderful to see SHADOWS again, real snow too. I missed them without knowing it, in England; that gradual attrition! I don't know what to think of your return to U.S.A.[3] I should think, on the whole, it would be a good thing. The only thing that matters is

256

health, and that means food and some reserve of strength to draw on, in emergency.

I am so interested in the Pater.[4] I have found myself very happy, going on from the earlier German poets, some of which I had a slight knowledge of, to contemporary German, that is, most fortunately, HERMANN HESSE, the latest Nobel poet, though a German of the old-school and the old tradition, came before WAR I, to Switzerland, was more or less ostracized by friends and, I judge, prosperous family, lived here and in Italy, going through various phases of illness and poverty and in old age, that is about 70, he emerges as Nobel poet. He has the best diction I have met; I tried Thomas Mann in original but found him pretty stodgy, though I like 'Death in Venice'.[5] Hesse writes most lovely <u>Märchen</u> or sort of phantasy tales, much poetry, several sorts of novels – do you know if there are any translations? I have heard what there are, are not good. Perhaps Mr Frere could tell you.[6] I have asked several people, but no one seemed to know much about Hesse – such a real WAR II German name, the idea of a Hesse AND a Hermann being there in the Tessin, still living and writing after all that <u>Sturm und Drang</u>, has delighted me more than I can say. I turned from most of my English-writing contemporaries with a sort of malaise, my own fault and laziness, no doubt – but it is almost too good to be true, this discovery of a born-German living in Italian Switzerland and a Nobel poet! His books were impossible to get in German-speaking Switzerland, but I managed to collect about half of them, this French side. I will go into my book-shop and see if I can find any French Goethe for you.[7]

What a pity you can't all come here. The walks are beautiful above La Rosiaz and Chalet-à-Gobet. I am trying to find a XII century Abbey in the forest at Montheron[d], but so far have not succeeded. Do let me hear soon again. With love to you all,

Dooley/

1 H.D. did not need to worry at this point in her life about financial security and could depend on a modest but steady income. Although she made little money from her books, she had inherited some funds from her parents, which her brother Harold Doolittle had invested wisely for her in the United States. Bryher had also settled on H.D. a regular quarterly allowance and in addition paid for all hospital bills and 'special' items, such as travel or luxuries, which she frequently doled out as presents to H.D. as well as to other friends, among them later even Aldington and his daughter.

2 On 18 January 1947 Aldington had written to H.D.: 'It has troubled me that I have been unable to write, but twice in the past six weeks I have gone down with particularly vicious attacks of influenza. Apart from the fact that I have to take care this doesn't reach my lungs, one is left so depressed by it, that the arrears of things to be done appear quite mountainous.' Throughout his life Aldington took on huge amounts of work, often contracting for several books at once in addition to writing literary essays and maintaining a large professional and personal correspondence. This demanding workload exacerbated his bouts of winter colds and flu – illnesses made worse because of the danger of bronchitis, from which Aldington had suffered since the Great War. He was never hospitalized for gas inhalation, but like many soldiers in the trenches, he had breathed in a combination of poisons, and was subsequently prone to lung infections, particularly in chilly or damp weather.

3 Aldington wrote to H.D. on 18 January 1947 that he anticipated a screen writing offer from Hollywood, which for financial reasons he might need to accept, although he did not want to return to the United States. Probably the offer never materialized; in any event, Aldington remained in France.

4 Aldington's *Walter Pater: Selected Works* was published in 1948. It was in connection with this collection that Aldington was reading Goethe.

5 H.D. read and spoke German with some ease, having learned it in school. Her facility was probably also nourished by her mother's Moravian family with its German traditions.

6 Alexander Stewart Frere (1896–1984) was Aldington's good friend and editor at Heinemann. H.D. knew him because of his attempts to intercede for Aldington during the divorce.

7 On 18 January 1947, Aldington had written to H.D. that he was having difficulty finding translations of Goethe's work. Unlike H.D., Aldington could read German only with difficulty, although he could and regularly did read French with ease and appreciation. In a letter to Bryher on Christmas Day 1959, Aldington wrote: 'I read medieval Latin, French, Italian, Spanish and Portuguese, but not German, damn it. My fault, but I hated them so much for what I myself saw of their beastliness in France in 1918 – nasty people, criminals'.

≫ 112 ≪

24 January 1947
162 Boulevard Montparnasse
Paris 14

Dear Dooley,

Thank you so much for sending the Werther. If by any chance you should run across the Italian Journey and Sojourn in Rome I should be very grateful for them. I think I have all Goethe's other important prose, including the Eckermann conversations and Schiller letters. He is a most intelligent critic – obviously the source of many later writers. He was also very intelligent in his life, and it is distressing to think how few Germans have emulated him; but then one must think of the enormous numbers of British cows since Shakespeare.

My birthplace is Portsmouth, Hampshire. Date 8th July, 1892. You should give my name as: Edward Godfree Aldington, known as Richard Aldington. I hope you have no trouble over money. The British are clearly in a state of hysteria about their miserable money, and I wouldn't be surprised if the pound took a fearful tumble. During the war I sent food parcels to an old friend with three young children. Recently he got to U.S. on a ten pound a day business man's trip, and sent Catha some powdered milk and candies. Would you believe it, the Treasury found it out, sent for him, gave him hell, and made him pay them in dollars! To me it is beyond words that a once great country can stoop to such petty meanness and spying on a man who risked his life a hundred times to help during the bombardments.

My return to the U.S. is conditional on a Hollywood job, though from a letter just received from my agent the job looks nearer. (There has been a long strike now ending.) The fact that my novel on Casanova has subscribed 22,000 copies in London is the sort of fact which determines an engagement.[1] If I go, I shall go alone for the first six months. Then, if they keep me on, it will be at a salary of $1250 a week, so that the girls can come back to H'wood if they want or find something comfortable in Europe. I think I must take this job, Dooley, because sterling just isn't money any more. Since September I have earned on paper about 4000 pounds, but how much shall I get after payment of income tax? How much of the small remainder should I be allowed to take out? As a matter of fact I have sent it to my brother, Tony, to keep in case Catha wants to go to an English university. But she might prefer to go somewhere else.

By the way, is there no possibility of your regaining U.S. nationality? As a native American I think you wouldn't have the slightest difficulty, and I believe Uncle Sam would force them to give you back your money. You'd have no further passport and money troubles. True, the State Dept. is mean about passports at present, but only because travel is so difficult. Why don't you go see the U.S. Consul at Lausanne and ask his advice? Or at any rate your friends at Yale?[2] I would get my American friends to do all they could to back you. Think about it. Believe me, I feel awfully guilty at having wished this unlucky nationality on you. True, I didn't naturalise American as I could have done, but you don't need me to tell you what an absurd lie that would have been.

Hermann Hesse – a deadly sort of name among the multitudes of fools these days.[3] Yet there are bound to be American translations – publishers would rush to buy a Nobel prizewinner. I will ask Frere.

Yes, I wish we could be at Lausanne for a time, but we are held here by the schools and by my waiting on the perhaps-never-to-arrive cable from Hollywood.[4] It would be so nice to see you.

With love to you,

Richard

1 Aldington's last novel, *The Romance of Cassanova* (1946).
2 That is, Norman Holmes Pearson (1909–75), who had met H.D. during her visit to New York in 1937. Pearson, Professor of English at Yale, served with the OSS in London from 1943 through 1945, and during the war had been a regular visitor at H.D.'s flat. From this period onward he championed H.D.'s work, and after the war began to collect and preserve her books and papers in what has today become a vast archive at Yale. Pearson was both a personal and professional friend, and his advice would certainly have extended to such areas as regaining US citizenship.
3 While H.D. freely associates this alliterative name with the German romantic past and with the writer's biography impressionistically apprehended, Aldington connects the name more specifically and exclusively with recent historical events, calling to mind here the Nazis Hermann Göring and Rudolf Hess. These different patterns and tendencies of association are characteristic of H.D. and Aldington.
4 When Catha began school, Aldington found himself bound by her schedule, which he was invariably careful to respect, and his travels were suddenly limited to school holidays.

≈ 113 ≈

7 February, Friday [1947]
Alexandra Hôtel
Lausanne

Dear Richard,

Thank you so much for your two letters [24 January and 6 February 1947]. I think I felt a little uneasy about Maria as I was told that letters had come to me, from her or Olga or both, while I was so ill. It was thought better not to tell me of this, at the time. I never saw the letters but imagined the very worst. However, I did write friends in New Jersey who knew the whole history and they finally told me that Maria was going to be married to an Italian-Russian – and they believed she was all right. They also told me that Dorothy was near, outside Washington, I think – anyhow, I don't think now I need worry. Thank you all the same for the news.[1] I also want to thank you for the birthplace. Yes, I could get and could have got USA papers back at any moment before or during the war, by banging down a dollar; I think that is all. In fact, I had difficulty as they said I was American, when I went for my last pass-port, anyone born in USA is. But I came under a marriage-law that has been practically forgotten. I didn't want to take out USA papers again, as Perdita has her British ones, and I thought there might

259

be trouble. I am afraid I am rather attached to the old Lion and Unicorn [England] after all these years, maybe the effect of my early infatuation with Alice [in Wonderland].

It has been cold here too, but we have a pulse of steam-heating as we used to call it in America – and I have a nice, small, narrow room with a large wide balcony, facing the sun-rise over the Savoy Alps, where the gulls from the lake come and perch. There is a garden table there but so far, I have not had the temerity to sit out of doors; also, there is an awning, so far un-rolled, but a happy augury. I feel very selfish when I hear of this sort of black frost that has fallen on England. I don't know if Paris is so bad. I really have no trouble with money, as I have an affable Swiss doctor, whom I have seen only once, but he produced proper papers for me. Compared with people I left in London, I suffer from 'rude health', but it is a good excuse to draw a living allowance and I can go on till April – if the very worst came to the worst, I could get the USA papers and my brother says he would send me money. Now, the dollar is frozen. Yes – Hermann Hesse is as you say a 'deadly sort of name'. But his poetry and tales are an antidote not only to the Hesse and Hermann but an anodyne, as well. I have one French translation, SIDHARTHA. If you are prowling in book-shops, just ask if there are any others to be had; there are other translations but very hard to get – none in English. I envy you the Japanese prints.[2] I had a little Fujiyama collection. I think we found it in Kenniston, about 100 years ago. I believe it is about somewhere, still.

I do hope you are keep[ing] well. How is food now? I am so happy about the thought of a possible trip to Lugano, in April. It would be no more expensive than here and now they have opened the Simplon, Domodossola cross-cut or short-cut, through Italy. It was a deadly journey before, up to Zürich and then back from Zürich, eight hours. But I won't be going yet. I believe it is pretty un-spoiled and it would be wonderful to hear Italian again and to prowl in some of the old churches. It is really not so far from Milan and some of the Verona and Venice painters came from that district.

Again with all best wishes and do keep well –

Love from
Hilda.

1 On 6 February 1947, Aldington had written to H.D.: 'A letter has just arrived from my friend Halcott Glover, whose wife was a great friend of Olga Rudge. He says: "We have just heard from Olga Rudge's brother that she is safe and at present at Siena on musical affairs. Had a hard time earlier, teaching English for a bare living. The daughter by Ezra was married the other day."'

2 On 18 January 1947 Aldington had written of his two bouts of influenza: 'I entertained myself during my forced stay in bed with some lovely Japanese colour prints (Toyokuni, Hiroshige, Kuniyashi).'

≈ 114 ≈

18 April 1947
162 Boulevard Montparnasse
Paris 14

Dear Dooley,

This Pater is an ever toiling up a toiling wave job, and I'm heartily sick of it – particularly as the Americans are only doing it with great reluctance and I hear from Heinemanns that the 50% cut in paper rations will delay it.

One begins to feel a goddam all governments resentment, until one meets (as we did yesterday) a Scottish anarchist-nationalist, a most unholy spectacle.

You know, old Ez does sound a bit crackers. Frobenius cannot be anyone but Froben of Basle, the great Renaissance printer – you may remember I once burdened your life with a vast folio of Caelius Rhodiginus printed by the said Froben. But Frobenius never wrote anything, so far as I know. For prefaces etc. he usually applied to his friend Erasmus. So either Ezra sends you to non-existent works or to a vast farrago of classics and humanists – if he means the works published by Froben. Of course, there may be writings of Froben I don't know.[1]

May Sinclair has bequeathed Ez, you and me fifty pounds each, one or two specified books, and a choice from her library. She has bequeathed you her Euripides and Aristotle's Poetics in Greek. To me her ink-stand, Rabelais and Aeschylus. I have chosen 28 books. Ezra chose 11 – most modestly – but perhaps out of scorn, as he chiefly chose fat Ford, H. James and a work on Genetics! The list is frightfully misspelled. Your Palimpsest appears as Palmforest (!) and Ez's Quia Pauper Amavi as 'I'm a Pauper Marvi' (!) Oddly enough he seems to have made no comment on the list, though perhaps they had to make a new one, as they beg me not to mark this one.[2]

I have told them to communicate directly with you, and I gave Bryher's address, as you may have left the Alexandra [for Lugano]. I had better send this there.

We have lovely weather here, soft and poetic such as never happens in that hard California.

Catherine has the makings of a literary critic. I offered her [Charles] Kingsley's Westward Ho! [1920], but she disliked it, and when I asked why said: 'Oh, it's got too much cowboy stuff'! This is as bewildering as any pundit I ever heard.

With love.
Richard

1 Pound was in touch with H.D. through her friend Violet Jordan in Tenafly, New Jersey. H.D., in a letter that has apparently not survived, had written to Aldington about Pound's request. H.D. wrote to Aldington on 28 April 1947 that she had 'consulted the head of the Lausanne shop, as I was really wondering if Ez. had invented this. He told me quite solemnly that Frobenius was called Leo, that he was a quite-well-known mystic (are mystics ever well known? and by what or by whom?)' Aldington responded on 2 May 1947: 'I am very glad you settled that Frobenius mystery, for I should hate to think old Ez was really nuts.'

2 On 24 April 1947 H.D. responded: 'I am deeply touched that May should have remembered us all that time. I saw her, about 1927. She was ill then, and later moved out of London, I think. I tried to find out where she was but Dorothy Richardson seemed to think she was in a rest-home somewhere.' On 26 April Aldington wrote H.D.: 'I saw May as late as about 26–27, but then she disappeared. I wrote several times and had no answer. I wish we could have assured her of continuing affection …'.

≈ 115 ≈

25 May 1947
Minerva Hotel
Lugano

Dear Richard,

Thank you so much for your letter. I didn't know Helen Hoyt but will write a friend who was in touch with most of those people – she may know why H.H. landed in

Calif.[1] I am interested in the Michael Field; old Havelock Ellis used to talk of them.[2] As I remember, we both met Pearsall Smith at the Whitalls'.[3] I heard that T.S.E. was in America. I never followed his Milton points; the Milton seemed to be a peg to hang Eliot jokes on; I don't know; heard one student before the war, I met in London, say that Eliot went on about 'Milton and his green hair'. Whether Milton's green hair was meant or the green hair of the Comus sylph [in Milton's poem 'Comus'], I don't know – it was too erudite altogether for my taste. He did lecture at the Churchill Club in London during the war, with the Bishop or a Bishop in the chair. The Bishop was very flighty and remarked, 'we will ask Milton himself these questions when we get to heaven; for I hope to meet Milton there and surely Mr Eliot will be there'. This also may or may not have been irony!

I have not been in Philadelphia since I left – I mean since I set sail [for Europe in 1911]. I did once find my way to Horace Traubell – was taken there by an older 'girl', a member of the W[alt] W[hitman] Society – those were the days. I can't say that Traubell impressed me, he was rather done up like the good gray poet – with longish hair, cultivated to a Whitman wave but no beard. He was one of Whitman's youthful group – Camden, New Jersey.[4]

It is good of you to say that you will glance over the MSS. I have sent it to London to be typed, but hear now that the elderly typist is about to go off for three weeks holiday. However, she may have got the MSS just in time – I will hope to see typed sheets in about ten days, in that case. Otherwise, it will be about six weeks. But I will let you know about it, in the meantime.[5]

This is just to thank you for your offer of practical advice. I hope you are having a summer Whitsun, as we have here. It was cold and raw for about a week, I think it was that eclipse! I hear from Capri, too, that they had wind and sultry weather for their great saint day.

Love,
Dooley/

1 On 23 May 1947 Aldington wrote H.D. that while he was in California he had bought some books from Helen Hoyt's library. It seems likely that these had inscriptions which identified Hoyt (1875–1944) as a Bryn Mawr student (A.B. 1897, M.A. 1898) or faculty member (she taught in the English department from 1897 to 1904 and again from 1905 to 1907). H.D. attended Bryn Mawr in 1905–6, but she was not in Hoyt's section of the required course in Composition and Rhetoric. Hoyt moved to Santa Barbara in 1920.
2 Aldington mentioned in his 23 May letter that he had bought *Stephania* (London: E. Mathews and John Lane, 1892) by Michael Field, the pseudonym for two English women, Katherine Harris Bradley and Edith Emma Cooper. The book is a tragic trialogue in blank verse; the speakers are The Pope, The Emperor and a courtesan.
3 In his letter to H.D. on 23 May, Aldington reflected on Logan Pearsall Smith (1865–1946), the American author who had settled in England:

> Perhaps he was the person who mentioned Marcel Proust to me in 1917. He – Smith – had a good life within slightly old-maidish limits. And his mind can't have been too hot in the end. In 1940 he wrote me to New York asking about Ezra's first appearances in London. He had poor Ez hopelessly mixed up with Frank Harris, and nothing I could write would convince him that Ezra did not go about London dressed as an Idaho cow boy! I described him as well as I could, the dark suit and rolled double waistcoat, the very neat-waisted grey overcoat of Regency cut, the black cane, the hat jauntily on the side of the head – entre nous, a little Whistlerian, but let us not admit it publicly – but would Logan take it? He would not.

4 Horace Traubell (1858–1919) was Walt Whitman's literary executor and cared for him during the poet's last years in Camden, New Jersey. Traubell wrote an important early biography (*With Walt Whitman in Camden: A Diary*, in three volumes, 1905, 1908 and 1914). After Whitman's death in 1892 Traubell maintained his home as a sort of shrine.

5 On 14 May 1947 H.D. had asked Aldington if he would be willing to look at a draft of her still unpublished novel 'The Sword Went Out to Sea: Synthesis of a Dream'. The typescript is among H.D.'s papers at Yale.

≫ 116 ≪

Sunday, 1 June [1947]
Minerva Hotel
Lugano

Dear Richard,

I have the type script of SYNTHESIS of a DREAM, from London. Please do not undertake reading, if you are busy now. If you just happen to be free, it is not so very long, will you let me know, then, I will post, in two separate envelopes, with enclosed envelopes for return.

I satisfied myself, but it is so difficult to assess this prose, as it takes in the last-war London scene and one's own conclusions about it all, may seem exaggerated, hysterical and probably mad – but the whole lay-out or set-up of the present is so crazy. ....[1]

I use the name DELIA ALTON in the book and thought I would sign it so – *Synthesis of a Dream, by Delia Alton*. The point is, the Oxford Press set up three books of poems of mine, during the war – a Trilogy – and they asked me for some prose. But the poetry was H.D., of course, and you will see, if you read this, that I do not want it to appear too blatantly 'historical' – though I have published prose a bit, this is quite, I think, different, terse and short sentences and sequences. It really gets in a lot – but does not, I feel, twist the threads or muddle the mind – though the IDEA is rather gigantic, the expression is concentrated and almost meager at times. Well – I do not want to submit this to Oxford, that is all. Nor do I want to enter into explanations as to WHY H.D. is not used. I think taking the name of the woman who tells the story, the narrator, and signing the book with it, rather solves a number of problems. Anyhow, if you have no time, just now, I will understand. If you have time, I will send the two envelopes of MSS, on hearing from you.[2]

Love,
Dooley./

1 'Synthesis of a Dream', the subtitle for H.D.'s unpublished autobiographical novel 'The Sword Went Out to Sea', a work she later described in her unpublished journal 'Compassionate Friendship' (18 February–25 March 1955, Yale) as 'a reconstruction of my contact with Lord Howell, through and because of the messages we had received' (20 April 1955, 79). The novel is a companion piece to 'Magic Ring', another unpublished *roman à clé*; together, the two works explore H.D.'s spiritualist experiences in London during and just after the Second World War. The novels include accounts of seances in H.D.'s London flat, but the context for these spiritual experiences shifts from the 1940s to the historical past – medieval France or the England of William Morris and his circle. At the same time, encoded characters (whose names sometimes shift from sequence to sequence in the two novels) reflect important figures in H.D.'s life (Lord Dowding, Bryher, and Aldington among others).

2 Throughout her life H.D. struggled with the issue of artistic identity, even before Pound 'named' her 'H.D.' when he submitted her poems to *Poetry* in 1912. She signed manuscripts and published work with several different pseudonyms (Edith Gray, Rhoda Peter, John Helforth, D.A. Hill,

Helga Dart, Helga Doorn) as well as Delia Alton, most of them variations on her full name (Hilda Doolittle Aldington), so that they both mask and reveal her biographical self. The issue here seems to depend primarily on her idea of her public self as poet ('H.D.') and her awareness of the more obviously autobiographical ('historical') nature of her prose narratives. For a discussion both of her use of pseudonyms and this distinction between her verse and prose, see Susan Stanford Friedman's *Penelope's Web: Gender, Modernity, H.D.'s Fiction*, Cambridge: Cambridge University Press, 1990. Oxford University Press published H.D.'s *Trilogy* (*The Walls Do Not Fall, Tribute to the Angles*, and *The Flowering of the Rod*) in 1944, 1945 and 1946. Although some of H.D's stories had appeared in avant-garde periodicals, her published book-length fiction at this time included only *Palimpsest* (1926), *Hedylus* (1928) and the children's 'novel' *The Hedgehog* (1936). She had also experimented with novellas, some of which were privately printed, such as *Kora and Ka* (1934) and *Nights* (1935), and had among her papers several autobiographical fictions which she had not sought to publish.

≈ 117 ≈

Friday, 6 June [1947]
Minerva Hotel
Lugano

Dear Richard,

Thank you so much for your letter and offer to read the MSS. I am posting it, registered in two envelopes, this afternoon. The DREAM is, as I said before, fantasy-cum-reality. But the five year 'reality' of bombs, fly-bombs and V2 was by far the less stable or 'real' than the world of imagination that I tried to hold on to, those years. I don't really care who or what knows that H.D. wrote the DREAM. It is, as you will see, concerned with other people, with one in particular about whom I didn't 'tattle' outside.[1] It just happened that he happened to be next to Monty [Lord Montgomery of Alamein], perhaps the most popular (though unlike Monty, rather retired) personage of World War II. Of course, I might have made him up – or imagined the whole sequence. But whether made-up or imagined or 'real', there is a sort of protection in taking the name of the person in the BOOK – it does not really matter WHO wrote the DREAM! It stands or falls or falls or fades on its own merit or its own 'message' – the 'message' being simply, that the world was, perhaps is and possibly will be 'crashing to extinction', if these in authority, no matter where or who, don't stop smashing up things with fly-bombs, V2 and the ubiquitous (possibly) so called 'atom'. They could do something with the atom – better than smashing cherry orchards … that is all I am trying to put over in the DREAM. If it is to be put across, someone will eventually take hold of it. I don't want to send it to my Yale people, until I have had an opinion this side. And then, it has to do chiefly with England – and the scene of the two wars!

Yes – if you have any idea that my rather intense prose and <u>idea</u> would be kindly taken to, by any special publisher, I would be glad of a hint. I feel USA is so far away, and it takes so long for book-post to get there – can hardly afford air. Then there is the reading that side. I have only one blurred carbon and the original, otherwise, I could send both out together. I can get another copy made when my little old typist gets back from her holiday. Fortunately, she got this through quickly. I have another MSS, an or a H.D. one, that I would like to have you look at later – it is a life-synthesis of my feeling for Elizabethan poetry and is not very long – was part of the body of notes I was working on for Bryn Mawr when I collapsed.[2]

Don't worry about the MSS if it bores you. Just keep in mind, that what I HAD to say at that point, with whatever paraphernalia I had right at hand, was that WAR had got to stop – or we had got to stop. Well – I almost did. This I hope is not my last will and testament but it is a will and testament.

Love,

Dooley./

1 The 'one in particular' was Hugh Caswall Tremenheere Lord Dowding (1882–1970), Air Chief Marshal during the Second World War, who is credited with winning the Battle of Britain in September 1940. He retired at his own request two months after the victory. His abrupt departure, mysterious to the general public, generated much speculation and a longlasting controversy over his strategies – conservatively defensive – and his temperament – aloof, out of touch with internal RAF personality conflicts and politicking. After a short stint in America in 1941 as Churchill's emissary, he returned to private life and was made baron in 1943. He began lecturing on spiritualism in 1942. H.D., who had been attending seances since December 1941, heard him speak in October 1943 and initiated correspondence with him. He deprecated her romantic view of him as a spiritual leader, but came to tea at her flat several times. In early 1946, he politely refused her insistent request that he join her at her seance table to hear messages concerning post-atomic bomb disasters. H.D.'s interest in the occult, which led during the war years to her participation in seances and fostered her interest in astrology and mystical experiences, as well as her sense of Lord Dowding's rejection, certainly contributed to her breakdown in 1946. I am grateful to Jane Augustine for these details about H.D.'s friendship with Lord Dowding, a relationship that is the subject of her forthcoming dual biography, *The Poet and the Airman*.

2 It seems likely that this 'MSS' became *By Avon River*, published in 1949. It contains two parts: 'Good Friend', a long poem H.D. probably wrote during the spring and summer of 1945, and 'The Guest', an essay H.D. worked on during the autumn of 1946.

☙ 118 ❧

10 June 1947

162 Boulevard Montparnasse

Paris 14

Dear Dooley,

I have received and already read your Synthesis of a Dream. It is a remarkable piece of work, to me very interesting, particularly Part I, though the scenes at the Philadelphia 1903 epoch are perfectly done. Since you quote 'wings' and William Morris together, but do not refer to his poem, Golden Wings, I am sending a extract in which the word is frequently repeated. Perhaps this symbolism will interest you.[1]

I must think a little about the practical aspect. Am I right in assuming the following to be your wishes

(1) You would like it published in the British Empire and U.S.A., with of course all translation rights reserved.

(2) You wish it to be issued under a pseudonym (in which I now agree with you) but it will be necessary to tell the publisher.[2]

I'll let you hear again later when I have been able to form some sort of plan.

Love,

Richard

1 Aldington is aware of the importance of this matter to H.D. Earlier the same day he had written her: 'Be assured I shall try to carry out your wishes as exactly as possible. The script has not yet arrived, but I'll write you as soon as I am able to read it.' Aldington copied out for H.D. the ten stanzas from Morris's 'Goldens Wings' in which a woman beckons her knight to come to her from 'across the sea' and vividly describes the autumn wildlife (a swan, a moorhen, a stoat, a bat, a wasp) and nature (the wind, wheat, grass, apples) in a foreboding atmosphere of moonlit romance.

2 On 6 April 1947 Aldington had shared his reservations about this issue: 'I think your idea of assumed name is punk. You lose the value of your H.D. reputation in sales, and if your idea is real secrecy you won't get it. A publisher won't take it without knowing the real author, and will certainly tattle about it, so that the other publishers and the "groups" will find out. Thus you will be known to your enemies and not to your friends.'

ᚠ 119 ᚠ

11 June 1947
162 Boulevard Montparnasse
Paris (14)

Dear Dooley,

I am rather bedevilled these days by extra people who must be attended to, given that profusion of one's nervous energy which makes such people think it is they who are alive. My publisher from London is here [A. S. Free] – I have Albatross representative to see for lunch to-day; the French publisher must be entertained as I have a book coming out in French; letters about 'business'; an old sweetheart of Netta's who became a hero in Burma and is bringing his new bride to Paris. It is hard to concentrate, impossible to make anything. I shall have to go further away.[1]

This is to explain a letter I foresee will be 'scattered'.

First – do you remember that the 'hero' of W. Morris's The Glittering Plain is called Hallblithe? Howell is not an English name – it is an old Welsh name. You have accidently written 'Apocryphal' for 'Apocalyptic' – one or two other lapsus calami [slips of the pen], I'll note them.[2]

This book is going to be difficult in its present form – I mean from the commercial publisher's angle. Always the problem is: How to present new non-popular material in a form which the publisher will and the public must accept. You have not done it. Publishers all believe in Napoleon's dictum – they like 'clear-cut genres'. 'How are we to classify this?' they ask anxiously. If the answer is 'Fiction' or 'Biography' they are enchanted – if 'Essay' gloom! Now, from the publisher's point of view this is part fiction, part essay and can only be classified as 'Occult'. Difficult – the field is instantly limited.

The style of Part I, though a little staccato, is perfectly all right – Part II a little diffuse and even repetitive. (I speak only from the commercial standpoint.) If you had made the book 'straight' fiction, gone back one step and written of Delia in the third person – you looking on from outside, intervening if you like but always projecting Delia away from yourself – if you had worked it up to this climax, that Delia has the warning that will save England and Lord Howell rejects it, refuses to pass it on (a motive must be found) then you have the possibility of a great success. Delia's post-climax reflections would be shortened but would round the book out. Of course the illness would coincide with or immediately follow the neglected warning.

Can't you see what a new story you have there? But it must be more objective, and constructed – artificially if you like, but built up to the tragic climax, with Delia's soft profound musings afterwards. You would not be either for or against spiritualism (cut that brilliant piece of analysis at the end) but simply telling people – this happened, just thus, perhaps it is all a dream, but it <u>did</u> happen, Delia did and suffered and heard just this, so did Howell, so Gareth. The present title should be at best a sub-title – you need the idea but not perhaps the name: Cassandra – though I think most would get that.

I write frankly as one old comrade to another, so do not be froissée [offended]. Perhaps you do not want to be read by tens of thousands, but here I think you have the chance. In its present form the book is publishable but has little chance of popular success. It will be well reviewed but not sell. Of course I cannot guarantee success if the material is re-cast and dramatised, but there is a very good chance of it. The only piece of material to be supplied is Lord Howell's motive – he has saved England once, has the chance to save her a second time, why doesn't he? He is jealous of Delia's priority? There is another woman? Or what?

There are very few experiences of an author more dreadful than to receive this sort of comment, which you may wholly reject off-hand. I think in its present form the book does say what it sets out to tell, but only to the prepared inevitably few readers. There is the chance of many if the form though not the substance is modified. It is what Browning says somewhere about Men and Women following his other inaccessible work 'I have written not what the few must but what the many may like.' Of course, more than ever the book as 'straight' novel would have to be pseudonymous.[3]

Tell me what you think – your 'reactions' as they say. If you prefer to leave the material as it is I shall try to think of some way of getting by with it.

You explain the Ezra tragedy perfectly – 'they had to live.' Of course. Someone told me that at one period they were so poor Olga had to go to England each winter to stay with friends (her brother, perhaps?) because they could not afford her fuel and food in that little hut place above Rapallo. Last night somebody told me that Schuschnigg is in Rapallo.[4] 'Perhaps in Ezra's flat', I said. They seemed to think that would be fine. It hurts me very much to think that he became just a commonplace tool in the hands of these vile politicians. One must avoid that.

Love,
Richard

1 Albatross published Aldington's novels in their Modern Continental Library series. The forthcoming book was likely either the French translation of Aldington's *Casanova*, published by Nicholson and Watson in 1947, or the French translation of *The Duke*, Aldington's biography of Wellington, which appeared from Nicholson and Watson in 1948.

2 For H.D., Aldington's reference to Morris's hero is perhaps the most important he makes in all his letters to her. She felt it conveyed both his understanding of this novel and of how she worked in her writing more generally. Perhaps even more significantly, she felt the name 'Hallblithe' revealed the enduring intellectual, emotional, and spiritual bond between them. Aldington's use of the word here short-circuited, as it were, all that had occurred between them since 1918, reinstating the period when they had worked together as artistic partners in the earliest days of their relationship. Throughout the rest of her life, she would return to this moment as a turning point, a re-quickening of their relationship. Reflecting on Letter 119, she wrote to Norman Holmes Pearson on 8 May 1951: 'Richard, just like Richard, seemed to cancel out all psychic debts with his one word, <u>Hallblithe</u>. How did that happen, and how did it become a double miracle, coming through Richard?' But H.D. was more restrained in her response to Aldington; she added in her letter to Pearson, 'I do not write him like this.'

3 In a letter to H.D. on 15 July 1947 Aldington amplified this point:

> It is very much indeed a question of form and presentation. In its present shape I cannot hold out much hopes of a large audience. But if it were re-shaped into a novel of an objective kind, expressing all its sensations and ideas, its emotions and beliefs through action and character, then I think it would have the chance of a very big success. You wilfully put obstacles between yourself and the common reader. Why do you? It is so much harder to be lucid, to put things in such a way that any educated reader of good will can, indeed must, follow you. You are a lord of language and can so easily make speech obey you. ... [*sic*].

I have been unable to trace Aldington's quotation of Browning.

4 Kurt van Schuschnigg (1897–1977) was Federal Chancellor of Austria from 1934 until the *Anschluss* in 1938. He rejected National Socialism, but was forced into a policy of concession to Hitler. Interned in Austria after the German invasion, he was sent to Dachau in 1941 and remained in concentration camps throughout the war. In 1947 he left Austria for the United States.

🌿 **120** 🌿

20 June 1947

162 Boulevard Montparnasse

Paris 14

Dear Dooley,

I see that your last letter was written a week ago.[1] Here I have been snowed under with proofs, visits from London, and desperate efforts to get some introductions finished. What an epoch! The working classes are so completely in control that naturally all work is shoddy. For instance, printers send out sloppy proofs, and the author has to do their work for them – and with a book like the anthology that is something! By the way, it has taken six years to get that book out in England, and I still wonder if they will 'make' it this autumn. They started setting on the 1st January, and still have not sent all the proofs![2]

Do you hear any rumblings of a great financial crash in Western Europe? I get some disquieting rumours, but let's hope they're false.

Among the visitors here was the chairman of Heinemann, my old friend Frere. I sounded him out about the possibilities of Synthesis of a Dream, without revealing you, but telling him frankly what it is. He wouldn't touch it himself (this singular prejudice against 'mixed genres') and didn't think we could hope to get it out before 1950. The publishers are held to 60% paper indefinitely, it seems, and may be cut more. Heinemann alone have 1500 more or less 'live' books out of print. A publisher will within a year get out a book he knows will sell 10,000 copies in a week, or he will print or reprint a very slender book for which there is a steady demand. But no publisher can now afford to 'carry stock'. He must put his paper into what will sell at once.

This is not so true of the U.S., but the publishers there are mad for best-sellers and nothing but best-sellers. It is going to be tough, I foresee, to place the book in its present form; and I think it can only be done by a London publisher in partnership with an American. The book would have to be printed in Holland, part of the edition going to England, part to U.S. Forgive all these squalid details, but they are the essential framework of any publication. Now, less than ever does literary merit count.

There is one way in which it could be done quickly. Any new company with a proved registered capital of 1000 pounds can start publishing, and get a basic allowance of 6 tons of paper. This would produce about 15,000 copies of your book; you could spread it over others. They would not allow you to export sheets to U.S., only bound copies, and these are so heavily taxed as to be almost unsalable, and you lose U.S. copyright.

Well, there we are.

Meanwhile, I shall make the few corrections, and see what can be done on the practical side.

'Hallblithe' comes from the Glittering Plain, which is one of Morris's prose romances. You should not have any difficulty in getting copies of Morris, at from 10/- to 25/-. If you have a second-hand bookseller, send him your order. You will be allowed to pay out of funds in England, without having to send back from Switzerland. Here is a list of Morris:

> Earthly Paradise. In I vol. Longmans Green
> Poems by W.M. (Includes Jason) World's Classics.
> Sigurd the Volsung
> Odyssey
> Aeneids [check pl.]
> Poems by the Way
Prose: The Water of the Wondrous Isles
> The Well at the World's End
> The Story of the Glittering Plain
> The Roots of the Mountains
> The House of the Wolfings
> The Sundering Flood

and the Socialist things, which are not interesting. I have all these except the Odyssey, and can lend them to you if you can't get them or if you prefer. Let me know. Gerard Hopkins (Of the OUP [Oxford University Press]) said when he was here that he would try to get me any Oxford books I need, and I'm quite sure he'd do the same for you. I think you might find Morris very soothing – he is so absolutely remote from these ulcerating times we live in. I re-read Jason and Earthly Paradise in Hollywood, and the prose romances in Jamaica – strange places.

We are thinking of returning to our old stamping ground at or near Le Lavandou, in spite of the fact that it was knocked about so heavily by the Allied landing. Paris is delightful in spring and we've enjoyed it, but it is an absolutely dead city in August-September, and then the winter chill gives me one bad cold after another. It is a shame to move the child from school where she is happy, but it won't help her to have a bed-ridden or deceased father. I lost four months work last winter, and haven't nearly made up. Another move is a bore, but perhaps I can get books etc. installed, and not have to drag them around each time I move.

All these boring things press on one so.

With love,
Richard

1 Unfortunately, this letter in which H.D. evidently responded to Aldington's reading of 'Synthesis of a Dream' has apparently not survived. H.D. did, however, respond further in her letter to Aldington on 22 June 1947:

About the book – thank you so much. I feel that I struck a sort of oil-well or gold-mine –

my own – I have not plumbed the depth or yet veined the ore. I have started well on with Volume II [that is, Part II], and it might be indicated to bring them out later together, or one to follow on the heels of the other. In any case, I feel that the book is so very precious to me, that having satisfied myself, I am satisfied to have two or three readers – until/if the time comes, when it could be set up by someone who really WANTED it and believed in it, and who would do the business part altogether.

H.D. continued, asking Aldington to entitle volume I 'Wintersleep', moving 'Synthesis of a Dream' to a subtitle, as he had suggested. The second volume she added be called 'Summer Dream'. She then indicated various other corrections to phrasing and section breaks. For his part, Aldington was careful in his criticism, but he continued to offer H.D. additional comments, revealing his abiding interest as well as his frustration with her modernist prose that seemed to him intentionally and needlessly obscure.

2 Aldington's anthology of verse, entitled in England *Poetry of the English-Speaking World*, was published by Heinemann in 1947.

≫ 121 ≪

Monday, 4 August [1947]
Minerva Hôtel
Lugano

Dear Richard,

I would have written sooner but knew you would be busy getting settled in. I wonder if it is very hot – it is here, and everywhere, they say, but one can trail about in suitable clothes in these places.[1]

I will send you back the broadcast later, when you want it.[2] I would like to read it again. I found you had stressed the main points and condensed the whole, while giving an easy approach to the subject [the history of Imagism]. How well I remember that bun shop. I went back there during the war, this last war – it was much the same – but food everywhere then (and now worse they say) was most uninspiring. I think it was 'waffles' originally that Ez. was after. I hear from Viola Jordan that Mrs Ez [Dorothy Pound] is there now and writing round as his 'secretary' to all and sundry, re political, soi-disant, matters. Viola thought she ought to 'warn' me but I do not think Dorothy has [my] address; I believe Olga wrote several times, or the child [Mary Rudge de Rachewiltz] – now a mother, I am told, she married a Russian, my New Jersey news bulletin announced – well, anyway, the letters were sorted over last spring and I literally did not receive them.[3]

I read Wood Beyond the World and was renewed and refreshed. It is just as well that I did not read much during the writing of my Synthesis – and during the table-sessions there in London. It was so much more dramatic you finding Hallblithe like that, for me. I am so happy now to have the book. I am reading it again.[4] I have been recovering from visitors, very nice, but I did not like the motor-trips we took. It was interesting of course, but I was greatly saddened by the famine-look in the Italian faces – both the Como and the Maggiore trips upset me. Now, I won't go over the frontier again for some time, if I can help it. I wish we could do more for them.

I am a bit lost as due to visitors and heat, I cannot get on very fast with the typescript of the Synthesis, Summerdream part. I will feel better when this heat breaks.

I was thinking – is there a good 'life of William Morris'? I do not know of one. It would be a blessing if you could write one. There are a great many things I want to know about him. I thought of him as so ancient – but if he had lived, he would have been Professor Freud's age – about. It is true that Freud was 77 when I first met him. William Morris, I think, would then have been about 80, but a not-impossible-to-meet age. I just 'missed' Andrew Lang, but I regret the fact that I MIGHT have met him – and Morris? When did he die? Everyone always spoke of his Viking carriage and his exhilarating manner ... was he ill long? And so on? If you have any of these facts, please let me know. Did he give up his 'romantic' work when he took up socialism?⁵

I do hope to hear from you again. I am really pretty limp with this heat-wave – but will write again later.

Love-
Dooley./

1 Aldington and his family moved to south-eastern France at the end of July 1947; he would continue to live here until April 1951.
2 On leaving Paris, Aldington sent H.D. a copy of 'The Imagists', a script he wrote for the BBC. It was broadcast on 13 July 1946, and opened and closed with readings of poems by H.D.
3 In 1946 Pound's daughter Mary married the half-Russian, half-Italian Boris Baratti (in 1947 he took the title of Prince de Rachewiltz). Their first child was born in 1947.
4 H.D. refers to William Morris's *The Wood Beyond the World* (1894). Aldington had sent her a copy of Morris's *The Well at the World's End* (1896) and noted in a letter to H.D. on 22 July 1947: 'It is not the Hallblithe one, but in much the same vein.'
5 H.D.'s reliance here on Aldington for information – her idea that he would write the biography in this case that she needs – is characteristic of her and probably of the working relationship she and Aldington have had since the earliest days of their courtship in 1912. Her questions here and his subsequent responses reveal a pattern of intellectual exchange that persists throughout their correspondence. Andrew Lang (1844–1912), a Scottish scholar, poet and folklorist, also translated ancient Greek writers.

⊰ **122** ⊱

7 August 1947
Villa Aucassin
St Clair
Le Lavandou
Var

Dear Dooley,

We had a good enough journey. France looked disquietingly sun-browned from the air – reaped fields and woodland and little pasture. Only 3 hours from Le Bourget to Marignane, and since we could not have the real pleasure of going by car in freedom and really enjoying the land, I was grateful to be whisked on the wings of the mechanic fiend. Lunched on the old port of Marseille, almost intact, but with ominous piles of ruined stone in the distance. Restaurant Florida crowded, excellent unrationed food – Dives and Lazarus once more, except that Dives has ceased even to pretend that he is a gentleman and Lazarus carries a gun in his pocket.¹ What a déchéance [falling away]! It is true that wars are the opportunity of the insignificant – those who have no other gifts can learn thieving and hatred.

And here it is as if one had never been away – blue sky, blue sea, gold-furnace sun, baked mica-spangled hills, the endless cri-cri of the Cicadas ...

I hope Dorothy Pound will not torment you with Poor old Ez's 'case'. It is not your affair, and he deliberately put himself into this impasse. He even had his chance to get out with honour after Pearl Harbour. He could have said, I hate England and France but I can't go against America – I think the Italians would have agreed to let him alone. It is strange to me that Ezra failed to understand the stamina of England, the immense power of America, the size and populousness of Russia. Here I have been saddened myself by reading the official British reports on the destruction of art in Italy. The reports are intolerably smug and so carelessly edited that they contradict each other, but one can see the destruction is immense and irreparable. It is a great sorrow to me, and I have kept it to myself. The English merely sneer. They don't care a damn, and I don't believe they ever did – except for the few – [John Addington] Symonds, and [Walter] Pater and [John] Ruskin and that period [c.1850–90], but later it was only a pose. Osbert Sitwell cares – he sent me a really grieved letter from Florence last year. But the patriotic English are very loathsome. ...

When, if my books arrive here I will sent you the two volume Life of Morris by [John] Mackail. Regrettably it is not nearly as good as Mackail's name would imply, but it is sympathetic and has the facts, though Mackail has no gift as a biographer and (like many scholars) could not construct and vitalise a book – he could write scraps, essays, poems, but not energise 500 pages and re-create a living man. Is it not strange that two years ago I began re-reading and re-collecting Morris? I have nearly everything except some scraps, two of the translations, and the Socialist stuff about which I care nothing. Anything of his you can't get I'll be very happy to loan you indefinitely. There is a very good little essay by Pater on 'Aesthetic Poetry' which is an analysis of Morris as poet. It was suppressed, and I found it among those Mosher Biblot collections. I read it in my bath in Hollywood, and went out and searched in bookshops, started finding Morris at once. H'wood was filled with English books second-hand thrown out contemptuously by German Jews. I have brought a lot of them back to Europe at vast expense, but I feel European books are lost forever when they get to America – either locked away in iron 'stacks' or contemptuously scribbled on and dogseared by hideous young students who actually hated nothing in the world so much as beauty, the beauty of Europe.

Morris died in 1896, much too early for you, while Lang lived on until 1912. It is strange that for a time Morris was a fanatical Marxist, because he owed everything – his art, his poetry, his craftsmanship, his pretty wife, his typography, his collection of books – to the fact that he inherited shares in a copper mine. Man is a strange animal, and it is odd that Morris was preaching revolution while labouriously reprinting Chaucer at 40 guineas a copy. But the early poems and the Earthly Paradise stories are lovely, and the prose romances charming I think. The translation of Virgil is disappointing, and I'm not struck on the Icelandic or Volsunga Saga versions. The Odyssey is better – it has that 'hair crisp-curling as the flowers of the daffodil'. Perhaps I am under-stating, for I have read or re-read them all with delight, but the Poems and Earthly Paradise and prose romances with great gratitude. Morris was a lovely person.

Here I have read most of The Ring and the Book again with new appreciation. The merit lies in the power of creative construction, the building of character – wonderful. Very few quotes, but I marked these:

> ... Whose lot fell in a land where life was great
> And sense went free and beauty lay profuse.

and, sounding so like today:

For I find this black mark impinge the man,
That he believes in just the vile of life.
Low instinct, base prestention, are these truth?

I am now on Red-Cotton Night-Cap Country, and find this for you:

... Rome
Out in the champaign, say, o'er-rioted
By verdure, ravage, and gay winds that war
Against strong sunshine settled to his sleep.

I have guests – Frere and his family – in the house, and must go down to them. I'll write more about Morris. He was ill for about a year, declining energy and sadness. For many years he walked over and had breakfast alone every Sunday with Edward Burne-Jones (no wives) and one day E.B.-J. saw with a pang that Morris sat almost in silence leaning his head on his hand. He died about a year after. Jane Morris was in love with Rossetti, and I think was his mistress. Mackail married Margaret Burne-Jones [Edward's daughter], and so was given the biography of Morris. ... I must rush.

Love,
Richard

1 Dives was the rich man at whose door the beggar Lazarus was laid in Luke 16: 19–31. Failing to take the opportunity to comfort Lazarus, Dives was sent to hell after death while Lazarus was welcomed into heaven.

❧ 123 ❧

24 August [1947]
Minerva Hotel
Lugano

Dear Richard,
Thank you so much for your letter. I have been thinking of that William Morris Biography. You should really do something with the period, I feel. There is such magnificent material for a PLAY. I wonder it has not been done. Did you ever see Violet Hunt's Wife of Rossetti?[1] They said it was historically out of focus, but I found the book delightful, she described the little things, materials and dresses they wore. I gave her the title of the book, oddly enough; she wanted to call it Elizabeth S[iddal] – but I said the majority of the people wouldn't be taken by the name. I expect you saw the book. I should have talked more of these people to V[iolet], but saw her only a few times, about three or four in ten years.[2] I have not seen the Allingham Diary but am more or less free now, to read.[3] I asked a friend in London to lend me the Mackail and was surprised yesterday when two well-printed, small Longman Green volumes appeared. I am taking it very slowly – I am glad I did the SYNTHESIS before I began re-reading Morris and before I had the Mackail. It is confusing sometimes, to read of things and people of which you have a visual picture – have the familiar portrait in the Mackail.[4] I somehow 'lost' Morris for more than 20 years though occasionally dipped into the Defence.[5] That was very good, as I unearthed my adolescent enthusiasm when I began to dig – or when the Blitz broke into the past. The future, I think, should have a 'stunner' in the way of a 'grind'[6] – a play, I think, would take like anything in a year or so in London. I am so afraid that someone else might push in, that I am not speaking of

273

any of this outside. I can SEE those people, and hear them talking. All you have to do is a little home-work. You could just toss off the biography – and do the play at 'odd moments'. An idea?[7] That rather insipid Barretts of Wimpole Street ran for years in London, and I believe USA swallowed it whole.[8] I will, as I go along, just make out [a] list or lists of dramatis personae. I am afraid it would have to be a pretty big cast – or not? I can see Ralph Richardson in the part – possibly! [Laurence] Olivier would make an excellent Rossetti. I must say the stage was wonderful in London – things in that line improved enormously during the war. I really cherish the Midsummer [Night's Dream], Hamlet, [Duchess of] Malfi and others in London as well as the Stratford Romeo [and Juliet], Othello, Twelfth Night, Antony [and Cleopatra] and so on, in a special way. Do think about this. As I say, I won't breathe of it. It should be done – what costume possibilities! I agree – the Socialist side of the Morris life does leave me rather dim and indifferent. I agree about newspapers and the crisis, but actually I have been so interested in the psychological reactions, and being here, so far removed, I can see the drama – alas! A great deal is Gone with the Wind, I do agree. But this is the time – or will be – to re-create the eternal. ... I must say people were very 'keen' on the best stage productions. Though one heard odd remarks, for instance, waiting in the crowd in the corridor, for precious Oedipus place, I did hear this: 'My dear, it isn't exactly gay – but it turns out all right in the end. Yes, it's quite all right in the end – he does marry his mother.'

Well, thank you for all the Morris gossip. I am thankful to have time now to read and properly browse or 'dream' over and into the period.

Love,
Dooley,/

1 Violet Hunt's *The Wife of Rossetti: Her Life and Death* (1932). Aldington wrote on 31 August 1947: 'I heard of that book of Violet's, but missed it. I'll try to get a copy from England. I rather mistrust her accuracy, though of course she was not a congenital and incurable liar like Ford.'
2 H.D. frequently saw Violet Hunt during her early years in London, but she had not seen Violet often since moving to Switzerland in the 1920s.
3 In his letter of 20 August 1947 Aldington had recommended William Allingham's *Diary* (1907): 'He has, among other things, a story about Rossetti's barmaid mistress who, when other men were present, affected much propriety and prunes and prisms. When Rossetti swore, which he frequently did, she would say simpering: "Rissitti, if you say them words agine, I shall hev to go into the garding." She was the luscious blonde with the lovely breasts in his later pictures.'
4 Of this picture, Aldington wrote on 17 September 1947, 'I think he was much handsomer and more attractive as an old than as a young man. That kindliness is delightful in the old man, but the look of pain and weariness very sad.'
5 William Morris's first book, *The Defence of Guenevere, and Other Poems* (1858).
6 On 20 August 1947 Aldington had given H.D. more information about Morris on which she is drawing here and in subsequent letters and in her own work. Aldington had written:

> M.'s father was a successful bill broker. M. went to Oxford with a view to holy orders, met Burne Jones, then Rossetti, then Swinburne etc., and decided for art. Under D.G.R.'s influence they all affected slang and heartiness as an offset to their very aesthetic art. Girls were 'stunners'. Morris was called 'Topsy' and poems 'grinds'. 'Read us one of your grinds, Top', and growling M. would read Golden Wings or something of the kind. He found a 'stunner' in Jane Burden, a butcher's daughter (I think) but a lovely creature, and married her at about eighteen. For her M. built a house in Kent, and the start of the Morris art and craft movement arose out of the fact that he couldn't get the furniture or stuffs or colours he wanted. He worked very hard for the company, though there were quarrelling and bitterness

as later. He taught himself weaving, and most of the earthly Paradise was composed while working at the loom – he would compose and memorise 50 to 100 lines a day, then write them down in the evening. When they moved to Kelmscott, Rossetti came to live with them. Then there was a bust up, R. went to Chelsea, and W.M. hardly ever saw him, though Jane went regularly. Later in life, after translating Homer, W.M. was bitten by the Norse-Icelandic sagas. He learned Icelandic from Magnusson, visited the saga country, and translated the Volsunga and other sagas – not very well. The Volsunga Saga is so terrific that it is best in prose, and awfully primitive with the hero the product of brother-sister incest, witch women able to change shapes, wives buried alive with husbands, and fearful drama of jealous egotism and revenge. The Niebelungenlied is chivalric and medieval – clearly much later and belonging to a civilised and christianised Germany. Morris was a big burly fellow, red-faced with much hair and beard, and very kindly eyes – 'looking like a sea captain'.

7 H.D. seems quite serious here: she has a vivid sense of this project and appears willing to collaborate if Aldington will write it. Aldington, in his turn, was overwhelmed with work for which he already had contracts, and wrote H.D. on 31 August 1947 that he felt he had 'no real gift for the stage'. Alternatively, he proposed, 'As to a play – since you "see" it so clearly, why don't you do that? I can help in any way you suggest.'
8 Rudolf Besier's play *The Barretts of Wimpole Street* (1930).

⁂ 124 ⁂

3 September [1947]
Minerva Hôtel
Lugano

Dear Richard,
   Thank you so much for your letter. I am afraid I 'see' the play in rather a literary way, but I am reading now the Mackail and making notes of sorts; what was the name of Lady B-J?¹ I have the three men, Gabriel [Rossetti], Edward [Burne-Jones], William [Morris]; Gabriel, Ned, Top;² then Elizabeth [Siddal], ——, Jane [Morris]. I cannot 'see' the interworking until I have the name of ——; she seems to me, finding out nothing at ALL about her, in the Mackail, to suggest the Cathedral close. Elizabeth was, we know, poor, sickly, a milliner's assistant, lived along Brixton way, I imagine, or that is impression I get. Jane, you say, was a butcher's daughter; I heard she was part of a 'circus' but that sounds too mad even to be a trusty rumour, or a lie with a clue. I feel that Lady B-J was the one 'lady' of the crowd, and very long-suffering and broadminded about Elizabeth at any rate and maybe [about] Jane as well. I read in the Mackail that Gabriel stayed at Kelmscott while W.M. was in Iceland on that first trip; W.M. seems to have had a tiny bed-room in the furniture shop or house, and he seems to me to have spent most of his time there, though much is made in Mackail of those visits to Kelmscott. They gave up the Red House, Kent, after it was furnished with much beautiful built-in or original furniture and after he had spent the 'five happiest years of his life' there and in the garden. Jane Alice and Mary [his daughters] were born there, 1861, 1862. Then 'circumstances' over which they had no control caused him suddenly to give up the house. Why? It might have been something to do with his 'socialism' which I believe translated now would be 'communism'. He started a novel, which 'abortion' he flung aside and never attempted anything 'in modern dress' again. The novel was presumed to have been intended as a 'tragedy' about two brothers who fall in love with the same woman.

We know about Jane. But was there perhaps another woman, or more than one? I mean another woman that the 'older brother' (Gabriel) loved or possessed first. Do we know anything at all about W.M.['s] feeling for Elizabeth?

Why did W.M. connive at Gabriel being there at Kelm. so often while he was away?

Was Gabriel a 'father substitute'? We hear much of his powerful influence on W.M. in early years and how it was he who brought B.-J. and W.M. to painting.

W.M.['s] feeling about Gabriel seems to me to be contradictory and inconsistent.

Elizabeth was older and as the then companion of Gabriel, would perhaps have had some strong and subtle influence on the younger W.M.

There is a catch somewhere.

W.M. begins to write his real or emotional 'romances' at the end of his life. I see that Glittering Plain was the first MSS that was set up by the Kel[mscott] Press.

W.M. rails in these later pure fairy-tales against the yellow-haired witch-lady or sorceress. She overcomes him (in the form of Squire Arthur) in the Wondrous Isles; but this is temporary; is she not the yellow corn-goddess of the Rossetti Lilith? And others?

W.M. came to the dream or allegory late in life, after [the] death of Rossetti. There are the three knights in Isles; those three; but I think he doubles Gabriel and makes him the slain Sir Baudoin and, as well, one of the captains of the Red Hold, the Black Knight.

Well, this is only a faint sample of the way my mind is working on this. But I will also try to assemble notes, dates, scenes, people in a more reasoned order. If you cannot undertake this and I am not able to, someone else might come along who would find some clues, at least, in the fabulous character.

I see a good many English types here. Or rather two types. There are the girls with dyed hair, from the lower end of Oxford Street sweat-shops, who spend all their time on the Loido or Lee-doe and sit in the garden sun-tanning. I don't think they have ever been out of England and one is glad that they get a bite to eat. The others are mostly very hungry, shabby, pale 'country' or better class Londoners who say grimly 'it's not really so bad.' It is bad. Bryher went over on business for a week, but spent four of the seven days in Cornwall as she said literally she was starving, and the struggle for food made her too sick to eat afterwards, queue at Harrod's reaching out into the street. I will let you know if she has any illuminating gossip, but she just has given up hope for England unless there is possibly to be some new standard, not gold; she thinks the radio-atom medicine and possibly heating innovations (of the possible future) may yet save the situation; something in the way of a material miracle. The people I knew during the war who were all very wonderful, have become completely apathetic, as far as I can judge from letters. I have here now Bryher, for her birthday [on 2 September], and an Austrian friend with his Czech wife; she has set up her shingle in New York; they are both doctors and she returns to N.Y. where she is doing very well and is trying to force him to go over, but he had a bad time in [the] war, is British by passport; he is just recuperating here and simply won't move; he had to go over to London to see one of his old patients last winter and returned absolutely and literally ill, because there had been no change at all in the rubble and ash dumps left during the blitz. There is a young Welsh journalist also of the party, he has connections in S. Africa and talks of that or Canada; he looks ill and hungry. They all have gone off to Locarno this afternoon, so I take the opportunity of answering your letter at once. I am glad to hear of the Australian poet [Alister Kershaw], and sorry that the attitude of Mr F-R [A. S. Frere-

Reeves] has shocked you.[3] I am afraid you are right, that it is a question of this National Socialism; it is heart-breaking!

I wonder how long you plan staying at St. Clair?[4] I will stay here until the Signora closes down in November – at least, that is now my idea. Then, I will probably winter again in Lausanne. I would like to see people in London, but know I would go right to pieces. I cannot tell you how unhappy I am about it all. I know you must feel it deeply. I am interested in your Miracle play.[5] I have not heard of it. What was it all about? Well, thank you again for your interest in the play and I do hope that later, you will be free to undertake some more work on the P[re]-R[aphaelite] brotherhood.

Love,

Dooley./

1 Aldington informed H.D. on 17 September 1947 that 'Her name was Georgina Macdonald, daughter of a dissenting minister.'

2 These are the names by which the three men were known to their friends.

3 On 31 August 1947 Aldington had written H.D. about A. S. Frere and his family and about Alister Kershaw:

> We are beginning to recover from the visit of the Freres. I used to be fond of them both, but they have changed so much that friendship is out of the question and even a visit from them a penance. This new mixture of violent chauvinism and imperialism, plus the quite untrue British legend that England saved the world (it was in fact saved by the U.S. and Russia), combined with social climbing and Socialist politics is disgusting. It is Nationalist Socialism of a British brand, capable of being just as nasty as the German variety.
>
> By way of a change we have a happy-go-lucky and gifted young Australian poet, who belongs to one of the 'good' families there, but who is totally without snobbery and affectation. And intelligent.

In all fairness to these house guests, it should be noted that both Freres had become Aldington's good friends in the late 1920s and early 1930s when Aldington's circumstances were different. In contrast, Kershaw had just entered Aldington's life and was an energetic youth of twenty-six, willing to serve as Aldington's 'secretary' in exchange for room and board and the privilege of being part of the household of a man whose work and values he greatly admired.

4 While H.D. is under the impression that Aldington and his family have gone to Provence only for the summer, Aldington plans to stay in the south of France indefinitely.

5 This 'play' was in fact a movie treatment about which Aldington wrote to H.D. on 31 December 1947: 'The Miracle film-script was written in 1943–44 for Warner Bros, who paid me 25,000 dollars for it. By the terms of the agreement world film rights belong to them. If they don't produce it nobody can. Young Reinhardt was unable to convince Jack Warner that it would pay, though Warner personally complimented me on the draft scenario.' The subject was a medieval legend shifted to the seventeenth century and set in southern Europe.

H.D. continued to work on 'Synthesis of a Dream' throughout 1947. Aldington and she did not 'collaborate', nor did Aldington write the biography or the play H.D. suggested. Instead, H.D., who clearly 'saw' the material, claimed it for herself. In his turn, Aldington served as a resource, both a mine of information and a sounding-board, offering constant and informed encouragement. While H.D. felt 'free' to devote herself to reading and writing during these months, Aldington was distracted by house guests and the demands of numerous contracted projects; increasingly restless, he felt harried both socially and intellectually as he struggled to earn a living and to establish a home for his child.

In his work, Aldington was turning towards biography: in 1948 he published the short study *Jane Austen*, as well as *Four English Portraits: 1801–1851* (which included biographies of George IV, Disraeli, Dickens and the eccentric naturalist Charles Waterton), *Walter Pater: Selected Works* (which included a good deal of commentary), and his final collection of verse, *The Complete Poems of Richard Aldington*; in 1949 he published a full-length biography, *The Strange Life of Charles Waterton: 1782–1865*. Aldington continued to write for a wide variety of periodicals and to oversee the translation of his earlier work into several languages. His letters to H.D. and others detail his pressing obligations to publishers and his plans for future anthologies and biographies.

On 10 October 1947, H.D. wrote to Aldington:

I have been very happy and busy going over the last type-script of Synthesis, Book II, Summerdream. ... will you care to read Summerdream? Part II or rather Book II of the Synthesis? ... I would certainly like you to glance it over.

I enclose list of chapters. You will see that I cut up the long 'Philadelphia' chapter into four, Part II, that is of Wintersleep. Summerdream goes on into märchen or story-book world – with the same scene of the Round Table episode, taking place with variations, in Greece, Rome, Normandy, etc. – I trust you will not mind my quoting from your first letters, re Synthesis. [In the book] I send the ms. Wintersleep to Paris to a friend, connected with publishing world, called Randolph Spencer. But you can comment on that after (when/if) I get the Summerdream to you.

Randolph doubles on Geffray (so spelt in Normandy – the names of the children of the Lady Duchess' Company are all taken from William Morris Early Romances and poems of the little Everyman book). This same Geoffrey comes into the chapter The Queen, which is set in Elizabethan England. Geoffrey is so spelt except in the Normandy section, so that is not a mistake as I had so carefully to explain to the typist in London. Geffray is the William Morris spelling, for that section.

H.D. concluded with a comment on her creative process: 'I am glad you have a friend-secretary. I spend hours just arranging pages and sorting. But then it is just as well, as otherwise I get too embedded in creative work, and don't give my real heart to the sometimes restful business of the grand final assembling.'

The 'list of chapters' that H.D. enclosed further suggests the process which she obliquely describes to Aldington: she draws on historical material, gathered from specific literary sources (in this case primarily from Morris) and from her sense of history more generally (Greece, medieval France), and on her own past (in this instance, primarily her 'seances' in wartime London). Generically, the work becomes a modernist combination of the historical novel and the *roman à clé*, but the matter is even more complex for H.D.

as the layering process involves multiple doubling – that is, for example, Geffray is Geoffrey is Randolph is Aldington just as Delia Alton is H.D. is Hilda Aldington is author is character. This multiplicity is complicated further in that Delia is not only the 'author/character' of this work, but also the 'author' of, for instance, *Bid Me to Live*, in which the central character is Julia is H.D. is Hilda Aldington and Rafe is Aldington. Howell in 'Synthesis' is Lord Dowding but also – as the agent who brings Delia into contact with a spirit world and a spirit past – Delia's companion, a variation on Geffray/ Geoffrey and in turn a variant of Randolph/Aldington. Thus the work becomes both a novel and an intricate psychological study, both a 'grand final assembling' and the record of an intense process of self-examination which resonates throughout against the H.D.-Aldington relationship. H.D.'s 'list of chapters' is worth reproducing in full:

SYNTHESIS OF A DREAM

by

DELIA ALTON

BOOK I

WINTERSLEEP

For in that sleep of death, what dreams may come.

Part I

I.   Viking Ship
II.   Round Table
III.   Closed Circle

Part II

I.   Iphegenia
II.   Lost and Found
III.   Crashing Rocks
IV.   Revenant
V.   Traces of direction
VI   Chapel Perilous

BOOK II

SUMMERDREAM

We are such stuff as dreams are made of.

I.   Sempione
II.   Albatross
III.   Acropolis
IV.   The Road to Daphne
V.   And Five Others
VI.   Athens
VII.   The Queen
VIII. Ariadne
IX.   Delphi
X.   Rome
XI.   Distant Island
XII.   Normandy
XIII. The Story
XIV.   Goldwings

Aldington was, as always, a receptive reader. He wrote on 13 October 1947: 'Of course I should like to have Summerdream to read, and hope that down in this more peaceful part of the world I can give it more attention and concentration than was possible with Wintersleep in Paris.' While he wrote on 18 November 1947 that he liked the title, he was shocked by the complexity and obscurity of the novel once he had read it and confined himself to practical matters in his comments on 24 November 1947:

> I have read the second part of the Synthesis. There is no need for me to tell you that this is too allusive and subtle for what I must call 'the popular publisher'. Only a few with considerable education and specialist interests will be able to follow the arabesques – shall I call them? – or understand your folded pleats of Time – excellent metaphor, by the way. The 'story' of Part I could have been made available to a fairly wide public, but I don't see how Part II can. Perhaps I am wrong. What I mean is that the structure and method of narration are too 'difficult' for the person Dr. Johnson called 'the common reader'.

He concluded, however, with his support: 'If there is anything practical I can do about the book I do beg you to call on me unreservedly.'

H.D. was not offended; going over her work on 7 March 1948, she wrote to Aldington:

> I have been pretty swamped with my own untidy MSS, but now I think I have reached a pause on the road and am really beginning to enjoy them. I look like having written too many barrels-full but when I consider that I did not do much publishing (considering I was writing more or less all the time) I don't think the work disproportionate. I am glad, too, that a lot of the stories have waited, as they might have been merely thought stylized or of-the-moment. The same holds with the <u>Synthesis</u> that you were so good to comment on. All these things can wait – so long as I enjoy them now myself. Which I never fully managed somehow to do before.

As H.D. concentrated on 'Synthesis' and Aldington on his own writing obligations, their letters of late 1947 and early 1948 became shorter, less intense, less frequent, and more mundane. Catha was now nine years old and H.D. sent her chocolates; the child learned to ride a bicycle and her father noted on 13 October 1947 that 'of course we are in constant apprehension'. Aldington wrote affectionately on 18 November 1947: 'It is very sweet of you to send Catha some candies, which I hope come in time for Thanksgiving. I need hardly tell another American girl that she scorns the French for not having "punkins" on Halloween, and bawls the hell out of me for not having a twenty-pound turkey for Thanksgiving. I suppose you can manage the turkey in Lausanne, but how about the cranberry sauce and the sweet potatoes?'

H.D. for her part continued to share with Aldington news about mutual acquaintances and to ask him for information. On Christmas Day, 1947, she wrote: '... I get deeper and deeper into the Pre-Raff scene and have been making notes for another possible volume. A book first – maybe a play after – I see it in scenes and the costumes fascinate me. My setting, so far, is just roughly a hundred years ago, easy to think things out from that angle, well 1850–55, up to or including Crimea, upon which I am or have been very vague, except for Florence N[ightingale] – what is the school-book or the text-book date for the Crimean war?'

Aldington answered at characteristic length. On 31 December 1947 he sent H.D. a detailed account of the Crimean War (an entire single-spaced typed page), concluding: 'This will give you something of the international background of the 1850's, which we are apt to think of as so peaceful. 1851 was the Great Exhibition; 1852 the Duke died; 1853 Gladstone introduced his first budget; 1853 wars in Burma and South Africa; 1854 the University Reform Bill; 1855 Palmerston Prime Minister; 1856 "difficulties with America"; 1857 Indian Mutiny.' H.D. took from Aldington's accounts whatever bits she may have needed, but certainly must have been overwhelmed by the floods of information which regularly poured forth in answer to her simple questions.

In summary, the letters omitted here between September 1947 and April 1948 are friendly but less intense than the preceding correspondence whose core is the writers' shared interest in William Morris. By the spring of 1948, however, Aldington had in large measure fulfilled his contractual obligations and was ready to move on to new work, the challenges of which he reported to H.D.

⤞ **125** ⤝

29 April 1948
Villa Aucassin
St Clair
Le Lavandou
Var

Dear Dooley,

You will be at Lugano or on the way to-day; and I hope all has gone well.[1] Travel has been made so unpleasant that one shrinks from it. I understand so well your reluctance to root up, yet Lugano sounds so wonderful and it is a sort of Italy with the solid Swiss life backing the landscape and the old art. Fruit of professional neutrality! How often I wish I could be a professional neutral in all these meaningless fights.

I am sending you a little book you must have read long ago — the Ballades, Rondeaux etc. It may seem trivial in your present mood, but I find such utter trifles rather reposeful, and I've used a few of them in the Aesthetes book.[2] That is still not ready for the publisher. My secretary is constantly interrupted by 'business' letters. One of the innumerable little annoyances recently was this — a Hungarian firm called Athenaeum bought the rights in Casanova and options on other books; a second firm went to them and asserted quite falsely that they had the rights; without stopping to make sure, Athenaeum write me an indignant letter cancelling agreement; Kershaw had to go through our files to discover and copy out correspondence showing that we refused the second firm; he had also to write a London agent for confirmation, copy reply and send to Buda Pesth. Meanwhile, as Athenaeum don't answer, we have to draft a case to present for Tony to take action.[3] Just as it is completed, Athenaeum belatedly apologise and say I am quite right — having wasted about ten weeks of production time and hours of Kershaw's typing time! Then, getting money transferred from Italy, Spain and all the 'iron curtain' countries is a nightmare of weary dunning and complex negotiations and worse than nightmare 'regulations' and 'controls'. I sometimes wonder, when Kershaw shows me these things, whether I am not insane and imagining the modern world from a lunatic asylum! The alternative is the somewhat complacent feeling that a large part of the world is mad! What do they want? What do they think they're doing?

I have just been down to Kershaw's room to take him the little book to wrap up for you — and, as I feared, he has several letters before he can start on the book typing.

By the way, did you hear about the Australian writer, Robert Close, fined 100 pounds and sentenced to three months in Melbourne for an alleged obscene book?[4] I haven't read the book and only know about it because some of the dreadful English newspaper reports reached me from Durrant's, owing to the fact that they reported (quite falsely) that Death of a Hero is banned in Australia.[5] I believe The Colonel's Daughter and All Men Are Enemies were banned, but not the war book. But is not this sentence a new piece of savagery? Kershaw and his Australian friends staying here say that ordinary pornography is sold everywhere in Australia, and this Robert Close is attacked because he is a real writer. [D.H.] Lawrence over again on a small scale.

I have been meditating a short biography of D.H.L., trying to put it down sanely and coolly and to persuade people once more to read his books. But I don't want to get involved with Murry and Carswell and Frieda and Brett and E.T. and Helen Corke and Mabel Dodge.[6] Trouble is that most of them are nothing in themselves and never had anything in life but their association with D.H.L. and so cling on most fiercely to their little property and resent anyone else touching it.

The University of New Mexico has just sent me a large book, a very careful and commentated bibliography of the D.H.L. mss in Frieda's possession. (She wants to sell, I surmise, perhaps unjustly.) Among the mss is a set of rough financial and other memoranda from Feb 1920 to November 1924. You may remember he left England in Nov 1919 with only about 20 pounds and got landed in that appalling Picinisco. I had always felt they must have suffered great poverty, and so Frieda gave me to understand. But these notes show that as early as Feb 6 1920 (that is less than 3 months after exiling himself) he received a cheque for 100 guineas from Pinker [a literary agent]; on 10th Feb, 8.12.9 from Huebsch [a publisher]; on the 12th Feb, Amy [Lowell] sent 1300 lire (about 60 dollars);[7] on Feb 21st, 10 pounds from Oxford Press; and so on. On Dec 14 he got 100 pounds for the James Tait Black Prize (last year I got 180, so it has increased nominally).[8] During 1922 he earned 5,439 dollars in U.S. alone. And in spite of that incessant rushing about in Oct 1924 had 300 pounds in his English Bank and 2285 dollars in Chase National, N.Y.!! Their real bad time was clearly 1915–20, which must have been dreary indeed – starving in Cornwall and Berkshire. In Nov 1928 he told me himself that he had over 1000 pounds in his English bank and also I saw he received half-year royalty statements of 151 pounds from Secker [his English publisher]. You will think this a squalid way of approaching a poet, but it is interesting to see how it was still possible to be a poet and a nomad in the twenties.

What do you think of the wisdom of doing a Lawrence book at this date?[9] I had in mind about 75,000 words, the story of his days, and as much favourable comment on his work as possible – leaving the bad side, the 'dark abdomen' and the interpretation of same to Middleton Murry. It might help to get his books back in print in U.S. and so help Frieda, who must be rather hard up. Or do you think it a mistake? I still feel he was the greatest writer of our epoch, though a bit of a blackguard in some ways and horribly treacherous and gossipy. But he was – and still is – something, and what is the use of being a great writer if you can't be a blackguard too? Shelley was, they say, and certainly Verlaine.

Evans Bros. the education publishers like my Four English Portraits so well they want me to expand the one on Waterton into a full-length biography. This I shall do if Heinemann's will consent. Then I hope to do some novels again. They tear one up emotionally, but are less of a dull grind than biographies where you have to check facts. The bliss of a novel is that you invent any facts you like within reason.

Tell me how Lugano is looking. I pine sometimes for the feel of Italy, but dread the smashedness of it. As I wrote you before.

Love,
Richard

1 Until ill health in the late 1950s prevented her travelling, H.D. routinely alternated between living in Lausanne during the winter and Lugano during the warmer months.

2 Aldington's *The Religion of Beauty: Selections from the Aesthetes* was finally published in London by Heinemann in 1950.

3 From 1945 until his death, Aldington relied on his younger brother Tony for legal support.

4 Robert Close (b. 1903). In 1945 the first edition of his first novel, *Love Me, Sailor*, sold out in a few weeks but was banned for obscenity. After two trials and much publicity, Close left Australia in 1950 to live in France where the translated novel (*Prends-moi, Matelot*) became a best-seller.

5 Durrant's was an agency which regularly scanned papers throughout the world for mention of an author's books, then sent clippings on.

6 John Middleton Murry (1889–1957) was Katherine Mansfield's husband and a close friend of D.H. Lawrence; he wrote an early biography of Lawrence, *Son of Woman* (1931). Catherine Carswell (1879–1946) was another close friend of Lawrence and wrote *The Savage Pilgrimage: A Narrative of D.H. Lawrence* in 1932; her husband John also knew Lawrence well. Frieda Lawrence was living in New Mexico in 1948 as was Dorothy Brett, the English painter who met the Lawrences in 1915 and followed them to Taos. E.T. was Jessie Chambers, whom Lawrence portrayed as Miriam in *Sons and Lovers* (1913) and who under this pseudonym wrote *D.H. Lawrence: A Personal Record* in 1935. Helen Corke (b. 1880) was an early friend of Lawrence and his circle. Mabel Dodge Luhan (1879–1962) was also a Lawrence follower who lived near Frieda in New Mexico.

7 This was probably at least in part a gift, for the amount seems too large to have been royalties from Lawrence's part in the Imagist anthologies, small sums which Lowell routinely distributed.

8 Aldington received the James Tait Black Memorial Prize in March 1947 for his biography of Wellington.

9 H.D.'s letters during the spring of 1948 have apparently not survived, but Aldington suggests her positive and informed response to this question in Letter 126.

≫ **126** ≪

11 May 1948
Villa Aucassin
St Clair
Le Lavandou
Var

Dear Dooley,

Don't worry about the legal machinations of Ezra Karkus (cousin, I suppose, of the English legal luminary, Harvis Karkus) for the joining of our names in the notice is a mere formality. As your brother is cited he will deal with anything that has to be dealt with. The action would appear to be by the city of Rahway, N.J. to sell land for nonpay-ment of City Taxes.[1] People seem to do this in U.S. when land becomes a nuisance to them – i.e. refuse to pay taxes and force the city to take over the land. There was an enormous house with a lot of ground on Hollywood Boulevard, just near me, in that condition – a constant expense to the Country of Los Angeles, who could find nobody to buy it, and were compelled to put up the price every six months by adding the amount of unpaid tax! American Law is a marvellous thing – keep away from it!

Turning to matters vastly more important and more pleasant – you'll be glad to know that Rachel Taylor is still alive.[2] My excellent friend, Bill Dibben, who is a positive wizard in finding me rare books, discovered that she is living 'in a street off the Euston Road'. Alas, poor Banavahrd (if that is how it is spelled)! Dibben had arranged for her to be invited to dinner by a friend of his, and promised more news, which I shall pass on to you as soon as it arrives. I feel excited about this, as I should like to tell her how greatly I admire her work. Did you know that D.H.L., when at Croydon, gave a lecture on her? His notes for it are published in Orioli's edition of Ada Clark's book, but not (for some reason) in Secker's and Heinemann's.[3] Although D.H.L. afterwards jeered at her, he then admired her.

You are absolutely right about the 'screaming Maenads' and D.H.L. Frere, who hopes to put D.H.L. back into print eventually, is very anxious to counteract these 'hysterical females', as he calls them. E.T. (Miriam) is about the best, and Frieda about the worst. The M.M. [Middleton Murry] book you speak of is the greatest obstacle. Murry knew Lorenzo through and through, and that book is really a deadly piece of literary murder – far more thorough than the open enemies, who hated L. either from instinct or pretended to because it suited their journalistic ends, but had not closely read him. Murry had, and though his book is dull, as you say, it is deadly. Briefly, Murry's thesis is that L. tried to substitute physical for spiritual love, sex for Christianity, and utterly failed, being driven back into impotence, despair and murderous hate. Finally, in The Escaped Cock, Lawrence resurrects Jesus to try and show that Jesus was wrong and Lawrence was right! Murry is pretty devilish, and he is not altogether wrong.

It is going to be a difficult job, but while I am meditating it I have another and quite easy and congenial short biography (about 75000 words) commissioned. My Aesthetes book is done. I now call it The Religion of Beauty, and think it rather a useful little collection of rare and sometimes almost inaccessible texts. I have to see that through the press, as well as my Complete Poems – proofs due in June – and the revise of Pater, as well as one or two other things. So I shall have enough to do. Heinemann made a lot of mistakes in the Pater. One was in tacking the first version of the conclusion to the Renaissance on to the rare essay (about Morris) 'Aesthetic Poetry'. This means renumbering pages from 86 to 550 or, alternatively, sandwiching the Conclusion between Aesthetic Poetry and Rossetti! I have left them the choice, though in normal times I should have insisted on their correcting the mistake. Another thing – they have absurdly used two different founts of Greek type for Pater's Greek quotes. This looked so grotesque that I had to insist on uniformity. If I can get a clean duplicate to the Pater revise in bound sheets I'll send it along. I am sending at this time a Tauchnitz of J.A. Symonds New Italian Sketches you may like to have. It is something of a bibliographical curiosity. I turned it up in the back shelves of Libreria Arcadia in 1937. You will see by the dates on the back that it must have been there since 1929; and actually it is a bind-up of the original sheets printed in 1884! It seems impossible that Tauchnitz never reprinted, so perhaps it merely means that in reprinting they kept the original date '1884'.

The new Complete edition of Jane Austen, with an introduction by me, which has been postponed about six times, is once more postponed, to 'May 26th'. This time I think it probably will come out on that date, as the publisher has paid the advance. But what appalling muddlers they all seem to be. All part of this ridiculous socialism, of course.

It is full summer here now, and as we are really not far distant in a straight line, I suspect you will have much the same weather at Lugano. Your thunder-storm corresponded with an unusually late short wet spell here. I am glad of it for it keeps these sometimes dried-up hills green and fresh, and our two little cataracts still running. Beautiful, beautiful wild flowers – so many, I didn't know or have forgotten grew here. In one place I found many wild gladiolus, tall slim with blood-like blossoms, so incomparably more graceful and lovely than the garden ones. All the wild lavender in flower, with long stick-up petals like blue rabbit's ears. Wild mignonette, delicate, and many poppies, the white cistus flowers as abundant on the hills as a storm of snow.

With love,
Richard

1 H.D. is concerned about a threatened lawsuit connected with land ostensibly owned by her (and thus also nominally by Aldington, whose name she still uses). H.D.'s brother Harold Doolittle managed her investments in the United States. H.D. now often shares the details of such relatively small issues with Aldington, from whom she seeks reassurance and explanation.
2 Rachel Annand Taylor (1876–1960), a British writer whose work on the Renaissance Aldington championed in the 1950s. He and H.D. knew Taylor, whom they nicknamed 'Banavahrd', when they lived in London before 1920.
3 D.H. Lawrence's sister, Ada Clarke (1887–1948), wrote with G. Stuart Gelder *Young Lorenzo: Early Life of D.H. Lawrence* (1932).

≫ **127** ≪

10 June 1948
Villa Aucassin
St Clair
Le Lavandou
Var

Dear Dooley,

The Paris trip was tiring, and rather curious than rewarding – though I managed to snatch an hour in the Louvre, which is gradually re-opening.[1] I went in at the door just inside the Perrault façade, walked through the Egyptian and Assyrian rooms, and came suddenly on the Greek sculpture. After being away so long the feeling of passionate sympathy and admiration is poignant. Not to respond to those statues must, to my way of feeling, imply an inability to respond to high art. The long gallery is open as far as the Rubens room (not yet ready) and many of the old familiar lovely things are back once more. So many immortal things from the so-called Cimabue – far more beautiful in colour than I remembered – to the Georgione Fête champêtre and that superb Raphael, with the beautiful young Baglione en archange Michel swooping down on an admirable Satan, and the Caracci too. I came on two little panels, quattrocento, by someone di Giovanni, imitation Piero di Cosimo – the gods en Renaissance, gold helms and fluttering robes and nudities, quaint centaurs and nymphs escorting Thetis. The Leonardos all back, but in new places, a heavenly Bellini I had forgotten, but no Veronese or Tintorettos – where are they to be?

How well I understand the hatred for art in the contemporary world – the Russian moujik, the American farmer, the German bully, the British lout, the French fribble, the Italian politico – what have they to do with thirty centuries of art which is an ever-lasting reproach to their barbarism? How well, too, I understand the common agreement of the brave airmen to bomb the babies and the art towns!

Frere insisted on staying in a Champs Elysées hotel just opposite Unesco, and near the concrete Gestapo headquarters now appropriately occupied by American Army bureaucrats. I had plenty of opportunity to watch the innumerable brand-new 'official' Cadillacs, Buicks, Rolls, Bentleys, Oldsmobiles, etcetera 'purring up', as the stylists say, or parked in great blocks. For all of which you and I and all the people not in on the racket are ruthlessly taxed, and insulted to boot. Innumerable other brand-new cars waft up and down the profiteers – the war supply profiteers, the black market profiteers, and these new profiteers of war, the favoured untaxed government-supplied bureaucratic parasites. Thousands of 'em – Americans, Brazilians, Argentinians, Swedes, Swiss, Belgians, Portuguese, Canadians, Australians, and the hordes of British 'officials'. Culmination – the cadets of St. Cyr, pipers of the Scots Greys, a company of Royal Fusileers as guard of honour to a government delegation laying wreaths on the Unknown Soldier – the said delegation consisting entirely of <u>Swiss</u>!!! An equal peak, the Travellers Club, full of drunken, mouldy, betting, foul-mouthed titled British and French and rich Americans in a house which had been built a century ago by a wealthy German for his beautiful French mistress. Under the panels of naked goddesses and sculptured nymphs, these brutes have hung pictures of race horses. In an alcove which once held a statue (now removed) they set up a cocktail bar; and behind the bar is a 17th century tapestry they didn't trouble to move. It represents 'Triumphis Marci Aurelii'! Could you better it? Had you seen the bestial, dissolute faces of those British and French 'aristocrats' (all genuine – Stanleys and Throgmortons and Montmorencys and even a Romanoff) – well silence and exile between the mountains and the sea are all that is left me.

I have been back two days and have not yet managed to start work again, though I was easily knocking off 1500 words a day before I left. It is so characteristic of the English publisher to imagine that a writer can just 'throw off' anything wanted at any old time. Yet I must not be unjust to Frere. No other publisher in England or America would at this time do the Pater and the Aesthetes. He is doing them only out of friendship, and will lose money on both! The Americans will only take 1000 copies of the Pater. I must do the [D.H.] Lawrence biography as soon as possible to atone for this lapse into unpopularity.

I am glad you like the Pater foreword, though it is hopeless to expect anyone else but a very few even to read it without prejudice. Still, though the reviewers will put up their nets and traps to stop the book, I have a hope it will get through to some. After all, I have a fairly large public now, who evidently do disregard the cliques and the reviews, or I should hardly be able to sell 15,000 to 40,000 of every full-length book I do. May they not prove fickle! I so much want to bring them to Pater and the Aesthetes. (Frere, by the way, stated frankly that Pater bores him!)

If your Talbot is <u>the</u> Talbot, you will at once recollect the name in Froissart and Shakespeare's Henry VI.[2] He was the great English general fighting the losing battle against Jeanne d'Arc – I believe he captured her. Both father and son were killed in the Hundred Years War. They had estates near Bordeaux, and there is still a vintage claret, Château Talbot. (In 1938 it was 10 francs a bottle. It is now 400.)

Yes, <u>Miss</u> Blind.[3] She had a social conscience unluckily, and was not content to thank the gods for and enjoy being beautiful and rich and young while it lasted, but must needs write about ejected crofters ('The Heather on Fire') and a pseudo-Lucretian poem on Darwinism, 'The Ascent of Man'. But she had a mind – unlike Andrea's Lucrezia – and there is both intellect and charm in some of the lyrics. How so lovely a creature escaped matrimony, I know not. Perhaps she was fortunate enough to be one with Anactoria and Erinna.[4] She knows a lot about Egypt and seems to have spent her winters there. I must try to find more about her. She was very kind to the blind poet, [Philip Bourke] Marston [1850–87]. She translated Strauss, edited Shelley, translated Marie Bashkirtseff [1890], biographised Madame Roland [1886] and George Eliot [1883], and wrote a novel 'Tarentella' [1884]. Her sonnets are good. Why are women so good at sonnets?

I must rush. (No news yet of Rachel.)

With love,
Richard

1 Aldington had written to H.D. on 1 June 1984 that 'Frere has cabled me to meet him in Paris on Friday [4 June], and there are no reservations to be had on the train bleu, so I have to go on a 2nd class couchette in a slow train which makes me mad. And it's all about some mare's nest old Frere has suddenly discovered about getting a house in Antibes for us both, and I don't think I want to live in Antibes ... [sic].' The Louvre was closed during the war and its contents stored for protection.

2 H.D. has obviously asked Aldington, in a letter now lost, to identify 'Talbot'. Aldington is, again, serving as her library in providing information, but whether he is correct in giving H.D. what she wants to know is unclear. Jean Froissart (c. 1337-c. 1410), historian and poet, came to England in 1361. He chronicled the principal occurrences in the French and English battles of the Hundred Years War.

3 On 25 May 1948 Aldington had written H.D.: 'Did you ever read Mathilde Blind? Not a very good poetess, but her photograph is that of one of those handsome English ladies of the 1880's who have become extinct – unless perchance a few still linger in Boston and Philadelphia.' Blind (1841–96), a feminist, left her money to Newnham College, Cambridge.

4 Anactoria was a woman of Lesbos passionately loved by Sappho and portrayed by Ovid. Erinna (fourth century BCE) died at 19 and was famous for her poem 'The Distaff', written in memory of her friend Baucis from whom she had been separated by Baucis' marriage and death.

⤞ 128 ⤝

16 June 1948
Villa Aucassin
St Clair
Le Lavandou
Var

Dear Dooley,

Under another cover I sent you this morning a copy of H.C. Beeching's Anthology, A Paradise of English Poetry [London: Rivington, 1897]. I liked the book very much, and asked my English book-buyer if he could find another copy for you. And the excellent man has done so. Beeching's taste is limited, but within those limits admirable, I think, and he makes discoveries. He is good with Browne of Tavistock, for instance, and I like his Donne selections. He is better on the 17th century than I am. The book is nicely printed, don't you think?

I have still not quite recovered from the disturbance of that unnecessary trip to Paris. That club of English I described was so repulsive to me; and then it is so distressing to find what mean malicious whining nationalists the English have become in their loss of empire – as if it were not a good thing to lose and they could now possess their souls! The philistinism of America is one thing and the philistinism of England another. Which is worse? The English I think. The Americans are plain brutal barbarians, but the English deliberately want to sully and destroy.

A letter from Rachel Annand [Taylor]! The wonderful book-buyer (William Dibben) tracked her down, went to tea and took her a letter from me, to which she has just replied. Most excitingly she says she has just finished a big book on the Renaissance in France. Of course the vile publishers are hesitating, wondering if they have enough paper!!! Liars. All her books are out of print of course.

I think she was pleased that I like her work and apologised for not having recognised her quality sooner. Of course she finds 'post-war London dreary'. I wish to goodness I were rich enough to get her out and send her to live wherever she wants – Italy or France. When I think of the wealthy fools wasting money, of the money poured out for parasites and sycophants of these vile governments, and think of a sensitive artist like that imprisoned. ... Think of her learning, which has never received the least recognition, and the 'honorary' degrees lavished on people like [T.S.] Eliot and Jack Priestley and Morgan Forster!!' She says: 'You have an enchanting address. Somebody once said I was unable to write a book without mentioning Antinous and Aucassin; perhaps it was true. I have a passion for that prince of Beaucaire who described the way to hell so invitingly.'[2]

Here is something you must not mention. Frere is planning – plotting is better perhaps – to re-issue Lorenzo in the fall of '49. But only miserable Penguins – a million copies, made up of 10,000 copies of each of ten titles. He wants me to write a life to come out at the same time. Of course it would mean several thousand pounds to me from England and America, but I hesitate and feel inclined to refuse. I don't like this proletarianising of literature, nor the insolence of keeping L. out of print as long as it suits Heinemann's book, and then throwing him to the wolves when they see a chance of picking up some money – squeezing the orange dry – only to discard L. for good and all. What about Frieda? 'I don't give a damn about Frieda', says Frere. Only too plain he doesn't. I don't know what to do about it. When I offered in the first place to do the life, my idea was to provoke a reprint of the familiar 'little red books' of the Secker type. I never thought of Penguins, for until recently Frere and that sort of publisher spat at Allen Lane.[3]

Kershaw – my admirable secretary – is in London, and just when I need him. There are two sets of proofs due this month; royalties from Milan, Prague and London held up by 'exchange controls' (curse them); the Albatross edition of 'Rejected Guest' is due out to-morrow, needing correspondence and sending of copies to translators; my arrangements in America are in a mess, and need constant letters. Meanwhile, I am trying to write this biography of Waterton. And so on and so on. I hope to goodness the girl doesn't marry him – Kershaw – for I shall never find anyone half or a tenth as efficient and devoted. What says Racine? Vénus toute entière a sa proie attachée [Venus has completely entrapped her prey]!

This is a very whingeing letter, of which I ought to be ashamed. I am. If I had time I'd tear it up and write another. I must not let these exterior things be so shattering – 'the aim of culture is not rebellion but peace'.[4]

No chocs yet.

With love,
Richard

PS. I have been reading Fred Manning's 'Eidola' [1917]. His war poems are strangely akin to mine, sometimes on identical themes. His are very much better of course. I am glad to have re-discovered them.

1 The established British writers John Boynton Priestley (1894–1984) and E.M. Forster (1879–1970).
2 Antinous, Hadrian's lover; Aucassin, hero of the late thirteenth-century legend *Aucassin and Nicolette*, was the son of Count Garin of Beaucaire.
3 'Penguins' were the first British paperbacks. Allen Lane began the series in 1935 with ten titles, which he sold through Woolworth's for sixpence each. By 1941 there were eighty-seven titles; Penguins' popularity during the war increased production to seven hundred titles by 1945. These are certainly not 'beautiful' books of the sort that Aldington frequently recommends to H.D.
4 I have been unable to identify this quotation.

ᴥ 129 ᴥ

20 June [1948]
Hôtel Minerva
Lugano

Dear Richard,

Thank you so much for your letter – your letters, I should say. I do look forward to the Paradise of Poetry; it is good of you to think of me, I have time here to take my time over Elizabethans and 17th [century poets]. We are, however, in some sort of belt or pocket – I don't know what it's all about, but we have had unprecedented thunderstorms and now at lunch a group of people whom I said good-bye to, yesterday, turned up again, as there were landslides past Bellinzona. Our tiny lake, once it gets going, can act up – the Sailing School had all its pretty sail-boats turn turtle, such a fiesta as there was yesterday, with small boys in and out of the ordinary row-boats that were all dragged up on the pavements and into the street. Branches of chestnut and trails of flowering linden decorated the main square, trailed around our notable iron-balconies. I cannot quite make it all out – it has given me blitz-head and blitz memories. I do LOVE it so, here, have seldom been so happy. I dare say it will calm down again, but I may possibly be forced back to Vaud [Lausanne], earlier than I anticipated. However, there is a sort of gala about it all, and I love these Italians and the general come and go is heartening. I have been thinking about Rachel A.T.; does anyone know what SHE would like to do? Could she stand Italy or France – I mean on moderate means? And has she possibly a little income of her own? I know nothing at all. Was she in Scotland during the war? I have written to someone I know in London, on a committee of Authors' Society; they have a small travelling fund, as I understand, and elect someone from time to time, for a 'trip abroad'. I am getting particulars, sub rosa, of course. I will let you know at once, I find out anything. I am so happy that you got in touch with her. Is she very old? I cannot quite remember. I suppose she is about 65–66ish? She may have friends or a friend in England that she does not want to leave. Anyhow, it is most interesting, and I am sure she was really glad to hear of your interest in her work. I thought the reference in the Pater introduction most apropos.[1]

Perhaps your Kershaw is just having a little flutter of sorts. I cannot imagine he would like London. How interesting about Lawrence – but O dear. I feel sort of sick when I see him – only once – on a book-stall here; the First Mrs – no, Lady C. with an introduction by Frieda giving portrait of the artist as a great man, sitting in a bower, past the cyclamen slope–² but – but – Yes; Norman D [Douglas] said, 'he opened up a little window to people in the suburbs'. Somehow, how dreary that preaching of L., 'marriage is thus and so, but I myself, EGO SUM, think it should be, it must be thus and so. I will never ask you who was the father of your children, should you have any after we are married.' It is, isn't it, suburban?

I wish you all good luck, however, and there is the LITERARY side, the sheer writing!

I really feel a bit hay-wire what with our little Blitz, miniature channel with floating wrecks – they did manage to rescue the rudders, however, and I am off with most of the rest of the world here, to view the town below, after the havoc. I wonder if you have had it. Tramontane Sirocco and the other thing Transalpine seem to have met, locked in a struggle – Cis-Alpine, I believe we are? Here is Petrarca (is it true that he met Chaucer in Padua?): Solitudo transalpina mea jucundissima [my transalpine solitude is most pleasing]. I heartily subscribe – but I will write later when I am a little less hay-wire.

Love,
Dooley./

Choc from Manuel was sent, June 1. Do hope it has turned up.

1 In *Walter Pater: Selected Works* (London: Heinemann, 1948) Aldington wrote

> The most successful adaptation of Pater's methods and attitude is a book which has deservedly been most widely circulated in the United States, though it seems little known in England – I mean Rachel Annand Taylor's *Leonardo the Florentine*. This poetically written book disregards the proportions and principles of an ordinary biography to paint in brilliant hues a vast nostalgic fresco of the Italian Renaissance, a 'Prose Idyll' on a great scale, which should satisfy the most ardent yearning 'for something in the world that is there in no satisfying measure, or not at all' (25–6).

2 H.D. is probably referring to the Odyssey Press edition of *Lady Chatterley's Lover*, printed in Leipzig in 1933. It corrected many errors of the first edition and carried a brief introduction by Frieda.

≈ 130 ≈

27 June 1948
Villa Aucassin
St Clair
Le Lavandou
Var

Dear Dooley,

I was very sorry that you had to go through what was evidently a terrific storm. Here we had a day of heavy cloud with light rain, followed by a brief but violent mistral. However, if our weather is any indication, this long period of disturbance is over. We have cloudless skies, light 'halcyon' breezes, the sea is warming up, and the nightingales have handed over to the cicadas. I don't believe anyone really gets Italian poetry until he has lived on the Mediterranean, or Greek poetry for that matter.

I am sure Mrs Taylor has a private income. How otherwise could she have 'kept her integrity as an artist' – that being a pretty way of saying a writer has an unearned income? But I have heard no more, and don't even know if she wants to come overseas. I assume that any intelligent person would want to get out of that mess, and she certainly complained of its dullness. It is most generous of you to think of ways and means, and I'll let you know if she says anything. As she has just finished this big book she will obviously need to stay near the B M [British Museum] Library while it is going through the press.[1]

Kershaw was supposed to see her, but he has not reported anything, and is most conscientious in reporting the people he has interviewed for me in London. You've got that situation wrong. No sort of a 'flutter'. This is one of those heart-rending affairs which has now been going on for three years, separations due to war, economics, objections of parents, incompatibilities, then sudden reconciliations after flights across the world. And so on. I'm afraid the girl will marry him. He is a most handsome young man, straight as a spear, a first-rate boxer who knocks out Australian toughs, hates sports and patriots and les heros malgré eux [those who are heroes in spite of themselves], is a poet, very well read, and has the good or shall we say odd taste to believe that I am one of the best writers of the century. He is unbelievably efficient as a secretary – which of course he does out of kindness, not for the money. Should I not mourn the loss of such a phoenix? I shall.

The chocolates from 'la dame en Suisse' reached Catherine yesterday. 'I like that Pupier chocolate', she said. She will write as soon as the end-of-term examinations at school are over. Meanwhile she asks me to thank you for this very handsome present. Conditions are bit by bit easing in France, and the numerous stolen parcels from U.S. are being replaced, but a great box of pure chocolate like that is still a princely gift.[2]

I understand your revulsion against D.H.L. I had a similar feeling recently, as I think I told you, on re-reading St Mawr. I disliked intensely the acrid underdog hatred, not a generous hatred of indignation and scorn, but a hatred of envy and grudging – the very things his better self inveighs against! And then those ridiculous primitives – who are to save the world (from what, mon Dieu?) by going to bed with upper class women. But then there was greatness in him, more than anyone else in our time, I think.

Chaucer and 'Petrark'. I quote from the 1933 complete Chaucer, edited by Robinson, who is the great American Chaucer scholar and probably better than any contemporary British. He says: 'Chaucer's literary acquaintance may well have extended beyond England and France to Italy. For it would have been possible for him, at least, on his visits to that country, to see Sercambi, whose Novelle, like the Canterbury Tales, describe a pilgrimage; Giovanni da Legnano, the great jurist whom he praises in the Clerk's Prologue; and Boccaccio and Petrarch, to both of whom he is indebted for important material. But no record has been found of his meeting any of these Italians, and the passage in the Clerk's Prologue, which is often cited to prove his acquaintance with Petrarch, is not really valid evidence.'

The position is really rather like that of wonder-working images. The Church does not insist on a good Catholic believing the miracles, but if belief conduces to edification (marvellous word!) the Church will not object. So in the Temple of Culture, why should we not have our legends conducing to edification, like that charming story of the meeting of Chaucer and the divine Petrarch? Why not? Especially as Landor has made such stately talk up for them.[3] Even the appallingly erudite Robinson admits it was 'possible'.

Did you ever go to Certaldo? A bit of a disappointment, though one <u>imagines</u> Boccaccio there very vividly. Of course it was knocked to pieces in the war.

I do feel strongly with you that I should like to do something for R.A. Taylor. I have written her a fan letter, mentioned her in Pater (as you know) and retitled my Aesthetes 'John Ruskin to Rachel Annand Taylor'. I think her poems are very good of their kind. Unluckily it was a kind which was already out of fashion when she wrote, but enough time has now passed for them to reach timelessness. That Leonardo of hers is stupefying – so immense a sustained effort of imagination, eloquence and erudition! It knocks Pater and Symonds completely, for Symonds was a bad stylist and Pater had no 'souffle' [inspiration] – Marius drags terribly. I came across some twaddle of Max Beerbohm (he is a twaddler and a faker I think) in a periodical of 1896, when he remarks that 'Mr Pater writes English as if it were a dead language.' Something in that – it takes a worm to see that the gods have feet of clay.

With love,
Richard

1 On 18 July 1948 Aldington added that Taylor had written to him and that at 'over 70', she probably would not want to leave England. He arranged for his friends Kershaw and Dibben to take her out to dinner and wrote H.D. 'that they were charmed with her talk, and that at her age she drank level apéritif, two bottles of Pommard, … two Calvados and a Cognac. … They seem to have recited poems to each other for several hours.'

2 Catherine plays an increasingly important role in these letters, while Aldington carefully avoids nearly all mention of Netta; in fact, he seldom now writes of his wife to any of his correspondents. Exactly what Aldington has told Catherine about H.D. is not clear, but she obviously knows only a little about H.D.'s relation to her father and H.D. has the status and mystery for her of 'La dame en Suisse'. Catherine's English, it should be noted, is rapidly being replaced by a greater facility in French; she is becoming increasingly at home in Aldington's adopted country, while Netta, it may be imagined, is growing increasingly restive in the provincial Var.

3 'Chaucer, Boccaccio, and Petrarca' in *The Complete Works of Walter Savage Landor*, ed. T. Earle Welby, London: Chapman and Hall, 1927, Vol. II, 243–82.

⤳ 131 ⤶

1 August 1948
Villa ['Koeclin' is here crossed out] Aucassin
St Clair
Le Lavandou
Var

Dear Dooley,

I wonder why I wrote first the name of the villa I had here in the thirties? Evidently growing more gaga every day.

The wondrous box of chox arrived yesterday simultaneously almost with the arrival of the Frere children, so that was wonderful. But you really must not send any more, because the situation is easing here weekly and I can get her [Catherine] candy from U.S., along with a parcel for the poorer French children in the village, which Catha has been distributing. To try to keep her from being too smug I insisted that she say the food etc. came from an American lady qui aime la France and so forth.

I do wish people could stop hating each other so much. The English motoring through who stop off to call really upset me – they are so full of rancorous hatreds and envies. They're like refrigerators who've stopped being useful and just give off stifling fumes of moral ammonia.

Alister has sent off the two little books for you.[1] The Ruskin is not complete, but the last part is nutty as a fruit cake, and I thought that would be all you would want if you got through parts one and two. Some good writing, I thought, and perhaps some side-lights for Top, though perhaps not. Anyway, you will see. I much want to have your judgment on the Fredrick Tennyson – if you think the poems any good at all.

I am very glad indeed to know you are continuing with the book and that you are enjoying it, and hope it will last.[2]

A friend of Alister's (and mine too) is going to see Rachel and make another report. From what Alister says she must the nearly 80 and really too old to cope with foreign travel. But her letters are marvellously good and A. says her talk is excellent and her memory for poetry most remarkable. I don't yet know if anything has been done or planned about her new work and reviving the old. She has not written, and Mr Frere arrived late last night weary with driving and I didn't want to trouble him at once. But I'll find out. If Heinemann are no good for her I'll send her to another firm I think might be even better because more en rapport with her point of view. I don't think she is hard up in the sense of being destitute, but she is evidently poor though Alister thinks very happy among her books and quite astoundingly erudite. She seems to have made (and kept) quite a lot of enemies.

I hear Pater will be out at the end of this month. I expect very little of it, for I don't think people are any more intelligent and sensitive now than they were in 1890. But as the whole of W.P. is out of print and likely to remain so it seemed a duty – and a pleasant one – to give people a chance to read some of him. I suppose I shall be blamed for using so little of his Greek work, and perhaps I should have done. Wholly between ourselves for I would not whisper it abroad, I was disconcerted to find how ignorant he was of Italy. What I hope is that a few young or old or middle-aged people may find the book and learn a little to like W.P. But, as Max says somewhere, he writes English as if it were a dead language.

I think your idea of sending Rachel a Manuel box [of chocolates] is not only kind and generous but the very thing. She feels lonely and forgotten, so that the present would touch her, and surely that good chocolate would be an aubaine [windfall] for her. The Address is: 17 Jenner House, Hunter St., W.C.1.

You stagger me with the news that earthenware is still unobtainable in England. Here there is so much, both Provençal folk and commercial, some plain clay, most painted, that the place is covered with pots and plates and dishes and cups and saucers every Thursday, while there are several shops which have them. There is nice glass again too.[3]

I haven't looked at a newspaper for months now, and it is really wonderful not to care for such news as I couldn't help gathering from the Freres, such as the palpitating information that Molotov is out and Dewey the Republican candidate and Australia won the Tests and the Olympic Games are a flop – all of which could have been foreseen by a schoolboy and none of which is of the least importance. Politicians, unluckily, are the most easily replaced of human losses.

My wonderful book-hunting friend has sent some treasures lately, including all Fred Manning's poems (three books) and the first book of the Rhymer's Club. I now have both Rhymers. There were 300 copies of Vol 1 and 450 of Vol 2. They contain the first appearances of Lionel Johnson's Statue of King Charles I; Yeats's Man who dreamed of Fairyland; [Ernest] Dowson's Carmelite Nuns; [Victor] Plarr's charming Epitaphium Citharistriae; Yeats's Father Gilligan; J. A. Symonds's Javanese Dancers; Yeats's Fairy

Song and [The Lake Isle of] Innisfree; The Rose in my Heart; Dowson's Cynara; and many others.[4]

I am promised a complete set of Mathilde Blind's poems. Meanwhile I have her book, The Heather on Fire, the poem about the eviction of Highland crofters to make shooting places for English and American millionaires – a squalid business which not even her flaming indignation can make poetic. The 'crofters' were evicted by force, put on steamers and sent either to Canada or Australia without their consent and not knowing where they were going. One of the criminals who paid heavily to get the shooting was an American named Winans or Winant, who then (about 1850) lived in Brighton. Alas!

Your wine sounds excellent and probably better than ours here. I have drunk a Dôle in France, in queer stone bottles, a fragrant wine, and light. I thought Fondant was that melted cheese dish in which you dip bread, but there must be a white wine that goes with it. Do you get the Italian things like ravioli and gnocchi? We alternate two 'helps' in the kitchen, one who is French and one Italian, which is fun.

With love and thanks from Catherine for the box.

Richard

1 On 18 July 1948 Aldington had promised H.D. 'the Frederick Tennyson Isles of Greece and an odd volume of Ruskin's Praeterita'.
2 On 29 July 1948 H.D. had written to Aldington: 'I am deep in with Top and Gabriel now – the first part of White Rose and the Red was given over to Liz, more or less, and she was a bit sour-puss now and again. But Top and Gabriel get together after Liz sweeps out to Matlock, just before they do the Oxford Union, and they sit in Red Lion (Ted out of the way) and consume their Nostrano and talk shop. I am very happy with the book. I hope I do not finish it for some time, as I love it and live it so much.'
3 On 29 July 1948 H.D. wrote to Aldington: 'The Cappers, three, all got to Zinal, Valais. I heard from her that she hadn't a single matched cup or uncracked saucer and she had seen a tea-set at Brigue. I suppose it was the first one she set her eyes on, as I think Brigue is just a junction. I managed to send her a note [i.e. Swiss francs] and she got the tea-set and she is almost crazy with excitement about it, like a child with a doll-set.' Apparently, Jessie, her husband Athol, and their grown son John Capper have travelled to Switzerland for a summer holiday. While H.D. chooses to mention Jessie in connection with the topic of material scarcity in England, Aldington deftly avoids referring to his former neighbour. Capper and H.D. remained friendly throughout the 1930s and 1940s.
4 The Rhymer's Club was a group of poets who met regularly in London in the 1890s. Aldington is here acquiring familiar material, for his own library has repeatedly been collected and dispersed as he moves about.

❧ **132** ❧

16 September [1948]
[Hôtel] Minerva
Lugano

Dear Richard,

No, I am afraid I did not write.[1] Who was it who said, 'even if you have only invented a new mouse-trap, the world will seek you out in your wilderness'.[2] Ever since late-mid August, there has been a va è [sic] vient [coming and going] from England. I am sorry not to have acknowledged the charming picture of C[atha] and to have neglected her, but I have been dishing out Fr. 20-notes. I just have to draw the line at sending parcels to London – I am afraid I just cannot. But when they turn up on the door-step with their maintenance pittance, I cannot NOT give them their next Christmas present, for their extra tea or those doll-bottles of various red, green, gold liqueurs they find so fascinating. I have not sampled, but believe they are excellent, apricot, cherry and the rest. Two more are due to-morrow and, I expect, bang will go another two twenties. That will be the end of their summer – I do not mind the gifts, it is the sadness, the despair they bring, all bright and gay, of course, withal, but the screams over the croissants, the coffee, the cigarettes – not to mention the elbowroom and the postauto [car] trips in and through the hills, in and out of Italy and back to lake.

I am so glad to hear of all your various activities. I saw several good reviews of Pater but did not clip out as you have your press-cuts.[3] Thank you for mention of collections;[4] Norman Pearson at Yale has what he calls his H.D. shelf; I don't know what he has but he knows more about my editions than I do. Yes, the BY AVON RIVER (so-called) is due out in the spring; I have sent WHITE ROSE AND THE RED and THE SWORD WENT OUT TO SEA for them [her editors at Macmillan in New York] to comment on. I finished the ROSE with Indian Mutiny. I could go on and on for at least two more volumes, but I think it better to TRY to stop now. I am so terribly devoted to Tops; I get more and more peace and sustenance from him. I was sent a rare copy of [William Morris's] the Pilgrims of Hope, a Th[eodore] Mosher re-print from a re-print. I believe W.M. did not encourage the assembling of these poems from the Socialist papers he wrote for. They are pleasantly ordinary, and so comforting to find that he could NOT cope with the political, at all – just drab without Kipling's trumpet-ing. I am re-reading Paradise when I get back to Lausanne, I expect about late-mid October. I have not the books here, but am more and more intrigued by that break in time, those years after Earthly Paradise were filled with trans., which you and others tell me are not too good;[5] then, the hectic Red Lion business and design, then the Socialist upheaval (I believe he was arrested on one occasion); then the last years, those five very rewarding fairy-tale prose-romances in the last five years! But you know all this![6]

I will let you know when/if I hear, re the ROSE. I have told them I do not want SWORD set up for the moment. I made a few changes. But the book still lives for me and gives me life.

This is only just to thank you and to explain why I had not written. Perdita was here from New York for my 10th September birthday. She left yesterday. She is happy there, taking what she calls 'post-graduate courses' at Columbia and is part-time secretary in a literary agent's office. She is taking out her U.S. papers. Our air-mail, I think I told you, is what they call 'courtesy air'. That is, all the post is the same, but if there is room in the bag, they take along what they have of ordinary. However, I am sending in air-envelope, in the hope of 'priority'.

All the best to you all there.

Love from
Dooley./

1 On 11 September 1948 Aldington had written to H.D. to convey his concern at not having heard from her. He is always the more regular correspondent. H.D. is careful to answer his letters, but often writes one to his two, and she tends to write in spurts, in clusters of letters focusing on one topic, followed by as much as a month of silence.

2 Proverbial but attributed to Ralph Waldo Emerson. I am grateful to Fred D. Crawford for this gloss.

3 Aldington had written to H.D. on 11 September 1948 that 'The Pater is out. It had a very poor subscription. ... There were about a dozen reviews ... nearly all favourable, but very uninteresting and superficial.'

4 On 11 September 1948 Aldington had asked H.D. if any university was collecting all of her published work. He added: 'U.C.L.A. is doing this for me, and I regularly donate all new editions, reprints, translations and such older stuff as I find and they haven't got. ... Larry Powell, the head librarian, is a good chap, and a great fan of yours.'

5 Aldington responded on 19 September 1948:

> You must have got a slightly wrong impression of my views on Top's translations. I do think the metre of his Aeneid a mistake, and you cannot make 'folk' out of a poet so urban and scholarly as Virgil. I also think Top's versions of the Volsungasaga, the Grettirsaga and the other Icelandic work are almost as difficult as the originals. But his own story of Sigurd the Volsung, practically an original, is excellent, and I am a great fan of his Odyssey. I like that Morris Odyssey very much, almost more than any other English version I've read. Who, I wonder, has read his translations apart from you and me?

6 On 19 September 1948 Aldington commented to H.D. that he had read but does not now own a copy of *The Pilgrims of Hope*, adding: '... the Earthly Paradise is an endless pleasure – gives one so warm a feeling for the 1870's in England, with Pater hiding in Brasenose and Ruskin screeching from various platforms and young Mr Wilde of Magdalen writing aesthetic pieces, and everything very peaceful, and no Mogul hordes let into our midst by renegade German traitors to European civilization. I must say I look forward very much to seeing your two books in print, and I don't see why you should stop.'

⇜ 133 ⇝

> 1 October [1948]
> [Hôtel] Minerva
> Lugano

Dear Richard,

Thank you for your letter [19 September] – and the one before [11 September 1948], in which you mention Larry Powell and family coming over in 1950. Certainly I would be happy to see them, if they are anywhere near. At the moment, I am myself flirting with the idea of New York for a little trip; all very indefinite. I have now a new *Livret pour étrangers*, status B, which means I am in a sense now resident and have [i.e. am allowed] only 90 days out of the country. I had no urge to travel until I was rationed thus. I am, I am told, extremely luck to get this B. It started late July and made me wonder, for the first time, what to do with my 'rations'. I will let you know well in advance, if I make any move. It is not, perhaps, a bad idea to cross as Perdita is now getting her USA papers (she also is rationed) and she came this year; I might simply visit her, next.

I have just had a letter from James Laughlin of New Directions.[1] Do you know him? I met him in Boston when I was there, 10 years ago. I wrote him about the Spanish Anthology, among other things. He has not yet found it; poor E. [Ezra Pound] was anxious to have his copy. No one seems to have seen the book (such a really beautiful book) but H.D.[2] Laughlin writes me: 'I was down to see Ezra in Washington the other day and was pleased to find that in some ways he was considerably improved. His physical health seems good and he is able to concentrate a good deal better. He also seems to have been able to erect a kind of mental barrier between himself and his surroundings so that his own life is able to go on untroubled, and he is not too unhappy. However, his delusions seem to be somewhat worse than they were before. He himself has requested that we do not take steps to have him released until after the political changeover this year.'[3] Laughlin sent me E.P.['s] last book, Pisan Cantos, written while E. was at Pisa.[4] I sent E. a book of Botticelli Primavera in return. E. wrote me an appreciative letter, ending, 'benedictions; I have inordinate thirst for simple gossip – you get that way caged'. I did send cards and photographs of Venice etc. last winter through Viola Jordan, but I wrote E. this time, through Laughlin, to thank him for the book. I have, of course, the early scene to go back to, but I do not feel that I should mention any person in the way of 'simple gossip'; of course, I did not speak of you, but if at any time you came across a card that would please or help him, the address is: St Elizabeth Hospital, Washington, D.C.

I expect to leave here about October 20, though it is very hard to think of leaving now, just as there is this first gold leaf and pools of sun among the trees, warmer and more sustaining and nourishing even than summer sun. I was told before I first came in spring that the autumn was the time for Lugano. It is rather breath-taking with the vendemmia [grape harvest] now officially about to commence. However, I like my Hotel de la Paix in Lausanne and will be glad to unpack my stored books and belongings there.

All news is most interesting; I have been fairly quiet since the last visitors left, just two weeks ago. I really have now become swamped with Dante, I begin to see the fascinating pattern and day-light through the maze. I am very happy with this, as I never really seemed to have time or energy to tackle Dante in the original. I have made some most interesting discoveries – feel like Columbus. I guess I am destined to add to what Gabriel Rossetti, or one of the commentators, termed 'a whole literature to discuss the meaning of a single line'. Well – it will keep me busy.

Love,
Dooley./

1 James Laughlin (1914–97), who came to Rapallo to meet Pound in 1935, founded New Directions publishing house in 1936.

2 I have been unable to identify 'the Spanish Anthology'.

3 In a letter to H.D. on 21 January 1949 Aldington added to this portrait of Pound when he summarized for her a letter he had received from Laughlin: 'Result of election was great disappointment to E., who believed he was a Republican and would be taken to White House by Dewey as a sort of Harry Hopkins for China. E. violently refuses any suggestion of being transferred to a private asylum, being convinced his enemies would there kill or poison him, which they can't do where he is. Nothing to be done except try to alleviate necessary captivity. He sees Dorothy daily, is allowed "generous number of visitors", considerable correspondence, and "translates" Chinese Odes.'

4 Pound wrote these cantos while incarcerated at the United States Disciplinary Training Center outside Pisa in 1945; they were published as The Pisan Cantos by New Directions in New York in 1948.

4 October 1948
Villa Aucassin
St Clair
Le Lavandou
Var

Dear Dooley,

Yes, I did hear from Laughlin, and wrote him at once to say that I would support any effort to secure Ezra's release. I think E. is very wise to wait for a change of administration. Knowing nothing of these things, I can only guess that there will be a Republican administration. Between ourselves I wonder a little if it is wise to press for release? Of course, anyone confined would want to get out, but imprisonment of this sort usually makes people worse mentally, and then has Laughlin considered how E. is to live? Reprints of his old work will do little, and he seems not to have much that is new to offer. Do you think they would let him go back to Italy? And would that be wise? Well, those on the spot must decide.

I don't think it wise for me to write him direct and openly from here – sure to be noted, and I stand well with the French authorities at present, but they are still very sore with collaborators. But if anything seems possible I'll write undercover through Laughlin. Probably E. doesn't quite realise the feeling in ENG. and France. I had a fearful tussle with Heinemann to keep even those two poems of his in the anthology [*Poetry of the English-Speaking World*]. Those filthy newspapers did the harm. Poor old Ez, I am sorry for him.

Yes, that 90 day 'furlough' seems the idea everywhere now. Kershaw got a ten year carte d'identité to his delight – he doesn't realise that six foot Australians look good recruits in France! He has gone over to London to his girl again, but they would only grant him three months. If he overstays, he forfeits his residence, I suppose. So if you do go to U.S. don't overstay if you want to keep your Swiss residence.

By the way can you give me any clue to the meaning of E's Cantos? I simply don't understand what they're all about. *Is* there any plan, any structure? Or are they just at random? I really would like to know. I gave them up as I gave up Finnegan's Wake and for much the same reason, except that I think E. occasionally does write a line or two of real poetry.

Kershaw writes me that he dropped into the BM [British Museum] and found Banabhard working away cheerfully and in great form. She writes me most entertaining letters, full of scholarly wisdom and good sense and wit and excellent judgment. I believe I told you Heinemann are reading her new book [on the Renaissance]. Frere said it is the biggest script they have had since William de Morgan dropped 'Joseph Vance' on a protesting William H [Heinemann].[1] I am trying to get one of her books into the Pelicans, but so far without success.

We have had wonderful days here for about two or three weeks, but there are scirocco clouds on the hills to-night. The wind is from the S.W. so probably won't affect you. How late your vendemmia is! Ours was over three weeks ago. Only average, they say. But those picturesque ceremonies sound enchanting. Once they existed all over Europe. Why did the world let them die?

I have done 25,000 words of the [D.H.] Lawrence biography. It is, so far, not as difficult as I feared, but then the early part is the easiest, and then in his young days he was really rather attractive. Later on, when he got portentous about his mission and angry with the world, he is less pleasing. It is one up to old Ford that he instantly recognised the merit of those first poems and published them unhesitatingly. I ought really to have someone look up the English Review files and see what was published, but there is so much material I groan under it. Nearly as much as the Duke of Wellington!

Have been working all day and feel tired. Catha goes back to school to-morrow so is grumpy and sorry for herself to-day – also she smashed her kite. Life, life, as Gogol says.

Love,
Richard

1 William de Morgans's *Joseph Vance: An Ill-Written Autobiography* (London: Heinemann, 1908) is 509 pages long.

➣ 135 ➣

17 October [1948], 21 October [1948]
Hôtel Minerva
Lugano
Hôtel de la Paix
Lausanne

Dear Richard,

I have wanted to write but have had last-minute odds-and-ends. Difficult, too, to answer your question, Has Ezra any plan or central idea? I really did not read E. at all, during the in-between years, and during war, articles were sent me from Viola Jordan about his activities; they did not make me very happy. But Spirit of Romance[1] was sent me from my old London books by Bryher, who knew that I was after the 'answer', as we had read the last book with some surprise. I mean, I was surprised to find that it carried me along; I was leafing it over to get 'some idea', when I found myself caught up in it; I felt, almost for the first time, that E. had really genius: I say this, in the sense that I felt the lines ran along sometimes with an almost Elizabethan grandeur. I got the idea of some grand Elizabethan writing ABOUT a mad poet; a sort of King-Lear-cum-Fool-in-Lear; as if someone were writing lines for someone in a play; as if there were genius back of it; as if E. were not controlled but uncontrolled by this genius or daemon. I was actually very upset, as I had not bothered to analyze E. at all and my early impressions were mixed. Spirit of Romance, I find on re-reading after more than 30 years, is sound and has balance. I am, of course, more able to assess his findings now.

I really felt that I better get the book out of the way, so sent it on to Bryher; she wrote: 'I have re-read all of Ezra's poems very solemnly. Struck by three things, flashes of extreme beauty, an extreme coarseness, an obsession with "fame". Nobody comes in really as a person, he abuses people or accepts dead people, troubadours, etc. (not that they are dead in the mind) but it seems he cannot bear to surrender anything to a living human being. It's awfully interesting and sad. Eliot has pity, Ezra the lightening of genius and the desperation of the narcissistic mania.'

I could say a great deal more and will hope to, later. I was struck by your contrasting him with the [Finnegan's] Wake. I am interested in your work on Lawrence, too. There is, in some way, an interesting parallel between him and Ezra. They both rushed along; mountain torrents. E. is the more rugged, a sort of post 49-er, blasting up rocks, giving up his gold-field in a mad rush on; sifting stones and pebbles for a gleam of gold (and the gleam is there), not properly 'panning' the gold-sand when sifted, dangerous, undecorous, no dulce et decorum, potentially magnifico, disguised in harlequin rags? Or harlequin disguised as Magnifico? Well. ... I could go on and on this way. Lawrence a more native torrent, also rushing, but in valley and predicted channel, if rugged, yet still with European precedent; not so rugged; beautiful tender approach to cyclamen, narcissus, anemone; cottage, rural, village Miracle Play, tempestuous 'adultery' – what is adultery? Concern for some sort of Puritan formula, what is sin? And so on. ... But you did not ask for thesis; as I said, re Lawrence, some time ago, I would hope to write of him; perhaps I will later. I think the parallel in time and space of the two, is a help. They were (are) almost of an age, there is only about six weeks between Lawrence, Sept. 11, and Ezra, October 30, both born 1885 – if the 'stars' have anything to do with it.

Now I am not forgetting the pleasure of receiving the Bilder and 50 Romance and Lyric Poems.[2] In fact, this is a god-send; I am greatly indebted to you for the 'post-cards', beautiful and most 'thesaurus' in character; jewels. I will write further; I am always a little shattered at 'journey's end'; a new term begins for me and I am disassociated a bit until I get settled again in La Paix.

By the way, can you tell me anything of the connection of Margaret of the Paris tragedy that we 'witnessed' – was it 1912? I mean, I remember her being a niece or cousin of an American poet – was it Sydney Lanier? I am even uncertain if there is any such poet, of south, mid or deep south.[3] I am reminded as I had in mind a girl I knew at Bryn Mawr who was not unlike Margaret (and her name?) I was asked to look up this Pleasaunce (a dream of a name) Baker, during terrible Blitz time; Pleasaunce had married a Junker and I did not really feel I was, at that time, able to cope; she came back or was sent to England; friends wanted me to see her; by the time I had time to turn round, Pleasaunce was dead. There was something of the same repercussion, emotionally, I mean as in the case of Margaret.[4] Margaret I presume was from some south state, I remember her French was perfect; Pleasaunce was from Florida. There was just a suggestion of semblance in their appearance and background, though I have no reason to suppose that Pleasaunce died other than of pneumonia, as reported.[5]

I hate this air-paper, my last fragments; I will, as I say, hope to write further when settled again. And I do appreciate the little books.

Love –
Dooley./

1 Pound's *The Spirit of Romance* (London: J.M. Dent, 1910) comprised the texts of the lectures he gave at the London Polytechnic in 1909 on medieval southern European literature up to Lope de Vega. Humphrey Carpenter writes that '*The Spirit of Romance* does not suffer from [the] ... failure to explicate anything like as markedly as his later prose writings. There are passages in the book – for example his description of Dante's life – which are lucid and conventional narrative, though they lack the true Ezra fire and are merely lecture-room stuff. However, the preface to the book is typical of him, both in its dismissive attitude to conventional scholarship and as a statement of his own attitude to the literature of past eras ...' (*Ezra Pound: A Serious Character*, 125).

2 Aldington has sent H.D. copies of his *Bilder* (Hamburg: A Keune, 1947) – German translations of a selection of his poems – and *Fifty Romance Lyric Poems* (published in New York by Crosby Gaige in 1928 and in London by Chatto and Windus in 1931), a collection with commentary.

3 The 'Margaret of the Paris tragedy' was Margaret Cravens. She was born in Indiana, not in the deep south, but she was indeed related to the American poet Sidney Lanier.

4 H.D. and Aldington were both very upset by Cravens's sudden death. H.D. wrote about her as Shirley Thornton in *Asphodel* and returned to the incident of her suicide in her late journal 'Compassionate Friendship' (Yale).

5 Aldington responded on 9 March 1949: 'Was it not Margaret Craven[s]? I think so. I don't know where Ezra met her. Off hand I should have said "at a university dance" – much like that mysterious Mary Moore of Trenton over whom we used to laugh. I did not know that unlucky Margaret was related to Lanier. Yes, yes, he was Old South – fought, in whose Corps I forget – one of those romantic southern generals, like Beauregard. Lanier is a good poet, not great as Herman Melville is (who is so great that America has not yet published him) but good. I like Lanier.'

⤜ 136 ⤛

14 February [1949]
Hôtel de la Paix
Lausanne

Dear Richard,

Thank you so much for your two letters and the press-note enclosed in the last of February 11; it is most amusing though grim. I will pass it round; there is so little of this intelligent riposte to be seen these days.[1] It is all so sad and hopeless in England. I have the greatest affection for the Warwick and Glos. [Gloucester] country that I fortunately saw, in 1945. But a friend from Stonehouse, Glos., now writes that things are more and more depressing, even there.

Thank you for news of Rummel. I heard again, via Nadejine, that Walter had German affiliations, I believe he had German birth-certificate; that Rummel was back in Paris, as you reported, rather to the embarrassment of his old friends.[2]

I have heard again from E., but it is almost impossible to answer his flighty, disconnected little notes. He speaks of people of the pre-1914 war as if we were all in touch still; people I had forgotten.

By the way, I heard from my Glos. friend that he had seen a good deal of Fred Manning there in Glos., before his death, and that Fred had spoken of the old crowd with affection.[3]

The Paris book-shop gals [Sylvia Beach and Adrienne Monnier] were asking me of Flint. Do you know whatever became of him?[4] No – I have given up 'poor dear Rimbaund' as I had galleys of my Macmillan book, a good deal of correspondence with Pearson at Yale about it; I have sent in your name for advanced copy; I am not sure when it will be out. I call the book, BY RIVER AVON; it is in two parts, poems and essays. I must tell you that the vol. is H.D., and Hilda Doolittle is mentioned on the jacketblurb, but they put in, in the 'all rights reserved' note, 'Copyright, 1949, by Hilda Aldington'. This, I suppose, was indicated, I only hope it does not break in to your press reviews.[5] I do not think it will. I am very happy about AVON, as I did it from a few of my 'lecture notes', but with only one rather old-fashioned Anthology beside me, in Seehof, Küsnacht, before I left there, Nov. 1946. The poems, it is true, I had done in London, after my Birthday Celebration at Stratford in April, 1945.[6]

Yes, there is much talk of electricity but here, we have had no cuts; there has been a little snow, and I suppose the snow melting from en haut helps, too. I am suffering a bit still from a shock I had about three weeks ago. Do you remember Frances Gregg? I thought she and her mother had gone back to US, but heard by way of Andrew Gibson (the Glos. friend) that Frances, Mrs Gregg and Betty, the 20 year old daughter, had all been killed at Plymouth in 1941, in the raids there. I was thankful I had not known of it during the Blitz days in London. Andrew only found out as they discovered old bundles of his letters to her, with his address. I am trying to track down the boy Oliver, he was in the Navy, but last heard of on a ship in Iceland.

I am glad to hear your work progresses. I have been getting old stuff re-typed, notes I did in 1941, all rather depressing, but once they are in order, I shoot them over to Norman Pearson for his or my 'shelf' at Yale. If he can place [publish] them, O.K.; if not, they are at least shelf-ed.[7]

All my best to you all there,

Love,
Dooley./

1 On 11 February 1949 Aldington had sent H.D. a copy of his friend Roy Campbell's letter to the Editor of the *Times Literary Supplement* in which he complained wittily that 'The review of Aldington's "Collected Poems" deserved more space and a different reviewer.' Campbell objects to 'those literary officials for whom the formalities of procedure have long ago eclipsed any interest in' real poetry.

2 'Nadejine' remains unidentified, but on 1 January 1949 Aldington had written to H.D. that he was sure their acquaintance, the American pianist Walter Morse Rummel, had safely survived the war and was performing again in Paris.

3 On 18 February 1949, Aldington responded, 'Curious you should mention Fred. I also saw a good deal of him in the twenties, particularly after [his companion] Galton died. But unluckily Fred became such a dipso, it became very painful to know him. ... I have one, perhaps two of Fred's poems in my Religion of Beauty.'

4 Aldington responded on 18 February 1949 that Flint 'will be remembered because of his association with us, but he had no real energy, no staying power. I understand he was "dispersed" to Manchester with the Ministry of Labour during the panic days, and is now probably retired. I think he is still alive. I wrote him from Florida twice in '41, but had no reply.'

5 H.D. apparently has several concerns here: she is worried that Aldington subscribes to a press-cutting service that will send him reviews of her book (and charge him for doing so); she is uncomfortable with the revelation that H.D. is Hilda Doolittle is Hilda Aldington, information which seems to undermine her poetic persona; she is unhappy at being linked publicly with Aldington – not so much because she does not want him to be linked with her as because she does not want to trespass somehow on his career. Aldington responded on 18 February 1949, explaining that 'your legal name must appear on the book as copyright holder, but as I've had no sub[scription] for U.S. clippings since 1930 I shan't get your reviews'.

6 That is, H.D.'s celebration of Shakespeare's birthday (23 April), not her own (10 September).

7 On 26 November 1948 H.D. had written Aldington in greater detail about this work:

> I have been going over about 20 old note-books, of slapped-down impressions, Vienna [about analysis with Freud], London, Paris, New York, and combing out all sorry, unpleasant, unhappy references to anybody, more or less. I get in a few digs at the élite and the high-brow but personal revelations, I really do bar. This sounds as if my 'For Remembrance' may read pretty insipid. If I ever get Vol. I [of my memoirs] shaped, I will send you a copy. It will take some time. I use, of course, the Ophelia Rosemary lines on the title-page. I am happy doing this, I am only so grateful that the dear Lord spared me, so I can tidy up this mess of papers.

Much of H.D.'s writing after the war stemmed from this process of going over earlier material, retyping, revising, reworking, remembering and reconstructing. Often, it would seem, the revisions were minor — entire works at Yale exist in several typed versions with only occasional changes of words — but no matter how slight the changes may now appear, this process of going through her writing was vital to H.D., for only over time and through a complex series of revisions (of which we may have only the final stages) was she ready to seek publication for her writing.

≈ **137** ≈

23 February [1949]
Hôtel de la Paix
Lausanne

Dear Richard,

Thank you for your letter of Feb. 18. I am so glad that the letter [from Roy Campbell] is going in to the *Times*. There should be more of these old-time protests. I see the *Sunday Times* about mid-week but I will look out for it, here or possibly elsewhere. I was surprised to find on Sunday, when I was having morning-coffee downstairs in the La Paix café, a notice in the <u>Tribune de Lausanne</u>, to the effect that Ezra had been given a thousand dollar prize for his Pisan Cantos by the literary society of the Library of Congress. The Reuter, front-page report headed the news, <u>Prix Littéraire Américain ou une leçon d'objectivité</u>. The notice simply stated the facts of the 1943 events, and the later <u>asile</u> [asylum]. I did finally write E., as I had this cutting for him.

Yes, the apple-tree is very comforting.[1] I just sent a poem to Pearson with my last batch of papers, with a refrain <u>Georgius Sanctus</u>, a sort of conventional, metrical short litany, for W.M. [William Morris].[2] I am interested to hear of the book of Beauty [Aldington's *Religion of Beauty*] and glad that Fred [Manning] and Bvd. [Rachel Annand Taylor] are to be included. No, I do not feel all that young but I do think that E. and H.D. did come from a different vibration, and a vibration that did dart ahead, for all the zig-zag and the bogged-down periods.[3]

I have been feeling curiously deflated and elated at getting off several sets of my war sketches and pre-war long-short and short stories to Pearson. I have carbons of them all and will hope, one day, to have the joy of tearing up the rough originals. I keep them, for the moment, as there are a few of the carbons that I want read this side.[4]

There is one novel that took me exactly 20 years to get right. It is not quite as long as the Synthesis of a Dream volumes. It has a nice title;   MADRIGAL   I sign it
(Bid Me to Live)
Delia Alton, though I don't know yet how any of that will work out. Now, I do not think Pearson will want to substitute it for the Rossetti, White Rose and the Red, only the Rose book is as long as the two parts of the Dream book; you know what these publishers are. In any case, nothing will be done with any of the MSS, without consulting me, without my consent. The Madrigal is so oddly apposite; it is War I, but the whole scene and scheme is pure undiluted WAR II. I worked on and off at the thing, as I say, for exactly 20 years. There is a very concise sample of MADRIGAL in the Synthesis of a Dream, which you read. In fact, except for the names being different, the theme is the same, only it [Madrigal] ends before the war ends and 'Rafe' [the Aldington character] (this time) is still in France.

———

Feb. 24

Cuttings this mornings, from US, about E. 'Wins prize for verse he wrote awaiting treason trial'. And so on. ...

I am posting you the Imagist broadcast;[5] thank you again so much; I have noted down some of it; I expect you keep a file of these things for reference, I should have returned it sooner. I am, now, trying to get my bearings again, after some months of nothing but the old MSS. I hope to get off to Lugano soon after Easter; I am going to the <u>Croce Bianco</u>, D.V.[<u>Deo Volente</u>, God willing] – no, I am not taking the veil; it is the <u>Hotel Croix Blanche</u>, Lugano, but I will write you later, actually time of going and so on. <u>Croce</u> is difficult to get in to, so I have to arrange well ahead. I loved the old Minerva but it was set back in a garden, rather higher up the slopes and by mid-August, we got the heavy shadows soon after tea, actually at the end, Oct., soon after lunch.

I am anxious to get away from old MSS, once I DO get away; I have a lot of Dante queries, and they have a wonderful library, I have already written of it, at Lugano.

I will send you the MSS of MADRIGAL, later, if you would care to glance over it. Once you have it, there will be no hurry, as I am very anxious to get this Dante thing into line with my Shakespeare, AVON book – it will take me years, but it is beautiful work and I love the Italian but need an incentive to keep me at it. It is notable that Dante spent his exile in Shakespeare Italy, Verona, Venice – really, my dear Lugano is part of that very Lombardy.

I can post MADRIGAL before I leave or sooner; you need make no comment on it; simply – if there is anything that you especially dislike, I could always subdue or tone down. I did this book so many times; I have destroyed a sequel, a sort of post-war-I scene, it did not really come true and anyway, this MADRIGAL has the best, and I think I pay tribute in it, to that England, to that particularly Bloomsbury scene and those people;[6] it ends with a sort of good-bye to Frederico, old Rico [the D.H. Lawrence character]; I never wrote anything of Lawrence, though I was asked to. I do think I have a very authentic Frederico, and that pleases me as I did not want to let all that go, without a sort of hail and farewell.

I did the book the last summer in Vaud, 1939, but I left the MS here [in Switzerland] and was about to destroy it with some other old things, but I could not; so I boiled it down and tightened up the last chapters, the hail and farewell, and 'presented' the Rosigran scene as semi-platonic, which in fact it was[7] – but there is only that one Rosigran chapter and then the last two chapters [in the form of a letter to Rico] from Rosigran, summing it all up, 'a nice novel, eh, Rico?' and leaving the episode as a friendship.

All this is rather untidy; I have really been reading too much script.

Love -

Dooley./

1 In his letter to H.D. on 18 February 1949 Aldington had quoted William Morris's 'Pomona':

> I am the ancient Apple-Queen,
> As once I was so am I now.
> For evermore a hope unseen
> Betwixt the blossom and the bough.
> Ah, where's the river's hidden Gold!
> And where the windy grave of Troy?

Yet come I as I came of old,
From out the heart of Summer's joy.

Aldington commented: 'How beautiful that is! It haunts me.'

2 'To William Morris (1834–1896)' was published in *Life and Letters* (Vol. 65, No. 152, April 1950, 50):

Enemy of earth's desolation,
Husbandman, guardian of peace,
Raise your gonfalon over us,
    Georgius Sanctus,

Illuminated Book of Hours,
Thrones, Powers, and Dominions,
Chevalier of the Golden Fleece,
    Georgius Sanctus,

Marshal of Knighthood,
Sceptre of fleur-de-lys,
Holy champion of beauty,
    Georgius Sanctus,

Protector of shrine and sanctuary,
Soldier-Saint and Crusader,
Herald of Chivalry,
    Georgius Sanctus,

Saviour of sacrificed,
Maiden and Princess,
Shelter us and redress
    (*Georgius Sanctus*)

Wrong, the poisonous Serpent;
Return and defend us,
    Georgius Sanctus.

I am grateful to Cassandra Laity for helping me to locate this uncollected poem; her book, *H.D. and The Victorian Fin de Siècle: Gender, Modernism, Decadence* (Cambridge: Cambridge University Press, 1996), explores H.D.'s fascination with the Pre-Raphaelites and draws on the H.D.–Aldington correspondence on this topic to which both refer frequently beginning in 1947. Laity perceptively contends that these letters recapitulate the intimacy contained in Aldington's correspondence with H.D. during the First World War.

3 Aldington had written to H.D. on 18 February 1949 that 'Both Fred and Banabhard looked back, and belonged to the past. Ezra was a puzzle, but I think he belongs to the new rather than the old in spite of his immumerable imitations.' He added that he had not included any of H.D.'s verse in his *Religion of Beauty* because 'you are too young and belong to the future'.

4 This paragraph explains to some extent the curious collection of multiple copies and carbons of H.D.'s work among her papers at Yale. It also addresses the issue of the note 'DESTROY' written in H.D.'s hand on several of her original typescripts at Yale. Robert Spoo suggests in his introduction to his edition of *Asphodel* that H.D. intended to obliterate such works for aesthetic reasons, although he is aware of H.D.'s method of retyping and saving only a final version. Friedman has suggested that H.D. may have intended to suppress, censor or destroy her writing for psychological reasons – the lesbian relationships which H.D. explores, for example. The matter may be simpler, however, and more an issue of filing directions, for it would seem that H.D. does not in fact intend to 'destroy' her work. Rather, she intends to save a 'clean' and

finally revised copy at Yale, but keeps others, which she now perceives as redundant, to share with friends 'this side' of the Atlantic. Eventually, after H.D.'s death in 1961 or Bryher's death in 1983, some of these 'rough originals', which H.D. hoped to have 'the joy of tearing up', as well as extra carbons found their way to Yale.

5 See Letter 121.

6 Here H.D. does not mean the Bloomsbury of Virginia Woolf and her circle but rather the Bloomsbury of Mecklenburgh Square and the circle of people she and Aldington knew in 1917–18.

7 In this *roman à clé* H.D. substitutes 'Rosigran' for Bosigran, the cottage where she lived with Cecil Gray between March and August 1918.

❧ 138 ❧

4 May [1949]
Croce Bianca
Lugano

Dear Richard,

I must thank you for your letter of April 11. I have been here almost two weeks; was stunned and exalté[e] by my welcome of sun and swallows wheeling round the tower or campanile of San Lorenzo, out of my window. I got into sandals, a summer frock and straw hat and began to return to life … when we had the most blighting recrudescence of winter. In fact, the winter rain waited until almost May-day. They needed rain so badly – and I am snug here with most, most excellent food and happy surroundings, also busy with MSS, so I don't mind terribly. I am beginning to thaw out now; the sun is really trying to break through. There are one or two rather lost swallows instead of 1000 around the tower. They reminded me at first of Can Grande's tower – you remember your poem![1]

I am very anxious to know more of the D.H. Lawrence memoirs. When does it come out? I hope you will let me see the final version, as soon as may be. I am happy about Lawrence, now I finished my *Madrigal*. My first version of it was never satisfactory … but when I got a sort of Hail and Farewell into my last chapter (of the soi-disant heroine to the Frederico of the narrative) I felt that I did not have to worry any more to 'place' old Lorenzo, having 'placed' him in time and space and eternity, at last, to my own satisfaction. However, I am keenly interested in the actual story as you knew it and lived it.[2] My 'story' ended (that is *Madrigal*) before the ending of the last war, though I had a few letters at the very end, about the [1930 Imagist] Anthology. It was you, as I remember, who gave me the address and asked me to write. I have only one letter that I can find … I think the only one I have left from Lawrence. It is from Palma de Mallorca and dates 20 May, 1929.[3]

Thank you for the Jean Sedaine. My friend was delighted … a (lady) Dr. Ashby.[4]
All good wishes to all there,

and love
from Dooley./

1 In 'At the British Museum' Aldington writes of being transported by his reading from

> The heavy musty air, the black desks,
> The bent heads and the rustling noises
> In the great dome …

to the lush world of medieval Spain where

The sun hangs in the cobalt-blue sky,
The boat drifts over the lake shallows,
The fishes swim like umber shades through the undulating weeds,
The oleanders drop their rosy petals on the lawns,
And the swallows dive and swirl and whistle
About the cleft battlements of Can Grande's castle ...

(*Complete Poems*, 45, lines 4–6, 9–14.)

2 H.D. is under the false impression that Aldington's biography is a 'memoir', a highly personal account of Aldington's relationship wisth Lawrence. In fact, the book is discreet and achieves a good deal of intentional objectivity. It is worth noting, however, that the two writers come to their separate terms with Lawrence both as writer and friend at the same time; certainly their correspondence with each other about Lawrence influenced their different 'stories'.

3 This letter is not at Yale and has apparently not survived.

4 On 26 March 1949 H.D. had written Aldington: 'I have a doctor-lady or lady-doctor who has written a bit under a ps[eudo]-nom. She quoted O Richard, O mon roi and told me she had an old libretto opera of the story. She says the author is one dramatic poet Sedaine, of whom I have never heard. 18th c., I believe. I told her I thought O Richard was an old chanson and I associated Ronsard with it. She says now she doubts "if the famous song really is a chanson". She doesn't somehow "feel it is". I said I would try to find out where O Richard came from. You used to quote it.'

On 11 April 1949, Aldington responded to H.D.'s queries: 'Your friend is quite right about O Richard, O mon roi. Nothing to do with Ronsard. It came out in 1790 in the light opera Richard Coeur de Lion written by Jean Sedaine (1719–1797) with music by Grétry. It was taken up by the royalists, but did not alas save the king.' H.D. was embarrassed by her misquotation and commented to Aldington on 24 May 1949:

> You must forgive my dumbness over the one French quotation, I was under the impression that O Richard was near-contemporary with Elizabethans. However, I call it the blot on me scutcheon and I doubt if many people will notice my frightful remark [in *By Avon River*, New York: Macmillan, 1949, 72–3] that the song was sung outside the tower 'where the Saracens held the Prince captive'. My dear Dr. Ashby remarked, 'it must have been a slip of the pen on your part', and went on about the opera. I did ask Norman Holmes Pearson (my Yale 'Professor') to vet the MSS for me, though I don't blame him – and must say I enjoyed my little touché from Ashby, she was so pleased that my 'critic', as I called you, proved me wrong. There may be other frightful blunders, but as I pointed out to Dr. A., I did the essay with only one old-fashioned Anthology to hand, and a few notes I had done, as toward my USA soi-disant lectures. I am devoted to AVON and do long for you to see it –

Aldington consoled H.D. on 31 May 1949: 'Well, it is rather a boner, especially as King R. was not captive to the Saracens, but to the Austrians who held him to ransom and bankrupted England of its gold and silver to pay it. Such was the Age of Chivalry at its zenith in the 12th century. But you should not worry one second about it. In the first place everyone makes such slips; it is a trifle anyway; and reviewers of late are so ignorant that they know nothing but Eliot and Auden. So they won't even notice it.'

8 May 1949
Villa Aucassin
Le Lavandou
Var

Dear Dooley,

I was glad to hear and to know that you are installed in the Croce Bianca – sounds delightful in spite of the spell of bad weather. We had similar days of dark skies and rain following a long drought. I believe our weather here is much more influenced by the massif of the Alps than by the innumerable 'depressions moving in from the Atlantic' which deluge England and northern France.

I had hoped to get along to Venice, but I have work which ought not to be delayed which will keep me here until the end of next month. And then it is too late to travel until autumn. These hideous governments have made travel so beastly with their frontiers and controls that one just gives in and stays at home. And I should hate to see Italy smashed and degraded by the vileness of war and modern soldiery.

Still, I wish I could have had a little rest and change, though when I hear from other writers of how little they make and what poor response they get from the public I realise I am exceptionally lucky to have more demand for books than I can fill. The trouble here is that while nature is lovely and the human animal intrusive for only a few weeks, all the lovely art and beauty of the past simply are not. The mere word 'campanile' fills one with nostalgia. And then always one comes back to the horrible fact that the military brutes of the world have smashed Italy and the political fanatics Spain. I'm glad I saw both before the débâcles.[1]

The publication date for the Lawrence is not yet fixed, but I'll let you know when I hear. I believe there is still further confusion in the publishing trade, owing to the fact that the printers' unions have succeeded in cutting down their working hours to 40 a week with no decrease of wages. This means still further delays in production. I shall know more about all this when Frere comes down in August.

We are rather over-run with people at the moment, several at St. Clair and Henry Williamson and his newest wife in Lavandou.[2] There are two Americans whom I dislike very much, the kind of mongrel breed created by their idiotic 'democracy'.

I had forgotten about that Can Grande poem of mine, as Alister did the proofs of that 'Complete Poems'. Not much of a thing, valuable to me only as a note of happy days before all this vileness conquered the world.

I heard from Prague a few days ago that the Czech translation of my Romance of Casanova has sold 49,000 copies – would have sold more if paper had been granted. Remains to be seen whether I can get the royalties or be cheated by yet another government. Hitherto the Czechs have come through handsomely if belatedly, but this time the sum involved is so considerable I fear their cupidity may invent some excuse for not paying.

Let me hear how life goes at Lugano, which must be most beautiful at this time of year. Hope you are not swamped with people. One is so tremendously vulnerable to unintentional intrusions when putting out nervous energy and perception continuously in a long book.

Ever affectionately,
Richard

1 Aldington's mood here contrasts sharply with H.D.'s delight in her new surroundings: he is overworked and the tensions in his family life, though he does not mention them, are increasing. Netta was unhappy with her life in provincial France, and Aldington was dispirited by her frustration. He conveys his feelings to H.D. a bit more explicitly if still with humour in a short note on 21 May 1949: 'Warm and sunny here today, everybody bathing except Richard, the convict of the typewriter!' He reiterated ten days later, 'I am nearly dead with overwork, but hope and believe I shall be free in 4–6 weeks. I have promised then to take a holiday, even if it is only on the beach here.'

2 Henry Williamson (1895–1977) was an English writer known for his rightest sympathies as well as for novels about animals and for *The Wet Flanders Plain* (1929), a work based on his own experiences during the Great War.

≈ 140 ≈

5 June [1949]
Croce Bianca
Lugano

Dear Richard,

I hear from Rural Route 3, Waukegan, Illinois, asking for your address. It seems to be a 17 year old whose guidance teacher suggests his hobby being writing to 'great' people for their signatures. I was about to drop it in the basket when I realized that he got my address from Pearson and it suddenly struck me as very funny, as he has already collected signatures from Robert Frost, Carl S [Sandburg], [Edgar Lee] Master[s], Pound, Fletcher, Eliot, [Conrad] Aiken etc. I felt it a pity to be left out so gave him the signature on an enclosed card, returned his coup for eleven cents post, and addressed letter. Funny – how long it took me just to do that, also I gave him your address, hope you do not mind.

I also got the AVON blurb jacket which has rather staggered me. I must say I am not in the least responsible for it or for taking your name in vain. They remark on the inner leaf, 'In 1913 she married Richard Aldington, the poet and novelist. At that time she began with him the translation of Greek poets, which, since her divorce, she has carried on alone.' They also say she was an editor of the <u>Dial</u> and that 'in 1938 she won the annual Helen Haire Levenson Prize offered by <u>Poetry</u>'. This in the general hub-bub of War II may have escaped my notice, but I have no memory of it. Anyhow, poor old <u>Richard O mon roi</u> does not really worry me now, what with this jacket of 'haunting music' and 'immortality'.

They have set up a sort of booth-tent on the Lorenzo platform for <u>Pentecoste</u>. I was tempted to sneak in for a bit of the organ this morning but I wasn't dressed proper. I sometimes sneak in after dinner with a wisp of veil like Princess M [Margaret] wore for the Pope to see them light the candles and sing a sort of Sant Lucea anthem to Maria. Perhaps that is over now … anyhow, I manage to escape before the funny little man with his row of small boys starts to talk … it is all mate-y and informal.

Love,
Dooley/

27 July 1949
Villa Aucassin
Le Lavandou
Var

Dear Dooley,

I had hoped to be able to give fresh undivided concentration to By Avon River but just as I thought I had won through to leisure there was dropped on me some extra work which I did not want but could not refuse for complicated reasons too tedious to enumerate. So I have had to read the book by snatches in the evenings after a hard day's work, and feel my opinion therefore is hardly worth giving you.

The part I enjoyed most was the opening poem or poems, particularly the last on which I congratulate you most heartily – you know how much I despise Francis of Assisi and all his tribe![1] But it is a very fine poem, masterly. With The Guest you gave yourself a very difficult problem, inasmuch as the texts you deal with are as familiar as household words to all students of poetry and practically unknown to the vast public.[2] I wish so much you could have done as you intended, delivered it as an opening discourse to a university audience of students, for whom it is admirably calculated. Of course it goes far beyond the usual scope of such a discourse, and is really a compact anthology of Tudor-Stuart lyrics with a running commentary. You have extricated yourself with honour from a most difficult situation. I suppose the learned will or may quarrel with some of your inferences and generalities, but these are minor tribulations which are easily endured. I hope the book is selling well. Are you issuing it in England?[3]

I hear Pelican Books have just issued a cheap edition of Dover Wilson's Life in Shakespeare's England, and I have sent for a copy. It has been almost unobtainable for years. The Oxford Press also does a valuable Shakespeare's England, but that is hard to find second-hand and costs a couple of guineas.

Kershaw – my secretary – is just back from a week in Rome with his fiancée. They were utterly delighted with the place, but report it more fascist than ever – but then everybody under thirty is nowadays unless he is a tardy communist. They began by talking French in public and got such a frozen mitt they went back to English – and found a smiling welcome. Your ex-compatriots beyond the Atlantic have reached a peak quotation of culture by plastering Rome with enormous coloured ads of co-eds boozing Coca Cola. Swine, beasts! May they perish. They will.

I suppose you have the same heat we have here? It is really hot here, but luckily we have the Mediterranean and can bathe frequently. Is your lake possible or is it polluted? I wish there were many fewer people in the world.

With love,
Richard

1 In 'Claribel's Way to God', the third and final part of 'Good Frend', the verse section of *By Avon River*, H.D. explores the character and teachings of St Francis.
2 'The Guest' is the prose essay section of *By Avon River* in which H.D. discusses and quotes at length work by Shakespeare's contemporaries.
3 The book has never been printed in England.

18 August 1949
Villa Aucassin
Le Lavandou
Var

Dear Dooley,

Our letters seem to have crossed, with the usual result of smiting both writers dumb!

I had expected to finish the work I was on and to take a few weeks of idling about the 10th July, but in fact one little task has gone budding out of another, so that only yesterday did I really finish and clear my desk. But in all the pressure I cannot remember if I ever thanked you for sending the two snapshots of yourself, which I am very glad to have. I wish they were clearer. Evidently the hand of the potter shook! You look ever so much younger than you are supposed to be in anthologies.

How goes the book [*By Avon River*]? Never let yourself be troubled by the trifles which reviewers pick on to make such fusses about. It is obviously not true to say that all reviewers take to the job because they have failed or have not yet succeeded at something creative; but it is often the case. Nobody who can live by writing his own stuff is going to waste much time writing about the work of others. The fact that the reviewer is inevitably a kind of parasite on the work of which he sets himself up as a judge results in a curious ambivalence – a self-induced belief that he is a better and more important writer than his author, which the reviewer deep down knows perfectly well is false. Hence the irresistible temptation to make some perfectly potty and unimportant little 'point' against the author, and hence too the absurd attitude of condescending superiority on the part of the person who can't write towards the person who can! There is a little psychological knot there to be untied.

The truth is of course that while the romantic notion of the supreme importance of literature still persists, writers and literary talent of a kind have become so common as to be rather a nuisance than a cause of joy. Almost anyone now can write a book, and almost everyone does. There are too many books. Strangely enough, literary genius is as rare as ever, and whenever it shows itself however modestly it always incites dislike and derision from the 'literary'. One comes to dread praise as the hallmark of failure or, at any rate, the phoney.[1]

I wonder how you have survived these last weeks. Here it has been very hot, with a shortage of water, and hordes of people pouring in and out. The water company here has been 'nationalised'. For at least three years the Mairie [mayor's office] and residents have been urging a better supply, and at the same time spending money on advertising Lavandou as a 'resort'. The Government Water Supply starts sinking a well this month, after the acute lack of water has driven away in disgust hundreds of the tourists for whom they advertised! And the 'season' is only a few weeks. The smart bureaucrats will get the water here long after everybody except the few residents has gone. Indeed, Alister tells me some of the hotels already have empty rooms. At any rate, with lake and mountains you are not likely to have a water shortage.

However, the worst of the heat and of the crowds is over, and we shall soon be back to our usual quiet. Catherine is brown all over from sea and sun bathing, and looks very well indeed. The French schools work them hard, but this long holiday of three months seems an eternity to children and sets them up wonderfully. She still has over six weeks. She has a great passion for history and historical novels, both French and English. She is deep in Scott's Kenilworth at present, ferociously cross-questioning me to know if it is 'all true'. Her great ambition is to see Rome and Pompeii, which she imagines to exist as she reads about them in Quo Vadis and The Last Days of Pompeii and some French book about the Palatine. Isles of illusion! She is better off dreaming about them here than seeing the shattered reality at her age. I believe the hero boys [the Americans] contrived to ruin the ruins of Pompeii, remarking that anyway they'd rather have a corner drug store and a coke. I'm sure they would!

Our love to you,
Richard

1 Such thoughts as these are in part responsible for Aldington's unfounded reputation as at least a curmudgeon and at worst a mean-spirited and embittered old man. These ideas also lead him, finally, to valuing negative reviews (as in the case of those elicited in the 1950s by his biography of T.E. Lawrence), as if evidence of moral and literary success were substantiated by the establishment's rejection.

≈ 143 ≈

21 August [1949]
Croce Bianca
Lugano

Dear Richard,

Thank you for your letter of August 18 that came after lunch to-day. Yes – I did think of writing and felt sure our letters would cross again, which apparently they would have done. I am suffering from a number of frustrations, chief of which at the moment is stockings, as I have forgotten how to put them on, after these months of tropic heat. Now it is cooler, but we had an intermediate period of cool winds plus what someone called 'wind from the desert', a sort of sirocco cutting through or into our first real touch of moderation. Well, I usually like the heat but never in my life have I had to give up reading and writing because my glasses misted over. That was a new one on me, also the rooms were shuttered everywhere and yet one was too limp to explore the out-doors. Usually, I can forget myself in a heat-wave, indoors in my own armchair with books – but this all has left me a trifle deracinated. I gave up the type entirely, wrote in my usual corner of my favourite confisserie, in pencil; I think I wrote you last from there.[1] This is one of my first typed letters, and will be very untidy and disintegrated.

But we HAVE water. I have never seen such a lovely display as the spray or shower outside the long dining-room windows across the balcony-garden. The pipes are running along under the wisteria and below an array of old-pottery jars of vivid white and blue butterfly-petunias. There is another, a flowering tree rose purple, I have never seen it anywhere and it only appeared mid-summer, so I guess it is a real tropic. It flowers against a tamarisk (I think) that waves like green moss, beyond the wall of water. I wonder if this is some memory of the old Roman occupation? Everyone in England writes of devastated gardens. I should not complain of my poor old glasses and hateful stockings!

We have curious relays of people. When the cool came (plus sirocco) crowds pushed into the town; rather smarter than our usual tourist type. It appears they were driven down from the stylish resorts because of the SNOW. The passes were snowed over and I suppose that tempered our level here. Anyhow, I should never complain. Only, now suddenly, the days are so much shorter and my summer, though happy, as I say, was unproductive... though I shouldn't say that either.

I think I told you Norman Pearson was turning up. It was terrible in that heat, his live-wire intellect. He rushed on to Florence and Siena and saw everything there, for the first time, though he knows Spain and Norway. It was wonderful getting his cards, old towered San G. [Geminiano], Osbert [Sitwell]'s Monte G. and so on... that first enthusiasm seems inevitable and one lives back. He was good, too, about my MSS; oddly, he seems to think that the <u>Sword</u> should be set up [published], but I am in no hurry for it, and D. [?] now writes he likes the historical or fancy-dress Part II sequence but wants some changes in Vol. I. I cannot imagine what... but am postponing that anyway, as I want the Rosetti <u>ROSE</u> book to come out first; Norman P. wants me to add to it, and now that looms, a beautiful prospect but one must have just the mood.

I think your C. must be very advanced. I read [The Last days of] Pompeii a number of times, but I think I was about 14 when I embarked. I never myself got far with Scott at that age. Dreadful to confess, I loved Dove in an Eagle's Nest but not Daisy Chain. There was a thing called Four Girls, I could never find that book; I had it in an old Chatterbox [edition] and some of the chapters were torn out – but that was about C.'s present age. I am afraid I was an Alcott fan, Eight Cousins, Rose in Bloom, Under the Lilacs, when I was going-on eleven or twelve. Yes, do keep her away from 'ruins'.[2]

I think <u>Avon</u> is O.K.; Pearson wants me to let them run it on till over Christmas before we offer another script. Thank you for all comment on reviewers.

Love-

Dooley./

1 If so, this letter has apparently not survived.
2 The English novelist Charlotte M. Yonge (1832–1901) wrote both *The Dove in the Eagle's Nest* (1866) and *Daisy Chain, or, Aspirations: A Family Chronicle* (1856). I have been unable to identify *Four Girls*. The American writer Louisa May Alcott (1832–88), best known as the author of *Little Women* (1868–69), also wrote *Eight Cousins* (1874), *Rose in Bloom* (1876), and *Under the Lilacs* (1877–78).

⁂ 144 ⁂

31 October [1949]
Hôtel de la Paix
Lausanne

Dear Richard,

Just to thank you for your delightful butterfly letter and to say that I have got back, as per above, finally.[1] I had a most dramatic trip [from Lugano on 27 October], as we neared Gottard, the mountains appeared from the mist, snow-deep, down to the green line; much rain, torrents, a great treat really, coming up; the rather languid torrents had come to life over-night. It went on for about two days; here, it is blazing sun but very cold. We had such an odd second summer in Lugano, those great clusters of white blossom and the fiery Virginia-creeper, mingled with the pomegranates and persimmons, rose and pale orange. Now, I seem to be in – well, what? It does seem so startlingly somehow northern and modern, alive, out-of-the-dream, with the students in their picture-caps, like old Heidelberg, or a velvet tam or beret like Rembrandt portrait of self in youth. Well – I will go on inquiring about German and schools.[2] I felt singularly cut-off at the end, in Lugano, as I could not explain the sterling nor why with Marshall aid, England was letting or might let (that seemed the implication) 'us down'. One cannot argue nor explain. I can feel no panic here in Lausanne. I myself must just wait and if the worst comes, dodge over to New Haven. Perish the thought! I wonder if this place is like Stockholm? I was trying to find a proper comparison or companion. Perhaps I am reminded of Stockholm as I am always rather amazed, when I get on my train at Lugano, to see it labelled <u>Rome–Stockholm Express</u>. One must change at Lucerne and again at Bern, it is almost too long a trip, seven hours.[3]

Well, I am only just settling as I was given the wrong room, and had to wait around half-packed for two days. Now, I am really very happy, perched on the 4th or 5th (US) floor, with a wide platform of a balcony, out of my double French windows. There is a suggestion of gull-shrieks now and again; we had just a sprinkling at the end in Lugano or on Ceresio.

I am so interested in the Lawrence book and trust you will keep me informed as to time of publication.[4]

This is Hallow-e'en; we made much of it as children, with false-faces and later masquerade dances. They 'keep' All Souls here, both denominations; I like the gay evergreen wreaths and, most of all, the huge pine-cones with a candle stuck in the top, to take to the grave. It is so sort of Christmas-y.

I have a great pot of cyclamen and some enormous roses are dripping petals all over my desk. They made much of me, I suppose, for having made me wait for my room; this is my 4th winter in Lausanne. I really feel as if I had finished my University 'seminars'. Well, I will give myself this winter, as last term, for tidy-ing up. I do feel as if I could rest now, having done so much writing the last years, though much unpublished, as yet.

Your list of translators makes me positively dizzy.[5] O, did I tell you, I met Hermann Hesse last summer? He has a delightful home, at Montagnola, very remote from the madding crowd. I know so little (conversational) German, but we managed somehow; he refused to speak anything but German. Have you seen his monumental *Magister Ludi*? We had tea in the forest with some cats; Madame Hesse has quite a job, I imagine. A very intelligent woman, house-keeper, chauffeur and so on. He is 72, she about 52. A most interesting if rather alarming encounter.

This is just to hope all is well there. Forgive rather jerky letter. I am just beginning to get the feel of my desk and double window.

Love from
Dooley./

1 On 16 October 1949 Aldington had written H.D. a long letter in which he discussed the weather and the local flora and fauna. Such reflections – which for other correspondents might simply serve as filler when there was no 'news' – are important elements here. The passage which most impressed H.D. concerned the geography of the Var and concluded:

And we have had a near plague of butterflies, especially the ubiquitous Cabbage Whites. Yes those migrations of Painted Ladies (surely Thistle butterflies in U.S.?) are wonderful. I remember motoring a whole day in California with the butterflies drifting by like a sparse coloured snow storm. And again at Santa Monica thousands of Monarchs (Plexippus) slowly flying south, hovering around tree tops. Texas is marvellous for butterflies, in the spring when those vast semi-arid plains are covered with brilliant (and to me unknown) wild flowers for hundreds of square miles. And everywhere butterflies like flying flowers, and among the flower stems horned toads, which are really lizards.

Aldington's descriptions are partially in response to H.D.'s memories of the United States as she muses about her feelings towards a possible visit to America. On 12 October 1949 she shared with him her concern that for financial reasons she might have to return to the United States permanently: 'I don't suppose I really will go to USA, it just hangs over me and when there was that new atom blight, I felt I could not cope any more. ... I once saw a really good subdued colour-film of the swamps and sea-reeds, all along the coast; in London, it was, and I must say it pulled at me innards though I always protest about a visit over.' H.D. then wrote Aldington about flowers, 'butterflies in Vaud', butterflies in Italy, England and Pennsylvania'.

2 On 20 September 1949 Aldington had asked H.D.'s advice about Catherine's education: '... in addition to French and English, ought she not to learn German?' He wondered if H.D. could recommend a school in German-speaking Switzerland, even though 'I am not particularly sold on education, and think it should not be taken too seriously as it only forms school teachers. It seems to me that if she really knows three languages, has the reading habit, realises early that music, the fine arts and natural sciences exist, is kept healthy and exercised and free from British ball games and snobbery, American movies and comic strips and journalism – that's about all. The rest is up to her.'

3 H.D.'s rapid and disjunctive associations and shifts in this passage are typical of her mind – both of her poetic gifts and of her bizarre, sometimes psychotic patterns of thought. Her association of Stockholm with Lausanne here may be triggered in part by her train trip, but also by her association of New Haven with Norman Holmes Pearson, who does not know Italy but does know Norway, Scandinavia (as she wrote Aldington on 21 August 1949). Pearson's middle name also echoes 'Stockholm', suggesting the schizophrenic's echolalia, as does H.D.'s statement, 'I was trying to find a proper comparison or companion', which we may read poetically, but which we should also realize is simultaneously suggestive of psychotic thought processes, particularly in the context H.D. establishes (in which she had felt 'cut-off', unable to explain or justify her American identity, near 'panic').

4 On 16 October 1949, Aldington had written H.D. that he had finally finished his biography of D.H. Lawrence and was waiting for publication: 'The job was a fierce one, and in addition I had a good deal of extra work. Penguin books are bringing out in Feb-March 100,000 copies of each of ten D.H.L. books, and also reprinting White Peacock. They got into a jam, and asked me to make the selection of his Letters and Essays, and finally to write eight of the introductions.' On 9 November 1949 Aldington gave further details of his work on Lawrence, adding, 'This great million-copies reprint was decided on in this house in August 1948, about two months after I had begun my biography, when Frere and Allen Lane came to verbal agreement about it.'

5 On 16 October 1949 Aldington had written to H.D. that he was enjoying the new French edition of *Seven Against Reeves* (1949) and looking forward to Mondadori's *Figlia del Colonello* (1950) and *Il Romanzo di Casanova* (1950). He commented on the good sales of the Czech translation of *Casanova*, and noted that the West Germans were now interested in translations and that a Dutch *Casanova* (1950) was due out shortly.

≫ **145** ≪

9 December [1949]
Hôtel de la Paix
Lausanne

Dear Richard,

Thank you for your letter of November 9, just a month ago. I did not realize how the time had gone. Now we are getting very festive here, with trees in the shop windows and a beautiful St. Nicholas festival when a charming tot in 18c. costume (why 18c.?), very, very elegant, rode astride a white donkey, bringing in the Advent bundles of switches and promises of future rewards.

I go down to Ouchy on clear days; there, the pansies are in rather un-seasonable array but they bank them in with pine-branches when really in danger. The swans have become a little savage and trail after one's hand-bag, pecking. I took the hint and last time spared a breakfast-bun, endangering my life, it seemed, for they are ungainly with their swan-necks and can't race the sparrows and gulls, with crumbs on the floor; so taking the hint from a monster who still had his brown-coat but as big as a house, I fed him with my own fair hands; he grumbled and hissed at me when I dropped the crusts. I did not know they could TALK, but maybe this was all a Swan Lake fairy-tale. Anyhow, I suppose people do feed them, so to speak, without gloves, but I have since been sending up thanks for my deliverance. They look so HUGE when they beg on land. I never knew them so close-at-hand, literally.

I am interested in all your news and glad the D.H.L. is progressing at such gigantic strides. I will be interested, of course, to see the final volume [Aldington's biography].

I get letters from odd people and societies for poems for anthologies; I am letting MSS rest over a bit, I am so happy to have shaped these things, the 4 Delia Alton's especially; you did not want to see the MADRIGAL, really a very lovely story of the War I;[1] then I have the Rossetti and another that I don't need to finish about Prague, 18c; these I look upon as sort of shock-absorbers for the SWORD; then, with that four-square, I can afford my love-poems, as they call them, they always seem to print the ones I seem to have out-grown, but now I can say with Dante that I have an affection for my youthful VITA NOVA!

People here are very nice and there is a huge international sort of do, literary political; it gives us quite a high-brow feeling, here in Paix. Most of them are parked here [at the hotel]. I believe [Stephen] Spender and Elizabeth Bowen are due out for it, but they are not here, not now; it would be a joke if they walked in.

Now it is raining, but we are all very glad as per electricity and the lake really does look itself again; looking straight out from the island-like quai at Ouchy, you can see no land (that is, if there is a hint of mist) straight side-ways through the gap left by those monster Savoys. I watch the Evian boat go out and always want to take it, but one must stay 4 full hours until the return, and that seems almost too much for an afternoon trip. Still, I must go over one day.

Hermann Hesse has gone for some sort of cure; I am afraid our dear Tessin let us down a little last summer, much as I love it.[2] I got that tropic germ at the end but fared better than many. I was glad to be here in this clear, high space, and have been well, but know my good Dr. Herzog would cheer me up, if I got grumpy. They wanted me to go to the R.C. Santa Anna in Lugano, but I hung on; once in one of those places ... but it was just what everyone had, alas; water excellent ... I don't know what happened.

Well, let me hear again —

Ever affectionately

Dooley/

1 H.D. is under a false impression here; I have discovered no evidence to suggest that Aldington did not want to see *Madrigal*. On the contrary, he is invariably eager to see any work H.D. chooses to share with him. While she has earlier described her work on this book, she has yet really to ask him if he would like to see it.

2 Tessin or Ticino, the Italian-speaking corner of Switzerland which includes Lugano.

8 January 1950
Villa Aucassin
St Clair
Le Lavandou
Var

Dear Dooley,

We went over to Monaco for Xmas week at Catha's wish. She was taken there by Arthur Barker (the publisher) and his wife last summer – very British, to come to Lavandou and really want 'Monte'! Anyway, off we trotted and are now experts on the aquarium, the fishing expeditions and pickled catches of good Prince Albert I of Monaco, on the Grimaldi and Cro-Magnon skeletons; and saw the Paris Opéra-ballet in that charming Garnier-baroque theatre which is quite intact – not even written about by Sachie Sitwell. Had very fine weather until the last moment – a first drop of rain fell just as the train came into the station. There are practically no British except a few, a very few decrepits, but hundreds of cheerful Italians with plenty of paper money! There are also plenty of Belgians and Swiss. So the three 'glorious victorious' nations are well represented. Only a few Americans and that of a type you and I have never met, i.e. the kind of American who thinks it is democratic to bring street women into a first class restaurant.

Arrived back here I found plenty – the Penguin proofs of DHL's Selected Essays, American page proofs of my biography, and I think more permission requests from anthologists than I ever found in one batch of mail. I think they must wait for the Xmas holidays to send out their letters! The Lawrence Essays make a wonderful and living book, such a complete wipe-out of sterile highbrowism of the self-conscious, straining for effect type. There are of course some absurdities and some prolixities. I think you will particularly like the section I call The Spirit of Place. There is an almost unknown essay on Flowery Tuscany which is so beautiful and so sensitive in its appreciation of wild flowers that you'll love it. And the de-bunking of Ben Franklin is one of the wittiest things imaginable. As a good Philadelphian you'll feel you ought to rally to Ben's defence, but it's a masterly wipe in the eye for the smug 'be-good-and-you'll-make-money' religion of the Friends and so forth.

Of course, as you realise, English publication waits on this absurd election. I don't myself believe it will be until June, but the Tory papers of course want it as early as possible and are bally-hooing in consequence. Unluckily, the publishers listen to them and dilly-dally. But nine of the ten Lawrences are either printed or printing, and the English edition of the Life goes on the machines Monday. But an early or March election would hold everything up until April or May.

I liked hearing about the St. Nicholas procession. It is odd that the Swiss who are supposed to be so prosaic have kept the only really charming processions in western Europe. I never saw a prettier one than the vintage festival in Vevey. And those Ouchy swans! One hears fearful bugaboo stories about swans breaking people's arms and what-not with their wings, but I believe the birds are perfectly harmelss and that the stories were spread by the Thames conservators to try to protect the swans from the Cockneys. All the same a large male swan, hissing and ruffling, is a formidable sight.

All very quiet here, no tourists and no visitors.[1] I have come to like it best in the winter when one is really peaceful. In the summer the tourists flock in and occupy everywhere, and there are so many callers. The wild jonquils are full out, and the sweet alyssum seems to flower perpetually. The English daisy seems to flower all the year round too, except in the August heats. Those pretty little arum lilies are all out, and the wild lavender. When I was up in the hills the wild thyme was flowering and very fragrant.

Ever affectionately

Richard

1 The household quiet was not only the result of the end of the tourist season. Aldington does not mention here that on 2 January 1950 Netta travelled to London on the way to Jamaica to visit her mother. On the same day as this letter to H.D., Aldington wrote to Lawrence Powell that Kershaw had also left and 'it looks as if I shall lose him, for he is probably getting married this month' (Gates, 244). By 1 March it was clear that Netta had left for good; on that day Aldington wrote to Frere: 'She went away cheerfully, leaving many clothes and all her drawings etc; wrote one very affectionate letter from London, then … a brief and flurried letter saying she thought she would get a job. I wrote her at once to Jamaica suggesting she think again. … Something happened in London, but what?' (Gates, 245). Aldington found himself in the awkward position of sending Netta money and regular parcels of items left in Lavandou without understanding the nature of her decision and estrangement. After a period, Netta occasionally visited Aldington and her daughter in France, and Catha later made a few visits to England to see her mother, but from now on Aldington and his daughter essentially lived by themselves.

≈ 147 ≈

14 February [1950]

Hôtel de la Paix

Lausanne

Dear Richard,

Thank you for your letter of 8th January; I had not realized how the time had passed until this morning I actually received an old-fashioned Valentine. I believe they are collectors' pieces now; this was from US, I need hardly say. George Plank sent me an old-lace one that he must have cherished for ages; that was back in the thirties; I don't think I have had one since. I have been looking for the old-lace one but can't find it in my collection of old cards. I go over them from time to time, and I have sent E. [Ezra] several packets of Venice and Greece. I hear from him, begging for news. 'Benedictions. Thirst for news quite unslakable.' I would write more and oftener but one really cannot be gossipy about people who may not want 'news' picked over (as I suppose it is) by various authorities. There was a page review of his last Faber books in the T.L.S., done by a certain NINE editor, called Peter Russell – or so he told me; he wrote me asking me to do an article for NINE on E. but I could not attempt it.[1] It seemed odd to be on the list of a 'little magazine' again. They are very erudite and seem to carry on from E. and T.S. E. [Eliot], which is a better tie-up, I think, than Spender-Auden Co.; I don't know if you know any of them.

People are already writing, asking where I will be this summer. So I have more or less decided to make it Lake Thun for a time, just out of Bern, about half-hour by rail, I believe. I have to get a place where I can be at least half-independent and this, I believe, is scattered with small villages and one can park the visitors round about, not right in one's pocket. It seems odd to have to begin planning – but I love Lugano and may go there for a shorter visit later, September maybe. Do you know Thun?

I shall be interested in the DHL. I remember especially his flowers in one of his travel-books – Etruscan?[2] I forget the name. Perhaps that is what you refer to. Every-one is a-gog about the election. I dare not hope too much. People out here at Christmas depressed me very much; I hate to be selfish but one can only take so much. The war was bad enough but there was the stimulus and the constant gratitude that one was 'spared', and then things were really not so bad, as to food etc. We had plenty of cigarettes and the BBC encouraged smoking during, after, and between raids, 'for the nerves'. I read of some poor RAF boys who had their little ship confiscated and huge fines for having managed to get out far enough to sea to pick up bags of cigarettes. It is all so bitterly sordid.

We have been having snow, not very heavy, flowers did pop up a bit, but now everything is wintry again. Comfortable hotel, heating etc., and I have much to read and old MSS to sort over. This is just a line; I get more and more lazy about writing letters.

Love from
Dooley./

1 H.D. wrote very few 'reviews' or essays of the sort Aldington and Pound regularly contributed to periodicals throughout their lives. The exceptions are her work for *The Egoist* when Aldington was at the front during the last years of the war and her short essays for *Close-Up* in the late 1920s and early 1930s.
2 H.D. is thinking of D.H. Lawrence's *Etruscan Places*, London: Secker, 1932.

≈ **148** ≈

21 April [1950]
Hôtel de la Paix
Lausanne

Dear Richard,

Thank you for your last letter, I received it almost a month ago. Since writing, I have been in a state, as Perdita announced her engagement on March 31 [her birthday], when she was 31, to John Schaffner (36) in whose Literary Agent's office she has been working for some time. They seem to have tastes in common and I am really very glad she has chosen a stolid, settled sort of person, or so I gather from his letters to me and her description and his people, German of the '48 exodus, he writes, and old New England;[1] one grandfather, Daniel Webster Daniels ... somewhat her own American background; father is tree and forest expert, entomology, with laboratories near New Haven, a gvt. consultant expert – and so on. They expect to be married in June at the home of a Mrs Pulsifer of 'Little Ponds'; he was a protégé of her when he was at Bowdoin College, Maine. Well – well – I did not want to dash across and be a property mother in dove-gray – so now, at last, after a number of cables and long heart-to-heart letters from them both, I feel that I can wait here until the fall and will again try to get across.[2] They will spend their two weeks honey-moon there at 'Little Ponds', Maine. They wouldn't come across, he doesn't feel he can leave the office, just two years established; he was in Navy in war.

So now I no longer plan a summer trip of any length of time; I may rush down to Lugano for a few weeks, but won't pull up stakes for the six months, as I did the last three years. I will do charades of myself being – well what? Something or other – I must work it out – in New York, in the fall. Let me know well in time if I can do anything there for you. But this is in the future ... thank you for hints about Austria. Myself, yes, I am here, very bourgeois, I fear – or it was Schweiz that you called that.[3] And our spring is naught to write home about this year. Your descriptions of flowers (and from friends in Italy) surpass our somewhat late crop of blossom ... and I rejoice with you there. I see now, your letter is March 24, and our blossom is just arriving at the state it was with you then. The lake, too, is very low still – or again. But I must not get too tugged away, as it takes me a long time to get to USA – I mean it takes years of planning. This trip was planned spring 1946 ... sorry this is so dull. I just want to keep in touch. I saw review in Times of your D.H.L. book, I judge you get all these reviews so I did not cut it out. How terrible about Banabhard ... after all that war blitz, it is most ironical! Her Leonardo is, as you say, amazing.[4]

I am so relieved that I don't feel that I must to go to USA and Maine, at that, for the June doings, that I am a bit light-headed. It is beautiful here – for all I have been running it down. This cold, someone from London wrote me, was 'ghostly'; there, they thought the special effect was due to moon eclipse. I don't know!

More anon, when I come to....

Love from
Dooley./

1 That is, part of John Schaffner's family arrived in America in 1848 when, the revolution in Germany having failed, many dissidents fled to the United States, settling predominantly near Baltimore.

2 Aldington supported H.D.'s decision not to travel to the United States in June. On 3 May 1950 he wrote: 'I can understand your feelings at this news of Perdita's wedding, but I must say I think you are very wise not to be present at the ceremony. The right thing is to see them later as you propose.'

3 On 24 March 1950 Aldington had written H.D. suggesting that she consider going to Austria, which he had heard was 'very cheap' and 'all so much nicer than Schweiz – gemütlich and non-bourgeois'. He recalled his visit to Austria during the summer of 1934: 'In Feldkirch there was a girl in the Gasthaus who played so charmingly on the zither – Austrian songs, Wolkslieder, which made one weep for the Europe that is no more. And the place is bright with window-boxes of petunias.' He reflected: 'Why do you let those British oafs bully you into sticking in Switzerland? Pluck up spirit, answer them back, and INSIST on a liberty. They'll give in.' By 'oafs', Aldington means those government administrators who set and enforce rules for nationals resident abroad. It is likely, however, that Bryher was also urging upon H.D. the 'safety' (and medical attention should she require it) of Switzerland.

4 On 24 March 1950 Aldington had written H.D. that 'Poor Banabhard is very unhappy. Seems there was a fire and many of her books and unpublished MSS were destroyed. A tragedy for her. Apparently, her life is so pivoted on the B.M. library that she doesn't want to travel. ... She has always lived in a dream Italy which has no real existence, nor ever had. It is a wonderful dream – her Leonardo is the greatest novel about him ever written, far better than Merejkowski, but it is a dream, and the actuality of Italy would simply crush it.' Rachel Annand Taylor's *Leonardo the Florentine: A Study in Personality* (London: Harper & Brothers, 1928) is not in fact a novel but a vivid, well-documented if impressionistic biography which the author called a 'psychical history' (xi).

23 May 1950
Villa Aucassin
St Clair
Le Lavandou
Var

Dear Dooley,

False alarm. The extracts from my letters in the prof's book turn out to be only about 15 brief quotations from correspondence bequeathed to Harvard and Chicago Universities by Amy [Lowell] and Harriet Monroe respectively.

Nothing about you in any of them.[1]

Rather regrettable jokes about Ezra and Lorenzo which the campus proletariat may take au pied de la lettre [literally], but who cares?

I was a little apprehensive that private and personal matters might have been revealed, but such is not the case. So I have given the bon à tirer [go ahead to print] without worrying you with such trash.

I am just about to send to press my Religion of Beauty, Ruskin to Rachel Annand Taylor. I believe and even hope that it will annoy everyone including Rachel Annand.

I had a letter from Frieda yesterday, in which she wrote: 'Hilda; how is she? I shall always be grateful to her.' I kept your name and person out of my book [on D.H. Lawrence] as I thought that was what you want, except for a passing reference so that they couldn't remark on a complete absence. For what it is worth to you, what you did for Lorenzo in 1917 [in giving him and Frieda lodging] is remembered with gratitude by many who think he is the one great writer in English in this century.

I do hope Perdita will be happy, but who is? We go through life looking forward to a future happiness which after a certain age we look back upon wistfully in the past.

Love
Richard

1 See Stanley Coffman, *Imagism: A Chapter for the History of Modern Poetry*, Norman: The University of Oklahoma Press, 1951. Aldington was very concerned lest anything negative about H.D. or about Perdita's irregular birth appear in print. On 3 May 1950 he had written to H.D.: 'Do you know anything about this man Coffman? I don't suppsose there is anything very awful in those letters, but I think that published extracts should be approved by me and by you. ... This being mauled over is very disagreeable to me. I haven't yet forgiven Mabel Dodge Luhan for quoting a personal letter of mine to Lawrence without my permission.' On 8 May 1950, H.D. responded: 'I honestly think these many universities are reliable and there does seem to be an improvement in the way of discretion and asking permission hither and yon; though I must say, I am more and more surprised at the amount of stuff they seem to acculcate [*sic*; H.D. probably means 'accumulate'] and treasure. I don't know Mr Coffman or anything personal about him – or impersonal. It all does seem so impersonally-personal. ... But I agree, this "being mauled over" is a trial and unbelievable.' Both Aldington and H.D. are sensitive to the issue of publicity, the revelation of the private, but in this instance Aldington seems the more temperamental: he feels protective of both their reputations, even apprehensive, while H.D. is more willing to trust others' judgement and maintains her sense of humour. Aldington and H.D. thus to a degree here reverse their frequent roles of protector and distressed. H.D. demonstrates increasingly in these late letters a capacity to reassure and comfort Aldington, to play a role she probably played in some measure from the very beginning of their friendship in 1911.

22 June [1950]
Hôtel de la Paix
Lausanne

Dear Richard,

Thank you for your letter of May 23. I am glad that the quotations from the letters turn out to be comparatively unimportant. Apropos Lorenzo jokes you speak of, I have seen a number of very interesting reviews of your book [on Lawrence]; I do not send them to you, as I imagine your people keep you well supplied with your own press, both sides of the Atlantic. When you write Frieda, please remember me to her. It is nice of her to speak of me. I was literally sickened when I was last in U.S. by stories of ashes of Lorenzo − I don't like to repeat, even at this late date; I expect you know the sort of thing. I was really very shocked; also, by one fatuous party at a party, who would pick on me, 'O, D.H., I do love your novels etc.' Then, a long tirade from someone else, 'you're talking to the poet H.D.' 'Never heard of her ...' and so on. Somehow or other, just at that time (1937 − was it?), this Lorenzo story was going the rounds. I was in N.Y., at the turn of the year, '37–38, it must have been.

Now Perdita is due to be married on St. John's Day, this Saturday, in Maine. She said she wanted you to have a notice, so I gave her your address, I trust O.K.; she was pleased, apparently, as I wrote her you had sent your good wishes to them both. I am glad that I did not go over as, for this 'simple' wedding, apparently all his old college pals are congregating from along the coast, our friend Norman Holmes Pearson is giving her away, their hostess Mrs Pulsifer insists on the full marriage service; P chose sky-blue and sent me a snippet but J.V. Schaffner wanted her also to wear a hat, with VEILS! All this has somewhat shattered me.

Love from
Dooley./

151

28 June 1950
Villa Aucassin
St Clair
Le Lavandou
Var

Dear Dooley,

By now the marriage is a fait accompli. You were so wise not to go. American weddings are well-meant but to me a little depressing − everyone present is a lovely person and there are gallons of ice-cream. I hope Perdita will be very happy. You won't forget to send me news after you reach the U.S.[1]

'It is full summer now, the heart of June.'[2] The green shutters are closed, the cicadas in the garden sound like a perpetual shrill fountain, bathing becomes prolonged for hours. These are the last best days. On the 1st come the tourists et les campeurs, and our solitary plage [beach] is invaded.

I have had Alister back here all this month. His new wife joins him on Saturday, they go to stay at Cap Ferrat, then to Milan to see my Italian publisher for me, then back here. An Oxford friend and his wife have one of the cottages here, and Roy

Campbell and his family are at Bormes. A great fellow, Roy, physically a colossus, though crippled with the war wounds and malaria which did not somehow reach the heroic defenders of the B.B.C. A good poet, but above all a man – rather a rarity in modern England. True, he comes from S[ou]th Africa.[3]

Yes, malice and envy have done their damnedest against Lorenzo's memory, even to the invention of horrific stories about his dead bones – as if that would matter even if true when his soul goes marching on. As a matter of fact, Cholerton, Times correspondent at Nice, was here to interview me a few weeks back, and assured me from personal knowledge that they are all lies. Certainly few men have gone on living so vividly in their writings as he does.

Perhaps I am wrong, but I think perhaps you are inclined to give more importance to newspaper comment and highbrow periodicals than I do. I don't subscribe for clippings, barely glance at those which people are good enough to send me. But I do care very much about the response of the public, and that is satisfactory, especially since there is a fierce slump in the book market. The Penguin Lawrences are selling very well indeed – I think they are already near the half million. The Heinemann Pockets are already re-printing in three cases. The biography is now approaching 10,000 in England, and in U.S. – where it appeared later – is selling 500 copies a week steadily. There are many enquiries for translation, and the usual haggling, which Alister is good enough to deal with for me. It is odd that the first translations definitely clinched on are the Japanese and the Italian, with the German nearly completed. This is just an accident, as the greatest number of requests came from France.

I shall pass on your message to Frieda. She has a great regard for you – 'Hilda is Somebody!' she says in her very German voice. I had a very generous letter about the biography from Somerset Maugham, though he still (naturally) coughs a bit over Lorenzo's scorn of him. He cleared up their spat in Mexico, D.F. Willy, as you know, stammers badly, and always has his telephoning done by his secretary. This Lorenzo, with his morbid feeling of social inferiority, construed into an insult.

Next week is Catha's 12th birthday, which calls for a burnt offering of cash and time. On the whole, though, children are only happy with their contemporaries, and parents are required merely as bankers and social references. I am better at the first than the second.

Lausanne must be lovely just now, and I hope you go [on] trips on the lake and eat fritures de poisson at the lakeside restaurants and drink that excellent beer. Alister and I yearn for some German or Swiss or Czech beer. This French stuff is awful, and the wine is so bad one is reduced to eau minérale in sheer despair.

With love,
Richard

P.S. Campbell tells me he hears from Ezra, long rambling letters about Catholicism and rather piteous requests to 'get Unkel Ez out'. It is always wretched to hear of the dear fellow being incarcerated, but from what I am told (perhaps wrongly) he is now so ill he would have to be in some institution. So why not at the expense of Uncle Sam? So far as I know it is the only contribution made by the U.S. govt to any of America's poets. What porridge had Walt Whitman?

---

1 Although H.D. stated her intention in Letter 148 to visit the Schaffners in the autumn, in fact she did not travel to the United States until April 1951.
2 I have been unable to identify this quotation.

3 Roy Campbell (1901–57), the South African poet who spent most of his life in Europe. He fought on the side of the fascists in the Spanish Civil War and in Africa during World War II. Aldington particularly admired Campbell's extroverted poetry, his scorn for literary intellectuals, and his passionate affirmation of life.

⫷ 152 ⫸

1 July [1950]
Hôtel de la Paix
Lausanne

Dear Richard,

Thank you for your letter. It's all been a bit of a shock. I had my own card yesterday and am rather staggered to read

'Mrs Hilda Aldington

has the honour of announcing …'.

She did write rather touchingly, did I mind? But I have never seen myself so starkly engraved; she wrote she sent yours off the last hour as she was waiting to go to Maine, having packed her blue wedding-dress. Norman Homes Pearson gave her away and I hear from him full details; I cannot take it in, it all seems to go back to her grandmother's generation – but I believe they are now being over-conventional. Bless them! At least, I am nicely placed here and don't know about when/if I take the trip over. It will seem Wolf-wolf by the time (when/if) I do manage to get there. I would like to see the dogwood again – that would mean waiting till spring when they are having one of those comic exhibitions at Yale; this time, I am paired off with Marianne Moore; they collect old copy-books, one's school reports and so on; of course, I have none, but managed to find some old note-books that I had thought destroyed before I left Suisse in 1939. It will have to do – and some frightful old photographs! They had one of Stephen Benét, that is how I heard just WHAT they produce. His was posthumous – is that the word? And I am grieved to hear his brother, whom I liked, William Rose Benét, just died – also [John Gould] Fletcher!

My best wishes for Catha's birthday. It is yours too, very near, as I remember? To you, all bounty too and blessings. I am sorry about the beer. I noticed visiting English here – a very few and on the whole 'superior' – howl for beer; I would expect them to ask of the local wine, and our AIGLE is most delicate, a white wine, exquisite, refreshing, sustaining. I have two decies, a tiny carafe, about two glasses every evening. It comes to about the same as a bottle of beer – but I can't go on telling people; anyhow, now I feel it's explained. I suppose the beer IS good here.

I don't go about much, except over to Burier to see Bryher, about once a week.[1] I do go down to Ouchy and sit under a marble plaque which delights me; to the effect (Hotel Angleterre) that a certain MILORD BYRON sat thereunder when he authentically wrote a poem about our local Chateau.[2] Enclosed the same; it is, or was, on the blue stamps but they are always changing them. Riant Chateau, Territet, [the apartment building] where I was after World War I, is about ten minutes walk, this side of Chillon. I like Lausanne better – but everywhere we have, as a certain modest Swiss lady remarked to me once, 'nos coins' [our corners].

Love from
Dooley./

1 Burier-la-Tour was a suburban village not far from the city of Lausanne, to which H.D. regularly travelled by local train. It is worth emphasizing that during this period, from 1946 on, H.D. and Bryher lived apart and, although they continued to write each other and to chat regularly on the telephone, they saw each other only about once a week (and less frequently when H.D. lived during the summer in Lugano) and led quite separate lives.

2 Byron's famous poem about the medieval château two miles south of Montreux is 'The Prisoner of Chillon' (1816).

⇘ 153 ⇚

1 October [1950]
Hôtel de la Paix
Lausanne

Dear Richard,

It is a long time since I heard from you.[1] I hope you are all well. I have been a little uneasy, quite foolishly, about the future, as Perdita writes she hopes for a baby, late spring. At least, that put my mind at rest about going this winter to N.Y.; I go, D.V., if I ever manage to go, late spring or early summer, for or after the event. All this has been such a rush, the getting engaged, married, and myself in the grand-mother class. In the meantime, I am snug enough with old scripts and papers, books, a few friends, the happy round of tea-shops in rain or sun, my eleven [o'clock] coffee, or ten rather, in a brilliant and rather pretty new 'Dome' (actually, it is called the Dome) where there is music, elegant candelabra, concealed lighting and masses of, at present, gladiolus; there were sun-flowers and Michaelmas daisies in rotation. There is a really charming shop, called Mutrux, with a lively roof, now closed alas, many bright umbrellas, fish in a pond and a lovely crazy-pavement garden, especially wonderful in hyacinth and tulip season. The roof is level with the house-gardens at the back; this town is, as you know, very crazy-pavement altogether.

What do you read? I have found a rather good <u>Table Ronde</u> collection, I am afraid Malory always mazed me a little. In the French (this is more or less modern French from the originals) I can follow it much better, the old fairy tale <u>Ronde</u>.

Do let me have a line, unless a letter was lost in between; I wrote last, about early July [Letter 152].

Love from
Dooley./

1 Apparently Aldington has not written to H.D. since 28 June 1950 (Letter 151).

⇘ 154 ⇚

2 October 1950
Villa Aucassin
St Clair
Le Lavandou
Var

Dear Dooley,

Today is our wedding day isn't it?[1] Strange thought. And Perdita is going to have a baby. You are quite right to go to USA.

I have had another breakdown from over-work and the infinite worries which arose from trying to deal with things while Alister was in London. I was told not even to write a letter, and have had already to start work on a book.[2] (Didn't know until lately that literary overwork is a classic way of procuring nervous collapses.) Alister has been back some time, dealing admirably with everything, but naturally I couldn't send you a secretary's letter. Latest trouble is this. He married in London last Jan, and Mrs. is supposed to be helping run the house. The delicious French bureaucrats in London gave her only a 3 months visa (Australians have to have visas, but not Brits! he has a ten years carte d'identité!) and she had to go back to London. They treated her very rudely, said the application would be considered and reported on in six weeks (!) and didn't even read her recommendation from the Director of Australia House. Of course the girl can't hang about indefinitely in London, so is coming back on another 3 months visa. The people here at the Mairie and the Préfecture were most charming and have written letters, but it seems to depend on some sickening little swine in London.

There you are, you see! I get worked up over such things the moment I start writing or see anyone except Catha and the Alisters. Netta is in London to get a rest from me. Catha I have just sent to Cannes for a little holiday before she goes back to school.

With all love
Richard

1 Aldington is misremembering: he and H.D. were married on 18 October 1913. On 14 October 1950 H.D. gently corrected him: 'I think we were married on the 18th, as my mother used to remind me of it, it being also my brother's birthday.' Aldington's confusion is perhaps in part attributable to the overwork he describes but also to the same psychological pressures H.D. notes in her recent letters. Perdita's marriage and anticipation of motherhood brought back to both of them memories of their own marriage and early years together. Netta's desertion in early 1950, signalling the essential end of his second marriage, also threw his past and present relationship with H.D. into a kind of relief for Aldington, giving it an enduring primacy.

2 In early 1950 Aldington had begun preliminary research for his biography of T.E. Lawrence. Throughout the year, financial problems increasingly pressed upon him; despite the relative success of *D.H. Lawrence: Portrait of a Genius, But ...*, the Patmores' demands for regular payments agreed upon as part of the divorce settlement became increasingly difficult to meet. On the continent as well as in England, translations and reissues of Aldington's books were not selling well. His financial difficulties were exacerbated by his perception of them. On 24 February 1950 Aldington had written Kershaw, 'it is ruin ...' but added in the same letter either what his wife had told him before she left him in January or what she was writing him in letters that may have been in part designed to accuse him of incompetence in an awkward marital separation: 'Netta is quite right – my career as an earning writer is finished, owing partly to my own imprudence, partly to political events, partly to the malice of enemies ...'. Aldington concluded, '... as Netta so sweetly says, even if I could "squeeze out another book" it would "probably not be worthwhile economically"'(SIU). On 23 September 1950 Aldington wrote Leonard Bacon and confessed that the overwork and 'nervous collapse' of which he writes H.D. here had been going on for some time: 'probably you know that Netta unable to stand the strain has left me' (Yale).

29 November 1950
Villa Aucassin
St Clair
Le Lavandou
Var

Dear Dooley,

I write at once to thank you for sending me the poems (which I had never seen) and pre-war memories were blasted away by the barrages, night firing, bombings, machine gunnings etc. of 1916–1918. It is with a start of wonder that I recall the things of which you remind me and I have totally forgotten – the watch on Capri, for example. Strange! Banabhard told Alister that she saw us in Kensington Gardens in 1914 – a blank to me.[1]

With this I enclose a set of Catha's poems for you, begging you to overlook the obvious fact that she has not at all begun to master the strict rules of French versification. Also that she has sometimes to make herself masculine to avoid an inconvenient 'e' mute! Nothing much is made of this poetry writing, except that it is a nice game to play, like painting and modelling (she has made a marvellous clay old woman with sticks for the Xmas crèche) and so there is no 'stunt' about it. I don't want any Gene (was it?) Untermeyer business, poor child.[2]

The stamps, I know, will cause much rapture when she comes home from school this evening. As the collection so far is only about 500, many of them France and French Colonies, those you sent will be all new to her and some of them particularly important because they help to fill up series. Altogether this was a most handsome and unexpected gift, which will give much happiness. You can imagine us this evening, huddled over the album, to the tune of 'do look at this one, daddy, it's wonderful!'

I'd quite forgotten about that ban on stamps. I don't think it can amount to much, as I (in all unconsciousness) often popped them into letters for England.

At last I have found out what is the real trouble with me – overwork for too many years. For so long I've worked 12 to 14 hours a day for weeks on end without a single day off. Well, I can't do it no more. I've got to cut down to 5 days a week, and not more than 5–6 hours a day at that. This of course means a rather serious cut-down in output and reduction of income, since it is the new book which really earns. So I've had to construct (reluctantly) my own austerity plan, for I've made up my mind that Catha shall not suffer. I had cut out most things, so practically all that remains is guests, books and wine. I gave up smoking nearly ten years ago.

This is a brief note just to thank you again for your generosity, which I know will give the child so much pleasure.

Love
Richard

---

1 The letter to which Aldington responds here and several others from H.D. during this period have evidently been lost. Exactly which poems H.D. has sent him is unclear. The images which follow suggest *Bid Me to Live*, in which H.D. refers repeatedly to Rafe Ashton's military watch, and echo material in her unpublished journals in which she recounts the story of Aldington's watch, broken while they were at Capri in 1913. The sparrow recalls H.D.'s first meeting with Bryher, recounted by both women on several occasions; debating whether to invite Bryher to visit at Bosigran in Cornwall, H.D. supposedly determined to see her because a sparrow flew into her room.

2 Richard Starr Untermeyer (Louis Untermeyer's only son with his wife Jean) determined to become a writer. The young man hanged himself in early 1927 during his sophomore year at Yale. The *New York Times* suggested on 26 January 1927 that 'he committed the act while a victim of over-emotionalism due to a desire to write poetry which would bring him fame equal to that of his father'. Untermeyer writes at length about his gifted son and his suicide in *Bygones: The Reflections of Louis Untermeyer*, New York: Harcourt, Brace and World, 1965.

≫ **156** ≪

16 December 1950
Villa Aucassin
St. Clair
Le Lavandou
Var

Dear Dooley,
    Ever since I mailed that Ring and the Book I've had a dreadful feeling that I've dumped a green elephant on you. Don't hesitate to dump, give away or sell the set if it's a nuisance. There are often odd vols of this first edition, but a complete set is getting rare; and I thought you might like it for the sake of old memories. I discovered only recently that RB [Robert Browning] had the poem issued one volume each month over 4 months because he didn't want them to skip and read the end first! Rather naive if he expected to be read for more than a few months. I also meant to send you a copy of his magnificent bit of invective to [?] Fitzgerald for insulting EBB [Elizabeth Barrett Browning]; but you know it? If not I'll send a copy.[1]
    Thank you so much for the stamps. They are very pretty and Catha will be delighted when she comes home from school. I hope, though, that the sour-faced old gentleman in the yachting cap isn't meant as a specimen of Swiss youth.
    That whole Ezra affair makes me sick. Russell runs a Catholic-Fascist periodical called Nine, which is mostly written by prigs. They have taken up Ezra for motives mainly political and self-interested, and of course they know nothing about the real Ezra. Russell asked me to write for his damned book, and I told him I didn't intend to hack out something in five minutes.[2] The late invitations to us and Bill Williams were surely intentional. We had nothing to do with the creation of modern poetry. It was all T.S. Eliot, John-the-Baptised by Ezra. Well, in my opinion, Ezra, who was not only a charming person but a real poet in his younger days, ceased to be so when he began imitating Eliot.
    Curious. Not ten minutes before your letter arrived I was going through some old papers and I came on a letter from Ezra dated 7 August Anno 18 (1940) written in answer to my request for three of his poems for The Viking Book of Poetry. He addresses the letter 'To R. Aldington', demands 25 dollars for American and five guineas for English rights. All very upstage and highhat! Including 'Hope to see you when Churchill has been hanged out of the Gold Exchange window!!!' That during the battle of Britain! Ezra adds: 'I hear some of his' (i.e. Winston's) 'friends have already arruv in N. Yok.'!!![3]
    That annoyed me so much that I have never written to Ezra since.[4] You know the Viking people are Jews, and Harold Guinzburg was already working for some dept in Washington, knowing US would come in sooner or later.[5] They weren't much pleased at having E.P. anyway, and when they heard his terms (high for those days) they suggested dropping him. I compromised by dropping from three to two [poems], and

persuaded them to have him in. But didn't I catch it from some of the U.S. fellow-travellers (communists) for including him! But that's not the end. When H'mann [Heinemann] got around to sparing the paper for that [British edition of the] Anthology, it was already post-war, E. was in jug; and Frere, though an anti-Semite, had become a Picadilly socialist, as violently anti- the unfortunate Ez as Rebecca West herself. He was very angry with me for insisting that E's poems must go in. Incidently, I got visited by the F.B.I. because of the praise of Ez I put up in my book of memoirs [Life for Life's Sake] in 1940. Where were Mr. Russell and his fascist friends then?[6]

Incidently, for that book (the anthology) 3000 dollars and 400 pounds were paid out in fees. I got little but abuse for it from poets.

Of course there are good things, flashes in E's later work, but to me the Cantos seemed the product of a diseased mind long before the Yank doctors said he was paranoiac. I came to that conclusion when Brigit and I spent the winter of 1928–29 with him at Rapallo.[7] He was still very sweet at times, but certainly suffering from delusions of persecution and of grandeur. I saw him afterwards with Olga in Paris and in Venice, and each time felt miserable afterwards, and what a tragedy it was. If I ever get around to writing anything on Ezra, I want to try to revive the memories of those magical early years in London.

Well, once more a happy Xmas. And do forgive me if the Ring and the Book is the book and the burden.

Love
Richard

1 On 8 January 1951 Aldingtson explained his decision to send this book to H.D.:

> There is something in reading these books in the original edition, if only because (in Browning's case especially) the modern edition is heavy, closely printed and academic....
> One reason I felt that the Browning in 4 vols might be a nuisance was that just as I sent it I had news that Lady Harmsworth wants to return to this place in May and I have to leave. The problem of disposing of my books in an epoch when packing cases and transport and manual labour cost immensely is painful. ... As nobody here will buy English books I can see no way out except to burn all the bulky and less valuable ones. It is after all only an anticipation of their probable fate in the new war to make heroes of everybody.

2 Peter Irwin Russell (b. 1921), the English poet and literary critic, published *Nine* in London from 1949 until 1956. He developed a friendship with Pound, which continued when Russell moved to Venice in 1964.

3 Such statements or variations on them appear frequently in Pound's letters to several of his correspondents at this time. Aldington latched onto them as catch phrases which typified Pound's mental instability, his misunderstanding of both war and economics, and his peculiar iconography. Ironically, Aldington himself came to repeat the statement about Churchill and the 'Gold Exchange' and often echoed it in his descriptions and censure of Pound in letters to H.D. and others.

4 H.D. responded on 18 December 1950: 'E abused me in slightly indecent terms for not getting Bryher to give money to something or other....[sic] I, too, stopped writing but in Lugano had the Cantos sent me and began writing; his letters are almost in or undecipherable and I haven't written lately ...'

5 Harold Guinzburg (1899–1961), an American publisher long associated with Viking Press.

6 This story of being visited in California by the F.B.I. became an Aldington chestnut to which he frequently returned in his later letters to H.D. and others.

7 After the period at Port Cros during the autumn of 1928, Aldington spent several weeks in Paris, then travelled to Rapallo in early 1929. He had not in fact quite 'spent the winter' there, for he was back in Paris by mid-February.

1 February [1951]
Hôtel de la Paix
Lausanne

Dear Richard,

Thank you for your letter and the beautiful verse of Catha's.[1] It is really very remarkable that she writes as she does. P [Perdita] did some quite good prose at one time, but she never burst into meter or rhyme, that is when she was about Catha's age; she became more self-conscious later and the little stories were more derivative. She wrote a bumper 'novel' just before WAR II; it was not at all bad but we prayed it would not be published and it was not.[2] What did she call it? I can't remember, Pre-War, I think! It was chatty and clever and well-written, but a bit telling the world what she thought of us — which included people like [Norman] Douglas and Freud. Well, I don't think I put her off exactly, just suggested that she keep the MSS and let it simmer or ferment a bit. It was a great problem at the time and a head-ache, as I myself had always been so careful not to spill the beans or whatever; I had been asked for instance to write on Lawrence and personal reminiscences of 'other great writers' I had known. However, poor child, she was pushed into the Foreign Office [during the war]; fortunately, I suppose, at that, a miracle really and afterwards Norman Pearson took her on as secretary with her French and German and proper typing (not like Ma) to Germany [in 1946], then she got out and away; as ex-US, she got free classes, and 'finished her education', as it were, at Columbia writing-courses etc., which has always seemed so funny. But her US crowd was doing it — and — and — it led to John Valentine Schaffner and we can only pray all progresses happily [with her pregnancy] this spring.

I had my preliminary forms at Geneva the other day — all seems in order but I have to go again. It is a bit grim, that Geneva-end [of the lake]. Here, we have had unprecedented cold and avalanches, as the world knows.

The Browning has been a great delight. I had that fat edition with dreadful double-columns and tiny print. I do wonder that I read it ALL, in those days.[3] It is strange going over it now, and occasionally recalling a patch. I am surprised to find that your letter is dated January 8. I lately had to get new glasses, or did get them, as towards USA; had not changed for 15 years and [was] told I should have come sooner. Result was, I was put off [typing] machine for some weeks until I re-adjusted; a book can be slanted about, near or far, but type was different. I hope you will write sooner than that and give me more news and any English or French anthems that C produces.

I am extremely sorry to hear that you may have to move. I don't suppose I could keep anything for you? Not here — but I have a book-case at Villa Kenwin. I don't get over very often but they are very careful of the books.[4] I wonder where you will go? Near, I presume, or there in another house or villa. There is nothing worse than this sort of move. Yes, I feel that 'uneasiness' you speak of in your letter.[5] But I must materialize or externalize myself a bit more, have lived like a hermit-crab for almost five years. Do you know Martha's Vineyard? I have been asked there for part of the summer — at least, it has been suggested to me. But I will probably stay nearer New Haven, at a quiet place, not far from where the Pearsons have their summer cottage. Well, I must get there first. Yes, D.V., I have decided to fly. They say it is wonderful now; I had one or two dreadful bumpy channel-crossings in the very early days and the trip out from London to Zürich in 1946, but I don't really know the new air-liners. You must copy out some more of the Xmas book for me.

Love from
Dooley./

1 On 8 January 1951 Aldington had written that Catha had given him for Christmas a small book of her own poems in French and English, one of which he copied out for H.D.
2 The typescript of this 'novel' is at Yale.
3 On 1 January 1951 H.D. had responded 'I have been taking a volume in my bag, down to meals. ... I have skipped a bit but am re-reading. I read it through when I was end-school and I really wonder now how I followed or pretended to follow it. The nuances depend so much on the memory, the FRAGRANCE of the memory of the places themselves. Yes, I do long for Italy now.'
4 It is worth emphasizing how independently H.D. was living during this period and the diminished intensity of her relationship with Bryher. On 1 January 1951 H.D. wrote Aldington that 'I had Xmas dinner at Kenwin, not very far for me but quite a trip, only ½ hour by train but one has to get to the station and back after. The last time I was there was for the September birthdays – Bryher's is near my 10th.'
5 On 1 January 1951 H.D. had revealed to Aldington that 'I am worried all the time about the up-rooting in the spring.' On 8 January 1951 Aldington had responded that his anticipated move 'makes me all the more sympathetic to your uneasiness over the uprooting of the American trip'. H.D. and Aldington tended in some measure throughout their correspondence to identify with one another as illustrated by such explicitly paralleled experiences.

⤳ 158 ⤳

24 February 1951
Villa Aucassin
St Clair
Le Lavandou
Var

Dear Dooley,

All congratulations to you and above all to Perdita on the new Valentine.[1] This will be a motive for your visit. But please don't forget to have the doc test your heart. Those big Pan-Ams go high, and there is a strain on everybody. The thing is to loll around and have the 'hostess' look after you, sleep as much as possible. Pity you can't go direct. But can't you FLY Lausanne or Geneva to Paris and simply change planes at Orly?

Obviously summer hotels in USA are awful, and so are all the resorts. But if you take to the open road in a car, head south and west, stay in motels, avoid ciddies, there is wonderful country yet. I realise I was very lucky doing it in war time. But if you take the coastal roads from say Tampa, Fla. to Brownsville, Tex. on the Mexican border, there are literally hundreds of miles of open country with sea and sky and birds. It would all depend if you knew someone with a car and leisure and a knowledge of the highways and off the highways. But of course my idea of hell (and doubtless yours) is to be found in Jones Beach, Atlantic City, Miami. I think I was just in time to see the last of the great open spaces. I wish I hadn't missed that skyline drive down the Shenandoah Valley, but it was under snow when I left Washington, and I never had another chance. But the west can't be crowded. Hell! On that Jeff Davis Highway between Orange and El Paso, there are stretches of 100 miles without even a shack. There is a motel at a little place called Marathon, just on the east side of the Great Divide, which is about as remote as the moon. But that was five years ago. But ah guess you got too much Eastern culchur, Miss Hilda, to like the wild west. I've just been looking at my road map – from San Antonio to El Paso is close on 500 miles with nothing but a few motels and 'shack' towns. I remember Sierra Blanca, and the hugest sun I ever saw going down flaming crimson over the desert and the mountains turning blue. And Wyoming. I remember coming up from Boulder, Coloraydo, to Laramie and Medicine Bow, and stopping off at Rawlings, Wy., found a saloon with pictures of all the famous cattle brands in the West, and photos of all the famous hold-up men, including Calamity Jane. And they were very sweet to us, and gave us wonderful beef steaks, and whipped up ice-cream for Catha, and told us lots about cattle rustlers. And after we left the place I found out it was the entrance to the local brothel! Sure are hospitable, them folks out West.

But Europe hath its charms too, of a less strenuous nature, and I love your little hints and sketches of Lugano. Horses and cypresses and lilies, you won't find them ('cept horses) in Texas.[2]

We have to leave here end of April at latest. So far I have found nothing suitable, though on more than one trail. I <u>hope</u> to get a place I've heard of a little further along the coast. Anyway, I am burning duplicate and unnecessary books, but even those left will fill 25 cases. These I must store, either with various friends here or in a warehouse at Hyères or Toulon. Then we take to the open road in a Simca–5, and be culture fiends through Provence. Maybe we shall go north to friends on the Loire, maybe not, especially if the place near here turns out. Anyway, after about 20th April write care of Wm Heinemann, 99 Great Russell St, W.1. My idea was to take C. to Germany and Italy for a year each at least, but that looks hopeless in the obstructionist States of Europe.

Once more it rains here dismally and endlessly streaking. What a winter! I hear that London claims it is their worst winter in 70 years, or rather the wettest – what must it be!

Catha sends love and would be happy for stamps – and all our best wishes to the young mother and new little one!

Richard

P.S. These universitaires are becoming a bore. On top of that Minneapolis guy (who sounded all right) comes a most impudent creature from Rutgers (N.J.) practically demanding for NOTHING the right to reprint a 5000 word article on Willy Maugham I wrote. And a librarian in Ashville, N.C., calmly demands 'a long letter' containing all my reminiscences of Tom Wolfe. I feel like asking them back: Who paid the rent for Mrs Rip van Winkle when Rip van Winkle was away?[3]

1 H.D.'s grandson Valentine Schaffner was born on 21 February 1951.
2 Characteristically, Aldington here serves H.D. as an entertaining authority on a subject about which he knows far more than she. On 22 February 1951 H.D. had written Aldington that she now planned to spend only about a month in the United States. Anticipating her return to her summer home in Lugano after her American trip, she wrote of the 'precipitate rock shelves with pomegranate, cypress and white lilies in their season' and concluded, 'I am already homesick for the old tassled horses and the somewhat (they say) Sicilian atmosphere' of Lugano.
3 On 2 February 1951 Aldington had written to H.D. that '... a Minneapolis thesis writer wants dope on "the influence of Japanese poetry on the Imagists". A grown up man might be better employed one would think, but I gave him what little I can remember and suggested he write to you. Didn't Amy [Lowell] "translate" with someone else The Pillow Sketches?'
    H.D. responded on 22 February 1951: 'I heard from your Minneapolis. Just sent off a brief note; you are right, one wonders why they pick on these ephemera. Amy did translate with Mrs

Florence Ascough – that is somehow the pronunciation – but the spelling is not right. I mentioned [Arthur] Waley and E.P. but said I was not "influenced", that everyone took these things in their stride at that time.' Aldington and H.D. were willing to answer letters from scholars and admirers if they seemed specific, informed and sincere. Neither had patience for demands that appeared time-consuming, invasive or forward: Aldington, as here, resented writing without payment; H.D. refused requests which she felt invaded her privacy.

ᔗ 159 ᔕ

9 March 1951
Villa Aucassin
St Clair

Dear Dooley,

I understand so well your feeling of upset at this American trip and your wish to get back to Lugano, since I myself am in an even worse pickle. I am still suffering from two acts of altruistic folly. One is that, as I could live by US and S[ou]th American royalties and earnings during the war, I gave up my English quota of paper to other writers and published nothing there between 1939–1946. In other words, 7 years income were lost, and all the thanks I got was abuse from reviewers and the B.B.C. for hogging too much paper (true!) in that big Anthology, which you will confess was not over-burdened with <u>my</u> poems.[1] The second is that in trying to revive the unjustly neglected Aesthetes in the Religion of Beauty, I have burdened myself with about 1500 books which are not worth sending to England to sell (although they are so rare) and I hesitate to destroy because after the fearful destruction of books, particularly poetry, (to make newspapers) by the British government during the war, mine may be almost the only copies left. I only have them because a little bookseller, horrified at the ruthless destruction, hid them in sacks in a cellar, from which they were picked out by a bibliophile friend of mine. But in trying to save them for the future I've burdened myself with a very large white elephant.

So, you see, trying to sort and pack these books, plus another 1500, is one trial. Then, the difficulty of finding a suitable place. These little old Riviera towns are not civilised in the way Lugano is. They are pleasant, small shopkeeper, grasping hotelier, and in summer are invaded by noisy crowds of war profiteers scattering 500 fr notes as if they were sixpences. Then for months the places relapse into utter torpor. What I like and want is a place a little back from the sea, with a piece of wild maquis round it, and a little car to be free to shop where one wants. In addition I must be not too far from a school for Catha. There <u>are</u> places, but in the general system of grab they are priced either to rent or to buy at fantastic prices!

Your system of having rooms permanently in a hotel and moving to others is perfect. But it doesn't do for a child or for a man who has to have a reference library. I think I made a mistake in dropping novels for biographies. I should say a biography is about five times as laborious a piece of work as a novel, and you know from experience how a novel haunts one and takes one's energy. I could of course raise two or three thousand pounds between New York and London by <u>promising</u> a novel, but I boggle at that, because I might not be able to produce one in time, and because I wrote all the novels for fun primarily.

You remember [James] Laughlin? Perhaps you hear from him. Anyway, he wrote recently about reprinting an old translation of mine, and tells me en passant that Ezra occupies himself in writing to various people, 'and really seems to hope that one day his dreams will come true'. Well, anyone who shatters that illusion will be cruel indeed. I feel only too thankful, as I feel sure you will, that he has this fortunate illusion. Is it so much madder than the frantic nightmares of Truman, MacArthur and Co? It costs less anyway!

Inducing the baby is very common now. What happens is (at least in Catha's case) Mom is X-rayed, and when it is seen that the baby's skull is getting close to the size of the pelvis, a drug or drugs are administered, which 'induce' labour without tedious waiting on Nature and the probable Caesarian. It is all very modern and correct! The Americans are really good at this sort of thing, having the sense to learn from the Germans.[2]

Of course you are right about Heinemann's address. It is W.C.1.[3]

You ask me if I know the word 'lustre'. Dooley! After Ezra published an immortal work called LUSTRA, with a definition of same on the half-title! How will you atone for this injustice to classic American literature?[4]

You remember Mark Twain's jest – that everyone talks about the weather but nobody does anything about it. Well, it has been much in my mind this winter, for we have fared just as badly as you in our own way. No snow, but cloud, rain, cold for weeks. There have been those ominous southern thunder storms which always mean long disturbances. The sun is out this morning, but already (10 a.m.) the sky is clouding. It really is discouraging.

Yesterday (Thursday) I drove Catha to Hyères through heavy rain storms, and rather regretted it. The Frenchman is a queer coot. When roads get slippery with rain and visibility bad, instead of going slower as a precaution, he hurries to get the hell out of it to his destination. Result: we passed three accidents in 25 kilometres! Catha thanks you <u>very</u> much for 'the lovely stamps' and sends her love to you and to Perdita and the baby.

And so do I,

Richard

1 Aldington is not admitting here to being truly a paper-hogger but is emphasizing that the reviewers and the B.B.C. truly made this trivializing objection.

2 On 6 March 1951 H.D. had written to Aldington: 'Perdita was to go home [from hospital] on Saturday, she seems very happy, but baby was "induced" (I don't know the word nor the process) and all this worried me.'

3 H.D. had corrected Aldington in her letter of 6 March 1951. Usually it is H.D. rather than Aldington who makes this sort of error. She generally appears the more ethereal, he the more orderly and rational. It is worth noting how in this case, as in others, they complement each other.

4 On 6 March 1951 H.D. had written: 'I can't seem to settle anything nor to think rationally. I run round like a rabbit in a hutch, making out lists, sorting MSS; this is a five-year-end spring-clean; here, I have been a <u>lustre</u>. Do you know the word? I found in my dic. that it means, five-year period.'

April [1951]
Hôtel de la Paix
Lausanne

Dear Richard,

Thank you for letter, waiting for me, of 18/4. I risk this to Aucassin, though you did give me London address, as for after 20th. Thank you for return of photographs.[1] I am so glad to be back, left a week earlier than booked, but got place and even sleeper on return. We came direct, Paris, N.Y., not stopping at Shannon at all, a little over 12 hours. I had two nights in Paris but did not go anywhere – feel all right except but as to knees. Also fingers are more awkward than usual with the keys. I saw, of course, a great many people and went to the little family almost every day.[2] The baby is very mature and charming. I saw Mr [Pascal] Covici [the publisher] one afternoon, we spoke of you. He wants me to do a 'straight biography', I ask you. I told him I would think it over, as I want him to pronounce on some of the other things. He also suggested a volume of the last poems – but all that, in time. Saw Marianne Moore, the Gregories;[3] he spoke with appreciation of your book of essays, French masterpieces?[4] I had not seen it; Horace Gregory, I don't know if you know him. I did not get to Washington and did not even have the energy to accept their offer to 'set-up' for me in N.Y.;[5] Conrad Aiken came in one morning.[6] I don't know what or who else. I was sleep-walking most of the time, could not sleep, nor wake, I felt that five hours difference – but you are right, a boat seems, as you say, now, 'a floating (bad) hotel'. This may not reach you, I hope it does, just to let you know I am back.

Love,
Dooley./

1 On 17 March 1951, just before she left for her visit to America, H.D. had sent Aldington photographs of the Schaffners taken during their honeymoon in Maine in the summer of 1950.
2 When in New York, H.D. did not stay at the Schaffners' house but 'in a hotel across the street, Beekman Towers' (H.D. to Aldington, 6 March 1951).
3 The American poet, critic and editor Horace Gregory (1898–1982) and his wife, the poet Marya Zaturenska.
4 Probably the essays collected in *French Studies and Reviews* (1926), but possibly *Artifex: Sketches and Ideas* (1935).
5 On 6 March 1951 H.D. had written Aldington that she had 'been asked to do some recording at Wash, D.C., but I don't think I can face it …'. At Pearson's request in 1955 H.D. made her only recording: readings from *Helen in Egypt* (Watershed Tapes, Washington, D.C.).
6 Conrad Aiken (1889–1973) was Consultant in Poetry to the Library of Congress in 1950–52 and had, with other Fellows in American Letters of the Library of Congress, recommended Pound for the Bollingen Prize in 1948.

29 May 1951
Les Rosiers
Ancienne Route de Castelnau
Montpellier (Hérault)

Dear Dooley,

This address may perplex you, but after a good deal of wandering (by car) and seeing many places I have decided that this at any rate solves the education problem. Catha has been accepted by the Lycée de Jeunes Filles and started yesterday. Of course there are only a few weeks left of the scholastic year but I hope it will be enough to enable her to make some friends for the holidays and to get her through the October exam.

This is an old-time pension, fearfully run down but under new management which promises amendments. Its great asset is a large old garden with fine trees, very quiet, yet only ten minutes on foot from the centre of the town. It is, as you know, a university and medical centre, hence good bookshops, a municipal opera and concert hall. The Musée Fabre is a very good collection of pictures and sculpture – several very fine Houdons, and a miscellany of paintings, even a Bonington and a Sir Sloshua [Sir Joshua Reynolds]. How good the French portraitists of the 17th [century] are! There is a little 'Goethe in the Roman Campagna' by his friend Tischbein, showing the great man in much the same dress and pose as the Raphael Mengs Portrait. Too small to show the features. There is a pseudo-Botticelli with the super-Berenson-pedantic attribution 'École de l'Amico de Sandro'! There are some Ingres and Courbets. Not many of the contemporary École de Paris, whereof I am so heartily weary that I welcome anything as a change.

Our motor trip was spoiled to some extent by bad weather, but I think Catha enjoyed it. The place which delighted me was Glanum, the lately excavated site of a Greek village, afterwards Gallo-Roman, on the slope of a Provençal hillside near St. Rémy. There are only the usual broken walls and columns, but there remains a lingering faint aroma of Hellenic days – or was it but my fancy? There was the beauty of the site, reminding me that the people who chose sites and planned cities were most honoured among the Greeks. The place was brutally sacked by German invaders in the 3rd century. Why?

Then the Musée Arlétan in Arles, founded by Mistral and the Félibre, is a most intelligent and complete set of exhibits showing the life of the Provençaux which still existed as late as the 90s – the costumes, customs, arts, métiers, dwellings, etc. all perfectly represented and reproduced. There is a large scene (like those rooms in Basle but with human figures) of Xmas Eve in the Camargue, the exact lay out of the table, down to the eight or ten kinds of dried fruits, the log on the hearth where the oldest male sprinkles it with wine at midnight (the others standing to watch) and prays 'If possible let us be gayer this year than last, but in any case as gay?' (Can't remember the Provençal, but that is the gist.) We saw Aix, Lourmarin, Fontaine de Vaucluse (a huge underground river, not a mere fount), Avignon, Villeneuve, St. Gilles, Pont du Gard, Beaucaire, Tarascon (Catha disappointed not to see Tartarin), Nimes, Aigues Mortes, then Béziers, Carcassonne, St. Bernard de Comminges, Agen Auch, Périgueux, Bourges, Sancerre, Bourganeuf, Villefranche-en-Rouergue (a complete bastide), Cordes (another, almost intact), Albi, and St. Guilhem de Désert. The Albi cathedral is wholly painted to the vaults by Italians; there is a huge last judgment fresco imitating the Flemish, and a marvellous coro with statuettes in the Burgundy style. Most amazing that it escaped the Huguenots (destructive bastards) and the 1789 Revolutionaries, who managed to do some damage just to console le peuple souverain.

At St. Bertrand they have a dragon brought back by a Crusader and hung up in the church. Its head has dropped off and the stuffing is coming out. Worldlings base insist it is a Nile crocodile. St. Guilhem is quite overwhelming – a very early Romanesque basilica founded by one of Charlemagne's paladins, his cousin Guilhem le court-nez, no imaginary Roland but the hero who drove the Saracens from Languedoc and Gascony. The church still has a bit of the True Cross given to Charlemagne by the Pope in 800! The village pure mediaeval, and hardly tourist at all. The almost unique sculptures from the old church and cloister were bought for the Metropolitan [Museum of Art in New York]. I remember them – most remarkable. For lunch at the tiny inn they pull out of the deep blue stream a basket of flapping trout, and we sat on a terrace high above the river to eat them.

I have got to write a damned book I don't want to write, but when it's done I'll never again let myself be tempted by large advances to undertake anything my daimon doesn't suggest.[1]

I send to Lausanne, though you may by now be in Lugano. Hope you have good weather. One thing, the rain has made the wild flowers in the Midi simply wonderful.

Love
Richard

1 Aldington is probably referring to his *Lawrence of Arabia: A Biographical Inquiry*, published in London by Collins in 1955. He began this project in the spring of 1950 at Kershaw's suggestion. For a detailed account of the difficulties Aldington encountered during the course of writing this book, see Fred D. Crawford, *Richard Aldington and Lawrence of Arabia: A Cautionary Tale*, Carbondale: Southern Illinois University Press, 1998. Crawford concludes that Aldington encountered

> ...practically every obstacle that a biographer might face. With a minimum of resources and in virtual isolation, he overcame organized and dedicated opposition from powerful and influential friends of TEL, an uncooperative literary estate, a reluctant publisher, limitations on access to significant material, and severe restrictions from libel and copyright laws, all of which hampered his ability to tell the truth as he saw it. That he succeeded was the result of incredible courage, intellectual rigor, and determination even as he coped with crises of confidence, domestic troubles, financial woes, and failing health. His passion for truth gave him little choice. Had he foreseen the high personal cost of his TEL book, he would have written it anyway. (206)

⁂ 162 ⁂

21 July 1951
Les Rosiers
Ancien Chemin de Castelnau
Montpellier
Hérault

Dear Dooley,

You will not recognize the fact but this is written on a historic typewriter – one which I bought from Ezra in 1929. As it was made pre-1914, when 'workers' and 'bosses' were still compelled to be comparatively honest, it still works, and I keep it as a stand-by. My 1939 American typewriter is already done for, and my 1949 French breaks down every two months. On sent le progrès [One can see how things progress].

You know Mable [Dodge Luhan] and Frieda have deposited Lorenzo's typewriter (which he rarely used) in the memorial chapel. What must I do with Ezra's? Bequeath it to the Smithsonian? Or Library of Congress? Or Union of Fascisti?

Apropos I have had some correspondence with Ezra about a relative (male) of his in London for whom Ezra demanded letters of introduction! I needn't stress the absurdity of the situation. Except that he persists in writing like one of the Katzenjammer Kids, Ezra sounds no more insane now than in 1912. How do you account for the Katzenjammer Kids style? My own theory is that it began with the influence of James Joyce (Mr Shame's Choice), was developed under the 'fear of the cliché', i.e. fear of saying anything in a simple and natural manner, and was standardized from patriotism, the comic strip being America's greatest contribution to world culture. Anyway, he sounds well and fairly cheerful and good-natured. If Washington makes a pact with Franco what excuse is there for incarcerating Ezra? He should be sent to Madrid to lisp for his country.

The hot days have started here, and we are suddenly crowded with visitors. In this very small road a large monastery has housed all week La Semaine Sociale de France, which is a Catholic conference of priests, monks, Jesuits, in which they learn what of modern science they can no longer resist and how to pretend it is all in Thomas Aquinas. At the same time enters the Tour de France, a long stream of idiots on cycles led by the maillot jaune, and accompanied by hundreds of press cars and advertising cars (with loud speakers) of the various 'sponsors'. It costs millions of francs a day, often kills off the racers with heart disease at an early age, and vulgarises the inhabitants along the route, preparing them for the extension of advertising. Anyway, what with the sky-pilots and the road-racers we are crowded out, and they are sleeping – some of them – on the dining-room tables!

Later I was interrupted and meanwhile have recovered my mended French typewriter – only 8/- for a 6d repair to the new machine. ...

This letter was really begun – but got side-tracked – to thank you for the very lovely picture card of Lugano. There can be no doubt that the country has a peculiar quality, something both romantic and classical, if you see what I mean. There is nothing of that suavity here – all is mountain and garrigue and moyen âge except for the miles upon miles of vine and mulberry and plane in the flat lands. Yet there are bits so ancient-Rome they take one's breath away. I think I know now what was meant by a Roman 'villa' – the house, the farm, the outbuildings, the cottages, all built in brown brick round a court and forming a sort of defensive block.

There is a village called St. Martin-de-Londres near here which delights me. You come on it by an ordinary enough road, and find a little place, triangular shaped like a forum, with a powerful four-jet fountain under three magnificent planes. You climb a little hill of old houses to a point where a half-effaced sign says Monument historique, and find yourself in a 13th century arcade with a couple of hay carts, just beyond is a little open space crowned with a fortified Romanesque church of the XIth century (interior wrecked by the revolution) and round about forming an outer defence a ring of mediaeval houses, in one of which is a lovely Renaissance doorway with pilasters. I give you such a poor impression. Though it has of course been repaired it is all genuine with a wonderful feeling of age. Yet it seems totally unknown. Over the church porch is a rough relief of St. Martin of Tours – whose abbey comes much into the stories of St. Guilhem d'Orange and du Désert, so I suppose it derived from the abbey. But why Londres? Near at hand is the Mas de Londres, an old villa-farm, and Notre Dame de Londres, which I suppose was the convent answering to the monastery. These little places are all so old – if not Greek, then Roman or Gallo-Roman. By the way, lately they have found the Phocean fortress which guarded the old Greek colony of Marseille – so utterly lost and forgotten that even the name has gone unrecorded.

There is a whole cycle of chansons de geste about Guilhem, including Le Moniage Guilhem which relates his founding of the monastery. It is full of local names, including St. Benôit d'Aniane who I believe was a Visigoth! That, as they say, takes one far back.

Hope it is not too hot with you.

Love,
Richard

☙ 163 ❧

29 August [1951]
Hotel Bristol
Lugano

Dear Richard,

Thank you for your very interesting letter. No, you must not write when you are 'writing.'[1] I am rather in an end-of-season mood and want to go to Kenwin, where Perdita and John have left Valentine. They came here on the way through to Rome and I miss them now, so much. I hope to get to Kenwin about mid-September, I can't get away earlier as I promised to be here for some tardy visitors. P won't be back there till mid-September, I go to join her, as John is flying back and she taking an early October boat with Valentine. I think you know Bryher's address: Villa Kenwin, Burier-La-Tour, Vaud. But the [Hôtel de la] Paix, as per above, always reaches me.[2] P and John took the trip to Rome in sight-seeing stages as it is his first trip 'abroad'. I have new delight in their cards, Giotto's tower (of course) and so on.[3] I am being urged to join some people in Rome for October. I don't think I can face it, but this talk of Italy makes me very nostalgic or home-sick for the old scene.[4] Well – it is here too – but this compares to Garda, Vincenza and so on, not the older, first, over-whelming impressions.... Susan Pearson [Norman Holmes Pearson's wife] was here, too. She found Rome very hot and I think she was rather intimidated by it all. I had fun doing this all over as for the first time, helping her buy the ivory ear-rings, daisies, edelweiss, roses or gentians – the same sort of ideas as the Naples, but there it is all coral and tortoiseshell, as you remember. We have, too, some rather tourist-y yet authentic sort of Florentine silver work, yes, all very jumbled and pure bazaar in the arcades – but oddly Susan and John couldn't get over the joke of it all. P knew it from other summers. I have been reading Summer in Italy by Sean O'Faolain – don't think I could face the real summer....

I have Ezra's Fenollosa. I suppose you have it, too. Surely, they should get him or let him out? I worry about it. I don't know what I can do. Washington – I think you know it better than I – is a blast-oven in summer; I never liked it, but don't know all the seasons. I heard Dorothy had a little room or rooms, where she does the usual thing of serving tea as per on a gas ring or I suppose spirit-lamp. It all goes back so far, so far – it is fun in Paris when one has first begun to be on one's own. At the age of 65 – all but a few weeks (she and I are almost the same age) it must be – well what? Words fail. I hear he has disciples camped near who are allowed to interview him, with D as sort of secretary or nurse always there – also, heard from someone who wanted to get news of Maria to him that he was never to be seen alone. But, but poor Dorothy. What a fate. I always feel she is the heroine of Eliot's smash hit Cocktail Party. Poor Ezra – I sent a card with this address and have stressed <u>Paix</u> as more or less permanent, but he always writes me to <u>Croce Bianca</u>. I went in with Susan to show her where Norman had stayed in 1949 and the porter handed me the Fenollosa. I suppose the <u>Croce</u> rings a bell, is more Italian.[5]

I am so interested in your Lawrence of Arabia book. Is it L of A? I always wondered if there were any 'mystery' about his death; Shaw seemed to disappear; yes, I knew of the boats. Did you know him?[6] This is a very untidy note and does not need an answer, an in interim, as they say, as I am between seasons, as I just said. All the best to you all there and good luck

and love from
Dooley./

1 On August 9, 1951, Aldington had written H.D.:

> When I don't write the only reason is that I am so tired with work that I've no energy for anything but reading and little motor excursions to the many fascinating places near here. This book is the hardest nut I ever had to crack – a life of Colonel Lawrence. You'll think enough has been done on him! So do I. But much is left to say about that mysterious creature....
> I shall be most thankful when it is done.

Aldington included in this letter a lengthy account of bull-fighting in the Camargue and added, 'I have heard again from Ezra, and owe him a letter. He seems cheerful, except that he says – quite without ostentation – that his "mainspring is busted." Well, after the way he was treated by those thugs it isn't surprising. Poor Ezra. Still, he did behave like a chump.'

2 H.D. continued to use stationery from her Lausanne hotel even when, as now, writing from Lugano.

3 Giotto's multicoloured campanile stands next to the cathedral in Florence.

4 That is, the pre-war Italy H.D. and Aldington discovered together in 1912–13.

5 Working from Ernest Fenollosa's translations of Japanese versions of early Chinese texts, Pound had produced a number of oriental poems in 1913. He has sent his friends a recent pamphlet on Fenollosa's work.

6 H.D.'s mention of 'boats' here is not clear. Her mention of 'Shaw' is also confusing: she may mean George Bernard Shaw, who befriended Lawrence, or she may be referring to Lawrence's assuming the surname of Shaw during his last years. Aldington and T.E. Lawrence never met.

≈ 164 ≈

15 September [1951]
[Hôtel Bristol
Lugano]

Dear Richard,

Thank you for your letter of August 31. I am leaving in a few days for: @ W. Bryher, Villa Kenwin, Chemin de Valon, Burier-La-Tour, Vaud. I visit there with Perdita and Valentine, then above [Hôtel de la Paix, Lausanne], old address reaches me, even if I go to Rome – which is very much on the carpet.[1] Your encouragement impels me at least to keep the October trip in mind. I may yet do it.[2] I usually had October here and don't want to begin the winter, as it were, so early [by returning from Kenwin to Lausanne at the end of September]. Don't worry to answer this or any letters when working. I am so supremely smug in my self, to feel that I have written FINIS to my creative out-put, though I could spend years (and probably will, if the Lord spares me) niggling and picking and re-embroidering the old themes and MSS.

I had a Fenollosa booklet from E.; I have written him and had some odd letters. When I said that the messenger from Mary could not see him alone, it was not because of 'attendants', but this girl told Viola Jordan that Dorothy was always there, as sort of secretary-companion, during his visiting hours. A friend of Pearson's said he had this group of disciples and held forth professorially, as it were, in his own private room. But that he slept in a common dormitory and found this naturally distasteful. I do know that both Laughlin and Eliot have done much to help him.

I am interested in L. of Arabia. I did not know that poor W. Lewis was so afflicted. I have since heard that there was a talk or write-up of him in the B.B.C. 'Listener'. I did not see it.[3] I was surprised to see, last winter, a reference to a memorial exhibition of [Edward] Wadsworth [1889–1949], at Tate. I did not know he had gone. They do seem to be slipping away. I am feeling so home-sick already for Lugano, though I have not yet left – and am, of course, ambivalent about it all, as I am so anxious to see Master V [Valentine] and visit with P. She is now in London, seeing John off on his plane.

It has been a lovely summer though our storms seem to have made head-lines in England and in Italy – some bridges broken up the valley. I am taking the <u>Centovalle</u> trip back for the first time. We cross through Italy, thus shortening the trip; those long valleys are beautiful but Lausanne-Lugano is almost a day trip. I have heard this is remarkably beautiful, but means several changes and duane at Domodosola. This is in the Italian vibration a bit longer, the trip is shortened by some hours but the train is slower, almost a mountain-train, with little carriages and no wagon-restaurant but they bring through baskets of grapes and Chianti, I am told. I was amused by your marvelous dinner – what news of Catha? Is she still writing?

This is Battle of Britain Day and I have sadly celebrated by packing my first suit-case with books and MSS. I carry too much with me, always intend to get into Dante, and have glanced over some pages but not too thoroughly. Also, a dictionary or so take up so much room and MSS that I bring along to read to myself – the 'Delia Alton' sequence, <u>Sword</u>, you know. I went on back into time and know that I have done a real portrait of WM [William Morris] in <u>White Rose and the Red</u>. But I don't want to publish <u>Rose</u> without <u>Sword</u> as introduction. Then, my last, <u>The Mystery</u>, an 18c. reconstruction in Prague just before the French Revolution.[4] Other MSS I left at La Paix. Well – all blessings on your work

and love from
Dooley./

1 H.D. has used stationery from the Hôtel de la Paix, her 'above, old address', even though she is actually writing from the Hôtel Bristol, where she is currently staying.

2 On 31 August 1951 Aldington had suggested:

> But why not try Rome in October? It is so lovely then, the heats over, the vendemmia coming in, the wine carts, the Campagna refreshed by the first rains, the tourists rapidly departing. I loved so much the Octobers of 1922, 24, 26 I spent there – came to feel that the

autumn in and about Rome is better than the spring. The castelli, alas, have been badly damaged, but ROMA is intact. If ever I can wrest the leisure and devises from the bitter world I am going once more to Rome – those Vatican marbles, and the Papa-Giulia, and all the churches, and palaces. I think hooting of motor horns is still forbidden, so the town is not nerve-racking like the places in the Midi. Think of it. You could buy uva di Calabria again! Remember them?

Aldington continued to encourage H.D. on 17 September 1951:

You really should make the Roman effort – find a quiet or comfortable hotel or pension, plan what you want to see, and not too much. I always find it a good idea to take a taxi to the door of the church or palace or gallery, and then to walk back for the exercise – one arrives fresh. Also, you get much less tired in galleries, if about every five minutes you stop and do some deep breathing. A lot of fatigue comes (I am told) because in the interest of looking at pictures, statues etc. one forgets to breathe properly. ... There are plenty of fleas in the churches frequented by le peuple, so remember to have a bath and a complete change on returning. (The Santi Apostoli used to be very bad.) Water in Rome is perfectly safe, as you know, but squeeze a lemon in your last glass of wine, and avoid fried things especially in small restaurants. They are said to be the origin of those hideous 'disturbances'. If you should get one stay in bed and send for a doctor at once – they can fix you in two days. ... Wine (white) of the Castelli is best – but there is a white wine called from the grape Trebbiano which if good and chilled is delicious. After 25 years I still remember a flask in a restaurant of Piazza San Eustacchio – and I don't mind confessing that I finished the flask and went home in a cab! ... DON'T MISS ROME!

Aldington's advice (as his pronouns shift back and forth from 'you' to 'I') suggests not only his support of H.D. in a venture she finally did not have the confidence to undertake but his own vicarious pleasure in planning a trip which he would very much have enjoyed but could not afford. To a degree, Aldington's 'travelogues' functioned for H.D. as entertaining substitutes for direct experience; in turn, H.D.'s projected travels (to Italy, to America) allowed Aldington to recall his own past (both with and without H.D.) and to join her in fantasizing journeys they would never take together. These possible but impossible trips in conjunction with the vivid descriptions of local colour and seasonal changes which both writers regularly included in their letters are thus complex and highly charged elements in this correspondence.

3 On 17 September 1951 Aldington sent H.D. a copy of Wyndham Lewis's article 'The Sea-Mists of Winter' (*The Listener*, 19 May 1951, 765) in which Lewis movingly described his loss of sight: first he became aware that he was apprehending the world through 'a sea-mist', then that he could only perceive vague shapes and colors, finally that he could 'no longer see a picture'. Aldington commented: 'He certainly puts a very good face on it, though there is simply no consolation in a misfortune like that.'

4 By 'the 'Delia Alton' sequence' H.D. means 'The Sword Went Out to Sea (Synthesis of a Dream)' and its companion piece 'White Rose and the Red', but she may also intend *Bid Me to Live* ('Madrigal') as well as the reflective personal essay 'H.D. by Delia Alton' (entitled 'Notes on Recent Writing' by Norman Holmes Pearson, this piece was written in 1949 and 1950 and finally published in *Iowa Review* 16 [Autumn 1986]: 174–221).

4 October 1951
Villa Les Rosiers
Ancien Chemin de Castelnau
Montpellier
Hérault

Dear Dooley,

This comes slam back [in response to a letter dated 3 October], because I am just at a day's 'rest' between chapters and because I want to put to you a 'situation' concerning our old friend "Banabhard" (R.A. Taylor) of which I learned only this morn.

Briefly – you know some of this – she has written a stupendous work on French Renaissance, about 1,000,000 words I believe (holy smoke!) – turned down by Hamish Hamilton and Harper's. I got Frere (H'mann [Heinemann]) to read it, and he behaved with clownish insolence – refused to do anything about it, sat on the MS for a year, and finally Alister Kershaw took it back. Discouraged her and stopped her writing to me – so much for the British Piccadilly socialist, damn him.

Well, I now hear that Yale Press has/have written her THREE letters asking to see the script, and she has seemingly not even replied. She is over 70, very poor and lonely, in a miserable little flat where lately she had a fire which burned a lot of her books. Says no good sending her script to USA – nobody will print it.

Could you discourse all this to your friend (Norman Pearson, isn't it?) and ask him to pass the information on to the relevant person at the Press? I suggest myself that perhaps the best way would be to have some American – Yale – scholar-gentleman in London write and ask if he might see her about the script, and offer if entrusted to have it wrapped, addressed, insured, and despatched to Yale. Dooley, it's a book which <u>ought</u> to be published, and if Yale CAN do anything about it [, it] will make all the difference to her last years. Think about it, and if it won't bore her ask Bryher's advice. Banabhard has had a difficult life, but she is a great Renaissance scholar, and those disgusting little pigs of journalists in England sneer at her as 'Pater in petticoats'! Alister introduced her to MaCurdy – the supposed great authority on Leonardo and editor of L's note-books. A. says Banabhard simply wiped the floor with MaC. who is, however, about the 2nd great authority on Renaissance and a charming old man.

You see there is no room in the modern book world for people who [are] not either journalists or professors or thesis-writers.

So glad to have your news and snapshots. The baby looks strong and sane – about all one can say at that age! And I am happy to see you looking so well. I shall be very glad to see the Perdita snaps.[1]

I was near Creeley lately, but didn't call. It was Catha's end of the holiday car trip. We got to Aix just about noon – [The American poet Robert] Creeley and his wife are at Font-rousse (Ezra says) some[where] back behind Aix. I dementedly said she might choose her own lunch. She chose pâté de grives, a trout, a tournedos and a pêche Melba! I shall know not to do that again! After lunch I suggested a visit to the Americans, sleep in Aix and on to St. Clair next day. But no! she must see her friends at once, including 'a concierge de Madame Simone, les enfants de la gare, et le marquis de Poubelles' – the last disrespectfully named by me because he is really the village garbage man. So we did not see Creeley. Fantastic that they are "down" on poor Dorothy, who has obviously a devilish life. E. is safe in what he calls BUGhouz, but she has to go out daily and face the sneers. Poor girl.

Ezra is really a comic. In his latest he tells me I am old enough to 'start thinking about something more than café celebrities and blue chiny.' My recent café celebrities are Wellington, Charles Waterton, Lorenzo, and L. of Arabia in progress. E's letter contains references to Ford, [the British poet T.E.] Hulme, [Herbert] Read, Brooks Adams, Marie Menken, Creeley, Cocteau, Fritz Vanderpyl, 'yung Igor'? and 'Henriettaaahhh'?!!!² But I think it amuses him to get letters, and I just ignore his attempts to 'convert' me to his particular brand of economic fallacy and political violence.

Back to Banabhard – she doesn't need and won't take money (I tried) but needs boost, real appreciation. Being a woman you will know better than I if my idea of a <u>call</u> from Yale representative is the right procedure or a horrible mistake.

By same mail I get a Yale University Press ad of 'Gertrude Stein: A <u>Biography</u> of her <u>work</u>'. Really, America is impossible. Its 1st–2nd University sponsors a howler like that!

Love,
Richard

1 H.D. described these photographs in her letter to Aldington on 3 October 1951: '...enclosed is me, looking like Stonehenge on my balcony, with one of the guests. ... It gives the elevation and the town below like a cup or bowl that absorbs and holds the sun. Also, Bryher and me in the garden. Valentine speaks for himself with Fi-fi, an outsize boxer, and his rubber rabbit.'
2 Marie Menken was likely the American journalist H.L. Menken's wife; Fritz Vanderpyl, Igor and Henrietta remain as unidentified to us as to Aldington.

➳ 166 ⤨

9 October [1951]
Villa Kenwin
Burier-La Tour
Vaud

Dear Richard,
    You might note: Professor Norman Holmes Pearson
        233 Hall of Graduate Studies
        Yale University
        New Haven, Conn.
I think I did give you the address. I have written him to let me know about Yale Press. I said if they had not an 'agent' or someone suitable to call and ask for the MSS, that it might not be a bad idea to appoint an 'agent' pro tem, with a letter from him or them, to that effect. I suggested: Miss Ellen Hart
        37 Holmefield Court
        Belsize Grove N.W. 3.
She is Oxford, or was, well informed, lived in Crete as tutor, at one time, travelled in Greece, loves Italy, France etc. She, by the way, was more or less (I understood) commissioned to do a book on the founder of the Red Cross – Duchet? Ducrois? Anyway, she got permission to explore archives at Geneva and even went to Italy to visit the Solferino (1859) district – it is Dunant, I find it now. Well, it was a year or more work and I understood commissioned but Chatto (it was) just about refused it, though she is given option of more or less re-writing and shortening it all. Just that sort of thing – this, not so important. Ellen Hart is 55 plus, perhaps. Anyhow, this struck

344

me, she is very well-bred and tactful and reverential toward ART in its true sense. Or you might suggest another 'agent' or some other plan – yes, I am glad you wrote me and I am sure the only thing is to get the MSS away, on the way. Things do seem to die or pine when left too long – not that this would. But Banavahrd might, at least, have the fun of seeing it in print, if possible. But I will wait to hear from Norman before any other move – though I have written Ellen that there might be a tactful visit required from her later. She just about lives in the old B.M.; I thought she might be reading R.A.T. while there.

Thank you for all news. I am really rushing this out to noon-post. Catha sounds delightful – Perdita used to eat sausages from a stand in the market-square with ice-cream cone, one in each hand! Yes, it staggers one!

I do feel that poor Dorothy has had a tough time, I wrote her at some length and said I had heard from you that you were in touch with Ezra.

I did speak to Bryher about B [Rachel Annand Taylor] a year or so ago when you sent me the books. We might have 'wangled' something from a fund that is or was associated with Authors' Society, but you said that was not indicated. Bryher is in England now, I am really waiting here for her return in about a week. But I think Norman is the right person to consult and I will report at once to you.

Yes, Stein! Americana or some-such. I think they have bales of her note-books but I don't grumble as I have found it a great relief to wish unto Norman for his 'shelf', odds and ends and duplicates – some of your May Sinclair lot [of library books], I think I told you, that I already had. N was most grateful for them as a back-ground of the period. I told him that R.A.T. linked up with Violet Hunt and Ford Madox [Ford] and so on. I did not tell him of Ezra's impertinence, 'her poetry is paste-jewels in molasses'. Impossible... how one remembers!

Love
Dooley./

⤜ 167 ⤛

13 January 1952
Les Rosiers
Ancien Chemin de Castelnau
Montpellier
Hérault

Dear Dooley,

I have a dreadful feeling that while I have been expecting a letter from you, I have all the time owed you one! If so, please forgive the silence. I had to go to Paris to look up govt. archives; had just got settled, when I had to go to Nice to see the 'Albatross' ([the publisher] John Holroyd Reece) who is putting some of my books back into print. Then, ever since I have been slogging away trying to get through this interminable book [on T.E. Lawrence].

Did I thank you for the duck and stamps to Catha, which she very much admired and liked. It was kind of you to send.

16/1/52 I continue with this, to show at least the futile virtue of good intentions. But I really am very tired and over-worked, and the whole situation is a problem. For every reason I want to get (and indeed must) the book done, but yet can't risk another breakdown.

How very well the Americans have developed colour photography! Instead of being garish and false, it is now quite beautiful. The little boy [H.D.'s grandson, Valentine Schaffner] looks very sweet, and I am so happy to think that you will be seeing them again so soon. Perdita looks very well, I think.

Catha has a half-holiday because of the funeral of de Lattre.[1] At breakfast she remarked: 'Oh, I do wish a general could die every day!' It is rather how I feel myself – one each day on each side of the iron curtain.

Well, you have a wonderful experience at Chartres, for the glass there is really the best in the world, and the three sculptured façades quite extraordinary. But remember to dress warmly and to take a good overcoat if the wind is east, for that cathedral is like an ice-box and the cold wind round it is deadly. Alister and I stopped off there last month, and simply had to quit, it was so cold. Shall you go by car? I wish I had read Ambelain's book on cathedrals, but I never saw a copy.[2]

Banabhard and her book are a problem. Of course she is the uncrowned queen of the Brit Mus, but that's not getting very far. What I had in mind was that when some member of the [Yale] Press or Faculty or Pearson himself next go to London, they might try the personal approach. B. is still very lively and even skittish over a bottle of good wine, Alister tells me. She needs to be flattered and allowed to talk out her ideas about the book. Then, to be told tactfully the publishing realities. I wonder what she's working at now.

My own view on England – which is no doubt mere prejudice – is that it can never recover from the wars and the 5 or 6 years of socialist misgovernment. Not that the idea or fact of all-out government charity at the expense of the wealthy is necessar[il]y fatal, but because just at that time the whole experiment was fatal. The only salvation was, as Churchill saw, in two or three years more of coalition govt – he dealing with the Americans and the Labourites with the trade unions. He has just managed to save the pound, which otherwise might have crashed again with consequences too appalling to think of. But I don't think he can really save the sinking ship this time. One trouble with socialists is that they are so damned insular and provincial – they don't realise that England of all countries is the most vulnerable, being dependent on trade which always fluctuates and always shifts to new areas. England is worked out. What they'll do with that huge population, heaven knows. But no doubt you will write this off as pure pessimism.

Your swans across the roses – hasn't Morris a poem with the refrain 'Two red roses across the moon'?[3] My book-buyer sent me a 1st edition of The Earthly Paradise for Xmas – very nice. It seems that Morris and Rossetti firsts have not fallen anything like Swinburne, Browning and even Tennyson. ... The only flowers out in the botanic garden here are the dwarf iris and daffodils. I expect the freezias are coming out in the Var. We have had lovely sunny weather ever since Xmas, with early morning frosts, but no real cold. It is so pleasant after all that dreary wet weather.

All love,
Richard

1 General Jean de Lattre (1889–1952) was Commander of the First French Army, which liberated Paris in the summer of 1944.

2 On 15 January 1952, H.D. wrote Aldington that she anticipated a visit from Perdita and her family in the early spring: 'I am trying to bring myself to face going to Paris and staying a bit, meeting them, seeing Chartres, which I have never seen, and Notre Dame from a new angle,

got from deep reading, very deep, a wonderful book called <u>Dans L'Ombre des Cathédrales</u>, by Robert Ambelain. Did you ever hear of him? He was suspect, his books banned during occupation, this was published 1939 and is almost unobtainable, but Sylvia Beach ran it to ground for me. I have been trying for years to get it.' Characteristically, this proposed trip remained for H.D. an imagined one: on 25 April 1952 H.D. wrote Aldington from Kenwin that Perdita flew from Paris to Geneva where Bryher met her.

3 On 15 January 1952 H.D. wrote to Aldington that she hoped to get out for a short walk along the lake when the weather was good; from her window she could see '... astonishing, rather nipped but perfect red-roses, not one or two but beds of them – why? ... one looks over the red-roses to the Savoy snow-slopes – very Japanese ... [*sic*] seven, I ask you, seven swans flew across the "screen" last time, in perfect classical formation ... [*sic*]'. The William Morris poem to which Aldington refers has its title as its refrain, 'Two Red Roses Across the Moon'.

≫ **168** ≪

22 February [1952]
Hôtel de la Paix
Lausanne

Dear Richard,

Thank you for letter of January 13. Continued January 16. With return of the colour photograph. Yesterday was Valentine's first birthday. I cannot seem to settle-in to anything, the sun is brilliant but I tried to leave off heavy coat a day or so ago, and seem to have done it too soon – wanted to walk and walk in this sun but it is cold and heavy coat frustrated me. So came back to room full of flowers – Valentine's and some candles that I lighted yesterday – and for us all. For I have been smothered in newspapers, sets sent out from England and I have bought many of the French and Italian picture-papers here. The pictures of them all are surprisingly romantic, I mean, of them 'all' of this new age or era – and I wanted to write you some time ago to wish you all happiness and prosperity. All this has been exaggerated or made personal by Kenneth Macpherson turning up here with a friend [the photographer, Islay Lyons], with all details of Norman Douglas' end and before-end and terrific ceremony in the Protestant Cemetery, all mixed up with true 'South Wind' detail – how they had to get a private grave-digger, how three German nuns (angels, he said) were in constant attendance and N would either chase them away or ask 'who are those ghosts?' or offer them snuff – relays of well-wishers and the whole island trailing through to say good-bye; Norman Douglas died a few days after the King [George VI]. Then, their reactions and desire to get clear away. They stay about a week, I believe. But it brought Capri into new-old perspective, the stone-pines. Norman, too, I saw a bit of him in London. But he was very ill and his brilliant mind wandering, toward the end. I did not know that Cecil Gray had died in Rome, some months back [in 1951] – all that, too. He had taken [the British writer] Compton Mackenzie's Villa <u>Solitario</u>, and was there with a youngish pretty wife – SHE died in Capri. O – this 'South Wind' – about a year later, G. was taken with liver complications, rushed to Rome. One would think he would have left Capri and that Villa (haunted, I was told by Faith Mackenzie) after the death of Marjorie (I believe her name). What a saga – all this has left me strangely untouched – yet deeply wondering – I mean, it reads like a story, someone else's story – yet there is the scene from yesterday, the almond-trees, the lemons and their clustered blossoms together, the smell of the long grass. ...[1]

All your news is interesting and, of course, I know 'Three Red Roses' – it [the landscape] was all deep in snow my last trip. Now snow has melted a bit but trains were being held up – this is all very disjointed. I have heard no more of Banabhard. I will let you know of any news. I hope you are no longer over-worked. Do not hurry to answer this.

We have new stamps again, 100 years electricity. I will paste on the last of the set next time. There are just the four. I have not really answered your letter – but all this – all this –

Love
Dooley./

1 H.D. seems confused in this letter. She was invariably upset by special occasions and indeed by any event which altered her usual routines: the sun in February, Macpherson's arrival, Valentine's birthday, the king's death, and the news of the deaths of two close friends from the past (Douglas and Gray) have clearly merged here and disoriented her. She is at once trying to convey information to Aldington and to reorient herself as she takes in new information. In the process, boundaries seem to have broken down; she lights candles 'for us all' and is unsure of what is happening to her and what to other people, of what is 'someone else's story' and what her own life as present and past, life and fiction seem to her to interpenetrate one another. This kind of reaction is typical of H.D. and contributes to her special sensibility and angle of vision.

❧ 169 ❧

23 February 1952
Les Rosiers
Ancien Chemin de Castelnau
Montpellier

Dear Dooley,

So glad to hear from you – it seems 'quite a whiles' since you wrote. Situation here unchanged and not satisfactory. I have now done 300 pages out of the 400 of my Colonel Lawrence book, but realise that even after two writings, much revision and some re-writing is needed. A hundred pages – 30,000 words – doesn't seem much. And it wouldn't be in purely creative work, but when every paragraph and practically every sentence has to be documented by reference to one or more of 70 books and documents, and nearly 1000 pages of notes, the exact references checked and recorded – well, you see what it is. Only another writer can even guess the work involved. I calculate that by the time it is done it will have cost 4000 hours of hard work – and England and America will treat my pay as 'unearned income' and tax accordingly!

The king! Well, his father (mistakenly) called me [in a standard reference to soldiers of the Great War] 'trusty and well-beloved', so discretion is called for. I too had papers dumped on me – several languages. Not one told the truth – that he presided honourably but impotently over the most disastrous epoch in English history since the Great-Rebellion-Great-Plague-Great-Fire epoch. George Lackland. Did we have to let the Americans cheat us out of India, Burma, Palestine? Perhaps I should say, Clem Lackland. And now having had Elizabeth the Great, must we have Elizabeth the Little? Romulus Augustulus was also young and a little pathetic.[1]

I heard about Cecil Gray's death at the time, but did not mention it. Really, it is all so far away that it is quite unreal. The other day I was reading that chapter in Aaron's Rod where Lorenzo made fun of us all, and wondered if it is my passport to 'immortality'. I did not know it was 'liver complications'. G.'s heart was so bad in the

348

war – perhaps for war purposes? – that I was much surprised he lived so long. My friend and 'secretary', Alister, met him in a London pub – introduced by Roy Campbell – mutual interest in Heseltine (Peter Warlock) who never much interested <u>me</u>. Did I ever tell you that Alister and a man named Warman (to whom I introduced him) drove down into Surrey to Heseltine's grave, drank to his memory from bottles of beer, and poured the remainder on the turf! All the time keeping an eye for possible irruptions of the sexton or parson. I rather liked that. Heseltine, of course, was a soak – and Alister, alas, is an Australian. But a very sweet person – I wish you knew him.[2]

And Norman. I am very glad to have the inside news. The inevitable epitaph – we could have better spared a better man. He had long outlived himself, a ghastly misfortune. But never do the immortal gods fail to know one another – he was certainly an infinitely more important contribution to life than the dismal bureaucrats who persecuted and the innumerable little parasites who tried to flatter him into accepting them in his later days. I give you one memory which I think will recall the real Norman. He was staying with me at Le Canadel (Var) and I suggested a run in the car to the little hill town (then unspoiled) of Bormes. We descended at the one café. I explained that it was only a village place so we'd better have a vermouth. 'I'll go and see.' Off he went and in about ten minutes returned with the patron, a plate of English ham sandwiches (where did they get the loaf?) and <u>two</u> bottles of vintage champagne – for which needless to say I paid. Dear Norman.

Snuff to the nuns – perfect.

Yet I loved Pino more.[3]

Ezra writes, I may say, incessantly. Do you know, Dooley, I am coming to think once more that he <u>is</u> a bit cracked? At first I thought his letters were just Ezra plus the Katzenjammer Twins, as I wrote you. But as I utterly refused to take the slightest taint of the jargon, he has more and more dropped it, and he seems quite the old Ezra, except that he unaccountably drops into a rage over nothing or hands out some mouldy Fascist chestnut as an immense novelty and contribution to human thought! Amazing, as his friend Whistler used to say. I have got into touch with Dorothy through an interest in her cousin, Captain Shakespear of the Indian Army, who was one of these unknown English officers who explore and then administer vast areas (Arabia this time) on 15/6 a day and the ingratitude of government. She sent me, without comment, a post-card of a Washington National Gallery picture of 'A Tired Old Woman with a Book'! Pathetic. They seem to be very poor. Ezra sends naive proposals for me to get his works reprinted – ignoring the fact that there is still much prejudice against his broadcasting, that his 'works' are highbrow stuff of no interest to the public, and that Tom Eliot would deeply resent my butting in on his preserve. It is on the cards that I may be given control of a projected series of reprints with a big publisher – but could I sponsor Ezra in justice to my employer? I doubt it. Ezra doesn't know that when Heinemann published that big anthology of mine in 1947, I found in the proofs that he had simply been cut out! I had almost the worst row of my life with Frere to get him back – and if Ezra did hear this he would think it was less than his due. Edith Sitwell refused a poem, and wanted one of 1944, though the original (USA) edition was 1941 and didn't go beyond 1939. Made a fearful fuss in the Times. I couldn't tell the truth, as a cable from Viking warned me that by accident we had pirated her in 1941! I paid out 400 pounds and 3000 dollars in fees to living poets or heirs over that book, and will never again have anything to do with living 'poets'! Never.

Well, there's a new turn, a new phrase, but it won't be any better. Man is a silly animal who breeds too much and loves too little.

All love,
Richard

Thanks from C. for 'wonderful stamps'.

1 Romulus Augustulus (475–6) was the last western Roman emperor, a usurper not recognized in Constantinople. The diminutive comes from his having been a child when raised to the throne by his father, Orestes. He was overthrown but spared by Odoacer because of his youth.

    H.D. responded to Aldington's evaluation on 18 March 1952: 'I am shocked, too, when I look back...[sic] don't know how Albion survived at all, perhaps that is the mystery, the miracle of the George VI reign, like the "miracle of Dunkirk" when we were waiting for the invasion barges. That is the great gift, making a miracle of defeat. ... it is heart-breaking but my heart cannot break any more, having had two-wars of it.'

2 Philip Heseltine (1894–1930), who composed and wrote under his own name but also used the pen name Peter Warlock, was a British musician and a friend of Cecil Gray's. Eric Warman (1904–92) was an English writer and bookman and a close friend of Aldington's from 1932. Numerous letters to Warman are included in Gates, *Richard Aldington: An Autobiography in Letters*.

3 Giuseppe ('Pino') Orioli (1884–1942) was a Florentine bookseller and publisher and a close friend of both Norman Douglas and Aldington.

⤜ 170 ⤛

24 April 1952
Villa les Rosiers
Ancien Chemin de Castlenau
Montpellier

Dear Dooley,

Well, after all these strenuous months I finished the book [*Lawrence of Arabia*] on Sunday, and mailed it off next day. It covers 456 pages, at least 150,000 words, with about 1500 exact references to author, book and page arranged chapter by chapter with a small number in the text corresponding to the number in the list. Reviewers of my Lawrence complained that it would take 'months' to verify my quotations, not observing that the remark hardly qualified them to sit in judgment. But since when has ignorance deterred either the literary parasite or the literary amateur? At all events, in this case I have done their work for them. Any reference which escapes their learned memories can instantly be traced to its exact author, book and page. All they will need will be the sixty-five books I have collected which form my main sources. I hope they have them.[1]

Meanwhile, I hardly know for the moment what to do with my recovered freedom. I have spent extra time at the Fabre museum here and at the library which <u>does</u> contain Alfieri's books – I have seen and handled 16th century Decameron and Castiglione with 'Vittorio Alfieri' written in them. The library also seems to have a good collection of rare books and pamphlets on local history, topography etc. The sort of place for Norman [Douglas] in his younger days, for Bas-Languedoc is almost as neglected by writers now as old Calabria was forty or fifty years ago.

I continue to hear frequently from Ezra, more really than I want – he is still so coterie-minded, so full of blind prejudices based solely on personal motives. Thus, he pretends that he never heard anyone mention Norman (who did <u>not</u> admire Ezra!)

except you, me and Brigit! Which, if true, suggests that he (E.) moved among rather illiterate and undiscerning people. Again, he keeps urging me to write something or sponsor an omnibus of the work of his old buddy, Ford [Madox] Hueffer [Ford]. To please him, I had my book-buyer send out some early numbers (first 12) of the English Review and some of F.'s work. And it just won't do. When F.'s work isn't the dullest hack writing (as e.g. his quite unendurably jejeune Rossetti) it is painfully imitative, as e.g. his Fifth Queen which is a mixture of Hewlett and [Robert Louis] Stevenson. The E.R. is no doubt as good as could be expected in 1908–9, but what do you say of a periodical which takes up a quite snootily 'critical attitude' and prints in its first number as its first star prose contribution a sentence like this:

'He admitted himself with his key, as he kept no one there, he explained, preferring, for his reasons, to leave the place empty, under a simple arrangement with a good woman living in the neighbourhood who came for a daily hour to open windows and dust and sweep.'

Now, really! Did you ever read anything so dismally uninteresting, more banal, and in worse English? I defy you to discover anything as bad as that anywhere in Norman. And yet the author is the 'great' Henry James, in my opinion a dull, pretentious, clumsy writer except occasionally in his travel notes. As a rule he had nothing to say, knew nothing of life outside conventional parties, and was too conceitedly self-conscious to be able to put that down either clearly or convincingly! Am I too cantankerous about him? Perhaps, but it annoys me to see these dreary Americans foisted on the literary world over people 'immensely' their betters. The world of Henry James! Poof! my dear, what next?[2]

I took Catha over to Lavandou for her Easter holidays, and she ran wild on the hills and beach, while I sat in a little room and toiled over the correction of my script. Anyway, she seems to have had a lovely time, perhaps too lovely, for she hated leaving, and shed tears at the thought of returning to jography, algebra and instruction civique! I must say I deeply sympathise. But what is one to do? A girl can't be a barmaid nowadays without a university degree.

Is it true that Norman was penniless at the last? A. S. Frere tells me that N.D. said so to Graham Green[e] and F. advanced some money on the security of that old Venus in the Kitchen chestnut, which Pino showed me in the early 30s. But if N. was hard up, it's pretty disgraceful. I suppose his American editions were mostly piracies?[3] Talking of which, what do you say to this? You know, the Viking pride themselves on being such wonderful publishers etc. and are supposed to be such friends. Well, looking about for an easy job after this chore, I suggested that I should do them a Voltaire Portable. They write back condescendingly to say they did one in 1949, and send a copy to enlighten my ignorance. I find that without asking my permission or paying a cent, they appropriated my translations of some of V.'s letters, and also my translation of Candide which they printed without my name as translator! Of course, it's the pirated one which for years could be bought in every drug-store and was issued by the Peter Pauper press and heaven knows who else – always without my name. Nice people American publishers. By the time I'm through with them they'll wish they hadn't!

Turning over my notebooks I came across this which seems worth noting when you think of Henry Miller: 'There are no Breton ballads, no Cymric mabinogion, nor Gaelic sgéulan, which deal ignobly with petty life.' Perhaps that is why they are forgotten and Miller and Joyce literary heroes.[4]

Do write when you have a moment.

Love,
Richard

1 Aldington's comments here suggest both the state of scholarly books in 1952 (when by convention the footnote was rarer than today and considered less necessary) and his own position as a
writer outside the academy, used to addressing a general educated audience and to writing
biographies and critical appreciations without recourse to the technical paraphernalia which
scholars now take for granted as essential elements of responsible research and writing.

2 Ford founded *The English Review* in 1908 and edited it for several years thereafter. Aldington
refers to Ford's *Rossetti: A Critical Essay on His Art* (1902) and *The Fifth Queen Trilogy*, historical
novels based on Ford's idealized interpretation of the life and times of Catherine Howard,
Henry VIII's fifth wife; the trilogy included *The Fifth Queen* (1906), *Privy Seal* (1907) and *The
Fifth Queen Crowned* (1908). The English man of letters Maurice Hewlett (1861–1923) wrote
historical novels. Aldington quotes here from Henry James, 'The Jolly Corner', *The English
Review*, Vol. 1, No. 1, 1908, 9.

3 On 25 April 1952 H.D. wrote Aldington that 'No – . ... There was a written controversy in
TIME, I sent on what clippings I had to Kenneth Macpherson, he and Robin Douglas [Norman
Douglas's son] both wrote contradicting various rumours of "poverty" and so on.'

4 Breton Ballads, Welsh epic lore, and Gaelic tales are at a distance the precursors to modern
literature in English. Aldington is being a bit cryptic here. He seems to be saying that he once
felt that this early folk literature dealt only with large themes and grand subjects expressed in
admirable language. He now wonders, humorously, if he was wrong, implying that merely the
admirable material survived, those utterances dealing 'ignobly with petty life' having fallen
into obscurity. A reading public, insensitive to 'great' writing and responsive only to what is
sensational and low, has accordingly entirely forgotten this body of significant literature. As a
result, James Joyce and Henry Miller, whose work recalls not what is admirable in these earlier
writings but the 'petty' material and 'ignoble' expression of lost Breton, Welsh and Gaelic
literature, are thus regarded wrongly as 'literary heroes' in being innovative (which Aldington
suggests they are not) and important (rather than 'petty', which Aldington thinks they are).

≫ 171 ≪

10 October [1952]
Hôtel Bristol
Lugano

Dear Richard,

Thank you for your letter of September 18. I send you a line in a slightly muffled
state, a sort of polite grippe that has been hanging on for weeks, but just enough to
make me feel lazy and give me an excuse to sit in the sun – of which, mercifully, we
have now an Indian summer plenty. Trees are magnificent this year. The Venda[n]ge
[grape harvest] is at the far end of the town, so it seems more serene now than earlier;
though crowds and crowds come in on special trains, we hardly notice them here. I
think I will stay on for most of the month, as I hear the grippe is rampant around
Lausanne, plus cold and snow almost down to the lake, or creeping down from the
Savoy Alps opposite.

I hear from my old-timer friend Viola Jordan, who has been seeing E. and D. [Ezra
and Dorothy Pound] for some days, afternoons 'in the garden'. She has sent me post
cards from Washington and says she is writing at length. It will be interesting to hear; I
don't think she has seen E. there in Saint Elizabeth's before.

I don't know the book you speak of but just feel dizzy when I think of it – it's explosives in a cathedral – you can pick up bits of broken glass-pictures but it is so depressing.[1] Perdita seems well and happy – I only hope she gets a girl, as she is already talking of dolls – the boy has had a hair-cut and I suppose is much too hearty for dolls, has a sand-heap in their little back garden and generally throws his weight about. I really write so soon as P sent me a letter she had from Patricia Aldington. P did not know what to do about it. Pat asked her to write to May Aldington, as her mother felt lonely and could not often get to see her.[2] Should I write Pat (as she was then called)? I have not her address, I sent back the letter; Perdita's address – but I don't know what address, N.Y. or London – had come to Pat in a 'round-about way'. Perdita found it rather mysterious though she wrote and said, if I would explain, she would write to M.A. – but I told Perdita to hold it over, that I would ask you. Perdita just wondered what it was all about … and I don't suppose it's all that important, only if you do write, and it seems indicated, say that Perdita appreciated Pat writing but is very busy, getting settled in their new home (they moved, but just around the corner, for the sake of this miraculous little square of garden, for the 'children'). Also, if indicated, that Perdita expects her second baby, late winter – or what you will. But don't worry, just as it happens – I found it touching that Perdita was anxious to do the friendly thing and asked me what was indicated.

This is not much of a letter, don't let it add a weight to your un-answereds, just having written me – and thank you for all news.

Love
from
Dooley./

1 H.D. refers here to Aldington's comments about Pound in a letter to her of 18 September 1952:

> He has sent me that Kulchur book of his, and I wonder if you ever read it and if so what you think of it. 'Farrago' seems the word. His mind is like a mirror broken into fragments – it is still bright but the reflections are fragmentary and broken up. It is like the Cantos – no linking of ideas or thoughts – nothing leads anywhere – and yet the detail is not uninteresting. It seems a real tragedy, especially as he makes one blush for him by talking so self-importantly about himself. And yet there is something in it. I suppose the psychiatrists would have something to say. He goes out of his way to commend Wyndham Lewis for having praised Hitler! I wonder how Lewis will like that, since he has spent much time trying to explain away that little blunder.

2 Aldington explains many of the references here in Letter 172: Patricia Aldington (b. 1908) is his much younger sister; May Aldington (1874?–1953) is his mother. What is clear from H.D.'s quandary, however, is that neither Pat nor May Aldington knows that Perdita is not in fact Aldington's child. Perdita is willing to continue the ruse, even if it means taking on duties towards Aldington's querulous relatives.

12 October 1952
Les Rosiers
Ancien Chemin de Castelnau
Montpellier

Dear Dooley,

I have just received your news of the 10th, and reply at once. I have no idea how Pat Aldington knew about Perdita or got her address. She certainly didn't get either from me – indeed I don't know Perdita's address. Will you please tell Perdita from me that she is to forget the whole thing, and do nothing about it, and not to answer any letters from any Aldingtons. I am much ashamed that she should have been troubled. Be absolutely firm – Perdita is to take no notice.

My mother has been a most infernal nuisance, continually 'borrowing' money and squandering it, and you may be sure (I am!) that if she gets Perdita's address, there will be continual begging letters. I have had to stop writing myself, and my lawyer brother (Tony) has had the humiliation of having to put her in some sort of institution where she is looked after and cannot continue to waste our money and damage our reputations. It is very hard on him, for a lawyer has to be so Caesar's wifey, whereas a mere writer, out of England at that, is not much affected.

Dooley, all the time I was in USA and before and after, I gave up things to send her dollars (thinking it was tough for her in besieged England) only to learn that at that time she had quite enough, and spent the money she whined for to me on gambling and drink! Well, why not? But why should I and little family go without to finance them?

Pat (my sister) has become a violent R.C., but is very much in her mother's control. Margery [Aldington's other sister] and her husband have taken jobs in Tripolitania to get away from May!

Do make all my apologies to Perdita and her husband, and warn him (women have no sense) that my mother is now an accomplished begging-letter writer. I think she has now attacked every one of my friends, including my puzzled publishers! And don't you write to any of them. Send their letters (if they write) to me, and I'll give them one of my broadsides. It is damnable that you and Perdita should be bothered by them.

You will understand, dear Dooley, that whenever I've been asked I've always said that Perdita is my daughter, and it is doubtless on that they found this intrusion.

Ezra and Dorothy – I have found the card of the 'Tired Old Woman' D. sent me, and find it very touching and rather distressing! I have a memory of going up those flights of stone stairs to their Rapallo flat (1928) with D., and hearing E. from afar making that strange hum-groan he used to utter when composing. And D. exclaimed tragically: 'Oh, if E. does that again I think I'll throw myself out the window.' Or words to that effect.

I also enclose a copy of me as a Lance-Corporal from a 'lately-discovered' photograph in England.[1] Catha has a large-sized one in her bedroom, and is always asked if it is Stalin. Clearly, I missed my destiny.

Don't worry about that Aldington business. Just be tough and tell Perdita to be so.

Much love
Richard

1 This photograph may have been sent to him by his brother Tony, who would have gone through his mother's possessions when preparing 'to put her in some sort of institution'. The picture is probably the one reproduced in this book on p. 20. Aldington referred to this

photograph again in a letter to H.D. on 28 October 1952: 'If you have any photos of me, other than that one I sent, I'd be glad to have them. Owing to various accidents I seem to have none older than 1928. I am going to tell Heinemann to advertise me as the only author on their list who looks like two dictators. There exists a snap of me with a Chaplin moustache taken in Paris about 1930. Small French children looking over Catha's snap-shots invariably exclaim: "Itlair!" ... I must shave clean and put in for Hirohito.'

≫ **173** ≪

4 November 1952
Les Rosiers
Ancien Chemin de Castelnau
Montpellier

Dear Dooley,

I return the letter about Ezra, and am grateful to you for letting me see it. I have now read it several times, and each time with growing horror. It is a document straight out of Huxley's Brave New World – and what seemed the wild fantasy of a dyspeptic pessimist in 1932 is the every day of 1952. The sketch of Ezra is really more terrifying done in this curious garrulous style than it would have been if more 'sophisticated'. And the glimpses of that autostrada with rushing cars every 100 feet, the motels with TV, the ice creams continually, and all the rest! And the one person of something near genius shut up in a bug-house![1]

The letter with the lugubrious picture of me and the two cards has just arrived, and I know Catha will be very happy to see them, and place among her store. I think that she most likes the 1930 photo which Charles Prentice used to call 'the rowing blue', in a muffler with turned up coat collar, which Chatto used for years. It was selected from a lot of others by the sardonic suggestion from somebody that the photos should be sent down to the girl typists to vote on! They chose this choc-box personage unanimously. And now Catha falls for it. The lugubrious young soldier is reproduced in a work of reference I found in almost every American library – so reproduced that it is even more dreary-looking.[2]

I had utterly forgotten the R. Sussex card. I wonder who did that sketch? It has little artistic merit, but it brings back suddenly the sensation of all that weight of equipment and the memory of a Lancashire voice from the darkness during the confusion of a night relief: 'Eh, laad, hasta seen ma fookin ayversack?'

By the same mail as your letter came Catha's first passport from <u>Her</u> Majesty's Consul-General. The stamp unfortunately still has the King's head, for C. was very particular in ordering a passport from the Queen. By the way, they are very insistent on making us register with the Consulate annually. Do you find this, or do you ignore it? The notice says that failure to register in certain cases may mean loss of nationality.

Did you know that the Royal Sussex is also Winston Churchill's regiment? I wonder why I was given such a good regiment? I think it was due to a mistake and a disdain on my part. In ignorance I filled up an officer-cadet form and gave my mother as next of kin in case of casualty instead of giving you (she lived at Rye) and out of sheer indifference said I was prepared to go to any regiment or unit they cared to post me to. Now, about 99.9% of fellows tried to get into a regiment near their homes, and I can imagine the surprise of the bureaucrat who looked over that paper and found that astonishing piece of patriotism. I can see him taking it to the Colonel-Bureaucrat and hear the dialogue:

'Remarkable thing here, sir – young feller just passed out – says he's willin' to go anywhere.'

'Haw; haw. You don't say so. Most commendable. Where's he come from?'

'Rye, sir. Seems to be only support of a widowed mother.'

'Umph. Is he a gentleman?'

'Dover College, sir.'

'Haw. One of the new military public schools, eh what? Post 'im to the Royal Sussex.'

Much love,
Richard

P.S. Catha has now read both the books on the Norman invasion, and thinks Bryher's much more <u>interesting</u> than the earlier one.[3]

1 H.D. has sent Aldington a letter from Viola Jordan, dated 18 October 1952, about her visit to Washington.

2 On 3 November 1952 H.D. sent Aldington various 'R.A. souvenirs' from her own scrapbook. Among them were a photograph, a photograph in the form of a postcard, and a Christmas card.

3 On 15 October 1952, H.D. sent Catha 'a little novel of Bryher's'; exactly which of Bryher's historical novels is unclear. On 19 October Aldington thanked her and noted that Catha also had Hope Muntz's *The Golden Warrior* (1948) 'but has read neither'.

The 'choc-box' photograph of Aldington in 1930,
selected as particularly attractive by the typists at
Chatto and Windus

20 December 1952
Les Rosiers
Ancien Chemin de Castelnau
Montpellier

Dear Dooley,

I return the picture of the little boy, who looks very sweet. The bit about the child from the institution in Olga's letter rather hurts, doesn't it?[1] Which reminds me – a few days ago I was with Catha in a collection of very dull, respectable people, so I whispered [to] her: 'What would these people say if I suddenly gave a yell and threw you on the floor?' 'They'd say you are a père indigne, and put you in prison!'

Which brings us to Ezra. Of course this Olga letter is completely futile and beside the point. I didn't listen to E.'s broadcasts, and I suppose you didn't, so how can we have any opinion on his guilt or otherwise? BUT, Uncle Sam's monitoring service did listen to them, and the Roosevelt government took so serious a view that they sent the F.B.I. to interview me in Hollywood and find out what were my relations to E. I told them – and being decent Americans they believed me – that I had known E. before 1914, that he had been very kind to me and that I felt always an obligation to him, that I thought he was a paranoiac, that I had not seen him since 1929 or written a letter to him since early 1940 when he expressed a hope that the Italians and Germans would hang Mr Churchill 'on the Gold Exchange'. I said he was no doubt entitled to that hope, I was entitled to have nothing more to do with the person who expressed it. They asked if I listened to his broadcasts, and I said No, and showed them my 59 dollar radio.

I should want to hear the recordings of those broadcasts before I do anything publicly for E.

He is in a peculiar position, namely, he stands indicted as a traitor to USA, but has pleaded insanity, and consequently is confined for life to a lunatic asylum. Can the President quash such an indictment? I don't think he can, any more than the Queen could in England. If E. now claims to be sane, and is in consequence released, then he must stand his trial, for the indictment still holds. And if his lawyers advised that plea 7 years ago, what would they do now, when the spirit of the American public is worked up to panic heights about traitors and spies?

The claim that E. wasn't anti-Semite is simply untrue. I have myself heard him insult Jews in the abstract until I protested. I have recent letters from him with idiotic anti-Semitism. The idea that 'the Jews' have E. in prison is simply one more of their crazy anti-Semitic ideas. It is all part of E.'s muddle-headed burblings, which I still think are the product of paranoia, like those of his anti-Semitic friend Wyndham Lewis.

And the Irish! Fine judges they are, when thousands of British and American sailors died because they would not allow the Anglo-American Navies to use Cork and Waterford (which Neville Chamberlain under American pressure foolishly gave them back), when 'Eire' was a hot-house of Axis spies, and the Dublin intelligentsia openly regretted the end of the War and its victors because they were thus deprived of the wonderful 'spreads' given by the Nazis' and Fascists' Embassies in Dublin! Sputiamo sull' Irlanda [Let's spit on Ireland]!

No, Dooley, you keep out of this mess, as I have done and intend to do. And I feel pretty sure Bryher will give you the same advice. If anyone is to put his finger in the fire let it be the great Mr Eliot, who stole our thunder and got himself called Zeus. Let him get on with it![2]

I have two young Americans motoring down from Paris to spend Xmas with us, and I hope they are bringing Alister and his wife. Alister has now a very good job [as a press analyst] on MSA [the Mutual Security Agency], but they don't give much leave, and he has been absent a good bit with tooth-troubles.

I am just completing a little book of notes and memories of Norman and Pino, with a few letters I have from them, and notes on our publisher Charles Prentice.[3] Can you tell me who is actually Norman's legal literary executor? In a late edition of South Wind, Willy King says he is. The Times says it is Kenneth Macpherson. I have to ask permission for some short quotes from N's writings, and to print my letters. (Nothing scandalous in them!) Also, do you know who is Pino's executor? Is it Carletto? I suppose there is no hope of my recovering the script I felt with Pino pre-1939. Doubtless sold long ago. Let me know if you can about this. The book is in no sense a biography, you understand, just an Ave atque Vale to the old days.[4]

Would you care for Catha to send you a note, or would it be a bore?

Well, all good things for 1953,

Richard

1 H.D. has apparently sent Aldingtson a letter from Olga Rudge asking H.D. for help on Pound's behalf. The 'little boy' is probably Mary de Rachewiltz's son.
2 H.D. wrote to Aldington on 22 December 1952: '... no, I never listened to a broadcast and will keep out of it all, anyway. ... As you say, let Mr Eliot carry on.'
3 Aldington's *Pinorman: Personal Recollections of Norman Douglas, Pino Orioli, and Charles Prentice*, London: Heinemann, 1954.
4 On 22 December 1952 H.D. told Aldington that Kenneth Macpherson was Douglas's executor and added, 'I think your book would be excellent.'

≈ **175** ≈

27 December [1952]
Hôtel de la Paix
Lausanne

Dear Richard,

Thank you for your letter of 23rd; I had already posted the ER II [calendar]; then the book came and I have been making excuses to be alone so that I can get into it; no trouble, that.[1] It is by far the most consistent book on DHL that I have seen. I did not of course read all [the other recent books], but did read Luhan, Carswell, Frieda and the letters.[2] Please give my love to Frieda when you write. It is an astonishing portrait of her, too. The Mexico saga was all rather confused in my mind; now, I have sorted it out. I am afraid I read a bit backwards, but have the middle-first half left and will write of that [later]. There WAS a blob of lapis, L. gave it to me that time they stayed at M [Mecklenburgh] Square. He said or F said that the 'Ott' had hit him with it.[3] I unfortunately had the lapis cut, gave half away and lost the other half. Symbolical? I worked off and on on a shortish novel, <u>Madrigal</u>; I wrote you of it. I think I started it in Cornwall [in 1918], but it wouldn't 'come true'. I had to get the period off my chest or, in some way, 'perfect' it, project it. I have the top copy and two good carbons and the original, and Pearson has an early typescript. I felt that the book shocked him. I got right into it, the summer of 1939 before leaving Vaud for England; left the MSS out here, was about to destroy it – and golly – there it all was and now IS. I am not keen to publish this or anything – but I do think it gets a lot into a small space and it is alive. You might hate it, of course. I won't send it at once, as I want to re-read the script; one always finds ludicrous slips in the best copy. You can keep the copy as long as you want, or even keep it [permanently], unless you hate it – then, sling it back. You need not comment on it. I kept the 1939 version, only scrapped the last chapters; they did not ring quite true and brought in 'others', if you know what I mean.[4] But I made the 'happy ending', if it could be called that, the fact that Julia (this time) somehow knows that she will live in the gloire, as she calls it, will, will, will sometime write, as she wants to write, not just slim volumes of Greek Chorus quality, but something else. It took a long time to do it, and the final theme, of course, is the War II one. But this stands on its own.

Thank you for the news cutting. I have not seen the new Immigration laws. I will look out for this. Just have not had time to leaf over the usual weeklies.[5]

This in a hurry.

It is snowing really beautiful fine drift-snow now.

Love,
Dooley/

1 Aldington has just sent H.D. a copy of his *D. H. Lawrence: Portrait of a Genius, But* ....
2 Mabel Dodge Luhan, *Lorenzo in Taos* (1932); Catherine Carswell, *The Savage Pilgrimage* (1932); Frieda Lawrence, *Not I, But the Wind* (1934); Aldous Huxley, ed., *The Letters of D. H. Lawrence* (1932).
3 H.D. is apparently responding here either to Aldington's book or to an earlier letter, but this incident was sufficiently important to her that she recounted it further in *Bid Me to Live*. Julia is thinking of Frederico and recalls 'The lump of lapis-lazuli that someone had given him, that he had given her one day, "Take this, do you want it?" "Isn't that what Lady Ottobourne gave you?" said Elsa. "Yes – I'm sick of the Ott, she bores me", he said, leaving the lump of lapis there on the table, where Julia had been sitting, writing' (139). 'The Ott' was Lawrence's nickname for Lady Ottoline Morrell (1873–1938), whose patronage he both appreciated and resented.
4 H.D. apparently means 'other characters'. In all likelihood she means specifically Bryher, whom she met in July 1918, but who is excluded from this autobiographical novel set in 1917–18.
5 On 23 December 1952 Aldington sent H.D. a clipping about Robert Best, who died in an American prison while serving a life sentence for treason; he was convicted of broadcasting Nazi propaganda in Germany during the war. Aldington also mentioned the new Macarren immigration laws. He was outraged that, under this legeslation, the US had reportedly accepted immigration applications 'from 6000 ex-Nazis!'

᠄ **176** ᠄

31 December 1952
Les Rosiers
Ancien Chemin de Castelnau
Montpellier

Dear Dooley,

Herewith a letter from Catha – a bit prunes and prisms, but there is nothing like a child for being formal on what seems a formal occasion.[1]

I would have sent the DHL book to you when it came out if I had thought you would be interested. Yes, I was pretty sure there was a bit of lapis, but I did not know it went to you. Observe the difficulties of biography! Frieda was vague about it, and Carswell in her mutterrecht omniscience was sure that Frieda also 'biffed' him with a soup plate.

I am not wholly sure that the soup plate story isn't Carswell's blundering version of the lapis! Those Carswells sound awful people. She got into several libel actions with her first version of Savage Pilgrimage, and Chattos withdrew it. I mentioned in my book her story about Mrs Belloc Lowndes and the money for the War fund for DHL, and Rebecca West (who was pro-DHL and a friend of Mrs Lowndes) wrote and told me it was a malicious invention! If the book is ever re-set I must remember to cut that out. Most of the 1930s books on DHL did his reputation much harm, because they were so partizan, and people were repelled by Murry, Luhan and Brett and Carswell, and the books by Ada and Frieda are feeble, though Frieda's has some of his best letters.[2]

Yes, by all means send me your novel, Madrigal, which I shall be very happy to read. I hope to finish work on my Pinorman in about ten days to a fortnight, and then shall have time free until the proofs of my Lawrence of Arabia start coming in.

Apropos DHL and the ranch – in the summer I met a British naval officer and his wife who went to Taos in 1948. They met Frieda, and stayed at the old ranch (Frieda and Angie [Angelo Ravagli] have built a bigger house with the money from L's books! below the old one) but did not meet Mabel Luhan, who was having a fearful feud with Frieda and not speaking to her or her friends! I think it may have been this which forced Frieda to marry Angie [in 1950], as Mabel otherwise could have got them expelled for mor'l turpitude. Nize peeple!

Much love,
Richard

P.S. Elizabeth the Little a great success with Catha, and hung on the wall beside an enlarged picture of me as soldat. I notice the people in London who send one reproductions of Picasso as Xmas cards all use George stamps, and those who send old masters, snow scenes &c all use Queen stamps. A mere coincidence?

1 Catha is thanking H.D. for the gift of a calendar featuring Queen Elizabeth II on the occasion of her accession to the throne.
2 The books to which Aldington refers here include, in addition to those H.D. refers to in Letter 175, John Middleton Murry's *Reminiscences of D. H. Lawrence* (1933), Dorothy Brett's *Lawrence and Brett* (1933), and *Young Lorenzo* (1931) by Ada Lawrence and Stuart Gelber.

≈ **177** ≈

2 January [1953]
Hôtel de la Paix
Lausanne

Dear Richard,

I enclose letter from Pearson about E., with note, also cutting [about the young Queen Elizabeth] for Catha if suitable and she has not yet seen it. Her letter is completely and entirely delightful. I have a box of maple-sugar, I don't feel that I can cope. I WONDER if it would go through, without duty? I have already paid slight duty, this end. I will ask at P.O. when I take the script [of 'Madrigal'] this afternoon.

I have read now all of the DHL and think it really an achievement; you keep the balance and relate his early life to the last days – it reminds me of Ezra, not personally – but the Ezra I knew when I was 15 and he 16, really, really is the same, as this, per enclosed from Norman Pearson. Your irony is delightful, I mean your quotes for instance, from Brett – I did not read her book – am glad you put that in about the dagger – I did read the Dane book.[1]

Don't worry or hurry about <u>Madrigal</u>. You will understand it is a PATTERN, and came out that way, and much is condensed into its 197 typed pages. I am thrilled literally about all your Taos or Chaos news. Think of it still going on! It takes thirty years off my life. Don't send <u>Madrigal</u> back; I will ask for it if there is any question of Norman [Holmes Pearson] wanting it, as he has early rough copy only. But he never mentioned <u>Madrigal</u>, except for just acknowledging script. I think he thought I had TOO MUCH – all the finished War II sequence, then this, which I could not finally shape until I got the War II off my chest. How long I worked on it – destroyed maybe, ten to twenty – or approx. [–] 'beginnings'. So this was finally, in its limited way, an achievement. This is just to go with the enclosed letter and to thank Catha for hers. I will write again.

Love
Dooley./

Kenneth and Islay are staying on till mid-January, if there is anything more I can do about the Douglas Ave atque. ...

I remember N D saying in Florence to me, after a notable row with DHL, 'he has grit, and the fellow can write'.

1 Pearson's letter, dated 22 December 1952, appears in *Between History and Poetry*, 130–5. In his biography Aldington notes that Lawrence found Dorothy Brett '"a little simple but harmless", while in Taos the Indians said of her: "Señorita with the dagger very dangerous"; for she pluckily carried a dagger to protect herself' (*D. H. Lawrence: Portrait of a Genius But ...* , New York: Collier Books, 272–3). By 'the Dane book' H.D. means Knud Merrild's *A Poet and Two Painters: A Memoir of D. H. Lawrence* (1938).

✐ 178 ✐

6 January 1953
Les Rosiers
Ancien Chemin de Castelnau
Montpellier

Dear Dooley,

I am returning Mr Pearson's letter – though I should have liked to keep it a day or two – because I am afraid of mislaying it in the mass of letters, papers and typescript on my work table. It is most interesting. Did you notice that it begins like one of the Gospels with 'that Mary who is John's sister'? But a grisly, grisly picture of poor old Ezra in that awful place. 'The air-conditioned nightmare' – everything from US sounds a bit nightmarish these days.

I am very glad to hear of your publication in US. There should be a standard book of your poems. I notice Mr Pearson speaks of 'the Imagist Label'. I should think he was quite right – it was a 'label' which never should have been attached. It gave a little contemporary réclame and a lasting misunderstanding. I have never forgiven E[zra] for pinning that second-rate tag on you. But all comes straight in time, and good work can no more be kept down than a cork will stay under water.

Talking of which ... in looking for Mr P.'s letter I turned up the enclosed 'Check-List' of DHL since 1931, and thought you would like to see it. (Return, at your leisure, as I might need it later.) To me it reads like reports on a battle, and a hard fight it has been, with few allies and many enemies. A good many of these books and articles in the earlier years were very hostile, and you will see that in 1942 it looked as if they and the highbrows had won. Nearly all L's books were out of print in the later war years. It was so lucky I persuaded Frere in Dec 1930 to buy up the whole lot, for he has fought hard too. Finally we got the million Penguins, and there are now also about twenty of the Heinemann 'brave little red books' back in print, and you can see how the US universities are going for him. I can sit back and say my nunc dimittis.

Incredible that Mabel Dodge set-up, and how American! In order to 'help' the Indians she has to exploit them as a show for those hideous 'tourists'. To prove her love for remote Taos she makes a business success of her real estate there, and turns it into a more awful 'artists' colony' than Carmel. Finally, to show her respect for DHL she has his poor bones dug up and placed in the 'Memorial Chapel' as a 'shrine' for tourists from Hollywood, Detroit and what you used to call Squawbunksville.

That DHL's work has survived all this seems to show uncommon vitality.

I haven't been able to look at your script, still working all day on my book [*Pinorman*], but as soon as that is done I shall sit down to it happily. The first page looks really marvellous!

Love
Richard

≈ **179** ≈

7 January 1953
Les Rosiers
Ancien Chemin de Castelnau
Montpellier

Dear Dooley,

I finished that book [*Pinorman*] yesterday and then found energy to put on the new [typewriter] ribbon I should have put on long before. Then with the unusual luxury of a morning not pre-empted I sat down to Madrigal, and have now read 120 pages. It is awfully good, Dooley, really good, authentic and concentrated, better than the equivalent chapters in Aaron's Rod where Lorenzo was in one of his fits and guying us all. I was so much a bemused visitant from another world that there are still things that puzzle me. Jack White for instance. Where did he come from? (Ezra? Yeats? Lorenzo?) and why did you all like such a chump? Or seem to like him? That hitting a sick man like Lorenzo was surely below the D.S.O.?[1]

You bring out splendidly L.'s mimicry, and you were right to do so. It was something much more than monkey tricks, because he could also do it on paper, when it becomes genius. It was that plus his refusal to take people at their own valuation and his seeing through their self-deprecations which made him so much hated. I think David Garnett was quite right to say it was class hatred, 'the impotent hate of the upper class for the lower'. Did you see that screech of unappeased hate Bertrand Russell set off in the Listener recently? It seemed to me to miss its aim, for it merely proved that L. was not something nobody ever thought he was – namely, a plausible doctrinaire with a don's education.[2]

'From another world' – I thought of sending you a collection of rough sketches called Roads to Glory, not that they have any merit as writing, but simply for the curiosity of seeing how simultaneously in Time there may be such utter contrast of experience in Space. But why should I worry you?[3]

I think it a great pity that book wasn't published. But perhaps that didn't matter to you.

There is snow over Montpellier to-day, the first I have seen for several years. Catha of course is enchanted – I suppose I was at her age. 'Odd how one changes' as Mr Hueffer [Ford Madox Ford] remarked. ... That makes me think of Ezra again. I did not mean to be impatient with him, but I get a little bored with his trying to bring me into his three-ring-circus and turning on me his tedious 'young men'. He is very peremptory that I should do a book on, or make a selection of, his friend, Ford, and show what a great man Ford was. Well, I've had some of his stuff picked up and have read it, and if those books were ever alive (which I question) they're dead enough now. There is, exceptionally, real vigour and life in those four war books, though lots of padding and stuffing. All the rest are dead, though one might pick out a few poems. I was irritated too when I sent them [the Pounds] the Lawrence life to receive a note from D[orothy] (great man couldn't be bothered) 'we are not interested in Lawrence.' But wouldn't they lap up a tenth of his posthumous fame and success!

The upward glare off this fallen snow gives me a slight headache. I must stop.[4]

Much love,
Richard

1 During the Great War the Irish patriot James Robert White was awarded the Distinguished Service Order.
2 The English novelist and editor David Garnett (1892–1981) was a friend of D.H. Lawrence. Bertrand Russell's 'Portraits from Memory III: On D.H. Lawrence' appeared in *The Listener*, 24 July 1952, 135–6. Apparently motivated by jealousy, Russell attacked Lawrence's ideas, finding them fascist in implication, but paid no attention to the quality of Lawrence's writing. Noting the vast differences between them, Russell admitted Lawrence's energy, but found him finally 'a positive force for evil' (135) who placed 'an excessive emphasis on sex' (136).
3 Aldington agrees with H.D.'s sense that he came to see her at Mecklenburgh Square during this period on which the novel draws as if 'from another world'. His *Roads to Glory* (1930) contains war stories based on his own experience. While accepting her view of their experiences, Aldington here comes unusually close to defending his behaviour, and his slightly bitter if finally kind 'why should I worry you?' suggests that he is restraining himself.
4 Aldington is not being petulant here: on 17 January 1953, he admitted to H.D., 'I am only just out of bed, feeling wretched, but got sick of lying like a pig in straw. I finished reading Madrigal with a temp of about 101°, which probably accounts for the fact that towards the end I found myself rather exhausted, by the intensity of all these rather self-absorbed emotionalists.' It is also worth noting that Aldington often experienced a physical collapse after finishing work on a book.

≫ 180 ≪

14 January [1953]
Hôtel de la Paix
Lausanne

Dear Richard,

Thank you so much for your letter. I meant to write you that I had sent on that maple-sugar; afterwards, I was rather upset, as I remembered how I had asked in Manuel about sending on some sweets; they said it was not worthwhile to France, as the tax was exorbitant, moreover they insist now upon an equal weight of 'groceries' going with it; it is true, 'groceries' can be raisins, dates and so on, but it seemed quite out of the question. They advised me not to send – but the poor old sugar will come under the same rule of thumb – so please be kind and let me know what they charge at duane, as I would not feel happy otherwise, would just have to make up a sum and send it, on chance.

I have written Pearson to send me what pictures of you he has. It will take some time (with some old ones of mine) – then I can go into that matter of re-prints.

I am happy that the <u>Madrigal</u> got across to you. You must not think I minimize your out-put and your years of hard work. I just had to do my own work and was from the first, even with Ezra, in danger of being negated by other people's work. I speak of this in regard to DHL in the book. I would like to have given my gift to someone but it was just not possible; no one could 'take it', in several senses of the phrase. And I went on and on. <u>Madrigal</u> was literally on the hob for 30 years. I added and subtracted and worked and destroyed till I got the 'perfect formula'. It is true, I may have seemed to dash off the long Howell sequence and the two books that followed, on the same theme, in different periods (circa 1850 and circa, no exactly, 1788) but I had the subject, and the years and years of hard work behind me. Now, I am happy with all this and, in time, the things will be placed. It must be just the right moment and the right publisher – but that will come, when indicated.[1]

I should be interested in the 'Roads to Glory'. I will take care of the MSS and return to you or to any address you give.[2] Yes – I thought that B R <u>Listener</u> article really false and patronizing. I read it in Lugano. I was really deeply interested in the check-list you sent. I am amazed and happy that the work has obtained so much notice – even if not all sympathetic. At any rate, it kept and keeps Lorenzo's name and fame, spirit or *geist* alive – although as Julia says in <u>Madrigal</u>, 'ghosts don't die'.

Good-luck with the new book and books. Yes – I find the snow a little distracting – though it is so pretty on the Hans Anderson roofs out of my window, and it drives the birds to my sill.

Love from
Dooley./

1 If H.D. is remembering accurately, she began work on this novel much earlier than Friedman indicates in her important chronology 'Dating H.D.'s Writing' (in *Signets: Reading H.D.*, ed. Susan Stanford Friedman and Rachel Blau DuPlessis, Madison: University of Wisconsin Press, 1990, 46–51). Friedman states that the work was begun in 1939 and finished in 1950. H.D. suggests here that she was at work on it at least as early as 1923 or, if Friedman is correct and the novel was completed in 1950, then as early as 1920 – a date which would make *Bid Me to Live* the earliest of H.D.'s fictions, at least in conception. Indeed, it seems likely that H.D. began work on this book in Cornwall during the summer of 1918. By 'the long Howell sequence' H.D. means 'The Sword Went Out to Sea' (Parts I and II) and 'White Rose and the Red'. In response to H.D.'s apparent willingness to see 'Madrigal' in print, Aldington began immediately to try to interest publishers. On 17 January 1953 he wrote her: 'Madrigal as it stands is excellent, yet I don't know who would publish it. I will think about it. May I show the script to Alister? He is excellent about such things ...'.

2 H.D. does not realize that *Roads to Glory* has already been published as a book and thus is no longer a 'MSS'.

181

[30 January 1953]
Clinique Cécil[1]
Lausanne

Thank you for suggesting your friend read <u>Madrigal</u> — there is no worry about publicity, but it is a beautiful, tragic + basically anti-war story — I will be here two weeks anyhow, but they say I have been dragged down for years + years by some internal tangle, they have straightened now inside — an unexpected shock to be ordered here but it is a heavenly place. I will write, later. The Sister is severely telling me I must stop —

Nicholas [Schaffner, Perdita's second child] arrived at 3:09 night before last. The 2<u>nd</u> belongs more to me, I feel — dark + chunky, more as his mother was — V[alentine] was so ethereal + fair —

More later + thanks for M. — [comments on 'Madrigal'] + love to all

from
Dooley

1 H.D. was operated on for abdominal intestinal occlusions and remained in this clinic until March; she returned for further treatment in June 1953.

182

22 February [1953]
[Clinique Cécil
Lausanne]

Thank you for letter of 20th. I am so very sorry to hear of illness. How odd that we both collapse from 'fall of innards' + same symptoms, 'aches + depressions'. Mine, too, had been accumulating for years, but I kept myself going on the 3 novels, the <u>retour</u> of <u>Madrigal</u>, notes + general re-typing + arrangement of old papers. I did work very hard, too, but feel satisfied now.[1]

I can stay here or return to <u>Paix</u> in about two weeks — but must have along my really terrific Dragon of a <u>garde-malade</u> to change bandage or belt; the thing is to remain open until June, when with proper diet I am supposed to be strong enough for final re-setting of 'innards' and final sewing-up. So I, too, am going into 'Prinney's stays' soon, an advance from the swaddling-clothes state, they tell me. I suffer nothing but weakness + claustrophobia. All the best convalescence to you. Sorry about the bronchitis. Best to you all + love

from
Dooley./

1 On 20 February 1953 Aldington had written, 'I've been so dreary for so long that after three days in bed on milk and viandox (for about the 6th time!) I had a diagnosis specialist. Chronic bronchitis in right lung (which I suspected) and, strange to relate, a slight fall of the innards which has caused all these tummy-aches and depressions, aggravated by overwork over a number of years. No operation, but I have to wear a sort of belt — like Prinney's stays!'

H.D. returned to her room at the Hôtel de la Paix for the winter and spring of 1953; in April, she travelled to New York to visit her daughter; in June, she re-entered the Clinique Cécil, then moved during an extended period of recovery to the Klinik Brunner in Küsnacht five miles outside of Zürich. Aldington remained in his pension in Montpellier. From this point on, ill health and social isolation play an increasing role in the correspondence. H.D.'s letters are generally shorter in length, but both correspondents now write more frequently, sometimes even daily, and their relationship is best illustrated by selected clusters of letters about particular or representative subjects, as the following exchange at the end of the year should suggest.

≫ 183 ≪

24 November [1953]
[Klinik Brunner
Küsnacht]

Dear Richard,

Thank you for letter and most interesting and helpful rhyme.[1] I am now going to cadge some more information. I have no reference books at all – HOW many plays did Shakespeare write, generally in groups, comedies, historical, tragedy. I know the sequence ... of course, roughly. The worst has happened. I suggested <u>Midsummer</u> for the reading sessions; Dr. H. got copies, then said he could not possibly conduct this Sh. [Shakespearian] English, and I was roped in. It is great fun, a bit over-stimulating; a Mr Bernosconi, mad to read and reads not very well, got Oberon's part for a time and I was wild to switch it on to someone else, or do it myself, but he flung himself into it with such gusto. A pretty little Belgian did Hermia very nicely, an old Lady, half-German, did Lysander but she wanted to do a romantic woman, so I switched her on to Helena – this had to be shared with the rather prim Zürich manageress; the other Belgian got coy but finally condescended to Quince. I got the little English occupational-therapy (basket-weaving etc.) girl to do Puck. Do [Doctor] H was very good as Theseus and Bottom. Now they are going too fast and I am supposed with Miss Holder, my accomplice Puck, to put on the brakes and 'talk' to them about the play in general. This is so funny. I have never laughed so much and they seem to love it.

The message from E [Ezra]; M Barnard is a girl or woman who got in touch with E., through Viola Jordan, I think. NO NEED TO WRITE HER or about her. I suppose the 'translations' are the ones I did not do on Callimachus. I sent E for his birthday a postcard of the temple at Sunium. I suppose the photograph is for me, but it only makes me sad. I don't know. I gave address as Villa Kenwin, as I do not know where I am going or when to Lugano.[2] Also, I am so happy here and staying <u>NOT because I am not well</u>, but because I have this pleasant room and books and time, and time, and time to read – the Anthology (yours) is really being appreciated; papers and new books come from Bryher.

I have such fun in Zürich, did see <u>Crin Blanche</u>, a lovely film, I thought. I will write again. Do hope the cold and tiredness is better. We are foggy and raw here. Br returned from her N.Y. trip, but held up by fog, and had to land Geneva, instead of Zürich, as I had hoped. But she is coming over one day soon again.

I wish you could conduct my 'class'!

Love
Dooley./

1 H.D. has joined a reading group at the clinic and characteristically is turning to Aldington as a source of historical and technical information. On 7 November 1953 she told him of her literary discussions with the resident psychiatrist Erich Heydt, a sensitive young man whom she looked to as both a friend and a doctor for intellectual and social stimulation as well as psychological affirmation. She wrote Aldington that Heydt 'holds an evening once a week – so far I have dodged it, but he wants me to supervise the Shakespeare reading. And how had they best begin?' She added that Heydt 'plagues me with erudite questions of rhythm and so on. I find I don't know the NAMES of anything. Iambics yes – can you list me roughly the lot with metres …'. Aldington responded on 10 November with a page-long treatise on poetics and concluded by copying out with his own scansion marks Coleridge's poem 'Metrical Feet'.

2 On 10 November 1953 Aldington wrote H.D.,

> I have a mysterious message from E. which for once does baffle me. I promised him to send (and have sent) one or two snapshots of St Blaise, supposed to be a Greek site near Martigues. In return E. sends me a snap of the Parthenon and two other Greek ruins sent to him by 'M.B.' Then in E.'s letter I find this:
>
> 'main porpoise of these presents is that Mr Barnard iz larning to use her koDAK, and H.D. said she Wuz moving to frogland, but address on bak of Gk/ foto is NOT clear/
> so
> cause enc/ to cirCulate as they belong in her dept.'

> Who is M. Barnard? I suppose you know. I suppose that the 'she' moving to France is M.B. and not yourself (to whom it grammatically refers) but am I supposed to send the 'fotos' to you or to M.B.? And what does he mean by asking me to read 'her' translations? If yours, most happy, If M.B.'s then can an over-worked man who begins to feel very old be spared?

❧ 184 ❦

11 November 1953
Les Rosiers
Ancien Chemin de Castelnau
Montpellier

Dear Dooley,

Strange to relate there is no agreement on the Shakespeare canon, and the one I send is from Everyman, and therefore embodies nothing more startling than the opinion of our old friend Ernest Rhys. What the pundits and the public cannot understand is that Shakespeare was a journalist, a hack, a re-write man for a set of actors, an up-start much scorned by the University wits (Greene, Peele, Marlow) and the genteel highbrows – Philip Sydney, Gabriel Harvey, Lady Pembroke. There was a Hamlet and a Lear before Shakespeare's. About 90% of the 'learned' and 'philosophical' trash about Hamlet (particularly the Germans') disappears in smoke when you realise that the reason Hamlet couldn't kill the king in the original was because of the royal bodyguard; for reasons of economy the stage manager suppressed the guard, and Shakespeare had to find more or less plausible reasons for prolonging the agony through five acts. It was all done for money, and as soon as he had saved enough Shakespeare dropped the whole thing and pushed off to Stratford. One of the few things we really know about him was that he was prosecuted for non-payment of taxes. Once you get the highbrow nonsense about

367

Shakespeare out of your mind, there is simply no end to the enjoyment and admiration. He was the greatest journalist who ever lived, far greater than Dickens and Scott and Victor Hugo and Edgar Wallace. Apart from his marvellous sonnets and rather piffling Lucrece and Venus, he never wrote a line except for money. This is the way it ran: Shakespeare solus, drinking tobacco. Enter an irate Actor.

Actor: Hi, Bill!

Sh: Nah whatser matter?

Actor: Well, ye know when Lidy Macbeth – my missus – croaks off stige, all I gotta sy is: 'She shoulda died 'ereafter, There woulda bin a toime fer sich a word.'

Sh: Well, swop me bob, what's wrong with that?

Actor: It ain't enough.

Sh: Whaddyer mean 'it ain't enough'?

Actor: Well, I tell yer, Bill. There's a lidy taken a bit of a fancy ter me, and I'd like to 'ave a nice bit there to 'ave 'em all lookin' at me, yer know. Write me in suthin'.

Sh: Nerts.

Actor: Nah, down't be so bad-tempered, Bill. Tell yer what – I'll give yer five bob on the nile, stright I will, if yer'll write me in something to please that lidy.

Sh: Or' right. Gimme the dibs. (Writes) Ah abaht it?

Actor: (Reads) Tomorrow and tomorrow and tomorrow Creeps in this petty pace from day to day &c. Well, it could be better, but I s'pose it'll 'ev ter do. So long, Bill.

Thank you much (as Catha used to say) for clearing up the mystery about Ezra's female translator. One thing I cannot endure is E's passion for pushing on to me his friends and admirers. I have begged him not to, but he goes on. The last time I protested, he said I was just like Eliot and [Wyndham] Lewis, utterly unfriendly! I daresay you have the same trouble. Lately I had a letter from an ex-B.B.C. pansy who was motoring to Pakistan (in imitation of Geoff Dutton and his wife – you'll have seen his A Long Way South)[1] with a Moslem General, and asked me 'to write a message' of goodwill to the Pakistaners. As my opinion is that they are a pack of bastards and I hope the Afghans cut their throats, I said nothing, and once more am written down 'unfriendly'. The BBC man was actually put on to me by Ezra!!!

I have just sold (or rather the good Kershaw has) the French rights of my Lawrence of Arabia for half a million francs.[2] We tried for a million but couldn't quite bluff them. However, they agreed to serialise in the provincial press, including the Midi Libre, so Catha will at last feel Pop is somebody she doesn't have to go down side streets to avoid when she is out with her friends. We are now trying to swindle what Ez would call the 'dagos' and the 'Huns'.

Talking about Shakespeare … You know that when George V. changed his name from Saxe-Cobourg-Gotha to Windsor some wit at the Foreign Office pretended that the Kaiser had ordered a command performance of a Shakespeare play. 'Which one, your Majesty?' 'Oh, the Merry Wives of Saxe-Cobourg-Gotha.'

A young man from England who was down here last summer looked over some of my unpublished trash, and picked out a light-hearted lecture I gave at Columbia in 1939 making fun of Ezra and Eliot and showing up the two of them as charlatans. He keeps begging to publish it, promises beautiful type and paper, etc. not to mention money for Catha's ski-ing expenses. Ought I to accept?[3] It is really rather wicked. I have sent the whole thing to Kershaw for him to decide – as I have all the world my enemy, it doesn't really matter. Quite coldly and abstractly, the little piece is much wittier and more readable than anything Tom or Ezra ever wrote – but who but I will recognise that important fact?

I am old and tired, very tired, but I think the stuff I have in the press at this moment (if we include the Ez-Tom lecture) will suffice to infuriate practically everyone from Winston Churchill to Mrs Grundy.[4]

Much love,
Richard

1 Geoffrey Dutton (1922–2002), an Australian writer and Kershaw's friend, whose account of his journey from Europe to Australia appeared in 1953.
2 This translation, *Lawrence L'Imposteur*, appeared in 1954, three months before *Lawrence of Arabia: a Biographical Inquiry* (London: Collins, 1955).
3 The 'young man' was George Sims, a rare book dealer and owner of the Peacocks Press, which published *Ezra Pound and T.S. Eliot* in 1954. I am grateful to Norman T. Gates for this identification.
4 By 1953 Aldington had an unfounded reputation as a peevish and resentful old man. He sometimes enjoyed this public impression, but came to regret it bitterly when the uproar he anticipates here erupted in response to the appearance of his *Lawrence of Arabia* in England. This reputation finally resulted in financial disaster.

⁂ 185 ⁂

28 November 1953
[Klinik Brunner
Küsnacht]

Dear Richard,

I must thank you for the list of plays. I ask you, by way of a royal command, to write a book of essays on 'Bill', just as you wrote me. I agree with you. It is such FUN. I have never had such a revelation as this 'class' of mine, wild horses can't hold them, when they get going. Now, tell me. I know this but want to explain. Blank verse? Was it lifted straight from Virgil? Did Homer have roughly the same line? Arma virumque cano is as far as I can get. Will you give me one Latin tag with metre indicated, then tag of Marlowe or 'Bill'.

This Erich Heydt is a German, mirabile dictu, somewhat of a mystery. He is only 33, a very old head on young shoulders. I cannot help wondering of his past there, we never speak of this. There was a rumour he was half-Jew, but as he went to the top universities, I can't quite see it. He is an accomplished musician and had me over to his room to Mozart sonatas, played with a visiting friend, an American doctor violinist, in the American forces there [in Germany]. I mention the German, as I have never been put through such a quiz test, and desperately try to link up, where I can, the German poetry with 'Bill'. Of course, except for Luther's bible, there doesn't seem much to go on, till Goethe's Faust, and what about Marlowe, some centuries earlier? I managed, however, with Oberon, supposed to be original Erlkönig, then on to France, Auberon, in a romance, Huon de Bordeaux. Spenser then, in Faerie Queen. Now Tamburlaine? Just two lines on historical original. (I am about to change ribbon and want to get this written first, in case of snarls; also, will be glad to hear; my session is Friday and your last letter came just in time.) I am glad to hear of demands or/and commands as to books, and would love to see the Ez/Eliot.

Hope Catha enjoys her winter sports – how like Perdita with whom there was constant procession of such accomplishments. But of course Br saw to it. This is just a line to thank you. Do you think my 'class' should tackle <u>Julius Caesar</u> next? The film will be here, I presume, fairly soon and I hear from London that it is very good.[1] I am sorry you are old, I am six years older. I think one gets a re-birth somewhere along the line, about now. I was deep in my philosophical 'novels' those years, after my first stay here, was just 60 that September [1946]. Now, I am resting on my (sic.) laurels and catching up to the past.

Love from
Dooley./

1 Joseph L. Mankiewicz's <u>Julius Caesar</u> (1953) starred John Gielgud, Marlon Brando, James Mason, Deborah Kerr and Greer Garson.

❧ 186 ❧

1 December 1953
Les Rosiers
[Ancien Chemin de Castelnau
Montpellier]

Dear Dooley,

Though blank verse derives from the classical Renaissance it has nothing in common with the Hexametre of Homer and Virgil. It is a rhymeless Iambic metre, if we are justified in using 'iambic' of English verse. It originated with the Italians, and the earliest example known is the tragedy, Sofonisba, of Giangiorgio Trissino (1487–1550) which appeared in 1515, and starts the many wearisome imitations of Seneca. The 'blank verse' is an imitation of the tragic iambic pentametre of Seneca, itself derived of course from the Attic tragedians, especially Euripides. But Dante had so firmly fixed the hendecasyllable on the language that the Italian 'pentametre' was always 'catalectic' i.e. had an extra syllable. This is the metre as handled by Trissino:

> 'Le grazie e le virtù, che 'l ciel v'ha date,
> Non sono mai per usciri de la mente,
> Mentre che viverem sopra la terra;
> Ond' ornerem la vostra sepoltura
> De la lagrime nostre e dei capelli ...'

It was then taken up by Giovanni Rucellai (1475–1525) and applied to non-dramatic poetry, which he described as '... verso Etrusco dalle rime sciolto'. (By 'Etrusco' of course he means Tuscan, Italian). Hence 'versi sciolti' which the English rendered 'blank verse'. His poem on bees is an imitation (in theme) of Virgil's Georgics (Bk 4). Rucellai starts off:

> 'Mentr'era per cantare i vostri doni
> Con altre rime, or verginette caste, (i.e. bees!)
> Vaghe angelette de le erbose rive,
> Preso dal sonno, in su 'l punta de l'alba ...'

It chiefly went into dramatic poetry in Italy, and Tasso's Aminta and Guarini's Pastor Fido (beautiful pastorals you should read) have all dialogue in versi sciolti with choruses and soliloquies in the almost vers libre which Milton took over in Samson Agonistes.

The first example of blank verse in English is Surrey's translation of Virgil – or

370

rather two books of Aeneid – from which there's a quote in my anthology. It is a pure accident that the form got associated with Virgil, for in 1564 (year of Shakespeare's birth) Annibale Caro (1507–1566) issued his beautiful translation of the Aeneid which is still widely read in Italy. The passage from Surrey's version of Bk IV in my anthology begins thus in Caro:

> '... Udito ch'ebbe
> Mercurio, ad eseguir tosto s'accinse
> I precette del Padre; e prima a' piedi
> I talari adattossi, Ali son queste
> Con penne d'oro, ond'ei l'aria trattando
> Sostenuto da' venti ovunque il corso
> Volga, o sopra la terra, o sopra 'l mare,
> Va per lo ciel rapidamente a volo.'

If you'll compare you'll see that beautiful as the Italian is, it is diffuse – the Italian needs 7 lines for what the English says in 4.

Blank verse appears first in English drama in Sackville and Norton's 'Gorboduc' (1562), in my humble opinion a dreary performance, which is why I give no example [in the anthology]. I see that in my copy I have feebly marked these lines:

> 'For cares of kings, that rule as you have rul'd,
> For public wealth, and not for private joy,
> Do waste man's life and hasten crooked age,
> With furrowed face, and with enfeebled limbs,
> To draw on creeping death a swifter pace.'

Pretty punk. On pages 136–7 of anthol, you'll find quotes from Peele's Arraignment of Paris (1584) – still in rhyme, though there is blank verse in the play – and from David and Bethsabe in the blank verse Marlowe had by 1599 given to the world. I always like:

> 'God, in the whizzing of a pleasant wind,
> Shall march upon the tops of mulberry-trees,
> To cool all breasts that burn with any griefs.'

Which to my mind is more like Plato's Eros walking delicately on hearts than that horribly old jealous Iavhe.

Turn now to pages 171–179 which give the Marlowe blank verse discoveries, which are the great ones. (Though Chapman's blank verse comes earlier in the book that is only because he was born a little earlier.) I don't know why the dates are omitted from Marlowe – I think I began with him, and had not then decided to fag after the dates. Tamburlaine was 1589, and you can hear them bragging about how they defeated the Spaniards!

After that comes Shakespeare, and you have a rough chronological list. Notice that in the earliest plays there is a lot of rhyme still. Shakespeare and Milton are the great masters of blank verse and indeed of all English verse harmonies. When Ezra and Eliot sneer at Milton they simply prove they are cockneys with no ear for beautiful English. There has never been such blank verse since. Wordsworth made a sad hash of it. You know Tennyson invented as a joke a perfect Wordsworthian line of blank verse:

'A Mr Wilkinson, a clergyman.'

As to German poetry, I think you are on fairly safe ground that it had very little originality until the time of Goethe. In Zürich there should be plenty of German stuff. Pre-Goethe I like best the Minnesingers (esp Walther Von der Vogelweide) and the Volkslieder. Of course they got their Faustus drama from Marlowe!

In old French (Frankish) legend, Oberon is a Merovingian magician. Then he got into the Nibelungenlied as a treasure-guard, then into Huon of Bordeaux and so on.

Julius Caesar [is] a bit tough for foreigners, isn't it? If you do it, make them read the life of Jules in North's Plutarch, where they can see how Shakespeare cribbed.

You must be firm with your German [Erich Heydt], and point out that miscellaneous facts about poetry (such as this letter contains) are of no importance, and in fact interfere with real aesthetic appreciation.

Much love,
Richard

⇛ 187 ⇚

19 June 1956
Les Rosiers
Montpellier

Dear Dooley,

I think a letter of mine got lost owing to your moves, for I wrote some time back, and was getting anxious at not hearing.

I am so glad to know that the German Avon [*By Avon River*] got a good reception. It is a constant annoyance and cause of fury to me that the English-speaking countries don't make much more public fuss of your really unique contribution to modern poetry. But the whole thing has become a matter of cliques – most of them sods – and there is no disinterested love of the art. Auden boosts Cocteau and Cocteau boosts Auden. The B.B.B. Brigade of British Buggers. Not that Cocteau is [British], but he ought to be … Could you send me translations of a few things from the reviews. I'd love to see them.

There is too much of his baby-production nowadays. These philoprogenitive females are swarming the world into starvation and every kind of overcrowded wretchedness. Every woman who has more than 3½ babies (the average necessary to maintain the population) should be publicly castrated. The half baby is rather a difficulty, but no doubt with the advance of science and statistics that can be dealt with. What is the good of Perdita producing more and more Americans? You must point out that there are far too many already.[1]

Your puritan ancestors seem speaking when you denounce the softening delights of Lugano. If you are able to live there, warum nicht? as Norman [Douglas] used to say. Now, if the Romans and the Carthaginians had both wintered in Capua and both got 'soft', think what a lot of lives and trouble and useless distress might have been spared. But the fun of Switzerland is that by judicious hopping from bough to bough one can get the impression of being in Germany, France and Italy, without the inconveniences of those countries. An ideal arrangement.

I got a little story from an Australian friend of mine [Denison Deasey] in a letter to-day. He is a very cultivated man (as the Aussies sometimes are) and a prof; and is building a shack in the 'bush'. He has a French wife who had made them a lapin sauté with mushrooms and tomato and garlic and wine. They offered this to the hired man who refused and produced a 'healthy' sandwich. My friend then offered him a glass of red wine. 'Nao thenks, Denison, oi never drink anythin' when I'm eatin'.' Those are the people who rule the world to-day. Bastards!

We are to affront the first of the Bac exams on Thursday morning. What happens after that I don't know. I suppose we ought to move, but where? It is all too complicated.[2]

Let me hear about Perdita as soon as you get news. Take care of yourself and don't get virtuous about enjoying life!

Much love,
Richard

1 H.D. had informed Aldington that Perdita was expecting her third child; Elizabeth Bryher Schaffner was born on 29 June 1956.
2 That is, Catherine, now almost eighteen, is about to take her final school (university entry) exams, and Aldington is wondering if they ought to move to a community with an appropriate institution at which she can complete her education, whose goals are still undefined.

⤳ 188 ⤳

22 January [1957]
[Klinik Hislanden
Zürich]

Dear Richard,

To continue this saga; I said, a young sister had broken her leg, but she is about 50 – broke lower leg in two places + is in bed for three months. On Xmas Day, an 84 year old old-fellow was brought in for broken leg – wonder at times at my own good luck, as I am in a chair now, for about two hours.[1] I said, this vibration did not concern the young – I have only heard of this calamity for the over-50 group – rap on wood – they are all right. I expect Catha knows more German already than I do! And is probably home now or soon.[2] I have a little Xmas-tree that Dr. Rudolf (Brunner) brought in – he, by [the] way, was a year in Cantonal Hospital for broken leg – why do I tell you this? It was years ago, but leg was re-broken twice – he, of course, has been most kind and helpful. I am getting the little tree un-picked [sic] tomorrow, agony, not to be able to do this + other things myself. I do hope your friends in Paris are getting on, I can not imagine – why all this.[3] I laugh so over your letters + your rage.[4] I don't know what I must do, but feel more + more the human comedy or what-not, the nearness + the smallness of our interests – the excitement that America brings in, to me, is enhanced 50 percent by the surroundings + reactions here. They have 'Guys + Dolls' + are taking it very seriously, as they did 'Porgy + Bess'.[5] I have seen neither, but love Luxembourg, Liechtenstein reactions (as well as Swiss), which I get now indirectly, for the most part, via Dr. Rudolf + Dr. Heydt, who is now in Rome. I am lop-sided, writing in bed, but no excuse – + I do hope you will laugh at this letter. Again a Happy New Year + love

from
Dooley./

1 In November 1956, H.D. fell and broke her hip; she was moved to this clinic where she remained until February 1957.
2 Catha had gone to Austria to ski over the Christmas holiday.
3 This catalogue of injuries is in part in response to Aldington's similar catalogue, which included the sad situation of the medievalist Gustave Cohen (1878–1958), who as a result of wounds suffered during World War I was confined to a wheelchair. On 22 December 1956, Aldington

had written H.D. that 'Léa Cohen, wife of my dear friend Gustave, has had precisely the same accident as yourself! She slipped on the waxed floor of her studio, fell and broke her left hip! … So there they both are in Paris and only able to communicate by telephone!'

4 For instance, Aldington had written on 5 December 1956, in response to the Suez crisis, 'The hero boys have really got us into a mess. Perhaps Sir Winston will at last realise that England can't afford the money for any more of his finest hours. We shall be lucky if we get out of this without some major economic-financial crash. I see they have already had to suspend service of the interest on the American and Canadian loans. And the assertion that they won't devalue naturally makes one think they will.' On 19 December 1956 Aldington asked H.D., 'Do you remember Nina Hamnett? She "fell" from an upper floor and died next day in hospital. Obviously suicide, though the hypocritical English papers pretend otherwise. She was a good soul, and I honour her memory – a whore, of course, but in every other respect a really honest woman for whom there was no place in the Welfare State.' In a postscript to this letter, Aldington added yet another example of the 'rage' which so amused H.D.: 'Suez? "Give me back my legions." In 1918 we (the bloody British infantry) could have swept the lot of them into oblivion. Personally I shall never shake hands again with an American.'

Aldington made real efforts to entertain H.D. On 18 January 1957 he wrote:

Did you see that Mrs Truman fell down, and broke a bone in her foot? And I had a nasty shock on Tuesday – a fool on a Vespa knocked down an elderly woman with an awful crack close to me as I walked on the pavement. Of course if I'd been Norman [Douglas] I should have been delighted, but as I am not a Grand Man I must confess with shame that I was upset for the rest of the day …

I really dread to open my mail or the newspapers in case of finding news of some further female accident! …

Now I learn that the mysterious marriage at 68 of Tom Eliot with his landlady's daughter (or rather his confidential secretary) is due to his 'having spells of wretched health, breakdowns and the like.' I'm sorry to hear that he's ill and marrying (presumably) to get a nurse, for I hoped this was a last flare-up and spree.

5 H.D. is probably referring to Joseph L. Mankiewicz's film *Guys and Dolls* (1955) and a local stage production of George Gershwin's *Porgy and Bess*, which was not filmed until Otto Preminger's version in 1959.

⤞ 189 ⤝

21 March 1957
Les Rosiers
Ancien Chemin de Castelnau
Montpellier

Dear Dooley,

As you speak so warmly of the Swiss flowers I send you under separate cover a book of Australian wild flowers which please keep if you like it. The Poinsettia of course is introduced, but all the rest are native, and very spectacular, don't you think? They make one think of Texas and the Rockies.

There may be some hitch about the private clinic for E. [Ezra Pound], but I understood it was simply lack of money. Now there may be a complication in the sense that E. proudly refused to leave St. Elizabeth's unless declared not guilty. But there are surely enough people in USA with means to put up the money for him to have peace and decent attention during his last years?

The story of me is more odd than interesting.[1] The Russians, as you probably know, pirated four of my novels pre-1939 as anti-bourgeois propaganda. The Russian readers evidently thought otherwise, as they have been very popular. I hear from the Moscow Writers Union that they are to be reprinted and perhaps others added. With this comes a promise of payment and an official invitation to Russia. (They pay roubles, and exploit you as a supposed enemy of 'capitalism'.) Well, I thought if they would pay my air-fare I might go and see what I could get from them. But I have chronic bronchitis, and any ordinary cold is liable to bring on acute bronchitis. I therefore went to see the MD here and ask if I could risk such a fatiguing journey and round. He gave me a full examination, and tests &c, and warned me that I am on the edge of a nervous collapse from overwork and worry. I am also too fat. (A plague of sighing and grief, it blows a man up like a bladder!) Not only I can't go to Russia, I must follow a strict régime and also a treatment of various drugs both for the nervous system and fatigued brain cells. No alcohol whatsoever. Six months rest. I can't afford six days, but the trouble is it takes me two days or more to do one day's stint. I suppose this was to be expected, as I have been journalising and hack-booking it for close on 50 years. I have to follow the MD's directions until 6th April when he will examine again. One of the drugs I am taking is American for 'depression due to over-work' and claims that it has 'immediate, progressive and durable' effects on the nervous system. I have most faithfully taken the better part of a small bottle of these comprimés, and don't find the slightest sign of improvement!

Curious that you should mention Brigit and her wistful letters.[2] These highly sensitive and delicate consciences! At the time of Netta's divorce damages for 5000 pounds were given against me, the usual vindictive English judge laying it on one of these damned writer fellows. Of course the Ps. [Patmores] knew I hadn't 5000 pounds, but they refused to make the decree absolute (so that C. would have been illegitimate) unless I signed an undertaking to pay B. 250 a year. She has now bled me of at least 4000 pounds. Owing to the terrific press attacks on me over the Lawrence book my sales in England have dropped and after 40 years the US won't take any more! (How they love a fraud.) Consequently I haven't been able to pay of late, and my latest 'wistful' contribution is a writ (served by the British consul at Marseille) to attach my English royalties! That came the day after I saw the MD. Please consider this as wholly confidential, and do not speak of it even to Bryher.

Brigit lives in London with the novelist Marguerite Steen. Of course she believes or affects to believe that I am living in luxury on the Riviera, instead of in a pension in Languedoc! And this is bolstered by the British press which will describe me as living in my villa at Montpellier! This latest bit of spite is all the more annoying since her solicitor has been told the situation, so it means I am a liar. It is all the more annoying (in view of the irreparable damage which newspaper reports of this would cause) since there is a move towards making some amends to me, particularly by the Times. (I enclose two cuttings which please return.)[3] My anthology has just been reprinted. I have a new study of Louis Stevenson in the press for Sept, and contracts (if only I can fill them) for two more biographies and a book of biographical studies.[4] Of course, if the Americans would come through all would be well, but the great Lowell Thomas and CBS have been offended.[5]

This is a lugubrious letter, but it can't be helped. I rejoice indeed to hear of you making excursions to an 'Ermitage' on the lake. It makes me (the Ermitage does) think of Jean Jacques [Rousseau]. I suppose he was there?

Love from us both,
Richard

against that. It is a great, great consolation to me to think that you too will fight for the poetry which is accessible to the many without in any way lowering standards and ideals.[2]

I can't afford to send you a copy (it costs 400 French francs) but perhaps your doctor friends could borrow you a copy of the French 'Problèmes' for Mars-Avril 1957, which deals with Les Enfants Abandonnés. I have in it my first article written in French! Mainly on Savage and Dickens, but when I mentioned d'Alembert and Rousseau I didn't know others were to treat them. Try to get it – a most interesting number, though I think excessive as medical people always are.

Gustave is ill again – signs of diabetes. Léa is better and allowed to fly to Nice on the 15th May. I have warned Gustave about the need to make sure her fracture has healed, for she is much heavier than you. The doc says I shall get over this – the injections of vit B.12 are the great help. A woman from Unesco came down here, has had exactly the same illness and treatment; we both think it due to exploding atom bombs!

Love from both,
Richard

1 The spring of 1957 was a difficult period for Aldington. Not only was he in ill health, financially pressed and concerned about his daughter's future, he had discovered, as he wrote to H.D. on 22 December 1956, that 'this estate has been sold to build a large block of workmen's flats. ... Where we shall go I know not, but I think Catha must end her lycée in 1958 whether she passes her Bac or not. I wish I knew what to do.' On 6 January 1957 he reiterated: 'The menace of having to leave here is very disturbing, for places are very hard to find and the absence of gas [for the car] makes it impossible to look.' In fact, Aldington stayed on in Montpellier until July 1957.

2 On 27 April 1957 H.D. had written to Aldington, 'I am really out of myself, scribbling a sort of "popular" love sequence. ... I am sure Pearson would be shocked...'. In fact, this sequence probably became the poems collected in *Hermetic Definition* (New York: New Directions, 1972). Although these poems contain informal language and snippets of colloquial conversation, they are certainly not 'popular' in the ways Aldington hopes for here.

⤞ 191 ⤝

3 May 1957
Les Rosiers
Montpellier

Dear Dooley,

I have written to Rob Lyle – one of Roy's closest men friends – but have not heard. I can't yet brace myself to write to his daughters. I will, I will. I'll even dare to ask them to think of me – if they can – as a little bit of their father, loving them as he did. Perhaps that is cheek. Mary is evidently recovering.

I know that road from south Portugal to Lisbon via Setubal. Have driven it several times. In the 1930s it was a mere dirt track through various soils, and in wet weather one arrived at Setubal (the inn was kept by a Nazi spy!) with the car so splashed with coloured muds that it looked like the palette of a painter of the anti-beauty school. Mary was quite incapable of driving safely on such a road.

Later, if you wish, I'll send you his last letter – in deepest confidence because he speaks of an affair of his daughter which upset us both.

Enclosed Roy's review of my Mistral, an attack on Roy, and my defence. I loved him – 40,000 Ophelias!!

Yes, I have written Gustave to warn him about Léa. I am sure she is older than you, and not nearly so light. She is flying to the south on the 15th. Gustave goes by car on the 10th, to be there to meet her. It is a curious ménage. Both had children by defunct spouses, and she (Léa) married him to look after him because she admires his talent and superb courage so much. And now she is a cripple too! Did I tell you that Gustave in his chair was present at the prise d'armes at the Invalides when General Koenig gave him the accolade and his insignia as Grand Officier? Why grown men value these toys is a mystery.

I am very pleased you liked the Poussin. I send you with this rather a naughty one of a different kind, which I expect you know. It is said to be Diane de Poitiers in a bath with one of her girl friends. The King unexpectedly came in, saw the scene, was enchanted by it, and insisted that it be immortalised in paint. It was hidden for centuries, and turned up somewhere in the store-rooms of the Louvre. The one on the left is Diane. You will notice that the background is imitated from Titian's Duchess of Urbino.[1]

Excuse brief letter. Very tired and ill, though I hope recovering.

Love from Catha and
Richard

1 Aldington regularly sent H.D. postcards of works of art, some of them erotic, particularly when he felt too ill to write at length or when he felt they might amuse her, as in the case of the 'naughty one' he describes here. H.D. enjoyed these pictures: on 1 May 1957 she wrote to him about the Poussin. 'I love photograph'; on 13 May 1957 she thanked him for 'the delightful cards. I am glad to feel that you were having a little binge (your old word) + gather that you must feel better. I am writing more about the cards –'. On 19 May 1957 she continued: 'Thank you for the interesting cards – all you have sent are stimulating and exciting.' Although H.D. was not willing to comment very specifically or to shift the level of discourse to a more personal or erotic level, she did respond in kind. On 15 May 1957 Aldington wrote, 'Your Hindu girl-lovers are most beautiful and charming. Exquisite. If I am ever in Paris again I'll try to see them at the Guimet. How very charming.' He enclosed two postcards of pictures by Toulouse-Lautrec and Moreau, then continued: 'I am adding (for you alone, but keep her) a Breton girl sent me by a woman I know in Paris, who has lately abandoned her husband and turned to her own sex. I cannot make out whether the Bretonne is really her amie or whether she represents the type my friend is seeking. The Bretonne seems to me infinitely attractive, but I would much like to know exactly what is your expert judgment.' H.D. commented on the Bretonne on 19 May 1957, in psychological terms, protecting herself personally in a 'scientific' discourse: 'I would know more about the effect she has had on your friend if I had some idea of her. The girl may be a substitute for her mother in youth, or some school-friend ...'. This sort of response was probably not what Aldington had hoped to receive, although he answered on 21 May 1957, 'What you say about the Bretonne is most wise and illuminating to me.'

⤞ 192 ⤝

9 May 1957
Les Rosiers
Montpellier

Dear Dooley,

I return the H. [Horace] Gregory letter. Most interesting, and (I think) almost entirely the truth. You may remember that when I suggested E. might be released, I was careful to stress the 'IF' his 'wealthy American friends' would provide for him. Obviously they have no such intention (I think it would cost 6000–7000 dollars a year) and he has to remain a pensioner of Uncle Sam – the strangest way of providing for a poet yet thought up. But I do think Mr. Gregory's letter calls the bluff of Banabhard and all the other 'Leftist' or 'Rightest' persons trying to cash in on the situation. I know that you and I will say, write, or do anything which we feel SURE would be for Ezra's benefit and that he wanted it; meanwhile 'silence is most noble to the end'.[1] Banabhard's letter riz my dander – she obviously has never thought of what that long captivity has meant in suffering and frustration. But more than ever I feel you and I must do nothing without full assurance from E.'s American friends that it is the right time. I don't believe Tom Eliot has thrown E. over, even after those H-Tribune articles.

As to the 'Institute of Arts and Letters', will you tell Bryher and Gregory that I think it a racket and refused to belong when invited? I think they are American phonies operating from Suisse but mailing from Germany because the postage is less. I refuse to touch them.

I am delighted you liked the card. I hope the 'story' might be true, but fear not. Speriamo! I send two Poussins which I'm sure we've seen together, for you always had that wonderful gift of making one see a picture or statue as no-one else could. I think you always liked Poussin, and I am more and more delighted with him. I send you another girl, an alleged 'Naïade' of the dix-huitième, but, subject to your correction, I think her arms and legs too thick, her belly button too big, and her breasts too little! Excuse my brutal frankness, but I wonder much if you agree or if you rally round. I must try to find you some more to amuse a minute or two of your enforced leisure.

On Saturday (11th) Catha and I drive to Chateauneuf du Pape to lunch with Gustave at La Mère Germaine – and how much I wish you could be there to savour the good things and look across the great stretch of country to Avignon as we drink the Clos des Papes! I shall take care to warn Gustave once again about the danger of Léa's moving so soon. Your bone structure is doubtless more fragile, but she is at least three stone heavier than you; and I worry very much about this air flight. I shall try to get Gustave to describe the prise d'armes at the Invalides when he received his cordon de grand officier from General Koenig. Curious how the French hold by such toys. I only wish you could send better news of your poor leg, and that you are running about the Alpine slopes gathering gentians![2]

Love from us both,
Richard

1 Swinburne writes in 'Atalanta in Calydon', Chorus, Stanza I, 'For words divide and rend; / Silence is most noble to the end.'
2 H.D. sent Aldington regular reports of her slow progress. On 18 April 1957, for example, she wrote, '... I am trying sort of mental + psychic gymnastics + planning (a cosmic task) to get hold of my shoes + hobble to a chair, as I am told I can do – can't wear bed-room slippers, as one can't hop in them – + where are my shoes – + I must have a coat – + how to get at it – a fury of minor frustrations!'

193

13 May 1957
Les Rosiers
Montpellier

Dear Dooley,

I have at last heard from Rob Lyle about the Campbell tragedy.

It was a front tire blow-out which, as you are not a car driver, you may not know is virtually uncontrollable if the car is going at any speed. (You will see in to-day's paper the smash of Portago and Nelson in the Mille Mighlie – due to the same thing.) The result of the blow-out is to turn the car violently to one side or even capsize it. They smashed into a tree, and were both picked up unconscious from the wreckage. Roy died before reaching hospital – fractured skull and internal injuries. Mary has a broken rib, two cracked ribs, dislocated foot, cuts and bruises. She has made an astonishing recovery and is already back with the girls at Linho.

As I guessed, Rob Lyle was phoned for from Lisbon. His first pleasant job was to break the news to Anna who had gone to London for a holiday! Owing to pressure on the air lines (this was on April the 24th) they had the additional torment of having to fly first to Brussels, then change to a plane for Madrid, and then change again for the Lisbon plane!

Rob was able to see Roy's body. His face was almost uninjured – which for some reason comforts me a little, for though I've seen so many soldiers with bashed heads and faces I didn't want it to happen to Roy, great soldier that he was. Rob says he looked peaceful and still and 'infinitely noble'. His daughters and Rob buried him in the little cemetery of San Pedro in the Sintra hills, and his gravestone will carry the lines from the Canadian Boat Song which Roy loved and so often quoted:

'From the lone shieling of the misty island
Oceans divide us and a waste of seas,
But still the blood is strong, the heart is Highland,
And I in dreams behold the Hebrides.'

I don't expect you to feel as I feel. I loved and admired the man, a real hero, a real poet. I wish I could believe that the 'holy angels' of his Faith did really receive him, as the Catholic burial service proclaims. If they did they'll have to make some changes in Heaven!

I enclose a flower piece I hope you'll love as much as I do. And two cuttings, which return at leisure.

With my love,
Richard

20 May 1957
Les Rosiers
Montpellier

Dear Dooley,

Why can't those Swiss doctors make you well again? It makes me <u>miserable</u> to think of you laid up like that. Can't you get a specialist opinion from outside? I worry about you through sleepless hours. They <u>must</u> get you well.

Enclosed cards of girls to cheer you.

Much love, my dear,
Richard

P.S. Shall I get together some old soldiers and come and beat them up? Command us.

≈ **195** ≈

24 May 1957
Les Rosiers
Montpellier

Dear Dooley,

I am a little comforted by your letter, but I still think you are laid up too long, and that the MDs should really make an effort to help you, so that you can move about and enjoy the spring and the flowers. Here the nightingales are incessant, and I see a hoopoe from my window nearly every day. Alas, I have become suddenly so feeble that it is the greatest effort to walk the 1½ miles to the post office and back. But I am resting, working only a little each day, and hope.

Since you are still laid up I send letters and cuttings which may amuse a few minutes. The letter from Anna Campbell is touching, I think. I suppose all these masses for Roy are because of his sudden death. I don't pretend to understand Catholic theology, but his death was so sudden there was no time for confession, absolution and viaticum or even for 'an act of perfect contrition'. So dear old Roy might be innocently damned unless they make interest in Heaven on his behalf. Crudely, I wish the money went to those two grandchildren.

You will think me very imprudent to have gotten myself and Catha into a state of virtual destitution, but such is the case. I am short between four and five thousand pounds <u>promised</u> me on the TEL book and on the Stevenson book. The press attacks have killed me as an author pro tem. Mistral sold 625 copies, as against 10,000 to 30,000 of its predecessors. The Frauds book is refused by America, and Nude Erections (as Ezra amusingly calls them) have refused Mistral on the ground that 'he does not rate a whole book'. Imbeciles.

There are signs that this is breaking down, but unluckily just when I ought to be working I have this unfortunate illness. But I can work and I will work. Only I must have a little more rest. We are saved from despair by our Australian friends. Alister is buying a cottage in which we can live rent-free and I can rest (and do the cooking and gardening for him) and a wealthier friend in Australia [Geoffrey Dutton] is making a handsome loan. But it needs time to get the money through the 'restriction', and then Alister thinks the franc will be devalued in a month or two, which of course would be a great help. Anyway, any (even five!) dollars you could lend us would be most gratefully received, and I can reply by assignment on USA royalties – my Boccaccio and Alcestis still sell there.[1] The Russians and East Germans also promise to pay me, but you know how uncertain they are. The Italians (Mondadori) owe me royalties, but delay paying endlessly.

I hope you got the Rétif, Picasso and Matisse reproductions – which please keep. I had read about the Rétif in H. Ellis, but had not seen those illustrations. It is a most curious 'ideal' of feminine beauty, and I suppose it's my coarse nature which makes me think real women preferable. I thought the Picasso and Matisse the most cleverly suggestive drawings I had ever seen. Don't you think so?

381

Thank you very much for the charming lady wilderness with her antelope (is it?) and the lovely three and the lions (?) not much bigger than hares! But the lady is too thin and needs her friend rather than the prettiest antelope. How charming and in what perfect taste these Persian artists always are.

Yes, you <u>must</u> get back to your books and your writing of poems, escape from Herr Wolfensberger and sun lamps. I didn't known ladies had male masseurs (they wouldn't let me have a woman at Feldkirch!) but I am sure it is more efficacious.

On Sunday we have a hunting Mass in the Cathedral, with an hallalli of silver horns from the huntsmen of the Duchesse d'Uzès. If I can drag myself there, I'll go and put up a candle for you to St. Martha who slew the Tarasque.

With love,
Richard

1 Aldington's translations of Euripides' *Alcestis* and Boccaccio's *Decameron* were both published in 1930.

❧ 196 ❧

27 May 1957
Les Rosiers
Ancien Chemin de Castelnau
Montpellier

Dear Dooley,

I know not how to thank you for the cheque, which at this moment is a god-send.[1] An Australian is sending me 750 pounds sterling, but the immense difficulty is to circumvent these 'controls'! Blast them. It may be months before I can get the money smuggled through.

If you can, get the N. Statesman for April 13th, and read the series of articles and interviews on publishing. It will show you how the socialist revolution, the inflation &c, make it impossible for an author like me to earn an adequate income. The change happened only last year, but it is decisive. There is nothing to be done about it.

Later I will try to expand all this and answer any questions.

Thank you also for the lovely flowers. They are such a refeshment. I am very happy that you liked R. [Rétif] de la B. and the Picasso and Matisse reproductions. I found them very exciting, and felt almost sure you would. I will look for others for you, but doubt there are more as good. I think they have the perfect balance of sex and art, like the Greek and Graeco-Roman things. Do you remember that in Naples [in 1913] they would only let me into the Gabinetto Segreto? These prohibitions are too damned silly. You would have understood and been inspired far more than I.

I wish I could 'keep well' but I can't.

This is just to acknowledge and send most grateful thanks for the cheque. I'll write again.

Love,
Richard

1 Aldington was not able immediately to cash H.D.'s cheque, however, for her impulse to help him was more sympathetic than pragmatic; Aldington returned her cheque later the same day explaining that she would need to write another for she had dated her cheque 'March' instead of 'May' and had signed her name in pencil rather than in ink.

8 June 1957
Les Rosiers
Montpellier

Dear Dooley,

In my humble opinion those Swiss doctors have taken you for a ride. Certainly you are delicately and sensitively formed – who should know it better than I? – but you have the strength and health of a good stock and a good family. I think they're exploiting you. Ask for a French specialist. Obviously, I have never seen Léa naked, but she is much heavier and clumsier than you & aged 70, and I hear from Gustave that she is now 'much better and able to take her meals again with us'. Why can't you be well again? Don't let them exploit and rob you. Ask Bryher to get a French specialist.[1]

I had such a strange dream. I was with Alister and vague unidentifiable female in one of those New York (N.Y.) apartment houses where there is a restaurant. I was talking to Alister, and suddenly on the floor there was 'manifested' the body of a man. He lifted his head, and we gasped: 'Roy!' He was wearing a red (!) shirt and khaki trousers with a leather belt, got up, and shook hands with his usual warmth. His hand was <u>deformed</u>, but I didn't mind, because it was his. I said: 'How did you get here, Roy?' He said: 'Flew in last night from Lisbon, man.' Then it became a frustration dream – we lost him – wandered eternally – and at last found him – characteristically! – at table enjoying his lunch. We joined him, talked, I forget all, and then I thought that I must buy him the best bottle of port in the place. (Imagine getting vintage port in America!) Well, I couldn't get the waiter, and it again became a frustration dream. I had to stand at a desk and look through an immense wine list, and I couldn't turn the pages. Meanwhile, a couple of riotous Teddy boys [young hoodlums] kept bumping against me until I told them (imitating the old Roy!) that I'd knock their silly blocks off if they didn't clear out. And still I couldn't turn the pages, and the waiter (or whoever) sneered: 'You're looking at the gins, now!' I was so angry I woke up in a sweat and a rage with a temperature. Perhaps Roy wanted to tell me something, and I was too stupid to understand? Tell me what you think.

Documents enclosed in case you may be interested. I'll send any pictures I can find. But I am so feeble, the walk into town leaves me exhausted when I get there – but I will look over the cards.

Much love and all grateful thanks,

Richard

P.S. I find I have the Sonnetti Lussuriosi of Aretino – they are fearfully sexual!!! Shall I translate them for you? Or would they repug you?

1 H.D. was slowly recovering. On 8 June 1957 she wrote Aldington, 'I feel much relief that I can walk a little, but I must go slowly, with sticks.' She added that Bryher and Dr Heydt were so pleased with her most recent X-ray that they took her to an inn for a meal. H.D. was thrilled to be outside once more: 'I was a little hysterical with joy, <u>really</u> wanted to get out of the car + eat the very, very green grass.'

12 June [1957]
[Klinik Brunner
Küsnacht]

Dear Richard,

You can translate the dream on several layers. To me the creative layer appeals most. You are looking for Roy, he is (dream) cow-boy or bohemian, artist. You can translate his image as a dramatic exteriorisation or as a subjective identification. He was killed, his hand (his pen) was useless. You feel your work (excellent as it is) 'repugs' you. You have spoken of yourself, at times, as a journalist. You know this is not true. There is the classic 'transference' to consider. Without bothering with h [homo] -sexual matters, there is only one woman + she is a shadow – of you? of Roy? Or/and you get tough with 'Teddy boys'. Are they determinatives of Alister + Roy. That is, you who feel so ill +, at times, helpless, are bossing them about. <u>You</u> are the stronger. I don't know the expression, Teddy boys, so this may mean something else. There are all the text-book layers, people you may have liked or hated at school, your father or some father-image. You would get <u>vintage port</u> – inspiraition, creation, again red. I could write a book on this, but I think you should – Roy, not too historically presented, the poet, an objective yet subjective self.[1]

This is most superficial. But I want to get it off at once.

Love
Dooley./

1 Aldington responded to H.D.'s interpretation on 15 June 1957: 'Your commentary on the "dream" is most fascinating and ingenious! Most likely all true, but to me it (the dream) is just grief.' He amplified on 16 June 1957 ('I have brooded long over your wonderful interpretation …'), but he declined H.D.'s suggestion that he write at length on Campbell, feeling that he did not want to appear to be 'cashing in' on his friend's death (as Aldington was accused of doing in D.H. Lawrence's case) nor to tangle with Campbell's family.

199

18 June 1957
Les Rosiers
[Montpellier]

Dear Dooley,

Amid infinite distractions and worries I have at last managed to find time to read (or rather re-read, for I knew nearly all of them) your selected poems.[1] Of course I would rather have your Opera omnia, but in these miserable days we must be thankful to get anything, and I think the selection is a very good one. I have of course to guard myself against favouritism towards the earlier poems with which I am so intimately connected, but standing back and trying to be purely objective I think there is no falling off in the later poems, but on the contrary an opening out of taste and feeling, and a 'wider horizon'. You are much more sure of yourself and your art, and so less 'taut' without losing any of the wonderful acuity and compression of the first poems. I am understating when I say that there are at least a dozen of the first order, and that not one of them falls below a very high standard. One's difference of appreciation is simply a matter of personal limitation and power of response. Making all homage to Tom Eliot and Ezra, I think that their work doesn't come up to this. They are too full of quotations, too much slaves of the city and the library. Eliot is a pedant and a plagiarist, and so is Ezra, compared with this entirely pure and lovely work of yours. In this century I have put everything on three poets – DHL, Roy and you. After a tremendous battle I've been proved right about DHL and Roy, and I am right about you.

I was interested to see in the blurb that the writer stresses the importance of your experiences on the N. [New] England sea coast. Now, that was a point I made in my Columbia Extension lecture on you and DHL in 1939. I said I thought that though the Greek influence is clear and the quality of the poems attains something Hellenic, the essence of the poetry is American and above all New England. I should have suspected this, but felt it very strongly because by then I had spent two summers on that fierce New England coast. There are two 'American' schools, in my opinion. The 'urban' to which Ezra and Eliot belong, and the 'out-door' which includes Whitman, Thoreau, Melville and yourself. I can never get up any enthusiasm for those millions of little poems of Emily Dickinson, and besides they are neither urban nor out-of-doors, but village – sort of American Cranford if you see what I mean.[2] I found Eliot was interested in the wild birds in Berkshire, but in a rather academic way. He never felt the ecstasy of life as you and DHL do.

Still struggling with wretched affairs here, and unable to get away as I hoped, so please forgive these disjointed and quite inadequate words.[3] What I want to do is repeat that I am sure those poems will remain as long as the language survives and there is any response to poetry. The purity of the English is wonderful. Amazing that it is not more recognised!

Love,
Richard

1 H.D.'s *Selected Poems of H.D.*, New York: Grove Press, 1957.
2 That is, like Elizabeth Gaskell's *Cranford* (1853). It is worth noting here that Aldington is reacting to various bowdlerized versions of Dickinson's work; he is unaware of Thomas H. Johnson's three-volume edition of Dickinson's poems, the first publication of the poems in their original form, which only appeared in 1955 and which transformed readers' impressions of this American poet.
3 Aldington is trying to tidy up his financial affairs (he owes his landlady for months of back rent, for instance), to pack up his books, to bring to closure a variety of writing projects, to gain some control of his physical and mental health, and to prepare generally to leave for Kershaw's cottage near Sancerre. Aldington is suffering, apparently, from a possible heart condition and emotional depression related to his physical health but also, psychologically, to his real financial and work-related distress; his handwritten signature on the letters written in July 1957 is often a bare and wiggly scratching.

At the end of July Aldington finally moved into the small cottage near Sancerre about a hundred miles south of Paris. His last days in Montpellier were hectic and embarrassing, and he was only finally able to leave because of generous cheques from both H.D. and Bryher, whom H.D. had petitioned on Aldington's behalf.

Bryher had occasionally written to him about H.D.'s situation: in 1953 they had exchanged a few letters about H.D.'s abdominal operation and the possible publication of 'Madrigal'; in June 1957 Bryher had written him of the slow healing of H.D.'s fracture. On 16 June 1957 Aldington responded in a letter which begins 'Dear Mrs Bryher' and concludes with 'Yours sincerely' and a spidery signature, 'Richard Aldington'. By 8 July 1957, however, although Aldington maintained his dignified formality, he responded gratefully and in detail to Bryher's 'assurance of aid': 'I have only one debt in France … and that is our pension here, which fell into arrears simply because I did not receive the money I had been promised [from publishers], and because the boycott has cut my sales in England badly and in USA completely. It covers 10 months and runs to 800,000 French francs.' After explaining the difficulty he was having getting money into the country from his Australian friend Geoffrey Dutton, he indicated that even Gustave Cohen had offered him funds. He concluded: 'In the midst of all this my daughter passed her written Baccalauréat on the 3rd, and has the oral on the 12th. I wanted to get away then, and had a chance to send off my books free – or most of them. The packing of these aroused the suspicion and cupidity of this very avaricious landlord, and led to the[ir] seizure. Without my books and typewriter I am helpless. …' After trying to explain further his problems with book sales, money and customs, Aldington attempted to respond to Bryher's news of H.D., but his own difficulties were clearly overwhelming:

I am grieved to hear that Hilda has been suffering from the heat, and do hope the X-ray will be favourable.

Forgive me if I sound a bit rebellious, but this is a nice way for me to celebrate my 65th birthday after nearly 50 years of hard work, out of which I have been largely cheated by publishers.

And my thanks to you for your sympathy and aid. If I can get out of this mess and place to Sury, I shall be all right. I think I can live on my foreign royalties. …

Trying to meet this situation, I have not taken a holiday since I realised the power of the Establishment attack, nor once been to theatre, opera, concert or movie; or bought clothes; or even taken more than a very few local excursions. The only times I have been to 'good' restaurants is when friends have taken me. But so far Catherine has not suffered much, I think.

On 20 July 1957 Aldington was able to thank H.D. and to inform her that his situation was at least under control: 'This is to tell you that at last I got the cash for the 600 and 200 has come by mandat, of course from Bryher to whom all my thanks. … I feel I have never thanked you enough for the 1000 Swiss francs and 200 dollars, which quite literally saved us from destitution. Since then prospects have changed for the better, but that was a nasty time.'

Once in Sury, Aldington settled slowly into an empty house surrounded by boxes of books (for weeks he had no shelves and little furniture). He wrote H.D. on 16 September 1957, 'To get Catha through her last year [of school in Montpellier] I have sold my interest in the Viking Book of Poetry for a million francs. They are going to wreck it by cutting down all my choice moderns (including yourself) and including all the people I carefully kept out.' Aldington spent most of his days in housekeeping tasks, reading, resting, and reflecting. In response to re-reading John Ruskin's autobiography, for example, he wrote H.D. on 10 December 1957 that he marvelled at Ruskin's 'enormous belief in his rightness ... and his blindness to the beauty he praises so much ... When I think of what our brief time in Rome [in 1912–13] has meant to me – confirmed by later visits – I am simply staggered.' He thanked H.D. for her 'generous Xmas gift' of more much needed money, then told her how he intended to spend it: the Kershaws 'are pro tem hard up, at least until Feb, as much of their joint salaries goes to paying off the loan for buying the house. So I have decided to use the French francs from your 100 dollars as follows: One quarter to make a better Xmas for my friends when they have their brief vacation here; one quarter to Catha for pocket money; and the rest to get her a winter coat and shoes, for it is cold this year, and she will feel the change from Montpellier.' On 10 January 1958 he described his daily schedule:

I go to bed about 8 p.m. and stay there whether sleeping or waking until about 10 a.m., getting up only to stoke the furnace and take in the morning milk from the little girl. I then drive (for I can't walk that far) the mile to Sury P.O., collect mail, newspaper, and bread etc., return, and about 11 a.m. take my first meal of 'brunch', which is simply a good English breakfast of eggs and bacon. I walk a little when it is not raining or too cold, and about four drive to beautiful old Sancerre, where I usually mail letters, and do main shopping either there or at St. Satur. About 6 I have a second meal – soup and fish or vegetables. The water here is not safe, but wine is too heating, but one can now get a light bock for about 1/- or rather less a litre. And with that plus some Evian or Vichy I make out.

Aldington's ill health persisted, not improved by the northern cold and damp, and by the end of the year he decided that he would need to give up his present project, a biography of Balzac. He put aside the work of several months and repaid his publisher's advance. He would not write another book.

For her part, H.D. was slowly adjusting to what would be permanent lameness as a result of her fractured hip. On 18 June 1957 she wrote, 'My days are crowded, oddly, masseur, sun-lamp + now twice I get down the hall on my "ski-sticks" to a wide balcony or terrace ...'. She had frequent visitors, among them of course Bryher, but also Norman Holmes Pearson and George Plank. Her letters to Aldington are primarily reactions to his letters to her, and her world seems narrower than his; she gets about less, reads less widely, and has a smaller number of correspondents. She continues to go through her own papers and to write poetry and journals, much of her creative energy going into *Helen in Egypt*. As Pound's release from St. Elizabeth's grew to seem a real possibility (he finally left the hospital in the spring of 1958 and returned to Italy that summer) she began in March 1958 the memoir that would become *End to Torment* (1979).

Pound persists as a subject of interest for both Aldington and H.D., as do other mutual friends, Perdita and Catha, nature, memories, their health, and pictures of 'girls'. Catha did not pass the second part of her 'Bac' and several letters concern her future and Bryher's interest in advising her. Aldington was now in the awkward position of being beholden to Bryher and, while benefiting from her financial generosity and sincerely grateful for her help, he was also obliged to attend to her general advice (initially relayed through H.D. but by 1959 directly through letters of her own) and specifically to approve

Aldington, taken by his friend Frédéric-Jacques Temple in
Montpellier in 1955

her attention to Catha as an educational challenge which in addition to worrying
Aldington piqued Bryher's interest.

While Aldington's letters remain lengthy, H.D.'s letters often seem a bit rushed ('This is
just to thank you ...' and 'I will write again' are frequent comments). She is invariably
sympathetic to Aldington's problems and interested in his thoughts; she seems artistically
productive if physically restricted, and emotionally sensitive but controlled, although her
comments are sometimes fey – on 6 January 1958, five months after Aldington left the
south of France, she asked, 'Please tell me where S. en V. [Sury en Vaux] is, as I cannot
place even Cher [the département] on my small Atlas map. How far are you from Paris –
from Montpellier?' If Aldington in his letters seems in contrast practical and domestic,
H.D. remained more rational and less bothered than Aldington about what others might
write of their friends or her past. His letters frequently detail his concern that authors
such as Harry T. Moore in his edition of D.H. Lawrence letters (1962) or Patricia
Hutchins in her *Ezra Pound's Kensington* (1965) might say something untrue, indiscreet,
even 'libellous'. And their correspondence usually contained enclosures, keeping both of
them in touch with the world beyond Maison Sallé and Küsnacht. On 18 January 1958
H.D. forwarded to Aldington a letter from Athol Capper informing her that his wife,
Jessie, had committed suicide.

H.D. on a balcony of the Klinik Brunner in Küsnacht in the late 1950s

21 January 1958
Maison Sallé
Sury en Vaux

Dear Dooley,

This is a dammed business about poor Jessie. Of course she never recovered from that unfortunate fact that her first lover was a pederast. And then Athol had that ghastly wound at Ypres, and in consequence was partially blinded. What will become of him? You know, Aldous [Huxley] was even more dependent on Maria, and just before she died Frieda wrote me that she had seen him and that he appeared quite 'lost' without Maria! (I must look for that letter for you – everything still in such confusion here.) It makes me speechless when I think of good, innocent people like the Cappers, in their millions, paying for the spurious réclame of Lloyd Georges and Churchills, Haigs and Montgomerys, and all the rest of them. Did you know that for weeks now the Spectator has carried a correspondence about Passchendaele, in which the 'experts' (including Haig's son and the friend of the bogus prince of Mecca, Liddell Hart) have discussed it as if it had been a mixture of a game of checkers and a 'chance for promotion'. Well, Hindenburg said 'The British Army broke its teeth at Passchendaele' (400,000 casualties for nothing); and a great many English families broke their hearts, not to mention the fact that the brilliant English politicians and generals broke the man power of England. Well, no use grumbling. Pah.

Thank you for your enquiries about me. After about three weeks of complete rest I do begin to feel better. The pain in my arm has diminished, and I can begin to use it more normally again. I sleep fewer hours per day (12 instead of 14) and more tranquilly. Alister saw my London agent in Paris, and I hope and believe the Balzac business can be settled amicably. What I regret is that I have worked so hard and so conscientiously in my life. A little cheating and flattery would have been so much more profitable. Anyway, if 'crime doesn't pay' I know that honesty and hard work pay less.

Ezra is silent. Well, I tried hard to make my last letter as 'tactful' and friendly as possible, but I simply did not know what he meant!

If that James Joyce and Ezra-Pound's-Kensington woman comes here shall I tell her you are not well enough to receive visitors? Or would you rather let the janitor deal with her? I shall of course be very careful what I say.

You will be amazed to know that my books are still not all unpacked, partly because we can't get the carpenter to work on shelves, partly because Alister has been here so little, and partly because I am so drearily decrepit I can deal with only a very few at a time. Things keep turning up. Did you ever read an essay by Frederick Myers on Greek Oracles, in which he argues most convincingly that the priests and priestesses at the various shrines were really <u>mediums</u>? It was an utterly new idea to me, though the first (and completely ignorant) American to whom I mentioned it, said it had 'always' been known in US! Anyway, it does give me (ignorant as I am) a new 'slant'. Myers's essay on Virgil is beautiful, and consoles me so much for the denigration of the Eliots and tutti quanti. How persons loudly calling themselves 'poets' can affect to despise Virgil … !

Forty-five years ago today we were in Rome, and life seemed hopeful, however poor one was. On Washington's birthday we moved to Naples, and I remember the huge cold room I had with a wonderful hanging chandelier of 60 candles, only one of which I was allowed to light! And my poor 30/- a week didn't come from England, so in zero temperature I lived daily on a few oranges and a roll ('bun' as you used to call it) until the cheque arrived and I could go to a cucina borghese, and revel in hot minestrone and piselli con riso. By the same token, wondering what to make for my supper a few days ago, I made a riz au lait which would not have wholly disgraced the crémerie in the Rue du Four.

My love to you
Richard

I do wish you would tell me how you progress – if the leg is quite mended and you are skipping upon the hills like Queen Victoria.

⤳ **201** ⤶

30 August 1958
Maison Sallé
Sury en Vaux

Dear Dooley,

I return Mary's letter, with many thanks for allowing me to see it. Very good to know that Ezra is settled comfortably in an adoring family. He needs a little relaxation after those ghastly years. Rather hard punishment for a lot of silly broadcasts which probably no one in USA heard except the monitors.[1]

By now you will have had my letter about [Harry T.] Moore [the D.H. Lawrence scholar], and you can tell Dr Pearson that the letter will not be published. M. wants me to write a note pointing out the untruths in the L. letter, for publication after we are dead. Pouf, my dear. Who cares? He is also bringing out some sort of DHL periodical ('world of crazes') and asks me to do a bit about the Lawrence-[Bertram] Russell row during the war. Perhaps I should. They both made infernal asses of themselves, and Russell's extreme vindictiveness even 30 years after is mainly wounded vanity. Russell says DHL nearly made him commit suicide. More fool he. It would take a damn sight more than DHL at his beastly worst to make me contemplate such a compliment.[2]

I enclose the letter I had from [Edward] Nehls [the American academic] about the introduction I wrote for Vol III of his Composite Biography of DHL [1957–59]. I am glad he is pleased. But I wonder what DHL would have said if he had ever known he would be 'taught' in Wisconsin?

Hot here after a cold wet summer, but we are under threat of storms from the weather bureau.

Do you remember sending me Bryher's <u>Fourteenth of October</u> for Catha? I find that she has kept a book of notes since 1956 about her reading, and says of this: 'Histoire d'un jeune Saxon et de Hastings. Le mélange moderne et d'épopée montre bien que quelque soit le temps la vie est toujours la même. Il n'y a pas d'historie, il y a la vie; il n'y a pas de souvenir, il y a la mort.' [The story of a young Saxon and of Hastings. This mixture of the modern and the epic shows that whatever the period, life is always the same. There is no history, only life; there is no memory, only death.]

Not very profound, no doubt, but appreciative.

Much love,
Richard

1 Pound was now settled in Italy with his daughter's family.
2 Despite an initial friendship, Russell's desire for secular and humanist reform finally clashed violently with Lawrence's ideas about the necessity for a spiritual revolution.

∽ 202 ∽

7 September [1958]
[Klinik Brunner
Küsnacht]

Dear Richard,

I return the E. Nehls letter. it will be interesting to see your essay – of course, your own book on DHL was simply head-and-shoulders above <u>any</u> other. I am rather shattered and scattered by a hectic week – Norman Pearson was in Z. [Zürich] + came out every day – helped me with my stacks of old MSS + so on. Br had her birthday here on the 2nd + mine, the 10th, means a sort of octave of letters, greetings + so on. I should be + am very grateful – really – but so much has been un-earthed or gone over – I will write again. I am still using my two 'sticks' but am getting more ambitious about motive and/or motivation. I do hear of more bone breaks – why? Two near acquaintances have recently slipped + broken arms. Do be very careful –

I hope things march with Catha. No more news from Merano. ALL good luck, with love
from
Dooley.

Br was charmed with Catha's comment on her book. Later, I will have Bryher's <u>Gate to the Sea</u> sent. It is a short historical romance about Paestum, our old Poseidonia, with some remarkable pghotographs – how it brought back our visit there!

➶ 203 ➴

14 September [1958]
[Klinik Brunner
Küsnacht]

Dear Richard,

The book is beautiful + contains endless food for thought – + for dreaming.[1] I could have got about on one [stick] in the past but I had my compulsion to stay put, if that is what I mean, to <u>write</u>, to record – well, anyhow, that is over + my mind is singularly free + I can travel far in + with the Myth or Mythologie! I had finally to give in to the arguments + affections of Norman Pearson + Bryher, + after painfully collecting documents, birth, marriage, divorce etc., I was taken on September 12 by my good doctor to the American Consulate. After signing endless papers, declaring Allegiance etc., the deed was done. It really upset me very much, before the final pontifical blessing, 'Yes, ma'am' (that was <u>lovely</u>) 'now everything is in order.' Let us hope so. I stay here anyway. The argument was, 'if anything should happen – of course it won't but it <u>might</u> – you run the risk with British papers of being returned to England' – + so on! Well, this is just to let you know how I stand – though with difficulty – + to thank you for the infinite treasures of the Myth.

With love
from
Dooley./

I do hope you are well – + Catha is not too worried with apprehension about her work ...

———

I was surprised to find Ezra Pound, with my parents, as witness on our marriage license. ...

1 On 9 September 1958, Aldington sent H.D. for her birthday 'a book I have been keeping for you on this occasion. It is the Mythologie Générale of Larousse, and even if the text doesn't interest you, I think you may like the photographs.'

➶ 204 ➴

4 September 1958
Sury en Vaux
Cher

Dear Dooley,

At our age we live so much in letters – so I venture to send you a most charming one from Tom MacGreevy. I had forgotten that you met him in Florence (Italy) – do not confuse, yank, with Florence, N.C.! Poor Tom, he had a coronary thrombosis, and has been sent to Suisse just to wander, and NOT TO TALK, which is his life (a brilliant talker). Unluckily, he has given me no address in Suisse, and evidently letters are not to be forwarded from Dublin (Ireland). Otherwise, I should have asked you if you would care to see him. But you will see I can't catch him. The 'message' as he charmingly calls it was of course the money he sent me out of his travelling allowance.

I have a letter almost of despair from Catha in London (Eng.), and I have written her to come 'home' at once. She wants to go back to Montpellier and to try to find a job at once. I have told her that it is a mistake to hurry – she must take time. (I can live here very cheaply, and if I can a bit stop the publishers cheating me, I can have something for her.)

Catha, unluckily, doesn't like her mother, and I was perhaps wrong in thinking she ought to try. (How can one?) Anyway her letter has such phrases as 'madly longing to get away as soon as possible', 'feeling lost, lonely and thoroughly dreadful', 'getting to France and being able to EAT something again seems incredible'. And so on.

Well, I am to blame – perhaps I should have stayed in Hollywood (Calif) with the Thrifty Drugstore and the Radio (she was on the radio with Art Linklater!) and all the rest of it.

You MUST somehow get hold of a book 'Goethe et l'Art de Vivre' par Robert D'Harcourt (Payot, 1939). Certainly you will know more of it than I did, but it is such an encouragement when one feels battered and broken. And ... I hesitate, for I remember how Ezra wanted you to translate the untranslatable Callimachus ... but there is in existence a Conversations of Goethe, collected by Woldemar von Biedermann, TEN vols; Leipzig, 1889–1896. Would you not select and translate from them? You write such beautiful pure English, and Goethe has been translated by the vilest pedants and fools. Such a great man. Do think about it. If, as I perhaps wrongly assume, you are not now doing creative work, this Homage to Goethe would surely be the Crown?

I wish I could attempt it – but I am a know-nothing. And that war prejudiced me against German ... Slonimsky had offered to teach me. I like Goethe so much – the one really civilised man. Please like Goethe!

And you must get Lawrence Durrell's last book, Mountolive.

It is really very good indeed, wonderful.

DON'T get Alister Kershaw's book the Guillotine, which is having such good reviews in England. It would harm your fine susceptibility – but send copies to your enemies.[1]

I want to get Catha settled – and then to die. I am not interested in living in this filthy political mess, and after the insults I have had from Yankosachsendom [the English-speaking world]. Once she is settled, I have nothing to live for. I shall write no more.

But you – think of that Goethe book. It would be wonderful.[2]

Love,
Richard

P.S. Let me have Tom's letter back. I must have a letter waiting for him in Dublin.

1 *Mountolive* (1958) was the third volume of Durrell's *Alexandria Quartet* (1957–60). The British writer (1912–90) was a close friend of Aldington's and lived in the countryside near Montpellier. The Durrell-Aldington correspondence, beginning essentially in January 1957, was published as *Literary Lifelines*, ed. Ian S. MacNiven and Harry T. Moore, London: Faber and Faber, 1981. Kershaw's first book, *The Guillotine* (1958), details the history of this machine and suggests that it was the ideal symbol of the French Revolution.

2 On 13 October 1958, H.D. responded: 'I have been greatly impressed by the Durrell novels ... + the Goethe suggestion is, of course, tempting, but I must not go too deep there – + my German is not <u>that</u> good!'

21 November 1958
Sury

Dear Dooley,

I worked most of yesterday and this morning, and think (hope) I have got the script right for the printer.[1]

'Border bard' is, I suppose, all right for Swinburne. The family certainly were of Northumberland, though ACS was born in London, and the Admiral's home was in the Isle of Wight. But I believe the bard did spend part of his childhood in N'land, doubtless while his father was at sea with the R.N.

Brzeska – I laughed, remembering how Ford, complete with top-hat, took me aside and censured me severely for allowing Brzeska to 'sit in the same room with H.D'.[2]

Are you sure about the Museum tea room and the Imagist 'revelation'? My memory is of both of us with E. in the Fuller tea-shop in Kensington; but very likely he arranged it first with you in the Museum, and then re-staged it for my benefit in Kensington.[3]

How bitterly and deeply do I regret having had anything to do with it! Why did I have to be dragged in? An attendant lord, I suppose.[4]

I have corrected the Morris quotes from the Oxford edition of his Poems, so you may rely on what I put.

Do you remember that day we met Katherine Mansfield with the Lawrences in the Vale of Health, and how much we disliked her? In his latest and valedictory book, Points of View, [William Somerset] Maugham has some interesting remarks on her talent. I took down and re-read the Bliss stories and her Letters, and was rather moved. That portrait of Carco in Je ne Parle pas Français is a slasher – a revenge. The Prelude, the children's wonderful phantasmagoria as they move from the old home to the new – if only I could just once write something so true and so unaffected and so vivid! Why did Lorenzo write her that appalling, that unforgiveable letter – 'I hate you, stewing in your consumption, I think the Italians were right to hate you etc ...'?[5] How could he? And why? How much it meant to her in all her miseries when she had an affectionate letter from her father. I must remember that. She describes – so beautifully – the Luxembourg Gardens as they were during the guerre de quatorze. I remember wandering there in August 1946, agonizing over the destruction, until I came on the statue of George Sand – there was one mark on it, a bullet through her heart.

Much love,
Richard

Do you remember – Algernon [Swinburne] had a 'controversy' with the philologist Furnivall, who sent him an angry letter addressed 'Dear Mr Pigsbrook'? Algy was so delighted he made it up at once.

1 On 11 November 1958 H.D. had sent Aldington a copy of *End to Torment*, commenting that it was 'typed by Lausanne French-Suisse girl'. She continued:

End to Torment was written on the strength of the *Weekend* article you sent me [David Rattray, 'Weekend with Ezra Pound', *The Nation*, November 16, 1957, 343–9, one among many pieces exchanged during the time of Pound's incarceration]. It achieves for me a balance between my first + my last 'attachment', Ezra oddly + the London Air-Marshall – with the nostalgic entry of June 19 ... – 'We don't care any more' – only there is 'le Paradis ... [*sic*] of the orange-groves of Capri' etc. This, with the help of Erich Heydt, was getting the

whole Ezra complex out into the open. ... Pearson was very keen – but it can't be published
– not yet, anyhow – it comes so bang-on-top of the journalists.

Aldington is responding to *End to Torment* as an editor preparing the typescript for publication.
When he first received a copy on 14 November 1958 he wrote more generally:

> I have already 'wolfed' it down with the utmost interest, and approval. I think perhaps,
> though, you are right to delay publication for a time. ...
>
> I must re-read carefully before sending more than generalised praise and encourage-
> ment. But, my dear girl, I hope Pearson corrects you in matters of detail? Your William
> Morris misquotes must be seen to be believed! Always verify your quotations, even when
> you are quoting yourself!
>
> One thing I never told you. The reason I was 'annoyed' with poor old Wyndham
> [Lewis] for using my shaving things is that I found out he had venereal disease at the time. I
> thought that was a damned dirty trick to play on a man with a young wife. Of course, the
> risk of infection may have been slight, but it was there. ...
>
> I'll write again about the End to Torment. It is a most subtle text which must be re-read
> and brooded over.

2 Henri Gaudier-Brzeska (1891–1915), the French sculptor killed during the Great War, tended
to perspire heavily.

3 In *End to Torment* H.D. recalled meeting Pound

> ... alone or with others at the Museum tea room. ... 'But Dryad,' (in the Museum tea
> room), 'this is poetry.' He slashed with a pencil. 'Cut this out, shorten this line. "Hermes of
> the Ways" is a good title. I'll send this to Harriet Monroe of *Poetry*. Have you a copy? Yes?
> Then we can send this, or I'll type it when I get back. Will this do?' And he scrawled 'H.D.
> Imagiste' at the bottom of the page. (*End to Torment*, New York: New Directions, 1979, 18.)

4 H.D. responded on 24 November 1958: 'How sad I am that you so regret having had to do with
the old Imagist saga.' She added that although the label had once bothered her, the 'saga' no
longer did: '... at 72, it is part of my youth.'

5 This letter ('? 6 February 1920', *The Collected Letters of D.H. Lawrence*, Vol. I, London:
Heinemann, 1962, 620–1) consists of fragments which Mansfield quotes in a letter to John
Middleton Murry, who destroyed the original after Mansfield's death, and reads in its entirety,
'... I loathe you. You revolt me stewing in your consumption ... The Italians were quite right
to have nothing to do with you ...'.

🖎 206 🖎

10 April [1959]
Villa Verena
[Klinik Brunner
Küsnacht]

Dear Richard,

I am so glad to have your notice of the Prix. It does sound romantic and most
ésotérique. I really am glad + will send the notice to Br – though perhaps you sent her
one? Anyhow, congratulations – + again on the Hero which came yesterday. I re-read
it with more depth of understanding – how fascinating the notes look – if we could only
read them! I 'hinted' to Pearson about E.P. books – I wonder what he would like?[1]

We have howling wind here – but I had two little outings this week – the blossom
against the dark pine woods is curiously ghost-like here – I felt I was in a dream. I had
not been really 'out' since before Christmas – but am now really making an effort + can

walk better. I must put on some kind of show for Perdita's arrival, April 30.

This is just to thank you for the <u>Hero</u>. Part III is especially important and Sophoclean. I will write again. I had to do some 'copy' for Pearson.

Love (+ to C)
from
H./

1 On 6 April 1959 Aldington sent H.D. an announcement indicating that he had been awarded Le Prix Frédéric Mistral for 1959 for his *Introduction to Mistral*. On 13 April 1959 Aldington tactfully responded to her query here: 'I didn't send Bryher a copy of the Mistral prize notice because I think she is not interested in the Midi nor in modern Provençal literature.' H.D. is perhaps unaware of how carefully Aldington has constructed his relationship with Bryher; he is still proud, sensitive, and wary. Additionally, H.D. seems not to realize how very important Aldington's letters to her are to him; he shares information with her he would not consider for a variety of reasons sharing with others, among them Bryher. Aldington has also sent H.D. a copy of his *Death of a Hero*, recently published in Russia. On 13 April he commented: 'English language books are still not imported there for the public, so they publish their own texts [in English with Russian notes] for students. I rather approve of this as they (sometimes) pay the author and never the publisher.' On 6 April Aldington told H.D. that he had learned Pound was not regularly receiving periodicals and books; although the difficulty might be merely the Italian postal service, Aldington suggested that she write to Pearson about the problem.

≫ 207 ≪

19 April 1959
Sury en Vaux
Cher

Dear Dooley,

Under separate cover (imprimés [printed matter]) I send you Two Cities with the bits on Durrell.[1] Will you pass it on to Bryher if you think it worth her attention. I must admit I am disappointed. The amount of space given to Durrell is much less than I was led to expect. Then I was led to expect that a genuine effort had been made to interpret Durrell's genius, which hasn't happened. Miller and the other American are more occupied in talking about themselves than about their nominal subject. The best is the 'interview', and that is rather factitious as it is obviously all written by himself. The best I think is the brief but sincere and affectionate note by [Frédéric-Jacques] Temple. My own effort is all tatters and hurry. I was given only a few days, told copy must be in by the 15th Feb at latest, as they were appearing in late Feb. In fact they appeared yesterday! Heaven preserve us from the amateur editor!

The rest of the thing isn't 'two cities', it is a bit of 'this quarter' about a quarter of a century too late. What is the need for these people to print their insincere and unnecessary opinions? Kifka-Kafka, Rimbaud-Bimbaud, Gidey-Weedy. They have only second-hand views to air, and don't know how to write.

I <u>am</u> disappointed, as I had hoped for something more worthy of Durrell's gifts. But what can one expect of Parisites?

I enclose for you also a piece on Roy by the translator of his poems. There is a far better one by Maurice Chauvet (a real writer, he) but I had to send it [to] London to help along the Hommage.[2] It is curious how sloppy and inaccurate these very self-satisfied critics are! In [Armand] Guibert's article, note that Roy was born 1902 (not

396

1901); it is T.E. Lawrence, not T.H. Lawrence, and he wrote no Memoirs (apart from 7 Pills and Mint, which don't mention Roy) and the words quoted don't appear in L's letters! If not supposititious they must have been on the blurb of Flaming Terrapin or in one of the numerous unpublished letters.

Had a letter from an unknown in London professing great admiration for my Portrait of a Hero. Restrained myself from replying that he must have meant Death of a Genius, But. …

I have in front of me something I never expected to see, namely the ad. for a pamphlet The Colour Question in Britain!!! When you think what a frightful affliction it has been to the USA (certainly one of the causes of that dreadful destructive war) you would suppose no government would be so idiotic as to create the problem gratuitously and needlessly in G.B., simply for the vanity of keeping the flag flying over a number of derelict sugar islands which could have been kept prosperous if the sugar contracts had been made with BWI and not with Cuba.

And they are not happy in England, which is over-crowded anyway. You know Tony, my brother, served first at sea during the last war, and then when invalided out was the only solicitor to stay in Dover throughout the bombardment. Consequently he got and still handles the Admiralty legal business. Lately he told me the case of a Trinidad negro, penniless, trying to stow away to get back home. He was found, arrested, tried, condemned, and as he couldn't pay the fine imprisoned. When he left prison he could only ask for (and get) relief. Tony worked out that the cost of the proceedings up till the day the man left prison must have been nearly double the first-class fare to Trinidad! And the poor devil is now forced to stay in a place he doesn't want to be and where he can't earn a living, after being lured over with false promises.

Catha very cheerful, and recovering from being knocked down by the bullock at the ferrade.[3] I suggested she might perhaps see a doctor, and she replied 'only for the pleasure of showing off my bruises'. She seems to have had a decent horse to ride before she invited this catastrophe – she hates a slow horse.

How is your weather? Here we have had three days of cloud, rain and cold, and in spite of optimistic forecasts today is overcast and the wind still chilly. I do hope it is better with you, and that you are able to walk. You must be as strong as possible for the meeting [with Perdita] at the end of the month, which I'm sure will go off well.

I am struggling between avarice and discomfort – not wanting to re-light the furnace so late in the year, but not very hopeful of any warming up of the day. When these 'depressions' come off the Atlantic, the persistent and endless drive of cold grey clouds seems almost as if meant as a personal attack.

My friend Tom MacGreevy has written a short book on Nicolas Poussin, I suppose as an introduction to a book of reproductions. Have you got any book on him? All I have is the small Collections des Maîtres but it has some perfectly lovely drawings and 'classical' themes with beautiful nudes. There is a most elegant Bacchus in a picture of Bacchus and Midas in Munich. A magnificent triumph of Galatea is in – Leningrad! (Why can't they let us have this product of fascist bestiality and capitalist hyena-ism?) I only wish the old masters would not take such upsetting subjects as the Massacre of the Innocents and the Judgment of Solomon. Would you like me to send you this little book? I can easily get another copy here if you would. But I don't like to litter you with books you can't throw away. There is in the book also a Leda with the Swan (Chantilly), a beautiful picture but also distressing. I can't imagine why I used to think that subject exciting. That hard beak and scratchy feathers and huge wet webbed feet and ice-cold penis – it must have been a dreadful experience for the girl! But I expect that, woman-like, your sympathies are all with the infatuated bird – these hussies!

To-night I make my weekly feast – a small shoulder of lamb. It is dreadfully expensive, about 17/-, but it lasts three days (hot and cold) and I get so depressed if I do without meat wholly.

I do wish it would be real spring.

Much love from us both,

Richard

I send the Poussin because you won't ask for it & you can give it away!

1 Jean Fanchette launched his journal, *Two Cities: La Revue Bilingue de Paris*, with a tribute to Durrell consisting of five essays and an interview.

2 Frédéric-Jacques Temple edited *Hommage à Roy Campbell* (Montpellier: La Licorne, 1958), a collection of pieces by Aldington, Durrell, Sitwell and others; Chauvet's tribute was not included.

3 Catha, who had returned to Montpellier to try to earn a secretarial certificate, was visiting her father briefly. She felt the south of France was her home and had many friends there with whom she enjoyed the local sports.

⤳ 208 ⤶

28 April [1959]
Villa Verena
[Klinik Brunner
Küsnacht]

Dear Richard,

Do you want the M. Harald article?[1] I will re-read + send it, if you do. It is exciting + concise. I also have been reading Part I of <u>Hero</u>. I will hand over the magazine + article to Br tomorrow. I am glad you see my idea about <u>Volkswagen</u> etc. I <u>have</u> to look ahead, but it will probably be some time before I get on with my plan. By the way, Br has been agin' my driving a car – she was, years ago, when I was better able to undertake it, 'you are too old to begin now'. Heydt is all for it, but says I ought to have everything under <u>hand</u> control – Volks may not do, but he is looking into it, + I am not sure that he is right. Can you sometime give me, on separate page, general list of terms used, 'clutch' etc. I got mixed up or Heydt did – we both did – with English-German. I don't know what sort of instructor I could get, I mean, re language.[2]

I think I agree with you + 'Sheila' about B.B. [Brigit Bardot] – but thank you for the cutting.[3]

Thanks for Rapallo 'guide' – I don't think Br will like that either + she has been so staunch + loyal, it is hard for me to argue about it + the car. But I will go slowly, tactfully. I just suddenly visualized Fla. as a vacuum – I would be so out of touch. I have tried so hard to believe in it, really – but my files and roots are here.[4] No – I don't think you would be happy in England, even if there were not risk of pneumonia.[5] I am always jotting down the year the <u>Mona Lisa</u> was stolen, my first time 'abroad', + then can't find the note – 1911? I have just been through my address-book again. It is a long time anyway, almost 50 years!

I will write N.P. [Pearson] about the package etc. at the <u>Schloss</u>.[6] Norman writes of

398

Donani, head of Italian Centre of Culture in N.Y. Donani said it was he, through Italian ambassador, who got Ezra released. ('How many of us each really did more than anyone else to spring Grandpa!') Donani said ambassador asked 'if Pound was really a great poet'. '"Oh yes", I said, "Well quote me ...". My memory fumbled ... then,

> Oh, to be in England
> Now that Winston's out ...

that clinched it.'

Anyhow, I am glad the pullover [in the package] was found. I will tell Norman. And all thanks for help about plans.

Love

Dooley.

1 H.D. may be referring to Michael Harald's article on Pound which Aldington indicated, on 30 April 1959, appeared in 'Mosley's paper'.

2 On 23 April 1959 H.D. wrote to Aldington, 'Heydt thinks it [learning to drive] would help me get away psychically (?) as well as physically. Aldington was eager to fill any of H.D.'s requests, however unusual, and wrote her in characteristically pragmatic detail on 30 April 1959:

Steering wheel	Steuerrad Ienrad
Gear	Ubersetzungsgetriebe
Gear box	Getriebekasten
First, second, third, reverse gear	Same in German
Brake	Bremse
Clutch	Lederkupplung
Clutch-pedal	Kupplungspedal
Ignition-lever	Zündverstellhebel
Ignition	Zündung
Ignition-key	?
Tire	Reifen
Inner tube	Luftschlauch
Radiator	Kühler
Battery	Trockenelment
Carburettor	Karburator

He concluded with bits of advice, revealing inadvertently that he himself was finally more comfortable with French terminology: 'You always have to verify that there is water in the radiator, oil in the engine, energy in the battery. ... Sparking-plugs have to be renewed occasionally. The wind-shield has a mechanical screen-wiper to keep the glass clear when driving in rain. ... Turning signals are now no longer made by hand but by clignotants. ...'

3 On 24 April 1959 Aldington had written that Sheila, Kershaw's second wife, 'gets wild with jealousy because Alister always says how "sweet" B.B. looks etc. I tried to soothe by saying that I think her thighs are too thin and her bottom too small and "uncongenial"!'

4 Throughout early 1959, H.D. considered moving from Küsnacht, possibly to some place warmer such as Nassau, Florida, or Rapallo. On 17 February 1959 she wrote Aldington, 'I don't think I can make a move – not yet – but I brace morale, thinking about it. ... This Flo. is, as I say, just an idea – but I don't want to get stuck here forever.' On 18 March 1959 she continued to voice her restlessness: 'I almost feel, as you do, Florida etc. is a "cutting off". I just don't feel that I can stand another winter here.' Aldington's supportive letters during this period provide information in the form of reminiscences and travelogues.

5 On 24 April 1959 Aldington wrote to H.D. that Pound and his daughter 'keep urging me to go to England, as you to USA. What they don't realise is that during 17–18 I picked up so much

phosgene and mustard gas (without ever being really knocked out) that since my late thirties I have had chronic bronchitis. (Just 42 years ago this month, we had about 30,000 German gas shells fired "experimentally" on our very small area.) If I go to England I catch a head cold at once (on the <u>boat train</u>). ...'

6 On 23 April 1959 Aldington had written that 'it looks as if the hold-up of [Pound's] mail was only temporary and due to the servant at Brunnenburg' (the Alpine castle where Pound had settled with his daughter) and related a story of a parcel turning up in a bottom drawer.

⇗ **209** ⇖

18 June 1959
Sury en Vaux
Cher

Dear Dooley,

What do you think of <u>her</u>?[1] I cut the photo from this morning's local paper, Le Berry Républicain. She seems to me ever so much more attractive than the B.B. I sent you, which Alister thinks so wonderful.

It is disturbing that Ezra is wanting to sell Williams and Santayana proofs, but perhaps he asked Pearson about this before the Hem [Hemingway] cheque arrived? I do hope so.

Is it unfair to suggest that a more humane and realistic attitude towards poor old E. would be reached if only these fans of his would realise that he <u>is</u> crackers. If they would read up modern psychologists on Tasso and Rousseau they would see it at once. But there! I mustn't boast. Lately I received a long and embarrassing letter from him, and really feel at a loss how to reply. I am only required to produce (1) a reprint of Little Review on [Remy de] Gourmont, if not the whole periodical, (2) an anthology of English prose 1890–1920, containing chiefly E's friends, (3) interest Sir Wm Haley [editor of the London *Times*] in E's schemes for saving humanity, (4) state who is present editor of Time and Tide, (5) read the Square Dollar series[2] and pass on to Sully André Peyre (whose interest is Mistral!), (6) state who are the Franco-Italian 'Lions' who are staging a Convegno dell'Amicizia Italo-Francese [a convention of Italian-French friendship]. This is a bit much for 'old Aldington' (cf. casebook, p. 107!) to tackle all at once.[3] Curia vult adversari [the senate wishes to oppose], as the lawyers say.

Mary's resentment against the frank discussion of her father is very natural and sympathique, but after all if you attack you must expect a counter-attack – only in sacred fiction do the walls of Jericho fall down to a trumpet blast. And then, the most damaging part of the casebook is what he said himself, as recorded in the last 3 pages.[4]

To-day 18th is not only the anniversary of Waterloo and of le Général's BBC appeal from London (Eng.) but the first day of Catha's Bac exams.[5] I urged her to make yesterday a full holiday, and to take her vélo-moteur and ride to Palavas beach, and spend the day bathing and basking. But I bet she stayed in over-tiring herself.

Once more Alister and his wife have had the dates of their holidays changed! Of course, it is difficult to synchronise. However, my arrangements remain unchanged. I leave here on the 30th June, and shall be with C. [in Montpellier] for her 21st birthday on the 6th, and shall stay through much or most of July. My friend Temple offers free his rather luxurious flat in Montpellier – too good for the likes of us, who are only miserable writers! I shall try to get back in time to have this place ship-shape for the Ks when they come down on the 31st July.

Bryher has been more than generous, and I can give Catha now a month's complete rest and holiday, and also pay her plane fare to fly to Zürich. Bryher very wisely thinks that she (C.) should be examined by the 'orientation' psychologues (who, I am told, are very good) and IF Catha has any aptitude and would like to study on that line Bryher most super-generously offers to help me get her the training. If a girl can possibly fit herself for some fair occupation, it is so infinitely preferable to life as cook and bottle-washer to some bloody man and his brats. I don't mean to say that she or any girl should avoid marriage and children, but the independence is so important. Don't you think? Where there is the old patriarchal family life, it is another matter. With the peasants here (still living in the 15th century) the man governs unquestioned, BUT all money is handed at once to the woman, who feeds and clothes the children first! Alister disapproves of this, though he greatly approves the custom (Roman!) of not allowing the women wine. 'Look what I should save', he says! Whereupon I come in and say, 'Yes; but Sheila pays for her own wine, and very often for yours too!'

How are you getting on? You say nothing about yourself. A friend of mine in the Midi – a man – tells me he has completely eliminated all symptoms of Rheumatism by sun-bathing. (He also prays to Apollo beforehand.) You might do both? Questions are (a) can you sunbathe privily at the clinique? (b) is there enough continual sun in Suisse? It may be worth trying. I remember long ago an Austrian officer I met in the Tyrol telling me that he was captured by the Russians and sent to some ghastly humid place where he got fearful rheumatism. They then transferred him to (I think) Turkestan, and allowed him to sunbathe, with the result that he too was cured.

I forgot to ask – when Catha comes to Suisse would you care to see her, or would you rather not? Say frankly. According to tentative arrangements, this should be in the second week of Sept.

How very wise Bryher is to go sailing and fishing for a summer holiday. It is one of the few means of avoiding the dreadful crush and noise and over-charging of 'les vacances'.

We shall not know the news of C's Bac for some time. There are so many extra students and no increase in profs that a week or more will elapse before we know the result of the écrit. And if she passes that there remains the oral in the first week of July, and more waiting after that.[6]

World of frustrations! I had decided to give Catha the money of my Prix de Gratitude Mistralienne, whatever it amounted to. But though I was officially informed of this 'award' nearly three months ago, not a sign of a cheque or hint that one will come! It is like winning the caucus race in Alice – remember? – 'we beg your acceptance of this elegant thimble.'

Love from us both,
Richard

1 The enclosure is missing, but in the margin H.D. has commented: 'Fat bathing "beauty" – joke?'
2 This was a quirky series of booklets masterminded by Pound in 1950.
3 *A Casebook on Ezra Pound*, ed. William Van O'Connor and Edward Stone, New York: Thomas Y. Crowell, 1959. The volume included a variety of material related to Pound's incarceration. Pound is quoted in 'Weekend with Ezra Pound', reprinted here, as saying that 'old Aldington' was an authority on Greek and Provençal.
4 These pages of the *Casebook* include excerpts from Pound's broadcasts over Rome Radio in 1942–43.
5 General Charles de Gaulle addressed France over British radio on 18 June 1940.

6 Aldington asked H.D. on 25 June 1959, 'Will you tell Bryher that I have this moment received a letter from Catha to say she has PASSED her written Bachot ...'. She also passed her oral in July.

☞ 210 ☜

7 September 1959
Sury en Vaux
Cher

Dear Dooley,
Last week I was (as the stylists say) COMPLETELY SHATTERED by receiving this:

'Cher R/
amid cumulative fatigue, and much that has gone to muddle, thinking of early friendship and late. This is to say I have for you a lasting affection.
E.P/

25 aug 59
Came on some notes of first walking tour in France, amid the rubble a week or so ago. Quanti dolci pensier [So many sweet thoughts].'

It upset me greatly – seems to have something far too valedictory about it. I would rather have had (for his sake) one of his bravura letters. It seems to indicate surrender – although I never doubted the warmth of his heart.

The deuce of it is that the letter arrived just at the beginning of one of my damnable semi-comas ('whoreson lethargies' Falstaff calls them) and I simply couldn't answer, although an immediate response was the obligatory thing. After two days, still hardly able to see type-paper, I did manage to reply, and I hope with all the affection and warmth I (and you) would have wished.

But I like not this too reasonable sweetness.[1] He drops his sword – bad, bad. I don't think that at his age he should go swimming with young females called Marcella. Take it from me all Marcellas are w xxxx s! Still, if it cheers him, and the angelic D. [Dorothy] doesn't mind – she must be beyond caring much about anything. Did ever woman suffer such a dismal martyrdom? You know, her cousin, Captain Shakespear, was one of the real English heroes of that Arabian desert? He crossed it by camel – from Baghdad to Suez – when such a feat was unheard of for a European. (He got the R. Geographical Soc's gold medal.) He was killed with Ibn Saud's Arabs – they bolted from an attack by the Shammar tribes, and he told them 'A British officer never retires' – killed trying to mend a stoppage in his Lewis gun with which he had been holding up the whole issue! Dorothy has the same spirit.

Krankengymnastik is a wonderful word. Of course you must have massage. After my broken knee I had a terrible man, a Boche, who was delighted to torture an Englander: 'Es muss weh, es muss weh!' [It must hurt.] And he saw it did. I hope your fraulein (or frau) is less of a nazi. But, as I found, a little bit of walk on my own was worth a week of the massage. Is there an (unwaxed) corridor in which you can walk, and perhaps look over the lake? It is true you have a weight of years, but consider all those tough old yankees and boches your ancestors! Remember how spry [your father] Charles Leander was on our never-to-be-forgotten tour [in 1912–13]? He wasn't in Sherman's army? No, they were cavalry. Under Grant anyway. Funny that 'modern'

Americans are for secession in all countries but their own. BUT, if only you can get the old pins waggling again, the world is all before you.

Bryher is the kindest and most generous of friends – this extra holiday in the Camargue has made Catha wonderfully happy. I get only scraps of notes – a sure sign that she is enjoying life – but it will all be poured out when I see her next. She is now alone in her cabane, reading and writing, when she is not riding in the Camargue, and cooking her own meals over a fire of vine roots. The rain has been so heavy the whole Camargue is under water, and the horses splash up to the saddle-girths. It is a grand farewell to her childhood, and without Bryher's help and yours it could not have been done. It is a pity that she must dwell in a Paris office, which MILLIONS of girls long to do, instead of being a gardian [cowboy] de Camargue which not one in a million could do. But that is the cussedness of life. Curse the Establishment and the Lawrence Bureau. Apropos, there is a comical little book just out in French 'The Uncrowned King of Arabia' etc. all the old lies. Pah. Did I speak of Varsittart's memoirs? He shows that Hart and Churchill lied about 'Egypt' and Hankey.[2]

I don't think the ref to my books in 'Henry's' wire means anything but good intentions.[3] The yanksachsen censorship is very strong in Germany. Amazing that Ez's translation got through. Apropos, Larry [Durrell] and his girl have gone to Bournemouth (angels and ministers of grace defend us) for THREE weeks – the time between a sentence of death and the hanging, and also that required of the third time of asking. I only infer this – no word from them. But otherwise, why go to the Bourne at which no traveller arrives?[4] My last letter was from Claude – 'the children' had dropped chewing gum in Larry's typewriter and put it out of action! They have the 'modern' pose of pretending to dislike their children (all by different spouses) and in fact giving up everything to them. Can human folly go further? Of course it can!

I am sending you (which please return at leisure) a MS of Catha's, written here last spring, and confided to the Durrells. She seems to have summed up a certain type of youth rather well.

Attention! Univ of Arkansas on the prowl over J. G. Fletcher. Old iron, old iron! Pearson will stave them off if they attack you.

Much love,
Richard

P.S. What is the news of Perdita? Does all go well? How about a little birth-control? Nicht?[5]

1 I have been unable to identify this quotation.
2 T.E. Lawrence's cousin Lord Robert Vansittart, in *The Mist Procession* (London: Hutchinson, 1958), denies Lawrence's contention that he was ever offered the job of governing Egypt (327); Lord M.P.A. Hankey also wrote about the campaign in Egypt in *The Supreme Command: 1914–1918*, Vol. II (London: Allen and Unwin, 1961, 500–1).
3 On 27 August 1959 Aldington had sent H.D. 'an amusing telegram' from Henry Miller to Lawrence Durrell.
4 Aldington is punning on Hamlet's 'bourne from which no traveller returns', *Hamlet*, Act III, Scene I, ll. 79–80.
5 Perdita was expecting her fourth child, born in February 1960. From their earliest associations in 1912 with *The Egoist*, in which such issues were discussed, both Aldington and H.D. were staunch advocates of 'modern' birth control. H.D. responded on 9 September 1959: 'I have much to say but don't say it. Surely three children is enough?'

8 September 1959
Sury

Dear Dooley,

I digressed in yesterday's letter, and omitted some literary points.

Your translation of the Lais epigram (I wonder if it is Plato's? doubt it) is now in the anthology.[1] But I can find nothing else in the Selected. I would gladly use the Anyte – but I just can't. This is to be a reference book, and translations must be translations, not re-creations and expansions. I regret infinitely. But for the same reason I have to exclude Roy's magnificent re-creation of Mistral's wild horses in the Camargue, and have been forced to use George Meredith's much inferior version which, however, is a translation. Ezra's Propertius is barred, and so too of course all the 18th century 'allusions to Horace' from Pope downwards. I have hesitated a lot over Byron's lovely version of Sappho's Hesperus, but I think it does pass, as also a few lines of Swinburne about Atthis. If you remember anything else of yours which can be used as a 'straight' translation, please let me know.

Apropos, did Pearson correct the proofs of that Selected? If so, what the devil does he mean by passing 'Callypso' for 'Calypso'?

Did I send you my copy of Larry Durrell's Selected [Poems] – also in Grove? He (L.D.) swears he sent me the book, and I know I've read it, but damned if I can find it. Perhaps Alister has it in Paris.

Have you read that amazing papyrus of Timotheus of Miletus in Vol. 3 of the Loeb Lyra Graeca? It is 4th century, and as Timotheus lived until about B.C. 348 it must be nearly contemporary. It is a sort of war-whoop of triumph over the defeat of the bicots (Persians) at Salamis – wonderfully eloquent and chauvinistic.

Also if you have not got the Loeb Select Papyri III, Literary Papyri: Poetry, ed. D. L. Page, you must get it. Wonderful things, including a fragment of the one longish poem by Erinna in lament for her dead girl-friend – very beautiful and touching – how they played dolls together and were frightened of the bogy-man, and then the friend got married and 'forgot all that you learned from your Mother' – it is assumed that E. was 'Mother' when they played dolls. E. must have been a priestess (Artemis?) for she could not go to the funeral. I am of course including this. Erinna must have been a wonderful girl and a great loss to world literature – only 18 when she died.

As to the Arabs and Provence-Dante. I forgot to send you the titles.[2]

For the Hispano-Arab influence on Provence:

The Dove's Neck-Ring. Professor A.R. Nykl; Paris 1931.

El Cancionero de Aben Guzman. Madrid 1933. edited A.R. Nykl.

Les Troubadours. Robert Briffaut. Paris 1945.

Nykl is/was prof of Oriental languages at Chicago, which is hot stuff on those studies – Breasted was their prof of ancient Egyptian. Nykl is the FIRST scholar to investigate that problem having a thorough knowledge of Arabic as well as of Provençal, Italian etc. This is of course rather unfair to his predecessors, who blithely asserted that the Arabs had no influence on Provençal, without knowing or being able to read one word of Arabic – rather like the famous Prince of Mecca [T.E. Lawrence].

For the influence of the Arabs on Dante read Dante y el Islam by Asin Palacios, Madrid 1927. There was an English translation by Harold L. Sunderland, entitled Islam and the Divine Comedy. You will be amazed how much D. took from the various Arab versions of Mohammed's Dream – his visit to Hell, Purgatory and Paradise. All those fanciful astronomical unfacts, most of the circles and grisly torments are not his but Arabic, and so too the paradise.

Another very interesting Loeb is the Duffs' Minor Latin Poets. Reposianus on Venus and Mars is clearly the origin of Botticelli's picture in the National Gallery. I used to think it was Poliziano, but no, Poliziano fished his version out of Reposianus. Of course they all go back to Homer. Yesterday I was re-reading the Odyssey scene when Hera deliberately sets out to tempt Zeus so that the Greeks shall come to harm, borrowing the famous girdle of her rival Aphrodite. A Parisian cocotte couldn't do more.

I must get on with 'work' damn it. Haven't yet answered the Arkansas prof about Fletcher.

I got an indication of how our alleged democratic world is in fact dominated by militarism. Had a call from my young friend at Nato, just off on a month's tour of Italy on full pay. He interprets for those generals etc. at NATO, and is paid a fabulous salary, all tax free, part of it in dollars banked in Suisse so that he can ignore currency restrictions. His car is a Mercedes, and he and the car have diplomatic status – C.D. on the car. In Rome free accommodation will be found for him. Now, he is a son of an old friend of mine, and I rejoice in his good fortune. But what are his services? He simply facilitates militarism and has a tiny share of the fantastic waste of money on armaments, H-bombs, shooting monkeys at the moon, and all the other insolent trash. What artist, writer, poet, philosopher, ever had any such privileges from government? All they get is threatening demands for income tax if they succeed, and contempt if they don't. And if there is another war NATO will no more protect us from being burned up than an old umbrella.

Love,

Richard

1 On 14 August 1959 Aldington had written H.D., 'Long ago I did a huge anthol of Poetry of Western World for Ency Britt. ... the editor was fired, scripts were canned for years, but now they have determined to issue. I have a few weeks "to revise and bring up to date" which I take to mean "insert pieces by y [your] friends".' Aldington was paid for his work on the *Encyclopaedia Britannica*, but his piece was never published.
2 In a letter which has apparently not survived, H.D. must have made a simple query to which the following paragraphs are Aldington's typically scholarly response.

≽ 212 ≼

23 September [1959]
Villa Verena
[Klinik Brunner
Küsnacht]

Dear Richard,

Br has, no doubt, written you that she is meeting Catha on the 29<u>th</u>, dropping her bag at the hotel, <u>Glockenhof</u>, bringing her here for talk + early tea with me, sending her on to a preliminary, informal session at 5. with Dr. Dori Heydt, who talks French, arranging for the formal sessions with a Dr. Schmid, on 30<u>th</u> + after, if advised.

I only fear that Catha will find it <u>very dull</u> here, en Suisse. But Heydt + his wife are both interested + it saved time, giving them an outline of your feelings – but Catha <u>must not know that</u>.

Now, thank you for <u>Madrigal</u>. I have the <u>Grove</u> contract but have not signed it. The book was + is by 'Delia Alton'. I think you agreed in the case of the later War II 'novels' that followed that the nom-de-plume was indicated. Now Pearson writes that <u>Grove</u> would wish to list it as <u>H.D.</u> This takes the wind out of my sails, as I was following <u>Madrigal</u>, in anticipation, by other of the <u>D.A.</u> series. I don't mind what they say on the blurb, Pearson says Grove might think it 'coy' to be <u>D.A.</u> This is <u>not</u> the point – <u>D.A.</u> stood and stands aside from <u>H.D.</u> Well, I need not publish the book, or any of the series. But I had to write them + I did sweat 'blood + tears' etc. to get the formula for <u>Madrigal</u>.[1]

Thanks for enclosed – the writer never wrote me, though he seems to imply that 'I have heard …'. I will send the letter, later, to Ezra.[2]

I will write again. All will go well with Catha our end, I only worry lest she find us too dull.[3]

Ever –

With love –

Dooley./

1 Aldington has just returned, at H.D.'s request, the copy of 'Madrigal' which he has had since 1953 (see Letters 177–182). He wrote on 17 September 1959 'I am very glad that Grove are putting this into print. I tried very hard with the commercial publishers in London, but they have the morals of moneylenders and the mentality of race-course bookmakers.' Despite her reservations here, on 1 October 1959 H.D. wrote Aldington, 'I finally signed my <u>Madrigal</u> contract, + told Pearson it can be <u>H.D.</u>'

2 On 21 September 1959 Aldington sent H.D. a letter from Charles Norman, who was working on his biography *Ezra Pound* (1960).

3 Both Aldington and his daughter were very grateful for this visit. On 9 October 1959 Aldington wrote H.D. that Catha found her '"so beautiful and so sweet"'.

❦ **213** ❦

13 October [1959]

Villa Verena

[Klinik Brunner

Küsnacht]

Dear Richard,

If you should include H.D. in the anthology, please choose anything you want – + don't include, unless indicated.

Thank you for news of Catha. Yes, I saw the delightful 'little piece', I am glad the Deux Cités will print it. You must let us have a copy. For my own sake, I too wish she would write more English. Of course, her speaking English is perfect, warm + unspoiled + uncontaminated. Dr. Dori Heydt said her French is impeccable.[1] I have been so long 'resident abroad' that I find myself struggling to keep English-speaking. As one <u>writes</u> English, one fears sometimes a crevasse may separate self-from-self. But I confess I felt the same anyway in England, + in a different way in the États.

I think that 'suspicious characters' was a joke of S.B., as Eliot was on the list – re Egoist, I think.[2]

I am glad that Catha has Alister to help her. The list as sent to Bryher seemed on the 'Histoire politique' + 'economique' side. But no doubt she and/or Catha have written.[3]

I haven't Catha's address, so tell her when you write how <u>very</u> happy her visit made me. She is very endearing + everyone here loved <u>das Mädchen</u>. Thank you so much for letting her come to us.

Love,
Dooley./

Let me know of the new medicaments.[4]

1 On 9 October 1959 Aldington asked H.D., 'Did Bryher show you that little piece [by Catha in French] about Cocteau and shooting his film [*Orphée*] at Les Beaux?' Aldington also asked, 'Do you think her English is very bad?'

2 On 9 October 1959 Aldington reported that 'Catha says Sylvia Beach describes us (you and me) as "suspicious characters". I always said she mis-spelled her name.' Catha has probably been reading Beach's memoir *Shakespeare and Company* (London: Faber and Faber, 1956).

3 It was decided that Catha would attend the Sorbonne and Alister is helping her to register and to move into a flat in Paris.

4 Aldington has been regularly reporting to H.D. his doctor's recommendations and prescriptions. She in turn has been discussing his treatment in detail, particularly in terms of medication, with her Swiss physicians, and reporting back to him.

⁂ 214 ⁂

30 October [1959]
[Klinik Brunner
Küsnacht]

Dear Richard,

The 2 volumes of <u>Walks in Rome</u> are very fascinating.[1] It is a personal return and understanding, after reading the new 'Queen Mary' huge biography.[2] <u>That</u> seemed 'foreign' but I am picking over the old story with its voluminous German connections. It almost seems that the Wars, War I in particular, was [*sic*] a Civil War. Do you remember how you + Cournos + I stood outside B-Palace, when War I was about to be declared, + the Family appeared, at various lighted windows, like dolls in a dollhouse? When the mob shouted, 'We want war', you or Cournos shouted back, 'We don't'. I thought we might get trampled to death.

Please collect <u>any</u> old stamps in an envelope + later send them to me. A youthful <u>Pfadfinder</u> [Boy Scout], son of a doctor here, asks for them. Eventually, they invite some foreign invalid child here with the proceeds of sale of stamps. Well, I find it an incentive to clearing up old stacks of letters – special stamps I give to a night-sister. By the way, Lisa [one of the nurses] wasn't very helpful, re new medicaments, as the two new ones are French + she doesn't know them. The first, Swiss <u>Tofranil</u>, she already praised highly, you remember, + has used for patients here. I will try to consult someone else.

Looking over letters, I found this from Ezra, 8 Sept. – 'Not since Brigit, Richard, the four of us, has there been any harmony around me. Their irritations with each other used to amuse me, never seeming to have any serious root. ... What, damn it, do you think is the reason why my friends don't get on <u>with each other</u>?' I couldn't really go into this at the time. And why suddenly, 'the four of us'?

Br is due now, for long week-end. I hope your cold is progressing – mine is so-so, and snow half-way down the opposite mountains.

All love + to C when you write,

from
Dooley./

1 On 26 October 1959 Aldington sent H.D. Augustus Hare's *Walks in Rome* (1871).
2 There are so many biographies of Queen Mary, the grandmother of Elizabeth II, that it is difficult to determine exactly which one H.D. is referring to here.

During the 'long week-end' of Letter 214, Bryher and H.D. must have talked seriously about H.D.'s relationship with Aldington. The visit from Catha had gone well: H.D. had genuinely liked her and Bryher was enjoying her role as benefactor with its scope for education and advice. H.D. was now particularly concerned about Aldington's health, another issue about which Bryher liked to think of herself as an authority. On 2 November 1959 Aldington wrote H.D., 'Bryher most sweetly suggests my coming to Suisse for medico consultations. I WANT to come, more to thank you and her for Catha, than for health. BUT I MUST get this super-damned anthology done. ...' While Aldington felt pressed to finish this editorial chore, his work is merely one of several matters that he felt needed to be attended to before he could travel to see H.D. for the first time since 1938. H.D. obliquely reiterated Bryher's invitation on 4 November 1959: 'We must arrange carefully about "medico consultations", if you do manage to come. Br spends to-day in Locarno, but I have tomorrow with her, to talk things over. She does have miraculous ideas – but is so far ahead of me in energy.' If H.D. worried that she would not have the 'energy' the visit required, Aldington had other excuses: on 5 November 1959 he protested, 'I'm so shabby you'd be ashamed for me to be seen, but under Catha's tyranny a corduroy complète is being made in Sancerre. ... If there is frost-snow I can't car it, but if there is only fog-rain, I can.' He also worried about the water pipes freezing in his absence, and his November letters are peppered with reports on road conditions and possible driving routes. But the conversational tenor of his correspondence persists (on 11 November 1959 he wrote matter-of-factly, 'Could you book me an appointment with an oculist?') and there seems never to have been a question that, having been asked, he would come.

For her part, H.D. sent him a flurry of letters and telegrams with maps and explicit directions about his hotel and appointments. On 16 November 1959 she confessed to Pound, 'I have not seen R.A. for 21 years + am terribly apprehensive. I mean, merely physically – will I come unstuck?' (Yale). Bryher was in London while the arrangements were being made and H.D. kept her informed of the details, but the two women had separate agendas. For example, H.D. wrote Aldington on 17 November 1959 that she had two problems: first, she was 'very anxious' that he meet one of her friends at the Klinik, 'but we must not discuss Catha in her presence ... she is very jealous of our contacts – + resents Br.'s interest in Catha'. H.D. continued, 'The second thing: Ezra was very anxious to come here. I want to talk to you of this, quite freely, but can't in Bryher's presence. He wants you to go to Brunn. [Brunnenburg] Merano, for a week's visit. I said that I would give the message. I suppose I should not have mentioned your coming here. ... I said no, of course, to his coming here.'

Aldington did manage to drive in his unheated Renault the 450 kilometres from Sury en Vaux to Zürich and saw H.D. amid a round of medical appointments between 24 and 30 November. He was relieved that the doctors found nothing seriously wrong with him and pleased with their new medication and diet for indigestion, insomnia, lethargy, depression, and generally 'nerves'. He wrote Lawrence Durrell on 4 December 1959, 'The trip to Zürich was rather pleasant, in fact very much so', and asked him if he could do anything to arrange publication of H.D.'s work, adding 'She is 73, crawling about still on crutches three years after breaking her femur, lonely in that Klinik.'[1] As soon as he returned home, he wrote to H.D. on 1 December 1959, 'How to thank you and Bryher for all you did I know not. I can only say that I am very grateful. The trip did me good ...'.

Aldington and H.D. are curiously silent in their letters to each other and to others about the details of their meeting. Aldington is oblique in affirming their sympathetic bond, closing his 'thank you' letter of 1 December characteristically, 'My green fields this afternoon are as misty as your lake.' H.D. was somewhat more explicit in responding on 4 December 1959: 'It was good for me to get out. And to have you bring a new vibration here – or a new-old vibration. Bryher was happy too. Any time you feel you want reassurance, you must let us arrange meeting [with the doctors]. ... All thanks for visit.' It is clear, however, that the encounter was significant for both of them. Bryher and Aldington remained guarded friends: in his letter of 3 December 1959, thanking her for the visit, he closes 'Yours sincerely, Richard Aldington', but indicates at the end of this letter that before leaving Zürich Bryher had invited him and Catha to return at Easter, a trip to which he was not yet ready to commit himself. Bryher then suggested he travel to Basel where they might all meet part way, for H.D. was eager to see him again.

1 *Literary Lifelines*, 108, 110.

≈ **215** ≈

30 December [1959]
[Klinik Brunner
Küsnacht]

Dear Richard,

Bryher just had your long letter forwarded from Vaud, she shared it with me. I did not think you would consider Basel – still, it was not wholly a bad idea of Bryher's. Why don't you come to Kloten [Zürich's airport] + escort me to N.Y.? Now, I can hear you howl. You could see Dr. Prutting + that would settle all sorts of anxieties. I am not in the least visualizing <u>myself</u> getting to Swissair at Kloten, Zürich, but it makes me laugh to think that I could even <u>think</u> of it. Poor Perdita will be in purdah with her 4th + you would not have to be on view. The Stanford – no, Stanhope [Hotel] is just opposite the Met. [Metropolitan] Museum [of Art] + you could stay there incog., with me, in the middle distance, also incog.

<u>Dec. 31.</u>

Do not be alarmed, Dec. 30 entry was written in an end-of-year frenzy to turn over a new leaf, to <u>get away</u>.

I enclose two <u>Helen</u> sections. They were set up in America – they are less abstract than the sections I gave you. I had to find out from Norman Pearson if they could be re-printed here. He said yes, <u>Licorne</u>, but I hear from Mr Temple and he speaks of <u>Two Cities</u> – It doesn't matter.[1] I wonder if the two enclosed would be more suitable? I had a charming letter from him. Should I write him?

Bryher was here for the week. The va + vient + confusion have been terrific. I will get back to papers + books after tomorrow.

Do you <u>want</u> to write poetry, romances? If you do, you <u>will</u>.

All blessings to you both.

From
Dooley./

I believe I have kept my title, Bid Me to Live (A Madrigal). I have been fighting hard. ...

1 Aldington, with the help of Durrell and Temple, is trying to place H.D.'s work in these small periodicals.

Aldington did not take seriously H.D.'s suggestion that he accompany her to New York to visit Perdita's family. He may well have felt threatened by the idea of being in some ways responsible for H.D. or even just by being in such physically close and regular proximity without the excuse or presence of physicians and other attendants. Additionally, the trip to Zürich had been a real effort; although he was feeling comparatively better, he was still unwell and an excursion to New York was simply out of the question. On 2 January 1960 he responded, 'New York. What next! My dear girl …'.

Aldington's intimate connection with H.D. depended on ties established in the past and on the exchange of daily and parallel experiences rather than on physical presence or a new phase of relationship. Thus he wrote her on 5 January 1960, 'I send you photos of 1916 and 1942. Although the 1916 one is pretty blurry, I must say you had a fairly good-looking husband.' On 12 January 1959 he wrote about the winter weather both were experiencing: 'You must be colder in Zürich. … Is your room really warm? By a prodigal expenditure of coal … I can keep this stout little place really warm. It is really very snug and quiet. … Then this evening I shall make a curry and put in some of the exotic spices Alister sent me.' He continued to send her detailed accounts of his varied reading (Ruskin, Pepys, proofs of Durrell's *Clea*), and concluded on 16 January 1960, 'Excuse long and silly letter – but I have written myself out of agitation into some calm. … All love, my dear …'. He also sent her extensive commentary on his cooking and on the local wildlife (particularly mice, birds and butterflies) and regular jokes from subtle to broad to naughty. On 29 January 1960 he asked her if she knew 'a book called "Love in Action" by one Fernando Henriques, a West Indian. … According to Geoff [Dutton], it is highly entertaining and instructive.' Three letters later, on 12 February 1960, he commented, 'I believe we ought to get that book, Love in Action. Geoff Dutton says it is a scientific treatise on (parm my sarong) "how the world fucks". I'll ask him to bring a copy.' In the same vein, on 6 May 1960, he wrote,

> I'm sure you admire the beautiful [Gina] Lollobrigida. Though she is vulgar she has the aristocracy of race in her very bone-structure. Well, in French baby slang 'Lolla' is milk, and she is pretty well-equipped in that respect. And now, I discover, that pretty little boy of hers is called Milko.
> Milk-ho!

During the winter and spring of 1960, H.D. readied *Bid Me to Live* for publication and prepared to visit the United States. She questioned Aldington about final matters of accuracy, writing for example on 20 January 1960, 'I speak of "separation allowance" in Madrigal, the money allowed a private soldier's wife. Pearson says it is the wrong term. … Then he queries "Vale of Health" … Wasn't Keats somewhere near that Vale of Health?' In the same letter she emphasized her apprehensions about the trip to see Perdita and the new baby due in February: 'I talk about America. I try to imagine myself there.' On 15 February 1960 H.D. wrote Aldington, 'I had a staggering letter from Norman Pearson. The "American Academy of Arts + Letters" gives a Litt. Award, once in five years… now H.D. is offered, if she will go + fetch it, $1000 + a gong [medal]. I am rather upset. I will have to make a speech. … I am rather un-nerved with gongs + babies.' As late as 21 April 1960 H.D. worried that parts of *Bid Me to Live* might be considered libellous (she was especially concerned about 'animosity' from 'Bella' and 'Ivan', that is

Arabella Yorke and John Cournos) and she remained upset about the trip: Bryher had booked a flight and arranged that Dr Brunner's daughter Blanche would accompany her, but H.D. wrote Aldington, 'I consented with proviso, <u>I may not go at all</u>. I am clearing out, books, papers etc., but feel I have Atlas' world on my head. I can't shake it off. I will go on, however, with preparations.'

Aldington was pleased and supportive about the publication of *Bid Me to Live* and H.D.'s award, offering advice about details in both instances, but his own mind was farther ranging than the immediate concerns reflected in H.D.'s briefer letters, and he rambled anecdotally and at length in his correspondence. For example, in recommending *Clea* to H.D. on 23 February 1960, Aldington describes a scene: 'When Darley gets her inanimate, half-drowned body to the beach, and is working on her lungs with artificial respiration, he suddenly feels the pathos of the fragility of her girl's ribs.' Aldington then contrasts Durrell with D.H. Lawrence: 'Lorenzo was always talking about "new tenderness" to women, which usually ended up in his pulling Frieda's hair and calling her "shit bag", but at that moment when the poor Clea is sicking up her lunch, it seems to me real tenderness.' On 3 March 1960 he noted, 'I saw some lovely wild violets yesterday – considered sending a few to you in an envelope – refrained because squashed flowers are useless, and there is so much destruction now of everything beautiful.'

In late March, after much planning, Aldington returned to Switzerland, this time accompanied by Geoffrey Dutton and his wife. H.D. was concerned that the Duttons would find her 'shattered', for as a result of publicity associated with *Bid Me to Live*, *Newsweek* wanted to interview her. Her response on 18 March 1960 to a wire from Pearson that 'they will fly man immediately from Paris' was to alert the Klinik office that she had 'gone away but left orders to forward letters'. She hoped she had done the right thing and asked Aldington, 'You <u>did</u> tell me not to give interviews? I shall quote you … as my "advisor here" (not by name) but I must write a stiffish letter to Pearson. He has been so terribly kind and tactful – why this <u>now</u>?' H.D. was eager to see Aldington again, however, advising him on 20 March 1960 to drive very carefully and to ring her at any time and in any event as soon as they arrived. She added a postscript on 21 March: 'Br wants me to see these people, <u>Newsweek</u>. She has wired them I have grippe (her idea) but if they <u>write</u>, I will try to arrange something, she said, she told them. I am sure you will agree that I cannot undertake this sort of thing. But we won't argue when you come – only tell the others that I have been worried – + I must be firm with Pearson + Erich Heydt is urging interviews, too.' Aldington supported H.D., sending 'a wire of protest' at the same time as his letter on 21 March 1960, and writing again the next day, 'I spent a very broken and uneasy night, worrying about you and this Newsweek affair.' But their meeting, again brief, went off well (on 25 March H.D. lunched with Aldington and the Duttons at their hotel). The *Newsweek* interview, with Lionel Durand, occurred – as Pearson, Bryher and Heydt wished – in early April and appeared on 2 May. On 12 May H.D. flew to New York for six weeks.

15 May [1960]
[Stanhope Hotel
New York]

Dear Richard,

We were shown a door on street-level, to [the Metropolitan] Museum, so we went up in a lift, yesterday, + I felt completely at home with Pompeii + archaic Greece, even if some were copies – such miraculous ones. Lunch by the pool! An attendant said to me, 'You better have a chair – no charge', so I was wafted along to the book-and-card room + bought about 100 cards + can go back there, even alone, at any time. Thank you for last letter +/or letters + all stamps are greatly appreciated. I have a lovely apartment, very quiet, + people in every day for tea – <u>tea</u>, as of old, which Blanche prepares for me in a sizeable kitchenette. Lots of flowers and <u>Bid Me</u> letters. This is just to let you know that I have arrived. It seems years since I left, May 12–13. Rather hot, + cornflowers + poppies from Perdita bring in the summer. We go to them this afternoon – all seems very well. Greet Catha, + look after yourself.

Love,
Dooley./

During the spring and summer of 1960 Aldington felt better physically, in large measure due to Bryher's generosity both to him directly and to Catha in overseeing and paying for her education and through various gifts – among them a new car and funds to permit holidays away from Paris and Sury. Because he felt financially more secure, he could at last rest from the round of work which had been making him so nervous. Evidence of his rallying spirits appeared in his renewed desire to travel. On 16 June he wrote H.D., 'I drove Alister and his wife and [baby] Sylvain to Fontainebleau. It is about 135 kilometres from here. We had a delicious lunch at a small restaurant, quite near the lovely old palace … trout, ham cooked in a sauce of Chablis wine, and goat cheese, with white wine of Sauvigny, and red of Bordeaux.' He added: 'Thanks to Bryher's generosity I shall be able to spend a fortnight with Catha at the Saintes Marie [in the Camargue]. I had intended to start today, but (1) the car must be overhauled before so long a trip, (2) I must get my washing, (3) the stay of my friends tired me, (4) I need a haircut!' By the time he left the south of France for Sury in early July he was already planning a trip to Rome with Catha over her Christmas holiday.

H.D. returned to Switzerland on 25 June 1960, and settled back into her relatively uneventful life at the Klinik Brunner. She was impressed with her reception at the award ceremony, charmed by her new grandson, stimulated by the positive response to *Bid Me to Live*, and sorry to leave the pleasures of the museum across the street. Encouraged by her trip to America, H.D. continued to entertain the idea of leaving the Klinik and now considered the possibility of southern California. She wrote Aldington on 30 June 1960, 'I wouldn't leave before end Oct., if I leave at all, but I don't want to get stuck here again.' On 4 August 1960 she was more hesitant: 'I have been trying to settle-in, destroying old MSS + so on. … Bryher goes or plans N.Y. in Oct. – she wants me to go with her, but it is too soon. I only dream of some coast-retreat.' Inspired, however, by the attention to her novel, H.D. began work on her last long poem *Hermetic Definition* in August and continued to write 'Thorn Thicket', the reflective journal which complements her other journals, 'Compassionate Friendship' and the 'Hirslanden Notebooks' (Yale). She also wondered now about publishing 'The Mystery' (Yale), written in 1949 and 1951, which she wrote Aldington on 9 August 1960 she thought of as 'the 3rd of the series' which included 'The Sword Went Out to Sea' and 'Red Rose and the White'.

⇗ **217** ⇖

6 August 1960
Sury

Dear Dooley,
I wrote you yesterday, but write again to say that the 'échantillon' arrived this morning.[1] I don't know whether to send it on to Li Santo [in the Camargue] or to keep it for her [Catha]. She will be delighted, because she has a very keen response to beauty. Apropos which – all this 'modern art' rot has brought about a situation in which I have the greatest difficulty in finding her photos or picture-books of Greek sculpture. IF we are able to get to Rome at or about Xmas, I'll try to get some there.
In past two days I've had a request from some Catholic institute in Buffalo for (free) permission to 'sound record' a poem for their 'deaf' pupils; and another from the Jewish

Hospital in Denver asking for a (free) copy of Mistral for their patients. It doesn't seem to strike these people that a writer hopes to be paid for his work before he gives it away. I think I'll write and ask if they'll give me a job as a janitor or garbage-man.

[Michael] Harald's idea was that Pitman [a journalist from the *Sunday Express*] should fly out to Zürich to interview you and get a 'pre-view' of Bid Me, with the idea of launching it in England. It annoys me very much that Pitman hasn't been out, and apparently hasn't rung Bryher. Why do they ask one to arrange these things if they don't intend to carry them out? Unluckily, as I told you, Michael is in Rome dragging tourists about to earn some money for his young wife and baby. But I'll get on to him, and blow him sky-high if they don't do something.

I am in a state of fury – a modern successor to Dodson & Fogg[2] in London is trying to bully and rob me, and of course everybody who might help is AWAY, and I can't get any answers.

Under separate cover I send you the copy of Mystery. It is in such a different mood and style from Bid Me that I would advise postponing publication until late in 1961. One isn't allowed to be versatile anymore. I remember Michael Arlen[3] telling me I was not a novelist because each of my novels was different from its predecessors – 'a real novelist chooses a milieu, a set of characters and certain situations as his genre, and never goes outside'. I think he's right. Look at P.G. Wodehouse and Graham Greene – perpetually plagiarising themselves.

My friend Robert Allerton Parker (whose wife is N.Y. editress of Vogue) says in answer to my queries: 'Tell H.D. all is exorbitant in price everywhere in USA. Even Sausalito where the fogs roll in from the Golden Gate.' I remember with pain how you used to suffer from London fogs, and though these Pacific fogs are at least <u>clean</u>, you won't enjoy. Louis Stevenson had to fly. Have you thought of the coast of Texas? What is wrong with southern California? Too much oil and too many Los Angelers of course. I loved the desert part of Texas for a very few days after the rains, such billows and seas of incomparably lovely wild flowers – oh, hashish-dreams of them! – and among them, as in Eden, multitudes of what the Americans ignorantly call 'horned toads' – they are really lizards. All <u>real</u> poets love lizards and snakes – sacred to Phoebus – Tom Eliot screams when he sees one!!

Much love,
Richard

1 Literally, 'échantillon' means 'sample'; here Aldington is referring to the gifts H.D. got for Catha at the Metropolitan Museum of Art: a tiny bronze head of a bull and a small statue of a cow.
2 The corrupt law firm in Dickens's *Pickwick Papers*.
3 Michael Arlen (1895–1956), author of the popular novel *The Green Hat*.

≫ **218** ≪

17 October 1960
Poste Restante
Aix-en-Provence
B. du R. [Bas du Rhône][1]

Dear Dooley,

The Cur-nos letter (herewith in a pair of disdainful pincers) is typical of the writer, of course not to receive any notice but a contemptuous disdain.[2] I could send him one of my 'stinkers' but why notice the Thing? He is so completely forgotten that only 3 or 4 months back I had a letter from a London publisher who wanted to reprint that very bad Sologub translation, which unhappily has my name on it.³ The publisher said all efforts to trace the Cur had failed – could I help? I couldn't. The motive behind the letter is a base envy – you are praised, printed, and prized – he is in what is known as the dawg-house. Poof, my dear.

We are in Aix, and, as they say, rather 'frustrated'. There is difficulty still over Catha's registration – sheer bureaucracy, of course – and I shall have to call in the big guns again. My daughter has no more sense than her father, and the two places she has chosen are not very comfortable. In the Camargue there are 3 meubles [pieces of furniture], 2 beds, a huge hearth, electric light, but no running water; and the difficulty of even moderate cleanliness is great. But the Mas [cottage] is old and the meubles (such as they are) authentic 18th century Provençal. One looks out across the great marsh, and there is no sound. This morning when Catha opened her shutters, two small bats fell out – apparently chilled by the recent cold. The sun was fairly strong, and first one and then the other recovered under its warmth, took to their wings, and went off to find a less chilly roost. We saw the flamingoes, numbers of egrets, sea-mews, gulls, and lovely little birds I can't name.

The place in Aix has a lovely view, downstairs kitchen and dining-room, upstairs two bedrooms; but the water is deficient, there is no electricity, and a mere presence of a shower-bath – what use without warm water? And it is 3 miles out of Aix, so how can C. get to and from the University except by taking my car, and leaving me to shiver over a poor wood-fire? So we are looking for a better place. If not findable, C. must get a student's room and I must go back to Sury. But I dare say we shall find something. The places are not at all bad – in 1913 we should have been thrilled by them, but my aged bones need more warmth, and my eyes can't cope with kerosene lamps.

I am very pleased indeed that you like Temple's DHL, which of course was written under my influence. The whole thing is a kind of battle, in which nobody wins. The Viking Press ('rich as Croesus, my dear, wish we had their income as our capital') disdainfully send me another 'token' 25 dollars for introduction to The Rainbow! Why not pay fairly, except that I am not an American journalist? May Allah blacken their faces.⁴

Temple is in USA, on some 'scholarship' to study American radio methods – he had better stay in France and study something else.

It is lovely to be back in the Midi, although at first it was appallingly wet and cold for October. In October 1928 Arabella, Brigit, Frieda and I all bathed naked daily together on one of the plages of Port-Cros, and then lay in the sun. So warm it was. They were charming – Frieda of course a Rubens, Brigit a Titian, and Arabella a Giorgione – that is, putting them in the highest class of their type. Even then Frieda naked wasn't really fat – just opulent like the other Rubens ladies! Anyway, to-night is less cold, and there seems hope.

Aix is very pleasant – a charming town – but one can't see the town for the traffic. You would laugh if you could hear Catha asking (as she drives) directions from the traffic cops, cheeking them, and of course getting the Frenchman's homage. Really it is the only country in which to be a woman.

Don't give another thought to that rat.

All love from us both
Richard

1 Catha had been unhappy in Paris and with her course at the Sorbonne. She has decided to transfer to the University of Aix-en-Provence and Aldington has left Sury to help her get settled. They planned to take a flat large enough so that Aldington could visit regularly and to locate a cottage in the Camargue for weekends and holidays.

2 On 11 October 1960 H.D. forwarded a vitriolic letter from John Cournos criticizing her treatment of factual material in *Bid Me to Live*. She wrote Aldington that Bryher 'thinks the letter is simply <u>insane</u>. A very slight shock to me, though!' Cournos was particularly angered by what he saw as H.D.'s unfair portrayal of Arabella in the novel.

3 Feodor Sologub (Feodor Teternikov), *The Little Demon*, trans. Richard Aldington and John Cournos, New York: Alfred A. Knopf, 1916. Aldington knew no Russian, so it was Cournos who actually translated this work; Aldington 'collaborated' by trying to polish the English prose.

4 F.-J. Temple's book was *D. H. Lawrence: l'œuvre et la vie* (Paris: Seghers, 1960), for which Aldington had written an introduction. It seems that Aldington is quoting in his parentheses a conversational quip by Norman Douglas. Aldington had written an introduction to *The Rainbow* for the Penguin edition of 1953.

~ 219 ~

18 November [1960]
[Klinik Brunner
Küsnacht]

Dear Richard,

Thank you for the <u>Venice</u>. Br is due to-night + I can discuss this with her – but now, I am already so depressed with the constant <u>Föhn</u> [wind], that I don't think I'll have the wit or grit to move out + into possibly more cold + floods. Anyhow, I will let you know.¹ It is as well that I got Heydt to go over <u>Die Tat</u>, Nov. 12 [1960] review of 'Ein Roman über D.H. Lawrence – H.D. "Bid Me to Live (A Madrigal)"'. I had missed this – it appeared so alien to the Julia of the book – but Heydt picked on it. This H.W. Häusermann brings up <u>Death of a Hero</u>. In the same paragraph, this Hilda Doolittle wishes to clear up her situation as described in R.A.'s 1929 autobiographical novel. After the separation + his death <u>verliert sie jeden Halt</u> (she loses all control or hold). Then directly he quotes R.A. in English, 'She travelled a good deal, always with a pretty large brandy flask, + had more lovers than were good for her – or for them.' I can later look this up, but will wait for Br – + I am sure you did not mean this for Julia or – I cannot recall the 'Hero'['s] name, if any. I think this man is a prof. of Eng. Litt. at Geneva – + really, I am a little amused, but let one such get past + it may become standardized for future reviews, if and when <u>Madrigal</u> appears here. Mrs Schnack, who wants to do the trans., told me she had lent her copy of <u>Madrigal</u> to a prof. at Geneva of whom she had spoken before. I suppose this is the man. I can write Schnack, but better let it rest now. It would be an amusing libel case – if they have them here – 'defamation of character', if ever there was such a thing. But case <u>against</u> the prof. not the 'Hero'. He does quote the DHL 'Nightmare' bits from 'Kangaroo'. It doesn't seem consistent with the brandy-flask. However, don't bother with this. I read a lot about the Lady C. [D.H. Lawrence's *Lady Chatterley's Lover*] + in a way it is good for the 'little people' that it [this misreading of H.D.'s novel] came up. To me, their peep-show seems as innocuous as Alice in Wonderland.²

All the best to you both.

From
Dooley./

1 Apparently H.D. earlier in the autumn gave Pound the impression that they might meet in Venice. She is continuing to think of possible trips she might take or places she might settle, but when she seriously contemplates the practical details of uprooting herself from Switzerland and choosing a site either for a brief or extended period, she recoils. Aldington wrote on 17 November 1960, 'I sent you a [postcard of] "Venice"' and commented, 'It is just as well you decide against Venice, for I suspect emotional complications [with Pound] there, which might distress you.' On 12 November 1960 he had advised her against this trip for other reasons: 'I think the Venice trip ... depends almost entirely on your <u>legs</u>, and your ability to endure the damp and possible cold of Venice in late Dec. ... If you can stand the fatigue, I think the change would do you good.' Aldington also worried that H.D. would have difficulty getting in and out of gondolas and finding a warm hotel, but he was invariably supportive of her projected travels. Bryher, in contrast, was not, and her response was always a hurdle for H.D. Still thinking about the trip to Venice and Pound's expectations, she wrote to Aldington on 23 November 1960, 'I dare not tell Bryher, but must speak of it, when she gets back. Mary de R. seemed very keen, but indefinite – + I can't plan everything – + I do not think that I can manage <u>with my legs</u>. ... + Br is going to scream anyway.'

2 The author of this German review has garbled Aldington's *Death of a Hero* in part by mis-quoting but particularly by falling into the trap of reading fiction as fact. H.D. is responding to several difficulties here. She indicates layers of personae or alter-egos. On one hand there is 'Julia', her autobiographical persona in *Bid Me to Live*, who, like H.D. ('I'), 'misses' the review because it seems as 'alien' to the real character of Julia as it is to H.D.'s true personality and experiences. On the other hand there is 'this Hilda Doolittle', Häusermann's incorrect representation of H.D., the author of *Bid Me to Live*, who has, according to the reviewer, written her novel in part as a corrective to Aldington's *Death of a Hero*.

   H.D. also responded to the further difficulty posed by Häusermann's equation of Alding-ton's Elizabeth, Winterbourne's wife, with H.D., something Aldington never intended and a reading that had not previously occurred to H.D. He answered on 21 November 1960, 'I wonder what gives a Genevan prof who has never met me and knows nothing about me the impudence to assert that D. of an H. is "openly autobiographical"? Certainly the third part is based on first-hand war experiences, and a certain amount of the pre-war is naturally based on life observed in England. ... The travelling, the brandy flask and the lovers were, I must admit, taken direct from Nancy Cunard. ...' While H.D. hoped that the reviewer's misinterpretations would not become 'standardized' for other readers, it is also important to realise that her predominant reaction was to be 'a little amused'. Ironically, as indicated in Fred D. Crawford's 'Misleading Accounts of Aldington and H.D.' (*English Literature in Transition*, 1890–1920, Vol. 30, 1987, 48–67), it has become common to misread *Death of a Hero* in this way and to see Aldington as hostile to H.D.

   On 21 November Aldington wondered if 'the Lawrence Bureau' was not perhaps respon-sible for what he called 'the attack', but he had long had a policy of not responding directly to reviewers in print; surely he had given up as futile any impulse to correct misinterpretations offered by those interested in discrediting him. He concluded: 'And for heaven's sake don't worry about Die Tat. Surely you can see that a divided press – calumny versus praise – is the very best thing for an author.' H.D., however, felt that she had to respond to the reviewer, and wrote Aldington on 29 November 1960 that with a friend at the Klinik she had 'managed to write a dignified short letter on Sunday, "I must ask you [the journal] to be good enough to refute this error" sort of thing'. Her concern, interestingly, was for the 'libel' which she saw as consisting of an unfair portrait of *Aldington* – not, as critics and biographers have suggested (misreading with Häusermann), her concern that she herself had been misrepresented by Aldington as Elizabeth.

H.D. remained at the Klinik Brunner for the winter: her travel plans persisted as absorbing projections, but the reality of her situation and the familiarity of her surroundings kept her in Switzerland. With Bryher's financial help and his moderately improved health, Aldington felt able to travel once more. His schedule was to a degree determined by Catha's school holidays, for he was eager to share his enthusiasms and depended on her as a traveling companion. She, in turn, was a willing pupil, but had a life of her own and increasingly wanted to spend her free time with her friends in the Camargue. They decided to spend two weeks over Christmas in Rome.

Aldington wrote to H.D. on 5 December 1960 that he wished he 'were going to the Rome of 1912 or even of 1922', but both Bryher and H.D. sent him extra funds as a Christmas gift and he and Catha thoroughly enjoyed themselves. Having returned to Aix, he wrote to H.D. on 30 December 1960 that 'It has all been a tremendous stimulus and "uplift" – one forgets how footling and dull this mechanised world is compared with the ancients and the Renaissance.' In February, he left Catha to pursue her studies and friendships in Provence and returned to Sury.

❧ 220 ❦

1 March 1961
Sury en Vaux
Cher

Dear Dooley,

If I don't mail these stamps to you I may lose them. I hope you will like the MILLIONS of South African water buffaloes, the most dangerous animal in the world – worse than a tiger, while the rhino is a pal. They always charge. Somewhere in his memoirs [*Light on a Dark Horse*, 1951] dear Roy has a marvellous story (wouldn't be him otherwise) of a battle with a water buffalo, which he told me viva voce long before that book. 'Well, you see, man, there I was with only one cartridge left in me rifle, and suddenly one of those bloody water buffaloes came at me ...'.

Of course, you are right about Harry T. Moore, and no doubt he and I could have mauled each other in print considerable.[1] But that would not have helped Lorenzo's fame, which is what matters – to hell with Angie [Angelo Ravagli, Frieda's husband] and [Lawrence] Pollinger [Lawrence's agent] and Heinemann e tutti quanti. So when he held out the olive branch I buried the hatchet – excuse mixed metaphor. You will have had the ghastly 'periodical' of his friend and disciple.[2] Before Frere decided Moore is the guy and I am no good I was silently correcting the misprints and misquotes in DHL's books as they were reprinted. Now everything will have to be brawled about.

Don't bother to return the Catalogue[3] or the pupil of Moore.

The enclosed from my London agent will give you an idea of the incredible cheating of non-best-selling authors which goes on. To save you doing arithmetic, Folio Soc proposed to take £9500 (approx) from the public and to give me £200, while dropping the Introduction which is the only authentic biographical-critical essay on Laclos in English.[4] After a fearful amount of wrangling Mrs Colin worked them up to £275 and the inclusion of the essay. Ma ché [nonsense]. It is true that three other editions (without intro) are in print in England and USA, but is that any reason I should be cheated on another? Do you know what Viking – Harold Guinzberg is a millionaire apart from that firm – gave me for each of those DHL introductions? All of 25 dollars, remarking with a sneer that I had omitted to take out US copyright (how could I when at the time, several years ago, they were spitting on DHL and wouldn't use them?) They proposed this as 'an ex gratia honorarium'. Poof my dear.

Non rag'iam di lor.[5] A fearful man with a stethoscope etc. says my acute bronchs are over but the chronic remain. I am not to diet against weight so much. So over last weekend Lucullus dined with Lucullus.[6] I bought a small duckling which I stuffed and baked, and ate with a Château Mouton-Rothschild which was delicious. Yesterday I wallowed in English haddock and an Anjou of 1959. And with fearful extravagance I have arranged for the shower here to be changed to a real bath. It's all very well for Alister, who is descended from convicts no doubt, to be satisfied with a shower, but I like a real bath; and I daresay his little son and his English wife may agree. Anyway, the order is given; and I hope to soak out in hot water some of the 'whoreson lethargy' left by the double flu and bronchs.

You do not say how you are, whether Bryher escaped the scourge [of tourists] in the Scillys, whether Perdita and little ones are all right. But sursum corda [lift up your hearts] – here it is really spring. We shall relapse of course, but the lilacs and quince trees are budding, there is a marvellous peach tree in flower under the hill of Sancerre, Alister's tiny judas tree and apricot are in flower. The [neighbourhood] children bring me violets.

Have you see Alec Randall's book on Rome? I don't think it's good enough for you, but if you wish, I'll send it.[7]

I read my Rowohlt DHL with difficulty and Bellows dictionary, realising how Germanic he was in many ways. I mean good Germanic, not Unser Grüss ist Heil. ...[8] I must say I think he was unfair to those girls, Jessie [Chambers] and Helen Corke etc. Mother-struck as he was, he was utterly embarrassed by the natural timidity and ignorance of virgins, and had the nerve to abuse them as inadequate, whereas the fault was his. Frieda, however, was a motherly type, and (between ourselves) a bit of a whore, which was what he could respond to. It's all in Freud!

Love,
Richard

1 On 27 February 1961, H.D. had written, 'It never seemed to me <u>fair</u> that he [Moore] should oggle + goggle + gobble the whole DHL saga, pre-digested or undigested – but I really, really should not judge – it's just an innate shuddering away –'.

2 Unidentified.

3 An unidentified English catalogue of second-hand books which Kershaw found for Aldington and which he passed on to H.D. on 24 February 1961.

4 That is, Aldington's introduction to his translation of *Les Liaisons Dangereuses* by Choderlos de Laclos, published by Routledge as *Dangerous Acquaintances* in 1924.

5 Aldington is quoting 'non rag'iam di lor' (let's not speak of it any more) from Dante's *Inferno*, III.

6 Aldington alludes to Lucullus, a man famed for his wealth and self-indulgence, depicted in Horace's *Epistles* II. 2.26.

7 Alec Randall, a friend of Aldington's since university, wrote of his experiences as an English diplomat in Italy in *Discovering Rome* (1960).

8 In 1959 the German publisher Rowohlt commissioned Aldington to write a monograph (in English which was then translated into German), published in Hamburg as *D.H. Lawrence in Selbstzeugnissen und Bilddokumenten* in 1961. While Aldington's 'Unser Grüss ist Heil' may

derive from an unidentified Nazi song, it seems more likely because of the unusual word order of the German that he is being generally descriptive. I am grateful to Wilhelm Bartsch for suggesting this possibility.

〜 221 〜

7 March [1961]
[Klinik Brunner
Küsnacht]

Dear Richard,

Keep the cutting if you want. I will return the Russians + H.T. Moore later.[1] I sent back the last lot before you wrote me not to. I must read HTM again carefully + Br must too, if you don't mind. About Alec's Rome – thank you. I have the old books + your folder – I don't think I want this – but give messages, as indicated. I don't know of your poet, but will ask Br if she does.[2] I allowed myself to read [Portrait of a] Genius, after a really serious siege with Rainbow. There is nothing to say: HTM is collecting; you, creating. How could HTM expect to understand the Englishness of England + the contrasting or compensating Sturm und Drang of the hochgeborene [high-born] – at home + abroad? I don't imagine that HTM has even the social sense to understand such as W. Bynner + Spud [Willard Johnson].[3] But I must not go on, I could write a book about him + 'the foothills of the Ozarks'.[4] But I must 'kill out ambition', as the Yogis advise. The Russian is really funny. I shall soon begin to love him. Thank you for saving the 'violets along the lanes' there for me.[5]

I enclose from Perdita. She writes terrifically + wants to 'write', but how can she + 'writing' could never approach her 'genius' for living – but there is time. I must send along her letters as they come.

This inadequately to thank you for all exciting papers.

Love
Dooley./

1 H.D. sent Aldington a 'cutting' of a review of the Rowohlt *D.H. Lawrence* taken from the front page of the Zürich *Feuilleton*. On 4 March 1961 Aldington had sent her 'in the hopes of giving you a laugh or two … a list of queries [by Mikhail Urnov] from the Soviet Writers' Union on the two books they are doing' (translations of Aldington's novels) and commented, 'so much good will, I feel, and such a lack of humour'. He had also enclosed a letter from Moore to Lawrence Durrell and 'a review of Moore's Rilke'.
2 On 4 March 1961 Aldington had asked H.D. if she knew 'anything about a dirty – I mean physically – English man of letters and poet called John Gawsworth', who had asked Aldington for financial help. On the basis of Gawsworth's friendship with Roy Campbell, Aldington has sent him ten pounds.
3 The American poet Witter Bynner (1881–1968) wrote of his friendship with Lawrence in *Journey with Genius* (1951). An American journalist, Johnson (b. 1897) travelled with Bynner and the Lawrences in Mexico in 1923.
4 H.D. may be under the impression that Moore grew up in the Ozarks (an unlikely origin) or that Southern Illinois University in Carbondale, where Moore now teaches, is in the Ozarks (it is not). Alternatively, she may be using this phrase merely to indicate what she sees as Moore's lack of sophistication. Her allusion here seems unclear.
5 On 4 March 1961 Aldington had written, 'Real spring here – wild violets along the lanes, and the first cowslip just out in the garden here. I was tempted to pick and send, but the plucked and crushed flower is such a corp when it arrives. Better leave, and not destroy.'

In February 1961 H.D. was notified that Dr Brunner intended to sell his clinic, and on 27 April 1961 moved to the residential Hotel Sonnenberg in the hills of Zürich. Aldington set off from Sury in mid-March to visit Catha in Provence, then left from Aix in mid-April for an extended visit to Venice where he wrote daily letters and postcards to H.D. Bryher characteristically provided funds, realizing the deep pleasure the experience would bring him, although the immediate excuse for the trip was a book of photographs for which Aldington hoped to write an introduction. On 7 March 1961 Aldington wrote H.D. from Sury, 'Bryher suggested it would be better just to rest and winter in Italy. And so indeed it would! But when I can go on working, I fell I should do so. And really … the prospect of doing a short book when I got back here would be a stimulus.'

꒰ **222** ꒱

21 April 1961
c/o Thomas Cook & Son
289/305 Piazzetta dei Leoncini
Piazza San Marco
Venezia

Dear Dooley,

There! But 'c/o Cooks, Venice' gets here just as well!

I am so glad you have a refuge in the Sonnenberg, which sounds rather nice – a lift! You should insist on one.

I got into a state of 'nerves' by over-walking & over-enthusing, & then finding the Savoia prices are for USA professors & not for humble British writers. But all is well – I have another 'stude's room', small but adequate, with a balcony looking over a court, and as quiet as Sury itself!¹

The Americans have made prices ridiculous – a dongola bird from stazione to hotel is 1500 lire, & 2000 an hour for 'trips'. Only Americans use them. But the vaporetti are excellent – & I did Accademia-Scalzi & Scalzi-Accademia for 150 only – 25 cents instead of $2.50! But it is the Americans who keep the whole place going, & they are so nice I am very glad to interpret for them when they get into 'jams'. In S. Zaccaria recently I was appealed to by a very nice middle-aged couple, who were in much confusion, since they thought they were in another church! When I explained to the Madame, & pointed out the lovely Bellini, etc., she said scornfully, pointing to her husband puzzling over his guide-book, 'Would you please tell <u>him</u> where he is – he doesn't know a <u>thing</u> about Venuss.'

I have 'gotten' out of Savoia, & away from Angles & Yanks to a real Italian & very clean little hotel. So my worries are over.

The D.H.L.-Meynell story….² In 1915, he & F. [Frieda] were given free lodging in a nice country house, by the Meynells. A grandchild hurt himself with some garden tool & became a cripple. DHL wrote a cruel & beastly story (England, Thy England) jeering at it, & blaming it on the feebleness and wishy-washy of the child's father. On the day (or near it) when the story appeared in serial, the father was reported killed in action on the French front. DHL at first was horrified at what he had done, repudiated his story; but then his conceit & malice came into action, & he added a postscript to his repentant letter saying: 'No, I am glad I wrote the story.' Alas that so great a genius should have also been such a dirty little cad.

I did not mention the name of Meynell [in *Portrait of a Genius, But* ...], merely said (I think) 'a friend who had helped him', & condemned his behaviour. Moore, of course, had to blurt out 'Meynell' & give his journalist-pendant version of what had happened – all done at high pressure between the lectures & the reviews & 'books' & cocktails & publicity & TV – with the result you read [in *The Intelligent Heart: The Story of D.H. Lawrence* (1954)].

I think so often how much you would love Venice again. BUT, one has to <u>walk</u> all the time (on account of expense of them dongola birds) and the steps or stairs are endless. The Serenissima decree & the building or re-building of the bridges in arch-shape, with <u>steps</u> to prevent horses! I go up & down, up & down, & my leg muscles <u>ache</u> at night. Very good for me – I was too fat & lazy.

As France is the last beleaguered citadel of European living, so Venice is the last little fortress of pre-machine times. And the machine-men & the money-men will destroy it. Terrible to see what has been done – or un-done already; & near the station more hideous pseudo-American atrocities are being put up, with as much noise & contempt as possible.

Well, I am enjoying what is left – & much is left – while it lasts, & it will outlast me. But I am sorry for the children, who will have nothing. But they will conform, & not care. What a Threnody might be written on:

The Death of a Culture

But who could write it? Not the author of Death in the Afternoon [Hemingway].

You asked me to write to Ezra from here. I am sorry, but after that terrible indictment by [the prosecutor, Gideon] Hausner of Eichmann, the Nazis, the Germans & their admirers, I <u>can't</u>, I just can't. It is too horrible, & I just can't condone it, I am cutting off all communication with pro-Nazis I know. If this is smug, well, it is, but it isn't vile, cold-hearted torture & murder.

All love
Richard

Tell me on which date I might write to Sonnenberg.

One gets such lovely cards here now – I long to buy you MILLIONS. San Marco ...!³

---

1 It took Aldington several days to settle in and to pace himself. He initially took a room at the Bella Venezia which, he wrote to H.D. on 18 April 1961, had '<u>rats</u> even in the daytime!' He then lodged in the Savoia, but had to leave after a week because tourist agents had booked the entire hotel.

2 Viola Meynell, daughter of Wilfrid and the writer Alice Meynell, lent Lawrence her parents' cottage in Sussex for seven months in 1915.

3 In the same vein Aldington had written to H.D. on 18 April 1961, 'So beautiful is Venice! I spent the morning in the Accademia – such lovely pictures. I wanted to steal them all for you!'

223

28 April [1961]
Hotel Sonnenberg
Aurorastrasse
Zürich

Dear Richard,

Thanks for the magnificent + many cards + letters. I was once caught in the Marco side-entrance + was unexpectedly blessed by Patriarch – Pierre della Fontaine, coming down the stairs, lace + all.[1]

We got away, as see per above. Br thinks of everything + worked so very hard, bringing bags and books from Verena [the Klinik Brunner]. The last days were, in a way, almost funny, two near-suicides, a girl breaks arm, old lady goes down with double-pneumonia. Br said, 'stay in bed – anything might happen', but I could not let her do the heavy packing alone + here I am with one full, stuffed book-case, radio, a large bath-room, a large balcony + the galaxy of Z[ürich] underneath at night + raging song-birds at dawn – all new furniture, but not ultra-modern + two lovely flower-prints + room, a garden, with lilac, muguet, red roses. Of course, I should have left months ago, but the time was propitious as this place is all, all booked up for early summer + all summer + before Easter. Telephone by my nice, low bed – I hardly know myself + feel that I have descended from space or up out of the horrendous depth. There are thick woods on one side + the open view ahead across the lake. The candles must have 'worked', thank you + them.[2]

Thank you for clearing up the Meynell story. I <u>was</u> shocked.

I sent Horace Gregory the German paper-book [Rowohlt's *D.H. Lawrence*] – he feels strongly on the subject of H.T.M. – as per enclosed.

Forgive long silence – all blessing on you + Catha

as always
Dooley./

1 H.D. is responding to Aldington's account of his experiences on 25 April 1961, St Mark's Day, and the '3 benedictions I collected this morning'.
2 On 21 April 1961 Aldington had written, 'so glad you have found a refuge in the Hotel Sonnenberg. I <u>knew</u> you would – have been putting up candles to saints for you, this morning to Santa Lucia.'

224

12 May 1961
as from Mas Dromar[1]

Dear Dooley,

Do you remember Huysmans' absurd phrase about having heard his last mass at Solesmes before the expulsion of the fathers (they are back again) 'J'ai bu ma dernière bouteille de plain-chant' [I have drunk my last bottle of plainchant]? Well, j'ai bu ma dernière bouteille de Venice, & finished my last dinner in Campo S. Maria Zobenigo. But (D.V., as you so wisely say) I shall come back & bring Catha.

I had a lovely 'last day'. Caffè-latte outdoors by the Rio del Ostreghe. Then to post to mail my Italian dictionary – lightening bag for plane. I had my shoes shined – lucky I remembered – not to shame Catha. Then took the slow boat as far as S. Stae

(Eustachio) which, you will remember, is the next stop after Ca' d'Oro on the other bank.

This was my third visit to S. Stae, & I still couldn't see those 12 allegedly 'remarkable' pictures of early Settecento. The light & angle of vision are wrong, & I don't like to go inside altar rails. I walked on and came to the Campo (the only one with trees) of S. Giacomo dell'Orio, so charming & remote & unspoiled, with a very tranquil church, where I found a pillar of <u>verde antico</u> – certainly Roman. Going on, I came to a courtyard & part of a Scuola, in perfect early XVth century Renaissance – delicately carved pilasters. Later I found myself near the Frari, I just strolled round once more, looking at the monuments & pictures – the great Titian, the splendid Baroque memorials of Doges. In a side chapel I found myself looking at a marble slab, simply engraved: Claudio Monteverdi.

Beyond that I came to the Carnivai, which I had not seen before. Do you know it? Gothic, with the longest nave proportionately I have ever seen, & rich with Sircuto paintings, & gilded wooden statues of saints. And as if that were not enough, there was the Scuola dei Cermini, still intact, with a stuccoed beautiful stairway (like the Scala d'Oro in the Ducale) and a whole series of decorative paintings by G.B. Tiepolo. They are lovely, but strangely secular for the headquarters of a religious fraternity – sort of holy Bouchers [butchers]! I have one or two photos for you – they are too big for my envelopes, but I'll send them from Dromar.

The noon bells rang me out, & I walked on to the Locardo Montin (the J. A. Symonds restaurant) and fared most sumptuously on a sole & wild strawberries, with a quartino of bianco. I later sat by the Grand Canal, beside the Accademia, over coffee; & then to San Marco for a farewell look round, seeing several mosaics I had missed. The Guida d'Italia says there are 4000 square metres of mosaics, so no wonder they can't all be seen at once.

Then I simply had to go back to the hotel & rest.

Well, I just don't know how to thank Bryher & you for these enchanting five weeks. Since I got away from that dreadful Hotel Savoia, all has been perfect. Dined, as I said, at Piccola Riposta, where the head waiter discourses of Tintoretto, Veronese, & Tiepolo with enthusiasm & knowledge; & the second waiter is an amateur painter.

The only troubles are those of <u>age</u>. The ruthless stairs of those palaces & galleries! (I suppose the noble ladies were carried up.) And it is a nuisance to have to put on glasses to read the Guide, & then take them off to look at whatever it is. These are small things, & I am infinitely grateful for all the enrichment.

I must to bed. Tomorrow I shall take the slow boat to Piazzale Roma, for a last, lingering look at the Grand Canal.

Love
Richard

I made a small offering on your behalf in the Frari, to the B.V.M. [Blessed Virgin Mary]

1 Aldington remained in Venice, aided by extra money from Bryher, until 18 May when he left for a week at Catha's Mas in the Camargue. He then returned to Sury.

225

1 June 1961
Sury en Vaux
Cher

Dear Dooley,

I was grieved indeed to hear from Bryher that the delayed shock of that sudden and brutal up-rooting from Küsnacht had made you so ill. How fortunate that Dr. Heydt was at hand with the specialist! Bryher says you are recovering splendidly, and that even on Monday you were allowed to sit up in your room. But you mustn't exert – so don't bother to write. Br. will send all news. But do get well soon.[1]

I expect that you have heard that Br. is giving Catha a car of her own. It is most generous, and of course will make Catha's summer for her, and also save her infinite fatigue in her next academic year – if she gets her Propédeutique [preliminary degree]. For the psychology course they have to go twice a week to the Medical School at Marseille (the University there is linked with Aix) and naturally the university doesn't provide transport. I wired her the wonderful news, but didn't expect a reply, as she is working overtime. The exams are on the 8th–9th, but we shan't know result for some days.

This morning I had an airmail from Geoff Dutton. On the 25th arrived Miss Teresa Rose Dutton, a strapping Australian lass weighing 9 lbs, 10 oz. There had to be another Caesarian, but when Geoff wrote all had gone well.

Alister, with wife and baby, are due here on Saturday, so I am trying to get the place a little less untidy. Meanwhile, Heinemann sent me the proofs of the DHL letters, which now run to 1200 pages.[2] I have read about 700, and can't help feeling how right Huxley was to select. Moore has turned a brilliantly entertaining book into a load of 'documents'. He opens with a lot of scrappy postcards, pre-1910, which are meaningless. Then there are a long set of letters to early women friends – some very interesting things in them, but there are far too many, and they should have been cut. Then we start on more mature letters, but there are ruthlessly too many, and somehow they often tend to stress the worst side of him. In his anxiety to gobble DHL all for himself, Moore is furious because Heinemann have insisted on retaining that excellent introduction of Huxley – his own is insignificant. And of course everybody's name is blurted forth, and while he rather sneers at some of DHL's real friends, he is very careful to flatter persons like Bertie Russell and Montie [Sir Compton] Mackenzie, who might be useful to him. American 'scholarship' is sometimes a dreadful thing. Yet he makes odd little blunders, such as calling Banabhard a 'novelist'! She would have sued him for libel. He says Russell was imprisoned in 1918 for 'pacifism'. That lets him off lightly. In fact he got 6 months for a criminal libel on the American Army, saying it had been sent to England to do what it did in USA, suppress strikes. As a matter of fact it was never the Federal Army, it was the State National Guard, whose duty it is to keep order. Trust a Cambridge savant not to know the difference.

Did I tell you that on my way back, not far from here, to my amazement I saw a beautiful American quail! Then I remembered that there has been an attempt to introduce them into France – to be shot by the beastly chasseurs [hunters], of course. Now there is a baby wild rabbit which bounds about in the garden here, and I am so afraid it may be killed by one of the farm dogs or cats. I wish I could tell it to run away fast, fast, fast, to the open fields.

It is still cold and grey up here, and I suppose it is even worse with you. The north wind blows as ruthlessly as Harry T. Moore.

All love, and take care of yourself,

Richard

1 On 16 May 1961 H.D. wrote Aldington, 'I have had the worst cold that I have had for many years.' On 25 May she again commented on her health: 'I have had a siege of sleepless nights, Br said due to suppressed anxiety or <u>Angst</u> about the Brunner break-up. But I think that I am out of the woods …'. On 4 June she indicated that she was receiving 'injections for what [the doctor] calls "cardial insufficiency"'.
2 Heinemann published Moore's *The Collected Letters of D.H. Lawrence* in 1962.

Coda

On 6 June 1961 H.D. had a stroke; she was initially paralysed on her right side, but soon regained a degree of mobility. She lost the power of speech, however, and could neither read nor write, though she continued throughout the summer to be able to understand what was said or read to her. Bryher immediately wired Aldington, and during the next few months Aldington communicated with H.D. through her. On 10 June 1961, not realizing fully the seriousness of H.D.'s condition, he wrote Bryher, 'I hope all goes well with Hilda. Please give her my love when she recovers enough to understand.' On 15 June he still did not completely grasp the extent of H.D.'s incapacitation and wrote to Bryher, 'I can see that she is really very ill, and wish that the next perilous fortnight were safely over. It is encouraging that she can eat, and that she has begun to speak [a few words] again. What a terrible misfortune if speech were lost ...'. Eating remained a major difficulty, however, and Aldington wondered if the problem were simply one of finding the right foods. He wrote Bryher solicitously on 21 June: 'I suppose we must feel the news of Hilda is good, though it is distressing that she is so greatly incapacitated and that progress will be so slow. I don't know what to suggest about tempting her so eat, as I suppose she has to follow a régime. Could the hospital perhaps try her with one or two American dishes? She used to like succotash (corn and lima beans) and lettuce salads with shredded apples. I suppose the Faculty would recoil in horror from fudge, which she used to make. A slice of smoked salmon? And doesn't she like Apfelkuchen in American style?' Aldington's frame of reference here goes back to the period of 1912 through 1918, as if he and H.D. had known each other on an uninterrupted basis since then, as if the letters they had exchanged over the years had come to substitute for an intimate married life together, as if the correspondence – increasingly like a daily conversation since 1946 – had obliterated distances of time and space.

Aldington regularly reported H.D.'s limited progress in letters to friends. On 29 July he wrote to Durrell, 'The news of H.D. is not so good. ... Pearson (of Yale) ... says H.D. is better physically and is even able to walk downstairs and sit in the garden, but there seems little or no recovery of speech. Shit, eh?' On 4 August Aldington continued, 'The news of H.D. is not good. She has made a remarkable physical recovery, but the speech centres seem badly damaged. And in the Swiss clinic they all speak German, which she hates. Bryher wants us to go to Zürich for Hilda's 75th birthday ([10] Sept) to see her, if the quacks permit, probably for the last time.'[1]

Anticipating the trip to Switzerland, Aldington sensed that time was running out and suggested to Bryher on 25 August, 'might it not be a good thing to let her have an advance copy of her new poem [*Helen in Egypt*] to look at now? If she can read at all, her own familiar words might help her to recover language ...'. The visit to Zürich was brief: Aldington and Catha arrived on 12 September and left two days later. The doctors decided that only Catha should see H.D., for she was very ill. Aldington reflected, 'I suspect she didn't want her former husband to see her in that state.'[2] But he may have decided earlier that he could not bring himself to see her, for he had written to Pearson on

29 August, 'I think Hilda might like to see Catha, but I doubt it would be wise for me to present myself. I think she would not like her ex-husband to see her with these disabilities' (Yale). On 16 August Catha herself wrote Bryher that Aldington was 'more nervous than usual. I think he is extremely upset by Hilda's illness. ... I suppose that when one's life has been so much attached to Hilda's as Daddy's is, it will be painful for him to see her unable to speak' (Yale).

H.D. died on 27 September 1961. Aldington was not prepared. He had lived with her for four years, been married to her for twenty-five, in love with her for fifty – and in vivid correspondence with her, despite hiatuses, from the time he left for the French front in 1916. As soon as he received the telegram, he wrote Bryher on 2 October 1961, 'It is a great shock and grief, although I have been trying to prepare for it, but I had hoped it would not be so soon.' Aldington wrote a friend, 'It was more of a shock and grief than I had expected, and I have been going quietly and refusing invitations.'[3] He reiterated the 'shock' in letters to his friends, explaining that 'It was far more of a shock than I expected, because in spite of separation one is still linked with an old love.'[4] On 21 October Aldington reflected in a letter to Bryher, 'It has been much more of a shock and loss to me than I had expected. I had got into the habit of noting things to tell her in letters and picking up postcard photographs I thought might interest her. So that I am constantly reminded of the loss.' Aldington received in turn many letters of consolation and was particularly moved by a note from Tom MacGreevy which poignantly conveys the relationship the letters in this book suggest:

> A copy of the London Times came my way to-day and I saw that H.D. has gone. I do so hope that you were able to go to her as you had planned to do and that she knew you were there. For – you will let me say it – your appreciation of her gifts and your tender thought for her have always been amongst the rarest and finest things in your own character. And I know enough to realise that she appreciated them and reciprocated them. So that if one always had regrets nobody's regrets in such circumstances could be more tempered than yours should be at this moment. It is not mere literary conceit to say that poetry that is poetry is essential truth, from the Holy Spirit (whether one calls it that or not), and at the level of poetry it seems to me that you and she never ceased to belong to each other.[5]

H.D.'s body was cremated and her ashes sent to the United States where she was buried in the family plot in Bethlehem, Pennsylvania. She had frequently imagined settling in America – in Florida, California, even South Carolina – but, as she wrote to Aldington, she had concluded finally that she was rooted in Europe. Bryher and Norman Holmes Pearson decided, however, that she should be buried in the country where she had been born although she had never been more than a visitor there since leaving with the Greggs for her summer tour of Europe in 1911.

Aldington spent the winter of 1961 in Sury en Vaux and in the spring accepted an invitation from the Soviet Writers' Union to celebrate his seventieth birthday in Russia. He and Catha travelled to Moscow in June and he was delighted with the Russians' obvious high regard for his work. Shortly after his return home, he died of a heart attack on 27 July 1962. For Aldington there was no question of a plot near Dover; he is buried in a simple French cemetery on a hill in Sury en Vaux.

1 *Literary Lifelines*, 185, 187.
2 Aldington to Harry T. Moore, 14 October 1962, quoted in *Richard Aldington: An Intimate Portrait*, ed. Alister Kershaw and F.-J. Temple, Carbondale: Southern Illinois University Press, 1965, 102.

3 Aldington to Alison Palmer, 16 October 1961, in Gates, *Richard Aldington: An Autobiography in Letters*, 309.

4 Letter from Aldington to Eunice Gluckman, 16 October 1961, Yale.

5 Letter from Thomas MacGreevy to Aldington, 29 September 1961, SIU, quoted by permission of MacGreevy's executors, Margaret Farrington and Elizabeth Ryan.

Index

436

Villon, François, 73, 75n, 143, 149
Vivien, Renée (Pauline Tarn), 143, 146n
Virgil, 144n, 272, 296n, 369, 370–1, 390
Voltaire, François-Marie Avouet, 92, 93n, 194n

Wagner, Richard, 99n
Waley, Arthur, 333n
Wallace, William, 88, 89n
Walpole, Hugh, 164
Warman, Eric, 127n, 236, 237, 349, 350n
Weaver, Harriet Shaw, 12, 23, 37n, 116, 117n, 123, 142, 150, 151, 151n, 155, 157, 158n, 160, 184
Weekly, Ernest, 90n
Wells, H.G., 227
West, Rebecca, 12, 329, 360
Westminster Gazette, 35n
Whistler, James, 349
Whitall, James, 13, 75, 76n, 80n, 83, 106, 142, 185, 262
White, James Robert, 50, 50n, 362, 363n
Whitman, Walt, 262, 263n, 323, 385
Wilde, Oscar, xi, 28, 59, 91, 129, 296n
Wilkinson, David, 34n, 190n
Wilkinson, Louis, 7

Willart, Paul, 246n
Williams, William Carlos, 179, 212, 213n, 218, 220, 221, 328, 400
Williamson, Henry, 308, 309n
Winter, Denis, 25, 38n
Wolfe, Thomas, 332
Wolle, Francis, 36n, 252
Woolf, Virginia, 186, 306n
Wordsworth, William, 53n, 371

Yeats, William Butler, 28, 50, 50n, 67, 79n, 153, 153n, 189, 293–4, 362
Yorke, Arabella, *see* Yorke, Dorothy
Yorke, Dorothy, 29, 30, 31, 33, 34, 38n, 43–4, 43n, 46, 49, 53, 77n, 84–5n, 88, 89, 98, 99n, 104, 106, 107, 110, 113, 113n, 115, 116, 117n, 118–19, 119n, 120, 120n, 121, 124, 126, 131, 133, 139, 148, 149, 158n, 158, 161, 162, 166, 168, 168n, 171, 172, 174, 178, 179, 184, 185, 186, 187, 188, 190n, 191, 192, 193n, 195, 200, 206, 208, 210, 215, 225, 227, 235, 238, 241, 411–12, 416
Younge, Charlotte M., 313, 313n

Zukofsky, Louis, 213n

P.S. I enclose also the blurb about the American drug. Could you ask one of your expert Swiss friends what they think of it?[6]

1 In several of the preceding letters, Aldington confessed to not feeling well. His handwritten signature is occasionally shaky now, and he indicates at the end of his letter to H.D. on 15 March 1957 that 'I can hardly hold up my head!' His confession here is in response to H.D.'s question on 19 March 1957: 'And do tell me just what is making you so ill? I am very distressed.'

2 On 19 March 1957 H.D. had written that Bryher had brought her to sort through a folder of 'strange, wistful letters' from Brigit (probably from the 1920s), and added, 'do you know what became of her?'

3 One of these, 'The Bard of Provence' (TLS, 8 March 1957, 146), was a review of Aldington's Introduction to Mistral (London: Heinemann, 1956). The anonymous author praises the book as 'a labour of love', adding that it should 'restore to Mr Aldington some of the public favour he lost by his treatment of two popular idols, the author of The Mint, and Norman Douglas.'

4 Aldington's study of Stevenson is Portrait of a Rebel: The Life and Work of Robert Louis Stevenson, London: Evans Brothers, 1957. Of the contracted books, Aldington completed only the collection of biographical studies entitled Frauds, London: Heinemann, 1957.

5 Lowell Thomas (1892–1981) championed T.E. Lawrence and was a well-known radio figure then broadcasting on the CBS network.

6 H.D. wrote the drug's name, 'mératran', in the margin and duly investigated, writing to Aldington on 25 March 1957 that 'Erich Heydt says he wants to help + advise, unofficially'. H.D. was concerned about Aldington's health and asked for more information: '... most important, blood-pressure – how, normal, high?'

➢ 190 ➣

29 April 1957
Les Rosiers
Montpellier

Dear Dooley,

Roy Campbell is dead, killed on the 23rd in a motor accident near Setubal on his way back from spending Holy Week in Seville. Mary [his wife] was driving, and is in hospital. I almost feel it might be better for her to die than to survive with so ghastly a memory. It hits me very hard, for I loved Roy and revered him – a great poet, I think, who swept away all the silly metaphysical nonsense of the Eliots and Audens. Pah, what do they matter? Roy is dead. Nothing can ever be the same again.

Banabhard's letter is no help to Ezra, and although well-meant only advertises her Left-Wing anti-American sentiments. I corresponded with her about E. nearly ten years ago, but then she was less sympathetic. He hadn't become a 'cause'. Am I unsympathetic to her about it? Perhaps. I feel certain that public agitation won't free him. I should much like to hear what Pearson thinks, especially about Dorothy's application.

My friends have been here, one has gone back to Paris, the other to Collioure and he will drop in on his return. I am to be moved to a cottage much nearer Paris, and they will try to get Catha a job. The change may bring on the bronchitis again, but down here I should never see her, and there she can come for week-ends. And I can live very simply alone, do my own cooking and housework, and feel free.[1]

I rejoice exceedingly that you are doing a popular poem or sequence, whatever the highbrows may think. It is the curse of 'modern' poetry that it cuts itself off from the people in sterile intellectual pride. I love Mistral and my dear Roy because they fought

376